Language
Development

Language Development

Erika Hoff-Ginsberg

FLORIDA ATLANTIC UNIVERSITY

Brooks/Cole Publishing Company

I(T)P™ An International Thomson Publishing Company

Pacific Grove • Albany • Belmont • Bonn • Boston • Cincinnati • Detroit
Johannesburg • London • Madrid • Melbourne • Mexico City • New York • Paris
Singapore • Tokyo • Toronto • Washington

Sponsoring Editor: *Vicki Knight*
Marketing Team: *Jean Vevers Thompson and Margaret Parks*
Editorial Assistant: *Jana Garnett*
Production Editor: *Laurel Jackson*
Production Assistant: *Mary Vezilich*
Manuscript Editor: *Barbara Kimmel*
Permissions Editor: *Cathleen S. Collins*
Interior Design: *Rick Chafian*
Interior Illustration: *Gloria Langer*
Cover Design: *Roy R. Neuhaus and Robert J. Western*

Cover Photo: *Erika Stone*
Art Editor: *Lisa Torri*
Photo Editor: *Robert J. Western*
Photo Researcher: *Susan Kaprov*
Indexer: *James Minkin*
Typesetting: *Graphic World, Inc.*
Cover Printing: *Phoenix Color Corporation*
Printing and Binding: *Quebecor Printing Fairfield*

For more information, contact:

BROOKS/COLE PUBLISHING COMPANY
511 Forest Lodge Road
Pacific Grove, CA 93950
USA

International Thomson Publishing Europe
Berkshire House 168-173
High Holborn
London WC1V 7AA
England

Thomas Nelson Australia
102 Dodds Street
South Melbourne, 3205
Victoria, Australia

Nelson Canada
1120 Birchmount Road
Scarborough, Ontario
Canada M1K 5G4

International Thomson Editores
Seneca 53
Col. Polanco
México D. F. México
C.P. 11560

International Thomson Publishing GmbH
Königswinterer Strasse 418
53227 Bonn
Germany

International Thomson Publishing Asia
221 Henderson Road
#05-10 Henderson Building
Singapore 0315

International Thomson Publishing Japan
Hirakawacho Kyowa Building, 3F
2-2-1 Hirakawacho
Chiyoda-ku, Tokyo 102
Japan

Printed in the United States of America

10 9 8 7 6 5 4 3 2 1

Library of Congress Cataloging-in-Publication Data

Hoff-Ginsberg, Erika, [date]
   Language development / Erika Hoff-Ginsberg.
      p.   cm.
   Includes bibliographical references and index.
   ISBN 0-534-20292-6
   1. Language acquisition.   I. Title.
P118.H64 1996
   401'.93—dc20   96-23849
                                         CIP

To Victor, Mark, and Alissa

About the Author

Erika Hoff-Ginsberg is Professor of Psychology at Florida Atlantic University in Davie, Florida. She has been teaching language development to undergraduate students for the past 10 years. Before joining the faculty at Florida Atlantic University, Professor Hoff-Ginsberg taught at the University of Wisconsin–Parkside for 14 years. She holds an M.S. degree in psychology from Rutgers–The State University of New Jersey (1976) and a Ph.D. in psychology from the University of Michigan (1981). Her own research investigates the process of language development in both typically developing children and children with language impairment. Her research has been funded by the National Science Foundation, the National Institutes of Health,  and the Spencer Foundation and has appeared in major journals, including *Child Development, Developmental Psychology, The Journal of Child Language,* and *First Language.*

Brief Contents

Contents

Preface

I have written this book in order to share with others a field of inquiry that I find endlessly fascinating. For me, studying and thinking about how children develop language is fun—not fun like a day at the beach, but fun like working on a puzzle. The fun comes both from the occasional feelings of success at finding pieces that fit together and from the constant feeling of wonder at the picture that emerges.

My aim in this book is to present the field of language development in a way that communicates the questions that are asked by researchers in the field, the answers that have been proposed, the evidence that has been collected to address these proposed answers, and the conclusions derived from this evidence that constitute the current state of knowledge in the field. Understanding the questions is crucial, because if a person does not understand the questions, often he or she will not consider the research findings that constitute the answers inherently interesting or particularly memorable. Also, in many areas, the questions are likely to outlive the tentative answers that the field can provide at this time. In discussing the theories that constitute the currently proposed answers, I have tried to present a balanced treatment that examines all sides of the arguments, even though this treatment is not strictly neutral. My goal is to help students understand the different theoretical points of view in the field and the evidence and reasoning that lead some to argue for and others to argue—often with equal vigor—against each point of view. I also think it is important for students to understand the research process. In presenting the findings in each area, I have tried to summarize the results from a comprehensive review of the literature and to show students where findings come from by presenting selected, illustrative studies in greater methodological detail.

This book was written for the course I teach to advanced undergraduate students. The text does not assume that the reader has a background in any particular discipline; therefore, it could be used in courses taught in departments of psychology, linguistics, education, and communicative disorders. The text should also be suitable for graduate courses—used as a background and framework for readings from primary sources. The instructor's manual provides an outline of the central concepts in each chapter, questions to promote student discussion, suggested supplementary student activities, and a test bank of multiple-choice questions.

Although this book does not assume any prior linguistic knowledge, it does not allow its readers to remain in that state. Some understanding of work in linguistics is necessary both to appreciate the magnitude of what every child accomplishes in acquiring language and to comprehend the research that asks how children manage to do this. However, I have made every effort not to intimidate the reader who is not linguistically inclined and to present the research in such a way that readers who miss the linguistic details can still appreciate the gist of what questions are being asked and why, and what conclusions the researchers are drawing.

The central focus of this text is on language development as a field of basic research. Chapter 1 provides an overview and introduces three major questions about language development that recur throughout the text: (1) Is language acquisition the result of nature or nurture? (2) Is the human ability to acquire language a specifically linguistic capacity, or is language acquisition one result of more general-purpose cognitive capacities? and (3) What is the relation between the communicative functions that language serves and children's acquisition of the formal structures of language? Chapters 2 through 5 cover the core of the field—language development up to the age of 5 years. Chapter 2 discusses phonological development; Chapter 3, lexical development; Chapter 4, the development of syntax and morphology; and Chapter 5, the development of communicative competence. Chapters 6 through 8 introduce more applied areas. Chapter 6 covers language development after early childhood, including language and schooling, the acquisition of literacy, and language changes typical of adolescence and old age. Chapter 7 examines language development in special populations; these populations include children who are deaf, children who are blind, children with mental retardation, children with autism, and children with specific language impairment. Chapter 8 discusses second language learning and bilingual development. Although the subjects presented in Chapters 6 through 8 are the applied areas of language development, the findings in each area are brought to bear on the three basic research questions that appear throughout the book. The focus of Chapter 9 is on understanding the biological underpinnings of the human language capacity, but this chapter covers a wide range of topics, including the process of creolization, studies of brain injury and aphasia, studies of neurological correlates of language processing in intact children and adults, "wild children," the communication systems of other species, attempts to teach language to chimpanzees, and the evolution of the capacity for language in humans.

Some instructors may choose not to use the entire book. Chapters 1 through 5 form a coherent whole that covers the basics of early language development. Chapters 1 through 5, together with Chapter 9, provide comprehensive coverage of the field, excluding the more applied topics. Depending on the audience, instructors could supplement either of these two sets of chapters with any combination of Chapters 6, 7, and 8. Students in elementary education would find Chapter 6 most relevant. Students in communicative disorders and special education would find Chapter 7 most relevant. Students in programs on teaching English to speakers of other languages would find Chapter 8 most directly relevant to their interest.

Acknowledgments

It is a pleasure to publicly acknowledge those who contributed to this book's coming into being. Marilyn Shatz first suggested (and persisted in suggesting) that I undertake this project. Friends and colleagues provided encouragement, intellectual stimulation, comments on earlier versions, and answers to specific questions. With apologies to those I am inadvertently omitting, I would like to thank Adele Abrahamsen, Susan Braunwald, JoAnn Buhr, Roberta Corrigan, Donna Kelly, Wendy Leeds-Hurwitz, Edith Moravcsik, Letitia Naigles, Amy Weiss, and members of the University of Wisconsin–Milwaukee Cognitive Science Reading Group. Many students at the University of Wisconsin–Parkside used earlier versions of this manuscript and provided helpful comments; Monika Momirov contributed to the glossary. I also appreciate Joan Koski's help in manuscript preparation and the help of Debbi Braun and others on the library staff at the University of Wisconsin–Parkside for their assistance in tracking down references.

For their help and careful attention to the quality of this book, I am grateful to my editor at Brooks/Cole, Vicki Knight, and to the many others who worked on producing this book, including Rick Chafian, Cat Collins, Jana Garnett, Lauren Harp, Laurie Jackson, Barbara Kimmel, Patterson Lamb, James Minkin, Roy Neuhaus, Margaret Parks, Jean Thompson, Lisa Torri, Mary Vezilich, and Bob Western. This book is much better than it would have been otherwise because of the valuable comments provided by several reviewers. They are Doug Behrend, University of Arkansas–Fayetteville; Judith Becker Bryant, University of South Florida; Nancy Creaghead, University of Cincinnati; Jane F. Gaultney, University of North Carolina, Charlotte; Katherine Kipp Harnishfeger, University of Georgia; Maureen Marx, Western Illinois University; Victoria L. Michela, University of Alabama at Birmingham; Mary Ross Moran, University of Kansas; Nickola Wolf Nelson, Western Michigan University; Twila Tardif,

University of Michigan–Ann Arbor; and Amanda Walley, University of Alabama at Birmingham.

Many of the examples of child speech in this book that are referenced as personal data come from my niece and nephews, who were learning to talk as I was writing this book. I would like to thank them for obligingly making just the sort of speech errors I was writing about at the time, and I would like to thank my sisters for their role in data collection. I know that my own children would also like credit for contributing some of the examples of child speech—they would willingly have done more, but they were well past that stage by the time I was working on this book. Last, but most certainly not least, I would like to thank my husband and children, both for putting up with the many hours that I worked on this book, and, more generally, for putting up with me.

Erika Hoff-Ginsberg

1 Introduction to the Study of Language Development

Examples of one child's speech:

At 1 year: Uh-oh (said when things fall).

At 2 years: Mine ball (meaning "my ball"; usually said to her older brother).

At 2½ years: I no want go in there (context not recorded).

At 3 years: I wish I could sit on a horse and ride him to every house in the world (context not necessary).

Somehow, in the span of just a few years, newborn infants who neither speak nor understand any language become young children who comment, question, and express their ideas in the language of their community. This change does not occur all at once. First, newborns' cries give way to coos and babbles. Then, infants who coo and babble start to show signs of comprehension such as turning when they hear their name. Infants then become toddlers who say "bye-bye" and "all gone" and start to label the people and objects in their environment. As their vocabularies continue to grow, children start to combine words. Children's first word combinations, such as *all gone juice* and *read me,* are short and are missing parts found in adults' sentences. Gradually children's immature sentences are replaced by longer and more adultlike sentences. As children learn to talk, their comprehension abilities also develop, typically in advance of their productive speech.

As children master language, they also become masters at using language to serve their needs. One-year-olds who can only point and fuss to request something become 2-year-olds who say "please"; later they become 4-year-olds capable of the linguistic and communicative sophistication of the child who excused himself from a boring experiment by saying, "My mother says I have to go home now" (Keller-Cohen, January 1978, personal communication).

This book is about these changes. It is about the *what* and *when* of language development—what changes take place and when they occur in the course of language development. It is also about the *how* and *why*. How do children learn to talk, and why is the development of language a universal feature of human development? This book is also about some other topics that are related to language development. It is about how language is related to literacy and school achievement. It is about language development in special populations of children who do not follow the typical developmental course. It is about acquiring a second language, and it is about the brain and how human biology underlies our ability to acquire language.

In the following chapters, we will delve into these topics in some detail. Before we get into the details, we should look at the big picture of the field we are about to study. The aim of this chapter is to provide that big picture.

WHAT IS THE STUDY OF LANGUAGE DEVELOPMENT ABOUT?

Language development as a multidisciplinary field

Language development is a subfield of several larger disciplines, each with its own reason for focusing on language development. Developmental psychologists study language development for what it can reveal about the processes of growth and change. Linguists study language development for what it can reveal about the nature of language. Neuropsychologists, speech pathologists, cognitive psychologists, philosophers, and anthropologists all have questions that can be addressed by studying language development. A quick survey of introductory psychology texts will give you an idea of the variety of ways in which people think the study of language development fits into the rest of psychology. In various texts, sometimes language development is paired with social development, sometimes it is paired with cognitive development, and sometimes it is discussed entirely separately from other aspects of development, such as in a chapter on language or on language and thought. Discussions of language development can also be found in textbooks on linguistics, anthropology, and neuropsychology.

Reasons for studying language development

Why are so many people interested in language development? Researchers who spend a large portion of their waking hours studying and thinking about language development generally do so because they find the subject intrinsically interesting. Some find it interesting because language development reveals the genius in all children; when you think about it, it is remarkable that 3-year-olds who can't tie their shoes or cross the street alone have vocabularies of thousands of words and can produce sentences with relative clauses. Some researchers find the study of language development interesting because they find the structure of language itself fascinating. (One informal poll of graduate students suggested that an individual's future interest in the study of grammatical development could be predicted in the elementary school years by his or her interest in diagramming sentences.) Some researchers (and some students) may not be particularly enthralled by the elegance of grammar, but they find language development interesting because of the window it provides for viewing social development. After all, instances of language use tend also to be instances of social interaction. The child who said, "My mother says I have to go home now" when she tired of being an experimental participant was demonstrating not just grammatical skills but social skill as well.

The reasons individuals study language development are probably as numerous and unique as the individuals themselves. However, the fact that language development is intrinsically interesting to many people is not sufficient to explain why you should study language development or why universities and funding agencies should let grown people earn a living studying language development. There also are important scientific arguments for valuing the study of language development.

From the standpoint of science, we can identify two reasons for studying language development. One reason is its potential value to basic research into the nature of the human mind. A second reason is its potential value to applied questions about treating language disorders, about designing education for young children, and about teaching second languages to those who want or need to learn them.

Language development as a basic research topic   A child who has acquired language has acquired an incredibly complex and powerful system. If we understood how children accomplish this task, we would know something substantial about how the human mind works. The modern field of language development emerged in the 1950s when it became clear that language acquisition would serve as a test for rival theories of how change in human behavior occurs (Gardner, 1985; Pinker, 1984). In the 1950s, two psychological theories that were pitted against each other were behaviorism and cognitivism. According to **behaviorism,** change in behavior occurs in response to the consequences of prior behavior. Most readers are familiar with clear examples supporting this view. For instance, rats who initially do not press levers come to press levers after receiving food pellets for producing behaviors that increasingly approximate lever pressing. The position of radical behaviorism is that all behavior can be accounted for in the same way. A central tenet of behaviorism is that it is not necessary to discern what goes on in the mind of the rat in order to explain the change in the rat's behavior; behavior can be fully accounted for in terms of things external to the mind.

Cognitivism asserts the opposite—that we cannot understand behavior without understanding what is going on inside the mind of the organism producing the behavior. From approximately 1930 to the early 1950s, behaviorism dominated American psychology. But in the 1950s, a "cognitive revolution" began (Gardner, 1985). Over the next two decades, behaviorism came to be seen as inadequate, and the focus of the search for explanations of human behavior shifted to internal mental processes. Studies of language played a crucial role in the cognitive revolution. The ability to speak and understand language is incredibly complex, and children acquire that ability without receiving positive reinforcement for successive approximations to grammatical sentences. Simple theories that may well explain why rats push levers, why dogs salivate at the sight of the people who feed them, and why humans get tense when they sit in the dentist's chair cannot explain how children learn to talk.

When cognitivism won over behaviorism, theoretical dispute concerning how to understand human behavior did not end. In fact, a new interdisciplinary field called **cognitive science** emerged from the cognitive revolution. Cognitive scientists now agree that it is necessary to understand how the mind works in order to explain human behavior, but they do not agree on how the mind works. The study of language acquisition still plays a central role in the debate over how to characterize human cognition for the same reason that language acquisition played a central role in the cognitive revolution. That is, it is so difficult to explain how language acquisition is possible that accounting for language acquisition is a test not likely to be passed by inaccurate cognitive theories. Language acquisition is the New York City of the field of cognitive science; if you can make it there, you can make it anywhere.

Language development as an applied research topic   The goal for many researchers who study language development is perhaps less grandiose than discovering how the mind works, but it is more immediate. Success in modern industrialized society depends on having good verbal skills, and acquiring the verbal skills society requires is problematic for some children. Developing the verbal skills necessary for success in school is difficult for some minority children and for some children from lower socioeconomic strata who enter school with language skills different from those that mainstream, middle-class teachers expect. Thus one area of research in language development focuses on understanding the nature of cultural differences in language use and how teaching practices can be designed to best serve children with a variety of styles of language use.

Acquiring adequate language skills is also problematic for children who have a variety of other conditions, including mental retardation, hearing impairment, or brain injury; and some children have difficulty acquiring language in the apparent absence of any other sort of impairment. A substantial body of research focuses on trying to understand the nature of the problems that underlie such children's difficulty and on finding techniques for helping these children acquire language skills.

A large number of people in the world need to learn a second language to participate fully in society. These people include immigrants who need to learn the language of their new country, people who live in a multilingual society who need to be able to converse with all its members, and people whose first language, learned in the home, is not their country's language of commerce or government. (This is true, for example, of many people in Africa whose first language is that of their ethnic group but not the official language of their nation.) Understanding how best to help people learn a second language and, for schoolchildren, how to combine second language instruction with instruction in other subject areas are questions of enormous practical importance.

The areas of basic and applied research in the study of language development are not wholly separate. There are important points of contact. For example, basic research on the process of normal language development is used to develop interventions to help children who have difficulty acquiring language (Warren & Reichle, 1992). Sometimes work on language disorders also informs basic research. For example, evidence that children with autism acquire language structure even though they have severe communicative deficiencies suggests that learning language involves more than learning how to fulfill a need to communicate (Tager-Flusberg, 1994). There are also important points of contact among the various disciplines that study language development. For example, anthropologists' discovery that in many cultures no one talks to babies is relevant to the work of developmental psychologists who study how mother-infant interactions contribute to language development.

Components of language development

The development we refer to as language development actually includes many subcomponents. Knowing a language includes knowing the sounds and sound patterns of the language, the words of the language, the grammar of the language, and how to use the language to communicate. Thus we can divide the study of language development into the study of *phonological development* (sounds and sound patterns), *lexical development* (words), the *development of syntax and morphology* (the grammar), and the *development of communicative competence* (language use). The knowledge that underlies successful and appropriate language use includes both *pragmatic knowledge* and *sociolinguistic knowledge*. We will define these components of linguistic knowledge further in later chapters. Readers with some background in language development or linguistics may be surprised not to find semantic development listed here. Semantics is the study of meaning, and certainly learning a language is learning a system for expressing meaning. Much of what is usually subsumed under the heading of semantic development is word meaning, which is discussed in this text in Chapter 3 on lexical development. The meanings expressed in word combinations are discussed in Chapter 4 on the development of language structure.

HISTORY OF THE STUDY OF LANGUAGE DEVELOPMENT

Big questions and studies of special cases

The language in the brain   The first recorded language acquisition experiment was conducted by the ancient Egyptian king Psammetichus and was described by the Greek historian Herodotus in the fourth century B.C. The issue at hand concerned who among the peoples of the world represented the original human race. To resolve the issue, King Psammetichus ordered that two infants be raised in isolation by shepherds, who were never to speak in the children's presence. The idea behind this experiment was that the babies would start to speak on their own, and whatever language they spoke would be the language of the "original" people. According to Herodotus' account, one of the children said something like "becos" at the age of 2 years. *Becos,* as it turned out, was the Phyrgian word for bread. In the face of this evidence, King Psammetichus abandoned his claim that the Egyptians were the oldest race of humans and concluded that they were second oldest, after the Phyrgians.

Although the assumptions underlying that experiment seem slightly comical now, and the method of the experiment is certainly unethical, the idea of asking about the language the brain creates when it is not given an existing language to learn has not been discarded. In 1978 Heidi Feldman, Susan Goldin-Meadow, and Lila Gleitman reported their study of gestural communication systems invented by children born deaf but who had hearing parents. Because the children's parents did not know any sign language (and were instructed not to learn or use any sign language, in accordance with the oralist method of instruction for the deaf), these deaf children were just as isolated from a language model as were the infants in King Psammetichus' experiment. These children did invent "signs" and combined them in two- and three-sign sequences, suggesting that putting symbols together to communicate is something that naturally emerges in the course of human development. In Chapter 7, we will come back to the specifics of what these children did and what it suggests.

"Wild children" and the nature of humankind   Occasionally there are children who are not only linguistic isolates but also social isolates, and these unfortunate children afford science the opportunity to ask an even broader question: What is the intrinsic nature of humankind? This question was hotly debated in the 18th century. On the one hand, there had been a long tradition of argument by philosophers such as Descartes (1662) that human nature (including having an immortal soul) was an innate endowment. On the other hand, the philosopher John Locke (1690) had argued that at birth the human mind was like a sheet of blank paper and that humans become what they become as a result of society's influence. What was needed to settle this question was a human raised outside of society. Such a human appeared in the winter of 1800.

That winter was an unusually cold one, and in January a young boy who had been living wild in the woods near Aveyron, France, approached a tanner's workshop on the edge of the forest (Lane, 1976). The child appeared to be about 12 years old. He was naked; he occasionally ran on all fours; he ate roots, acorns, and raw vegetables—but only after sniffing them first; and although he was capable of making sounds, he had no language. This "wild child" became the object of intense scientific interest because he provided an opportunity to examine the nature of the human species in its natural state. The young boy's muteness was problematic for theories of innate knowledge for two reasons:

(1) language was held to be one of the defining characteristics of humanity; and (2) his muteness made him a difficult subject to interview to determine whether he had an innate idea of God (Lane, 1976). However, the boy's muteness provided good support for the opposing idea that "man depends on society for all that he is and can be" (Lane, 1976, p. 5).

The wild boy of Aveyron, as he came to be called, was placed with young Dr. Itard for training at the National Institute for Deaf-Mutes in Paris. The scientific community watched to see whether society could provide this child with the human characteristic of language. Although Dr. Itard was able to teach the boy some socially appropriate behaviors, the boy never learned more than a few words, and to this day we cannot be certain why. Perhaps the child was impaired from birth, perhaps the training methods employed were not the best, and perhaps the boy was too old to acquire language by the time his training began (Lane, 1976). Although the success that Itard achieved was quite limited, this scientific enterprise yielded practical dividends. Dr. Itard went on to use the training methods he had devised for the wild boy of Aveyron in teaching the deaf, and some of the techniques for teaching letters that Itard invented are used in Montessori classrooms today (Lane, 1976).

Over the course of history, there have been other "wild children" who were discovered mute at an age when children in normal environments have learned to talk (see Brown, 1958; Curtiss, 1989; Gleitman & Gleitman, 1991). The most famous recent case is of a girl named "Genie," who became known to the public in 1970. She was 13 years old and had been kept locked in a room by her mentally ill father since the age of approximately 18 months. Her language remediation was somewhat more successful than the boy of Aveyron's, but Genie never acquired normal language (Curtiss, 1977; Rymer, 1993). Modern scientific evidence, including the case of Genie, strongly suggests that there is a critical period for language acquisition. That is, language learning is something done best by children, and language learning after puberty is never quite as successful; this is also a topic to which we will return in later chapters. However, the case of the wild boy of Aveyron remains something of a mystery. If the boy was abandoned—or wandered off, or fled his home—before the age of normal language acquisition, it is mysterious how he could have survived. If he began his solitary life in the woods after he had acquired language, it is curious that he retained nothing.

Baby biographies

Another approach to investigating "the nature of humankind" is simply to observe what emerges in the course of normal development. In this vein, several investigators in the late 1800s and early 1900s kept diaries of their own children's development. The most famous of these "baby biographers" was Charles Darwin (better known for his theory of evolution), whose description of his son's communicative development (Darwin, 1877) is similar to the child's speech excerpts presented in the chapter opening. Darwin's son said "da" at 5½ months, and, before he was 1 year old, the young Darwin understood intonations, gestures, several words, and short sentences. At 1 year, Master Darwin communicated with gestures and invented his first word, *mum,* to mean food. Other well-known diaries include Clara and Wilhelm Stern's *Die Kindersprache* (Stern & Stern, 1907) and Leopold's (1939–1949) four-volume account of his daughter Hildegard's acquisition of English and German.

Diary studies are not entirely a thing of the past. Child language researchers often have children of their own, and some researchers have kept detailed records of their children's language development. Some of the data we will refer to in later chapters come from such diaries (for example, Bowerman, 1985, 1990; Dromi, 1987; Halliday, 1975; Mervis, Mervis, Johnson, & Bertrand, 1992; Sachs, 1983). In addition, researchers have occasionally trained mothers to keep diaries so that the early language development of several children could be studied (for example, Bloom, 1993b; Gopnik & Meltzoff, 1987; Harris, Barrett, Jones, & Brookes, 1988; Nelson, 1973).

Normative studies

In the period between the end of World War I and the 1950s, the goal of most research on language acquisition was to establish norms (Ingram, 1989). Toward that end, several large-scale studies were undertaken to provide data on when children articulate different sounds, the size of children's vocabularies at different ages, and the length of their sentences at different ages. Consonant with the behaviorist orientation of the times, the goal was not to ask theoretical questions about either the nature of humankind or the nature of language development but simply to describe what could be observed. These studies are still valuable as descriptions of normative development (for example, McCarthy, 1930; Templin, 1957).

The Chomskyan revolution

In the 1960s, the study of children's language development changed radically. The catalyst for this change was the publication in 1957 of a slim volume entitled *Syntactic Structures,* written by Noam Chomsky, a young linguist at the Massachusetts Institute of Technology. That piece, along with Chomsky's subsequent prolific work, revolutionized the field of linguistics and, within a few years, the study of language development as well. Before Chomsky's work, linguists concentrated on describing the regularities of languages. Linguists could study their own language or, better yet, a little-known language, but the job was the same—to find the patterns in what speakers do. Chomsky caused a revolution by saying that what speakers do is not as interesting as the mental grammar that underlies what speakers do. Since Chomsky's writings, the work of linguists consists of trying to describe what is in the minds of speakers that explains how speakers do what they do.

The new goal of linguistics raises a question about children. If adults have a mental grammar that explains what they do when they talk, then children must have a mental grammar that explains what *they* do. Children's speech is different from adults' speech; therefore children's mental grammars must be different. What are children's grammars like, and how do children eventually achieve adult grammars?

In 1962, Professor Roger Brown and his students at Harvard University began to study the grammatical development of two children given the pseudonyms Adam and Eve (Brown, 1973). Somewhat later a third child, Sarah, was added to the study. Every week for Sarah, and every two weeks for Adam and Eve, graduate students visited these children in their homes and tape-recorded their spontaneous speech. Transcripts of the children's speech were then analyzed with the goal of describing the grammatical knowledge that underlay the speech they produced. That project, begun by Brown, along with just a few other projects (Bloom, 1970; Braine, 1963; Miller & Ervin, 1964), marks the beginning of the Chomskyan era of studying children's language. The graduate students who met with Roger Brown to discuss the analyses of Adam's, Eve's, and Sarah's language—along with a few notable others who were not at Harvard that year—became the first generation of child language researchers. We will discuss some of these pioneering projects when we discuss grammatical development in Chapter 4.

Chomsky focused on grammar (the structure of language), and the first new wave of research on language development in the 1960s was on children's grammatical development. Later, in part following theoretical trends in linguistics, child language researchers shifted their focus more toward semantics and the acquisition of word meanings. In the later 1970s, the domain of language development was further expanded. Again following developments in linguistics, language use was added to the field of inquiry, and child language researchers began to study pragmatic and sociolinguistic development. In the 1980s and 1990s, linguistics and language development returned to focus on syntax, but the other questions about the lexicon and pragmatics have not been abandoned (or solved). The study of phonology and phonological development has continued throughout this period, somewhat outside the center ring of linguistic debate. (For fuller accounts of the history of child language, see Golinkoff & Gordon, 1983; and Ingram, 1989.) Currently, the study of language development is a multifaceted field that includes a variety of very different research enterprises. One way of categorizing these different enterprises is according to their focus on the acquisition of either phonology, the lexicon, the grammar, or communicative competence. Another way in which child language researchers sort themselves is in terms of the views they hold with regard to the major issues in the field. The next section outlines the major points of controversy that sometimes give the field of language development the appearance of being separated into opposing camps.

CURRENT ISSUES IN LANGUAGE DEVELOPMENT

All child language researchers work on the problem of explaining how children learn to talk, and no one has a complete solution yet. Nonetheless, there are major disagreements in the field concerning what researchers believe is likely to turn out to be true. To understand the nature of those disagreements, it is necessary first to understand the problem researchers are trying to solve.

Think of the human capacity to acquire language as a device (residing in the human brain) that takes as its input certain information from the environment and produces as its output the ability to speak and understand language. (This model is presented in Figure 1.1.) Everything that is part of adults' knowledge of language must either be in the input, be in the internal device, or somehow result from the way the device operates on the input it receives. One basic issue in the field involves a trade-off between accounting for the end result of language acquisition in terms of information provided in input and information already in the device; this is the *nature-nurture* controversy. Another issue concerns how the device operates; is the device *language-specific* or is *general purpose cognition* applied to the language acquisition task? What counts as a plausible position on both issues depends on the description one adopts of the output. This is where issues in linguistics regarding the description of adults' linguistic knowledge enters into the debate about language acquisition. A third major issue (both in linguistics and language acquisition) concerns how the communicative functions of language fit into the picture, with *formalists* asserting that it is irrelevant and *functionalists* asserting that language function shapes both the nature of language acquisition and the form of language itself. All these questions will come up repeatedly throughout the text as we discuss the details of phonological, lexical, grammatical, and communicative development. In the next sections, we will preview these major issues in broad outline.

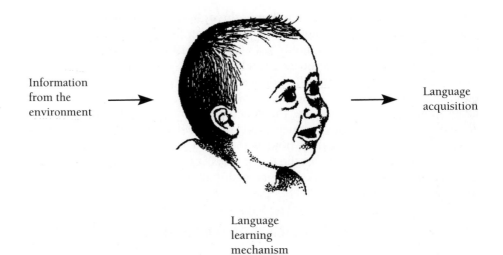

Information
from the
environment

Language
acquisition

Language
learning
mechanism

Figure 1.1   A model for studying the nature of the language learning capacity

Nature or nurture?

Is the development of language in children the result of human nature
(like the development of upright posture and bipedal locomotion), or is
it the result of the circumstances in which children are nurtured (like
the development of table manners or the ability to do calculus, both of
which depend on particular experiences)? The **nature-nurture** debate has
a long history that predates not only the modern study of language development but also the emergence of psychology as a discipline. This was
the ongoing debate when the wild boy of Aveyron left the woods in 1800.
The extreme experience-based position, known as **empiricism,** asserts that
the mind at birth is like a blank slate; all knowledge and reason come
from experience (Locke, 1690). The alternative view, known as **nativism,**
asserts that knowledge cannot come from experience alone. The mind
must have some preexisting structure in order to organize and interpret
experience (Gleitman, 1995; see the works of Plato and Kant for the original arguments). This debate still rages among those who study language
development.

The nativist view   For proponents of nativist accounts of language development, three salient "facts" about language development are that (1) children
acquire language rapidly, (2) children acquire language effortlessly, and (3)
children acquire language without direct instruction. Rapid, effortless, untutored
development seems more like maturation than like learning in the usual sense
of the term. As Chomsky (1987) put it,

Language learning is not really something that the child does; it is something that happens to the child placed in an appropriate environment, much as the child's body grows and matures in a predetermined way when provided with appropriate nutrition and environmental stimulation. (p. 519)

The modern-day descendant of the opposite, empiricist view is behaviorism. As mentioned earlier, behaviorism has not stood the test of time (or empirical evidence) as a theory of language acquisition. Behaviorist theories will be mentioned again in the following chapters, but primarily for historical completeness.

The interactionist view   In current debate, the alternative to nativism is not pure empiricism but rather **interactionism** (Braine, 1994). Like nativism, the interactionist position acknowledges that there must be some innate characteristics of the mind that allow it to develop language based on experience. But the interactionist position places a greater burden of accounting for language development on the nature of children's language learning experiences than nativists do. Research on the nature of the **language input** children receive and the relation of that input to the rate and course of development are relevant here (see, for example, Gallaway & Richards, 1994; Hoff-Ginsberg & Shatz, 1982; Morgan, 1990). The position known as **social interactionism** holds that a crucial aspect of language learning experience is social interaction with another person. For proponents of interactionism, the "facts" so salient to the nativists are not obvious and are, in fact, contested. A recent expression of the social interactionist position comes from Catherine Snow:

We on the other side think that learning language is a long slog, which requires from the child a lot of work. And the child is working as hard as he can, fifteen, sixteen hours a day. We think it requires a relationship with an adult, and a whole set of cognitive abilities. (quoted in Rymer, 1993, p. 37)

Another term for this type of position is *constructivism*. **Constructivism** as a view of development was first argued with respect to cognitive development by Jean Piaget, and *constructivism* remains a term in current use (for example, Quartz, 1993). According to the constructivist view, language (or any form of knowledge) is constructed by the child using inborn mental equipment but operating on information provided by the environment.

In 1975, Noam Chomsky and Jean Piaget debated their respective nativist and constructivist views of language development at the Abbaye de Royaumont near Paris. Nearly 200 years after the wild boy of Aveyron left his woods (and roughly 200 miles away), the debate about the essential nature of the human mind continued. In his foreword to the edited transcript of that debate, Howard Gardner (1980) summarized the two views:

> . . . Piaget saw the human child—and his mind—as an active, constructive agent that slowly inches forward in a perpetual bootstrap operation, Chomsky viewed the mind as a set of essentially preprogrammed units, each equipped from the first to realize its full complement of rules and needing only the most modest environmental trigger to exhibit its intellectual wares.(p. xxiii)

Language specificity or general cognition?

Granting that there must be some innate characteristic of the human mind that allows language development, theorists still disagree about the nature of that which is innate. One position, the **language-specific** view, is that the innate characteristic of the mind that underlies language development is specific to language. That is, children have inborn knowledge of the general form of language, and it is that inborn, specifically linguistic knowledge that allows children to figure out a whole language in only a few years. The alternative view, the **general cognitive** view, is that language acquisition is the result of general cognitive processes of learning applied to language experience (see Gunnar & Maratsos, 1992).

A language-specific module   The proposal that children have inborn knowledge of the general form of language may be more reasonable than it first appears. All languages of the world share many structural characteristics. These shared characteristics constitute the **Universal Grammar** of human language, of which each particular language is an example. (It's the different *vocabularies* that make languages other than our own incomprehensible.) Evolution seems to have equipped the human mind with other sorts of useful knowledge, such as the knowledge that the world is a three-dimensional place (our eyes alone cannot tell us this because our retinas are two-dimensional surfaces), and Universal Grammar may similarly be an innate endowment. The view that the human ability to develop language is specific to language is part of a larger theory known as the **modularity** thesis (Fodor, 1983). According to this thesis, the innate human ability to develop language is a self-contained module in the mind, separate from other aspects of mental functioning. Chomsky (1991), in fact, referred to the human language capacity as a functionally separate "mental organ," explaining: "The mind, then, is not a system of general intelligence. . . . Rather, the mind has distinct subsystems, such as the language faculty, a cognitive system, . . . " (pp. 50–51).

General cognitive skills   The alternative proposal that general cognitive processes can account for language acquisition is more difficult to summarize and attribute. Some early cognitive approaches to language development were based on Piagetian theory and sought to explain changes in children's language functioning in terms of stagelike developmental shifts in their non-linguistic functioning. The shift from the sensorimotor intelligence of infancy to the preoperational intelligence of the toddler years was a particular focus of research (see, for example, Sinclair, 1969; and see Corrigan, 1979, for a review). However, that sort of across-the-board relation between cognitive development and language development was not supported by the evidence (Corrigan, 1979).

Currently, there is no single general cognitive view. Rather, there are several proposals for how a variety of cognitive skills that are not specific to language contribute to language acquisition. The kinds of cognitive skills suggested as contributing to language acquisition include the capacity for symbolic representation (Bates, Benigni, Bretherton, Camaioni, & Volterra, 1979), memory skills (Braine, 1988; Gathercole & Baddeley, 1990), skill in segmenting chunks of speech into their constituent parts (Bates, Bretherton, & Snyder, 1988), and a variety of processes that might be grouped under the heading of pattern analysis (Braine, 1988; MacWhinney, 1987; Maratsos & Chalkley, 1980).

The plausibility of the general cognitive position hinges on whether the general cognitive skills available to the language learning child are sufficiently powerful to explain all the phenomena of language acquisition. Critics argue that they are not, but, on the other hand, it can be argued that we simply do not know very much about the general learning processes available to young children (Braine, 1994).

Connectionism   Another candidate for an account of language acquisition in terms of general learning processes comes from a new approach to modeling cognition known as **connectionism** (also referred to as parallel distributed processing or neural networks). In connectionist models, human thought is represented as the activation of nodes in a network, and human knowledge is represented as the strength of the connections among nodes. This view is starkly at odds with the previously dominant view of cognition as symbol processing. A little history may help explain the debate.

The idea that thinking is symbol processing goes back at least as far in history as the philosophy of Descartes and other rationalists of the 17th and 18th centuries (Bechtel, 1993) and, by some accounts, to the ancient Greeks (Dreyfus, 1988). It is a view that has dominated cognitive science since behaviorism was deemed inadequate. The basis of the cognitive revolution that occurred between the 1950s and the 1970s was the collective conclusion that human mental processes could be described only by positing that people have symbolic representations of ideas in their minds and that thinking consists of processing these mental representations in rule-governed ways. Thus, since the cognitive revolution, knowing a language has been conceptualized as knowing a system of rules, and language development has been conceptualized as the learning of those rules. So, for example, knowing how to form the past tense of regular verbs consists of knowing the rule of adding *ed* to the verb stem; apply this rule to *walk,* and you get *walked.* Learning to form the past tense consists of learning this rule.

In the late 1980s, a new view started to take hold—that human thinking can be adequately accounted for without positing symbols or processing rules. Instead, thinking consists of activating connections in a network. Ideas are represented in the mind as patterns of activation, and thinking is the process of activation spreading in this network along paths determined by the strengths of the connections in the network. With respect to language, the proposal is that adults' use of language can be accounted for in terms of the strength of the connections in the relevant parts of the neural network. Language development consists of forging and strengthening the relevant connections. Unlike the process of "figuring out" rules, strengthening connections happens automatically, based on contingencies in the input the network receives. So, for example, adults' production of a word's past tense is the result of a connection in the neural network between one sound, "walk," and another sound, "walked." This connection is formed by repeatedly hearing the sound "walked."

Part of the attraction of connectionist models is that they seem closer to biology than symbolic models, because we know that the brain is a set of interconnected neurons. If cognitive processing could be modeled in a system that is closer to what is termed the "wetware" of the brain (an analogy to a computer's hardware), we could eliminate the problem of determining how the brain represents symbols and rules. (For a more thorough introduction to connectionism see, for example, Bechtel & Abrahamsen, 1991; Martindale, 1991).

The kind of research that addresses the dispute between the symbol/rule approach and the connectionist approach consists of writing computer programs that instantiate a particular connectionist model, feeding the computer the kind of language input children are likely to hear, and then seeing whether the computer can mimic the course of human language development. The most optimistic view of the promise of connectionism is that it may offer an alternative to the trade-off between finding the structure of language in the input or building the structure into the acquisition mechanism. The most successful connectionist implementations suggest that complex linguistic knowledge can emerge from the operation of a device equipped with no specific linguistic knowledge that takes relatively simple examples of language as input. (See Bates & Elman, 1993; Elman, 1993; Plunkett, 1995. We will discuss some connectionist proposals in more detail in Chapter 2 on phonological development and Chapter 4 on grammatical development.)

The issue of whether language acquisition is supported by a domain-specific mental module or by general cognitive processes (connectionist or otherwise) is one contest in a larger ongoing debate in cognitive psychology. The debate concerns whether cognition in general consists of the activity of a general-purpose set of reasoning abilities applied to different tasks, or whether there are many cognitive abilities that are specialized to handle different kinds of information (Hirschfeld & Gelman, 1994). The modularity thesis asserts that the mind is a bundle of many special-purpose modules—one for language, one for perception, one for understanding spatial location (map making)—and that there is no such thing as a "general ability to learn" (Barkow, Cosmides, & Tooby, 1992; Fodor, 1983; Pinker, 1994). Thus the modularity issue is not an issue specific to language development but rather is an issue in cognitive psychology in which language plays a crucial, but not a singular, role. (For a discussion of modularity and nonmodularity in other domains, see Barkow et al., 1992; Cosmides, 1989; and Karmiloff-Smith, 1992.)

Formalism or functionalism?

In acquiring language, children learn a complex system which they then use to communicate. In fact, one might say that the value of language to the human species is the communicative power it enables. Although no one doubts that language is useful for communication, there are differing views on how important communication is to language and to language acquisition. The two extreme positions are (1) the **formalist** view that the nature of language and its acquisition have nothing to do with the fact that language is used to communicate, and (2) the **functionalist** view that both language itself and the process of language acquisition are shaped and supported by the communicative functions language serves.

Formalist views A starkly unqualified statement of the formalist position comes from Chomsky (1991):

> For unknown reasons, the human mind/brain developed the faculty of language, a computational-representation system [here more specifics of the nature of the system are spelled out]. . . . [This system] can be used . . . in specific language functions such as communication; [but] *language is not intrinsically a system of communication* [italics added]. (pp. 50–51)

For the formalists, language is an autonomous, arbitrary system whose form is independent of its function.

Another position asserts that language was shaped in the course of evolution by its communicative value, but the nature of that form cannot currently be derived from the functions it serves (see Pinker & Bloom, 1990). From the point of view of language learning children, this position asserts, as does the Chomskyan formalist view, that language is an external system that has to be figured out, and the use to which that system is put provides no clues about how the system is structured.

Functionalist views   The contrary view is that language "is not an arbitrary and autonomous system" (Budwig, 1995) but rather is shaped by the communicative functions it serves. And, one view holds, because the form of language reflects the communicative functions to which it is put, children are led to discover the form of language in using the system to communicate. As MacWhinney, Bates, and Kliegl (1984) state, "The forms of natural languages are created, governed, constrained, acquired and used in the service of communicative functions" (p. 128).

There are, in fact, a number of different functionalist views, and some make stronger claims than others about the usefulness of communication to language acquisition. We will return to this issue in Chapter 5 (for a recent summary of functionalist approaches to language development, see Budwig, 1995).

METHODS OF RESEARCH IN LANGUAGE DEVELOPMENT

Approaches to the study of language development

In addition to disagreeing about the kind of answer they think will explain language acquisition, child language researchers also disagree about the kind of approach they think is likely to yield an answer. The major difference of opinion is between those who adopt a developmental approach and those who adopt a learnability approach.

The developmental approach   For researchers working within the developmental approach, the basic question that needs answering is, "What is the course of language development and how can we explain it?" Researchers who work with this **developmental approach** start their investigations with data on what children do. They use the evidence of what children do as a basis for inferring what children know, and they use developmental changes in what children seem to know as a basis for explaining the processes of language development (Bloom, 1991). The goal of

the developmental approach is to account for the course of language development. However, at present, the evidence of what children do does not
add up to a full explanation of language development, and therefore the
developmental approach cannot now offer a complete theory of language
development.

The learnability approach For researchers who work within the **learnability approach,** accounting for the course of language development is *not*
the primary goal. Rather, the primary goal is to account for the fact that
language is acquired by children. Or, put another way, their goal is to explain
how it is that language is learnable by children. Researchers who work within
this learnability approach start with a theory of adult language and then
propose models of how children could achieve that adult state. Those working
within the learnability approach do not hesitate to attribute innate knowledge
of language to children when needed to account for language acquisition.
The combination of starting with a linguistic theory and the willingness to
posit innate knowledge allows the learnability approach to offer a complete
account of language acquisition. In fact, as Bloom (1991) noted, there are
several complete accounts, each working with a different theory of the adult
grammar (Hyams, 1986; Pinker, 1984; Wexler & Culicover, 1980). However,
those taking the learnability approach are to a certain extent in the same boat
as the developmentalists; the things we know about language development
from hard data do not add up to a full account of language acquisition. So
learnability theorists have complete theories that include assumptions (typically innatist) for which the primary evidence is that the theory won't work
without these assumptions.

The foregoing descriptions of the developmental and learnability approaches should not be controversial. That is, most developmentalists readily
admit they haven't got it all figured out, and most learnability theorists admit that
future research may prove some of their assumptions wrong. Eventually the two
approaches ought to converge, because the course of language development
does, after all, culminate in language acquisition. However, in the meantime,
practitioners of the two approaches strongly disagree about which tack is more
likely to be successful.

Cross-cultural and cross-linguistic research

The modern study of language development began with investigations of the
acquisition of English by middle-class American children. Initially this focus was
not seen as a terrible limitation because, so the thinking went, the processes
underlying language acquisition are universal, and thus discovering how
children in Cambridge, Massachusetts, acquire language is the same as

discovering how all children acquire language. Currently the study of language acquisition by children who live in other cultures and the study of the acquisition of languages other than English are considered crucial to discovering the universal processes of language acquisition.

Two insights provide the motivation for cross-cultural and cross-linguistic research. One is the realization that there are individual differences in language development, and there may be more than one route to language acquisition. This is true of different children within a single culture, but it may be especially true when describing language acquisition in cultures that provide children with different kinds of language learning environments (Lieven, 1994). Thus researchers no longer assume that if you've seen one child acquire language, you've seen them all.

The second reason for cross-cultural and cross-linguistic research is that different languages present children with different language learning tasks. The human capacity to acquire language works equally well whether the task is to acquire English, Chinese, or Walpiri (an Australian aborigine language). If researchers study only the acquisition of English and construct a theory of language acquisition that accounts for the acquisition of English, they run the risk that their theory could not account for the acquisition of Chinese or Walpiri. And a theory of language acquisition that cannot account for the acquisition of all languages is obviously not the correct description of the human language-learning capacity. Currently cross-cultural and cross-linguistic work is very much part of the mainstream of child language research. There is one central source for a great deal of this research, however, in a series of volumes entitled *The Cross-Linguistic Study of Language Acquisition* (Slobin, 1985, 1992).

Research designs

In their search for answers to the question of how children learn to talk, child language researchers make use of the same kinds of research designs that other sciences do. They engage in longitudinal and cross-sectional observational studies to describe developmental changes in children's language, and they analyze those patterns of development for what they might reveal about the process underlying that development. They do correlational studies in which they look for relations between different aspects of language development or between language development and other aspects of development or experience. They do experiments in which they provide children with different kinds of exposure to language and then look for differences in what children have learned. Sometimes researchers use computer simulations to test whether a hypothesized model of language development could work in principle. Sometimes researchers do case studies of individuals whose unique circumstances or pattern of development promises to shed light on some issue.

The focus of studies of children's language development can be on language production, language comprehension, or both. Researchers interested in comprehension have been very inventive in designing ways to get small children to reveal what they think a word or a sentence means. We will discuss the particulars of different methods in later chapters when the research is discussed. But one aspect of methodology in child language research is so often employed and so specific to this field that it is worth discussing by itself. The analysis of samples of spontaneous speech is the method Roger Brown used in his pioneering study of Adam, Eve, and Sarah, and it is a method that is still widely used today.

Assessment of productive language from speech samples

Speech sample collection   Child language researchers can often be identified by the equipment they carry. Videotape or audiotape records of spontaneous **speech samples** are the standard database for assessing children's language development. Typically the researcher picks a setting in which children are likely to talk—a meal time or toy play, for example—and then records interactions in that setting. The recording can be done in the children's homes or in a laboratory playroom. The children can be talking to the researcher or to someone more familiar to them, usually their mother.

The purpose of collecting speech samples is to find out the nature of the language children produce. Thus it is important that the speech sample collected is representative of everything the children say. Achieving representativeness can be difficult because speech may be different in different contexts (Bacchini, Kuiken, & Schoonen, 1995; Hoff-Ginsberg, 1991). Another concern is that the act of recording will alter children's speech in some way. This is probably more of a problem for recording the speech of adults than that of children, who tend to be less self-conscious than adults; but researchers typically spend some "warm-up" time with their subjects before turning on the tape recorder. One research project attempted to secure more representative speech samples by putting little vests with radio-controlled microphones on children (Wells, 1985). The children wore the vests all day, although the microphone was turned on only intermittently.

Collecting speech samples for the purpose of describing developmental changes also entails the issues of how much speech needs to be recorded to estimate characteristics of a child's language and how frequently speech needs to be recorded to capture developmental changes. Generally, a speech sample of approximately 100 utterances is considered large enough to yield reliable estimates of grammatical properties of children's speech. If the focus of interest is on some characteristic of language use not present in every utterance, then of course the sample would need to be larger. There are also no established guidelines for how often children need to be recorded (Bloom, 1991). Researchers select different intervals using the existing literature to make their best guess at what interval will reveal the sorts of developmental changes they are looking for.

Sometimes the focus of research is on a particular type of language use, such as storytelling. In this case, more directive techniques of elicited production can be used. As we shall see in Chapter 6, an enormous body of research on children's narrative development is based on studies using the same technique of asking children to tell a story using a book that has pictures but no words (Berman & Slobin, 1994).

Speech sample transcription   The invention of audio- and videotape recorders made it possible to collect a record of everything a child says, which made a central kind of language development research possible. However, there is a downside to tape-recording speech samples: the tapes have to be transcribed. Child language researchers are sometimes guilty of the sin of envy when they see their colleagues in other fields say good-bye to the participants in their studies and then turn to the participants' just-completed questionnaires to find numbers ready for analysis. When child language researchers say good-bye to the little participants in *their* studies, the task of data collection has only just begun.

The next step in data collection is transcription, which consists of writing down what was recorded. What makes that task difficult is that the children being recorded were not giving dictation but were engaging in conversation. In conversation, people do not speak in full sentences; they interrupt each other and even talk at the same time. Furthermore, especially if they are children, their pronunciation is less than clear, and their usage not quite adultlike. Creating a transcript that is a faithful record of what was on the tape is a difficult and time-consuming task. It requires training to be able to transcribe, and then it can take as long as five hours to transcribe each hour of recorded speech.

Transcript coding and analysis   After the speech has been transcribed, the researcher then has to code the transcripts. Coding consists of different things, depending on what the researcher is studying. For example, if the purpose of the research is to chart the development of verb usage, then coding the transcripts might involve identifying every verb in the children's speech. If the purpose of the research is to study children's conversational skill, then coding the transcripts might involve categorizing every utterance the child produces as related or unrelated to what was said before. Ultimately, for researchers to conduct the kinds of analyses that get reported in journal articles, the codes have to be turned into numbers. For example, a researcher might analyze changes in the number of different verbs in children's spontaneous speech or changes in the proportion of children's utterances that are related to prior speech.

When this sort of research started in the 1960s, transcripts were handwritten documents with columns for different codes. Graduate students in child language logged many hours over these transcripts, identifying verbs or whatever the research called for and adding numbers in the code columns. The advent of computer programs for analyzing child language transcripts has considerably lightened that load. It still takes a human being to transcribe and code, but the transcription can be done directly into a computer-based file, and the coding can be entered onto the transcript as well. Then, instead of the researcher having to count all the codes, the computer can do it—and far more quickly and accurately.

A few computer programs designed specifically to analyze transcripts are now available (see Miller & Klee, 1995, for a comprehensive review). Probably the most widely used is the set of programs associated with the Child Language Data Exchange System (CHILDES) (MacWhinney, 1991). Another is SALT (Systematic Analysis of Language Transcripts) (Miller & Chapman, 1985). SALT was developed specifically for researchers and clinicians in communicative disorders, but it is a flexible program that can be used for basic research as well. Its companion program, PEPPER (Programs to Examine Phonetic and Phonological Evaluation Records) (Shriberg, 1986), is designed for analyzing the phonological characteristics of transcribed speech.

CHILDES—A data archive

Another benefit made possible by computer-based transcripts is widespread data sharing. Although researchers have always been able to share data with colleagues by photocopying their transcripts, sharing is made easier when the transcripts are in computer-based files and when (as a necessary side effect of computerized transcription) the transcripts are in a standardized format.

The **CHILDES** project has taken the concept of data sharing even further by establishing an archive. In the early 1980s, the MacArthur Foundation funded a project, led by Brian MacWhinney and Catherine Snow, to establish an archive for transcripts of children's speech. Roger Brown contributed his transcripts of Adam, Eve, and Sarah, and other researchers contributed transcripts they had collected. Since then, more than 60 researchers representing more than a dozen languages have contributed transcripts to this archive. Now researchers whose questions can be addressed by looking at speech samples in the CHILDES archive are able to go straight to the coding phase of research. Researchers can access the archive through the Internet; workshops on how to use the CHILDES archive are offered periodically at major conferences and at Harvard University. Complete copies of the archive are housed at Carnegie-Mellon University in Pittsburgh, at Harvard University, and at three European centers.

Standardized tests and measures of language development

Sometimes researchers want to be able to describe a child's speech in terms that compare that child's speech to the speech of other children of the same age. Child language researchers are typically interested in such measures primarily for the purpose of describing the children they are studying, much the way researchers in cognitive development sometimes want to describe their samples in terms of IQ or mental age. By far the biggest users of standardized measures are practitioners in communicative disorders, who use such measures for diagnosis and for treatment evaluation.

There are essentially two ways to go about asking how a child's language development compares to that of other same-age children. One is to collect a speech sample and code it using a coding system for which norms have been collected. For example, the mean length of a child's utterances (MLU) is a good index of a child's level of grammatical development, and data that provide norms for MLU have been collected (Miller & Chapman, 1981; more on this topic will be covered in Chapter 4.) SALT will calculate MLU on an appropriately entered transcript and will indicate the child's level of grammatical development. Age-referenced norms for phonological features of children's speech are also available (Grunwell, 1981). The second way of getting a norm-referenced measure of a child's language level is to employ one of the many existing standardized instruments. One recently developed set of instruments that is coming into wide use in research is the MacArthur Communicative Development Inventories (CDIs) (Fenson, Dale, Reznick, Bates, Thal, & Pethick, 1994). There are two versions of the MacArthur CDI—one for infants between 8 and 16 months of age and one for 16- to 30-month-old toddlers. These inventories consist of checklists that parents fill out to report on the gestures, words, and word combinations that their children understand and produce. Data from nearly 2000 children have been collected using these inventories, thus providing a basis for evaluating an individual child's level of development. Many other examiner-administered tests of language comprehension and production are primarily used in the field of communicative disorders or speech pathology. A survey of these instruments is available in James (1993).

SOURCES FOR RESEARCH ON LANGUAGE DEVELOPMENT

Journals

One way students new to language development can get an idea of the range of topics, issues, and research methods in the field is to scan journals that publish research on language development. The titles of the articles in these journals give an idea of the topics being studied. The list of journals that contain papers on language development is long and includes journals from a variety of disciplines. The major sources are listed in Box 1.1.

Indexes

If you already have a particular interest in some topic, or if you find an interesting topic by scanning the journals, you may want to find other articles on the same topic. There are indexes that can help you track down everything that has been written on a particular topic in language development. Just as the index in the back of this book allows you to find all the places in this book that a particular topic is mentioned, these indexes allow you to find all the places a particular topic is mentioned in the set of journals they scan.

Psychological Abstracts is a service that covers over 1300 different journals in psychology and related fields and provides an index to material in those sources. Since 1987, *Psychological Abstracts* has also covered books and book chapters. **Linguistics and Language Behavior Abstracts** provides an index to material in 1500 journals in language and language-related fields. **Child Development Abstracts** does the same sort of thing for journals in fields related to child development. *Psychological Abstracts* and *Linguistics and Language Behavior Abstracts* are available in computer-accessible formats (*Psychological Abstracts* in computer-accessible form is called **PsychLit**); all you have to do is type in the subject you are interested in (such as "lexical development" or "sign language"), and you will get a list of articles on that topic drawn from the more than 1000 books and journals the indexing service covers.

Annotated bibliographies

A few times in the history of the field, enterprising researchers have compiled annotated bibliographies of child language research (Abrahamsen, 1977; Gelbart & Soederbergh, published annually; Leopold, 1952; Slobin, 1972). The most recent bibliography is *CHILDES/BIB: An Annotated Bibliography of Child Language and Language Disorders* (Higginson & MacWhinney, 1991). It is associated with the CHILDES project, and it is available in electronic versions that CHILDES committed to updating every six months.

SUMMARY

Language development is a multidisciplinary field that has as its central question, How is language learned? Because language is highly complex yet universally acquired, the answer to this question has profound implications for understanding the essential nature of the human mind. The study of language development

Box 1.1   Major journals that publish research on language development

Developmental psychology journals:

Child Development

Cognitive Development

Developmental Psychology

Journal of Experimental Child Psychology

Merrill-Palmer Quarterly

Cognitive psychology journals:

Cognition

Cognitive Psychology

Linguistics journals:

Discourse Processes

Language

Psycholinguistic journals:

Applied Psycholinguistics

Journal of Psycholinguistic Research

Language development journals:

First Language

Journal of Child Language

Language Acquisition

(continued)

is also of practical importance for education, communicative disorders, and second language teaching.

Acquiring a language includes learning the sounds and sound patterns of the language (phonological development), learning the vocabulary of the language (lexical development), learning the structure of the language (grammatical, or morphosyntactic development), and learning how to use language to communicate (pragmatic and sociolinguistic development).

The study of language development has a long history because questions of how children's language emerges have long been considered central to larger

---

Box 1.1 *(continued)*

Language disorders journals:

American Journal of Speech-Language Pathology

Journal of Communicative Disorders

Journal of Speech and Hearing Disorders (This journal was combined with the *Journal of Speech and Hearing Research* in 1991.)

Journal of Speech and Hearing Research

Language, Speech, and Hearing Services in Schools

Neuroscience journals:

The Behavioral and Brain Sciences

Brain and Language

Cognitive Neuropsychology

Second-language learning journals:

Applied Linguistics

Language Learning

Second Language Research

Studies in Second Language Acquisition

Other specialized journals:

American Journal on Mental Retardation

Journal of Autism and Developmental Disorders

---

philosophical and scientific debates. These debates have concerned the intrinsic nature of humankind and the role of experience in shaping human nature. The modern study of language development (or **developmental psycholinguistics,** as the field is sometimes called) began in the 1960s following the Chomskyan revolution in linguistics. Chomsky's argument, which revolutionized the field of linguistics, was that the study of language is the study of the mind. In turn, the study of language development captured the interest of researchers interested in the study of the developing mind.

Language development is a field divided on several fault lines. The major points of disagreement are (1) whether language is largely innate in the child or learned from experience, (2) whether the mechanism that underlies language acquisition is specific to language or consists of general-purpose cognitive abilities applied to the task of learning language, and (3) whether the communicative functions that language serves (for children and adults) contribute to the process of acquisition or are merely a benefit of learning a formal system, whose acquisition is independent of the use to which it is put. Another issue that divides child language researchers concerns whether the most useful approach to understanding language development is to focus on children and ask how they acquire language (the developmental approach) or to focus on language and ask how it is acquired by children (the learnability approach).

Language development researchers make use of a variety of research methods and designs. Central to a great deal of research is the collection of speech samples from children for the purpose of characterizing the children's productive language. Collecting speech samples involves recording children as they talk, and transcribing and coding the recorded speech. There are computer programs available to help in that process. For some purposes, researchers may not need to collect new speech samples if their question can be addressed by examining the speech samples contained in the CHILDES archive. For descriptive and assessment purposes, a variety of norm-referenced tests and measures of language development are available.

Because language development is a multidisciplinary field, articles and chapters on language development appear in widely diverse sources. Most of these are indexed in one of two computer-accessible databases: *PsychLit* or *Linguistics and Language Behavior Abstracts.*

KEY TERMS

behaviorism

cognitivism

cognitive science

nature-nurture

empiricism

nativism

interactionism

language input

social interactionism

constructivism

language-specific

general cognitive

Universal Grammar

modularity

connectionism

formalist

functionalist

developmental approach

learnability approach

speech samples

CHILDES

Psychological Abstracts

Linguistics and Language Behavior Abstracts

Child Development Abstracts

PsychLit

developmental psycholinguistics

REVIEW QUESTIONS

1. Describe the role the study of language development plays in cognitive science and applied fields.

2. Learning a language involves learning in several separable domains. List and define these components of language knowledge.

3. What questions can be addressed by studying children who grow up without exposure to language?

4. What was the Chomskyan revolution, and why did it have an effect on the study of language development?

5. Define and contrast the nativist and interactionist views of language development.

6. What is the modularity hypothesis with respect to language development? What is the alternative?

7. Define and contrast formalism and functionalism as theories of language development.

8. Define and contrast the developmental and learnability approaches to the study of language development.

9. What can be learned from studying language development in other cultures and other language groups that cannot be learned from studying the acquisition of one language in one culture?

10. Imagine you had to explain to your skeptical family (or roommate, or somebody) why you are taking a whole course just on language development. How would you justify spending this much time on such a narrow topic?

2 Phonological Development: Learning the Sounds of Language

2½-year-old: I'm pweet.

Mother: (not comprehending) *You're pweet?*

2½-year-old: No, I'm puhweet.

Mother: (agreeing, but still not comprehending) *You're pweet.*

2½-year-old: (growing irritated) *I'm puuhweet.*

Mother: (finally getting it) *Oooh, you're sweet?*

2½-year-old: Yes, I'm sueweet.

PHONOLOGICAL KNOWLEDGE IN ADULTS

Spoken languages are systems that express meaning through sound. Adult speakers know the sounds their language uses and how those sounds are used to express meaning. This knowledge can be described separately from the knowledge speakers have of the words and the grammar of their language. Knowledge of the sounds and the sound system of a language is **phonological knowledge.** In this chapter, we begin our discussion of language development with children's development of phonological knowledge. To describe how children develop knowledge of their language's phonology, we should have some background on what it is that develops. Thus we begin this chapter by describing the basics of adults' phonological knowledge.

The sounds of language

What are speech sounds?   Speech sounds are the acoustic signals languages use to express meaning. Of all the possible noises humans can produce, some 100 are used in language, and no single language makes use of all 100. For example, English uses 45 different sounds. If you have studied a foreign language, you are probably painfully aware that other languages use sounds English does not, such as the vowel in the French word *tu* (which mean "you") or the middle consonant in the German word *sprechen* as in *Sprechen sie deutsch?* (which means, "Do you speak German?"). The Zulu language has 12 different clicks (for example, the sound spelled "tsk-tsk") in its sound inventory (Ruhlen, 1976). Just as some French vowels, German consonants, and Zulu clicks sound exotic to English-trained ears and are often difficult for English speakers to produce, some sounds of English are unfamiliar and difficult for speakers of other languages. English spoken with a French accent reveals that the *h* sound is unfamiliar to French speakers, and English spoken with a German accent reveals that the German does not use the *th* or *w* sounds of English.

How do speech sounds represent meaning?   The phonological differences among languages are not just in *what* sounds are used but also in *how* the sounds are used. In some languages, the tone with which a word is produced (such as high or low, rising or falling) is part of how the word is pronounced, and the same sound uttered in different tones can be different words. For example, in Mandarin [ba] produced with a high tone means "eight," and [ba] produced with a rising tone means "to pull" (Li & Thompson, 1977).

Sometimes different languages include the same sounds but use them differently with respect to conveying meaning. For example, in English, the sound represented by the letter *p* can take two different forms depending on where it is in a word. When you say the word *pill,* the *p* sound is accompanied by a burst of air coming out of your mouth. (The technical term for this is *aspiration,* and it is represented in phonetic transcription as [pʰ].) When you say the word *spill,* the *p* sound has no burst of air. (It is unaspirated and represented in phonetic transcription as [p]). You may have difficulty hearing this difference, but you can see it. Hold a piece of paper a few inches away from your lips, and say the two words. You will see the piece of paper move more when you say *pill.* Although English has both an aspirated and unaspirated *p,* the form *p* takes depends on the sound that precedes it, and English speakers automatically produce the correct form. There is never a case in which two words differ only in the use of [p] or [pʰ]. Because aspiration is never the basis for a contrast between two words, aspiration is not a **distinctive feature** in English; it does not carry meaning.

Thai, the language spoken in Thailand, also has an aspirated and an unaspirated *p,* but the kind of *p* used makes a difference in meaning. In Thai, the word pronounced [paa] means "forest," and the word pronounced [pʰaa] means "to split." In Thai, aspiration is a distinctive feature, and Thai speakers have control over the production of aspiration in a way English speakers do not. The proper technical way to describe this similarity and difference between English and Thai is to say that both languages have [p] and [pʰ] as phones, but only in Thai are /p/ and /pʰ/ different phonemes. **Phones** are the different sounds a language uses; **phonemes** are the meaningfully different sounds in a given language. **Allophones** are phones that do not differentiate meaning; in English, [p] and [pʰ] are allophones. One task for the language learning child is to figure out which sounds of the language signal meaning distinctions and which do not.

Phonological rules

As a competent speaker, you not only know the sounds your language uses, you also know rules for how these sounds go together. For example, if you came across the words *kpakali* or *zloty,* you would not have to look them up in a dictionary to know that they are not English words. In English, the sequences *kp* and *zl* are not permitted. In other languages they are, however. In many West African languages, *kp* is not only permitted, but frequent. In Polish, *zl* is a permissible combination. In fact, *kpakali* is the word for a three-legged stool in the West African language, Mende (O'Grady, Dobrovolsky, & Aronoff, 1989), and *zloty* is a Polish word that refers to a unit of currency (Fromkin & Rodman, 1988).

Adult speakers' knowledge of English's phonological properties includes more than knowing that *kpakali* and *zloty* are not possible words. It includes rules that all native speakers follow when they talk, even though most adults would claim not to "know" anything about phonology. For example, say the words *bugs* and *bikes* aloud, and pay close attention to the final sound in each word. (Putting your fingers on your throat will help you become aware of the difference between the two final sounds.) The final sound in *bugs* is actually [z], and the final sound in *bikes* is [s]. The difference between the [z] and [s] is that your vocal cords vibrate as you produce [z] but not as you produce [s]. That is why your throat feels different to the touch as you produce the two sounds. This feature of sound production is called **voicing.** The [z] sound is voiced; [s] is voiceless.

We can demonstrate that the reason you produced two different sounds at the ends of *bugs* and *bikes* is that you were following a phonological rule of English—not that you have just memorized the different plural forms of *bug* and *bike*. If you were presented with a made-up word, such as *wug,* and were asked for the plural form, you would know to say *wug* + [z]. What you know is that the plural of a word is formed by adding one of the sounds represented by the letter *s,* and that the way *s* is pronounced depends on the sound that precedes it. You are consciously aware of the first bit of knowledge, but you are not aware of the second.

Stated in phonological terms, the second bit of knowledge is a rule that *s* is pronounced [s] after all voiceless consonants and pronounced [z] after all voiced sounds. In fact, this regularity is one example of a larger regularity in English. When two consonants are together in a word, they match in terms of voicing. So you have words with [k] and [s] next to each other in the middle of the word, such as *biscuit* and *trickster,* and words with [g] and [z] next to each other, such as the gangster nickname *Bugsy.* But it is rare to have a voiced and a voiceless consonant together, except in a compound word such as *dovetail* (Gleitman, Cassidy, Massey, & Schmidt, 1995).

It is interesting that children know this phonological property of English at an early age. In a very famous experiment, Jean Berko (1958) presented children with novel words like *wug* and *rick* and found that, by the age of 4, children were able to correctly indicate that the plural of *wug* was *wug* + [z] and that the past tense of *rick* was *rick* + [t]. (Following [k] with [t] rather than with [d] is another example of matching in terms of voicing. In contrast, the past tense of *rig* is *rig* + [d].) Children have been observed to obey this rule even when they get the rest of the word wrong. For example, children commonly have trouble producing the word *spaghetti,* and they frequently transform the first syllable from *spa* to *pas.* Often when they do this—although not always—the *s* gets pronounced [z], so the resulting word is *pazghetti.* Thus the word is not quite right, but the voicing rule is observed.

To summarize, when adults know a language, they know, among other things, what sounds their language uses, what sound distinctions signal meaning distinctions, and what sound sequences are possible. In discussing phonological development, we will be asking when children acquire this knowledge that adult speakers have and how they acquire it.

To answer the question of when children acquire phonological knowledge, we will describe the course of phonological development for both perception and production. Because phonological development begins well before children start to talk, we will begin by describing infants' perceptual and productive abilities. Phonological development continues after speech begins, and therefore our description of phonological development will continue past infancy into the second and third years of life, when children are producing words and rudimentary sentences.

In an attempt to answer the question of how children acquire the phonology of their language, we will describe what we know about the various factors that influence the course of phonological development. A recurring question concerns how much of the course of development is maturational and how much is influenced by children's experience with language. Finally, we will consider models that have been proposed to account for the process of phonological development. Before we can pursue these topics, however, we need to lay some groundwork for talking about speech sounds.

DESCRIBING SPEECH SOUNDS

Phonetics

As should be obvious by now, the letters of the alphabet are not adequate for describing speech sounds. (Remember, the letter *s* can be pronounced [z] or [s].) What we need is an alphabet in which each symbol can be pronounced only one way and every sound has its own symbol. The phonetic alphabet is just such a system. When a word is spelled in the phonetic alphabet, everyone who knows that alphabet can figure out how the word is pronounced, even if they do not know the language and have never heard the word before. When a word is being spelled phonetically, the standard is to enclose it in square brakets; so the English word *pill* is represented as [pʰɪl] and *spill* is [spɪl].

Phonemics

Often in describing how words sound, it is sufficient to indicate just the sounds that are phonemes. So in English, for example, information about aspiration could be left out. The standard way to indicate that phonemic transcription is being used is to use slashes. So the English word *pill* is represented as /pɪl/, and *spill* as /spɪl/. Table 2.1 presents the phonemic symbols for the sounds of American English.

Phonetic features

Speech sounds can be described in terms of their physical properties, such as frequency and amplitude, just as other acoustic signals can. Speech sounds can also be described in terms of how they are produced. Research on phonological development makes reference to both sorts of descriptions, but it relies more on the latter, known as **articulatory phonetics.** Using articulatory phonetics, it is possible to describe the 40-plus sounds of English (and also the roughly 100

36

Table 2.1   Phonemic symbols for the sounds of American English

		Consonants				Vowels		
/p/	pill	/t/	toe	/g/	gill	/i/	beet	/ı/	bit
/b/	bill	/d/	doe	/ŋ/	ring	/e/	bait	/ɛ/	bet
/m/	mill	/n/	no	/h/	hot	/u/	boot	/ʊ/	foot
/f/	fine	/s/	sink	/ʔ/	uh-oh	/o/	boat	/ɔ/	caught
/v/	vine	/z/	zinc	/l/	low	/æ/	bat	/a/	pot
/θ/	thigh	/c/	choke	/r/	row	/ʌ/	but	/ə/	sofa
/ð/	thy	/j/	joke	/j/	you	/aı/	bite	/au/	out
/s/	shoe	/k/	kill	/w/	win	/ɔı/	boy		
/z/	treasure								

sounds of all languages) as combinations of a smaller number of features of the articulatory mechanism that produces those sounds. These features are called **phonetic features.** For example, [z] and [s] differ in terms of voicing but are the same in terms of every other feature. As you produce [z] and [s], you can feel that your teeth, lips, and tongue stay in the same place; the only thing that changes is what you do with your vocal cords. Many other pairs of consonants differ only in voicing, such as [d] and [t] and [g] and [k]. (The fact that different speech sounds can be made without changing the position of the lips limits how useful lip reading can be.) Voicing is not the only feature that differentiates speech sounds. Because we will need to talk about the relations among different sounds in order to talk about children's phonological development, we need, at this point, to present additional information about phonetic features.

A basic distinction among speech sounds is between consonants and vowels. When you produce a consonant, the flow of air from your lungs through your mouth is obstructed somewhere along the line. In contrast, when you produce a vowel, the air flow is unobstructed. (That's why you can sing a vowel for as long your breath lasts.) There are also distinctions among sounds within the class of consonants and within the class of vowels that can be described in terms of how the sounds are produced. (We will focus here on consonants.)

Consonants differ both in where the vocal tract is closed (this feature is **place of articulation**) and in how the vocal tract is closed (this feature is **manner of articulation**). So, for example, in producing consonants like [b] and

Table 2.2   Classification of the consonant phonemes of American English

	PLACE OF ARTICULATION						
	Bilabial	*Labiodental*	*Interdental*	*Alveolar*	*Palatal*	*Velar*	*Glottal*
Manner of Articulation							
Stop (oral)							
voiceless unaspirated	p			t		k	ʔ
voiced	b			d		g	
Nasal (stop)	m			n		ŋ	
Fricative							
voiceless		f	θ	s	š		
voiced		v	ð	z	ž		
Affricate							
voiceless					č		
voiced					ǰ		
Glide							
voiceless						ʍ	h
voiced					j	w	
Liquid				l r			

[d], the airflow is completely stopped for a moment, and these consonants are called **stops.** In contrast, in producing [f] and [s], the airflow is not completely stopped; these are called **fricatives.** Although [b] and [d] share the property of being stops, they differ in where the airflow is stopped. To make [b] you put your two lips together; [b] is called a bilabial (i.e., two lips) stop. To make [d], you stop the airflow by placing your tongue against the ridge behind your front teeth. This ridge is called the alveolar ridge, and [d] is called an alveolar stop. Similarly adding place features to our description of [f] and [s], we would say that [f] is a labiodental (lip and teeth) fricative, and [s] is an alveolar fricative. All the consonants of English can be classified by how and where the airflow is obstructed. This system of classification is presented in Table 2.2.

We should understand one last distinction among consonants before we talk about children's phonological development: the now familiar distinction between voiced and voiceless sounds. As you can see in Table 2.2, two different consonants such as [b] and [d] sometimes have the same manner and place of articulation. The difference between them is in voicing. Voicing refers to the time the vocal cords start vibrating relative to the release of air. [p] is called voiceless because the vocal cords do not start to vibrate until after the lips have released air whereas in producing the voiced sound [b], the vocal cords start vibrating before air is released. Knowing that there is a system underlying how different speech sounds differ from each other is necessary for understanding phonological rules such as the voicing rule described earlier, and it will be important later in describing the systematic nature of children's early attempts at word production.

There is more to describing the sound of a language than simply describing the properties of individual sound segments (such as /p/, /ɪ/, /l/) and how these segments are sequenced in words. Languages also have meter (most obvious in the rhythm of poetry) and prosodic qualities (like the melody in music). Later, we discuss prosodic development in infancy, but the focus of this chapter is on the development of segmental phonology. (Readers who are interested in a more thorough introductionh to metrical and prosodic phonology as applied to child language are referred to Demuth, 1993, 1996; Dresher, 1996; Selkirk, 1996; and references therein.)

PRELINGUISTIC SPEECH SOUND DEVELOPMENT

Although children do not produce speech until they are approximately 1 year old, the development of the ability to produce speech sounds begins in early infancy, and important developments in speech sound production occur throughout the first year of life. The next sections will describe the changes that occur during this period of prespeech vocal development, using Stark's (1986) five-stage division of this period.

Stages of prespeech vocal development

Reflexive crying and vegetative sounds   Newborns cry. They also burp, sneeze, and may make a few other sounds that accompany the biological functions of breathing, sucking, and so on. In crying and in making these **vegetative sounds,** the infant's vocal cords vibrate, and the airflow through the vocal apparatus is stopped and started. Thus, even these unpromising sounds include some features that will later be used to produce speech sounds.

Cooing and laughter   At around 6 to 8 weeks of age, infants start **cooing.** Coos are sounds that babies make when they appear to be happy and contented. Social interaction in particular seems to elicit cooing. The first coos that infants make sound like one long vowel. Infants continue to produce cooing noises for many more months, and the quality of these coos changes with age. One change is that infants start to produce a variety of different vowel sounds. Another change is that, instead of producing a single vowel, the infant produces a series of different vowel sounds strung together but separated by intakes of breath. Although the infant isn't talking yet, more features of speech sounds are present in these prespeech vocalizations. Babies produce their first laughter around the age of 16 weeks.

Vocal play   The period between 16 weeks and 30 weeks has been called the period of **vocal play** (Stark, 1986), or the **expansion stage** (Oller, 1980). During this stage, the variety of different consonant and vowel sounds that infants produce increases. Infants seem to gain increasing control over the production of their growing repertoires of sounds, and they combine their different sounds into increasingly long and complex series. The long series of sounds that infants produce by the end of this expansion stage have been called **marginal babbling.** Other noises that infants produce during this period include squeals, growls, and a variety of "friction noises."

Because infants produce a wide variety of sounds that are not in the language spoken by adults around them, it was thought at one time that infants start out producing all the sounds in all the world's languages (Jakobson, 1941-1968). That turns out not to be true, however. In fact, the infant's repertoire is initially quite limited. In the first couple of months, the only recognizable speech sounds that infants produce are vowels. The first recognizable consonants are heard at around 2 to 3 months of age, and they tend to be the ones produced in the back of the mouth (velars), such as [g] and [k]. (So babies really do say "goo goo," although the vowel sound is not quite that distinct.) Around 6 months of age, infants start to produce consonants articulated in the front of the mouth, such as [m], [n], [p], [b], and [d]; and infants may stop producing the back consonants for a while (Ingram, 1989; McCarthy, 1954).

Reduplicated babbling   Sometime around 6 to 9 months of age, the quality of infants' vocalizations changes, and the infants start to babble. Technically speaking, what emerges is **canonical babbling** (Oller, 1986; Oller & Lynch, 1992). Canonical babbling is distinguished from the vocalizations that precede it by the presence of true syllables, and these syllables are typically produced in reduplicated series of the same consonant + vowel combination, such as [dada] or [nənənə]. Babies don't necessarily produce this **reduplicated babbling,** as it is sometimes called, in order to communicate (Stark, 1986). Babies will sit in their cribs or car seats and babble up a storm and show no evidence that they expect any reply at all.

The appearance of canonical babbling is a major landmark in the infant's prespeech development. All babies babble, and they begin to babble somewhere between 6 and 9 months of age. However, deaf infants do not produce canonical babbling (Oller, Eilers, Bull, & Carney, 1985). Deaf infants do produce sounds, and the sounds they produce are not noticeably different from the sounds hearing infants produce up to this point. Canonical babbling is the first development that distinguishes the vocal development of hearing children from that of deaf children.

Nonreduplicated babbling The appearance of canonical babbling is followed by a period of **nonreduplicated** or **variegated babbling.** During this period, the range of consonants and vowels infants produce expands further. Also, infants combine different consonant + vowel and consonant + vowel + consonant syllables into series, unlike the repetitive series that characterized the first canonical babbling. **Prosody**—the intonation contour of speech—becomes particularly noticeable at the stage of variegated babbling. Once prosody is added to the string of nonreduplicated babbles produced at this stage, infants sound as though they are speaking—until you listen closely and realize that the infant is producing the melody of language without the words. These wordless sentences are often referred to as **jargon.** Some infants produce much more jargon than others do, and some infants spend much longer in this stage than others do. Dore (1974) refers to children who produce a great deal of jargon and who do so for a long time as "intonation babies." In contrast, he refers to children who produce relatively little jargon and who move quickly on to learning the words to the tune as "word babies." An average time frame for children's prespeech vocal development is shown in Box 2.1.

Influence of the target language on babbling

Even babies who are babbling and not yet talking show that they are already learning to produce their particular target language. There is evidence that both the prosodic contour of babbling and the consonants and vowels babies produce when babbling are influenced by the language the babies have been hearing. Two techniques have been used in providing this evidence. One technique is to use the judgments of competent speakers to determine whether they can tell the differences among the babblings of babies who are acquiring different languages. This technique can tell you that differences in the babblings depend on the target language, but it cannot tell you *how* they are different. The other technique is to record babblings of children who are acquiring different languages and analyze them for the presence and frequency of features in the respective adult languages. This technique can potentially tell you not only whether babbling differs depending on target language but also how it differs.

Box 2.1   Milestones of prespeech vocal development

*Approximate
age in weeks*

0	BIRTH	reflexive crying and vegetative sounds
4		
8		cooing
12		
16		laughter; vocal play begins
20		
24		
28		
32		
36		reduplicated (canonical) babbling
40		
44		
48		nonreduplicated babbling
52	FIRST WORD	

Source: Based on Stark, 1986.

Using the first technique, de Boysson-Bardies, Sagart, and Durand (1984) found that French speakers could tell the difference between French babies' babbling and Arabic or Chinese babies' babbling. The researchers tape-recorded French babies, Arabic babies, and Chinese babies who were 6, 8, and 10 months old. Fifteen-second segments of babbling were isolated from these recordings. Then the recordings were presented to French speakers in pairs of either French and Arabic babies' babbling or French and Chinese babies' babbling. The French speakers were asked to judge which sample of each pair came from a French baby. French speakers were able to make that judgment at better than chance levels on the basis of the recordings of 8-month-olds. (They were correct about 70% of the time.) Trained phoneticians, who presumably are better at noticing differences between sounds, were able to make the discrimination from recordings of 6-month-olds. Interestingly, the recordings of the 10-month-olds were harder to tell apart. De Boysson-Bardies and colleagues concluded that this difficulty arises because in the more advanced babbling of the 10-month-olds, the consonant sounds are more noticeable. Thus the prosodic characteristics that differentiate the babbling of children acquiring different languages were less noticeable to the listeners. What the researchers are suggesting, as have others (Crystal, 1986), is that children learn to produce the melody of their language before they learn to produce their language's particular sounds, and it is easier to notice the melody in 8-month-olds' babbles than in 10-month-olds' babbles.

Using the second technique of actually analyzing the sounds in babies' babbling, researchers working in different countries have found that the particular vowels and consonants in babbling also differ depending on characteristics of the language spoken by others in the infants' environments. This fact can be observed in babies as young as 9 months of age (de Boysson-Bardies, Halle, Sagart, & Durand, 1989; de Boysson-Bardies, et al., 1992). For example, analysis of adults' productions of words infants are likely to hear showed that Japanese and French words contain more nasal sounds than Swedish and English words do, and analysis of the babies' babbling showed that Japanese and French babies use more nasal sounds in their babbling than Swedish and English babies do. De Boysson-Bardies and colleagues (1992) also consider it relevant that children start showing signs of understanding some words around the time when their babbling starts to show an influence of the sounds in the target language. The researchers conclude that babies pay attention to sounds that refer to things in their environment and that the sounds babies notice influence the sounds they produce.

Speech sounds at the end of the babbling stage

By the end of the babbling stage, children have made great progress from their first vowels to an increasingly large repertoire of consonants to knowing something about the prosody and sound patterns of their target language. However, phonological development is far from complete at the end of the babbling period. Just 11 different consonants, [h, w, j, p, b, m, t, d, n, k, g], account for about 90% of the consonant sounds produced by 12-month-olds who are acquiring American English, and children exposed to other languages have similar—although not identical—sound repertoires (Locke & Pearson, 1992). Children acquiring English rarely form consonant clusters, for example [kl] or [pr]. Also, some vowels are more likely to be produced than others. The vowels [ʌ], [ə], and [æ] are more frequent than [i] or [u] (Vihman, 1988). Another difference between the sounds children produce at this stage and the words in the target language is that children's vocalizations at this point are most frequently single syllables, with some two-syllable productions.

The transition from babbling to words

For many children, there is a transitional phase between babbling and the appearance of the first word. During this transitional period, children produce their own invented words. These invented words are sound sequences children use with consistent meanings but that bear no discernible resemblance to the sound of any word in the target language. Several researchers have discussed these transitional forms and have given them various labels, including **protowords** (Bates, 1976), sensorimotor morphemes (Carter, 1978), quasi-words (Stoel-Gammon & Cooper, 1984), and phonetically consistent forms (Dore, Franklin, Miller, & Ramer, 1976).

These transitional forms often express broad meanings, and their use tends either to be tightly bound to particular contexts or to serve particular functions. Sometimes, but certainly not always, the source of the child's invented "word" can be traced, such as a child's approximation of *yum yum* as a label for food. Sometimes a particular gesture is part of these transitional forms. For example, pointing gestures often accompany a sound that has the general meaning "I want" or "Give me." Sometimes the whole "word" is nonverbal. For example, "one 11-month-old child who observed adults blowing gently on the mobile above his crib apparently associated that gesture with the affective meaning 'delight' or 'wonder' and began using it to express that meaning; for example, he began blowing softly as he approached a Christmas tree" (Vihman, 1988a, p. 90).

To this point, we have described the course of vocal development over roughly the first year of the child's life. At the end of their first year, children typically have not really begun to talk, but much of what they will need to produce the words of their language is in place. That is, prior to the beginning of speech, children have developed the ability to produce many of the sounds speech requires.

Processes underlying infants' development of speech sounds

Three factors contribute to changes we see in infants' vocalizations over the first year of life: the physical growth of the vocal tract, the development of the brain and other neurological structures responsible for vocalization, and experience (Stark, 1986).

Physical growth and development   The newborn infant's vocal tract is not only smaller than the adult's, it is also shaped differently. For example, the tongue fills the entire mouth, severely limiting its range of motion. Growth of the facial skeleton during the period of vocal play gives the tongue more room and quite probably contributes to the increased variety of sounds infants can make at this time. Also during this period, the muscles of the vocal tract are maturing, and the sensory receptors in the vocal tract are changing. These changes also may contribute to an increase in the infant's control over sound production. Some have suggested that the vocal play of this stage is the result of the infant's exploring what this apparatus can do and exercising it.

Nervous system maturation   The cries and many of the vegetative sounds newborns make are controlled by very primitive structures in the brain stem. The fact that later neurological developments in higher brain structures happen at the same age as some developments in vocalization suggests that nervous system maturation is responsible for changes in infant vocalization. In particular, the onset of cooing at 6 to 8 weeks of age coincides with the beginning of functioning of some areas of the limbic system. This coincidence suggests a causal connection because the limbic area of the brain is associated with the expression of emotion in both humans and lower animals, and cooing tends to accompany a particular emotional state—contentedness. Further maturation of the limbic system may underlie the development of laughter at around 16 weeks. The maturation of still higher levels of the brain—areas of the motor cortex—may be required for the onset of canonical babbling at 6 to 9 months.

Experience   Two sorts of experience also play roles in shaping the course of prespeech phonological development. One experience is hearing the speech adults produce. Evidence that the ambient language influences prespeech vocal development consists of findings (discussed earlier) that both the speech segments (the phones) and the prosodic character of late babbling differ among babies, depending on the language they hear, and both have features of the target language. The other experience that contributes to prespeech vocal development is infants' experience hearing their own vocal output. In vocal play, infants seem to be discovering the correspondence between what they do with their vocal apparatus and the sounds that come out (Kuhl & Meltzoff, 1988). The absence of auditory feedback may explain why deaf infants produce less elaborate vocal play than hearing infants do and may help explain why deaf infants never reach the stage of canonical babbling (Oller et al., 1985).

PRELINGUISTIC SPEECH PERCEPTION

Human language and human perception

For languages to express different meanings with different sound sequences, the human users of those languages not only must be able to produce the different sounds, they also must be able to perceive those differences. For example, for a language such as English to encode different meanings with the words *pill* and *bill,* humans must be able to hear the difference between [p] and [b]. For students of language development, this fact raises the following question: Does learning English involve learning to hear the difference between [p] and [b], or can babies already hear that difference, and then use that ability in acquiring English?

Infants must have some capacity to make discriminations among speech sounds or they would never be able to get started on the language acquisition process. However, some learning must also be involved, because adults who are learning a second language often have difficulty with sound discriminations their native language does not require. Finding out just what the perceptual abilities of the infant are and how those perceptual abilities are affected by exposure to a particular language has been the focus of approximately 25 years of research on infant speech perception. The next sections review that research, beginning with the most basic question of what infants can hear.

Infants' hearing

Making discriminations among sounds in the ambient language depends, of course, on being able to hear the speech others produce. At one time, it was thought that babies were blind and deaf at birth and that basic sensory abilities matured only later. We now know that this is incorrect. Infants' hearing is not quite as sensitive as adults', but it is certainly adequate for hearing speech from the time infants are born (Kuhl, 1987). In fact, the auditory system is functioning in the fetus even before birth. There are two kinds of evidence to support this claim. One is that the fetus will move in utero in response to external sound (Kuhl, 1987). (Some pregnant women report that their babies were particularly active during concerts the women attended—although if this were the only evidence, we might be suspicious that internal responses in the mothers were the cause of the fetal activity.) The second indication that the fetus can perceive external sound is evidence that newborns have been affected by sounds that were in their environment before they were born.

In one study, DeCasper and Fifer (1980) found that newborns (less than 24 hours old) preferred hearing their mother's voice over hearing an unfamiliar female voice, and the researchers suggested that auditory experience before birth may be the explanation for that preference. (We will get to the methodological question of how infants demonstrate their preferences in the next section.) In another experiment, DeCasper and Spence (1986) demonstrated that newborns can indicate that they remember what they heard before birth. DeCasper and Spence had pregnant women read a particular passage aloud every day during the last 6 weeks of their pregnancy. When the babies were tested a few days after birth, these babies showed a preference for hearing that familiar passage over hearing a novel passage. A control group of newborns, whose mothers had not read either passage before their birth, responded equally to both passages.

Last, and what is perhaps most amazing, Mehler and his colleagues demonstrated that newborns can distinguish utterances in their native language from utterances in another language (Mehler et al., 1988). In this study, babies born to French-speaking mothers heard tapes of French and Russian speech, and the babies' sucking rate—as an indicator of their levels of arousal—was measured as they listened to the tapes. The babies showed more arousal when they heard French than when they heard Russian. When babies of mothers who spoke a language other than French or Russian were played the French and Russian tapes, these babies showed no difference in arousal to the two tapes. The results of this study suggest that French and Russian are not intrinsically different in how interesting they are to babies. However, if one language is familiar, it is more interesting, and newborns show evidence of familiarity with the particular language their mothers spoke.

The foregoing evidence suggests that babies hear speech before birth, they remember something about what they hear, and the something they remember distinguishes different target languages. The question then is, what do they hear and remember? The uterus is a noisy environment, and the fetus is surrounded by fluid—not exactly ideal listening conditions. The answer seems to be that babies hear and remember the prosodic contours of the speech their mothers produce while the babies were in utero. As evidence that prosodic cues are what distinguished French from Russian for the infants in the preceding study, when the French and Russian speech samples were filtered so that only the prosodic cues remained, the main findings of the study were replicated (Mehler et al., 1988). Having established that infants can hear speech, we can move to the question of what speech sounds infants can discriminate.

Studying infants' perception

Finding out what babies can discriminate is a tricky business; we obviously cannot just ask them. However, child language researchers have been very inventive in designing experimental procedures that reveal when babies perceive two sounds as different from each other. The two most widely used procedures are the *high-amplitude sucking technique* and the *head-turn technique.*

The high-amplitude sucking (HAS) technique The **high-amplitude sucking technique,** or **HAS,** makes use of three characteristics of babies: (1) babies like to hear sounds, (2) babies lose interest in a sound when it is presented repeatedly, and (3) babies who have lost interest in a previously repeated sound will become interested if a new sound is presented. Thus to find out whether babies can tell the difference between two sounds, researchers present one sound until the baby loses interest, and then they present another. If the baby shows renewed interest, the researchers infer that the baby can tell that a new sound has been presented.

In the HAS procedure, interest is measured by the baby's willingness to "work" to hear the sound played over a speaker. The "work" babies do consists of sucking on a nipple attached to a device that measures the pressure produced by the sucking. Every time the baby sucks with sufficient vigor, a sound is presented. After a while, the baby's rate of sucking declines; this apparent loss of interest is referred to as **habituation.** Once the infant demonstrates

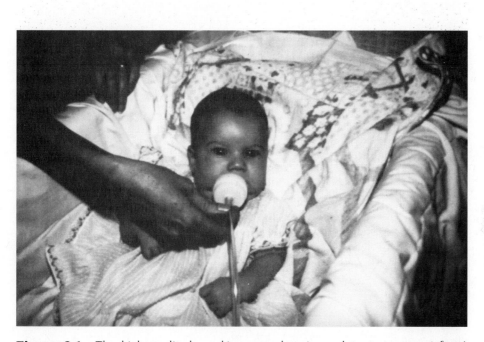

Figure 2.1 The high-amplitude sucking procedure is used to test young infants' perception of speech sounds. A sound is presented to the infant contingent on the infant's sucking with sufficient strength on a blind nipple. As the infant becomes bored, sucking declines, at which point a new sound is presented. If the infant begins to suck more, the inference is drawn that the infant perceived the new sound as different from the old.

habituation to the first sound, a new speech sound is played over the speaker, and the baby typically starts sucking more rapidly. This renewed interested is referred to as **dishabituation.** The sucking rate after the shift is compared to the sucking rate of a control group of babies who continue to hear the same sound. If the postshift sucking rate is higher for babies who heard a new stimulus than for the control babies, we conclude that babies can tell the difference. Figure 2.1 shows a baby whose sucking rate is being tested. An example of the kind of data produced by this procedure is illustrated in Figure 2.2.

One potential drawback to the HAS procedure is that, if the baby does not increase its sucking rate, the researchers can't know whether the baby was unable to make the discrimination or was just uninterested in the new sound, uninterested in the whole procedure, crying, sleeping, or doing other things that babies are wont to do. For this reason, a number of babies are usually tested, and the average sucking rate of babies who hear a new sound is compared to the average sucking rate of babies who hear the same sound continuously.

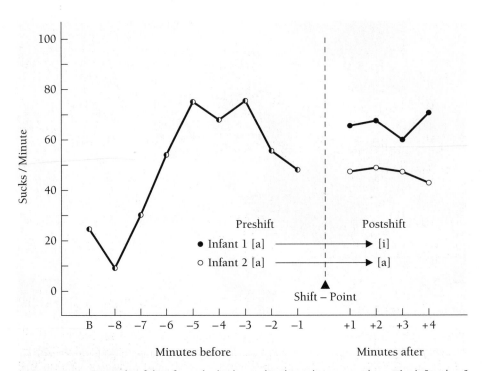

Figure 2.2   Example of data from the high-amplitude sucking procedure. The left side of the figure shows the average number of sucking responses for two infants presented with the sound [a]. The right side of the figure shows separately the sucking responses for the Experimental infant who was presented with [i] and the Control infant who continued to be presented with [a].

Source: From "Speech Perception in Early Infancy," by P. K. Kuhl. In S. K. Hirsh et al. (Eds.), Hearing and Davis: Essays Honoring Hallowell Davis, pp. 265–280. Copyright © 1976 Central Institute for the Deaf. Reprinted by permission.

Another problem with HAS is that it doesn't work very well with babies older than 4 months. Older babies get restless in the infant seat and tend not to be as interested in sucking on a nipple (Kuhl, 1987).

The head-turn technique   The second procedure for testing speech sound discrimination in infants is the **head-turn technique,** which is pictured in Figure 2.3. It is typically used with babies between 5½ and 12 months old. This procedure makes use of the fact that babies are interested in a moving toy, such as a monkey that claps cymbals together. Using the presentation of the moving toy as a reward, babies can be trained to turn their heads when they hear a change in a sound being presented. First, a sound is played over and over and then the sound is changed, followed by activation of the toy monkey who is

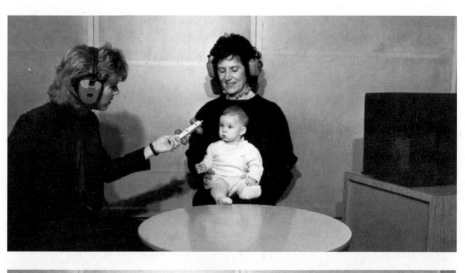

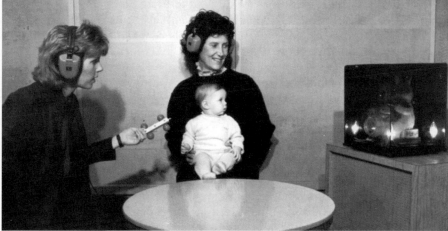

Figure 2.3 The head-turn procedure is used to test perception of speech sounds in infants older than 5½ months. Using easily discriminable sounds, researchers train the infant to turn her head when the sound being broadcast in the testing room changes. Once the infant is so trained, the infant's producing a head turn when the sound is changed is taken as evidence that the infant perceived the new sound as different from the old.

otherwise concealed behind dark plexiglass. The babies turn to look at the monkey when it is activated. After several trials, when the sound being presented changes, the babies turn their heads toward the place where the monkey will appear even before it's activated.

Babies are trained using sound pairs that we know they can discriminate, and then they are presented new sound pairs to see whether they can discriminate the new contrast. Babies sit on their mothers' laps for this procedure, but the mothers wear headsets to prevent them from hearing the sounds and inadvertently providing cues to the babies. A researcher is also in the testing room to get the baby's attention between trials so that the baby isn't already looking toward where the toy will appear before the stimuli are presented. Using primarily the high-amplitude sucking and head-turn procedures, child language researchers have learned a great deal about what discriminations babies can make among the speech sounds they hear.

Infants' discrimination of speech sounds

The results of 25 years of work testing infants' abilities to discriminate speech sounds are easy to summarize. Infants can discriminate essentially all the sound contrasts languages make use of. For example, infants as young as 4 weeks old can discriminate vowel contrasts such as /u/ versus /i/ and /i/ versus /a/ (Trehub, 1973) and consonant contrasts such as /p/ versus /b/ and /d/ versus /g/ (for a summary, see Kuhl, 1976). Furthermore, infants' discrimination abilities are language-general; they include the ability to discriminate contrasts not used in the ambient language. For example, English-learning babies can discriminate vowel contrasts that are present in French but not in English (Trehub, 1976), and they can discriminate consonant contrasts that are present in Hindi but not in English (Werker, Gilbert, Humphrey, & Tees, 1981). Many studies have established the range of infant perceptual abilities using contrasts from many different languages (for summaries, see Goodman & Nusbaum, 1994; Werker & Polka, 1993).

Categorical perception

One feature of infants' speech perception was the focus of intensive research during the 1960s and 1970s: infants' tendency to perceive some consonants categorically. So, for example, listeners hear one range of acoustic signals all as /p/ and a different range of acoustic signals all as /b/, but no acoustic signal is perceived as something in between a /p/ and a /b/. This phenomenon of categorical perception, more properly termed the *phoneme boundary effect,* was first discovered in adult perception and then investigated in infants. The next sections will describe the phenomenon, first as it is demonstrated in adults, and then as it has been observed in infants.

Categorical perception in adults   Demonstrating the phenomenon of **categorical perception** requires two steps. In the first step, stimuli are constructed to vary along an acoustic continuum. One example of an acoustic continuum is the one that differentiates /p/ from /b/. The difference between /p/ and /b/ is in the duration of the time lag between air passing through the lips and the vocal cords vibrating when producing a syllable. This lag is called

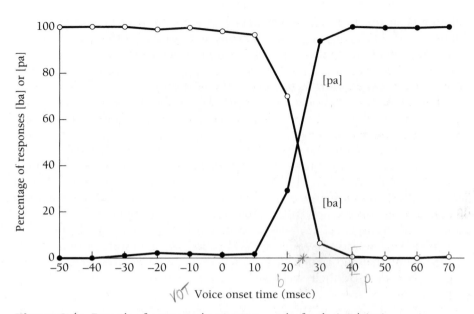

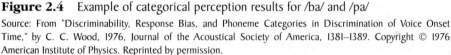

Figure 2.4 Example of categorical perception results for /ba/ and /pa/

Source: From "Discriminability, Response Bias, and Phoneme Categories in Discrimination of Voice Onset Time," by C. C. Wood, 1976, Journal of the Acoustical Society of America, 1381–1389. Copyright © 1976 American Institute of Physics. Reprinted by permission.

voice onset time (VOT). For /b/, the lag is very short—about 15 milliseconds (msec). For /p/, the lag is longer, closer to 100 msec. By using a computer, it is possible to artificially create sounds that vary along this VOT continuum, producing sounds in which the lag is 0, 20 msec, 40 msec, 60 msec, and so on. When these sounds are played to adults who then report what they hear, everything with a VOT of less than 25 msec is perceived as /b/, and everything with a VOT of more than 40 msecs is perceived as /p/. In fact, there is very little variation among listeners; the **phoneme boundary** between /b/ and /p/ is at about 25 msec VOT. This response pattern is depicted in Figure 2.4.

In the second step of the procedure, pairs of these artificially synthesized stimuli are played to adults who judge whether the two sounds in a pair are the same or different. Sometimes the two sounds really are identical; sometimes they differ by 20-msec VOT. The different pairs are taken from throughout the VOT continuum, so the adult judges are required to discriminate the 0-msec from the 20-msec sound, the 20 from the 40, the 40 from the 60, and so on. The result that emerges from such studies is that adults cannot distinguish between 0 and 20-msec VOT or between 40 and 60 VOT, but they can distinguish between 20 and 40 VOT. It seems, then, that not all 20-msec intervals are equal. Adults cannot detect a 20-msec difference within a phonemic category, but they can detect a 20-msec difference across a phoneme boundary. The phenomenon illustrated in the first step is categorical perception, and the phenomenon illustrated in the second step is the **phoneme boundary effect,** although the term *categorical perception* is frequently used to refer to both.

Categorical perception in infants   The next question asked in the course of research on this phenomenon was whether infants also exhibit categorical perception. In a now classic experiment using the HAS procedure, Eimas, Siqueland, Jusczyk, and Vigorito (1971) demonstrated that <u>infants do show categorical perception.</u> The researchers played artificially synthesized syllables to 1- and 4-month-old babies in three different conditions. In the first condition, babies habituated to a 20-msec VOT sound and then were presented with a 40-msec VOT sound. Babies in this condition increased their sucking when the new sound was presented. (Remember the phoneme boundary between /b/ and /p/ is 25 msec.) In the second condition, babies habituated to either a −20-msec VOT sound or a +60-msec VOT sound and then were presented with a new sound that had a 20-msec longer VOT lag. Babies in this group did not significantly increase their sucking. In a third control condition, babies were

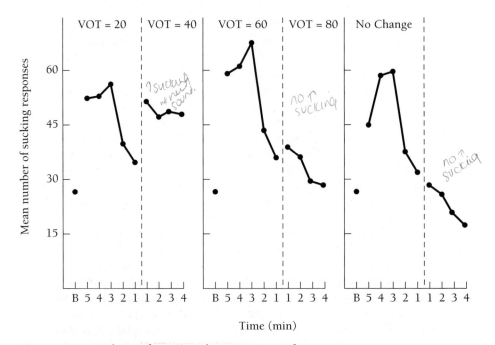

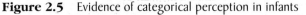

Figure 2.5   Evidence of categorical perception in infants

presented with the same sound even after they had habituated to it, and no increase in sucking occurred. These findings are depicted in Figure 2.5. They suggest that babies perceive the VOT continuum the same way that adults do. Everything on one side of the 25-msec boundary is perceived as one sound; everything on the other side is perceived as a different sound. These results suggest that infants sort sounds into phonemic categories, and they do so with little, if any, experience.

The significance of categorical perception   The initial discovery of categorical perception for speech sounds led to the claim that speech perception is special because, for most physical continua, perception does not change abruptly at some point, and the ability to perceive a difference between two stimuli does not change abruptly in the middle of the continuum. For example, if there were categorical perception for the pitch of a sound, it would be as if the first 44 notes on a piano were perceived as "low" and the second 44 notes perceived as "high," and the only difference you could detect was between notes on the "low" side and notes on the "high" side. Categorical perception of the VOT continuum packages sound into the categories relevant for speech.

For a while, the finding that even babies perceived VOT categorically was taken as strong evidence that human babies come into the world specially prepared to acquire language. The claim was made that language is unique among human abilities and humans have evolved mechanisms, including perceptual mechanisms, that specifically serve this special ability (for a more detailed history of this argument, see Kuhl, 1987).

Two subsequent discoveries have cast doubt on the significance of categorical perception for the argument that language is unique. (There may well be other arguments, and we will take that issue up later as well.) One finding that burst the uniqueness bubble was that some nonspeech sounds are also perceived categorically (Miller, Wier, Pastore, Kelley, & Dooling, 1976). A second finding that cast doubt on the notion that categorical perception is an example of human preparedness for language acquisition was that chinchillas also show the phoneme boundary effect for /b/ and /p/ (Kuhl & Miller, 1975), although chinchillas (small rodents whose main claim to fame is their soft fur) show no other signs of having evolved to acquire language. However, among audiologists, chinchillas are well known as research subjects because the chinchilla ear functions much the way the human ear functions, including—it turns out—perceiving the VOT continuum categorically. It seems that the phoneme boundary effect is a property of the mammalian aural system that language utilizes rather than a specifically linguistic property of auditory perception (Kuhl, 1987; Miller & Eimas, 1994). In fact, language may have evolved to take advantage of this preexisting property of mammalian audition. But whether this property is language-specific or not, it is clear that infants begin life with the ability to discriminate most phonetic contrasts that any target language might require, and their perception of consonant contrasts has a categorical quality (Werker & Polka, 1993).

Infants' mental representation of speech sounds

Although research on infant speech perception makes it clear that infants have the sensory capacity to discriminate between minimally different phones, that finding does not tell us that infants have separate mental representations for each phone. In fact, other evidence suggests that the syllable is the effective unit of infant speech perception. On this account, the infant hears /pa/ and /ba/ as different chunks of sound and would similarly hear /pa/ and /bu/ as different chunks of sound. The fine level of analysis that tells us that /pa/ and /bu/ are more different from each other than are /pa/ and /ba/ is not part of how infants mentally represent the sounds they hear.

The proposal that syllables are the units of representation for speech sounds is supported by the following evidence. Using a modified HAS procedure, Jusczyk and Derrah (1987) repeatedly presented a randomly ordered sequence of different syllables (bi, bo, bər, ba) to 2-month-old infants until the infants habituated to the sounds. Then the researchers altered the set of syllables, either by adding /bu/, /du/, or /da/ to the set or by changing all the syllables to begin with /d/. The result was that no matter how much or how little the syllables changed, the infants increased their sucking. Furthermore, the strength of the increased responsiveness was unaffected by the number of phonemes changed. For babies, it seems, a new syllable is a new syllable. A study of 4-day-old infants reached a similar conclusion, finding that the babies could distinguish a sequence of two-syllable sounds (such as *rifo, ublo*) from a sequence of three-syllable sounds (*rekivu, kesopa*); but they could not discriminate a two-syllable sequence with four phonemes (*rifo, ublo*) from a two-syllable sequence with six phonemes (*treklu, suldri*) (Bijeljac-Babic, Bertoncini, & Mehler, 1993). Again, babies seem to process the speech stream in terms of syllables, even though they have the sensory capacity to discriminate among phonemes.

Infants' recognition of speech sounds

Although the ability to hear the difference between sounds that mark meaning differences in the language is necessary for language acquisition, it alone is not sufficient. The language learning infant must also be able to ignore differences among acoustic signals that do not mark meaning differences. For example, the language learner must be able to recognize /b/ as /b/ and /p/ as /p/ every time they are produced, even if they aren't acoustically identical. The perceptual mechanisms take care of this distinction for acoustic continua that are perceived categorically. But what about acoustic differences that are not perceived categorically, such as the difference between vowels? And what about the acoustic differences that result from different speakers with different voice qualities? The answer to these questions seems to be that, by age 6 months, infants do treat acoustically different but phonologically equivalent speech sounds as equivalent. Young babies will treat as equivalent the same phoneme produced by a male and a female voice (Kuhl, 1980), and they will treat as equivalent acoustically different vowel sounds (Kuhl, 1983). In the case of vowels, the equivalence classes are organized around prototypes for each vowel (Grieser & Kuhl, 1989).

Infants' perception of multisyllabic strings

Even these abilities—to hear different speech sounds as different and to recognize the same speech sound as the same across acoustic differences—may be of limited use to the language learning child if the sounds must occur in isolation. Researchers test babies on contrasts presented in single syllables, such as [pa] and [ba], but the language learning environment presents sounds embedded in a stream of ongoing speech. Discriminating speech sounds embedded in multisyllabic strings is more difficult for infants than is discriminating isolated contrasts, and the more complex the string, the more difficult it is. This fact was nicely demonstrated in an experiment by Goodsitt, Morse, Ver Hoeve, and Cowan (1984). Using the head-turn procedure, the researchers trained 6½ -month-old infants to discriminate between [ba] and [du], a very easy contrast. Then [ba] and [du] were combined with other syllables to see whether the infants were still able to make the discrimination they made between the isolated syllables. The study found that infants could still tell the strings apart, but the discrimination was harder for infants to make when the [ba] and [du] were embedded in a complex sequence than when embedded in a redundant sequence. For example, infants correctly discriminated [kokodu] from [kokoba] 75% of the time, but they were able to discriminate mixed sequences such as [kotiba] from [kotidu] only 67% of the time.

This finding suggests that much of the speech babies hear must be a jumble for them. On the other hand, there is also evidence that prosodic features, such as stressing the contrastive syllable, can help (Karzon, 1985). So distinguishing [koti*ba*] from [koti*du*] is easier than distinguishing the same sequences presented with even intonation. This finding leads us to the topic of the prosodic features of the speech adults address to infants.

Infant-directed speech

The nature of speech addressed to babies   In many cultures, a particular way of speaking is used to talk to babies (Fernald et al., 1989; Grieser & Kuhl, 1988). This style of speech is sufficiently different from the way adults talk to other adults that it has been given its own name—**motherese** (Newport, Gleitman, & Gleitman, 1977)—although the terms **infant-directed speech** or

characteristic of baby talk

child-directed speech are currently more widely used. The prosodic characteristics of infant-directed speech are of particular relevance to prelinguistic babies. When talking to babies, mothers (and fathers and other unrelated adults) use a higher-pitched voice, a wider range of pitches, longer pauses, and shorter phrases (Fernald et al., 1989; Fernald & Simon, 1984). In sum, the intonation contour of normal speech is greatly exaggerated in speech addressed to infants and so is likely to highlight some features of speech for language learning infants.

Infant-directed speech as a universal signal system   It is not sufficient for scientific purposes, however, to assume that simply because a special speech register for talking to infants exists, it serves some useful function. A substantial body of research in the last 20 years has investigated how infants respond to infant-directed speech and what infants might learn from it. One finding from this research is that infants prefer to hear infant-directed over adult-directed speech. Anne Fernald (1985) recorded 10 different adult women talking to their 4-month-old infants and to an adult. These tapes were then played to 4-month-olds in an experimental setting in which the infant-directed speech tape was played if the babies turned their head in one direction, and the adult-directed speech tape was played if the babies turned their head in the other direction. The infants chose to hear infant-directed speech more frequently than they chose to hear the adult-directed speech. Cooper and Aslin (1990) also found a preference for infant-directed speech in newborns and 1-month-olds.

If we ask what it is about infant-directed speech that makes it so interesting to babies, the answer for 4-month-olds seems to be the exaggerated pitch contours. Fernald and Kuhl (1987) found that 4-month-olds preferred to hear infant-directed speech when everything but the melody had been filtered out of the speech signal. However, Cooper and Aslin (1994) found that 1-month-olds demonstrated a preference for infant-directed speech only if the full speech signal was presented—prosody alone was not sufficient. Thus Cooper and Aslin suggest that infants start out preferring something about the whole speech signal, but they come to prefer even the isolated pitch contours because these are associated with positive interactions with their mothers.

Whatever the relevant acoustic properties of infant-directed speech are, it seems that mothers naturally produce sounds that babies are naturally interested in. Fernald (1992) has referred to this kind of speech as a universal signal system, and she has proposed that it is based in human biology. That is, infant-directed speech is not just talk, it is also a system of calls that have effects on infants entirely separate from the meaning of the words produced. The immediate effects of these maternal calls are to direct the infants' attention and to calm or arouse them, depending on the particular call.

In support of this argument, Fernald points out that there appear to be universal correspondences between intonation and affect (the emotion behind what is said) that hold across languages. When mothers say things like "No!" or "Don't touch that!" the intonation is very different from when they say things like "Good!" or "Clever girl!"; and these different intonations for both prohibitions and praise tend to be much the same across different languages. Fernald (1989) has demonstrated that, on the basis of intonation alone, adults can tell the difference between prohibitions and approval statements addressed to babies.

The role of infant-directed speech in language acquisition   Some have suggested that, in addition to regulating attention and arousal, infant-directed speech also provides the gateway to language acquisition. The correlations between intonation and affect may provide infants with their first accessible sound-meaning correspondences. The exaggerated stress patterns may help infants isolate words in the speech stream. Another hypothesis is that the exaggerated prosodic contours of infant-directed speech may provide infants with the foundation for acquiring their language's grammatical structure.

Support for the notion that the prosodic cues of motherese might assist language learning comes from research that compared infants' processing of motherese and adult-directed speech. In one study, Hirsh-Pasek and associates (1987) presented 7- to 10-month-old infants with tape-recorded samples of motherese into which pauses had been inserted. In some of the samples, the pauses had been inserted at clause boundaries; for other samples, the pauses had been inserted within clauses. The researchers found that the babies preferred to listen to the speech samples that were interrupted at clause boundaries. This finding suggests that clauses are perceptual units for young infants. In a subsequent study, Kemler Nelson, Hirsh-Pasek, Jusczyk, and Cassidy (1989) repeated the same procedure, this time using samples of motherese with half of the infants tested and samples of adult-directed speech for the other half. Infants preferred only the uninterrupted clauses in the motherese condition. When the speech samples were adult-directed speech, it didn't matter where the pauses were inserted. These results suggest that prelinguistic infants can identify clauses in motherese but not in adult-directed speech. However, see Fernald and McRoberts (1996) for a different interpretation.

The proposal that infants find important clues to language structure in the prosodic characteristics of the speech signal is known as the **prosodic bootstrapping hypothesis.** A more encompassing proposal is that properties of the sound signal other than prosody contribute to language learning, a proposal known as the **phonological bootstrapping hypothesis** (for a comprehensive treatment, see Morgan & Demuth, 1996). We will consider how the phonological properties of language might be involved in lexical and grammatical development in Chapters 3 and 4. There we will also consider how properties other than the phonological properties of infant-directed speech might be involved in language acquisition.

When we consider the arguments offered regarding the role of infant-directed speech in language development, we also have to consider cultural differences in the speech addressed to children. Although it is often claimed that the special features of infant-directed speech are universal, there are dissenting voices (Ingram, 1995; Ratner and Pye, 1984). Furthermore, in some cultures, including cultures of Samoans (Ochs, 1982; Schieffelin & Ochs, 1986), Papua New Guineans (Schieffelin, 1979, 1985), and among U.S. African Americans in the rural South (Heath, 1983), adults simply do not address speech to prelinguistic infants. In these cultures, infants are loved, held, and cared for but not talked to, yet they learn to talk. The fact that language acquisition is universal whereas infant-directed speech may not be raises the question of how important the properties of infant-directed speech can be in explaining language acquisition. For our present purposes, we can conservatively conclude that in many cultures, infant-directed speech has properties that both make it interesting to infants and may help the infant identify linguistically relevant units in the speech stream.

The influence of the target language on infants' speech perception

Up to this point, we have focused our discussion of infants' speech perception on describing the initial state of the language learning infant. That initial state includes the perceptual abilities language acquisition will require, and it also seems to include a preference to attend to the kind of sound signal likely to be linguistically relevant—that is, infant-directed speech. Before leaving the topic of infant speech perception, we also need to consider the changes that occur during infancy. As was the case for prelinguistic sound production, we can see in prelinguistic speech perception that well before babies talk, they have learned something about the particular language to which they have been exposed.

The tuning of phonemic perception   Although infants start out able to make essentially all the discriminations language acquisition will require, they do not remain in that initial state. The infants soon become, like adults, less able to discriminate some contrasts that are not used in their ambient language.

An experiment by Werker and Tees (1984) demonstrated the influence of the linguistic environment on infants' speech perception. Werker and Tees took advantage of the fact that Hindi and Inslekepmx (the language spoken by the native Salish of British Columbia) have consonant contrasts that English does not. Using the head-turn procedure, the researchers found that 6- to 8-month-old English-learning infants could make these Hindi and Inslekepmx discriminations, but very few could do so by the time they were 10 to 12 months old. In contrast, 11- and 12-month-old Hindi-learning and Inslekepmx-learning infants were still able to make phonemic distinctions in the language they were acquiring. Regarding vowels, Kuhl, Williams, Lacerda, Stevens, and Lindblom (1992) found effects of the target language on vowel discrimination in infants as young as 6 months old.

Although experience with the target language results in a decline in the ability to perceive unused contrast, the loss of the ability to make nonnative discriminations is neither total nor across the board. Some contrasts remain easy even for nonnatives, and the perception of the difficult contrasts can be improved with training (Best, 1994). Also, regarding vowels, the effect of language experience on perception seems to be stronger in infancy than in adulthood (Werker & Polka, 1993). Thus the nature of the effect of experience seems to be an adjustment of attention rather than a change in basic sensory capacities (Best, 1994).

Learning the sound patterns of one's language   Earlier in this chapter, we reviewed evidence that even newborns seem to distinguish the language they heard in utero from an unfamiliar language. We also saw that babies appear to make this discrimination on the basis of prosodic contours. By the age of 9 months, infants are able to tell their language from another on the basis of sound patterns without relying on prosody. Just as English-speaking adults can recognize *geslacht* and *woestign* as foreign words based on their sounds, so too can 9-month-olds. Jusczyk, Friederici, Wessels, Svenkerud, and Jusczyk (1993) presented American and Dutch 6- and 9-month-old babies with American and Dutch words. At 9 months, but not at 6 months, the American infants listened longer to the American words and the Dutch infants listened longer to the Dutch words. When only the prosodic contours of the words were presented, there were no preferences. (English and Dutch have very similar prosodic characteristics.) This result suggests that, by 9 months, infants have learned something about the kind of sound patterns that characterize their language.

PHONOLOGICAL DEVELOPMENT DURING EARLY LANGUAGE DEVELOPMENT

We have thus far described the prelinguistic period in children's development of the production and perception of speech sounds. This prelinguistic period ends when children produce their first words, and at that point what could be termed the *linguistic period* begins. However, the appearance of a child's first word is not a major landmark in phonological development. Rather, phonological development proceeds relatively seamlessly through the transition from the prelinguistic to the linguistic period. The most important landmark in phonological development comes later, at the point where the child has acquired an approximately 50-word vocabulary. At that point, children seem to achieve a new kind of understanding of the phonology of their language that sets them on the path toward adult competence. An

Box 2.2   An overview of phonological development (with approximate ages)

Period 1: Prelinguistic (0–12 months)

Speech sounds gradually emerge, followed by babbling, long sequences of babbling with the intonation contour of the adult language, and some transitional forms. This period ends with the formation of the first true word.

Period 2: Prerepresentational phonology (12–18 months)

Articulation of first words is highly variable. Children appear to represent the sounds of words on a word-by-word basis.

Period 3: Representational phonology (18 months–3 years)

Children achieve a system for producing individual speech sounds, and children's productions become more consistent. Children develop phonological processes that alter the target sounds in systematic ways to conform to the children's limited articulatory abilities. Use of these processes gradually declines as children master the production of a wider range of speech sounds.

Period 4: Phonetic inventory completion (4–7 years)

Children master the remainder of the speech sounds in their language, including production of multisyllable words. Children acquire some of the morphophonological rules, such as the formation of the past tense and plural. Skills such as counting the number of segments in a word, rhyming, and appreciating puns develop.

Period 5: Advanced phonology (7–12 years)

Children's cognitive development and acquisition of literacy promotes conscious understanding of the relation between sounds and meaning.

Source: Based on Schwartz, 1983.

overview of the course of phonological development is shown in Box 2.2, which is based on Schwartz (1983). With that road map at hand, we resume our discussion of phonological development as it manifests itself in speech production. In this chapter, we cover the first four periods, reserving discussion of advanced phonology for Chapter 6.

The sounds in first words

Children's first words use the same sound repertoires evidenced in their late babbling and transitional forms. Leonard, Newhoff, and Meselam (1980) studied the initial consonant sounds in the first 50 words spoken by children acquiring English. The researchers found that the sounds most common in children's babble were also most common in these early vocabularies. Also, many sounds in the adult language were absent in children's productions. For example, [m], [b], and [d] were consistently present, and [θ], [ð], [l], and [r] were consistently absent. The researchers also found considerable variety across children in the phonemes in their first 50 words. This period of phonological development has been called **prerepresentational phonology** because children at this point do not seem to have a system for representing each sound in their language. Instead, when speech begins, the effective units for children are probably not phonemes but larger units such as syllables or whole words.

The argument that syllables are the units of sound in the child's mental representation of phonology is made on the basis of evidence that the different vowels and consonants children can produce do not combine freely. Instead, particular vowels tend to occur with particular consonants. Thus Oller and Steffens (1994) suggest that, in early speech, children are not producing sequences of phonemes but rather sequences of bigger, syllabic chunks. (Recall the evidence that syllables are also the effective unit of speech perception for infants.)

Another hypothesis is that once children are trying to approximate words in the target language, the children have mental representations for the sound of whole words—not even separate syllables. The support for this argument comes, in part, from the lack of consistency in how children produce sounds during this stage. The same sound may be produced different ways in different words in the target language. So, for example, the initial sounds in the words *purse* and *pretty,* which are the same in adults' productions, may be different in the child's productions (Ferguson & Farwell, 1975). Although Ferguson and Farwell presented this evidence in support of whole-word representations, it is also the case that *purse* and the initial syllable in *pretty* are different syllables. A particularly striking sort of inconsistency that suggests some whole-word representations is the production of **phonological idioms.** This term refers to words the child produces in a very adultlike way, while still incorrectly producing other words that use the very same sounds. Some frequently used phonological idioms persist into later stages of development, whereas less frequently produced words get assimilated into children's developing general patterns for producing speech sounds (Menn & Stoel-Gammon, 1995). Children's pronunciation of these assimilated idioms may actually become less adultlike for a while.

The emergence of a phonological system

A major development occurs in children's phonological progress sometime around 18 months of age, or about when a 50-word vocabulary has been acquired. A change occurs at this point that allows children to say most one- and two-syllable words after hearing them only a few times. The change has been described as a change from prerepresentational phonology to **representational phonology** (Schwartz, 1983). What children seem to have now that they did not have before is a phonological system. Changes in cognitive capacity may be the development that enables the child to come up with a phonological system at this point. Vihman, Velleman, and McCune (1994) suggested that increases in representational capacity allow children to increase the number of words they have stored in memory. When this mental store of sound patterns reaches a critical size, a system emerges. Children's phonological systems are typically not adultlike, but they provide children with a way of representing the sounds in their target language, albeit using only those sounds within their own more limited repertoires (Menyuk, Menn, & Silber, 1986).

Many aspects of children's systems are common to all children acquiring the same language. These common **phonological processes** that alter the target forms to fit children's production repertoires give young children's speech certain characteristic features. For example, pronouncing *bottle* as [baba] or *Mommy* as [mama] results from the process known as reduplication, in which one syllable, usually the first, is reduplicated. Another common process is the substitution of stops for fricatives, so that *church* becomes [tʌrč]. This particular example illustrates that a process can be applied to a sound in one position in a word but not to the same sound in a different position. Consonant clusters tend to be reduced, so *school* becomes [kul]; and glides are often substituted for liquids, so that *rabbit* is pronounced [wæbɪt]. Deletion, particularly of word-final consonants, is very common in children's early speech. Common phonological processes and some examples are listed in Box 2.3.

Often more than one process is applied to a word, making the relation of the child's attempt to the target language less than obvious. For example, one early "word" observed in the speech of a 2-year-old boy was [bu]. This child consistently used his word [bu] to refer to his urine and feces as he proudly flushed them down the toilet. The fact that [bu] doesn't sound like any related word in English suggests that maybe this was an invented, idiosyncratic form.

Box 2.3 Common phonological processes in children's speech

Whole word processes

Weak syllable deletion: omission of an unstressed syllable in the target word

> banana [nænæ]
>
> butterfly [bʌfaɪ]

Final consonant deletion: omission of the final consonant in the target word

> because [pikʌ]
>
> thought [fɔ]

Reduplication: production of two identical syllables based on one of the syllables in the target word

> Sesame Street [si:si]
>
> hello [jojo]
>
> bottle [baba]

Consonant harmony: one of two different consonants in the target word takes on features of another consonant in the same word

> duck [gʌk]
>
> tub [bʌb]

(continued)

However, it is possible to explain the derivation of [bu] from the target language word *poop* in the following way: First, apply the common process of deletion of the final consonant. That changes *poop* to [pu]. Then apply the less common, but certainly not bizarre, process of voicing initial voiceless consonants. That changes [p] to [b] and yields [bu]. Some children may have a great many idiosyncratic processes, making their speech difficult for unfamiliar people to understand, although it may be quite comprehensible to their mothers and quite lawful to the linguist.

In addition to these processes for transforming words in the target language to sound sequences within the child's articulatory abilities, children may adopt other strategies when confronted with a new word. One strategy is simply to

---

Box 2.3   *(continued)*

Consonant cluster reduction: omission of one of the consonants of a cluster in the target word

    cracker [kæk]

Segment substitution processes

Velar fronting: a velar is replaced by an alveolar or dental

    key [ti]

Stopping: a fricative is replaced by a stop

    sea [ti]

Gliding: a liquid is replaced by a glide

    rabbit [wæbɪt]

    Lissa [yɪ sə]

Whole-word processes, which alter the adult word most drastically, are especially typical of younger children (up to age 3 or 4), whereas in some normally developing children, some of the segment substitution processes persist into the early school years (Vihman, 1988).

---

avoid acquiring new words that use sounds that are not in their repertoires (Schwartz & Leonard, 1982). Alternatively, children may assimilate a new word to either another, similar-sounding word in their lexicons or to a preexisting whole-word sound pattern (termed a **canonical form**). For example, a child might modify all words to fit the pattern *consonant + vowel + /j/ + vowel + consonant*. One child pronounced the word *panda* as [pajan], the word *berries* as [bəjas], and the word *tiger* as [tajak] (Priestly, 1977, in Vihman, 1988a). Some children seem to modify all new words to fit a small set of canonical forms; other children use a few canonical forms along with a more elaborate system of phonological patterns. The need for these processes gradually declines as children become able to produce more and more of the sounds in their target language.

General patterns of phonological development

Some speech sounds seem to be harder for children to produce than others, and therefore there are some general patterns in the order in which different speech sounds appear in children's productions. We have already seen that some sounds are common in children's babble and first words. Other sounds still cause difficulty to many children at the age of 5 or 6 years. Normally, children sound adultlike in their phonology by the time they are about 7 years old. Sander (1972) summarized the data on the age at which different speech sounds appear in the speech of children learning English. His age estimates, shown in Figure 2.6, relate to what he terms the "customary" production of a sound, which

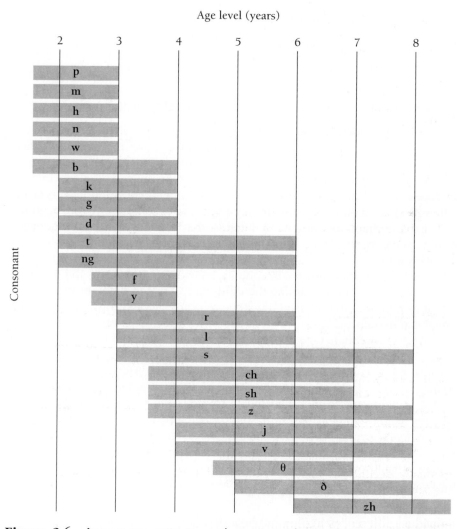

Figure 2.6 Average age estimates and upper age limits of customary consonant production in the speech of children acquiring English.

Source: From "When are Speech Sounds Learned?" by E. K. Sander, 1972, Journal of Speech and Hearing Disorders, 37, 55–63. Copyright © 1972 American Speech-Language-Hearing Association. Reprinted by permission.

he defines as the age at which a majority of children can clearly articulate that sound in two out of three word positions.

However, several factors limit the usefulness of such norms as descriptions of phonological development (Menyuk & Menn, 1979). First, the likelihood that a sound will be articulated depends both on the sound's position in the word and on the neighboring sounds in the word. Furthermore, the factors of word position and neighboring sounds affect different sounds differently. For example, fricatives, such as /f/ and /s/, tend to be produced first in word-final position and to appear only later as the initial sound in a word. In contrast, stops, such as [p] and [g], tend to be produced first in word-initial position. Other factors that limit the usefulness of such norms are the cross-linguistic and individual differences observed in children's phonological development.

Cross-linguistic differences in phonological development

The order in which sounds appear in children's speech is influenced by properties of the target language. For example, for children acquiring English, [v] is a relatively late-appearing sound. However, among children acquiring Swedish, Bulgarian, and Estonian, [v] is a much earlier acquisition (Ingram, 1988). Such cross-linguistic differences indicate that the difficulty of producing different speech sounds cannot entirely explain why some sounds are acquired earlier than others. Ingram (1988) suggests that the function different speech sounds serve in the language is another important factor. In English, [v] is relatively infrequent and children can get fairly far making different words sound different without mastering [v]. In contrast, in Swedish, Bulgarian, and Estonian, [v] is more important to marking the difference between different words.

It is important to understand that the relevant factor according to Ingram's functional hypothesis is not the frequency with which children hear the sound but rather the frequency with which the sound is used in different words. For example, in English, the initial sound in *the* and *this* is very frequently heard because it is used in a few very high-frequency words. However, because that sound is not involved in many different words, its functional significance is low. And it is interesting to note that the *th* sound (ð) is a late-acquired sound in children acquiring English. In sum, sounds that appear early may not always be sounds that are easy to produce. Rather, they may be the sounds that carry information in the phonological system. On the other hand, Ingram (1989) suggests that it would not be surprising to find that languages tend to assign the greatest functional loads to sounds that are easy to produce.

Individual differences in phonological development

Even children acquiring the same language vary in their phonological development; one difference is in the rate of development. Some babies start to babble earlier than others, and some babies acquire the ability to produce adult-sounding words earlier than others. Although severe difficulty in producing speech may be a sign of some underlying language or hearing disorder, there is a wide range in the rates of development associated with normal language development. Figure 2.6 gives a rough indication of the range observed.

There are individual differences in aspects of phonological development other than rate. As mentioned earlier, some children in the babbling stage are "intonation babies," who babble long strings of jargon with the intonation contour of the target language. Other children are "word babies," who tend to produce one short babble sequence at a time (Dore, 1975). Children also differ in the particular sounds they produce. Some children, for example, produce many nasals; others produce few. These differences may be due to differences in articulatory ability, but some children just seem to like certain sounds (Vihman, 1993).

At a later point in development, it becomes clear that children differ in the approaches they take to constructing a phonological system. Some children rely heavily on whole-word processes, assimilating adult words to a few patterns and avoiding unassimilable words. Other children have a larger repertoire of phonological processes. And children differ in the particular processes they use in transforming target words in their own speech. For example, children who like to use reduplication will be good at maintaining the multisyllabicity of adult words even if they cannot quite produce all the individual sounds. So, a child who reduplicates might produce *blanket* as [baba], whereas another child less inclined toward reduplication might say [bat].

Another difference is that some children approach the learning of phonology in a cautious, analytical manner, whereas other children are less analytic and more risk-taking (Ferguson, 1979). Cautious, analytical children will have less variability in the forms of their utterances, whereas exploratory, risk-taking children will say the same word many different ways. It seems that the cautious child figures things out first and then talks, whereas the risk-taking child plunges ahead using forms not quite mastered.

The development of linguistic perception

Linguistic perception, or receptive phonology, has been much less studied in older children than it has in infants. Some topics investigated include the development of the ability to discriminate words based on contrasting sounds and the relation of phonological development in perception to phonological development in production.

Word discrimination   The fact that two sounds are discriminable to infants does not mean that children will perceive two words that differ in only those sounds as two different words with different meanings. That is, just because children can tell two sounds apart doesn't mean they make such fine-grained distinctions when they hear new words. Children as old as 24 months (2 yrs) fail to treat as phonemic contrasts they were able to perceive as infants (Barton, 1976; Garnica, 1973; Menyuk et al., 1986; Shvachkin, 1973). Several studies have investigated the order in which different phonemic contrasts are acquired. The method, in broad outline, is to try to teach children new words that differ on only one contrast (such as [mos] versus [pos]) and see whether they can learn them. However, most of phonemic perception development occurs between the ages of 1 and 3, when children are extremely difficult to test. Beyond the initial statement that the ability to hear a difference between two sounds is not sufficient for phonemic perception, no clear conclusion has emerged from these studies. In fact, this question is not really investigated any more because it seems more likely that syllables, rather than phonemes, are the functional units of speech perception (Menyuk et al., 1986; Vihman, 1988).

The relation between perception and production   Children's perception and production of speech sounds are initially different from adults' perception and production of sounds in the language, and both aspects develop toward adultlike competence. One question about the causes of phonological development concerns the possible connections between changes in perception and changes in production. We have already reviewed evidence that the order in which particular speech sounds emerge in children's productions is influenced by which speech sounds are frequent in the meaningful units of the child's language (the words) (Pye, Ingram, & List, 1987). This evidence suggests that the change from acoustic processing of sounds to linguistic processing of meaningful units precedes and shapes speech sound production. According to this view, perception (or comprehension) is always more advanced than production, and production follows the trail that receptive development has blazed. In a sense, production never quite catches up, because we can all understand many more dialects than we can produce.

Other than the order of their development, there is another difference between receptive phonology and productive phonology that enormously complicates the question of how the two are related. Production potentially has motoric obstacles that interfere with children's demonstrating their phonological knowledge. Thus the fact that a child pronounces something in an immature way does not mean that the child is unaware of the difference between that pronunciation and adult pronunciation. For example, a child named Alissa pronounced her name as though it were "yitya" for a long time. However, if someone else teasingly called her "yitya," she became quite incensed. This phenomenon is sometimes referred to as the "fis" phenomenon, following an oft-cited example of one child's refusal to accept "fis" as the label for his toy fish, even though "fis" was how the child produced the word (Berko & Brown, 1960). Such anecdotes are common (see, for example, Butler, 1920), and they tell us that children's mispronunciations do not necessarily imply that children have incomplete mental representations of how the word is supposed to sound (see also Eilers & Oller, 1976, for an experimental investigation).

MODELS OF PHONOLOGICAL DEVELOPMENT

Having described the course of phonological development, it is now time to consider explanations of phonological development. We can organize the proposed explanations under four headings: (1) behaviorist models, (2) biologically based models, (3) cognitive models, and (4) connectionist models. Each model is a proposed answer to the question of how children learn to distinguish and produce the sound patterns of the adult language.

Behaviorist models

In the heyday of behaviorism in the 1950s, attempts were made to account for children's phonological development using the behaviorist mechanisms of imitation and reinforcement (for example, see Mowrer, 1960; Skinner, 1957). According to such an account, babies produce the particular sounds they do because they imitate the sounds they hear and because they receive positive reinforcement for doing so. Over time, the sounds babies produce come to match the sounds of the target language because these are the sounds babies have imitated and that have been reinforced.

There are a few problems with such an account. One problem is that it ignores the role of maturational processes in accounting for infants' changing sound repertoires. Some sounds seem to be late appearances in children's babbling because they are difficult to produce, not because children are not reinforced for producing them. This leads us to the second problem with the behaviorist account, and that is that parents do not selectively reinforce speech sounds. Many parents express delight at every burp and raspberry their babies produce, and those children acquire the phonology of the target language nonetheless. These babies may also burp and make raspberries with high frequency, but that does not seem to interfere with their phonological development.

The most serious problem for a behaviorist account, however, is that the development of phonology is more than just the development of a repertoire of sounds. It is the development of a system of regularities (such as the rule that adjacent consonants within a word match in terms of voicing), and it is coming to know the relation between sounds (such as knowing that the voiceless equivalent of /d/ is /t/). This knowledge is not conscious knowledge, and it is not available to be reinforced. Because behaviorist accounts of phonological development, and of language development more generally, operated with fundamentally mistaken notions of what language knowledge and language development are, behaviorist accounts were not taken very seriously for very long. Although there are many unresolved issues regarding how children acquire the phonology of their language, virtually everyone agrees that 1950s-style behaviorism is not a serious candidate for an explanation.

This somewhat harsh dismissal of behaviorism should not be taken to mean that responding to babies' vocalizations has no effect; it does. Bornstein and Tamis-LeMonda (1989) found that mothers who are very responsive to their babies' vocalizations have babies who vocalize more than do babies of less responsive mothers. Oller, Eilers, Basinger, Steffens, and Urbano (1995) found that babies living in extreme poverty, who tend to get less verbal stimulation than do more advantaged babies (Hart & Risley, 1995), also tend to produce less babbling. Rheingold, Gewirtz, and Ross (1959) demonstrated experimentally that smiling in response to a baby's vocalization causes the baby to vocalize more. Other findings suggest that mothers may encourage their children's language development by responding contingently to their infants' prelinguistic vocalizations (Velleman, Mangipudi, & Locke, 1989). Thus a responsive environment does seem to support vocal development and perhaps also helps language development proceed. (Other ways in which parents' responses to their children do and do not influence language development will be considered in later chapters.)

The problem with behaviorism is not that it is wrong but that it is insufficient. A theory of phonological development needs to explain why development follows the path it does (as opposed to other paths), and it needs to explain how the ultimate achievement of the phonology of a language is possible.

Biologically based models

There are persuasive arguments that biological factors shape both the course of phonological development and its ultimate result—namely, the phonological properties of the world's languages. According to Locke (Locke, 1983; Locke & Pearson, 1992), infants' first sounds are the sounds the human vocal apparatus is most inclined to produce, given its anatomical and physiological characteristics. Sound production is shaped by motor capacity, and the development of sound production is shaped by the development of motor capacity.

According to Locke (1983, 1993), the similarity of the early sound repertoires of children across different target languages is evidence that the biologically determined development of motor capacity shapes the development of sound production in infancy. There is evidence that these biological factors shape adult languages as well; sounds in infants' early productions are also common sounds among the world's languages, and sounds produced late in the course of development tend to be rare in the world's languages. For example, [m] is among the first sounds babies produce, and 97% of the languages studied have /m/ among their phonemes. In contrast, [r] is a sound that causes difficulty for children even into the school years, and /r/ is a phoneme in only about 5% of the world's languages. A related argument was made by Donegan and Stampe (1979), who claimed that the phonological processes young children employ are also seen in processes used in adult languages. For example, children commonly substitute voiceless for voiced consonants at the ends of words, such as pronouncing *bad* as [baet], and many languages have a rule that voiced consonants are pronounced as their voiceless counterparts in word-final position (Vihman, 1988).

Although no one would argue that motor capacity and its development are irrelevant to phonology and phonological development, there is disagreement about how important a role biology plays compared to the role of language experience. We know from studies discussed earlier that the sounds the target language uses influence the sounds in babies' babbling before the end of the first year (de Boysson-Bardies et al., 1984), and we know that how those sounds are used in the target language influences which sounds will be common in young children's early speech (Ingram, 1988; Pye, Ingram, & List, 1987). Thus an account of phonological development also has to explain how experience exerts its effects.

A somewhat different biologically based model was proposed by the Russian linguist Jakobson in 1941 (translated into English in 1968). This view, in its entirety at least, is generally considered to be primarily of historical interest. According to Jakobson, the distinctive features that define the relations among speech sounds (vocalic, voicing, labial, and so on) "unfold" in the child in a universal, predictable order as a result of maturation. For example, the first distinctive feature to emerge is the contrast between vowels and consonants, and so the first sounds children produce are [p] and [a]. Although Jakobson said maturation is the explanation of phonological development, he said nothing about what actually matures in the child. Unlike Locke, Jakobson did not start from anatomy and physiology to explain the course of phonological development. Jakobson started from linguists' description of speech sounds in terms of distinctive features. Because Jakobson's theory is based on a theory of the structure of the phonological system, this theory is often termed a "structuralist" theory. Jakobson's predicted order of emergence of features was intended to apply not to babbling but only to first words. According to Jakobson, babbling was random activity that had nothing to do with language acquisition.

Jakobson's theory has difficulty dealing with some of the data on early phonological development. First, there is substantial evidence that speech builds on the phonological developments that occur during the babbling period. A second problem for Jakobson's theory is the evidence of individual differences in phonological development. Jakobson's theory proposes to account for a universal course of development in terms of an unfolding genetic blueprint, but the course of phonological development itself seems variable.

One claim in Jakobson's theory still figures in current debate—the claim that children acquire phonemes from the start. As discussed earlier, the more widely held view of phonological development is that children initially have syllable-based or whole-word-based representations of how things sound; they only later analyze words into their component speech sounds and speech sounds into their component features. However, Ingram (1989) argues that children have representations of phonemes at the beginning of phonological development, and Ingram refers to his position as neo-Jakobsonian.

The cognitive problem-solving model

Probably the most widely held view of phonological development is that it is a problem-solving activity for children (Ferguson & Farwell, 1975; Macken & Ferguson, 1983). According to this **cognitive model,** children actively try to sound like adults, and they work on figuring out how to do so. One piece of evidence cited in support of this view is that children avoid saying words that use sounds they cannot produce.

Another tenet of the cognitive model is that there is a prerepresentational or presystemic stage of phonological development during which the units of representation are words, not phonemes or features. That is, children start out with ways to say whole words and only later break down words into their component sounds. Evidence for this latter claim is the inconsistency in how certain phonemes are produced across first words and the regression in the quality of some productions. The cognitive theory explanation for this regression is that, as children move from a word-by-word approach to production to a phonological system, some words that had accurate representations will suffer as they are produced through the child's new, but incomplete, phonological system.

Two aspects of the cognitive view are in conflict with a strong biologically based account of phonological development. One is the relative importance of the child's active problem-solving efforts. According to the cognitive model, active problem solving is the most important factor underlying phonological development. Often the extent of individual differences in phonological development is taken as the critical data for distinguishing between a predominantly biological and a predominantly cognitive explanation of phonological development. According to this logic, different children might, at least initially, solve the problem of figuring out their language's phonology in different ways; therefore the problem-solving view predicts that there will be substantial individual differences. In contrast, because all children share the same essential biological makeup, the biological view suggests that the course of phonological development should be more similar across children.

This controversy is difficult to resolve for two reasons. One is that different procedures for analyzing children's phonetic inventories give different pictures of how much variability there is. The second is that individual differences can result from individual differences in biological makeup. Children may vary in the anatomical and motoric underpinnings of phonological development, just as they vary in hair color, height, and other biologically determined characteristics.

A second point of disagreement is the difference between the neo-Jakobsonian view and the cognitive view regarding the units of phonological development. According to the neo-Jakobsonian view, children are acquiring phonemes—or even phonetic features—from the start. So, essentially, the information on phonemes in Table 2.2 develops bit by bit. On the other hand, the cognitive view holds that the initial units of phonological development are words. Again, the resolution of this conflict hinges on how children's productions are analyzed. Finding variability from word to word in how a child produces particular sounds is evidence for a word-based approach. However, according to Ingram, there is systematicity at the level of phonemes to be found from the start, if you look for it correctly.

The connectionist approach

Another potential source for a model of phonological development is connectionism. As we discussed in Chapter 1, connectionism is a relatively new approach to modeling all human cognitive processes. There are **connectionist models** of pattern recognition, of learning, and of other aspects of language development. Here we will try to give a flavor of how the phonological processes of young speakers and their eventual decline would be described in connectionist terms, based on an account by Stemberger (1992). Connectionism will come up again in Chapter 4 on syntax and morphology.

A central tenet of connectionism is that rules are not necessary to describe the regularities of human behavior. One example of unnecessary rules is the phonological processes described in Box 2.3 that have been proposed to account for the systematic differences between the sound of words in the target language and the sound of words as children produce them. Instead of the processes view that children systematically transform the targets and then utter this transformed word, the connectionist view is that children try to approximate the target word and make an error, saying [wæbɪt], for example, instead of [ræbɪt].

The test of such a model is whether it can account for the systematicity of children's "errors." According to the connectionist model, in the process of producing a word like *cat,* a mental unit corresponding to the word is activated (presumably by the intention to say *cat*). That mental unit is connected to units that correspond to the phonemes in the word *cat*—/k/, /æ/, /t/—and those units are connected to the features that make up the sounds—voiced, stop, and so on. The hypothesized units and their interconnections are depicted in Figure 2.7. When the *cat* unit is activated, that activation spreads downward and eventually reaches the units connected to the actual muscles involved in speech production.

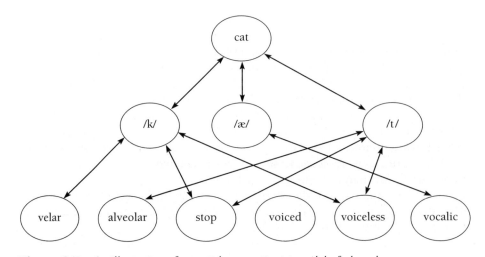

Figure 2.7   An illustration of a partial connectionist model of phonology

Source: From "A Connectionist View of Child Phonology," by J. P. Stemberger. In C. A. Ferguson et al. (Eds.), Phonological Development, pp. 165–189. Copyright © 1992 York Press. Reprinted with permission.

According to this model, children make errors because their connections are not yet adultlike. For example, *cat* is pronounced [tæt] because the connection from the phoneme /k/ to the feature velar is weak. In fact, some features may be weakly connected to everything initially—that is, some features may be inaccessible. (Inaccessibility could have a motoric basis.) In such a case, velars would be systematically absent from a child's productions, replaced by a sound that shared all the strongly connected features but was missing the weakly connected features; so /k/ would be replaced by /t/, and /g/ by /d/. The process of phonological development, according to this account, is the process of setting up the connections. This process begins in the vocal play that precedes babbling and continues until phonological development is complete.

To many people, connectionism sounds uncomfortably like behaviorism in that it tries not to talk about mental entities such as rules, representations, or knowledge. Behaviorism has not been a serious contender as a theory of any aspect of language development since the cognitive revolution that began in the 1950s. Since that time—until the connectionist approach was proferred—the universally accepted theory was that acquiring language consists of acquiring a system of rules. The connectionist approach attacks that basic dogma of the field. However, it would be false to equate behaviorism and connectionism (Seidenberg, 1992, 1994). It is too soon to tell how successful the connectionist approach to phonology, or to language more generally, will be, and we certainly have not considered it in enough detail to evaluate it here.

SUMMARY

Acquiring phonology consists of learning to "distinguish and produce the sound patterns of the adult language" (Vihman, 1988, p. 61). At birth, the child has the ability to distinguish virtually all the sounds all languages use, at least when the sounds are presented in isolation. The newborn produces no speech sounds, however. During the first year of life, speech sounds gradually emerge, beginning with vowellike coos at 6 to 8 weeks of age, followed by some consonant sounds, followed by true babbling. By the end of the first year, children are typically babbling sequences of syllables that have the intonation contour of their target language.

The factors that underlie these developments include physical growth of the vocal apparatus, neurological development, and language experience. Language experience shows its influence on both the perception and the production of speech sounds. Although 4-month-old infants demonstrate that they can hear the difference between all the sounds languages use, 12-month-olds cannot. Like adults, although not necessarily to the same degree, 12-month-olds have lost some of the ability to hear contrasts that are not in the language they are acquiring. Language experience shows its influence on early sound production as well. The babbling of 10-month-old infants has elements of both the prosodic features and the particular sounds used by the infants' target language. Also, which sounds are acquired early and which sounds appear later depends to a degree on how important those sounds are to marking distinctions in the target language. The full repertoire of speech sounds develops only gradually, with children typically sounding adultlike by about 7 years of age.

Phonological development is not just a matter of becoming able to produce and hear speech sounds. Phonological development more importantly consists of acquiring a system for mentally representing speech sounds and the relations among them. Although there are different points of view on how children come to achieve an adultlike representation of their language's phonology, the most widely held view is that children do not have such a system when they begin to talk. Only at about age 18 months—or upon achieving a productive vocabulary of about 50 words—do children achieve a phonological system in which words are represented in terms of their component segments or phonemes. Children's systems are not yet adultlike at this point. Rather, children seem to have achieved a system that maps phonemes in the target language to sounds within their own, more limited repertoires. This system allows children to approximate most one- or two-syllable words after only a few hearings. Many of these mapping rules—or phonological processes—are common across children, giving all young children's speech characteristic features, such as pronouncing *bottle* as [baba] or *rabbit* as [wæbɪt]. The use of these processes declines gradually as children's articulatory abilities develop.

The most widely held account of the process of phonological development describes it as an active problem-solving process for the child. Children try to sound like the adults around them and try to figure out a system for doing so. Individual differences observed in phonological development are the result of children's hitting upon different strategies for approximating the target language. There is also good evidence that biology plays an important role in shaping both the course of language development and its end result. Some sounds are harder to produce than others. These sounds are less frequently used by the languages of the world, and, on average, children acquire them later. However, another factor influencing the order of speech sound development is how important different sounds are to marking distinctions in the language. One new approach to modeling phonological development, the connectionist approach, proposes a radically different view of how phonology is represented and of what causes the transformations of adult sounds in children's productions.

KEY TERMS

phonological knowledge

distinctive feature

phone

phoneme

allophone

voicing

articulatory phonetics

phonetic features

place of articulation

manner of articulation

stops

fricatives

vegetative sounds

cooing

vocal play

expansion stage

marginal babbling

canonical or reduplicated babbling

nonreduplicated babbling

variegated babbling

prosody

jargon

protowords

high-amplitude sucking technique (HAS)

habituation/dishabituation

head-turn technique

categorical perception

voice onset time (VOT)

phoneme boundary

phoneme boundary effect

motherese

infant-directed or child-directed speech

prosodic bootstrapping hypothesis

phonological bootstrapping hypothesis

prerepresentational phonology

phonological idioms

representational phonology

phonological processes   biologically based models

canonical form   cognitive model

linguistic perception   connectionist models

behaviorist models

REVIEW QUESTIONS

1. How would you convince your friend, who claims to know nothing about phonology, that she knows the difference between voiced and voiceless consonants?

2. What is the difference between a speech sound (or phone) and a phoneme?

3. List and describe the five stages of prespeech vocal development.

4. What have 10-month-old babies learned about the sounds of their language?

5. Why is a normative description of the development of speech sounds (such as Figure 2.6) only a very rough description of phonological development?

6. What are phonological processes? How are they significant?

7. What evidence supports the view that phonological development is the result of biological processes?

8. What evidence supports the view that phonological development is the result of children's active problem solving?

9. What claims and evidence about phonological development are consistent with a nativist view of language development, and what claims and evidence suggest a greater role for input in accounting for language development?

10. What claims about phonological development are consistent with the notion that language acquisition is the result of language-specific mechanisms, and what claims and evidence are consistent with a general cognitive account?

3 Lexical Development: Learning Words

5-year-old: (singing, in the presence of his 2½-year-old brother) *A horse is a horse, of course of course*
And no one can talk to a horse, of course
That is, of course, unless the horse is the famous Mr. Ed.
Go right to the source and ask the horse
He'll give you the answer that you endorse
He's always on a steady course
Talk to Mr. Ed.

2½-year-old brother: What a Mr. Ed is?

LEXICAL KNOWLEDGE IN ADULTS

As an adult, you know tens of thousands of words. The vocabulary of an average English-speaking college student has been estimated at 150,000 words (Miller, 1977). What is perhaps even more impressive is that the average first-grader has a vocabulary of more than 14,000 words (Templin, 1957). What we consider in this chapter is what this word knowledge consists of and how children acquire it.

The mental lexicon

Think about what you know when you have a vocabulary of 100,000-plus words. You have in your head something like a dictionary with 100,000-plus entries. Each entry consists of a word and the things you know about that word. One sort of word knowledge you have is phonological; you know how to pronounce the word. Another sort of knowledge is grammatical; you know how to use the word in combination with other words. Another sort of knowledge, and the central information about each word found in a dictionary, is its definition; you know what the word means. This knowledge of words that adults have—this dictionary in the head—is termed the **mental lexicon.** The study of lexical development is the study of the child's acquisition of a mental lexicon.

There are many questions to ask about lexical development: When does lexical development start? What words do children learn first? Are some words easier to learn than others, and why? What do children know about the words they use? How do children learn the words of their language? Before we turn our attention to these questions regarding lexical development, we need to consider a very basic question about lexical knowledge in adults: "What is a word?"

What is a word?

A word is not just any set of sounds (or gestures) that communicates a meaning. If I point to something out of my reach and whine, you can probably figure out that I want what I am pointing to. However, neither my point nor my whine is a word. So what is a word? First of all, a word is a symbol. That is, it stands for something without being part of that something. Furthermore, the relation between words and what they stand for is arbitrary. Pointing and whining fail by this criterion. Many behaviors communicate meaning but are not symbols and therefore are not words. Babies' crying because they are hungry, dogs' barking because they need to go outside, and adults' shivering because they are cold all convey information; but neither the cries, the barks, nor the shivering are words because none is a symbol.

Words are not simply arbitrary symbols; they are symbols that can be used to refer to things. The notion of **reference** is difficult to define, but it is crucial to discussions of lexical development. For a word to be used consistently in combination with a particular object is not sufficient to qualify that word use as referential. To borrow an example from Golinkoff, Mervis, and Hirsh-Pasek (1994), "one can say 'yikes!' each time one sees a particular cat, but that is not necessarily the same thing as referring to the cat" (p. 130). That is, reference involves words "standing for" their referents, not just "going with" their referents (Golinkoff et al., 1994).

As adults, we use words referentially all the time, and nonreferential uses are the exception. (Greetings and social routines might be considered examples of nonreferential language use.) For young children, however, the referential status of the words they use is one issue that comes up in describing children's early lexical development. (It is also an issue in chimpanzees' language acquisition, but discussion of that will wait until Chapter 9.) As we shall see, describing lexical development involves more than just describing what words children say and when they say them. We are actually concerned with the development of children's mental lexicons—the knowledge inside their heads—and words children say are often our best, and sometimes our only, evidence regarding children's mental lexicons. However, in studying lexical development, we try to discern not just what words children know but what sort of lexical knowledge underlies the use of those words. With that in mind, we turn now to a description of lexical development.

THE COURSE OF EARLY LEXICAL DEVELOPMENT

First words

Children usually produce their first words sometime between 10 and 15 months of age (Benedict, 1979; Fenson et al., 1994; Huttenlocher & Smiley, 1987). These first words may be hard to distinguish from the earlier protowords described in the previous chapter on phonological development. The critical difference is that although protowords are sound sequences that seem to have consistent meaning for the child, the particular sounds of protowords are not derived in any obvious way from the language the child is learning. In contrast, true first words are approximations of words in the target language, even if somewhat rough approximations.

Many first words are context-bound   Like the protowords that preceded them, the first words children use are often tied to particular contexts (Barrett, 1995). One famous example of such **context-bound word use** comes from Allison Bloom as reported by her mother, a well-known child language researcher. Allison produced the word *car* at the age of 9 months, but she said "car" only when she was looking out her apartment window at cars on the street below (Bloom, 1973). She did not say "car" when she saw a car close up or when she saw a picture of a car in a book. Similarly, at the age of 12 months, Martyn Barrett's son Adam used the word *duck* only when he was hitting one of his toy yellow ducks off the edge of the bathtub (Barrett, 1986). He never said "duck" while playing with these toy ducks in other situations, and he never said "duck" while looking at real ducks. Barrett's interpretation of this behavior was that Adam "had not yet learned that the word *duck* could be used to refer to either his toy ducks or real ducks. Instead, his behavior suggests that he had simply identified one particular event in the context of which it was appropriate for him to produce the word *duck*" (Barrett, p. 40).

Even when word use is not limited to a single context, as in the examples above, children's use may be limited in ways that suggest their understanding of the word's meaning still falls short of adultlike representations of word meanings. For example, *more* might be used only as a request and not to comment on recurrence, and *no* might be used only to indicate refusal (Gopnik, 1988). Although these uses are more general than Allison's use of *car* and Adam's use of *duck,* these uses suggest that the child's mental representation of these words is only that words are what you say to accomplish a particular goal. On the basis of data from hundreds of American and Italian children, Caselli and colleagues (1995) concluded that children's first words may always be parts of routines or language games. Such situation-specific or function-specific understandings of word use are crucially different from adults' mental representations of words as symbols that refer.

Is there a prelexical stage of word use?   Because the understanding of word meaning that seems to underlie children's early context-bound words is so different from adults' mental representations of word meanings, it has been argued that these context-bound words are not really words at all. Behrend (1990) suggests that these words are merely responses elicited by particular environmental conditions, similar to the reaching and pointing gestures of prelinguistic children. Behrend terms these context-bound words *prelexical.*

But if these first words are not really words, then when do real words appear? This question is important, in part because we want to know if the context-bound nature of early words reflects some internal limitation in the child. Are word meanings tied to particular contexts because there is something about these particular words that children do not know, or is there something about words in general that children don't know? That is, are the words prelexical or is the child prelexical?

To answer this question, we need to know (1) whether there is a stage during which the child uses words only in these prelexical ways or (2) whether these prelexical words in children's vocabularies coexist with words that have true referential uses. Some researchers argue that context-bound words appear first and that truly referential words must await some cognitive development in the child (for very different versions of this hypothesis, see Gopnik & Meltzoff,

1987; Nelson & Lucariello, 1985). Other researchers have found evidence that suggests otherwise.

First words can also be referential An example of evidence of **referential word use** among children's first words comes from research by Harris, Barrett, Jones, and Brookes (1988), who analyzed the first ten words produced by four children using diaries mothers kept of their children's word use. Harris and colleagues were able to categorize children's first words into three groups, as shown in Table 3.1. The largest category was context-bound words, containing 22 of these 40 first words. Contextually flexible **nominals,** or names for things, were the next most frequent, accounting for 14 of the 40 words. Last, four words were contextually flexible in their use and were not nominals.

It is interesting to note that the same word that is context-bound for one child may be contextually flexible for another. For example, Jacqui, who participated in the study by Harris and colleagues (1988), said "no" only when

Table 3.1   Four children's first ten words

Word type	CHILD			
	James	*Jacqui*	*Jenny*	*Madeleine*
Context-bound	mummy	wee	choo-choo	there
	go	hello	bye-bye	hello
	quack	mummy	there	here
	there	here		bye-bye
	buzz	no		
	moo	down		
	boo	more		
		go		
Nominal	teddy	Jacqui	teddy	teddy
	ball	bee	doggy	shoes
			moo	brum
			shoe	woof
			car	baby
Nonnominal	more		mummy	yes
			no	

Source: From "Linguistic Input and Early Word Meaning," by M. Harris et al., 1988, *Journal of Child Language, 15,* p. 83. Copyright © 1988 and reprinted with the permission of Cambridge University Press.

refusing something that was offered by her mother, so for Jacqui *no* was a context-bound word. In contrast, Jenny said "no" while pushing a drink away, while crawling to a step she was not allowed to climb, and while refusing a request by her mother. For Jenny, *no* was contextually flexible.

Why are some words context-bound and others referential?   If children are capable of acquiring referential words from the start, then why are some words not represented that way? It could be that limited experience produces limited understanding. However, not all of children's limited understandings seem explainable in this way. Children seem to not make use of the full range of their linguistic experience. In their study of children's first ten words, Harris and associates also looked at how the mothers used these words and found that mothers used their children's first words in contexts other than the ones in which their children used them. So the children had extracted narrower meanings than their experience would have supported. The reason the children did not use their experience to build contextually flexible representations of word meanings may be that distilling the common meaning from a variety of contexts of use takes time for the beginning language learner. Some words get used before that common meaning has been inferred. The particular narrow meaning the children inferred does make sense given the children's experience hearing the word. Harris and associates found that for 18 of the 22 context-bound words, the child's sole use was the same as his or her mother's most frequent use.

Context-bound words become decontextualized   Words that are at first context-bound gradually become decontextualized (Barrett, 1986; Bates et al., 1979; Dore et al., 1976). For example, about two weeks after Barrett's son Adam first said "duck" while hitting toy ducks off the edge of the bathtub, he began to say "duck" in other settings as well. The description of the beginning of lexical development that emerges from studies of this early stage is one in which children start out with at least two kinds of lexical entries for the words they use. One kind of lexical entry is situation-specific; this is a word you can say in this particular circumstance. The other kind of lexical entry is more adultlike; this is a word that encodes this meaning, and you can say it whenever you wish to express this meaning. Although some words enter the lexicon as context-bound words and gradually become decontextualized, other words are contextually flexible from the time the child first uses them.

Vocabulary development from first words to 50 words

For several months after the appearance of their first words, most children plod along, adding words to their vocabulary slowly at first but with increasing speed as they approach the achievement of a 50-word vocabulary.

Sometime around 18 months of age, but ranging from 15 to 24 months, children achieve a productive vocabulary of 50 words. The results of Katharine Nelson's (1973) longitudinal study of 18 children can be used to illustrate the course of lexical development from the first word to the 50-word vocabulary. Each mother in Nelson's study kept a diary and recorded each new word her child produced, along with the date and notes about the context in which the word was used. All mothers kept records until their children had acquired 50 words. From these records, Nelson was able to analyze the content of children's 50-word vocabularies and the course of their lexical development to that point.

Nelson classified the children's words into six different categories:

1. *specific nominals,* such as *Mommy, Daddy, Rover*
2. *general nominals,* including common nouns such as *dog, ball, milk* and pronouns such as *he, this*
3. *action words,* such as *go, up, look*
4. *modifiers,* such as *big, all gone, outside, mine*
5. *personal social words,* such as *no, want, please*
6. grammatical *function words,* such as *what, is, for*

Nelson found that nominals were the largest single category of children's words, from the first 10 words to the 50-word mark. She also found that the proportion of general nominals in children's vocabularies increased as vocabulary size increased during this period. Her results are illustrated in Figure 3.1.

Vocabularies at the 50-word mark

The content of children's 50-word vocabularies   Many investigators have noted the predominance of general nominals, or common nouns, in children's early vocabularies (Bates et al., 1994; Benedict, 1979; Dromi, 1987; Goldin-Meadow, Seligman, & Gelman, 1976). The particular nouns children learn come, not surprisingly, from their experiences. Names for people, food, and body parts are frequent among children's first object labels. Also common are words for clothing, animals, and household items that are involved in children's daily routines (Clark, 1979).

However, some have questioned the universality of a noun-dominated early vocabulary. Not all studies find a strong noun bias, even among children acquiring English (Bloom, Tinker, & Margulis, 1993; Gopnik & Choi, 1995); and a noun bias seems to be even less common for children in other cultures acquiring other languages. Gopnik and Choi (1995) report that verbs appear earlier and are more prevalent in the speech of children acquiring Korean than in the speech of children acquiring English. Fernald and Morikawa (1993) report

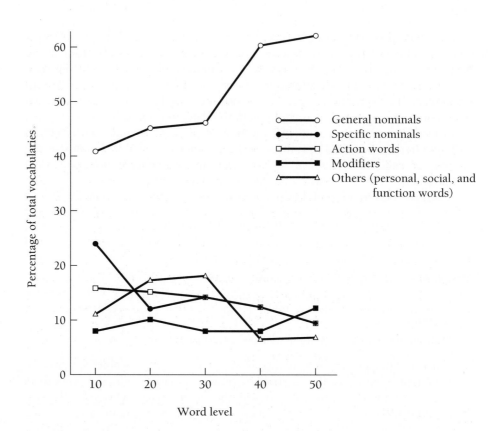

Figure 3.1 Lexical growth from l0 to 50 words, by word type

Source: From "Structure and Strategy in Learning to Talk," by K. Nelson, l973, Monographs of the Society for Research in Child Development, 38, Serial No. l49. Copyright © l973 The Society for Research in Child Development, Inc. Reprinted by permission.

that 12- and 19-month-old American children have larger object-label vocabularies than do Japanese children at the same age. Tardif (1996) reports that for 21-month-old children acquiring Mandarin (Chinese), the number of different verbs in their speech is equal to or greater than the number of different nouns.

What determines the content of early vocabularies?   One potential determinant of the content of children's early vocabularies is the nonlinguistic cognitive understandings children bring to bear on the word learning task. In explaining what she took to be evidence of a universal noun bias in children's vocabularies, Gentner (1978, 1982) argued that children acquire nouns before verbs (and hence nouns dominate early vocabularies) because the meanings nouns encode are easier for children to learn than are the meanings verbs encode. Nouns refer to entities or things (like tables, chairs, birds, or dogs), and young children can have an understanding of things based on their perception of the physical world. Verbs, on the other hand, express relationships among things; for example, *give* entails somebody giving something, and *go* entails somebody going somewhere. According to Gentner, the relational meanings encoded in verbs are less available to young children through nonlinguistic experience.

Cross-cultural and cross-linguistic evidence that the noun bias may not be universal has implicated other factors besides cognitive development in shaping early lexicons. One additional factor is the nature of the target language and how it illustrates nouns and verbs. In the Asian languages, where there doesn't seem to be a noun bias in children's early vocabularies, a verb is often the final word in a sentence, and this position may be particularly salient (that is, noticeable) to children. Also, the grammars of these languages allow noun dropping, thus making verbs more frequent in the input.

Not only the grammar but also the culture shapes input and affects children's vocabulary development. American mothers—at least the middle-class mothers most frequently studied—spend a great deal of time labeling objects for their babies. Fernald and Morikawa (1993) found that Japanese mothers do so much less frequently. Thus both the structure of the language and the sociocultural uses to which it is put shape the nature of children's input, which in turn appears to shape the content of their early vocabularies. Nonlinguistic cognition is a factor in lexical development, but only one of several factors.

The word spurt

As previously mentioned, lexical development starts slowly for most children. During the first months after speaking their first words, children add an average of between 8 and 11 words to their vocabularies each month (Benedict, 1979). During these months of slow lexical growth, exposure to a new word does not necessarily result in word learning. Another characteristic of this period is that words that were apparently learned at one point do not necessarily become permanent additions to children's productive vocabularies.

For many children, lexical development seems to shift into a different gear at about the 50-word milestone. In this new gear, the rate at which new words appear in the children's vocabularies increases from 8 to 11 words per month to an average rate of 22 to 37 words per month (Benedict, 1979; Goldfield & Reznick, 1990). In fact, one of the reasons Nelson's study of lexical development ended at 50 words is that word learning was too rapid for most mothers to keep up with it after that. In this later period of rapid lexical growth, children often learn a new word after only a single exposure.

A great deal of attention has been given to this increase in the word learning rate, which has been called the **word spurt,** the word explosion, and the naming explosion. This spurt occurs for most children some time around the achievement of a 50-word productive vocabulary or around the age of 18

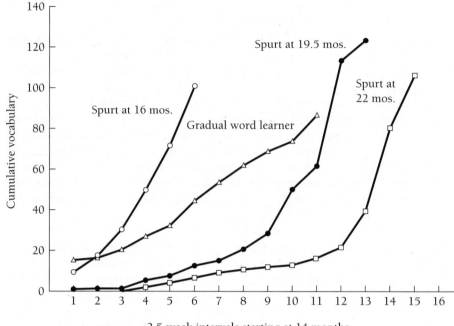

Figure 3.2   Patterns of lexical growth shown by four different children

Source: From "Early Lexical Acquisition: Rate, Content, and the Vocabulary Spurt," by B. A. Goldfield and J. S. Reznick, 1990, Journal of Child Language, 17, Cambridge University Press.

months (Benedict, 1979; Bloom, 1973; Nelson, 1973). We will first consider the evidence that some "shifting of gears" occurs and then consider proposals for what causes that shift.

What is the word spurt?   Many observers have reported this marked increase in the vocabulary growth rate (Benedict, 1979; Bloom, 1973, 1994; McShane, 1980; Nelson, 1973). However, there is some disagreement as to whether all children show this pattern. Goldfield and Reznick (1990) claim that some children show more even rates of vocabulary development and never show a spurt. These researchers carefully documented the rate of vocabulary development in 18 children whom they studied from the age of 14 months until each child achieved a 75-word vocabulary. Examples of four different growth curves shown by children in Goldfield and Reznick's study are illustrated in Figure 3.2. Thirteen of the 18 children showed a word spurt, or surge in the rate of vocabulary growth, which occurred at ages as early as 14 months and as late as 21 months. However, 5 of the 18 children achieved vocabularies of 75 words or more without any spurt at all. Instead, these five children showed a linear pattern of vocabulary growth in which their vocabularies increased at a constant rate. It is possible, however, that Goldfield and Reznick stopped their study too soon and that they would have seen spurts in all the children if they had followed them long enough. Mervis and Bertrand (1995) followed some apparent nonspurters past the 75-word point and found that these children eventually did show a vocabulary spurt. (But see Goldfield & Reznick, 1996, for an alternative view.)

One aspect of the spurt (whenever it occurs) widely observed among children acquiring English is that it is not a spurt in the acquisition of all kinds of words. Rather, it is a spurt in the acquisition of object labels. Children who show the word spurt concurrently show a large increase in the proportion of object labels in their vocabularies. In Goldfield and Reznick's (1990) study, the children whose vocabularies grew at a constant rate showed only a small increase in the proportion of nominals in their vocabularies.

What causes the word spurt?   Although words must be available in input for the child to learn them, something seems to change in the child that allows this sudden spurt in vocabulary. Several studies have found that children younger than 18 months or with vocabularies of fewer than 50 words are not as good at learning new words in an experimental situation as are older children or those with larger vocabularies (Lucariello, 1987; Oviatt, 1982).

Fast mapping   Mervis and Bertrand (1994) tested the ability of children between 16 and 20 months old to **fast map,** or to learn a word on the basis of a single exposure. For this test, Mervis and Bertrand used the following procedure: A child was presented with an array of five objects that included four familiar objects for which the child had a word (such as a ball, a cup, a shoe, and a toy car) and one unfamiliar object the child would not have a word for (such as an egg piercer or a garlic press). Then the experimenter asked the child, "Can I have the shoe?" After the child indicated the shoe, the experimenter asked, "Can I have the zib?" Children who fast mapped concluded at once that the new word *zib* must be the name for the unfamiliar object. In Mervis and Bertrand's experiment, the children heard the new word three more times in sentences produced by the experimenter; in fact, four new words were introduced to the children in this fashion. Later, the researchers tested the children's comprehension of the new words.

Some children were able to learn new words in this situation and some were not. Mervis and Bertrand (1994) compared these two groups of children in terms of their productive vocabularies—assessed by mothers' reports, using the MacArthur Communicative Development Inventory. They found that the children who were not successful at word learning in this situation had smaller vocabularies and (by inference) had not yet "spurted" in their vocabulary growth. In contrast, the children who were successful at learning these new

Figure 3.3   In her autobiography, Helen Keller (portrayed in this photo by Patty Duke in "The Miracle Worker") recalled the moment at which she realized that "everything had a name." It has been suggested that all children experience such a naming insight.

words had larger vocabularies and were (again by inference) "post-spurt." A longitudinal follow-up of the children who were not successful at the first visit confirmed that once these children's vocabularies had spurted, they were able to fast map. This correspondence between the word spurt and fast mapping ability was found a second time in children who were late spurters and had vocabularies nearing 100 words at the time of their word spurt (Mervis & Bertrand, 1995).

The naming insight   Several proposals have been made to explain what underlies the ability to fast map. The most dramatic hypothesis is that the child experiences a **naming insight.** The naming insight is the realization that words name objects and that all objects have names (Dore, 1978; Gillis & De Schutter, 1986; McShane, 1980). Helen Keller, who was blind, deaf, and without any language at the age of 6 years, recalled experiencing such an insight (Keller, 1902-1954) (see Figure 3.3). Before Helen achieved this insight, her teacher had been trying for a month to teach Helen names for things by using the manual alphabet and fingerspelling words into Helen's hand, but with little success. Helen's insight came as her teacher placed Helen's hand under water running out of a pump and spelled W-A-T-E-R into Helen's other hand.

> As the cool stream gushed over one hand she spelled into the other the word *water*, first slowly, then rapidly. I stood still, my whole attention fixed upon the motions of her fingers. Suddenly I felt a misty consciousness as of something forgotten—a thrill of returning thought; and somehow the mystery of language was revealed to me. I knew then that "w-a-t-e-r" meant the wonderful cool something that was flowing over my hand. . . . I left the well-house eager to learn. Everything had a name. . . . (Keller, 1902–1954, p. 36)

Although this scene is very compelling, it is important to note that Helen was 6 years old at the time, and she had had some language before she lost her vision and hearing to "brain fever" at the age of 18 months. Helen Keller refers, in fact, to a "returning thought." The critical issue is whether under normal circumstances children experience such an insight and whether that insight precipitates the word spurt. There is no doubt that adult speakers know that words name things and that everything has a name. The questions are, When do children achieve this knowledge? Do they achieve it gradually or suddenly? and Does it have anything to do with changes in the rate of vocabulary growth? One problem with the notion of a naming insight underlying the word spurt is that it does not explain how children could have truly referential words prior to this insight and the resultant word spurt, as they seem to have.

Other cognitive changes as preconditions of the word spurt Other proposals of cognitive changes that might underlie the word spurt are more compatible with the evidence that truly referential words precede the word spurt. One proposal offered by Nelson and Lucariello (1985) is that before children have a word spurt, they organize their experiences in terms of whole events, and words are attached to events. What allows the word spurt, according to Nelson and Lucariello, is that the child analyzes these whole events into components (such as objects) that can be individually labeled. If Nelson and Lucariello's proposal allows for some components to be less embedded in events than others, then different levels of lexical understanding could exist simultaneously.

The strongest experimental evidence of a cognitive change coincident with the word spurt comes from Gopnik and Meltzoff (1987). They propose that an insight underlies the word spurt, but it is only the second half of the insight Helen Keller experienced; the insight that every object has a name. Before the word spurt occurs, according to Gopnik and Meltzoff, children understand that words are names for things, and that understanding allows early words to be truly referential. But the child doesn't look for new words at this early point because the child doesn't know that there will be words for everything.

Gopnik and Meltzoff believe this second insight comes from cognitive development. The cognitive change that underlies the word spurt is the development of an understanding of categorization. To illustrate, if you give a set of objects—say, four blocks and four dolls—to a 15-month-old, the child may pick out all the blocks and leave the dolls or pick out all the dolls and leave the blocks. (The child may also just pick up one block and work on getting it into his or her mouth until the researcher decides it's time to end the experiment.) Although children's behavior remains variable and often unpredictable, a new behavior emerges at age 18 months that you do not see in much younger children. If you give an 18-month-old four dolls and four blocks, the child is likely to spontaneously make two piles, one of dolls and one of blocks. An important difference between the behavior of the 15-month-old and the behavior of the 18-month-old is that the 15-month-old shows evidence of recognizing similarities among the dolls. You might want to say that the child recognized that all the dolls were members of the same category. What the 18-month-old does, in contrast, is to put *all* the items into one category or another. It is this development of the nonlinguistic understanding that all things can be categorized that underlies the linguistic insight that all things have names.

Gopnik and Meltzoff have found good support for this view. They followed 12 children longitudinally, giving them cognitive tasks every 3 weeks between the ages of 15 and 20 months and monitoring their vocabulary development through records the mothers were instructed to keep. They found a strong relationship between the age at which children spontaneously sorted and the age at which children showed a spurt in their lexical development. A similar finding is reported by Mervis and Bertrand (1994, 1995).

Early word comprehension

At this point, we have described lexical development only in terms of the words children say. The course of word comprehension is another source of evidence about the internal changes that occur as children's mental lexicons develop. Clearly, word learning begins months before children speak their first words. Both anecdotal reports (Vihman, 1988) and experimental demonstrations show that children as young as 5 months selectively respond to certain words (Mandel, Jusczyk, & Pisoni, 1995). The first word children seem to respond to is their own name. Anecdotal evidence that infants recognize their own names includes such incidents as: a baby sitting in an infant swing ignoring the conversation going on behind her but turning around to look when someone mentions her name (personal data). Experimental evidence is supplied by Mandel and associates' (1995) demonstration, using the head-turn procedure described in Chapter 2, that 5-month-old babies preferred their own name to prosodically similar foils.

At around the age of 8 months, children begin to understand a few phrases, such as "Give me a hug," "Stop it," and "Come here" (Fenson et al., 1994). Shortly after that—between the ages of 8 and 10 months—children start to understand the meanings of individual words. Fenson and colleagues studied more than 1000 children in the United States using the MacArthur Communicative Development Inventory, which assesses children's comprehension and production vocabularies from mothers' reports, and found that 10-month-old children's comprehension vocabularies ranged from an average of 11 words (for the bottom 10% of children tested) to an average of 154 words (for the top 10%). At 16 months of age, children have comprehension vocabularies between 92 and 321 words. Compare this with production vocabularies that are typically zero at 10 months and under 50 words at 16 months and it becomes clear that comprehension vocabularies are acquired earlier and grow faster than production vocabularies. Other, smaller-scale studies have also found that early comprehension vocabularies are larger than production vocabularies (Benedict, 1979; Goldin-Meadow et al., 1976).

Comprehension and production vocabularies differ not only in size but also in content. Both Benedict and Goldin-Meadow and associates found proportionately more verbs in children's comprehension vocabularies than in their production vocabularies. Gentner (1978) suggests that this imbalance may be because communication works adequately with a minimal verb vocabulary. For example, the single verb *go* can be combined with *night-night, car,* and *park* to convey the meanings of three verbs: *sleep, drive,* and *play.*

Although, in general, the relation between comprehension and production in early lexical development is that comprehension precedes production and comprehension vocabularies are larger than production vocabularies, some words may appear in production first. When children have context-bound word meanings or word meanings that are narrower than the adult meanings, they tend to use those words correctly, even though they don't fully know what the words mean. Isolated words with context-bound meanings can coexist with a large and fairly adultlike vocabulary. For example, the preschool child who said he was "late" to school that morning defined *late* for the inquiring researcher as "when I get to school and everyone else already has their boots off" (Keller-Cohen, personal communication, 1978). Thus, if not pressed for definitions, children can sometimes appear more competent verbally than they really are.

INDIVIDUAL DIFFERENCES IN LEXICAL DEVELOPMENT

Thus far in this chapter, we have been trying to construct an account of the normative course of lexical development. That is, we have been trying to describe how lexical development generally proceeds. In describing this normative course, we always gave age ranges for the achievement of various landmarks because children vary in the rate at which they develop. But our focus has been on abstracting that which was common among all children. Now we will focus on the ways in which children differ in the courses of lexical development they follow and the rates at which they proceed.

Individual differences in language style

First words   Characterizing first words as context-bound seems to be more true for some children than for others. Some children's vocabularies consist almost entirely of referentially used words from the start. Other children acquire many context-bound words even as their acquisition of referential words proceeds. What underlies these differences? One factor, already discussed, may be the contexts in which children hear the words. Words taught as labels and given explicit definitions may be more likely to be used referentially from the beginning than words the child picks up from context. Particularly if a word is used almost exclusively in a single context, the child would have no basis for figuring out its more generalizable meaning. For example, Ferrier (1978) reported that her daughter thought *phew* was a form of greeting because that's what her mother said to her when she entered her room each morning. Her mother was responding to the smell of the diaper the baby had worn for the past 12 hours, but the baby didn't know that.

Another factor that may influence the number of context-bound first words is the child's approach to the language acquisition task. Some children seem to be more analytic about language learning than others. The most analytic children divide the speech stream into small bits (words or even phonemes), whereas other children proceed in a more holistic manner, acquiring big chunks (Peters, 1983). For example, *Don't do that* appeared as a single big chunk in the early vocabulary of one little boy (personal data). Such big chunks are more likely to be associated with certain interactive functions or with whole events than with particular referents. As we saw in the studies by Barrett (1986) and Harris and associates (1988), however, single words can have contextually bound meanings. So the distinction between analytic and holistic approaches does not seem adequate to fully explain individual differences in the use of context-bound words.

Another way in which children differ, which may have something to do with this difference in lexical development, is the extent to which children are risk takers (Peters, 1983; Richards, 1990). Some children may jump into talking with a minimal understanding of what they are saying, whereas other children may be more cautious, not using words until they are sure of what they mean. The more cautious children would be expected to produce fewer context-bound words—if children at this point in development know that their understanding of context-bound words is incomplete.

How social children are is one last way in which children may differ that might have something to do with who uses many context-bound words and who uses primarily referential words. A child who is very interested in social interaction would want a vocabulary of words to use in particular situations. Also, such a child might be more driven to use whatever means available for interaction and thus be more likely to talk when his or her understanding of word meaning was still incomplete and tied to particular settings. A child who is less social, or who is good at maintaining interaction nonverbally, may have little use for words that serve only a social function and so may wait longer to talk, at which point the child's understanding of word meaning is more likely to allow contextually flexible usage.

Referential and expressive language users Most of the work on individual differences in lexical development focuses on children's vocabularies at the 50-word mark. Nelson (1973) studied the lexical development of 18 children and found that some children's vocabularies had a much larger percentage of nominals than others' did. For example, one child had 38 nominals among her first 50 words, whereas another child had only 17. Nelson also argued that for the children who used fewer nominals, the difference was not made up evenly with words from other categories. Rather, children with fewer nominals tended to have more personal/social words. Nelson concluded that these two kinds of early vocabularies—one dominated by object labels and the other including many more personal/social words—represent two different styles of language use. Nelson labeled the children with more object labels in their vocabularies **referential,** and she called the children with relatively fewer object labels and more personal/social words **expressive.** The composition of the vocabularies of the referential and expressive children in Nelson's study is depicted in Figure 3.4.

Two things about the difference between referential and expressive children should be noted. First, these two types of language learners represent two ends of a continuum, and most children fall somewhere in between. Second, even when comparing the extremes, the difference is one of degree; all children have some object labels and some personal/social words in their early vocabularies. Nonetheless, the difference between a referential style and an expressive style has been the subject of a great deal of subsequent research on (1) what these differences actually reflect about the language learner, (2) where

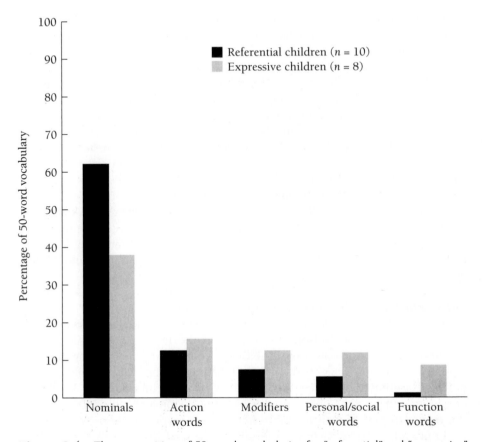

Figure 3.4 The composition of 50-word vocabularies for "referential" and "expressive" children.

Source: Based on data in Nelson, 1973.

these differences might come from, and (3) what other sorts of differences in language acquisition these styles might be related to.

Sources of the referential/expressive difference in lexical development   One proposed explanation for why some children have more referential vocabularies than others is that these differences in language usage reflect differences in children's language learning experiences. Some children's mothers spend a great deal of time teaching them labels, and these children accordingly acquire large numbers of object labels. Support for this view includes the finding that the proportion of nouns in children's early vocabularies is related to the frequency with which their mothers produce descriptive utterances containing nouns (Pine, 1994). Also, referential children are more likely than average to be the first-born of college-educated parents (Goldfield & Reznick, 1990; Nelson, 1973), and later-born children have a higher number of unanalyzed chunks in their vocabularies (Pine, 1995). More educated mothers may be more likely to engage in explicit labeling (Lawrence & Shipley, 1996) and are more likely to have the time to do so with their first children. Children who are not the first-borns of college-educated mothers pick up more of their language from context.

Some researchers have also proposed that individual differences in early vocabularies reflect differences in the children, not just in their input. Nelson postulates that the referential/expressive difference in the content of early vocabularies reflects differences in the views children hold about what language is for. Some children seem to regard language as a vehicle for making reference to objects. Perhaps these children are inherently more interested in the world of objects than other children are, or maybe their mothers play word games with them and thus teach them that reference is what language is for. In either case, a vocabulary dominated by object labels suits the function to which these children assign their emerging linguistic abilities. Other children seem to regard language as a vehicle for social interaction, either because they are inherently more social or because of the situation in which they are placed. Accordingly, a vocabulary of personal/social words best suits the function of language for them.

Others have suggested that the referential/expressive difference is related to the analytic/holistic dimension of difference referred to earlier regarding individual differences in first words (Peters, 1983). According to Bates, Bretherton, and Snyder (1988), children who approach language analytically are more likely to be referential, and children who approach language holistically are more likely to be expressive language users. Bates and associates also hypothesized that the analytic/holistic difference in approach may reflect differences among children in the parts of the brain doing the work of language acquisition.

The significance of the referential/expressive distinction   For whatever reason, referential and expressive children seem to follow different routes in their early lexical development. It is not clear, at this point, whether these are two routes to the same place or whether referential and expressive children will continue to differ in the course of their later language development.

One proposal that was made and rejected is that the referential style is superior to the expressive style and is associated with more rapid language development. The referential style initially may have seemed to be associated with more rapid learning for two reasons. First, Nelson (1973) found that the referential children in her study took less time between acquiring their first word and achieving a 50-word vocabulary. Second, Bates and associates (1988) found that among a group of 13-month-olds with vocabularies ranging from 2 to 32 words, the children with proportionately more object labels had the larger vocabularies. However, neither finding implies that the referential children should be more precocious language learners. In Nelson's study, both referential and expressive children reached a 50-word vocabulary at the same age. The referential children produced their first word later than the expressive children, so the time they took to go from 1 to 50 words was less. In Bates, Bretherton, and Snyder's study, the children's vocabularies were different sizes at the point when referentiality was assessed. Looking at the graph in Figure 3.1, it is clear that, up to a 50-word vocabulary, children with larger vocabularies would have proportionately more object labels. In sum, variation in style and rate of vocabulary development are separate phenomena, and the referential/ expressive distinction properly applies only when the size of vocabulary is held constant (Bates et al., 1994; Pine & Lieven, 1990). But if differences in style are not the source of differences in the rate of vocabulary development, then what is?

Individual differences in the rate of lexical development

Some children reach the 50- and 100-word milestones at younger ages than others. To put the same phenomenon another way, the vocabularies of children of the same age vary enormously in size. The MacArthur Inventory data referred to earlier (Fenson et al., 1994), for example, show that even if we exclude the top and bottom 15% of children, 16-month-olds have production vocabularies between 0 and 160 words, and 24-month-olds have vocabularies between 50 and 550 words (for a discussion of individual differences in these data, see Bates, Dale, & Thal, 1995). Although how all children acquire a lexicon is far more central to the field of child language than why some children do so more rapidly than others, there has been some research on the topic of differences in the rate of lexical development. That research points to both characteristics of the child and properties of the child's experience as relevant factors.

Characteristics of the child as an influence on rate of lexical development   Phonological memory is one cognitive skill that seems to contribute to vocabulary development. Phonological memory is the ability to remember a sequence of unfamiliar sounds. Gathercole and Baddeley (1989) tested the phonological memory skills and vocabulary size of 100 children, first at the age of 4, and then a year later at age 5. They found that children with better phonological memory skills had more advanced vocabularies at both ages. Even more important, phonological memory tested at age 4 predicted vocabulary one year later, even when earlier vocabulary and nonverbal intelligence were factored out statistically (Gathercole, Willis, Emslie, & Baddeley, 1992). It makes sense that remembering how newly encountered words sound is a prerequisite to learning what those words mean. In Chapter 7, we will see that phonological memory is also implicated in cases of impaired language learning ability.

Another finding that suggests there may be differences among children in word learning ability is the frequent finding of sex differences in vocabulary size or word learning ability. The sex difference is small and it is not always present, but several studies have shown girls to be more advanced in vocabulary development than boys (Fenson et al., 1994; Huttenlocher, Haight, Bryk, Seltzer, & Lyons, 1991; and for a review, see Klann-Delius, 1981). Also, girls sometimes demonstrate word learning skills that boys of the same age do not (Katz, Baker, & Macnamara, 1974; Naigles, 1995). Such a sex difference could reflect the differing maturation levels of girls and boys; as infants, girls are physically more mature than boys. There are also structural differences between male and female brains that may affect language development (see Chapter 9). Some studies have found that mothers talk more to girl babies than to boy babies (Cherry & Lewis, 1978; Halvorsen & Waldrop, 1970), suggesting a possible experiential basis to the observed sex differences. However, Huttenlocher and colleagues (1991) found a sex difference in the rate of vocabulary growth that could not be accounted for by different amounts of input.

Characteristics of the environment as an influence on rate of lexical development   It is clear that experience affects vocabulary development. In the next section, we will introduce evidence suggesting that the way in which adults talk to children influences children's word learning. There is also evidence that the sheer amount of talk that children hear is a predictor of their vocabulary growth. In a longitudinal study of 11 children who were followed from the age of 14 to 26 months, Huttenlocher and associates (1991) concluded that the amount of speech mothers addressed to children was a significant predictor of the children's rates of vocabulary growth.

We can also infer the effect of differences in amount of exposure to language from evidence that vocabulary development is affected by birth order and socioeconomic status. The effects of birth order are small and not always found, but when evident they consistently show that first-born children have a slight advantage in vocabulary development over later-borns. Fenson and associates (1994) studied more than 1000 children in the United States and found that first-born children have slightly larger production vocabularies than do later-born children at the same age. In another study, Pine (1995) used mothers' diary records and compared nine first-born children to their younger siblings. Pine found that the first-borns reached the 50-word milestone on average one month sooner than their second-born siblings did. However, he found no age difference at the 100-word mark. Hoff-Ginsberg (1993), using spontaneous speech samples collected at two points during the second year of life for 63 children, found that first-borns used a more varied vocabulary than did later-borns. The likely cause of this difference between a first- and a later-born may be the different amount of one-to-one interaction with an adult each experiences.

The effects of socioeconomic status (SES) on vocabulary development are also small at the beginning of language development, but these effects grow larger over time and always in the children of more educated parents having larger vocabularies than children of less educated parents (Fenson et al., 1994; Hart & Risley, 1995; Hoff-Ginsberg, 1993). These SES-associated differences suggest that the amount of speech children hear has an effect, because many studies have shown that more educated mothers talk to their children more than less educated mothers do (Hart & Risley, 1995; Hoff-Ginsberg, 1994; Hoff-Ginsberg & Tardif, 1995).

HOW ARE CHILDREN'S WORD MEANINGS REPRESENTED?

To this point, we have described the course (or courses) of early lexical development in terms of the words children say and, to a lesser extent, the words children understand. We considered the issue of how children represent the meaning of their first words when we discussed the difference between context-bound words and truly referential words. However, even when words no longer have the limited, context-bound meanings of children's very first words, the meaning representations children have may be different from the meanings of those words in adults' lexicons. That is, once it is clear that children's words refer, the next question we have to ask is, To what do the words refer?

If a 2-year-old points to a dog and says "dog," we tend to think the child has learned the word *dog*. In a sense, that's true; however, we cannot assume the child has the same meaning associated with his or her lexical entry for *dog* that an adult does. The child's meaning may be narrower if, for example, *dog* refers to collies and spaniels but not to chihuahuas. Such narrower meanings are called **underextensions,** and they may reflect either situation-specific understandings of word use or narrowly defined meanings that exclude atypical category members. It is also possible that the child has a broader meaning and might, for example, point to a horse and say "dog." In discussing the meaning representations in children's mental lexicons, a great deal has been made of the latter sort of errors, called **overextensions.**

Children's word meanings as incomplete lists of semantic features

One early theory of word meaning proposed that the child who calls a horse "dog" has learned some of the features that define *dog* (such as it is an animal and it has four legs) but does not know other definitional features of dogs that

Table 3.2   Examples of children's overextended word uses

Word	Referents
ball	ball, balloon, marble, apple, egg, wool pom-pom, spherical water tank (Rescorla, 1980)
cat	cat, cat's usual location on top of TV when absent (Rescorla, 1980)
moon	moon, half-moon shaped lemon slice, circular chrome dial on dishwasher, ball of spinach, wall hanging with pink and purple circles, half a Cheerio, hangnail (Bowerman, 1978)
snow	snow, white tail of a spring horse, white flannel bed pad, white puddle of milk on floor (Bowerman, 1978)
baby	own reflection in mirror, framed photograph of self, framed photographs of others (personal data)
shoe	shoe, sock (personal data)

distinguish dogs from horses (such as it doesn't have hooves). This proposal is known as the **semantic feature hypothesis** (Clark, 1973). The semantic feature hypothesis is both a theory of how adults mentally represent word meanings and a theory of what could be incomplete about children's representations of word meaning. According to the semantic feature theory, word meanings are represented by a list of semantic components (features) that together make up the word's meaning. For example, the meaning of the word *bachelor* can be defined as + male and − married.

Like all good theories, the semantic feature hypothesis was sufficiently explicit that it was possible to test. The hypothesis inspired a huge amount of research, but the findings were not favorable for support of the hypothesis. The componential theory of word meaning the semantic feature hypothesis entails is apparently not the best representation of either adults' word meanings or children's incomplete word meanings. For example, the sorts of overextensions children produce are not consistent with the idea that their word meanings differ from the adults' only in terms of a feature or two. Bowerman (1978) reported that her daughter used the word *moon* to refer to the moon, to a ball of spinach, to hangnails she was pulling off, to half a Cheerio, to curved steer horns mounted on a wall, and to a magnetic capital letter D she was about to put on the refrigerator, to list a few. Another child used the word *baby* first to refer to a framed picture of himself his mother had just labeled *baby*. Then he used *baby* in reference to his own reflection in a mirror, and then he used *baby* to refer to any framed photograph (personal data). In all cases, the overextended uses have some component of meaning in common with the original referent of the word, but the overextended uses defy explanation in terms of any single list of shared features. These and other examples of overextensions are presented in Table 3.2.

Children's word meanings as categories with single-exemplar prototypes

What better accounts for both children's overextensions and for adults' representations of word meanings is the theory that word meanings include both a **prototype,** or central category member, and things that bear a "family resemblance" to that prototype (Rosch, Mervis, Gray, Johnson, & Boyes-Braem, 1976). So, for adults, the meaning of *bird* is represented as some generic bird and things that are similar to it in some way; the meaning of *fish* is a generic or—more properly speaking—a prototypical fish and things that are similar to it. This model explains why robins and crows seem to be "better" examples of *bird* than are ostriches and penguins; robins and crows are more similar to our prototype of a bird. This model also explains why whales seem, at least to those of us who look at superficial characteristics, to be more like fish than like mammals, which they are. Learning the prototype for word meanings takes time. Overextension errors of the type in Table 3.2 suggest that the prototypes of the children's word meanings were the first things the children heard those words refer to, including, in the case of *baby,* the irrelevant feature of being in frame.

The whole enterprise of carefully documenting children's overextended word uses and then constructing theories of word meaning and word learning on their basis assumes that the central task of word learning is determining what a newly learned word refers to other than the original referent. However, a great deal of evidence suggests that figuring out the extensions of words is not usually a problem for children.

Children's word meaning as essentially adultlike

Most of children's word meanings may be very much like adults' word meanings from the beginning of lexical development. Evidence supporting this conclusion includes findings that overextensions are actually not very common in children's word use. Rescorla (1980) followed six children from age 12 to 18 months and reported that 33% of the children's word uses were overextended, but only a few different words accounted for a disproportionate share of those overextensions. Also, some have argued that when overextensions occur, they may occur for reasons other than that children have incomplete word meanings (Hoek, Ingram, & Gibson, 1986; Hudson & Nelson, 1984; Huttenlocher & Smiley, 1987).

That is, it's not that the child really thinks that the word for horse is *dog;* it's just that the child doesn't know or can't remember what the horse is called and wants to make some comment on it, and *dog* is the closest word the child can find in his or her vocabulary. Rescorla (1980) found that the incidence of overextensions declined as children acquired more differentiated vocabularies, for example, learning words for animals other than *dog.* Other findings indicate that overextensions in comprehension are rare and are not predictable from overextensions in production, which further supports the idea that overextensions are not reflections of underlying semantic representations (Chapman & Thompson, 1980; Fregmen & Fay, 1980; Huttenlocher, 1974; Kay & Anglin, 1982; Naigles & Gelman, 1995).

If most words are used correctly from the start, and if they are used in contexts other than the one in which they are first heard, then there is no long, gradual process of learning word meaning. Once children hear a word, they know what it means and they use it correctly. A great deal of evidence supports this view. But in solving one problem, we have raised another. How do children know what a word means from hearing it once? In fact, we could ask how children even identify separate words in the stream of speech they hear.

HOW ARE NEW WORDS LEARNED?

At first glance, word learning may seem to be a fairly straightforward process. Someone holds up a cup and says, "This is a cup," and then the child knows the word *cup.* Similarly, the word *ball* is uttered in the presence of a ball, and so on. The child takes the word uttered to be the label for the thing that is there, and that's all there is to it. But let's examine this scenario a little more closely.

The segmentation problem

The first problem for the child is how to find the word within the stream of speech. Someone says, "Thisisacup"; to learn what *cup* means, the child must identify *cup* as a word. In writing, we put spaces between words to separate them, but speakers do not reliably pause between words. The child must find the word boundaries some other way; this is called the **speech segmentation problem.** Of course, sometimes children make mistakes, such as thinking that *elemeno* is one letter in the alphabet (see others in Box 3.1); but children must get it right most of the time or they couldn't acquire language. How do they distinguish word boundaries?

One potential source of information about word boundaries comes from the rhythm of language. A variety of evidence suggests that infants are naturally inclined to attend to the rhythmic properties of speech; they learn the rhythm of their particular language, and they use that rhythm to segment the speech stream (Cutler, 1994, 1996; Mehler, Dupoux, Nazzi, & Dehaene-Lambertz, 1996).

Box 3.1   Examples of children's speech segmentation errors

Family interaction:

> Father: Who wants some mango for dessert?
> Child: What's a semmango? (Ratner, 1996)

Children's attempts to say the "Pledge of Allegiance":

> ". . . and to the flag of the nine of states . . . "

> ". . . and to the republic for witches stands . . . " (Chaney, 1989)

Child's version of a line from the Bob Dylan song:

> "The ants are my friends, they're blowin' in the wind."
> (Pinker, 1994)

Mother and child reading a book:

> Child: I know why he's called Don Quixote. It's because he's
>   riding a donkey. (personal data)

It's not surprising that children occasionally make such segmentation errors. What is more difficult to explain is how children usually succeed in identifying words in the stream of speech they hear.

For example, in English, a stressed syllable is likely to signal the beginning of a new word. If children pay attention to the contrast between stressed and unstressed syllables in the speech they hear, they will be able to identify word boundaries. Other languages have different rhythmic structures, and there is substantial evidence that the strategies adults use to segment the speech stream are shaped by the first language they acquired (Cutler, 1994, 1996).

Some of the special characteristics of child-directed speech might also help children with speech segmentation (Ratner, 1996). Utterances directed to children are short, so there are few word boundaries to find. Also, speech to children uses a small vocabulary, so the same word is presented in many different utterances. Hearing the same sound sequence repeatedly may help the child identify that sequence as a word. Furthermore, when adults are trying to teach children a new word, they tend to stress that word and to put it in sentence final position (Ratner, 1996). Both stress and final position seem to make a sound salient to young children (Echols & Newport, 1992). And there is evidence that new words presented in sentences produced with infant-directed intonation are easier to learn than are words presented in adult-directed speech (Golinkoff, Alioto, & Hirsh-Pasek, 1996). Part of the reason for this advantage may be that the exaggerated intonation of infant-directed speech helps the listener extract the word to be learned.

The mapping problem

When children successfully identify the sound sequence "cup" as a word, their word learning problems are not over. Do the children know what a cup is? If our simple story of word learning is to work, children must have the concepts of things that are labeled by words in the language and lack only the label for them. (This is a problem to which we will return. Let's grant for purposes of discussion right now that the child has the concept of a cup.) Still, how does the child know that it is the cup that is being labeled rather than the cup's handle, the cup's color, the material the cup is made of, or the contents of the cup? Or maybe the word being uttered in the presence of a cup is not a label at all but a command to do something, like drink. The possibilities are limitless. This problem is known as the **mapping problem.**

The philosopher Quine (1960) described the child's problem as follows: an infinite number of hypotheses about word meaning are logically possible given the data the child has. Yet children tend to figure out the meaning of the words that they hear. How do they do it? Several explanations for how children learn new words have been proposed, each relying on a different source of potential help to the child.

Internal constraints as a source of support

Word learning would certainly be facilitated if children did not have to consider all of the many possible meanings each time they heard a new word. Some contend that children do not, in fact, consider all possible meanings but instead enter word learning situations with several assumptions about how the lexicon works. These assumptions limit, or constrain, the possible interpretations of new words that children must consider (Behrend, 1990). Three proposed **constraints on word learning** have been the subject of a great deal of research: the whole-object assumption, the taxonomic assumption, and the assumption of mutual exclusivity (Markman, 1991, 1994).

The **whole-object assumption** is the child's assumption that words refer to whole objects. According to this proposal, children assume that every new word they hear refers to some whole object rather than to part of an object or to a property of the object. This eliminates "white," "handle," "being held in a hand," and the like as possible meanings of *cup*. The existence of such an assumption is supported both by evidence from word learning experiments (Markman & Wachtel, 1988; Mervis & Long, 1987; Taylor & Gelman, 1988; Waxman & Markow, 1995) and by errors young children make. For example, it is not uncommon for very young children to think that *hot* is the label for stove, given the common experience of hearing, "Don't touch it; it's hot." in reference to the stove.

The **taxonomic assumption** is the assumption that words refer to things that are of the same kind. This assumption—it is proposed—helps the child figure out what else, other than the particular whole object being labeled, is included in the meaning of the new word. A taxonomy is a system of classifying things into categories. So when the child hears the word *dog* in the presence of a dog (and assumes that it is the whole dog that's being referred to, thanks to the whole-object assumption), then the taxonomic assumption leads the child to think that *dog* will also refer to other dogs but not to things that are thematically related to dogs, such as collars, leashes, or bones.

This assumption about word meanings may be crucial for word learning, because preschool children show a preference for making thematic groups on many nonlinguistic tasks. For example, if you give children a jumble of toys—including toy people, animals, and vehicles—and ask the children to "put together the things that go together," children who are age 7 or older will sort the collection into groups of animals, people, vehicles, and so on. However, given the same toys and same instructions, preschoolers will put a person with a car because the person drives the car (Markman, 1989). But if preschoolers have this inclination to form thematically related groupings, why don't preschoolers hypothesize that words refer to thematically related sets of things? The answer offered by the taxonomic assumption is that children know that words don't work that way.

Evidence that children actually operate according to the taxonomic assumption in word learning comes from Markman and Hutchinson (1984), who found that preschool children override their inclination to group thematically related things when presented with a new word. Markman and Hutchinson used a puppet to present a picture (say, of a dog) to 2- to 3-year-old children, and then presented a choice between a thematically related item (dog food) and a taxonomically related item (a dog of a different breed). In the "no word" condition, the puppet pointed to the first picture (of a dog) and said, "Look carefully now. See this?" When the next two choices were presented (the other dog and the dog food), the puppet said "Find another one that is the same as this." In the "word" condition the puppet introduced the first picture by saying, "See this? It is a sud." And when presenting the other choices, the puppet said, "Find another sud that is the same as this sud."

Children in the "no word" condition chose the taxonomically related choice 59% of the time. In contrast, children in the "word" condition made the taxonomic choice 83% of the time. That is, even though these children think that thematically related things such as dogs and dog food "go together" (41% of the time), they don't think that words label things that "go together." Children assume that words label things that are of the same kind.

The **mutual exclusivity assumption** is the assumption that different words refer to different kinds of things. So, for example, members of the category labeled *dog* do not overlap with members of the category labeled *cow*. Evidence that suggests children actually operate according to such an assumption consists of experimental studies in which children are given an array of familiar objects for which the children have a label and one object that is novel and nameless. Given the instruction to "Show me the *x*," where *x* is some nonsense syllable chosen to function as a new word, children pick the object for which they do not yet have a word—seemingly indicating that they assume the new word cannot be a synonym for any of the words they already know (Markman & Wachtel, 1988).

Another consequence of the mutual exclusivity assumption is that it provides a basis for overriding the whole-object assumption, which children must do in order to learn terms for parts and properties of objects. So, if a child knows the word *cup* and her mother says, "This is a handle," the child won't take *handle* to be a synonym for *cup* but will look for something else to be the referent of the new term.

Pragmatic principles as a source of support

An alternative proposal to word learning constraints is that word learning is supported by **pragmatic principles** (principles about how language is used). Clark (1993, 1995) proposed the **principle of conventionality,** which is simply that the meaning of words is determined by convention that has to be agreed upon and observed by all members of a language community. Language wouldn't work if people just made up their own words for things, and children seem to know that; they try to learn the meanings of the words they hear. Clark (1993, 1995) also proposed a **principle of contrast,** which is simply that different words have different meanings. This principle is a close variant of the mutual exclusivity assumption but differs in that it allows for multiple labels with different meanings, such as *dog* and *animal,* whereas mutual exclusivity does not. As a practical matter, the two principles would have the same effect in many situations. When a child hears the word *cup* in the presence of a cup, the child would exclude possible meanings such as "container for liquid" and "juice" if the child already knows the words *bowl, glass,* and *juice.*

Arguments against attributing either the mutual exclusivity assumption or the principle of contrast to children are that the kind of response shown in word learning experiments can be explained in terms of weaker constraints or operating principles. So, for example, Gathercole (1989) proposed that children expect a novel word to have a new meaning, not because of some linguistic principle, but because they assume the speaker is trying to communicate and thus would not have used an unfamiliar term if a familiar one would have sufficed. Another proposal to account for the same basic phenomenon is that children operate under a novel-name–novel-category principle, according to which a new word is assumed to label the novel thing (Golinkoff et al., 1994; Mervis & Bertrand, 1994). This principle allows a thing to have two names, however.

Input as a source of support

It has been argued that the way in which people talk to children makes word meaning in context much less ambiguous than it seemed to Quine. Compared to speech among adults, speech directed to children is overwhelmingly about the here-and-now. We tend to talk to young children about what is currently going on rather than about past or future events. Furthermore, many mothers tend to label things the child is looking at, so children hear words when they are looking at the things the words label. And both naturalistic and experimental studies have shown that when adults follow the child's focus of attention and label what the child is looking at, children learn object labels better than when adults try to redirect the child's attention or label things that are not in the child's attentional focus (Dunham, Dunham, & Curwin, 1993; Harris, Jones, Brookes, & Grant, 1986; Tomasello & Todd, 1983). This evidence strongly suggests that children use the correspondence between the speech they hear and the nonlinguistic context as a basis for figuring out the meanings of new words. To the extent that adults ensure that the words children hear will match their perception of the nonlinguistic context, the nature of the input facilitates word learning, and the mapping problem is attenuated.

However, this evidence in no way implies that the correspondence between speech and context is sufficient. Even in our simplified cup example, the correspondence was perfect but there were still multiple possible meanings of *cup*. One possible solution to this problem might come from cross-situational information. That is, across many hearings of *cup*, cups would be the only constant in the situation, not the color or the contents. On the other hand, "handle" would remain a possible meaning. And another problem is that sometimes speech doesn't at all refer to the nonlinguistic context as the child perceives it. For example, a child's mother may open the door and say, *"Whatcha doing?"* not *"This is a door";* or the mother may say, *"Eat your peas"* when the child's thoughts are entirely elsewhere (for a more developed argument in this regard, see Gleitman, 1990). If children use the correspondence between the word and the nonlinguistic context to infer word meaning, then why aren't they hopelessly misled when the two don't match?

Socio-pragmatic cues to word meaning

One proposed explanation is that children don't merely match words with the nonlinguistic context; they match words with speakers' intended meanings. Thus, a child wouldn't be misled by the mother's saying, "Eat your peas" while

Figure 3.5 Joint book reading provides an opportunity for adults to label objects that are the focus of the child's attention.

the child was busy studying the edging on her bib because the child would be able to ascertain the mother's goal from social cues in the interaction. Thus the child would take the mother's words as expressions of those goals.

A variety of evidence supports the claim that children are capable of inferring speakers' semantic intentions from **socio-pragmatic cues** and then using these inferences to assign meaning to newly encountered words. For example, Baldwin (1993) found that by 18 months of age (but probably not before), children can follow a speaker's gaze and use it as a clue to word meaning. As another example, Akhtar, Carpenter, and Tomasello (1996) found that 2-year-olds will infer that a novel label produced with an expression of surprise refers to an object that is also novel to the speaker. And Tomasello and Barton (1994) found that 24-month-olds could distinguish accidental from intentional actions. If an experimenter said, "Let's go twang it" and then did something accidentally (that is, clumsily) followed by doing something intentionally, children took *twang* to refer only to the intentional action.

The socio-pragmatic account of word learning is like the input view in its claim that information about word meaning is available in the environment. But the socio-pragmatic view adds the social behavior of others to the richness of the environment, and it adds children's understanding of other people to their abilities to pick up that information (see also Tomasello & Akhtar, 1995; Tomasello & Kruger, 1992; and references therein). The strongest socio-pragmatic view of word learning asserts that the information children can glean from each word learning situation solves the mapping problem, and thus there is no need to posit internal constraints or principles that apply across all situations.

Syntax as a clue to word meaning

Thus far we have focused on the trade-off between what prior knowledge children might bring to bear on the word meaning task and what they might be able to figure out from the social and physical context in which a new word is heard. Another potential source of information about word meaning is the structure of the language itself.

Distinguishing different grammatical classes   A poem in Lewis Carroll's *Through the Looking Glass* begins, "Twas brillig, and the slithy toves did gyre and gimble in the wabe. . . ." Although you certainly have never seen a slithy tove, you can probably figure out that *toves* are things of some sort and that *slithy* is some property of those toves. Similarly, you can figure out that *gyre* and *gimble* are actions, although of what sort of actions you cannot be sure. It is a fact about language that different grammatical classes tend to have different sorts of meanings. Nouns tend to refer to things, verbs to actions, and adjectives to properties of things. Once children have acquired enough grammar to identify nouns, verbs, and adjectives (using the same cues you did to interpret Lewis Carroll's poem), children can use the grammar as a clue to meaning.

Children can identify nouns, verbs, and adjectives   Roger Brown (1957) demonstrated that children use grammar as a clue to meaning by showing preschool children a picture of a pair of hands kneading a mass of material in a container. He described the picture as *sibbing* to some of the children, as *a sib* to some of the children, and as *some sib* to others. Children interpreted *sib* as describing either the action, the container, or the material, depending on which form they heard. Other studies also have found that preschool children use grammar to infer the meaning distinction between proper nouns like *Lassie* and common nouns like *dog* (Gelman & Taylor, 1984) as well as between nouns and adjectives (see Figure 3.6) (Gelman & Markman, 1985; Hall, Waxman, & Hurwitz, 1993).

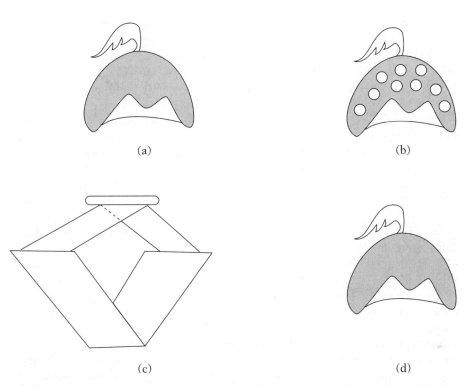

(a) (b)

(c) (d)

Figure 3.6 Syntax as a clue to word meaning. Four-year-olds pick (b) when told, "Find the fep one," and they pick (c) when told, "Now find the fep." These responses suggest that 4-year-olds can use the syntax of a sentence to distinguish between words that imply a contrast between members of the same category (adjectives) and words that do not imply such a contrast (common nouns).

Source: From "Adjectives vs. Nouns," by S. A. Gelman and E. M. Markman, 1985, *Journal of Child Language*, 12, p. 135. Copyright © 1988 and reprinted with the permission of Cambridge University Press.

It is important to note that children who demonstrate an ability to use syntax to distinguish word meanings (as referring to objects, actions, or properties of objects) are older than the children who make errors such as calling a stove "a hot." Any account of word learning, whether in terms of constraints, sociopragmatic cues, or syntactic cues (or some combination of those), will have to account for developmental changes in word learning. (For proposals in this regard, interested readers are referred to Golinkoff et al., 1994; Waxman, 1994.)

Children can identify different kinds of verbs   Syntax not only provides clues to whether a word refers to an object or to an action, but can also provide clues to what kind of action is being referred to. Verbs with different meanings can appear in different kinds of sentences. For example, a verb like *hit* means to do something to someone else; and it usually appears in a sentence like *Tom hit Jerry,* in which the verb is preceded by one noun, the doer, and followed by another noun, the recipient of the deed. In contrast, verbs like *laugh* that refer to an action with no recipient appear in sentences like *Tom laughed,* in which there is just one noun, the doer.

Letitia Naigles (1990) found that 2-year-olds used this correspondence between sentence structure and verb meaning to learn the meaning of new verbs. Naigles showed children a videotape depicting a novel action that could be interpreted as either something one person did to another or something two people did together. Different children heard different sentences with a novel verb accompanying the action, and then all were tested to see how they interpreted the new verb. It is no small feat to figure out how 2-year-olds are interpreting anything, so the experimental method had to be ingenious.

First, the children watched the action, which consisted of a rabbit repeatedly pushing a duck down into a squatting position with its left hand while at the same time both the rabbit and duck were making circles in the air with their right hands. (The rabbit and duck were actually people—probably graduate students—dressed in costumes.) Some children heard the sentence *The rabbit is gorping the duck,* and other children heard the sentence *The rabbit and the duck are gorping.* If these children used the sentence structure as a clue to verb meaning, the children who heard the first sentence should infer that *gorping* refers to what the rabbit did to the duck, whereas children who heard the second sentence should infer that *gorping* refers to what both the rabbit and duck did (arm circling). As expected, when the two different actions were presented separately, the children picked the meaning consistent with the sentence structure they had heard.

Naigles' method for eliciting the children's responses was to show two actions simultaneously on two TV screens. One screen showed the rabbit pushing the duck down and doing nothing else; the other screen showed the rabbit and the duck making hand circles. The children were asked, "Where's gorping now? Find gorping!" The children who had heard the initial sentence *The rabbit is gorping the duck* looked longer at the screen on which the rabbit was pushing the duck down. The children who had heard the initial sentence *The rabbit and duck are gorping* looked longer at the screen on which the rabbit and duck were making hand circles. The proposal that knowledge of language structure is generally useful for learning new verbs is termed the **syntactic bootstrapping hypothesis,** and it is supported by a variety of experimental and naturalistic evidence (see Fisher, Hall, Rakowitz, & Gleitman, 1994; Gleitman, 1990; Naigles, 1995; Naigles & Hoff-Ginsberg, 1995).

Multiple sources of word learning support

In the previous sections we have introduced several proposed sources of support for the word learning child. These are summarized in Box 3.2. Most people in the field would agree that each of the sources of information contributes something to an explanation of how the child learns the meaning of new words. The process of learning words surely depends on mapping words to the nonlinguistic context in which they are heard. Most would also agree that (1) the process is facilitated by children's biases toward certain interpretations of words over others; (2) some ways of talking to children may be more supportive of word learning than others; (3) children are good at figuring out others' intentions, and they use those socio-pragmatic skills in the service of word learning; and (4) children can use syntax as a clue to word meaning.

All this agreement notwithstanding, there are still deep unresolved controversies about how word learning occurs. The controversies in the field concern the relative contribution of each source of information to lexical development, whether the constraints (or principles) are specific to language or are domain-general, and whether the constraints are innate or are themselves part of the lexical knowledge the child acquires from experience (see, for example, Behrend, 1990; Markman, 1989, 1992; Merriman & Bowman, 1989; Nelson, 1988, 1990). The relative contributions of input and constraints and the domain-specificity of constraints are part of the larger nature/nurture and modularity controversies that pervade discussions of language development. The syntactic bootstrapping hypothesis is controversial in a unique way. In suggesting that children learn a great deal of syntax before word meanings, this hypothesis contradicts the long-standing view that children learn word meanings first and use that knowledge of word meanings to figure out syntax. This is an issue to which we will return in the next chapter on grammatical development.

The careful reader of this section on how children learn words may have noticed that we began with a vignette in which a child has to learn the meaning of a common noun, *cup,* and ended with a hypothesis about how children learn verb meanings. This shift follows the history of the field to a certain extent. The study of lexical development began with the study of how children learn object labels, and attention to verb learning came later. Although the basic question of how children figure out the meanings of new words is the same for nouns and verbs (and other categories of words as well), the tasks of learning noun meanings and learning verb meanings may differ in a variety of ways (Maratsos, 1991). The nonlinguistic situation is different for nouns and verbs because objects tend to remain in place for a while, whereas actions tend to be over and gone (Tomasello & Barton, 1994). Children's internal constraints seem to bias them toward mapping new words onto objects, at least initially (Waxman, 1994),

Box 3.2   Proposed sources of help to children learning the meaning of new words

Internal constraints

Children know something about how words encode meaning (words refer to whole objects—the whole object assumption; words refer to kinds—the taxonomic assumption; different words have different meanings—the mutual exclusivity assumption), and this knowledge narrows down the number of possible meanings they consider in each word learning situation.

Pragmatic principles

Children know something about how speakers in any community use language (words have meanings that all language users agree to—the principle of conventionality; speakers use different words to convey different meanings—the principle of contrast), and this knowledge of how language is used narrows down the possible meanings to be considered.

Child-centered input

Adults' child-directed speech makes the word learning task easier for children by focusing on the here-and-now and by labeling objects the child is looking at.

Socio-pragmatic cues

Children can use cues that come from speakers in the word learning setting (such as eye gaze, facial expression) to infer what the speaker is talking about, and children use these inferences about what's going on in the speakers' mind as clues to the meaning of the words they produce.

Syntactic bootstrapping

The syntactic structures in which words appear correlate with word meaning (for example, in *The zov blicked the flump to the grop, zov* is probably some animate being and *blick* is probably some action that involves transfer or motion), and children use the syntax of the sentences they hear as a source of information about the meaning of new words in those sentences.

but other biases may play a role in mapping verb meanings (Behrend, 1995). Also, the role of syntax in disambiguating possible verb meanings seems to be greater than the role of syntax in learning object labels. There is currently a burgeoning field of research on children's acquisition of a verb lexicon that asks how children learn verbs and how this process may differ from the process of learning object labels (see, for example, Gleitman & Landau, 1994; Tomasello & Merriman, 1995).

THE RELATION OF WORDS TO CONCEPTS

Up to this point, we have been discussing the acquisition of word meaning assuming that the child's problem is to decipher what ideas or concepts words encode, but we haven't considered how the concepts themselves might develop. In a sense this is proper, because this is a book about language development, not cognitive development. However, the relation between words and concepts is too intimate to do a good job of talking about one without talking about the other.

The meanings of words are functions of the **concepts** the words encode. Words with different meanings encode different concepts. To illustrate with our *gorping* example from the previous section, the meaning of *gorp* as "pushing into a squatting position" encodes the concepts of motion and causality (among others), whereas the meaning of *gorp* as "making circles with the arms" encodes motion but not causality. The task of determining what concepts words encode is simpler for common nouns. Concepts encoded by words like *juice* and *dog* are mental categories that include everything that is juice or dogs, respectively, and excludes everything else.

Words map onto preexisting concepts

To learn the meaning of the words *juice, dog,* or *gorp,* the child must have the concepts of juice, dog, or motion and causality. Usually the relationship between concepts and words is described as one in which the concepts develop first, independent of language. Some concepts may well be innate in the child. For example, motion is a good candidate for an innate concept because the infant's perceptual apparatus detects motion from birth. Other concepts develop as a result of the child's nonlinguistic experience in the world. In either case, the child's task is most commonly conceptualized as that of mapping the words heard onto this preexisting conceptual structure (for further discussion of this "cognition hypothesis," see Cromer, 1974). The kinds of word meanings children consider, according to such an account, are a function of the kinds of mental categories children have.

A study by Soja, Carey, and Spelke (1991) offers an example of just such an influence of prior nonlinguistic cognition on word learning. Soja proposed that 2-year-olds nonlinguistically make the conceptual distinction between objects (like cups and sticks) and substances (like sand and clay). Soja presented children with a new word by saying, "This is my blicket," as she showed them either an object or a substance. (The objects were things like apple corers and honey dippers and the substances things like face cream and hair gel, all of which 2-year-olds are unlikely to have words for.) After the initial word learning trials, the child was then given two things to choose from and was told to "Point to the blicket." The choices were constructed to make the children reveal the meaning they had construed for the new term, *blicket*. So, if the child first saw a plastic honey dipper, the child would then have to choose between a wooden honey dipper and pieces of plastic. If the child first saw a glob of face cream, the child would then have to choose between a similar shaped glob of hair gel and an arrangement of lots of little dots of face cream. Two-year-old children who first saw the plastic honey dipper chose the wooden honey dipper; they thought *blicket* referred to the form, not the substance. Two-year-olds who first saw the glob of face cream chose the arrangement of little dots of face cream; they thought *blicket* referred to the substance, not the form.

Thus Soja and colleagues concluded that 2-year-olds have separate mental categories of objects and substances. Therefore they see a plastic honey dipper as one example of honey dippers (the object), not one example of plastic; and they see a glob of face cream as one example of face cream (the substance), not one example of globs. Children then use this way of organizing the world (known as their ontological categories) to guide their inductions of word meaning. The researchers' conclusion, consistent with the constraints position, is that children take words as referring both to the whole thing present in the nonlinguistic context and to other things of that kind. The child's ontological categories are the kinds of things the child thinks there are. However, this process of using cognitive categories as a basis for inferring word meanings cannot fully account for the word learning process.

Lexical organization differs from conceptual organization

Words do not always map onto concepts in a one-to-one fashion. Sometimes children have concepts for which there is no word in their language, and so they may invent words to fill these lexical gaps. For example, one child invented the words *couch hole* and *pee mat* (personal data). *Couch holes* are the cracks between cushions that a 2-year-old has to be careful to avoid when walking across a couch. A *pee mat* is the bathmat in front of the toilet the same 2-year-old stood on when urinating. Lexical gaps, however, are not the biggest problem in learning how words map onto concepts. A far more pervasive problem is that words mark some, but not all, conceptually available distinctions, and children have to figure out how their language divides the world into word-sized packages (Bowerman, 1978).

The fact that there are many different ways a language could potentially map words onto concepts is best illustrated by comparing languages that do this differently. In Spanish, one word means both "fingers" and "toes." (In English, there is a single word for these things—*digits*—but it is not used very frequently.) In Navaho, there is one word for both "head" and "human hair" and a separate word for "animal hair" (Miller, 1981). English has a huge vocabulary of color terms (in addition to the basics, there are terms like *puce, magenta,* and *turquoise*), whereas some languages have fewer than half a dozen color terms. What verbs encode also differs across languages (Talmy, 1985). In English, verbs tend to encode both motion and the manner of the motion, so we have many different verbs for different manners of motion, like *run, skip,* and *slide.* In Spanish, verbs tend to encode direction rather than manner. (Again, English has such verbs, such as *exit* and *enter,* but they are less commonly used.) This difference is illustrated in the Spanish and English descriptions of the scene in Figure 3.7.

Figure 3.7   Languages differ in how they package meaning into words. To describe this scene, an English speaker would say, "The girl is running out of the house," encoding the manner of the motion in the verb. A Spanish speaker would say, "La niña está saliendo de la casa" (the girl is leaving the house), encoding the direction of the motion in the verb (Naigles, Eisenberg, & Kako, 1992). Thus, learning a lexicon includes learning how your language packages meaning into words—that is, learning lexical organization.

Source: From Acquiring a Language-Specific Lexicon: Motion Verbs in English and Spanish, by L. Naigles, A. R. Eisenberg, E. T. Kako. Paper presented at the International Pragmatics Association Conference, Belgium, November 1992. Reprinted with permission. Drawing courtesy of Qi Wang.

Learning lexical organization   In learning the lexicons of their languages, children must determine which cognitive distinctions are marked in their language and which are not. This level of organizing the world that mediates between cognitive organization and language is called **semantic organization.** Acquiring a language includes learning its semantics—that is, learning how meanings are linguistically realized. In this chapter, we discuss how children learn the semantics of their language with respect to the lexicon—that is, **lexical organization.** We will discuss semantics again in the next chapter with respect to the grammar.

The process children go through in figuring out the semantic level of organization is interestingly revealed in a word learning study by Carey (1978). Three-year-old children were exposed to a novel word in a naturalistic context. The word was *chromium,* and it was used to refer to the color olive. (Carey made sure that none of the children had a word for olive or knew the word *chromium* before the study started by giving them a pretest with color chips.) The children's preschool was equipped with two identical trays, one blue and one chromium. In the course of setting up for a snack, the preschool teacher asked each child to "Bring me the chromium tray; not the blue one, the chromium one." The children also had a second exposure to the word *chromium* a week later using the color chips.

The interesting finding of the study came five weeks later, when the children were tested by being presented with several color chips, including familiar colors and olive. The children were asked what color each chip was. None of the 14 children in the study had learned to call olive "chromium." But they had learned something because they changed what they called "olive." Two children who had called olive "green" on the pretest said that they did not know what to call it. Six children called olive a color term—gray, blue, or brown—they had not applied to olive before and did not yet use appropriately. What this shows is that although the children had not learned the word *chromium,* they had learned that olive was a color that had its own name.

Carey's study shows that children use input to figure out that a particular concept (in this case, the color olive) is lexicalized (has a name) in the language, even if they don't know what the name is. We can also ask whether children use input to figure out broader principles about what gets lexicalized in their language. For example, do children acquiring Spanish learn that verbs generally encode path, whereas children acquiring English learn that verbs generally encode manner?

The best evidence that children do learn language-specific lexicalization patterns comes from a comparison of the early description of motion by children acquiring Korean and English (Choi & Bowerman, 1991). In English, the same words are used to describe the path of motion (such as *up* or *down*) regardless of whether the motion is caused (He pushed me down) or spontaneous (I fell down). In Korean, however, the direction of motion is part of the meaning of the verb (like *ascend* and *descend*), and different verbs are used for caused and for spontaneous motion. This means that in Korean, path is lexicalized along with cause, and in English, path is lexicalized independent of cause.

Very young English and Korean speakers seem to know this. One-year-old English-speaking children commonly use the words *down* and *up* for both spontaneous and caused motion—to mean "put me down" or "I fell down." However, Korean children do not extend verb meanings in this way. Even children under the age of 2 respect the caused/spontaneous distinction in their use of motion verbs. That is, from the very beginning, Korean children seem not only to be learning Korean words but also to be figuring out how Korean words divide meaning into lexicalized components.

Words influence conceptual development

Thus far, we have been taking the commonly held view that cognitive organization comes first and that children learn semantic organization as they map words onto concepts. Other relationships between cognition and language are possible. For example, language might influence cognition. Spanish speakers might really think of fingers and toes as being more similar to each other than English speakers do. English speakers might consider manner of motion to be more central to action than Spanish speakers do. This hypothesis, that language influences thought, was first developed by linguist Edward Sapir and his student Benjamin Lee Whorf. Known as the **Whorfian hypothesis,** or the **linguistic relativity hypothesis,** this position states that the way our language "carves up" the world influences how we think about the world. This hypothesis has inspired a large body of research on the thought processes of adults who speak different languages. There is much less empirical work on children, but there are some suggestions that characteristics of the language children are acquiring exert an influence on their cognitive development.

As we discussed earlier in this chapter, some languages seem to make it easier to learn verbs than others. In Japanese and Korean, verbs are more frequent and more salient in input than they are in English, and children acquiring Japanese and Korean seem to acquire verbs relatively earlier in the course of lexical development than children acquiring English do. The Whorfian hypothesis would predict that children acquiring Japanese and Korean should acquire the concepts encoded by verbs at a younger age than would children acquiring English (Gopnik & Choi, 1990).

There is evidence to support this Whorfian prediction. Gopnik and Choi studied both early lexical development and early cognitive development in children acquiring Korean and in children acquiring English (Gopnik & Choi, 1995; Gopnik, Choi, & Baumberger, in press). They found that Korean-speaking children used verbs earlier and acquired concepts of means/end relations (the kind of things that verbs encode) earlier than English-speaking children did. In contrast, English-speaking children had larger naming vocabularies and also showed a more advanced understanding of object categorization. Thus this evidence suggests that characteristics of the input language make some concepts more salient and easier to learn than others. Although this idea goes somewhat against the more mainstream view of the primacy of cognition, such a notion has been proposed before.

In a classic article on children's word learning, Roger Brown (1958a) suggested that the particular words adults use when they talk to children can influence children's cognitive organization. For example, when a child points to a tree and says, "What's that?" it's up to the adult whether to say "maple" or "tree." The child whose parents say "oak," "maple," and "dogwood" will develop more differentiated mental categories of trees than will the child whose parents say "tree." The word the adult provides serves as "an invitation to form the concept." In actuality, the effects of parental naming practices on cognition may be hard to untangle from the effects of other information. It would be odd for an adult to label oaks, maples, and dogwoods individually without also pointing out some of their distinctive characteristics. Mervis and Mervis (1988) have argued that such demonstrations of important attributes play the greatest role in children's category evolution.

Words and concepts develop together

There is another proposed relationship between cognitive development and lexical development for which there is strong empirical evidence: the relationship of simultaneous development. Concepts don't develop first and wait for the words, nor do the words prompt the development of the concepts. Rather, words and concepts develop together. One piece of evidence comes from the same sort of research and the same researchers who found the relationship between the development of categorization and the naming spurt. The basic research strategy was to follow children longitudinally, measuring their understanding of particular concepts and also tracking their vocabulary. Using this method, Gopnik and Meltzoff (1984, 1986) found a close correspondence between the age at which children were successful on a non-linguistic task that measures understanding that objects are permanent (young babies seem not to fully understand that objects continue to exist when they are out of view), and the appearance of words that encode disappearance, like *gone*. Gopnik and Meltzoff also found a close correspondence between children's development of the understanding of means/ends relationships and the children's first use of words that encode success or failure, such as *there* or *uh-oh*. What Gopnik and Meltzoff proposed is that "children acquire words that encode concepts they have just developed or are in the process of developing" (Gopnik & Meltzoff, 1984, p. 495).

In fact, it has been suggested that the beginning of word learning itself may coincide with infants' mental individuation of the different sorts of objects they encounter (Carey, 1994; Xu & Carey, 1995, in press). Xu and Carey found evidence that before about the age of 11 months, infants' understanding of the world may be very different from ours. Imagine you saw a book emerge from behind an opaque screen and then return; then you saw a cup emerge from behind the screen and then return: What would you think was behind the screen?—a book and a cup, most likely. If the screen were removed and only a cup was there, you would be surprised. However, you would not be surprised if the screen were removed and both objects were there; that would be just what you expected.

When Xu and Carey performed this demonstration with babies, they found a difference between the responses of 10-month-olds and 12-month-olds. The 12-month-olds looked longer at the cup than at both objects, and looking longer is what babies do when they are surprised. Thus the 12-month-olds responded the way adults would. In contrast, 10-month-olds, as a group, showed no surprise at seeing only a single object and thus no evidence that they expected two objects to be behind the screen (Xu & Carey, 1995, in press). (There were actually several trials with different sets of objects.) It is as if 10-month-olds perceive things as "objects" but not as separate, different objects. Twelve-month-olds, on the other hand, share the adult view that a cup and book are two different things, not one thing that takes on different forms as it moves through space.

Xu and Carey's findings suggest a striking coincidence between the nonlinguistic development of concepts of books, cups, and other things as individual, countable things and the comprehension of words that label these categories of individual things (count nouns). A corollary of the claim that concepts of individual objects develop with comprehension of words for those objects is the claim that even the youngest word learners share the adult understanding of what count nouns mean; they refer to instances of countable things. This position contradicts some earlier proposals about the nature of children's first semantic representations offered to explain children's overextended word uses.

LATER LEXICAL DEVELOPMENT

We have spent most of this chapter discussing lexical development up to about the age of 3 years (although some of the sensitivity to syntactic clues to word meaning isn't solid until age 4). We have concentrated on early lexical development for two related reasons. First, the beginning of lexical development is the period that is currently being most actively researched. Second, the major issues concerning how lexical development happens are issues that concern developments during the early period. It is clear, however, that lexical development continues after the age of 3. We will consider lexical development in school-aged children in Chapter 6. Here we briefly mention some of the phenomena of lexical development during the period between the ages of 3 and 6 years.

Later word production

The most obvious feature of lexical development after 3 years is that children continue to learn new words. Templin (1957) estimated that children have vocabularies of approximately 8000 words by 6 years of age. More recently, Anglin (1993) estimated first-graders' vocabularies at over 10,000 words. The kinds of words children learn also change with age. Older children acquire new types of words that encode meanings that younger children do not express. Also, older children acquire words to serve new grammatical functions as their grammatical abilities develop. For example, children add to their vocabularies terms that indicate temporal and causal relations and that serve to link clauses in complex sentences (such as *if* and *then, because, then, instead*) (Bloom, Lahey, Hood, Lifter & Fiess, 1980; French & Nelson, 1985; Scholnick & Wing, 1991; Scott, 1984).

Later word learning

Children also seem to get better at word learning with age. In particular, at 3 years of age, children appear to improve in their ability to pick up new words (particularly object labels) from incidental exposure in context (Rice, 1990). This later-developing ability may be important because the characteristics of mother/child interaction that probably facilitate early word learning are not present, at least to the same degree, in the interactions older children experience. On the other hand, word learning in older children is supported by new kinds of experiences as children enter school and begin to read.

Later word knowledge

The process of lexical development after the age of 3 is not just one of acquiring more new words in new ways. Some late-appearing errors suggest changes are going on below the surface as well. For example, children correctly use verbs like *untie* and *unbuckle* for years before producing novel verbs such as *unstraighten* (meaning "bend") and *unhate* (meaning "like") (Bowerman, 1985). Children also produce errors like *broom the floor,* in which they take a known noun and use it as a verb. Both types of errors suggest that children learn something about how the language works but sometimes overextend these principles of word formation.

Other types of errors may indicate that children continue to reorganize the semantic structure of their lexicon well after acquiring the words. For example, Bowerman (1978) reports that her daughter substituted *behind* for *after,* in "Can I have any reading behind dinner," at the age of 3½. Both words had been used correctly prior to this error, so the reason for the error can't be that the child didn't know the words. Rather, the error seems to be like an adult's slip of the tongue, in which a related word is uttered by mistake. What the 3½-year-old had developed was the underlying lexical organization in which the meanings of *behind* and *after* were related.

These late errors are the basis for a very important claim about what motivates lexical development and what kind of process lexical development is. Bowerman (1985) argues that these errors suggest that the impetus for language development cannot simply be the need to communicate, because these errors indicate that the child has continued to think about how the lexicon works long after achieving communicative adequacy. Also, the process of lexical development cannot be simply a process of figuring out how linguistic structures (in this case words) map onto meanings; it is also a process of figuring out the system in the linguistic structures themselves. The question of the relation between the communicative function that language serves and children's acquisition of the system itself is an issue we will consider more fully in Chapters 4 and 5.

Later word comprehension

No detailed studies track the growth of both production and comprehension vocabularies after age 30 months (which is when the MacArthur Inventory ends), so it is difficult to make statements about the relative size of comprehension and production vocabularies later on. In fact, describing vocabularies of older children and adults becomes more complex because their reading and writing vocabularies may differ from their speaking vocabularies. It is probably true that children understand more words than they use throughout the course of lexical development (which may be a lifelong process). However, children may use some words correctly before they fully understand their meanings. This was true of early word use, and it seems to be even more true of some later-acquired terms, such as words that encode temporal or logical relations. For example, children correctly use terms such as *before* and *because* as early as 2 or 3 years of age. However, in experiments in which children are presented with sentences such as *The man clapped before the lady waved* (Ginsberg, 1976) or *The scissors moved because the pencil moved* (French, 1988), children may not be able to demonstrate perfect comprehension until the age of 7 or 8 years. The experimental tasks are probably more difficult both because they require children to contrast terms with similar meanings (such as *before* versus *until*) and also because the sentences describe unfamiliar events out of context (French & Nelson, 1985).

SUMMARY

Words are symbols that can be used to refer to things, actions, properties of things, and more. Adults' knowledge about words is stored in the mental lexicon. The process of children's lexical development is the process of learning the words in the target language and organizing them in the mental lexicon.

Children may begin to recognize some words as early as 5 months of age and to truly understand word meanings around 10 months of age. Children typically produce their first word around their first birthday. The course of vocabulary development is slow at first. On average, children take approximately 6 months to acquire a productive vocabulary of 50 words. At the point of achieving a 50-word vocabulary, typically around age 18 months, many children show a word spurt, in which the rate of vocabulary development increases dramatically. Cognitive changes in the child probably contribute to this word spurt.

From the beginning of lexical development, there is substantial variability among children in both the size and content of their lexicons. A great deal of research suggests that early vocabularies of English-speaking children tend to be dominated by general nominals, or object labels. However, there are individual differences in the extent to which this is true. Some children have proportionately fewer object labels than others and proportionately more words or expressions that serve social-interactive functions. Also, cross-linguistic and cross-cultural differences in the relative dominance of object labels in early vocabularies suggest that both the nature of the language and the sociocultural uses to which it is put influence the content of early vocabularies. Two factors that affect the size of children's vocabularies are their phonological memory skills and the amount of speech addressed to them.

The words children utter when they first begin to talk may not have the same sort of representation in the children's mental lexicons as adults' words have in adults' mental lexicons. The meaning of some of children's first words seem tied to particular events or contexts, and, even later, children may not fully understand the meanings of all the words they use.

Such immature word knowledge seems to be the exception, however. For the most part, children do a remarkable job of correctly figuring out the meanings of the words they hear. This accomplishment is remarkable because most situations in which a new word is heard leave room for many different possible interpretations of that new word.

Accounting for how children manage to learn words as quickly and accurately as they do is the main arena in the study of lexical development where different theoretical orientations clash. Proposals consonant with a nativist view of language development suggest that children know something about how words work before they learn any words. This prior knowledge then constrains the universe of possible solutions to the word learning problem and makes it solvable. Counterproposals claim that children can find all the information they need for word learning in the social context in which words are encountered, thus obviating the need for constraints.

Words are not the only things in the mind that represent things in the world. Children and adults also have nonlinguistic concepts. Conceptual development influences lexical development, as children acquire words for newly developed concepts. Lexical development may also influence conceptual development, as new words stimulate the development of new concepts. Because not every concept has a word, part of the process of lexical development is learning lexical organization, or how the words in the target language map onto nonlinguistic concepts.

The second and third years of life are the most active word learning years. However, lexical development continues throughout childhood, perhaps indefinitely, and the kinds of words children acquire change with age. As children develop new, abstract concepts, they acquire new words to encode those concepts. As children's grammatical abilities develop, they acquire new categories of words that serve new grammatical functions. In the period between 3 and 6 years of age, children also continue to learn how the lexicon works, allowing them to create their own novel words. And, finally, through the elementary school years, the internal structure of children's lexicons changes and becomes more adultlike.

KEY TERMS

mental lexicon

words

reference

context-bound word use

referential word use

nominals

word spurt

fast map

naming insight

referential and expressive language styles

underextensions

overextensions

semantic feature hypothesis

prototypes

speech segmentation problem

mapping problem

constraints on word learning

whole-object assumption

taxonomic assumption

mutual exclusivity assumption

pragmatic principles

principle of conventionality

principle of contrast

socio-pragmatic cues

syntactic bootstrapping hypothesis

concepts

semantic organization

lexical organization

Whorfian hypothesis, or linguistic relativity hypothesis

REVIEW QUESTIONS

1. Give examples of the kinds of questions we are asking when we study lexical development.

2. What is a word? Explain the difference between a baby's reaching gesture and true words.

3. What is the difference between context-bound word use and referential word use? Why is this an important distinction?

4. What kinds of words make up children's early vocabularies? Why do children learn these as opposed to other kinds of words?

5. What is the word spurt? Discuss the proposed explanations for the word spurt.

6. What is the relation between word production and word comprehension in early lexical development?

7. Describe the kinds of individual differences in lexical development style that have been observed. What might account for these differences?

8. What factors appear to play a role in accounting for differences in the rate of lexical development?

9. What's the mapping problem, as the philosopher Quine described it?

10. What are "constraints" on word learning? Define and illustrate with an example.

11. What claims are made by the socio-pragmatic view of word learning?

12. Give an example of how syntax provides clues to word meaning and an example of evidence that children use those clues in figuring out the meaning of newly-encountered words.

13. Define and explain the difference between conceptual organization and lexical organization.

14. Outline three proposed relations between the development of concepts and the acquisition of words that encode those concepts. What kind of evidence would support each view?

15. What's the significance of a 5-year-old child's producing errors such as "I'm going to *broom* the floor" or "*unstraighten* this" (meaning "bend this")?

16. Which proposed solutions to the mapping problem entail the most nativist views of lexical development? What are the most experientially based proposals?

17. Find examples of evidence in this chapter that support the views that (a) children's lexical development is guided by properties of the speech they hear and (b) children's lexical development is guided by internal properties of children's minds.

18. To what extent are the several proposed solutions to the mapping problem incompatible, and to what extent could they all be true to some degree?

4 The Development of Syntax and Morphology: Learning the Structure of Language

Do you are happy? (Mark, age 2 years 4 months)

When we go inside our hotel we can take our shoes and socks off can we go swimming? (Alex, age 2 years 8 months)

I did take a napped. (Alissa, age 3 years 0 months)

My hair tickles myself. (Alissa, age 4 years 11 months)

Thus far we have described children learning the sounds and the words of their language. Some time, typically between 18 months and 2 years, children start to put words together. The development of this ability to combine elements of the language is the next facet of language development we will consider. Because elements are not combined haphazardly but only in certain structures, we refer to this aspect of language development as the development of language structure. As we did regarding phonological and lexical development, we will begin our discussion of children's development of language structure with a description of the endpoint of that developmental process. We will not attempt a comprehensive description of adults' knowledge of linguistic structure but rather will focus on the basic aspects of grammar we need to understand the discussion of development that follows.

SOME FEATURES OF ADULTS' KNOWLEDGE OF LANGUAGE STRUCTURE

The productivity of language

When mature speakers talk, most of the sentences they produce are sentences they have never produced or heard before. When mature speakers understand the sentences others produce, it's almost always a matter of understanding sentences they have never heard before. This characteristic of language and of language knowledge—that speaker/hearers have the capacity to produce and understand an infinite number of novel sentences—is referred to as the **productivity** or **generativity of language.** The productive nature of language has a very important implication both for linguistic theories that try to describe adults' linguistic knowledge and for psychological theories that try to explain how children achieve that knowledge. The implication is that knowledge of language is not knowledge of a list of sentences from which to select as the occasion demands; rather, it is knowledge of a system that allows speakers to produce an infinite number of different sentences from a finite inventory of words. The two components of that productive system are syntax and morphology.

Syntax

Syntactic rules   Let's say that you want to communicate that John kissed Mary. Assuming you know the words that refer to "John," "Mary," and "kissed," you also need to know the order in which these words must be combined to produce the sentence *John kissed Mary.* If you said instead *Mary kissed John,* that would mean something quite different, and if you said *kissed Mary John,* that would be ungrammatical. (It is a convention in linguistics to put an asterisk in front of ungrammatical constructions.) So when you know a language, you know a system of rules for putting words together.

What do these rules look like? To account for your ability to produce and understand *John kissed Mary,* we could posit that you know a rule something like the following:

Sentence → *John + kissed + Mary*

However, this rule generates only one sentence. If each rule generates only one sentence, then to produce an infinite number of sentences you would need a grammar with an infinite number of rules. Such a system is not productive, and because we know that the system adults have *is* productive, the grammar must be of a different sort.

Syntactic categories   The solution to the problem of accounting for the productivity of syntactic rules is to posit rules that operate over linguistic entities that are bigger than individual words. For example, we could posit a rule something like

Sentence → agent of action + action + recipient of action

This would account for *John kissed Mary, Mary kissed John, John Wilkes Booth shot Abraham Lincoln,* and many more sentences as well.

Although categories such as agent and action allow a productive system, such categories cannot handle all the kinds of sentences speakers produce and listeners understand. For example, we would run into problems if we tried to use the rule "S → agent + action + recipient" to account for *John resembles Mary* because *John* is not an agent of any action, *resembles* is not an action, and nothing is being done to *Mary* at all.

To solve this problem, we could try to figure out a new set of categories that would handle this kind of sentence and add those categories to the grammar. A better way, however, would be to posit even more abstract categories— categories that would include *kiss* and *resemble* as instances of the same kind of thing and that would include *John* both when he was kissing and when he was resembling. These categories are the familiar categories of Verb and Noun. By writing rules that operate over categories such as Noun and Verb, we can account for all the sentence examples just listed with a rule like

Sentence = Noun + Verb + Noun

As you are very aware, more kinds of words than just nouns and verbs get combined in sentences, and more kinds of sentence structures than the simple examples just listed get produced. Although we won't attempt anything like a full treatment of **syntax** in this book, we need to establish two more pieces of information about adults' syntactic knowledge before we can talk about children's syntactic development. One piece is a further elaboration of the kinds of categories rules operate over; the other concerns the kinds of structures the rules build.

The categories that linguistic rules operate over seem to divide fairly neatly into two types. One type, termed **open-class words,** content words, or **lexical categories,** consists of the categories noun, verb, adjective, and preposition. (The different terms come from different linguistic theories. Here we introduce the terminology so that you will be able to recognize the terms in other sources, but we will not attempt a treatment of the linguistic theories themselves.) The words in these categories do most of the work of carrying the meaning of a sentence. They are called "open" classes because you can always invent a new noun, verb, or adjective and use it in a perfectly grammatical (if not particularly meaningful) sentence (for example, the blick gorped the fepish woog.) The other type of word category includes the **closed-class words,** also called function words or **functional categories.** These are auxiliaries like *can* and *will,* the complementizers like *that* and *who,* and the determiners like *the* and *a.* They are called closed-class words because you can't really invent new ones, and they are called function words or functional categories because their main role in the sentence is to serve grammatical functions rather than to carry content.

Syntactic structure   The last crucial feature about grammatical knowledge we need to establish concerns the nature of sentence structure. Sentences are not merely linear arrangements of content and function words; Sentences have hierarchical structure. Consider the following sentences:

John Wilkes Booth shot Abraham Lincoln.

A Confederate sympathizer shot the 16th President.

The clever runner stole second base.

The catcher swore.

Although each sentence would have a different description in terms of the sequence of nouns, verbs, adjectives, and so on, all these sentences are similar at another level of structure. They are all accounted for by one set of rules:

Sentence → Noun Phrase + Verb Phrase

Verb Phrase → Verb + (Noun Phrase)

Noun Phrase → (Determiner) + (Adjective) + Noun

What these rules say is that a sentence is made up of a Noun Phrase plus a Verb Phrase; a Verb Phrase comprises a Verb plus an Optional Noun Phrase; and a Noun Phrase comprises a Noun, optionally preceded by a Determiner and/or an Adjective. These three rules generate a large number of sentences (limited only by the number of different nouns, verbs, and so on in your vocabulary), and they also describe the hierarchical structure of sentences. Words are combined to form phrases and phrases are combined to form simple sentences.

Complex sentences are formed by combining simple sentences, and this is how the system acquires the capacity to generate an infinite number of sentences with a finite vocabulary. You can conjoin sentences (*The runner stole second base, and the crowd roared.*), and you can embed sentences in larger sentences forever. For example:

The catcher swore.

The umpire noticed that the catcher swore.

The crowd saw that the umpire noticed that the catcher swore.

In sum, then, the syntax of a language is a system of rules that specifies how words belonging to different linguistic categories can be combined into structured sentences. The rules we have discussed are far from constituting the entire system for English, but they illustrate some basic features of syntactic knowledge we want to account for in discussing language development. That is, we need to explain the origin of rules, of linguistic categories, and of sentence structure.

Morphology

It is easy for English speakers to think of sentences as combinations of words. However, the units that are combined in language include something smaller than words. To illustrate what is referred to as the **morphology** of language, consider the following:

One book

Two books

In English, a plural noun is usually indicated by adding an *s* to the end of the singular form. This *s* means something; it indicates the plurality of the noun. Even though the *s* conveys meaning, it does not stand by itself as a word. In linguistics, this kind of language unit is called a **bound morpheme—morphemes** being the smallest units of meaning. Most units of meaning in English are words that stand alone, and these are **free morphemes.** However, bound morphemes, such as the plural marker, must be attached to a word.

The English language does not have a very rich morphological system, and the bound morphemes in English are few. Other examples include the *s* that goes on the end of a verb to indicate a third person singular subject (he talk*s*), the *ed* that goes on the end of a verb to indicate past tense (he talk*ed*), and the *ing* that goes on the end of a verb to indicate progressive action (he is talk*ing*).

Other languages have very rich morphological systems. In such languages, the form of a noun is different depending not only on whether the noun is singular or plural but also on whether the noun is the subject of the sentence, the direct object, or the indirect object—and that would be just part of the morphological system. For example, compare the following English and Hungarian sentences:

The boy gave a book to the girl.

A   fiú   egy könyvet adott a   lánynak.
(The boy a   book   gave the girl.)

In Hungarian, the morphemes at the end of the nouns indicate the noun's role in the sentence. The *et* at the end of *könyvet* indicates the role that in English is the direct object, and the *nak* at the end of lánynak indicates the role that in English is the indirect object. (For readers who know other languages that have a similar system, these are the accusative and dative markers, respectively.) English has remnants of such a system in the pronoun system, where *he* or *she* indicates the subject of a verb and *him* or *her* indicates the object. However, English speakers primarily rely on the order of words in the sentence to indicate the words' roles.

For children acquiring languages with rich morphological systems, morphological development is a larger component of language acquisition than it is for children acquiring English. Although in this chapter we will focus on the acquisition of English, child language researchers also study children acquiring languages that are unlike English. This research is important because one of the goals of studying language development is to understand the mental processes that make language development possible. If we looked only at children learning English, we would run the risk of coming up with a description of mental processes that would be adequate only for acquiring English. Such mental processes are obviously not true of children, because children can learn whatever language is spoken around them.

To summarize, syntax and morphology are the systems for combining units of meaning. Syntax refers to combining words into sentences, and morphology refers to building words. All speakers of a language know the rules of both syntax and morphology as well as the categories and structures these rules operate over. But before we begin describing children's acquisition of the rules of language, it is important to understand just what sort of rules we are talking about.

Descriptive versus prescriptive rules

The knowledge of the rules of language that speaker/hearers possess is not explicit. Unless you have taken a course in linguistics, you don't know these rules in a way that would allow you to explain them. Rather, you know these rules in the sense that you always follow them. We illustrated this kind of rule knowledge with respect to phonological rules in Chapter 2, and the same thing applies here to the rules of syntax and morphology.

The implicit rules we address in this chapter are not like the prescriptive rules of grammar taught in an English class. The difference is that an English class teaches the current standard of language use for educated speakers and writers. Linguists, in contrast, take whatever people do as "correct" and try to describe the patterns in it. One way of seeing the difference between the **descriptive rules** that linguists write and the **prescriptive rules** taught in English class is to compare the outcome of breaking those rules. If you turn in a paper to English class that includes the sentence

Me and Tiffany went to the mall.

you will be corrected because that form is not acceptable in formal writing, even though it is a form that people say all the time. On the other hand, if you just string words together in violation of word order rules, you get

*mall the to went me Tiffany and

This is something that no one would ever say and that everyone would agree is ungrammatical. The study of language acquisition is the study of how children learn the language used by the adults around them. Thus, we are concerned with the acquisition of the descriptive rules that disallow *mall the to went me Tiffany and,* not the prescriptive rules that deem *Me and Tiffany went to the mall* "bad grammar."

Having thus established what this chapter is about, we will begin our discussion of children's development of syntax and morphology with a brief overview of the ground to be covered.

AN OVERVIEW OF GRAMMATICAL DEVELOPMENT

After several months of talking in single-word utterances, children begin to put two words together in sentences like *Daddy shirt, Off TV,* and *Pretty tower.* These first word combinations tend to be missing function words and the bound morphemes that mark plural, possessive, or tense. Next, children start to produce longer utterances, combining three and more words. As children start to put words together in longer sequences, they also start to add the function words and bound morphemes that were missing in their first word combinations. Children's first sentences are usually simple active declarative sentences; later, negative sentences and questions appear. The last major syntactic development is the production of multiclause sentences. This course of development usually begins some time before the child's second birthday and is largely complete by the age of 4.

The foregoing outline is painted in very broad strokes. It ignores completely the individual differences that exist and the development of grammar as it is evidenced in comprehension. Our next task is to fill in and supplement this sketchy outline. As we did for phonology and the lexicon, we will first describe the changes that occur in what children say as they learn their language's syntax and morphology. We will begin by describing the transition from single-word speech to the production of word combinations, and we will follow the course of development in production through to the production of complex sentences. We will then turn to the topics of individual differences in the course of development and the measurement of grammatical development. Following that, we will turn to studies of comprehension for what they can reveal about what children know about the grammar of their language at different points in the developmental process. Having thus described the course of development, we will then turn to the theoretical issues in the field regarding what sort of linguistic knowledge children actually have at different points in the course of development and how to account for the changes that occur.

THE TRANSITION FROM ONE-WORD SPEECH

Many children produce transitional forms between single-word utterances and the clear two-word utterances that mark the beginning of grammatical structure in their speech. These **transitional forms** can blur the distinction between the one-word and two-word stages of language production.

Vertical constructions

Before they produce two-word utterances, some children utter successive single-word utterances that seem to be related to each other in meaning in the same way that the words in a two-word utterance are related. For example, one little girl who woke up with an eye infection pointed to her eye and said, "Ow. Eye" (personal data). In this case, each word had the same intonation contour as if it had been said by itself, and the two words were separated by a pause. However, the meaning expressed clearly involved a relation between the two words. At this stage, children also sometimes produce a single-word utterance that builds on someone else's previous utterance. Scollon (1979) called these sequences "vertical constructions," because when researchers transcribe what children say, they write each utterance on a new line. A two-word sentence, in contrast, would be a horizontal construction and would be written on the same line in transcription.

Unanalyzed word combinations and "word + jargon" combinations

There are other transitional forms besides these vertical constructions. Most children have at least some multiword phrases in their repertoires that have been memorized as unanalyzed wholes; these phrases therefore do not reflect the development of the ability to combine words (Peters, 1986). *Iwant* and *Idontknow* are examples of unanalyzed wholes that are common in children's early language. Some children—typically those who have been producing long strings of jargon since their babbling days—produce utterances longer than one word by inserting one clear word into what is otherwise an incomprehensible babble sequence. The result can sound something like *mumble mumble mumble cookie?* To further complicate matters, all these transitional phenomena may exist simultaneously, so that one child's first multiword utterances may include some rote-learned wholes, some "jargon + word" combinations, and some truly productive word combinations.

EARLY MULTIWORD UTTERANCES

Two-word combinations

The beginning of a productive system   At some point, truly productive word combinations begin. We say that children have a productive system when they use the words in their vocabularies in different combinations. A sample of the two-word utterances produced by one child during a one-month period is presented in Box 4.1 (from Braine, 1976). The variety of utterances in this table suggests that the boy who produced these utterances was able to combine the words in his limited vocabulary productively. For example, he could say that anything is big or little; he could say that Daddy and Andrew walk and sleep. (And you would predict from the appearance of the utterance *Daddy sit* on this list that the child could also produce *Andrew sit.*) It's also a good bet—and crucial to the claim that the child has a productive system—that these utterances were not just reduced imitations of sentences he has heard adults produce. The test would be to introduce this little boy to a new person, Emily: if his linguistic knowledge were productive, he should immediately be able to produce *Emily sit, Emily walk,* and so on.

Box 4.1   Examples of one child's two-word utterances

Possessives

daddy coffee	Andrew book	daddy book	daddy eat
daddy shell	daddy car	mommy book	juice daddy
mommy shell	daddy chair	daddy bread	daddy juice
Andrew shoe	daddy cookie	Elliot cookie	Mommy butter
daddy hat	daddy tea	Elliot diaper	daddy butter
Elliot juice	mommy tea	Elliot boat	
mommy mouth	daddy door		this Nina

Property-indicating patterns

big balloon	little shell	all wet . . .	red balloon
big hot	little ham	mommy . . .	blue stick
big shell	little water	all wet	
big juice	little light	daddy all wet	hurt Andrew
big pants	little wet	daddy all	hurt fly
big lion	little step	wet	hurt knee
big water	little boy	all wet ball	hurt plane
big light	little bird	shirt wet	hurt hand
big step	little tobacco	wet nose	
big jump	little banana	shoe wet	old cookie
big boy	little spilt	wet diaper	old apple
big bird	little hurt		old cup
big tobacco		hot sand	old stick
big banana		hot fire	old egg
	all wet . . .	hot tea	
	water . . .	hot ball	
little hat	all wet	blue shirt	
little duck	all wet pants		

Recurrence, number, disappearance

more glass	two plane	two car	one daddy car
more boy	two stick	two diaper	
more raisins	two ducks	two tobacco	all gone big
more shovel	two spoon	two raisins	stick
more "O"	two fly	two daddy	all gone stick
	two shoe	door	all gone bee
other door	two bird	two daddy	all gone
other pin	two pipe	two mommy	stone . . .
other ball	two door	two squirrel	all gone
other hand	two cup	two bread	

Box 4.1 *(continued)*

Locatives

sand ball	"ON"	hand eye	"IN/TO"
hand hair	"IN"	stone outside	"TO"
ball house	"IN/TO"	key door	"TO"
man car	"IN"	raisin cup	"IN/TO"
fly light	"ON"	dog house	"ON"
sand toe	"ON"	feet light	"TO"
sand water	"IN/TO"		
sand eye	"IN"	in there . . . old apple . . .	
daddy . . . hot ball	"TO"	in there . . . old apple	
ball daddy	"TO"	milk in there	
stick car	"IN"	down there car	
rock outside	"TO"		

Actor/action

mommy sit	daddy work	boy walk	Andrew sleep
daddy sit	daddy sleep	man walk	daddy work
Andrew walk	daddy walk	Elliot sleep	stone daddy

Other combinations

have it egg	eat fork	back eat
have it milk	bite top	up bed
have it fork	bite block	
	bounce ball	mommy girl
dirty face	broke pipe	daddy boy
dirty mouth	ride car	
dirty feet	walk car	orange juice
clean socks	ride daddy	apple juice
spilt bread	walk daddy	grape juice
spilt raisin		drink water
	daddy window	butter honey
boom-boom tower	window byebye	sock shoe
boom-boom car	hat on	sit down
boom-boom coffee	socks on	lie down
boom-boom plane	out car	
boom-boom chair	out chair	
	back car	
eat dessert	back raisin	

Source: From "Children's First Word Combinations," by M. D. S. Braine, 1976, *Monographs of the Society for Research in Child Development, 41,* Serial No. 164. Copyright © 1976 The Society for Research in Child Development, Inc. Reprinted by permission.

Box 4.2   Relational meanings expressed in children's two-word utterances

Meaning	*Example*
agent + action	Daddy sit
action + object	drive car
agent + object	Mommy sock
action + location	sit chair
entity + location	toy floor
possessor + possession	my teddy
entity + attribute	crayon big
demonstrative + entity	this telephone

Source: Based on Brown, 1973.

Meanings in two-word utterances   Although we say that children's systems are productive when children can put words together in novel combinations, children's first word combinations are quite limited in the range of **relational meanings** expressed. (The term *relational meaning* refers to the relation between the referents of the words in a word combination. So, for example, in the utterance *my teddy,* the word *my* refers to the speaker and the word *teddy* refers to a stuffed animal; the relational meaning is that of possession.) Roger Brown (1973) proposed a list of eight relational meanings that he claimed accounted for the majority of the meanings children express in their two-word utterances, even children acquiring different languages. These meanings, with examples drawn from many different children, are listed in Box 4.2. According to Brown, the child's grammar at the two-word stage is a vehicle for expressing a small set of semantic relationships. The particular semantic relationships expressed at this stage reflect the level of cognitive development typical of children of this age. The particular words, of course, reflect the language the children have been exposed to. So, according to this view, cognitive development provides the categories of early **combinatorial speech,** and input in the target language provides the lexical items that fill those categories.

Three-word and more combinations

For some children, the two-word stage lasts for several months. For other children, the two-word stage is brief and barely identifiable as a separate stage before utterances with three and more words are produced. Of course, children continue to produce one- and two-word utterances. What changes with

---

Box 4.3 Examples of multiword speech

All the utterances longer than two words produced by one 2-year-old child during breakfast:

I want some eggs.
Where'd it go?
I watch it.
I watching cars.
Here it comes.
Daddy get you.
Put it table.
I see it.

Source: From data described in Hoff-Ginsberg, 1991.

development is the upper limit on the length of utterance children can produce. Box 4.3 is a sample of all the three-word utterances produced by one 2-year-old child in the course of having breakfast. This child had just started to put three words together; most utterances were one or two words long and only one was longer than three words. These sentences illustrate several typical characteristics of children's speech at this stage.

When children start to put three words together, many of the meanings expressed are combinations of the relational meanings in two-word combinations, with the redundant terms mentioned only once. For example, the sentence *I watch it* could be described as a combination of "agent + action" (I watch) and "action + object" (watch it). Another generalization that can be made about the meanings in children's utterances at this stage is that they are almost exclusively about the here-and-now. Even 3-year-olds rarely mention absent or imaginary events (Sachs, 1983). However, it is important to point out that these generalizations do not hold perfectly. Not all meanings expressed fit the description of combinations of the two-word relational meanings. For example, one of the sentences in Box 4.3 refers to an absent person, Daddy. (For a more elaborate description of the meanings in early multiword speech, see Bloom, Lightbown, & Hood, 1975.)

In terms of structure, two characteristics of these early multiword sentences are noteworthy. First, early sentences tend to be affirmative, declarative statements, as opposed to negations or questions. Second, certain types of words and bound morphemes consistently tend to be missing. Because the omission of certain words and morphemes makes children's utterances sound like the sentences adults produce when writing telegrams, children's speech at this point in development has been termed **telegraphic speech** (Brown &

Fraser, 1963). The telegraphic quality of children's early speech has been the focus of considerable research attention.

The telegraphic nature of early combinatorial speech

The words included in children's early sentences are primarily words from the major grammatical categories of nouns, verbs, and adjectives. The missing elements are determiners, prepositions, auxiliary verbs, and the bound morphemes that go on the ends of nouns and verbs. These missing forms are called **grammatical morphemes** because the use of these words and word endings is tied to particular grammatical entities. For example, *the* and *a* can appear only at the beginning of a noun phrase; *ing* can be attached only to a verb. Although these grammatical elements do carry some meaning, they seem to carry less meaning than do the nouns and verbs in the utterance (Brown, 1973).

The telegraphic quality of children's early word combinations has been reported in studies of children acquiring languages as diverse as Finnish, German, Luo (spoken in parts of Kenya), and Kahluli (spoken in Papua New Guinea (Brown, 1973; Mills, 1985; Schieffelin, 1985). However, it appears that syntax is not necessarily easier for children to learn than morphology. Children who are learning languages that have rich morphology seem to learn morphology earlier in the course of language development than do children acquiring morphologically impoverished languages, such as English (Berman, 1986; Peters, 1995). What seems to be particularly important in determining children's ease of acquisition is how regular or predictable the system is (Berman, 1986; Maratsos, 1983). Children acquiring Turkish, which has a highly regular, rich, and perceptually salient inflectional system, have been reported to produce inflected forms (that is, words with grammatical morphemes) before they combine words (Aksu-Koc & Slobin, 1985).

Exactly why these grammatical functors and inflections are omitted in the early sentences produced by children acquiring languages such as English is a matter of some debate. One possibility is that the omitted words and morphemes are not produced because they are not essential to meaning. Children probably have cognitive limitations on the length of utterance they can produce, independent of their grammatical knowledge. Given such length limitations, they may sensibly leave out the least important parts. It is also true that the omitted words tend to be words that are not stressed in adults' utterances, and children may be leaving out unstressed elements (Demuth, 1994). Some have also suggested that children's underlying knowledge at this point does not include the grammatical categories that govern the use of the omitted forms (Atkinson, 1992; Radford, 1990, 1995). We will return later in this chapter to the question of what grammatical knowledge underlies children's early sentences.

THE DEVELOPMENT OF GRAMMATICAL MORPHEMES

The missing forms in children's telegraphic speech begin to appear in utterances around the time that the first three-word utterances appear. In his famous longitudinal study of the three children known to child language researchers by their pseudonyms, Adam, Eve, and Sarah, Brown (1973) tracked the appearance of <u>14 grammatical morphemes of English</u>. Brown's careful study of the emergence of grammatical morphemes allows us to make some generalizations about children's transition from being beginning telegraphic speakers to having full command over the use of these forms. One generalization is that this transition takes quite a long time. Although the first

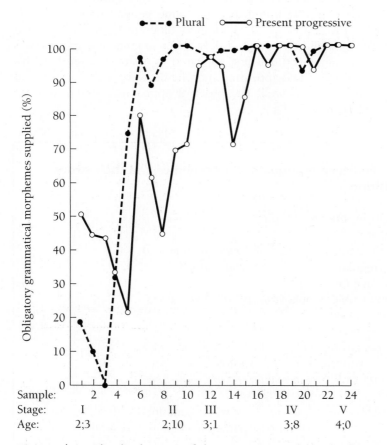

Figure 4.1   The development of the progressive and plural inflections in one child's speech

Source: Reprinted by permission of the publishers from A First Language: The Early Stages, by Roger Brown, Cambridge Mass.: Harvard University Press, copyright © 1973 by the President and Fellows of Harvard College.

grammatical morphemes typically appear with the first three-word utterances, all the grammatical morphemes are not reliably used correctly until more than a year later, when children are speaking in long, complex sentences. A second generalization is that the acquisition of grammatical morphemes is not an all-or-none phenomenon. A long period of time passes between the first time a morpheme is used and the time it is reliably used in contexts where it is obligatory. Figure 4.1 shows the gradual development of the progressive *ing* and the plural *s* in one child's spontaneous speech.

A third generalization that can be made is that the order in which the 14 different morphemes are acquired is very similar across different children. Brown found that Adam, Eve, and Sarah acquired these 14 morphemes in similar orders, although their rates of development were quite different. De Villiers and de Villiers (1973) found that that same general order of development was true in a sample of 21 children at different levels of language development. That is, children who had only a few grammatical morphemes were likely to have only those that first appeared in Adam, Eve, and Sarah's data. Children who had a late-appearing morpheme were likely to have all the earlier-appearing ones as well. The order of appearance found in these studies is presented in Box 4.4.

Box 4.4   Fourteen grammatical morphemes and their order of acquisition

1. present progressive (+ *ing*)
2–3. *in, on*
4. plural irregular (for example, *men*, regular + *s*)
5. past irregular (for example, *came, went*)
6. possessive (+ *'s*)
7. uncontractible copula (*am, is, are, was, were*)
8. articles (*a, the*)
9. past regular (+ *d*)
10. third person regular (+ *s;* for example, *she talks*)
11. third person irregular (for example, *does, has*)
12. uncontractible auxiliary (*am, is, are, has, have*)
13. contractible copula (*'m, 's, 're*)
14. contractible auxiliary (*'m, 's, 're* when combined with + *ing; 've, 's* when combined with a past participle such as *has been*)

Source: Reprinted by permission of the publishers from *A First Language: The Early Stages,* by Roger Brown, Cambridge Mass.: Harvard University Press, copyright © 1973 by the President and Fellows of Harvard College.

THE DEVELOPMENT OF DIFFERENT SENTENCE FORMS

Another syntactic development, which typically begins around the time the first grammatical morphemes appear, is the development of sentence forms other than the basic affirmative, declarative form. In English, forming negative statements and questions requires auxiliary verbs. Auxiliaries are among the last grammatical functors children acquire, but children do not wait until they have acquired the adult means of expression to make negative statements or to ask questions. Initially they indicate negation or questioning without auxiliaries. (Typically children use *can't* and *don't* long before they use *can* and *do,* and *can't* and *don't* seem to be used as unanalyzed negative markers, much as *not* is used. Therefore, *can't* and *don't* are not counted as auxiliaries.) As children's syntactic abilities develop, the form of their negative statements and questions changes.

Expressing negation

The earliest linguistic means of expressing negation that children acquiring English use is to tack on a negative marker (typically *no* or *not*) to the beginning or end of the sentence. Some children also mark negation nonlinguistically by shaking their heads as they utter an affirmative statement. Following the sentence-external means of marking negation, children produce utterances in which the negative marker is inside the sentence (such as *I no want go in there*), but the sentences are still not adultlike because auxiliaries aren't used. Finally, as children acquire auxiliaries, their negative expressions take the adult form. Examples of these different types of linguistic expression of negation are provided in Box 4.5.

Asking questions

English-speaking children's first expression of questions is also affected by the late acquisition of auxiliaries. Describing the development of question forms is a little more complicated than describing the development of negation because there are two types of questions forms. **Yes/no questions** are those that can be answered with either *yes* or *no*. **Wh- questions** are those that begin with *who, where, what, why, when,* or *how.* Children's first yes/no questions are typically marked only by intonation. At this stage, wh- questions are typically affirmative statements with a wh- word at the beginning, such as *What that is?* Next, auxiliaries appear in questions. In yes/no questions, auxiliaries are added to the beginning of the utterance, which suffices to construct a grammatical yes/no question (such as *Will it fit in there?*). At this stage, however, wh- questions are still not adultlike because children do not invert the subject and auxiliary, instead producing utterances like *What a*

Box 4.5   Children's negative sentence forms, in order of development

1. *Sentences with external negative marker*
   No . . . wipe finger
   No the sun shining
   No mitten
   Wear mitten no

2. *Constructions with internal negative marker but no auxiliaries*
   I can't see you
   I don't like you
   I no want envelope

3. *Constructions with auxiliaries*
   I didn't did it
   Donna won't let go
   No, it isn't

Source: Examples are from Adam, Eve, and Sarah, as reported in Klima & Bellugi, 1967.

Box 4.6   Children's question forms, in order of development

1. *Constructions with external question marker*	*Yes/no questions* Mommy eggnog? I ride train? Sit chair?	*Wh- questions* Who that? What cowboy doing? Where milk go? What a bandaid is?

2. *Constructions with auxiliaries but no subject-auxiliary inversion in wh- questions*	*Yes/no questions*
	Does the kitty
	   stand up?
	Oh, did I caught it?
	Will you help me?
		Wh- questions
		Where the other
		   Joe will drive?
		What you did say?
		Why kitty can't
		   stand up?

3. *Subject-auxiliary inversion in wh- questions*		What did you doed? What does whiskey taste like?

Source: Examples from Klima & Bellugi, 1967, and personal data

doctor can do? Once subject-auxiliary inversion has been acquired, wh-questions are adultlike in form. Box 4.6 lists examples of children's question forms in their typical order of appearance.

THE DEVELOPMENT OF COMPLEX SENTENCES

After the development of grammatical morphemes and different sentence forms is well under way, the next grammatical development is the appearance of sentences that contain more than one clause. There are many different types of **complex sentences,** and some appear in children's spontaneous speech much earlier than others do. Box 4.7 contains examples of the different types in their approximate order of development. The first complex sentences appear after children are regularly producing four-word utterances (Bowerman, 1976), typically around the age of 2½ years. Children use most of the different complex sentence types by the age of 4 (Bowerman, 1979; Limber, 1973).

INDIVIDUAL DIFFERENCES IN GRAMMATICAL DEVELOPMENT

Children differ in both the rate and the course of grammatical development. The differences in rate are the most obvious. Some children produce multiword utterances at age 18 months, whereas others do not start combining words until

---

Box 4.7   Children's complex sentences, in order of development

1. *Object complementation*
   Watch me draw circles.
   I see you sit down.

2. *Wh- embedded clauses*
   Can I do it when we get home?
   I show you how to do it.

3. *Coordinating conjunctions*
   He was stuck, and I got him out.
   When I was a little girl I could go "geek-geek" like that, but now I can go "this is a chair."

4. *Subordinating conjunctions*
   Here's a set. It must be mine if it's a little one.
   I want this doll because she's big.

Source: Examples from Limber, 1973.

they are 2 years old. Less obvious than differences in when children start to combine words are differences in the kinds of multiword utterances children produce. Some children's early multiword utterances are rote-learned as wholes; other children's are combinations of separate words from the start.

The different kinds of multiword utterances children produce seem to reflect different approaches to the task of syntax acquisition. The approach that results in many unanalyzed chunks has been termed **holistic** (Bretherton, McNew, Snyder, & Bates, 1983), or top-down (Peters, 1986). Children who take this approach can sometimes produce impressively long utterances with little combinatorial ability. For example, a 2-year-old who stores chunks in memory might be able to say "I don't wanna go night-night" by combining just two units—*Idontwanna* and *gonightnight*. The other approach of breaking down speech into smaller units and then combining them has been termed **analytical** or bottom-up. Although children eventually must figure out the smallest units and how to combine them, the holistic approach to combinatorial speech is not necessarily a dead end. Some children may "break into structure" (Pine & Lieven, 1993, p. 551) by starting with unanalyzed phrases and then identifying slots in these phrases that can be occupied by different lexical items. At this intermediary stage, a child may have a repertoire of rules that allow very limited productivity—for example, rules like:

Sentence → There's the + x

Sentence → Me got + x

Sentence → Wanna + x

A similar account of children's first word combinations was suggested by Braine (1976), who called such rules limited-scope formulae.

Most children make use of both the top-down and bottom-up strategies, and most children include both unanalyzed chunks and smaller units in their early sentences. However, children vary in how much they rely on one strategy versus the other, and the route to syntax some children take seems to be extremely holistic or extremely analytic.

Another difference among children is in the kind of word that is part of their early word combinations. Some children's word combinations depend on combining a few function words—such as *no, more,* or a pronoun—with other content words. Such a child's multiword utterances could be described as following the form "no + x," "more + x," or "x + it." At one time, it was thought that this was a stage all children go through. Children at this stage were described as having acquired a grammar that operated on only two categories of words. The function words were called pivot words and everything else was an open category (Braine, 1963). There has been some debate over whether a **pivot grammar** is the best way to describe the syntactic system of children who produce those kinds of word combinations (see Brown, 1973). What seems clear, however, is that not all children produce them. Some children combine content words from the start, producing two-word utterances like *kathryn sock* and *touch milk* (Bloom et al., 1975). These children use pronouns much less frequently.

Some authors have suggested that these differences in the nature of children's early syntactic systems are related to each other and are also related to the referential/expressive distinction in lexical development discussed in Chapter 3 (Bates et al., 1988; Nelson, 1981; Peters, 1986). According to this view, a holistic approach is characterized by heavy reliance on unanalyzed chunks, heavy use of pronouns in word combinations, and an expressive style of lexical development. In contrast, an analytic approach is characterized by word-sized units that are combined in multiword utterances, infrequent use of pronouns, and a referential style of lexical development. Although there is evidence that these different features of early language development may be related (for example, Bates et al., 1988), they are not welded together. And again, it is important to point out that all children use both approaches to language acquisition, although some rely more heavily on one and some rely more heavily on the other.

MEASURING GRAMMATICAL DEVELOPMENT

As children gradually master the grammar of their language, they become able to produce increasingly long utterances. This is true not only when length is counted in words but even more so when length is counted in morphemes. For example, a telegraphic sentence such as *I watch it* has a length of three words and a length of three morphemes. A nontelegraphic version of that sentence, *I am watching it,* has a length of four words and a length of five morphemes. Because length in morphemes is a good index of the grammatical complexity of an utterance, and because children tend to follow similar courses of development in adding complexity to their utterances, the average length of children's utterances (counted in morphemes) has been widely used as a measure of children's syntactic development.

The relation of **mean length of utterance (MLU)** to age for the three children Adam, Eve, and Sarah is depicted in Figure 4.2. Even within these three children, there were large differences in the age at which each began to show evidence of grammatical development. And because the range of individual variation in the rate of syntactic development is so great, age is not a good indicator of a child's level of grammatical development. Thus knowing that a child is 18 months old doesn't tell you very much about that child's level of productive language. It would be normal for an 18-month-old to be talking in single-word utterances or in three-word sentences. Describing a child in terms of MLU provides a sharper picture of the child's level of productive language—at least up to an MLU of 3.0 (Rondal, Ghiotto, Bredart, & Bachelet, 1987). After MLU exceeds 3.0, it is less useful as a predictor of the complexity of children's utterances (Klee & Fitzgerald, 1985).

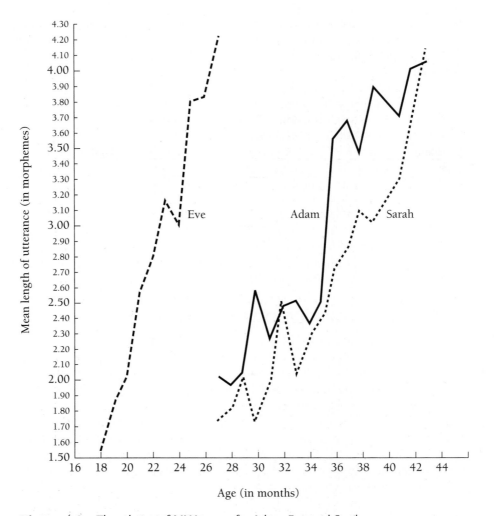

Figure 4.2   The relation of MLU to age for Adam, Eve, and Sarah

Source: Reprinted by permission of the publishers from A First Language: The Early Stages, by Roger Brown, Cambridge Mass.: Harvard University Press, copyright © 1973 by the President and Fellows of Harvard College.

MLU has also been used as the basis for somewhat arbitrarily dividing syntactic development into five stages. We can use this stage terminology to summarize the major developments in the course of children's acquisition of the syntax and morphology of English we have just described. In Stage I (MLU = 1.01–1.99), children begin to combine words. In Stage II (MLU = 2.00–2.49), children begin to add grammatical morphemes to their word combinations. In Stage III (2.50–2.99), children begin to use different sentence modalities

Table 4.1 Stages of grammatical development and normative age ranges

Stage	MLU	Age range
Early I	1.01–1.49	16–26 months
Late I	1.50–1.99	18–31 months
II	2.00–2.49	21–35 months
III	2.50–2.99	24–41 months
Early IV	3.00–3.49	28–45 months
Late IV/Early V	3.50–3.99	31–50 months
Late V	4.00–4.49	37–52 months
Post V	4.50+	41—

Source: From "The Relation between Age and Mean Length of Utterance," by J. F. Miller and R. S. Chapman, 1981, *Journal of Speech and Hearing Research, 24,* 154–161. Copyright © 1981 American Speech-Language-Hearing Association. Reprinted by permission.

(negative and question forms). In Stage IV (MLU = 3.00+), children begin to use complex sentences; new forms of complex sentences emerge in Stage V. Miller and Chapman (1981) collected data on 123 children to establish norms for the age at which most children reach each stage. The MLU boundaries and the age at which roughly two-thirds of children are at each stage are presented in Table 4.1.

THE DEVELOPMENT OF COMPREHENSION OF STRUCTURED SPEECH

Having described grammatical development in terms of what children produce, we now turn to studies of what children understand. The picture of grammatical development that can be constructed from studies of comprehension is not as continuous as the picture that emerges from studies of production. There is no such thing as a record of spontaneous comprehension that would be the counterpart to the transcripts that are records of children's spontaneous productions. Instead, to find out what aspects of grammatical structure children understand, one must devise a way of testing for comprehension of particular structures.

Simply talking to children and seeing whether they respond appropriately is not sufficient because children have a variety of ways of responding appropriately, even without truly understanding the structure of what they hear.

These strategies for responding are sufficiently successful that if you ask parents of 1-year-olds how much their children understand of the speech that they hear, most parents will answer, "Everything" (Hoff-Ginsberg, 1991). (The next most frequent answer is "too much.") Although it's not the business of child language researchers to delve into the details of what constitutes "too much" language comprehension for some parents, researchers have tackled the question of whether children understand "everything." In the next sections, we will first discuss the strategies children use that sometimes mislead parents and others into thinking children have more competence than they do. Then we will describe the course of grammatical development suggested by controlled studies of comprehension.

Strategies children use

Children have **response strategies** that enable them to respond to speech they only partially understand. Very young children are particularly likely to respond to speech by *doing* something (Shatz, 1978a, 1978b). This action strategy allows children to produce appropriate responses to much of what is typically said to them. For example, when a child's mother says "Why don't you play with your blocks?" playing with blocks will probably satisfy her; and when she asks "Where are your shoes?" getting your shoes is probably what she wants you to do. However, the success of this strategy depends on the child's ability to figure out the correct action without fully understanding the sentence.

Occasionally, children's strategies trip them up and reveal their syntactic ignorance, as in the following example provided by Robin Chapman (1978). Chapman's young son was standing in the living room when his father asked, "Do you need a dry diaper?" The little boy felt his diaper, ran to his room, and returned with a clean diaper in hand. At this point, the child appeared to have fully understood his father's question. After the boy was changed, his father said, "There, now you have a dry diaper," and the little boy ran to his room to return with more clean diapers. In doing so, the child revealed that all he really understood of what was spoken to him was the word *diaper* and that he knew just one thing to do with diapers. Chapman (1978) described children at this stage as deriving sentence meaning from knowledge of the world rather than from knowledge of syntactic structure.

To find out what children know about syntactic structure, it is necessary to set up a situation in which knowledge of the world is not sufficient to yield a correct response. Even then, children have strategies that they use before they have achieved full understanding. In this case, the strategies are sentence comprehension strategies rather than response strategies. One sentence comprehension strategy is a **word order strategy,** which treats whatever is mentioned first in the sentence as the subject and whatever is mentioned second as the object. This strategy allows children to correctly act out *The swing bumps* *the kitty* and *The kitty bumps the swing.* However, this strategy produces incorrect responses to passive sentences, such as *The swing was bumped by the kitty.* A similar strategy that children use in interpreting complex sentences with two events is the **order-of-mention strategy.** This strategy works for interpreting sentences such as *John played before Mary sang,* but it yields misinterpretations of sentences such as *John played after Mary sang* or *Before Mary sang, John played.* Another strategy children use, even at this later stage, involves recourse to world knowledge. This **probable-event strategy** allows children to correctly act out sentences like *The mouse was chased by the cat,* even though the word order strategy doesn't work here. However, children using this strategy will reverse the sequence of events when presented with nonprobable sentences, such as *I broke my balloon because I cried.*

In normal interaction, the strategies children use tend to serve them well, and for that reason children may appear to understand "everything" even when child language researchers can prove that they do not. But if children do not understand everything, they do know more about the grammar of their language than they reveal in their spontaneous productions. We turn now to a description of what children know about the grammar of their language and when they know it, based on studies of children's comprehension.

Children's comprehension of meaning in sentence structure

Comprehension of relational meanings in word combinations   Children who produce only single-word utterances appear to know something about the meanings that arise from putting words together. Sachs and Truswell (1978) found that children who were all one-word speakers (and between 16 months and 24 months old) could correctly respond to two-word instructions such as *kiss keys* and *tickle book.* Hirsh-Pasek and Golinkoff (1991) demonstrated comprehension of the relational meanings in two-word combinations in even younger children. Utilizing the preferential-looking paradigm used in the *gorping* experiment described in Chapter 3, Hirsh-Pasek and Golinkoff presented 13- to 15-month-old children with a sentence like *She's kissing the keys.* As the children heard this sentence, two videotaped scenes were presented simultaneously on two different screens. On one screen, a woman was kissing keys and holding up a ball; on the other screen, a woman was kissing a ball and holding up keys. Thus *kissing* and *keys* were depicted in both scenes, but *kissing keys* was depicted in only one scene. These very young children looked longer at the action that matched the sentence than at the nonmatching action. In doing so, these children demonstrated that they knew that words together carry a meaning beyond the meaning of each word individually. Understanding that meaning is carried not just by words but by word combinations is the kernel of understanding grammar. The next thing the child must learn is that particular sorts of combinations yield particular sorts of meaning.

Comprehension of meaning in the structure of word combinations   In English, the order in which words are combined carries meaning, and children learning English show that they are aware of language-typical word order patterns and that they are sensitive to the meaning carried by word order before they produce word combinations.

Using the sort of procedure described in Chapter 2 (in which an infant's preference between two sets of auditory stimuli is measured by how much time the infant does what is needed to get the experimenter to play that tape), Fernald and McRoberts (1995) found that 12- and 14-month-old infants (but not 10-month-old infants) preferred to listen to sentences presented in normal word order over sentences with scrambled word order—even with all prosodic features held constant. Of course, this doesn't mean that the 12-month-olds knew what the sentences meant, but it does mean they knew something about the word order pattern in their language; when Fernald and McRoberts presented normal and scrambled Spanish sentences, children learning English showed no preference, but children learning Spanish did. Children do show sensitivity to meaning carried by word order by the age of 16 months. Using the preferential-looking paradigm, Hirsh-Pasek and Golinkoff (1991) found that 16- to 18-month-old children, most of whom were one-word speakers, could distinguish between the meanings of contrasting pairs of sentences such as *Where is Cookie Monster washing Big Bird?* and *Where is Big Bird washing Cookie Monster?*

There's more to syntax than word order. Hirsh-Pasek, Golinkoff, and Naigles (1996) found, again using the preferential-looking paradigm, that 28-month-old children are sensitive to the difference in meaning among the sentences *Find Cookie Monster and Big Bird turning* (both creatures are turning), *Look, Cookie Monster is turning Big Bird* (only Big Bird is turning), and *Cookie Monster is turning with Big Bird* (they're both turning). All these sentences had *Cookie Monster, Big Bird,* and *turning* in them, but who is turning and whether he is turning independently or as a result of somebody else's action is signaled entirely by sentence structure. By the age of 28 months, when most children are still saying things like "I watching cars," children are sensitive to these structurally carried distinctions in meaning.

Children also seem to know that grammatical morphemes do something in a sentence before actually producing grammatical morphemes in their own sentences. Shipley, Smith, and Gleitman (1969) found that children who were telegraphic speakers were more likely to respond to a well-formed command, such as *Throw me the ball,* than to a command that matched their own productive speech, such as *Throw ball.* Of course, children in this case might know only that the telegraphic utterance isn't quite right, rather than understanding any information carried by the omitted morphemes.

There is also evidence that children actually derive information from the function morphemes that they hear before they have control over the use of these morphemes in production. Gerken and McIntosh (1993) found that children with MLUs over 1.50 were better able to find the correct picture when told *Find the dog for me* than when they were given an ungrammatical sentence in which the wrong function morpheme was used, such as *Find was dog for me*. Other findings presented in Chapter 3—that children use the presence of a determiner to decide if a new word is a common noun ("the zav") or a proper noun ("Zav") (Gelman & Taylor, 1984; Katz et al., 1974)—also indicate sensitivity to the meaning these grammatical forms carry.

Up to this point, we have described a course of grammatical development in which children show that by 12 months of age they have learned what word combinations in their language sound like (we say "learned" because the preference for normal word combinations is language specific and not in evidence at 10 months), by 13 to 15 months they know that words together mean something more than the meaning of both words individually, by 16 to 18 months they know the meaning carried by the basic word order pattern of the language, by the time they reach an MLU of 1.5 they know something about grammatical morphemes, and by 28 months they are sensitive to distinctions among more complicated sentence structures (see Hirsh-Pasek & Golinkoff, 1996, for a summary of much of this work). Two basic conclusions can be drawn from this account. One is that the sequence of grammatical development that occurs in comprehension is like the sequence seen in production, but it occurs earlier. [The duration of the lag between achievement in comprehension and evidence in production is different for different children. Thus an individual child's comprehension skills is not a very good predictor of that child's level of productive grammar (Bates et al., 1988).] The second conclusion is that grammatical competence is achieved very early. This latter fact places constraints on the kind of account of grammatical development that is plausible. However grammar is acquired, it is a process that is accomplished quickly and by very young children.

In addition to showing that children have grammatical knowledge earlier than they evidence it in production, comprehension studies offer the possibility of finding out things that children know about grammar that you would never see in production. At this point in our description of children's grammatical development, we are going to jump ahead to consider older children and more complex structures. Having established that children know the basics of grammar when they are still babies or toddlers, we now turn to evidence that children know a great deal more than the basics while they are still preschoolers.

Comprehension of complex sentences   Imagine that you were told the following story:

> Once there was a boy who loved climbing trees in the forest. One afternoon he slipped and fell to the ground. He picked himself up and went home. That night when he had a bath, he saw a big bruise on his

arm. He said to his Dad, "I must have hurt myself when I fell this afternoon." (de Villiers, 1995a, p. 23)

After hearing this story, suppose you are asked, "When did the boy say he fell?" There are two possible answers to this question: "in the afternoon" or "at night," because there are two possible interpretations of what *when* is asking about—the "saying" or the "falling." On the other hand, if you are asked, "When did the boy say how he fell?" then the only possible answer is "at night" because the only possible interpretation of what *when* is asking about is the "saying."

It would take more grammatical theory than we want to get into to account for why the first question has two interpretations and the second only one. We introduce this phenomenon here, however, to present a finding about children. When Jill de Villiers and Thomas Roeper (1995) presented 3- to 6-year-old children with stories and sentences like these, they found that even 3-year-olds knew that there were two possible interpretations of the first question and that the word *how* in the second question form made only one interpretation possible. Even without the linguistic theory that describes the knowledge underlying this phenomenon, children's performance in response to questions like these makes it clear that children know very subtle aspects of complex syntax at a very young age (de Villiers, 1995a).

Sometimes production precedes comprehension

Before we leave the topic of children's comprehension of grammatical structure, we need to point out that there are exceptions to the general pattern of competence in comprehension preceding competence in production. Sometimes children are unable to show that they understand the grammatical structures they produce in their own spontaneous speech. One reason for this inability may be difficulties in demonstrating comprehension in the way a particular testing situation requires. It is also possible for children to use structures correctly in a limited way without necessarily knowing everything about those structures. For example, young children can correctly use if-then statements describing contingent relations they are familiar with (such as, *If I'm a good girl and eat my beets, then I can have ice cream*), but these children could not understand the logical implications of all if-then statements that might be presented to them (such as, *If Socrates is a man and all men are mortal, then Socrates is mortal*). Also, it has been argued that children can demonstrate competence in the supportive context of describing familiar events that they cannot demonstrate in experimental settings (French & Nelson, 1985); and sentences presented in isolation may be more difficult to understand than sentences presented in context (de Villiers & Roeper, 1995).

In Chapter 6, we will consider later developments that may explain how the syntactic ability required to perform in comprehension experiments differs from that required to produce and understand speech in ordinary situations (Karmiloff-Smith, 1986).

WHAT IS THE NATURE OF CHILDREN'S GRAMMARS?

So far in this chapter we have simply described the different kinds of sentences children become able to produce and understand as they acquire the syntax and morphology of their language. We now need to back up and consider what children know about the underlying grammar at different points in the course of development. As we have seen, some of children's first multiword utterances appear to be partially or entirely memorized routines. We would not want to credit children at that early point with any understanding of grammar. However, this rote basis for producing multiword utterances doesn't last very long, and it doesn't account for very much of what young children say. When children can produce a variety of word combinations (such as those in Boxes 4.1 and 4.2), and when they regularly add grammatical morphemes to indicate plurals and past tense, children have some productive system underlying the syntax and morphology of their speech. By most accounts, the form of this underlying knowledge is a system of rules.

Evidence that children know rules

Three kinds of evidence support the contention that children know rules: (1) regular patterns found in children's word combinations, (2) errors children make that seem to reflect overapplication of rules, and (3) children's performance in experiments that shows they know how to use words they have never heard before in grammatical constructions. We will review each of these types of evidence in turn.

Patterns in early word combinations   There is order or systematicity in the way children put words together; their word combinations are not word salad. For example, if you inspect the two-word combinations in Box 4.1, you will find that possessive relations are consistently expressed in the form of "possessor + possessed object" (*my teddy*), actor/action combinations are consistently "actor + action" (*Daddy sit*), and so on. When psychologists and linguists find order in behavior, they tend to describe that behavior as rule-governed. We account for the consistent word order patterns across a variety of newly produced utterances in adult speech by attributing a productive rule to adults; similarly, the child's production of many different utterances that all have consistent word order seems to require a rule-based explanation.

Overregularization errors   Another piece of evidence that children know rules is that children make errors in spontaneous speech that seem to be overapplications of rules. For example, one 4-year-old consistently said "amn't I," as in *I'm a good boy, amn't I?* (personal data). This is not something that he heard, but it is a sensible overapplication of the rule that forms a tag question by inverting the subject and the form of the verb *to be*. In American English we say "You're good, aren't you?" and "He's good, isn't he?" but the ungrammaticality of *I'm good, amn't I?* is an exception to the rule. The 4-year-old who said "amn't I" had learned the rule, but not the exception.

In the domain of morphology, applying a rule to a word that is an exception in the language results in the production of plural forms such as *footses* or *toothes* or past-tense forms such as *goed* or *breaked*. These errors are called **overregularizations** because the child has made an irregular part of the language regular. One fact about these overregularization errors that has received considerable attention is that children will produce them after they have already been heard to say the correct irregular form—*went* or *broke*. So, in this case, it can't be that the children do not yet know the exceptions to the rule; they know the exception but apply the rule anyway.

Exactly why children overregularize when they already know the irregular form is a matter of debate. It has been argued that the same analytical tendency and search for patterns that allows children to learn the rule results in the rule's overriding the rote-learned exceptions. Some children overregularize more than others perhaps because they have a particular affinity for regular systems (Maratsos, 1993). However, overregularizations are always fewer than children's correct uses of the irregular forms, and overregularization errors are infrequent for most children. Analyzing 11,521 irregular past-tense verb forms in the speech of 83 children, Marcus and associates (1992) found a median rate of overregularization errors of 2.5%. In a similar analysis of plural noun forms, Marcus (1995) found a median overregularization rate of 8.3%. The explanation for overregularization errors that Marcus and colleagues suggest is that sometimes children, in talking, fail to retrieve the irregular form from memory. (According to this account, the retrieval failure rates must be 2.5% for verbs and 8.3% for nouns.) When retrieval of the irregular past-tense form fails, the regular rule for past-tense formation applies as a sort of default. Adults make overregularization errors too, although less frequently than children because adults have fewer retrieval failures.

Experimental tests of rule knowledge   Perhaps the strongest evidence that children have rules is that they know what to do with novel forms. In the domain of syntax, children who are taught a novel verb in one sentence structure show that they know how to use that verb productively in other sentence structures. For example, 4-year-old children who are told *The pig is pilking the horse* can later say, "The horse is being pilked by the pig" (Pinker, Lebeaux, & Frost, 1987).

Similarly, children who hear *I'm mooping a ball to the mouse* can then say, "I'm mooping the mouse a ball" (Gropen, Pinker, Hollander, & Goldberg, 1991).

In the domain of morphology, the classic demonstration of children's productive knowledge is Berko's wugs test, which was also mentioned in Chapter 2. Berko (1958) tested children's knowledge of inflectional rules by giving children nonsense words and asking them to supply the inflected forms (the forms with the grammatical inflections added). Berko found that children as young as 4 years old knew that the plural of *wug* must be *wugs* and that the past tense of *blick* must be *blicked,* thus demonstrating that "their linguistic knowledge went beyond the individual words in their vocabularies, and that they had rules of extension that enabled them to inflect the nonsense words" (Gleason, 1992, p. 10).

Questions about the nature of those rules

According to the preceding account, children's underlying grammatical knowledge is like adults' grammatical knowledge in that both consist of a system of productive rules. Some of the evidence for a rule-based system can be found in the regular patterns in 2-year-old children's first word combinations. Other evidence, such as evidence that children use verbs productively, comes from 4-year-olds. Although both kinds of evidence may indicate an underlying system of rules, the rules that 2-year-olds have when they begin to combine words may operate over a different kind of category than do the rules that 4-year-olds have when they produce passive sentences.

Is early grammar semantically based? It has been suggested that 2-year-olds have a **semantically based grammar,** in contrast to the **syntactically based grammar** of 4-year-olds and adults. To explain this position, it is necessary to review an important claim about adult grammars that was made in the first section of this chapter. That claim is that the rules adults have are rules for combining grammatical categories like *Noun* and *Verb*. Nouns and verbs are defined in terms of how they function in a sentence. A noun is anything that fills the Noun slot in a sentence. A noun can be a person, place, or thing, as you may have learned in elementary school, but it does not have to be. The first nouns in the following sentences include a person, an action, an internal state, and an attribute:

> Melissa is the class president.
>
> Swimming is good exercise.
>
> Hunger is a common problem in many parts of the world.
>
> Blue is my favorite color.

What makes *Melissa, swimming, hunger,* and *blue* all nouns is that they fill the same slot.

If you look at children's sentences, however, you find that the variety of meanings in words that fill the first Noun slot is clearly less than the variety of meanings adults express. For this reason, it has been proposed that the rules underlying children's early word combinations operate over semantic categories (Bowerman, 1973). This is essentially what Brown (1973) said about the system underlying children's first word combinations. The categories that are combined are semantic categories such as agent, action, and location, not Noun and Verb. Radford (1990, 1995) more recently made a similar suggestion, arguing that children's early sentences are purely combinations of lexical categories in thematic (meaning-based) structures.

Are early rules lexically based? Another proposal for how children could combine words without syntactic categories argues that the rules are lexically based, or specific to individual words. Some of the limited-scope formulae [to use Braine's (1976) term] or partially analyzed phrases [to use Pine & Lieven's (1993) term] may be examples of rules that are only partially productive because they are anchored by specific lexical items. Tomasello (1992) has made an even stronger claim, arguing that all of children's multiword utterances might initially be generated by lexically based rules. Based on the diary record of one child's first word combinations, he claimed that all the multiword utterances this child produced (at this early stage) involved words that would be categorized as verbs in the adult system; but there was little consistency across different verbs in the kinds of structures the verbs appeared in. Rather, each verb appeared in different structures.

Remember, the argument for having categories like *Verb* in the adult grammar is that a variety of words (such as *kiss* and *resemble*) appear in the same structure. Tomasello (1992) argued that at the age of 2 years, children do not have the category *Verb* at all. Instead, what 2-year-olds have is a vocabulary of particular verbs, each associated with its own possible structures. The other evidence on which Tomasello based this argument is the results of an experiment in which 2-year-olds were exposed to novel (nonsense) verbs (Olguin & Tomasello, 1993). In the course of play, an experimenter would say things to the children, such as *"Oh look, gaffing!"* and *"See that? Ernie's chamming!"* Later, the children used these newly learned verbs in their spontaneous speech but not productively with structures or even tense markings that had not been modeled. Bloom (1991) made a similar argument with respect to the knowledge that underlies young children's verb morphology. She argued that when children first begin to add inflectional endings to verbs, all that children know is that certain words can take different forms (such as fit/fits, play/playing), rather than that inflections apply to all members of a syntactic category.

In contrast to the doubts raised about crediting 2-year-olds with the category *Verb,* arguments have been made that 2-year-olds do have other syntactic categories. For example, Bloom, Lightbown, and Hood (1975) argued that the initial nouns in children's utterances do include some variety in expressed meanings. She observed that children produce sentences including the following:

Lois watch Gia

the bag go

Kathryn jump

Bloom and associates argued that, in these sentences, the first Noun slot is assigned the following different semantic roles: noticer (Lois), object (the bag), and actor (Kathryn). According to the researchers, a child who produces all these utterances has a system for combining categories in which the categories are not defined by meaning. Valian (1986), who also used children's spontaneous speech as the database, argued that 2-year-old children show evidence of the major syntactic categories (Valian didn't look at verbs) because children use words from these categories in a range of appropriate syntactic structures. Experimentally, Tomasello and Olguin (1993) found that children did use newly learned nonsense nouns in structures and with inflectional morphology that had not been modeled in their learning experiences.

In the foregoing discussion, we have really been asking two questions: (1) Do children have adultlike grammatical categories? and (2) Are children's categories semantically based? These are separable questions, because children's categories could be different from adults' without being semantically based. In answer to the first question, the data suggest that children initially have a less productive grammar than adults do. That is, they do not use all their words in the full range of grammatically permissible structures. One possible explanation for this limitation is that the categories over which children's rules operate are narrower than the adult categories. The evidence cannot be considered conclusive, however, because it is perilous to argue from evidence of what children do not do that they *could* not do it. First, what researchers record is only a sample of what children say, and second, what children say is not necessarily all that they *could* say.

The second question of whether early grammatical categories have a semantic basis is also difficult to answer on the basis of spontaneous speech. Again, children might have the competence to produce sentences they didn't produce or that the researcher didn't record them producing. In addition, it is always possible to take issue with the way in which spontaneous productions are interpreted. For example, although the initial nouns in the three sentences cited by Bloom and associates include some variety in meanings, they all fit the semantic definition of nouns as people, places, or things. There is another way to examine whether children start out with a semantically based grammar other than analyzing spontaneous speech. We explore this way next.

Do children look for a semantic basis to grammar?   Children are not likely to have a semantically based grammar if they don't look for a semantic basis to the regularities in the speech they hear. Thus one way of asking whether children have a semantically based grammar is to ask whether children seem to be looking for one. If they are, then they should have particular difficulty acquiring categories that have no semantic basis. Furthermore, in acquiring categories that have no semantic basis, children should make errors that suggest they are trying to find a semantic basis. One way of testing these predictions is to study children's acquisition of gender categories.

Many of the world's languages have two or more categories of nouns that take different forms of many grammatical morphemes. Although these categories are called **genders,** gender is not a very useful clue to which category a noun belongs. For example, in French, the words for necktie and man's shirt are feminine and the word for blouse is masculine. If children tried to construct grammatical categories on the basis of meaning, you would expect them to make errors in marking the gender of such words, but they do not. Children acquiring languages with gender systems do make errors, but not semantically based ones. In French (and Hebrew and other languages as well), a noun's gender can be predicted to a certain degree by its phonological characteristics. The gender errors that children make seem to be in those cases where the predominant phonological patterns do not apply (Levy, 1983).

There is also experimental evidence that children use phonological patterns rather than semantic information in assigning words to gender categories. In a French version of something like Berko's wug test, Karmiloff-Smith (1979) showed children pictures of novel animate and inanimate objects with nonsense labels and asked the children to predict each noun's gender. Children were able to use the phonological properties of the nonsense word to predict gender better than they were able to use clues to gender in the pictures. Interestingly, the children were unable to explain the phonological basis of their category assignments. This evidence does not mean that semantics plays no role in the grammatical categories that children form; but it does mean that when semantically based regularities are not present in the target language and phonological regularities are, children can extract categories from the phonological patterns in the speech they hear. Two implications of this finding will become relevant in the next section when we ask how children acquire grammar. One implication is that children can find patterns in the speech they hear even when the patterns have no semantic basis. The other is that phonological properties of speech are one potential source of information about grammar for children.

ISSUES IN EXPLAINING THE ACQUISITION OF GRAMMAR

In acquiring grammar, children acquire a productive system of rules and the categories and structures over which those rules operate. The previous sections described the developmental changes in the structures that children produce and understand and the nature of the underlying grammatical capacity. We now turn to the question of what kind of process could produce these developmental changes. In addressing this question, we return to some of the major issues in the field outlined in Chapter 1.

Nature or nurture?

It is obvious that children have some quality of mind that explains why they learn to talk but kittens, for example, do not (Pinker, 1984). It is not obvious what that quality is. One possibility is that children are much smarter than kittens. If that is the case, then somehow general cognitive processes must be sufficient to account for language acquisition, and there are several proposals to this effect. An alternative possibility is that children acquire grammar but kittens do not because the acquisition of grammar is preprogrammed in the human genetic blueprint but not in the cat's. There are proposals that significant aspects of grammatical knowledge are innate, the motivation for which in large measure is the view that there is no way to explain the acquisition of grammar otherwise. We will not resolve the debate over the innateness of grammar here, but we will review some of the evidence that has been marshalled on both sides of the argument.

Is innate grammar possible?   To many people, the idea that grammar is innate is preposterous. First, babies don't talk and second, how can something as specific as a grammatical rule be specified genetically? Also, many people believe that saying some aspect of language is innate is effectively to give up trying to explain it. However, many human characteristics *are* innate, even ones that are not present at birth and that are extremely specific. Take the example of motor development. At birth, babies cannot do very much physically. However, with maturation, babies go through a sequence of stages from rolling over, to sitting up, to crawling, standing, and walking. And fairly specific behaviors, such as smiling when one is happy, appear to have a genetic basis. Although we speak colloquially of babies' "learning" to walk, this development is not learning in the usual sense of the word. Both the development of smiling and the development of walking are the result of maturation.

Some have argued that "learning" to talk has much in common with "learning" to walk. Babies do not talk at birth, but they go through a sequence of stages in the production of prespeech sounds, words, and then word combinations. This reliable sequence of development cannot be attributed to any schedule of instruction the environment provides, and therefore it must reflect some underlying maturational process at work (Gleitman, 1981). It is true that no one knows exactly what a biological explanation of grammar would look like, but that shouldn't exclude innateness from the realm of possibility.

Is innate grammar necessary?   Most of the arguments for grammar's innate basis are not arguments based on evidence *for* such a genetic basis. Rather, the argument is that general learning mechanisms are too weak to accomplish the acquisition of grammar and that, regardless of the learning mechanism, the speech that children hear is inadequate to support the acquisition of grammar. Thus grammar *must* be innate because there is no way to learn it. The argument that input is inadequate was made first by Chomsky and is known as the poverty of the stimulus argument. The stimulus is the speech that children hear, and its poverty is its inability to support the acquisition of grammar. There are two aspects to the poverty of the stimulus argument. One is the assertion that it is impossible in principle for children to figure out the generative system under-lying language just from hearing examples of sentences. The other is a claim Chomsky made that the speech children hear is full of errors, false starts, slips of the tongue, and so on, so that children have a very bad database from which to work.

All these claims that support the contention that grammar must be innate have been countered, although the adequacy of the counterarguments is subject to dispute. The assertion that cognitive mechanisms are inadequate has been countered (1) with evidence that general cognition does contribute to grammatical development and (2) with proposals of how general cognitive mechanisms could achieve aspects of grammatical knowledge. The assertion that the input is inadequate has been countered with evidence that the speech children hear is not so impoverished as Chomsky had supposed and that it does play a significant role in grammatical development.

Can general cognitive processes account for grammatical development?

One approach to making the case that general cognitive processes contribute to grammatical development is to look for aspects of development outside the domain of grammar that are correlated with grammatical development. If the pace of grammatical development appears to be linked with the pace of other developments, then a common underlying mechanism is suggested. Any mechanism common both to grammar and to something else must be somewhat general. A large body of research, much of it produced by Elizabeth Bates and her colleagues, takes this approach and draws the conclusion that there are general cognitive processes at work as children learn the grammar of their language.

For example, Bates, Bretherton, and Snyder (1988) followed 27 children from the age of 10 months to 28 months, collecting data on several aspects of the children's language production and comprehension along the way. They then analyzed these data to see which aspects of development were related and which were not. They found that measures of the children's lexical development at ages 13 and 20 months were strongly related to measures of their grammatical development at 2½ years. Bates and colleagues argued on this basis that a common cognitive process underlies both.

Some researchers have also attempted to find relations between grammatical development and completely nonlinguistic aspects of cognitive development. Shore, O'Connell, and Bates (1984) investigated the relationship between children's ability to combine words in sentences and their ability to combine elements in symbolic play. They found that 20-month-olds who produced longer play sequences (such as *pretend to pour a drink, then pretend to drink it, then pretend to wipe your mouth* as opposed to *pretend to pour a drink* and then move on to a new activity) also produced longer utterances. This research approach starts with the statistical evidence that some common process or processes exist and then tries to infer what those processes might be. However, one problem with this approach is that although statistical analysis can tell you *that* things are related, it does not clearly tell you *why*. (For a discussion of some hypothesized processes see Bates et al., 1988.)

Another approach to making the case for general cognition as the mechanism of grammatical development is first to hypothesize a mechanism for learning grammar, or some aspect of it, that doesn't depend on innate grammatical knowledge or on any language-specific learning procedure; then directly test that hypothesis. Toward that end, several researchers have proposed ways in which children could figure out the grammar of their language by analyzing the patterns in the speech they hear.

For example, Braine (1992) and Maratsos and Chalkley (1980) proposed models to explain how children could learn grammatical categories. According to Braine (1992), children start out with categories, such as actor and action, that have their basis in general cognition. Then, as children hear sentences with other words filling the actor slot, children broaden that category until it includes anything with the same privileges of occurrence as "actors." At that point, the category is a formal grammatical category.

In Maratsos and Chalkley's (1980) account, the primary basis on which children construct grammatical categories is not the meanings of words but their distributional properties—that is, where in sentences they appear and what else they combine with. For example, children figure out that the words that take +s in the third person singular also take +ed to indicate past tense and take +ing to indicate present progressive. This correlation would be the basis for inferring the category *Verb* from properties of the speech children hear.

Another, not incompatible, view holds that the correlation between prosody and syntax helps children learn syntax (Morgan, 1986; Morgan & Demuth, 1996). For example, speakers pause at phrase boundaries, thus providing a clue to language structure. Such prosodic bootstrapping might be particularly helped by the exaggerated prosody of motherese. Connectionist models of language acquisition are another example of attempts to account for children's grammatical development by using learning procedures that apply outside the domain of grammar as well (for a review, see Plunkett, 1995). According to all these accounts, children find the information they need to figure out the grammar of their language in the speech they hear. Thus the plausibility of all these learning proposals depends on whether input does indeed provide adequate information and whether children use it. With that in mind, we turn now to descriptions of the speech children hear and evidence of its role in grammatical development.

The role of language experience

The nature of the speech children hear   Contrary to Chomsky's claim, the speech children hear is not full of mistakes. When adults talk to children, their speech has very few grammatical errors (Newport, Gleitman, & Gleitman, 1977). Speech to children has other characteristics that might make it a good database from which to figure out a language's grammar. Conversation with children tends to be about the here-and-now, so it is easier to understand what is being said from the extralinguistic context than it would be in most adult-to-adult conversations. Also, adults talking to children use gestures to secure children's attention, so the speech children hear is likely to be about the things the child is focusing on (Zukow, 1990).

Speech to children also has properties that may be more directly related to children's acquisition of language structure. Speech to children is very repetitious. Caregivers say things like, *"Put the doll in her crib. Yes, the doll. That's right, in her crib."* They also repeat and expand children's utterances:

Child: Milk.
Adult: You want some milk?

These repetitions and expansions of children's incomplete utterances might serve as little language lessons, revealing the component structures that sentences are made of. Also, prosodic features of speech, which tend to be exaggerated in speech to children, may provide cues to syntactic structure. For example, pauses and changes in intonation tend to occur at phrase boundaries (*Little Red Riding Hood* pause *lived with her mother* pause *at the edge of the woods*). Also, open-class words tend to receive stress and closed-class words tend to be unstressed, providing cues to that grammatical distinction. Additionally, there are phonological differences between nouns and verbs; nouns tend to have first syllable stress, and verbs have second syllable stress (compare the noun and verb versions of the word *record*) (Kelly, 1996). The hypothesis that children use these phonological cues to break into grammatical structure is known as the **phonological bootstrapping hypothesis.** Often, because prosodic cues seem particularly important, it is known as the **prosodic bootstrapping hypothesis.** (See Morgan & Demuth, 1996, for a full discussion of this hypothesis.)

The other side of the argument points out that some of these hypothesized cues to language structure are unreliable (Fernald & McRoberts, 1996; Pinker, 1984). For example, when the subject of a sentence is a pronoun, pauses don't separate the subject from the rest of the sentence but occur elsewhere (*She went* ~pause~ *to Grandmother's house*). Furthermore, these hypothesized little language lessons do not cover everything children need to know about their language's grammar. Even if children do use the properties of the speech they hear to learn the basic structural components of their language, where do they find the information that tells them that *When did the little boy say he hurt his arm?* has two interpretations but *When did the little boy say how he hurt his arm?* has only one (de Villiers, 1995b)? Last, a frequently made argument against attributing much importance to the role of input in grammatical development is the observation that in many cultures of the world people simply do not talk to prelinguistic children, yet these children acquire language too.

This last objection may not be as damning as it first appears. Lieven (1994) suggested a way to reconcile the fact that some children acquire language without being spoken to by adults with the hypothesis that adults' child-directed speech significantly contributes to grammatical development. One part of the solution is to point out that siblings and older children may talk to young children, although a variety of evidence suggests that the child-directed speech of older children does not have all the potentially supportive properties of adults' child-directed speech (Barton & Tomasello, 1994; Hoff-Ginsberg & Krueger, 1991). Another part of the solution is to suggest that children who learn language from the speech they overhear are more likely to learn grammar through rote-learning large chunks and then later analyzing their internal structure (Lieven, 1994). Finally, Lieven proposes that children in cultures where they are not directly talked to may learn to talk more slowly as a result. If children who are not directly addressed by adults acquire grammar in a different way or less rapidly than do children who are directly addressed, then the fact that they do acquire language does not mean that input plays no role when it is available. To the contrary, if differences in grammatical development are associated with differences in input, that suggests that input is playing a role.

The relation between the speech children hear and grammatical development   Even within cultures where children are talked to, children's language learning experiences vary. One approach to investigating the role of language experience is to look for relations between variability in experience and variability in grammatical development. Such research has yielded evidence that the input children receive contributes significantly to their acquisition of grammar. (No one doubts that the particular words children acquire come from the speech they hear; it's the acquisition of grammatical structure that is at issue.) At the most general level is evidence that the amount of speech addressed to children is related to the rate of children's grammatical development. McCartney (1984) found that children who attended day care centers that provided more one-to-one contact with an adult developed language more rapidly than did children who attended day care centers with less one-to-one adult contact. Other evidence indicates that first-born children begin to combine words at a slightly younger age than do later-born children (Hoff-Ginsberg, 1993). In both studies, differences in the amount of adult speech addressed to the children is a likely explanation for the observed differences in language development.

Particular properties of the speech children hear also seem to be related to grammatical development. For example, studies of mother-child conversation and its relation to child language development have shown that both the frequency with which mothers produce partially repetitious sequences (like *Put the doll in the crib. That's right, the doll.*) and the frequency with which mothers expand or slightly change their children's prior utterance are associated with more rapid grammatical development (Hoff-Ginsberg, 1985, 1986; Nelson, Denninger, Bonvillian, Kaplan, & Baker, 1984; Newport et al., 1977).

The relation between input and acquisition that has the best support in evidence is a relation between the frequency with which children hear questions that begin with an auxiliary verb (such as *Can you catch the ball?*) and children's acquisition of the auxiliary verb system. This relation has been found using both naturally occurring variation and experimentally created variation in children's language experience. Newport, Gleitman, and Gleitman (1977) found that children whose mothers asked more of these sorts of questions acquired the auxiliary system more rapidly than did children whose mothers asked fewer such questions. Shatz, Hoff-Ginsberg, and MacIver (1989) found that children who heard extra questions of this form in an experimental setting showed more rapid acquisition of the auxiliary system than did children in a control group, who received different kinds of language enrichment.

Although there is good evidence that children use the speech that they hear in figuring out the grammar of their language, there are also limits to what can be explained on that basis. The differences in the rate of language acquisition associated with differences in experience are small. Furthermore, the same studies that find that some aspects of grammatical development are related to input also find that many aspects of grammatical development are unrelated to input (Gleitman, Newport, & Gleitman, 1984; Newport, et al., 1977). Another problem with trying to explain the acquisition of grammar in terms of children's language experience is that experience might often mislead children, as illustrated below.

The role of feedback   Language is full of places where an active problem solver, trying to figure out the rules of grammar from the patterns in the sentences heard, would come up with overly general rules. For example, imagine you heard the following sentences:

John gave Mary the book.

Nicholas tossed Alex the keys.

Alissa threw Mark the ball.

You might, on the basis of this experience, construct a rule that allowed verbs to be followed by two objects. (The structures in the above examples are called double-object constructions.) The rule you constructed could lead you to produce the following ungrammatical utterances:

*John carried Mary the book.

*Nicholas said Alex something.

The verbs *carry* and *say,* however, need a different construction: *John carried the book to Mary* and *Nicholas said something to Alex.*

In fact, children do make errors of overgeneralizing the double-object construction to verbs that do not allow it; for example, *I said her no* and *Shall I whisper you something* (Bowerman, 1988). Any theory of language acquisition has to explain how children recover from such **overgeneralizations.** Just hearing examples of grammatical sentences is not sufficient. No matter how many times you hear *John carried the book to Mary,* that experience wouldn't tell you that it's not possible to say *John carried Mary the book.* One thing that would solve the problem for the learner is correction, or **negative evidence.** Because the availability of negative evidence has crucial implications for attempts to account for learning language from input, whether or not adults provide and children use this kind of feedback is hotly debated.

In 1970, Roger Brown and Camille Hanlon studied the mothers' speech in the transcripts of Adam, Eve, and Sarah, and they found that the mothers did not correct their children's ungrammatical utterances. The mothers did correct factual errors, mispronunciations, "naughty" words, and some overregularizations, such as *goed.* However, syntactic errors such as *Why the dog won't eat* passed without comment. On the basis of this finding, the general consensus for a long time was that children do not receive negative feedback.

More recently, others have looked more closely to see whether parents respond differentially to children's grammatical versus ungrammatical utterances in ways that are more subtle than overt correction but are nonetheless potentially useful to the child. Bohannon and Stanowicz (1988) found that adults were more likely to repeat verbatim children's well-formed sentences than their ill-formed sentences, and adults were more likely to repeat with corrections children's sentences that contained errors. Also, adults were more likely to ask for clarification of ill-formed sentences. Other studies have also found differences in the frequencies of different kinds of parental responses, depending on the grammaticality of children's speech (for example, Demetras, Post, & Snow, 1986). However, it is not clear how children use such parental behavior as a guide to language acquisition. Children clearly cannot depend on being corrected if they produce an ungrammatical utterance. Although researchers can find a statistical difference between responses to grammatical and ungrammatical utterances by looking at hundreds of children's utterances, it is not clear that children could ever discern a pattern in their parents' behavior. Marcus (1993) has estimated that a child would have to say the same ungrammatical sentence 85 times to have enough data to determine that the sentence was ungrammatical.

In sum, research points to ways in which children's language experience provides a rich database from which to figure out the structure of language. Furthermore, evidence that aspects of children's language experience influence the rate of their language development suggests that children are actually using that database in acquiring language. On the other hand, research on language experience has not demonstrated how language experience could be sufficient to explain the acquisition of grammar.

Continuity or discontinuity in grammatical development

Another issue, besides whether nature or nurture explains grammatical development, is whether development itself is continuous or discontinuous. We will illustrate the issue with the aspect of grammar that is the focus of much of this debate: the origin of grammatical categories. Remember, categories such as noun and verb are crucial to a productive system. Also remember that it is not at all clear that very young speakers have grammatical categories. Some have suggested that children's first word combinations are based either on structures learned word-by-word or on semantically based categories. If the latter is the case, then children start out with a very different kind of system than adults have, and somewhere in the course of development they undergo a qualitative change. Such a change has been likened to the metamorphosis that tadpoles undergo to become frogs (Gleitman, 1981; see Figure 4.3). Accounting for the change is known as the **tadpole-frog problem,** and how to solve the tadpole-frog problem is a central issue in accounting for grammatical development.

Figure 4.3 Tadpoles appear to be a different kind of animal from frogs—not just younger, smaller versions of the same animal. Similarly, it has been proposed that the system underlying early child language is qualitatively different from the adult grammar.

Arguments for continuity   Pinker (1984) has argued that continuity in development should be assumed unless the data prove otherwise. The argument for this **continuity assumption** is that the fewer changes a theory has to account for, the more parsimonious the theory will be. In keeping with the continuity assumption, Pinker proposed that children are innately equipped with grammatical categories, and thus there is no metamorphosis to account for. Such a proposal solves the tadpole-frog problem by saying there are no tadpoles; they're frogs from the very beginning (Levy, 1983).

There is another way to meet the continuity assumption, aside from crediting young children with formal grammatical categories. That way is to describe the endpoint of development differently. If the system the child ultimately achieves does not have rules that operate over arbitrary, formal categories, then there is no tadpole-frog problem because there are no frogs. Some functionalist and cognitive theories of language essentially redefine linguistic competence in a way that makes the tadpole-frog problem a nonproblem (for example, Van Valin, 1991; see Tomasello, 1992b). The connectionist proposals we will review later also fall into this category of avoiding the tadpole-frog problem by getting rid of the frogs.

Maturation as the mechanism of discontinuous development   A solution to the tadpole-frog problem that is equally as innatist as crediting children with inborn syntactic categories is the proposal that syntactic categories appear later as the result of biological maturation. This position accepts the evidence that children's early speech does not require crediting children with a syntactically based grammar and explains the change from a semantic to a syntactic system as a result of maturational processes. According to this view, children begin to combine words with whatever pregrammatical system they can figure out using general cognition and language experience; but their systems undergo a qualitative change when their innate grammatical knowledge matures, sometime during the third year of life (Atkinson, 1992; Radford, 1990). The analogy to the physical changes that occur at puberty is typically used to argue for the reasonableness of such an assertion. The genetic program for these changes is innate, even though the changes themselves occur well after infancy.

Learning from input as a mechanism for change   Another possibility is that children initially have word-by-word or semantically based systems, but they revise their categories on the basis of the speech that they hear. (Proposals to this effect were reviewed in the section on general cognitive mechanisms.) Discontinuity is not a problem if you can explain how the metamorphosis occurs.

THEORETICAL POSITIONS ON THE ACQUISITION OF GRAMMAR

We have outlined some of the issues any theory must address if it is to account for children's acquisition of language structure. We turn now to a discussion of the major theoretical positions taken in attempting to construct such an account.

The behaviorist account

If you ask the proverbial "man on the street" how children learn to talk, you are likely to get the answer that children learn to talk by imitating adults. This "folk psychology" belief somewhat resembles the explanation of language development that behaviorist psychology proffered in the 1960s. According to a behaviorist account of language development, children imitate what they hear, and they are reinforced when they get it right and are corrected—or at least not reinforced—when they get it wrong. Obviously, this account is inadequate because the adult language ability is not confined to repeating sentences that have previously been heard. Somewhat more sophisticated behaviorist accounts tried to handle the productivity of language in terms of "grammatical habits," or word-association chains in which each word uttered serves to elicit the next word in the sentence (Staats, 1971).

Such attempts to account for children's language development and adults' language ability in behaviorist terms were fairly short-lived and unsuccessful. In 1959, Noam Chomsky wrote a scathingly negative review of B. F. Skinner's (1957) attempt to account for language in behaviorist terms, and he was successful in convincing the scientific community that adult language use cannot be adequately described in terms of sequences of behaviors or responses (Chomsky, 1959). Because the behaviorists' notion of the endpoint of development was wrong, the behaviorist theory of achieving that endpoint was inadequate as a theory of language acquisition. In successfully arguing that the human capacity to produce language results from knowledge of a system of rules, Chomsky set the agenda for those who then took up the study of language acquisition. If knowing how to talk consists of knowing a system of rules, then the question of language development becomes how children learn this system of rules. With the exception of the recent constructionist proposals, competing theories of language acquisition are theories of how children could come to know a system of rules.

The social/cognitive position

According to the **social/cognitive view** of language acquisition, the starting point of language acquisition is provided by general cognition, as are the mechanisms of language development. The requisite experience for language

Figure 4.4 Social interaction with others provides the context for language learning, but the types of social interaction that children experience vary from culture to culture. One important question for child language researchers concerns how children make use of their varying experiences in accomplishing the feat of language acquisition.

acquisition is social interaction with other speakers (see Figure 4.4). This position is not one person's theory; rather, it is a school of thought that encompasses a variety of more specific proposals about how children's early language experience, in interaction with children's active efforts at figuring out language, results in the course of language development we observe (Bloom, 1991; Snow, 1989; Snow, Perlmann, & Nathan, 1987; Tomasello, 1992a). The social/cognitive position is also associated with the developmental approach to investigating language acquisition (see Chapter 1 and Bloom, 1991).

Much of the work that is relevant to an evaluation of this position has already been discussed in this chapter. The evidence that children's experience in conversation affects their language development supports the notion that social interaction contributes in an important way to language development. Arguments that children's initial grammars are not adultlike and that children could achieve adult grammar by analyzing the speech they hear are also consistent with—and in fact necessary to—this point of view. As we concluded earlier, there is substantial evidence to support the claim that language experience contributes to children's language development, and children's overgeneralizations—to cite just one example—suggest that children actively construct the grammar of their language. However, the problem of sufficiency remains. There is at present no explanation of how experience in combination with general cognitive abilities is sufficient to account for children's acquisition of the rules of grammar. This is perhaps to be expected in what is a fairly young field. The fact that there is not now such an account does not mean that sometime in the future, when we know more about how children use their experience, there could not be such an account. However, many people consider such an eventuality unlikely, and they have proposed different sorts of theories of language acquisition.

The innate grammar position

The **innate grammar position** is the view that the acquisition of language is significantly supported by innate syntactic knowledge and language-specific learning procedures. This view of how language is acquired, which differs radically from the social/cognitive view, is also associated with a different approach to studying how grammar is acquired—the learnability approach discussed in Chapter 1. It begins with a description of the endpoint, constructs a theory that fits known developmental facts, and fills in what is not known to arrive at a theory sufficient to explain language acquisition. In such an approach, there is no hesitation to attribute innate knowledge to the child if such knowledge seems necessary to account for the acquisition of grammar. We will discuss two different theories that have in common this strong commitment to learnability and the assumption that children start out with substantial innate syntactic knowledge.

Semantic bootstrapping and linking rules   We may be able to overcome the insufficiencies in accounting for how children could learn the syntactic categories of language and the rules for combining those categories if we give the child a head start in the form of innate knowledge. This is essentially what the theory of language acquisition proposed by Steven Pinker (1984, 1989) does. According to this theory, children innately know the categories of Noun and Verb, but they have to figure out the rules for ordering these categories in sentences. But they are helped here, too, because they know innately that agents are likely to be subjects, objects affected by action are likely to be direct objects, and so on. All that children need to figure out in the sentences they hear is which words are nouns and which are verbs, which noun is the agent that performs the action, which noun is the object that is acted upon, and so on. From that information, children can construct the rules for ordering these elements in sentences. Of course, the full theory is far more complicated, because sentences have more parts than just nouns and verbs, and sentence structures can be far more complex than just "subject + verb + object." But this little bit of the theory will serve to illustrate this position.

A crucial component of this theory is the assertion that children can identify the nouns and verbs in the sentences they hear. They can do this, according to Pinker, because they know that nouns tend to refer to persons or objects and that verbs tend to refer to actions. Thus semantics provides the entree into the system—hence the label **semantic bootstrapping.** However, semantic bootstrapping depends not only on what the child knows but also on what the child hears. If children hear *John throws the ball* in the presence of John throwing the ball, they could—assuming the postulates of this theory—correctly assign words to syntactic categories and even figure out that *John* is the subject of the sentence and *the ball* is the direct object. But if instead children heard *John, you'd better not break another window,* they would be in trouble. Some of this objection may be countered by the evidence that children learn language primarily from speech addressed to them, and that there is generally a good match between what adults say to children and the accompanying extralinguistic context. However, it is still the case that a mother coming home from work at the end of the day is more likely to say, "Hello, Alfred, whatcha been doing all day?" than she is to say, "Hello, Alfred, I'm opening the door" (Gleitman, 1990). The fact that even child-directed speech is not just a running commentary on the nonlinguistic scene is also a problem for many cognitive accounts of how children could figure out language by trying to match sentences to scenes. However, it is a fatal problem only for a theory that claims semantic bootstrapping as a crucial mechanism and that also claims to be sufficient to account for the acquisition of grammar.

Criticism has also been leveled at the proposal that children know innately that agents are likely to be subjects and affected objects are likely to be direct objects (this is one example of a **linking rule**). One sort of evidence against innate rules linking grammatical notions like "subject" to semantic roles like "agent" is that languages differ in the semantic roles that serve the grammatical function of subject. Some languages (called ergative languages) do not have true subjects, yet children acquire these languages without difficulty (Maratsos, 1988; Pye, 1992). Closer to home, children do not seem to produce sentences that conform to the supposedly basic "agent + action + affected object" structure any earlier than they produce sentences in which the subject is not a true agent and the verb is not really an action (such as *Ernie got spoon, Tasha have it*) (Bowerman, 1990).

Pinker's theory is the most complete and precise theory of how children might learn the rules of their language. As we have seen, there is reason to question some of its most important tenets. It is harder to find fatal flaws in the alternative social/cognitive position because that position's claims are less precise. If by now you have concluded that it is impossible to explain how children learn the rules of their language, you are in good company. The next two theories we will discuss eliminate the need for rule learning, albeit in very different ways.

Principles and parameters theory   Children do not need to learn rules if *all* the rules are innate. According to the **principles and parameters theory,** essentially all grammar is innate. This degree of innateness is possible, the argument goes, because almost everything about grammar is universal—that is, true in every language. For example, every language allows movement of grammatical categories, such as the subject-auxiliary inversion involved in question formation in English. Thus the possibility of movement is a universal principle. However, languages also vary in some of their structural aspects. For example, *what* can be moved and *to where* varies from language to language. The aspects of grammar that vary across languages are termed **parameters.** Languages do not vary in an infinite number of ways; rather, differences among languages are a highly constrained set of options. If children know that set of options, they can figure out which option applies to their particular language on the basis of their language experience. Thus the task of acquiring the language's grammar becomes the task of setting parameters, which is much less burdensome for the child than the alternative of figuring out the grammatical rules from scratch. To summarize, according to principles and parameters theory, the child has innate knowledge of **Universal Grammar.** This knowledge consists of a set of principles that hold for every language and a set of options, or parameters, that have to be filled in by experience (see, for example, Atkinson, 1992; Clahsen, 1990/1991; Hyams, 1986).

More than the other approaches to the acquisition of syntax, principles and parameters theory makes a strong commitment to a particular linguistic theory. After all, if a theory proposes to explain language acquisition by attributing innate knowledge of Universal Grammar to children, then the correctness of that theory depends on the correctness of its account of Universal Grammar, among other things. The principles and parameters theory of acquisition was motivated by the linguistic theory known as **Government and Binding theory,** first articulated by Noam Chomsky in 1981. By describing language in terms of a set of universal principles and parameters, this linguistic theory made possible a principles and parameters theory of language acquisition. We will not attempt to explain or evaluate government and binding theory here, but we will try to provide some idea of how research on the principles and parameters approach to acquisition is done.

If children come to the language acquisition task knowing the principles of Universal Grammar, and if the process of syntax acquisition consists of setting parameters, then we should be able to find evidence (1) that children know principles from a very early age and (2) that children's language changes in ways that conform to parametric variation in Universal Grammar. Research on what is known as the null-subject parameter illustrates this research approach (Atkinson, 1992; Hyams, 1986). This research starts with a set of facts about languages: some languages, such as English, require overt subjects in declarative sentences whereas others, such as Italian, do not. In Italian, if you simply say the first-person form of the verb, you have a grammatical sentence. Languages that require overt subjects also have some other properties that distinguish them from null-subject languages. Languages that require overt subjects also have constructions like:

It's cold outside.

There's a fly in my soup.

whereas null-subject languages do not. There are also differences between null-subject languages and other languages in how auxiliaries are used and, related to that, differences in how questions are formed.

The next set of facts relevant to this research are facts about children's language. Children who are acquiring English (which is not a null-subject language) tend, at an early point in language development, to produce sentences without overt subjects, such as *Helping Mommy,* or *make a house* (Bloom et al., 1975). These constructions are more typical of Italian. At this stage, children also do not use the type of construction that begins with *It's* or *There's.* And, at this stage, children acquiring English also do not have auxiliary verbs. According to one analysis within the principles and parameters framework, these different facts about children's early utterances are related to each other. That is, it is no coincidence that the features of language that hang together across languages also hang together in development. Rather, these features hang together across languages because they are controlled by the same abstract principle of Universal Grammar, and they hang together in development because development reflects Universal Grammar. In Universal Grammar, a parameter can be set as plus or minus "null-subjects allowed." The co-occurrence of different kinds of disallowed utterances in the early speech of children acquiring English is interpreted as evidence that children have the Universal Grammar principle that unites these features, but they have not yet set the parameter correctly. (For some reason, the plus "null-subjects allowed" setting is the default.) Once the parameter is set, all three aspects of children's language change.

Since the null-subject parameter was proposed, researchers have questioned both the "facts" that it explains and the nature of the explanation (Valian, 1991). Research on this, and on many other principles and parameters, is being actively pursued. There are at present hugely different opinions in the field on the promise that this line of research holds. To some, a principles and parameters approach is obviously the correct kind of theory, and the point of research is to determine the correct account of Universal Grammar. To others (such as those adopting the developmental approach), the principles and parameters approach of starting from a linguistic description of Universal Grammar and looking only secondly at children's speech, is the wrong order in which to do things (see discussions in Bloom, 1991; Tomasello, 1992a).

Connectionism

The last theory of syntax acquisition that we will discuss is the connectionist proposal. Recall from Chapters 1 and 2 that connectionism is a theory of cognition according to which seemingly rule-governed behavior—such as speaking a language—can be explained without recourse to underlying rules. Connectionism, then, solves the problem of accounting for children's rule learning by saying children do not need to learn rules because there are no rules. Rather, what underlies language is a network of interconnected units. The process of language development is a process of getting right the relative strengths of the connections in the network.

Connectionist models are tested in a way that other theories of language acquisition are not. A proposed model is programmed into a computer, and the computer is fed input that presumably resembles children's language learning experience. On the basis of the input provided during training, the system alters the weights of the connections among the units in the model, and then the model is tested in some task that requires the linguistic knowledge the selected input illustrates.

One line of work within the connectionist approach has tried to model the acquisition of the morphology of past-tense formation (see, for example, Daugherty & Seidenberg, 1994; Pinker & Prince, 1994; Plunkett, 1995; Plunkett & Marchman, 1991). A connectionist model of past-tense formation starts out with units that correspond to the sounds of verb stems and the sounds of verb endings. The model is fed "experience" in which certain stem sounds appear with certain ending sounds, and the model increases the strength of those particular connections. In its final state, the model can generate the past tense of novel forms based on the similarity of the novel form to stored forms. So, if we gave the model the Berko test and asked it to form the past tense of blick, it would produce *blicked* based on the similarity in sound of *blick* to *kick* and *lick* and past exposure to *kicked* and *licked*. Just how successful connectionist models are at mimicking what every 4-year-old can do is a matter of considerable debate (see references above).

Two types of criticisms are leveled at connectionist models. One consists of specific criticisms of particular models, which can and have been addressed by the proposers of these models revising how the model works or changing the input to the model. A second type of criticism ignores the specifics of any model and claims that connectionism cannot work in principle for the same reason that behaviorism could not work: its description of the end state is wrong. The argument is that we do not form the past tense of new verbs because of the similarity of their sound to verbs we already know. What we do, as adult speakers, is apply the rule, "add *ed*." It is easy to demonstrate this fact with what psychologists call an armchair experiment. Sitting in your armchair, you can easily retrieve the irregular past tense form of the verb *to ride;* it is *rode*. What happens if you imagine a new verb that sounds exactly the same as *ride* but isn't *ride?* If you want to say that someone was such an amazing pioneer that she matched and exceeded the accomplishments of the first female astronaut, Sally Ride, you would say that she out–Sally Rided Sally Ride. You would never say that anyone out–Sally Rode Sally Ride. This evidence suggests that we have a rule that applies as the default to new verbs even when they are phonologically similar or identical to old verbs (Marcus et al., 1992).

At this point, connectionism's potential to account for the acquisition of syntax and morphology is an open question. To some people, the connectionist approach is attractive because it holds the promise of accounting for language and language acquisition using the same mechanisms that could also account for other cognitive processes. To others, though, such an approach to language cannot possibly succeed because it assumes a theory that is wrong in its description of the endpoint of development (Marcus et al., 1992).

SUMMARY

Around the age of 18 months to 2 years, children begin to combine words. This milestone marks the beginning of structured language. Children's two-word combinations are followed by utterances that are three and more words long, and as children's utterances get longer, they also become increasingly complex. Children's first sentences tend to be simple declarative sentences lacking many of the grammatical morphemes, such as verb endings and auxiliary verbs, present in adults' speech. For this reason, children's early speech is described as telegraphic. Beginning around the time children start to put three words together, they begin to use grammatical morphemes. They start to produce questions and negative statements, whose form changes as children acquire the syntactic means of adult grammatical expression. By the time children are 4 years old, they can produce complex sentences, and it is said that at this point they have essentially mastered the grammar of their language.

There are individual differences in the early stages of the development of multiword speech. Some children rely heavily on rote-memorized phrases, and other children approach language more analytically—producing novel word combinations from the start. However, there is sufficient commonality among children in the course of syntactic development for the mean length of a child's utterances to be a useful measure of that child's level of grammatical development—at least up to an MLU of 3.0. Because the rate of syntactic development is extremely variable across children, age is not a good indicator of a child's level of grammatical development.

Children seem to know more about grammar than they demonstrate in their speech. For example, children who produce only one word at a time understand the relational meanings in two-word utterances. However, children often appear to understand everything that is said to them, and that is not the case. Children have a variety of strategies for interpreting and responding to sentences that they do not fully understand, and these strategies make children seem more grammatically competent than they really are.

Although the facts of the developmental changes that occur in children's speech are relatively clear, the explanation of those facts is not. One source of contention concerns how to describe the system of knowledge that underlies children's structured speech. Children's initial sentences seem to be combinations of semantically defined categories, such as actor and action. Children do not produce the kind of sentences that require knowledge of abstract grammatical categories such as noun and verb. However, if children start out with a semantic system and end up with an abstract syntactic system, there needs to be an explanation of how that change occurs. According to one view, the explanation is in the maturation of an innate grammar. According to another view, the explanation is in the learning procedures children apply to the speech they hear. Still other views argue that the adult system is not the abstract, syntactic system that most assume it is, thus redefining the problem. The debate over the innate and experiential contributions to the acquisition of grammar is fierce and unresolved at this point.

Current theories of grammar acquisition cover the spectrum from the most experientially based to the most innatist views. According to the social/cognitive position, the achievement of grammar is the result of children's applying general cognitive procedures for the acquisition of knowledge to the language they hear in social interactions. In contrast, the innate grammar view holds that significant aspects of linguistic knowledge are genetically preprogrammed. The most strongly innatist view is that of the principles and parameters approach, according to which the child has innate knowledge of Universal Grammar and uses language experience only to set parameters that vary across languages. According to the connectionist approach, the process of acquiring a grammar is the process of fixing the relative weights of connections in a network of interconnected units, and these weights are based entirely on properties of the input.

KEY TERMS

productivity or generativity of
language

syntax

open-class words

lexical categories

closed-class words

functional categories

morphology

bound morpheme

morphemes

free morphemes

descriptive rules

prescriptive rules

transitional forms

relational meanings

combinatorial speech

telegraphic speech

grammatical morphemes

yes/no questions

wh- questions

complex sentences

analytical versus holistic approach

pivot grammar

mean length of utterance (MLU)

response strategies

word order strategy

order-of-mention strategy

probable-event strategy

overregularizations

semantically based grammar

syntactically based grammar

genders

phonological bootstrapping
hypothesis

prosodic bootstrapping hypothesis

overgeneralizations

negative evidence

tadpole-frog problem

continuity assumption

social/cognitive view

innate grammar position

semantic bootstrapping

linking rule

principles and parameters theory

parameters

Government and Binding theory

REVIEW QUESTIONS

1. What is meant by the productivity of language, and what is its significance for the task of explaining language acquisition?

2. What aspects of language structure have children acquired and what have they not acquired when they produce telegraphic speech?

3. What is the difference between a holistic and an analytical approach to the acquisition of grammatical structure? What would be evidence for each in children's speech?

4. It often seems to parents that young children understand "everything." What is the evidence that this is not true, and why do children often appear to understand more than they do?

5. Based on evidence from comprehension studies, what is the developmental timetable for the acquisition of grammar?

6. What kind of evidence supports the claim that children acquire rules in acquiring the syntax and morphology of their language?

7. What are the differences among a lexically based, a semantically based, and a syntactically based grammar? Give one example of evidence for attributing each to children.

8. What is the tadpole-frog problem? Outline the possible solutions.

9. Outline the arguments for and against innate grammar as an explanation of the acquisition of grammar.

10. What assumption about children's language input is necessarily entailed by any proposal to account for the acquisition of grammar in terms of general cognitive processes?

11. What is negative evidence? Why is the availability of negative evidence to children an important issue?

12. What is semantic bootstrapping? What does semantic bootstrapping propose to explain? What does this hypothesis assume about children? What does it assume about children's language experience?

13. How is the connectionist account unique among theories of the acquisition of grammar?

5 The Development of Communicative Competence: Learning to Use Language

2½-year-old: (to his 5-year-old brother) *Hi, stupid butthead.*

5-year-old: You're a poopy butthead.

2½-year-old: We don't talk like that.

In the previous chapters, we described children's development of the sound system, the lexicon, and grammar of their language. Together, these accomplishments provide children with a system for expressing meaning by producing sequences of sounds. Children use this system to communicate with others. In this chapter, we focus on the development of language use, including a range of things children must know to use language to communicate—other than knowing the language itself.

Linguists and child language researchers refer to the distinction between knowing a language and knowing how to use language to serve communicative functions as the distinction between **linguistic competence** and **communicative competence.** Linguistic competence is the ability to produce and understand well-formed, meaningful sentences. Communicative competence is the ability to use those sentences appropriately in social interaction (Hymes, 1972). [Sometimes the term *communicative competence* is used to include linguistic competence (see Foley & Van Valin, 1984); we will use it in its narrower sense.] The knowledge that constitutes communicative competence consists of several overlapping domains of knowledge, including pragmatic knowledge, discourse knowledge, and sociolinguistic knowledge. **Pragmatic knowledge** concerns understanding the communicative functions of language and the conventions that govern the use of language in order to communicate. **Discourse knowledge** concerns the use of language in units larger than a sentence; conversations and narratives are two such larger units. **Sociolinguistic knowledge** concerns how language use varies as a function of sociological variables such as status, culture, and gender. In this chapter, we will consider children's pragmatic, discourse, and sociolinguistic development. As in previous chapters, we will begin with a description of the endpoint of the development, starting with what adults know when they know how to use language to communicate.

COMMUNICATIVE COMPETENCE IN ADULTS

Pragmatics

The first question to be tackled in trying to describe adults' communicative competence is to define communication. Just as we looked to linguists' analyses of language structure as a guide to what we must account for in describing children's development of language structure, we now look to analyses of communication as a guide to what we must account for in describing children's communicative development. Some of the most explicit accounts of what constitutes communication come from the the academic discipline of philosophy, specifically the philosophy of language.

Speech acts   The work of philosophers of language J. L. Austin and John Searle has been particularly influential in the study of children's pragmatic development. According to Austin, speaking is not just uttering sentences that

Table 5.1 Speech act components

Component	Definition	Examples
illocutionary force	intended function	request, query, promise
locution	form	declarative, imperative
perlocution	effect	obtaining requested object, directing other's attention

describe events but "doing things with words" (Austin, 1962). Each sentence a speaker utters is a **speech act.** Austin often illustrated this point with examples such as a judge uttering the sentence *I now declare you husband and wife* which, in the context of a marriage ceremony, has the effect of marrying two people. However, the notion that speaking is performing acts applies to all speaking. The kinds of acts performed are promising, requesting, referring, describing, arguing, demanding, and others (Searle, 1969).

A speech act has three components: (1) its intended function (its **illocutionary force**), (2) its linguistic form (its **locution**), and (3) its effect on the listener (its **perlocution**). Table 5.1 lists these components and some examples. We can illustrate these different components of the speech act using the following example of one child's communicative behavior (Rees, 1978): Dennis the Menace appears at his neighbor's front door and says, "My mother wants to borrow a cup of ice cream." In this example, the intended function, or illocutionary force, of Dennis' speech act is to request ice cream, and the form, or locution, is that of a declarative sentence. The effect, or perlocution, of this particular speech act is unknown. Dividing speech acts into components is useful for the study of communicative development because it enables asking separate questions about the development of children's communicative intentions, the development of the forms of language, and the development of the ability to achieve desired effects.

Intentionality   Of the three components of speech acts—intentions, forms, and effects—the intentions that underlie communication are the most difficult to specify. In fact, it could be argued that **intentionality** is irrelevant to the question of whether communication is taking place, and intentionality is not central to the concerns of some who study communication. For example, people who study nonverbal communication study messages that are often unintended (for example, Birdwhistell, 1970). However, in studying the development of communicative competence, we are not asking whether communication is taking place but rather whether *the child* is communicating. This focus on what's inside the mind of the communicator makes intentionality a crucial part of the definition of communication. Given that definition, then, it is not sufficient that a behavior be interpretable for it to be communicative. For example, if someone sneezes, you may be able to infer that she or he has a cold. However, sneezing is a reflex and not necessarily a communicative act. (If one pretended to sneeze in order to signal that one was feeling ill, *that* would be communicative.)

Beyond asserting that intentionality is necessary for communication, we can also ask what kind of intentions are involved in communication. It seems, for example, that the intention that is really behind communication is not just the intention to accomplish something. In the preceding example, Dennis' communicative intention was not just to get ice cream. Rather, the intention that underlies true communication includes the intention to create a belief in the listener's mind (Grice, 1957, 1969). If Mrs. Wilson had responded to Dennis that she didn't have any ice cream, we would judge the communication to have been successful even though the goal of getting ice cream was not achieved. Although the effort to obtain ice cream would have failed in that case, it would not have been a failure of communication. This distinction between the intention to achieve a goal and the intention to make contact with another mind will be an important distinction when we talk about the understandings that underlie children's development of communicative behavior.

Form-function mappings and the role of context   The example of Dennis talking to Mrs. Wilson also illustrates another important point about language use that speech act analysis reveals. Although Dennis' sentence was a declarative statement about his mother's need state, Dennis' purpose in uttering that sentence was to make a request. The intended function of language may be different from its form and its literal meaning. In fact, speakers use a variety of different forms for the same function. For example, the request that someone open a window can be made with any of the following utterances:

Open the window.

Would you open the window?

I'd love some fresh air.

It sure is stuffy in here.

These different forms of request for a window to be opened would not be equally appropriate in all settings. A parent might say, "Open the window" to a child but may be less direct when talking to a peer. Regarding the development of communicative competence, we can ask when and how children acquire a repertoire of different forms to express the same function and when and how they learn to use the form that is appropriate for the circumstance.

Box 5.1   Grice's conversational maxims

Quantity: Make your contribution as informative as is required; provide neither too much nor too little information.

Quality: Try to make your contribution one that is true; do not say what you believe to be false or that for which you lack adequate evidence.

Relation: Be relevant.

Manner: Be perspicuous (that is, be clear—be brief, orderly, unambiguous).

Source: From Grice, 1957, 1975.

Discourse

Using language to communicate typically involves stretches of speech that are much longer than a single sentence. These longer stretches can be the result of two or more people talking, in which case they are called **conversations.** Sometimes one speaker talks at length, as in a lecture, a sermon, or a **narrative.** Of these forms of extended monologue, telling narratives, or stories, is by far the most widely occurring. Communicative competence includes knowing how to participate in conversations and how to produce narratives.

Conversation   If a man were a guest on a talk show and answered each question with a single-word response, we would judge him to be a poor conversationalist. (And he probably would not be invited back.) Similarly, someone who never lets anyone else talk or who always talks about his or her latest vacation regardless of what others are talking about is also being a poor conversationalist.

What makes someone a good conversationalist? According to Grice (1957, 1975), there are two basic rules of conversation. The first rule is to take turns (see also Sacks, Schegloff, & Jefferson, 1974, for a description of turn taking in adult conversations). The second rule is to be cooperative. This cooperative principle of conversational participation includes four more specific maxims (or rules of conduct) having to do with the quantity, quality, relation, and manner of conversational contributions. These Gricean maxims are listed in Box 5.1. Like the rules of grammar that we discussed in Chapter 4, these rules are descriptive, not prescriptive. They are rules that describe how conversations work; when someone violates these descriptive rules, there is a breakdown in the interaction. The poor conversationalists in the preceding examples violated some or all of these rules. In studying children's development as conversationalists, we can ask when their participation in conversation starts to follow these rules—when they learn to take turns and when they become able to provide the right amount of relevant information in a clear manner. (Child language researchers have left the study of learning to be truthful to other disciplines.)

Narratives   There are also skills that children must acquire in order to produce text, or stretches of speech, on their own. Sustaining talk without a conversational partner and making that talk coherent place unique demands on a speaker's communicative competence. Children do not get very good at producing narratives until the elementary school years, and most of our description of narrative development will be in Chapter 6. However, the beginnings of narrative development can be found in the spontaneous descriptions of past events children produce in conversation, starting before the age of 3 years. We will describe the development of these early intraconversational narratives in this chapter.

Sociolinguistics

Registers   Language is used differently in different social settings. The way you talk to your friends in the dorm is different from the way you talk to the same people in a classroom discussion. Language is also used differently in talking to different people. For example, the ways in which you would talk to a child, a friend, a parent, and a professor are different. Styles of language use associated with particular social settings are called **registers** (Chaika, 1989). Learning to use different registers appropriately, depending on the conversational setting, is another task for children in acquiring communicative competence.

Dialects and cultural variation in language use   Language is also used differently by different social groups. For example, a typical conversation between New Yorkers might seem extremely rude to a southerner, and the kinds of conversations that occur among men are different from the kinds of conversations that occur among women (Tannen, 1990). The way adults talk to children is different among working-class African Americans than among mainstream, middle-class white or African Americans (Heath, 1983). **Dialects** are variations within a language that are a function of who the speaker is. Although some of the most obvious differences among dialects are in pronunciation, there is dialectical variation in the lexical, syntactic, and stylistic aspects of language as well.

The norms for how language is used in interactions vary widely from culture to culture, and these differences are separate from the fact that the cultures speak different languages. For example, conversations between mothers and children are different in Japan than in the United States (Clancy,

1986), and they take a third form in Samoa (Ochs, 1988). One thing children learn as they acquire communicative competence is to use language in the particular way their social group uses language. The process of learning the language style of one's particular group is called **language socialization.** In describing children's language socialization, we can ask when group-specific styles emerge in children, and we can ask how a culture transmits its particular style of language use to its children.

In this chapter, we will begin with the child as a newborn and start with the question of when communication begins. We will follow the infant to the beginnings of language and ask what communicative functions language serves when it first emerges. As children's language skills burgeon in the second and third years of life, children become increasingly competent communicators; we will describe the development of children's ability to fulfill their roles as conversational partners. As children's language skills progress, they become able to sustain increasingly long stretches of talk by themselves, and a new form of talk emerges—storytelling, or narrative production. As children are learning to use language, they are also learning that language is used differently in different social settings. We will review evidence that shows that even 3- and 4-year-old children show sensitivity to the social rules and contextual factors that govern language use. Finally, we will consider the thorny question of how learning to use a language is related to learning the language itself.

COMMUNICATION IN PRELINGUISTIC INFANTS

Most adults in Western culture believe that communicative interaction with infants begins well before infants begin to talk. Infants emit behaviors such as crying, fussing, and smiling that caregivers use as clues to infants' internal states. However, the fact that adults can interpret these signals—no doubt accurately— does not mean that these signals are intentional on the infants' parts. There is no reason to think that infants' early expressions of their emotional states are anything other than automatic responses to internal states, as is sneezing or coughing. In sum, young infants have effects on their listeners, but there is no evidence that they have intentional control over those effects (Bates, Camioni, & Volterra, 1975).

If very young infants do not intentionally communicate, when does intentionality first appear? Because we cannot know with certainty what another person's intentional state is, questions about the intentions underlying young children's communicative behavior are very difficult to answer. (Notice that we didn't say that infants are not intentional, only that there is no evidence that they are.) However, the difficulty of answering the question about infants' intentionality has not stopped researchers from trying.

The development of speech acts

Using the terminology of speech act theory, the question of when intentional communication begins is the question of when children's utterances or pre-speech behavior have illocutionary force. Bates, Camioni, and Volterra (1975) described the course of speech act development based on a study of three little girls, starting when the children were 2 months, 6 months, and 12 months old and following each for approximately 6 months until their developmental courses overlapped. The researchers went to the children's homes every two weeks with notepads and videotape recorders looking for spontaneous communicative behavior. On the basis of the development of these three children, Bates and associates described three phases in the development of speech acts.

Having effects   In the first, or perlocutionary, phase, children have effects on their listeners; but the signals that have effects are not produced with the intention of communicating to a listener. For example, the child who wants an object that is out of reach may try to get it and may make a fuss in the process. The mother may observe the child, infer the child's desires, and get the object for the child. In this case, the child's behavior had the effect of obtaining the object, but there was no effort to communicate with the mother. Bates and associates (1975) described such an example in one of the children studied when the child was 9 months old.

> In an effort to obtain a box that mother is holding in her arms, Carlotta pulls at the arms, pushes her whole body against the floor, and approaches the box from several angles. *Yet during the entire sequence she never looks up into her mother's face.* (p. 214; italics added)

Having intentions   In the second, or illocutionary, phase, children become aware that their behavior can be used to communicate with others. More specifically, what children come to understand around age 10 months is that other people can be helpful in satisfying one's goals and that it is possible to elicit this help by communicating with them. The evidence of this understanding is that a child who wants something will not just reach and fuss but will actively try to elicit another's aid in obtaining that object. Bates and colleagues (1975) provided an example by the same child described above, this time at the age of 11½ months:

> Carlotta, unable to pull a toy cat out of the adult's hand, sits back up straight, *looks the adult intently in the face,* and then tries once again to pull the cat. The pattern is repeated three times, with the observer refusing to yield the cat, until Carlotta finally manages to pull the object away from the adult. (p. 215; italics added)

Bates and colleagues describe such communicative behaviors as protoimperatives; that is, these behaviors serve the function of imperatives (commands). They have both the illocutionary force and perlocutionary effect of imperatives; all they lack is the locutionary content.

Another kind of communicative behavior that develops during this prelinguistic phase is the protodeclarative. In contrast to protoimperatives, in which adults are used as a means to obtain objects, children producing protodeclaratives use objects to obtain adult attention. For example, a child might point to an object while making noise to attract adult attention, being satisfied only when the adult looks where the child is pointing and acknowledges the child's gesture. Again, there is an important distinction between the behavior that counts as a protodeclarative, and therefore a communicative behavior, and earlier noncommunicative behavior. Before using a pointing gesture to direct adults' attention, children point to things when they are unaware of being observed, and they point to things without any effort to obtain adult attention (Bates et al., 1975).

Using conventional signals   The third, or locutionary, phase of speech act development begins when children's communicative behavior includes using language to refer. As we saw in the discussion of context-bound versus referential word use in Chapter 3 on lexical development, sometimes first words are not used referentially. Because first words can be used in a nonreferential way, the locutionary phase in speech act development does not suddenly begin with the child's first words. Rather, there are degrees within the locutionary stage. Sounds may first be used consistently in certain contexts but in somewhat idiosyncratic ways. For example, Bates and colleagues (1975) described one child using the sound "Mm" with a pointing gesture to indicate a request. Slightly more advanced, but still not referential, is using a word such as *bam* when knocking over constructions made out of blocks. The relevant distinction here is that "bam" is part of the activity of knocking down blocks, not a symbol that stands for and can be used to refer to the activity of knocking down blocks. Gradually children come to use language referentially, and at that point all three components of speech acts are in place. Box 5.2 summarizes these phases of speech act development.

The emergence of communicative intent

A major milestone in speech act development is the change from the perlocutionary to the illocutionary phase. It is important to note that several other researchers have also described a change in infants around the age of 10 months. According to Sugarman (1984), before this milestone is reached, infants are able to relate to an object or to another person but not to both at the same time. An example of relating to an object would be playing with a rattle or

---

> **Box 5.2   Summary of speech act development**
>
> *Phase 1: Perlocutionary (Birth–10 mos.)*
>
> Behavior has consequences but is not produced with communicative intent.
>
> *Phase 2: Illocutionary (10–12 mos.)*
>
> Behavior has communicative goals but does not use the forms of the target language.
>
> *Phase 3: Locutionary (12 mos. +)*
>
> Behavior has communicative intentions and adultlike forms.

looking at a mobile over one's crib. An example of relating to another person would be smiling or cooing. What emerges around age 10 months is the ability to relate to another person about an object. Sugarman-Bell (1978) described this development as the "coordination between actions and vocalizations" (p. 49).

Trevarthen and Hubley (1978) also described what seems to be the same change in infants at around age 10 months. Before this point, infants may share *themselves* with others; Trevarthen and Hubley call this **primary intersubjectivity.** After this point, infants share their *experiences* with others; this is **secondary intersubjectivity.** The convergence of the research suggests that a maturational change occurs in infants at around 9 to 10 months of age, and that change permits the emergence of intentionality. However, there is also evidence that caregivers may play a role.

The role of prelinguistic interaction in the development of communication

Maternal responsiveness and the development of communicative intent
In Western cultures, mothers typically treat babies as conversational partners from birth. Young infants do not do much in terms of holding up their end of the conversation, but mothers build conversational sequences around the smiles, burps, and other noises their infants do produce. The following example from Snow (1977) illustrates this kind of interaction.

3-month-old:	(*smiles*)
Mother:	Oh what a nice little smile!
	Yes, isn't that nice?
	There.
	There's a nice little smile.
3-month-old:	(*burps*)
Mother:	What a nice wind as well!
	Yes, that's better, isn't it?
	Yes.
3-month-old:	(*vocalizes*)
Mother:	Yes.
	Yes!
	There's a nice noise.

Snow suggested that such interaction may facilitate the child's communicative development, and she described mothers as "pulling intentionality out of the pre-intentional child" ("Baby Talk," 1984).

Other empirical evidence suggests that infants' experiences with responsive partners may help children discover that communication is possible. Bell and Ainsworth (1972) studied the responsiveness of 26 mothers to their infants' crying over the first year of the infants' lives. Observers visited each home at approximately 3-week intervals, recording the frequency of infant crying episodes, the length of time the infant cried without obtaining a maternal response, and the effectiveness of maternal interventions at calming the baby. Bell and Ainsworth found that infants who had the most responsive mothers when they were 6 to 12 months old cried less at the age of 12 months than did the infants with less responsive mothers. Also, the infants who cried less at 12 months were more communicative in terms of both their vocalizations and their nonvocal behavior.

In contrast, efforts to find relations between measures of mother/child interaction before age 6 months and children's later language development have not been successful (Kaye, 1979, in Golinkoff & Gordon, 1983). Bell and Ainsworth concluded that, at some point during the first year, infants' cries become communicative and maternal responsiveness to that form of communication benefits the development of communication more generally. What both Snow and Bell and Ainsworth suggest is that infants discover that communication is possible by observing the effects of their initially noncommunicative noises on the listener. This is one way in which early caregiver/child interaction may provide the foundation for communicative development. Others have made even stronger arguments about the role of caregiver/child interaction, suggesting that children not only learn that communication is possible but also learn something about the structure of communication in infancy.

Early interaction patterns and the development of conversation   The
nonverbal interactions that occur between mothers and babies have a structure
that some have described as like the **turn-taking** structure of conversation. For
example, when newborn infants nurse, they alternate between bursts of sucking
and pauses (Kaye, 1977). Mothers often jiggle either the nipple or the infant
when their infants pause. At first, mothers continue this jiggling throughout the
infants' pauses until the infant resumes sucking. By the time the infant is 2 weeks
old, however, mothers have changed their behavior so that they jiggle and then
stop, after which the baby resumes sucking. Kaye (1977) described this
phenomenon as "the earliest example of infants and mothers learning to take
and give turns." In these early interaction patterns, according to Kaye, is the
"origin of dialogue."

Patterned interaction between mothers and babies is not limited to feeding interactions. Mothers also vocalize (talk and make noises) to their young
infants. Mothers tend to alternate vocalizations with silent pauses and mothers
usually look at their babies when the babies vocalize. This interaction pattern
has been described as **protoconversation** (Bateson, 1975). However, Stern
(1974) found that when babies start to vocalize, they don't always do so during
their "turn." Sometimes infants vocalize during their mothers' pauses, but often
infants vocalize in unison with their mothers' vocalizations. In that case, these
early interactions are more like proto–choral singing than protoconversation
(Shatz, 1983a). Another example of patterned interaction between infants and
caregivers is the nonverbal games adults play with infants starting around the
age of 3 or 4 months. Peek-a-boo is one common game; another game is
Give-and-take, in which the mother offers the infant something and the infant
grasps it. Bruner (1977) described these games as **action dialogues.** He
argued that these joint interactions provide a scaffold that supports the acquisition of language (Ratner & Bruner, 1978). The term **scaffolding** is used
to describe these routinized formats for interaction because they provide
support that enables the child to do more than the child could do alone—
much the way holding a child's hand enables walking in a child who cannot
yet walk alone. However, the claim that Bruner and many others have made
(for a recent discussion, see Snow, 1989) is that this help not only supports
immediate performance but also facilitates the future development of competence.

As we discussed in the previous chapters, there is evidence that certain
kinds of conversational interactions facilitate the acquisition of words and
perhaps grammatical structure. However, the claim that preverbal interactions
facilitate language development is a different and probably stronger claim than
the claim that hearing language facilitates language development. Arguments for
a nonlinguistic basis for language development entail the notion that communication is the motivation for language acquisition and that there is continuity
between prelinguistic and linguistic interaction.

There are some problems with both notions. The fact that prelinguistic and linguistic interactions seem alike in some ways doesn't mean that one leads to the other (Bates, 1979). For an argument against continuity, see also Shatz (1983b). The relation between the communicative function of language and the acquisition of language per se will be discussed again in the final section of this chapter.

THE COMMUNICATIVE FUNCTIONS OF EARLY SPEECH

Transitional forms

Bates and associates (1975) described the emergence of two illocutionary acts—declaratives and imperatives—in the period before speech begins. Much more research has been devoted to describing the range of illocutionary acts

Table 5.2 Eight communicative behaviors produced by one child between the ages of 12 and 16 months *communicative schema*

BEHAVIOR		GOAL
Gesture	*Sound*	
Reach to object	[m]-initial	getting help in obtaining object
Point to or hold out object	[l] or [d]-initial	drawing attention to object
	phonetic variants of *David* or *Mommy*	drawing attention to self
Reach to person	[h]-initial	getting or giving object
	[n] or other nasal with prolonged falling intonation	getting help in changing situation
Waving hands, slapping	[b]-initial	getting help in removing object
Negative headshake	ʔəʔə	same as above
Smile	breathy [h] sounds	express pleasure

Source: Adapted from "The Development of Systematic Vocalizations Prior to Words," by A. Carter. In N. Waterson & C. E. Snow (Eds.), *The Development of Communication*, p. 130. Copyright © 1978 John Wiley & Sons, Ltd. Adapted by permission.

Table 5.3   Primitive speech acts at the one-word stage

Speech act	Definition	Example
Labeling	Uses word while attending to object or event. Does not address adult or wait for a response.	Child touches doll's eyes and *eyes*.
Repeating	Repeats part or all of prior adult utterance. Does not wait for a response.	Child overhears Mother's utterance of *doctor* and says *doctor*.
Answering	Answers adult's question. Addresses adult.	Mother points to a picture of a dog and asks *What's that?* Child answers *bow-wow*.
Requesting action	Word or vocalization often accompanied by gesture signaling demand. Addresses adult and awaits response.	Child, unable to push a peg through hole, utters *uh uh uh* while looking at Mother.
Requesting	Asks question with a word, sometimes accompanying gesture. Addresses adult and awaits response.	Child picks up book, looks at Mother, and says *book?* with rising intonation. Mother answers *Right, it's a book*.
Calling	Calls adult's name loudly and awaits response.	Child shouts *mama* to his mother across the room.
Greeting	Greets adult or object upon its appearance.	Child says *hi* when teacher enters room.
Protesting	Resists adult's action with word or cry. Addresses adult.	Child, when mother attempts to put on his shoe, utters an extended scream while resisting her.
Practicing	Use of word or prosodic pattern in absence of any specific object or event. Does not address adult. Does await response.	Child utters *Daddy* when he is not present.

evidenced at the onset of speech. The goal of such research is to describe the development of the functions language serves, or, as Halliday (1975) put it in the title of his book on the subject, "learning to mean." Research on the development of communicative functions has made it clear that children have a range of communicative intentions before they have the adult linguistic means of expressing those intentions.

For example, Anne Carter (1978) intensively studied one child during the period just before the child began to use real words. She found that the child systematically used particular sound-gesture combinations to express eight different communicative functions, including requesting help, directing the listener's attention, and expressing pleasure. Table 5.2 lists these communicative schemata (also sometimes termed sensorimotor morphemes). Halliday (1975) described a similar, but not identical, set of functions in the early vocalizations of his subject.

First words

Looking at a slightly later point in language development, Dore (1975) identified nine different functions served by the single-word utterances of two children, which he called primitive speech acts (see Table 5.3). Because the children's linguistic means were limited at this one-word stage, they used other, extralinguistic means to indicate illocutionary force. Intonation is one such means. Dore observed one child's use of intonation: *Mama* said with a falling intonation contour was used to label; *mama* said with a rising intonation contour was used to question; and *mama* said with an abrupt rising-falling contour was used to call his mother when she was at a distance (Dore, 1975).

The emergence of discourse functions

A new kind of communicative behavior emerges in children sometime around age 16 to 18 months, on average. Examples of this new function include the primitive speech acts of repeating, answering, and requesting. These utterances have functions that need to be defined in terms of the ongoing discourse; they serve either to respond to prior speech or to elicit further speech. These utterances still have communicative functions that can be defined at the utterance level—they request, they protest, and so on. However, unlike children's very first communicative behaviors, these newer types of speech acts need to be defined in terms of larger discourse context as well; the children are starting to be conversationalists. Another development in the meanings children express occurs by age 24 months, when children start to refer to absent objects and events and to use language imaginatively, as in pretend play. These first references to past events are the beginning of narrative development. We consider children's development of the discourse skills involved in conversation and narrative production in the next section.

LEARNING TO PARTICIPATE IN CONVERSATION

If you could be a fly on the wall in a preschool classroom, you would overhear conversations between children such as the following exchange, which occured between two 4-year-olds (Schoeber-Peterson & Johnson, 1991).

> Child 1:   I'm gonna put on my gloves.
>   Are you finished making your dog, honey?
> Child 2:   Almost.
>
> Child 1:   Good.
> Child 2:   I'm gonna get his nose on.
>   Some of the parts are the same.
>   This mechanical dog is more than I thought it was gonna be.
>   He's taking it back.
>   This will work.
> Child 1:   This is nice.
>   Oh, this is nice.

This conversation includes exchanges that seem to be examples of true dialogue, as when Child 1 asks, *"Are you finished . . . ?"* and Child 2 answers, *"Almost."* This conversation also includes a sequence of utterances in which Child 2 is talking to herself or himself about the toy dog being put together, and that stretch of speech is followed by Child 1's comments, which are unrelated to Child 2's speech. In discussing children's conversations, we start with the observation that conversations between children seem different and, in many ways, less successful than conversations between adults. We will ask two questions about children's conversations: (1) How are they different from adult-to-adult conversations?, and (2) What causes these differences?

Piaget's description of the egocentric child

The earliest answers to these questions come from the Swiss developmentalist Jean Piaget. According to Piaget, preschool children's speech is not really communicative (Kohlberg, Yeager, & Hjertholm, 1968; Piaget, 1926). On the basis of his own observations of the spontaneous conversations of young children, Piaget claimed that although children may take turns talking, each speaker's turn has little to do with the previous speaker's turn. Rather, each child is producing his or her own monologue, albeit with interruptions for the other child's monologue. Accordingly, Piaget termed such interactions **collective monologues.**

The preschool child does not participate in true dialogue because, according to Piaget, the child is "unable to place himself at the point of view of his hearer" and has "no desire to influence his hearer or to tell him anything" (Piaget, 1926, p. 9; Schoeber-Peterson & Johnson, 1991). Thus Piaget proposed two explanations for why preschool children do not engage in true dialogue; one had to do with "skill," the other with "will" (Kohlberg et al., 1968). The skill-based explanation was that children lack the requisite cognitive ability. In Piaget's terminology, preschool children are **egocentric.** This egocentrism is not limited to language use but is a general characteristic of children's thought at this stage. For example, preschool children have difficulty with tasks that require them to indicate what a visual array would look like from a different vantage point. (For a more complete description of Piaget's theory of childhood egocentrism and of research questioning that theory, see Gelman & Baillargeon, 1983.) The will-based part of the explanation Piaget offered is that preschool children are not trying to engage in dialogue. It is possible to pursue both explanations in subsequent work on the functions of young children's speech. One line of research pursues the explanation that children are not trying to engage in dialogue and focuses on the functions of children's self-directed, or private, speech. Another line of research investigates in greater depth children's abilities to participate in true conversation with others.

Private speech

Everyone talks to themselves sometimes, particularly when engaged in a difficult task (John-Steiner, 1992). However, young children talk to themselves more, and more obviously, than older children and adults do. Like adults, children talk to themselves when they are alone and engaged in a task or in play. Also, some children produce soliloquies alone in their beds before they fall asleep. Children also produce monologues in the presence of other people, in what would seem to adults to be a more suitable context for conversation. Research on children's nondialogic or **private speech** has looked at both solitary monologues and at monologues that occur in conversational contexts.

Solitary monologues   Researchers who have studied children's solitary monologues suggest that children use these monologues for language exploration and practice (Gallagher & Craig, 1978; Kuczaj, 1983; Nelson, 1989; Weir, 1962). In a famous early study of presleep soliloquies, Weir (1962) recorded the presleep narratives of her 2½-year-old son by means of a remote-controlled microphone placed in the child's bedroom. Weir found that the child produced sequences such as the following, which she termed a "substitution exercise" (Weir, 1962, pp. 135–136).

Mommy's too weak

Alice strong

Alice too weak

Alice too weak

Daddy's too weak

Mommy's too weak

Too weak with Barbara

Be careful Barbara

Barbara can broke

Careful broke the [rami]

Careful broke Anthony

Careful broke it

Careful broke the

Broke the finger

Broke the Bobo

Broke the vacuum clean

According to Weir, this child was practicing language. The notion that children practice language in their presleep soliloquies is also supported by Nelson's (1989) study of the presleep narratives of one 2-year-old girl (recorded by means of a microphone her parents hid in her bedroom). This child produced extended narratives about events in her day, and the narratives she produced when alone were longer and more complex than the narratives she produced in conversation with her parents.

The notion that children are practicing or exploring language doesn't mean that this activity is work for them. To the contrary, it is **language play.** The ability to play with language is itself a skill that is manifest in forms as varied as puns and poetry. The tendency to engage in spontaneous language play may be related to skill at language play. For example, kindergarten children who produce high amounts of language play in their spontaneous speech are also better than average at explaining verbal riddles, such as *"Why didn't the skeleton cross the road? He didn't have the guts."* (Ely & McCabe, 1994; Fowles & Glanz, 1977).

Vygotsky's theory of the function of private speech   According to the developmental theory of Russian psychologist Lev Vygotsky (Vygotsky, 1962, 1978; Wertsch, 1985), the primary function of private speech is not language exploration but behavioral self-guidance. This account of private speech derives from Vygotsky's theory that an individual's cognitive skills develop first in social interaction and then later are internalized. For example, a young child who is unable to perform a task such as putting a puzzle together alone can do so with the help of an adult who provides direction. At a later point in development, the child can do the task alone because the child has internalized the directions originally provided by the adult.

Private speech, in this view, is an intermediary stage during which the child is overtly producing the self-talk that will eventually be internalized. This explanation of private speech would not apply to presleep soliloquies but to situations in which children produce private speech as they are acting on objects. Other research supports the Vygotskyan view that first another person's speech and then one's own private speech guides behavior. Evidence shows that the kind of talk adults provide children does improve the children's task performance (Behrend, Rosengran, & Perlmutter, 1992; Wood, Wood, & Middleton, 1978) and that the private speech children produce during a task predicts their later performance on the same task (Behrend et al., 1992). This developmental sequence of first hearing the speech from another, then producing it oneself, and finally producing it internally has nothing to do with conversation per se. However, if children are engaged in a task while simultaneously engaged in conversation, the private speech they produce for self-guidance will intrude into the conversation.

Piaget and Vygotsky, then, provide two different accounts of why young children produce monologue in what most adults would construe to be a conversational setting. The Piagetian view is that the child lacks the requisite ability and interest to be truly conversational. The Vygotskyan view is that the child is doing something else with his or her speech. These two views are not necessarily incompatible (Warren & Tate, 1992). Monologue may be interspersed with dialogic speech for different reasons at different times.

The developmental course of nondialogic speech

Furrow (1984) analyzed samples of adult/child conversations in the context of toy play for twelve 2-year-olds and found that 36% of the children's utterances were private speech. That is, the utterances were not addressed to the adult at all. Schoeber-Peterson and Johnson (1991) analyzed the peer interactions of ten dyads of 4-year-old children—again, in play—and found that almost half of the children's speech was not dialogue. Schoeber-Peterson and Johnson (1991) found that some of the nondialogic speech produced was true private speech and some was made up of unsuccessful attempts at dialogue. This finding of different types of nondialogic speech suggests that multiple factors contribute to the presence of nondialogic speech in children's interactions. The frequency of private speech in children's peer interactions begins to decline around the age of 5 or 6 years (Berk, 1992; Kohlberg et al., 1968). According to the Vygotskyan view, private speech declines in frequency because children have internalized the self-regulatory function of language. According to the Piagetian view, private speech declines as children's egocentrism declines and their conversation skills therefore improve. The research on private speech and children's conversational skills suggests that both developmental changes play a role (Diaz & Berk, 1992).

In the rest of this section, we focus on describing children's development of conversational skills. We will see that although Piagetian theory motivated some of the early research on children's development of communicative competence, a more useful theoretical system for organizing the research on children's conversation comes from the work on the philosophy of language with which we began this chapter. Remember Grice's description of the rules of conversation: take turns and cooperate by making your turn informative, relevant, sincere, and clear. In this section, we discuss developmental changes that occur as children come to behave in accordance with that description. The topic of this section, then, is children's development of the mechanics of conversation, including the development of turn taking, the ability to initiate conversational topics, and the ability to sustain connected discourse with another speaker. We will start this description with evidence from observations of children interacting with adults—usually their mothers. We will find evidence that children know something about the mechanics of conversation from the age of about 1 year, but we will also see that mothers provide substantial support for their children's conversational role. We will turn then to descriptions of children's conversations with peers.

Children's conversational skills in interaction with adults

Although mothers and babies in Western cultures interact in formats that have the structure of conversations, babies do not do much to hold up their end of a dialogue. Very young babies do look at their mothers when their mothers vocalize; however, the turn-taking structure of early mother/child interaction (in those cultures where it occurs) appears to depend on mothers' building a conversational structure around their children's behavior, and it does not reflect infants' interactive skill (Shatz, 1983a). There is no clear landmark that signifies children's entry into conversational participation. Rather, the relative burdens carried by the adult and the child in sustaining conversation gradually become more equal as children develop an understanding that they have responsibilities as conversational participants, as they learn what is required of them to fulfill these responsibilities in different linguistic contexts, and as they master the linguistic devices for meeting those requirements (Shatz, 1983a).

Responding to speech   The first understanding about the rules of conversation children seem to achieve is the understanding that they are supposed to respond to another speaker's utterance. An early strategy that children employ to fulfill this conversational obligation is to respond with action. That is, when an adult says something to a young child, the child is quite likely to *do* something rather than to *say* something in response. This strategy allows young children to respond appropriately to much of what is typically said to them, such as *Why don't you play in the sandbox?* and *Where are your shoes?* The effectiveness of such a strategy in most everyday situations can mislead observers into thinking that children understand much more of what is said to them than they actually do. (See Chapter 4's discussion of sentence comprehension strategies.) However, clever experimenters can reveal when children are using strategic shortcuts to achieve appropriate responses. Shatz (1978a) asked 2-year-olds questions for which an action response would not be appropriate, and she found that sometimes 2-year-olds responded with action anyway. For example, when asked, "Why don't you wear shoes on your head?" one child promptly removed his shoes from his feet and placed them on his head.

Differential responding to different utterance types   Gradually, children start to respond more frequently to talk with talk and also to respond differently to different kinds of utterances (Shatz & McCloskey, 1984). In general, children are more likely to respond to questions than to nonquestions (Hoff-Ginsberg, 1990; Shatz, 1983a). Children under 2 years of age are more likely to respond verbally to *what* or *where* questions than to other question forms. Allen and Shatz (1983) suggested that the word *what* in particular serves as an early signal to the child that action is not an appropriate response. In contrast, *why* questions—perhaps because of their abstract meaning (Blank & Allen, 1976)—seem particularly difficult for children.

In some cases, children's abilities to take turns and respond in conversationally appropriate ways actually outstrips their understanding of what is being said. For example, children who cannot correctly identify any colors but who know several color words will reliably answer the question "What color is this?" with a color term, although the particular color term may have only a chance probability of being correct (Shatz, 1983a). A similar case is the preschool child who knows to answer the question "What time is it?" with a number, but who reveals her ignorance with answers such as "four-eighty" (personal data).

In other cases, however, children as young as 2 years old also produce appropriately different messages to different kinds of questions. For example, when adults fail to understand a child's utterances, the adult may indicate that failure with a general query such as "What?" or with a specific query, as in the following example:

    Child: Put it in cup.
    Adult: Put it where?

Anselmi, Tomasello, and Acunzo (1986) found that preschoolers were more likely to repeat their entire utterance in response to a general query and to repeat only the requested utterance part in response to a specific query. It seems, then, that 1- and 2-year-olds' abilities to participate in conversation are based on a mixture of partial understandings and strategies for participating despite only partial understandings. What children do seem to understand by the age of 2 years is that in conversation one takes turns, and what one says in one's turn is constrained by what the previous speaker has said. In some cases, children's understanding of those constraints is based more on the form than on the content of utterances.

Initiating topics   Another conversational skill is the ability to initiate topics. **Topics** are what conversations are about, so the speaker who initiates topics determines what the conversation will be about. Susan Foster studied the development of topic initiation using videotaped conversations between five children and their mothers, covering an age range in the children from 1 month to 2½ years (Foster, 1986). Foster observed three developmental changes in children's topic initiations: (1) With increasing age, children successfully initiated more topics, (2) the means of topic initiation changed from nonverbal to verbal, and (3) the type of topic children initiated changed. With respect to type, children's first topic initiations were about themselves. Next, children began initiating topics about things in the environment, and last (around the age of 1½), children began initiating topics about absent or intangible things.

Foster found that the acquisition of language proceeded in parallel with changes in the success and the type of topic initiations, and it no doubt contributed to these changes. However, Foster (1986) points out that the development of topic initiation skills is not solely a matter of developing language skill. She cites the example of a late talker who was nonetheless highly communicative at the age of 1 year and 10 months.

> On one occasion, when [the child] and her mother were looking at a book together, they came across a picture of a cat. Kate promptly pointed to the door to the back garden. Her mother responded with *Yes, there's a cat outside isn't there sometimes*. Kate then said *gone*, to which her mother replied, *It's gone now yes. We saw it yesterday didn't we?* (p. 246)

In this case, the child successfully initiated a conversation about an absent cat using only gesture. This example concerns a question that will come up several times in this chapter: How independent are communicative development and language development? Here Foster argues for some independence. This example also illustrates another recurring theme—the important contributions of a motivated conversational partner and of shared knowledge between speaker and listener to the success of conversation with young children.

Box 5.3   An example of the preverbal child's negotiation of a failed message

Child: (*vocalizes repeatedly until his mother turns around*)
Mother: (*turns around to look at child*)
Child: (*points to one of the objects on the counter*)
Mother: Do you want this? (*holds up milk container*)
Child: (*shakes head "no"*)
Mother: Do you want this? (*holds up jelly jar*)
Child: (*shakes head "no"*)
      (*two more offer/rejection pairs follow.*)
Mother: This? (*picks up sponge*)
Child: (*leans back in highchair and puts arms down; tension leaves body*)
Mother: (*hands child sponge*)

Source: From Golinkoff, 1983.

Repairing miscommunication   Even motivated conversational partners do not always understand what children are trying to communicate, and children's attempts at topic initiation are not always successful. A necessary conversational skill is the ability to respond to communicative failures by repeating or revising the message so that it is understood. Studies of children's responses to adults' comprehension failures describe the development of this skill. Beyond description, studies of how children respond to communicative failures may shed light on the intentions behind children's communicative efforts.

As is true for initiating topics, efforts at repairing misunderstood signals can be seen in preverbal children. When adults fail to understand children's noises and gestures, children often persevere, repeating or modifying their signal until they achieve the desired outcome. Golinkoff (1983) labeled such interactions "preverbal negotiations of failed messages." Golinkoff (1986) analyzed the mealtime interactions between three mothers and their children over the age range from approximately 1 to 1½ years. During the period studied, roughly half of the children's efforts at communication were initially unsuccessful; but by repeating, revising, or substituting a new signal, the children were ultimately able to be successful 55% of the time at 1 year and 72% of the time at age 1½. Box 5.3 illustrates one example of such a negotiation.

As children acquire language, both their messages and their repairs become more frequently verbal. There also may be developmental changes in how children repair their messages. Several, but not all, studies of older children's repairs suggest that young children (between 1½ and 3 years old) are more likely to simply repeat a misunderstood message, whereas older children (between 3 and 5 years old) are more likely to revise their message (Anselmi et al., 1986; Brinton, Fujiki, Lob, & Winkler, 1986; Furrow & Lewis, 1987; Gallagher, 1977; Tomasello, Farrar, & Dines, 1984; Wilcox & Webster, 1980).

What does such communicative behavior imply about children's communicative intentions and understandings? A strong claim has been articulated by Golinkoff (1986), who argued that the evidence of preverbal children's persistence suggests that these children have communicative intentions and that these intentions include not just achieving a goal but also getting their listener to understand. (Remember our definition of communication included not just achieving a purpose but also meeting another mind. Getting another person to understand what you have in your mind constitutes meeting another mind, and this is separable from whatever actions you might get the listener to perform.)

On the other hand, it has also been argued that before the age of 3 years, children's communicative goals are merely to direct another's behavior rather than to meet another mind (Shatz, 1983b; Shatz & Watson O'Reilly, 1990). These goals do not represent the child's selfishness or disregard for others. Rather, before the age of 3 years, children do not really understand that other people have minds. Young children do not know that other people have beliefs and intentions that guide their behavior. Young children know only that certain actions of their own (such as asking for something) are likely to result in certain actions by their listener (providing that something). Children do not understand the inner mental workings of other people. On this account, the intentions of a 2-year-old in making a request are something like the intentions of many (mechanically ignorant) adults in putting quarters in a soda machine. The adults have the goal only of obtaining soda. They can't possibly have as a goal causing some chain of events inside the machine because they have no idea how the machine works. Young children's understanding of the connection between their requests and the behaviors their requests elicit may be similarly limited. If this description of children's understanding of others' minds is true, then it's hard to imagine how they could have intentions of meeting another mind. You can't intend to meet an entity you don't know exists. The question we have raised here is, What theory about mind do children have? The topic of children's theory of mind is a large and difficult area of research and is a question of interest in its own right, separate from its implications for children's communicative understandings (see, for example, Astington, 1993; Astington, Harris, & Olson, 1988; Wellman, 1990). Here, we will limit ourselves to evidence from children's communicative behaviors.

If children's intentions are to communicate information to another mind and not merely to satisfy their wants, then children should persist and repair messages that are not requests just as often as they repair requests. To find out if that is the case, Shatz and Watson O'Reilly (1990) compared 2½-year-old children's responses when adults asked for clarification of the children's requests and assertions. They found that 2½-year-olds responded to 94% of the requests for clarification of their own requests and to 84% of the requests for clarification of their assertions. According to Shatz and Watson O'Reilly (1990), the finding that children more frequently responded to clarification requests when their own utterance was a request suggests that satisfying wants rather than meeting minds is part of why children repair their misunderstood utterances.

However, the fact that children responded to 84% of requests for clarification still needs to be explained if we are to believe that children's limited understanding of other minds precludes true communicative intent. Shatz and Watson O'Reilly offer two explanations of how this finding can be compatible with their claim than prelinguistic children do not have intentions to meet other minds. The first part of the explanation is that the children in this study were 2½ years old; other evidence suggests that children do have a theory of mind by the age of 3 years. Therefore, the behavior of the 2½-year-olds might reflect some nascent understanding of mind that would not be present in 1½-year-old children who demonstrate the persistence illustrated in Box 5.3. The other part of the explanation is that when the 2½-year-olds responded to clarification requests, they were doing so as a semantically empty way of simply keeping the conversation going. That is, the children were responding in order to take their turn, not because they cared about clarifying their assertion. In fact, Shatz and Watson O'Reilly argued that children may think that their mothers' clarification requests are themselves just devices for maintaining conversation, because mothers are often guilty of absentmindedly trying to satisfy their children's expectations of a response with questions that aren't sincere requests for information.

The issue of what children understand about communication and when they understand it is not just an issue of the appropriate description of children's communicative development. The communicative understandings attributed to children at different points in development have implications for possible accounts of the relation between communicative development and linguistic development. If children have full communicative understandings before the acquisition of language, then it is logically possible that language development depends on these communicative understandings. On the other hand, if children as old as 2½ years who have made substantial progress in acquiring their language nonetheless fail to understand some crucial aspects of communication, then such an account is impossible. For the moment, however, we will put this issue on hold and return to describing children's acquisition of the skills involved in conversation.

Sustaining dialogue and contingent responding   For conversation to be sustainable for very long, each party's contribution must be relevant to the previous speaker's turn. A salient change in children's conversational abilities

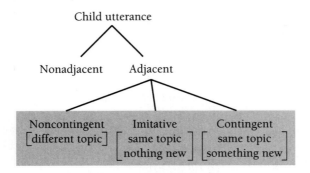

Figure 5.1 Categories of child discourse

Source: From "Adult-Child Discourse," by L. Bloom et al., 1976, Cognitive Psychology, 8, 521–552. Copyright © 1976 Academic Press, Inc. Reprinted by permission.

after the age of 2 years is an increase in the length of conversation children are able to sustain. Brown (1980) compared the conversations of 21 children who were all 30 months old but who ranged in productive language ability from an MLU of 1.0 to an MLU of 3.0. Brown estimated that the number of topically related utterances children can produce in sequence (related either to their own prior utterance or to intervening utterances by adults) changed from an average of less than 1 utterance at MLU = 1.0 to an average of over 20 related utterances at MLU = 3.0.

Bloom, Rocissano, and Hood (1976) have carefully investigated the development of children's ability to produce related replies. As their database, they used transcripts of adult/child interaction recorded for four children at three different points in the children's development: at Stage 1 (MLU < 2.0), at Stage 2 (MLU = 2–2.75), and at Stage 5 (MLU = 3.5–4.0). The age range covered was from approximately 21 to 36 months. Each child utterance was coded in the transcripts as either adjacent (occurring after an adult utterance) or nonadjacent (without a prior adult utterance or with a definite pause). Adjacent utterances were further coded as noncontingent (on a different topic), imitative (on the same topic but with no new information), or contingent (on the same topic and adding new information). The coding scheme is diagrammed in Figure 5.1.

At all stages, most of the children's speech was adjacent, and there was no clear developmental change in the proportion of adjacent speech. Thus Bloom and associates concluded that from before the age of 2 years, children followed the conversational rule of responding to another speaker. What changed with development was the kind of response children produced. Responses that were noncontingent or only imitative became less frequent as the children got older, and contingent responses became more frequent. The results from this study are graphed in Figure 5.2.

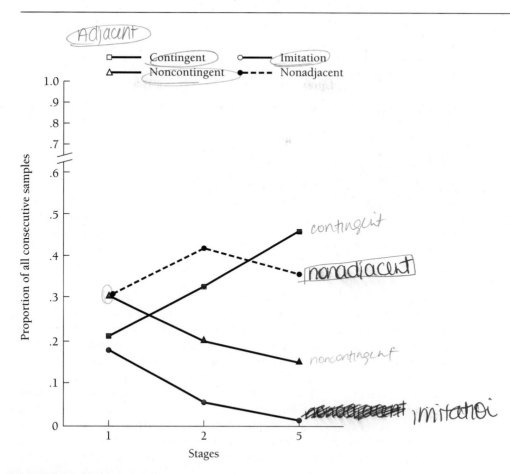

Figure 5.2 Developmental changes in the relative frequency of nonadjacent, contingent, noncontingent, and imitative speech

Source: From "Adult-Child Discourse," by L. Bloom et al., 1976, Cognitive Psychology, 8, 521–552. Copyright © 1976 Academic Press, Inc. Reprinted by permission.

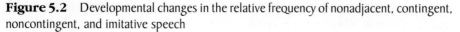

Apparently, initiating a new topic is actually easier for children than producing a response that shares the first speaker's topic and adds new information to it. Bloom and associates explained this finding in terms of the cognitive processing demands of producing each type of utterance. Producing a spontaneous utterance requires retrieving information from memory to formulate a message and attending to the ongoing interaction. Producing a contingent reply additionally requires attending to the content of the prior speaker's message. Paying attention to three things in formulating a message is more difficult than paying attention to two things.

Bloom, Rocissano, and Hood (1976) also found developmental changes in the kind of contingent responses that children produced. The frequency of contextually contingent responses declined with age, whereas the frequency of linguistically contingent responses increased. Contextually contingent responses refer to the same topic as the prior utterance does but are structurally unrelated to the prior utterance: for example,

Adult: Where's the other sock?
Child: See my sitting on it.

The linguistically contingent form of a reply would be *It is* followed by a prepositional phrase that describes a location. The answer in the example above provides the requested information but not in the linguistically contingent form.

In contrast, linguistically contingent responses not only are about the same thing as the prior utterance; they also use the sentence structure of the prior utterance: for example,

Adult: Pussycat is calling to wolf. Why?
Child: Because he's up in this building too tall.

Linguistically speaking, *because* is the appropriate form of an answer to a *why* question.

This finding of an increase in linguistic contingency suggests that learning to use the structure of language to link utterances in discourse is a later development than simply understanding that conversation requires producing semantically related utterances. However, remember from our discussion of children's turn taking that children seem to know something about the form their reply should take even without fully understanding the meaning of either the question or their answer. As was the case for topic initiating, topic maintenance skills develop along with language skills, but each component of development has some level of independence as well.

The role of the adult   A final point to reiterate about children's conversational competence as evidenced in mother/child interactions is that the mothers helped. In the example of nonverbal topic initiations presented earlier, the success depended as much on the mother as it did on the child. In verbal interactions, mothers also contribute to their children's ability to participate. For example, a generally observed characteristic of maternal speech is that it includes a very high proportion of questions, and children are more likely to respond to questions than to other types of utterances (Hoff-Ginsberg, 1990). Thus children's responsiveness is due in part to their mothers' efforts at eliciting responses. The children in Bloom and associates' (1976) study were also more likely to produce contingent responses to questions than to nonquestions; thus the frequency of contingent responding in those data depended in part on the mothers. Finally, in Bloom and associates' data, as the children's linguistically contingent responses to questions increased, the adults increased the frequency with which they asked questions, thus contributing to the observed developmental increase in the frequency of contingent responding.

Other researchers have identified additional means that mothers employ to sustain conversations with young children. For example, Kaye and Charney (1980) described mothers' use of "turnabouts," which both respond to the child's prior utterance and request further responding. More generally, mothers' efforts to follow their children's leads in conversation may contribute to sustaining dialogue. Hoff-Ginsberg (1987) found that children were more likely to respond to maternal speech that continued a topic in the child's prior speech than to speech that initiated new topics.

Children's peer conversations

If mothers help sustain conversation with young children, then a truer, or stricter, test of children's conversational abilities would come from examining children's conversations with each other. In fact, Piaget's description of children as egocentric rather than communicative was based on observations of peer interactions. More recent research on children's peer conversation presents a mixed picture. It is possible to find both examples of egocentric speech such as Piaget described and examples of dialogue that suggest greater communicative competence than Piaget attributed to young children.

Keenan (1974) conducted one of the first studies that challenged the description of preschool children as incapable and uninterested in true dialogue. Keenan recorded the conversations that occurred between her twin 2½-year-old sons early in the morning while the twins were alone in their room. (Babies of child language researchers should watch out for hidden microphones.) She found that the children did attend to each other's speech and produced related utterances. However, the children's ability to sustain a topic was limited, and the longest stretches of related exchanges between the children consisted of sound play with no semantic content at all. Box 5.4 presents examples of the Keenan twins' conversations.

Other evidence of conversational competence in 2-year-olds comes from Wellman and Lempers (1977), who studied naturally occurring instances in which 2-year-old children in a preschool setting initiated interaction by pointing out, showing, or displaying something. Wellman and Lempers found that 2-year-olds did initiate such interactions. Eighty percent of these initiations were directed to adults, and only 20% to other children. The children's initiations were successful in obtaining a response almost 80% of the time, and when they did not receive a response, they tried again with a revised message more than 50% of the time. Like Keenan's data, these data suggest that children as young as 2 years old are interested in and capable of engaging others in communicative interaction. Wellman and Lempers' data further suggest that

---

Box 5.4   Examples of 2½-year-old twins' conversations

A topically related sequence:

Child 1: tree
            see got grass
Child 2: yes I see it
            I see it

A sound play sequence (nonwords are written in standard orthography):

Child 1: wake up
            wake up
Child 2: hake ut *(laughing)*
Child 1: hake ut
Child 2: bake up
Child 1: break ut
            break up
Child 2: wake up
            week up *(laughing)*

Source: From Keenan, 1974.

children take into consideration characteristics of their listener, by preferring more competent adult listeners over peers and by adapting their messages to listener feedback.

Although such data indicate that preschool children have the will to enter into communicative interactions with others, their skills at doing so are still developing. Garvey and Hogan (1973) observed the free-play interactions of 3½- to 5-year-old children and found that children were able to sustain sequences of talk from 4 to 12 or more exchanges long and that between 21% and 77% of the children's utterances were contingent on the verbal or nonverbal behavior of others. Schoeber-Peterson and Johnson (1989) studied 4-year-olds' conversations and found that the percent of conversational segments that were dialogue ranged from 23% to 70%, across ten different dyads. The length of dialogue that a single topic was sustained by these 4-year-olds was shorter than 12 utterances for 75% of the conversational topics. On occasion, however, the 4-year-olds sustained topics for much longer stretches of dialogue—even up to 91 consecutive utterances.

One factor that seems to be an important influence on the success of preschool children's conversation is the context in which the conversation occurs. Nelson and Gruendel (1979) suggested that children's ability to sustain dialogue is facilitated when they share knowledge that provides a background for their conversations. In preschool settings, where much of the dialogue occurs in the context of pretend play, the background for interaction is the shared knowledge of routines such as planning a meal or going shopping. In support of this notion, French, Lucariello, Seidman, and Nelson (1985) reviewed evidence from several studies suggesting that when children share contextual knowledge, their conversations are longer and their language use is more advanced than when they do not share background knowledge.

LEARNING TO PRODUCE NARRATIVES

The conversational origin of narratives

Narratives are verbal descriptions of past events. In ordinary language, narratives are stories. Ultimately, adult speakers are able to tell relatively long, complete stories in an uninterrupted monologue. However, children's first narratives occur in the context of conversation. Eisenberg (1985) described three phases in children's development of the ability to talk about past experiences. In the first phase, children's talk about the past is typically elicited and maintained by an adult. The adult provides the scaffolding for children's reports of past experience by introducing a past event as a topic (*Did you go to the zoo?*) and then eliciting more information on the topic (*What did you see there?*). In these early narratives, most of the content of the narrative is supplied by the adult, and the child supplies single-word responses to the adult's questions.

In the second phase of narrative development, children depend less on the scaffolding of adults' questions, and the children's contributions are longer and introduce new information. However, children's reports of past events during this phase tend to be general descriptions of a kind of familiar event rather than specific descriptions of particular events. For example, a child's recounting of a birthday party might include things that didn't actually occur at that birthday party but that are typical of birthday parties in general. In the third phase, children's narratives depend less on either conversational support or general event knowledge, and they include more information that is unique to the particular event being recounted.

Adults' scaffolding of children's narratives

Some parents provide more useful scaffolding for their children's early narratives than others do. Reese and Fivush (1993) described two different styles in parents' elicitations of past-event descriptions from their 3-year-old children. An elaborative style is characterized by questions that help the child say something that moves the narrative forward. In contrast, a repetitive style is characterized by questions that seek the same information over and over again. These two styles are illustrated in Box 5.5. An elaborative style not only helps in the immediate production of a narrative, it also appears to influence the later development of children's ability to produce narratives alone. McCabe and Peterson (1991) found that children whose parents asked useful, elaborative questions when the children were 2 years old produced better narratives when they were 3½; and Fivush (1991) found that the complexity and structure of the narratives mothers produced in conversation with their 2½-year-olds were related to the complexity and structure of those children's narratives a year later. Reese and Fivush (1993) suggest that this evidence that the way mothers structure conversations about the past influences children's development of the ability to recount past events is an example of the developmental process described by Vygotsky (1962). That is, what children first do in collaboration with an adult, they internalize and later do on their own.

Developmental changes in children's narratives

In addition to the growing independence from adult support, other developmental trends in children's early narrative production include increases in the frequency of spontaneous mention of past events, increases in the length of the narratives produced, increases in the remoteness of the past event, and increases in the structural complexity of the stories told (Miller & Sperry, 1988; Umiker-Sebeok, 1979). For example, Umiker-Sebeok recorded the peer interactions of 3-, 4-, and 5-year-old children in preschool settings and found that the proportion of conversations that included narratives increased from 23% in the 3-year-olds to 35% in the 5-year-olds. The average length of the 3-year-olds' narratives was 1.7 clauses, compared to 2.8 for the 5-year-olds. With respect to complexity, the 3-year-olds' narratives tended to be simply a mention of a past activity. In contrast, the longer narratives of the 4- and 5-year-olds were more likely to have the plot elements of a story. These developmental changes are illustrated in the examples in Box 5.6 (page 221).

Another feature of children's early narratives noted by Miller and Sperry (1988) is that they are frequently about negative, emotionally charged events. This characteristic is true both when children's stories are elicited by a researcher (Pitcher & Perlinger, 1963) and when children's spontaneous intraconversational narratives are examined. One possible explanation of this finding is that emotionally charged events are more likely than neutral events to be remembered (Howes, Sigel, & Brown, 1993). Also, children may be more inclined to talk about emotionally charged events than about neutral events either for their own intrapsychic reasons or because raising emotional topics may be a particularly successful way of securing a listener's attention (Miller & Sperry, 1988).

The example of a 4-year-old's narrative in Box 5.6 is an unusually good narrative for a child of that age. Although children's narrative skills increase

Box 5.5   Examples of elaborative and repetitive styles in parents' elicitations of past-event descriptions from 3-year-old children

Elaborative style elicitation

Parent: Did we see any big fishes? What kind of big fishes?
Child: Big, big, big.
Parent: And what's their names?
Child: I don't know.
Parent: You remember the names of the fishes. What we called them. Michael's favorite kind of fish. Big mean ugly fish.
Child: Yeah.
Parent: What kind is it?
Child: um, ba.
Parent: A ssshark?
Child: Yeah.
Parent: Remember the sharks?
Child: Yeah.
Parent: Do you? What else did we see in the big tank at the aquarium?
Child: I don't know.
Parent: Remember when we first came in, remember when we first came in the aquarium? And we looked down and there were a whole bunch of birdies in the water? Remember the names of the birdies?
Child: Ducks!
Parent: Nooo! They weren't ducks. They had on little suits. Penguins. Remember, what did the penguins do?
Child: I don't know.

Repetitive style elicitation

Parent: How did we get to Florida, do you remember?
Child: Yes.
Parent: How did we get there? What did we do? You remember?
Child: Yeah.
Parent: You want to sit up here in my lap?
Child: No.

(continued)

Box 5.5 *(continued)*

Parent: Oh, okay. Remember when we went to Florida, how did we
get there? We went in the _____?
Child: The ocean.
Parent: Well, be—, when we got to Florida we went to the ocean,
that's right, but how did we get down to Florida? Did we
drive our car?
Child: Yes.
Parent: No, think again, I don't think we drove to Florida. How did
we get down there, remember, we took a great big _____?
Do you remember?

Source: From Reese & Fivush, 1993.

notably from their first descriptions of past events around the age of 2 years to their more structured stories at 4 and 5 years, there is still much that is lacking in 5-year-olds' narratives. Often the narratives 5-year-olds produce are difficult to fully understand unless the listener is already familiar with the event being described, because young narrators fail to provide enough information. At the age of 5 years, children have not fully mastered the tense system, and thus it is sometimes hard to know exactly when events in their stories occurred relative to each other. Often the referents of pronouns are unclear. These and other aspects of narrative performance continue to develop during school years. We will take up the topic of these developments in the next chapter. Another part of the story of narrative development we have not yet told concerns cultural differences. Cultures vary in the kind of narrative they value, and children's narratives vary correspondingly. We consider some of those differences later in this chapter, under the heading of learning culture-specific language styles. For now, we continue our discussion of the early development of communicative competence by looking at sociolinguistic development during the preschool years.

LEARNING SITUATIONALLY APPROPRIATE LANGUAGE

Communicative competence includes the ability to use speech that is appropriate to the circumstance. For example, it would be inappropriate for a child to say to a parent, "Gimme five bucks"; and it would be absurd for an 8-year-old to say to an infant, "It would be awfully nice of you to get out of my way, my dear Mr. Jones" (Becker, 1982). In this case, the social status of the listener determines the appropriate use of language.

Box 5.6   Examples of 3-year-olds' and 4-year-olds' intraconversational narrative

3-year-olds

Child: You know what I was doing?
Adult: What?
Child: I was doing my work.
Adult: Your work?
Child: Like I do at home.

4-year-olds

Child: . . . I have two sisters, one with blond hair like me 'n the other with long black hair. 'N the one with black hair, when she was four like me, she cut her hair with scissors that aren't for cutting hair. 'N now she has short hair.

Source: From Umiker-Sebeok, 1979.

Social status of the listener is not the only factor relevant to language use. It would not be particularly communicative to answer a 2-year-old's question about how a car works the same way that you would answer a 10-year-old's question. In this case, the cognitive capacity of the listener is the relevant variable. In Samoan, there are two speech registers (referred to as "good" speech and "bad" speech), which differ in phonological, lexical, and grammatical features. Which register is appropriate depends on the setting (such as church versus home), the addressee (family member versus Westerner) and the topic of conversation (food preparation versus the Bible). "Good" speech is used in church, in talking to Westerners, and in talking about things like the Bible; "bad" speech is used at home, in talking to family members, and in talking about informal, everyday topics (Ochs, 1988). In this case, the choice of register depends on multiple factors. Using language appropriately requires control over the different styles that different situations require, and it requires knowing when to use what register. Appropriate language use also requires attention to the relevant features of the situation.

The egocentric child

Until at least the 1970s, the Piagetian position that preschoolers are egocentric led most people to assume that children had quite limited abilities to attend to the relevant features of the social setting and to modify their speech accordingly.

Support for this pessimistic view of children's communicative competence also came from experimental work on children's **referential communication** skills. In the task used in much of the referential communication research, children are asked to describe one item in an array of objects so that a visually separated listener with the same array can identify the item referred to. Four- and 5-year-old children (who are typically the youngest children tested with this procedure) are not very successful at this task. They provide clues like *Daddy's shirt* as a description of a geometric form and then describe another form as *another Daddy's shirt* (Glucksberg, Krauss, & Higgins, 1975). Such inadequate descriptions have been attributed to children's inability to take into account the needs of their listener. However, when children's language use in naturalistic settings is examined, there is often evidence of more competence than the Piagetian view would predict.

Evidence of children's sociolinguistic competence

The use of request forms　　One way to examine children's ability to modify their speech to fit the social situation is to focus on one speech function and look at the different ways in which children express that function in different situations. Children's use of requests has been sufficiently studied to provide useful data in this regard (Becker, 1982). The first step in describing children's use of different forms as requests is to identify the different forms children have available to them. Ervin-Tripp (1976) proposed a system for categorizing request forms based on how direct the form is. For example, imperatives are the most direct (such as *Give me a fork.*), need statements are somewhat less direct (*I need a fork.*), question-form directives even less direct *(Can I have a fork?),* and hints are the most indirect *(Someone forgot to set a fork at this place.).*

With a system for categorizing request forms, it is then possible to ask which kinds of forms children know how to produce. Researchers have found that even telegraphic speakers know more than one way to form a request. For example, they can state their goal *(More juice),* they can issue direct imperatives *(Book read),* or they can state the problem that needs solution *(Carol hungry)* (Ervin-Tripp, 1977). Two- and 3-year-olds who have mastered the syntactic form of questions also use question-form requests (such as *Would you push this? Can you give me one car, please?),* and 3-year-olds use hints *(You could give one to me, You can make a crown)* (Ervin-Tripp, 1977). Other researchers have also supported the conclusion that preschool children (between 3 and 5 years old) have different forms for expressing requests at their disposal (Dore, 1977; Garvey, 1975).

If even very young speakers have multiple ways of requesting available to them, then it is possible to ask whether children select different forms from their repertoires depending on the circumstance. The literature clearly suggests that they do. The earliest differential use of request forms has been observed in the study of one 2-year-old girl (Lawson, 1967, cited by Ervin-Tripp, 1976, 1977). This child used simple imperatives in talking to other 2-year-olds at preschool, she usually modified her imperatives by adding *Please* in talking to 3-year-olds, and she used questions when making requests of 4-year-olds. In talking to adults, she used primarily desire statements or questions. At home she also differentiated between her mother and father, being much more direct with her mother. [In this case, it's not clear that perceived status was the relevant factor; her mother may have been more familiar to her (Becker, 1982).]

Politeness Perceived politeness is at least one of the differences between more and less direct forms of request that explains why both children and adults are less direct with higher status addressees. There seems to be a conversational rule to be more polite with higher status listeners, and indirect forms are more polite than direct forms. (For a discussion of other understandings implicated by children's use of request forms, see Becker, 1982.) Children not only use less direct forms with higher status listeners, they also switch to less direct forms when they are asked to be "nicer." Bates (1976) investigated children's productive control over degrees of politeness by eliciting requests from them. Bates introduced Italian children to a hand puppet of an elderly gray-haired woman named Signora Rossi (Mrs. Rossi), who had lots of candy. The children were told that Mrs. Rossi would give them a piece of candy if they asked for one. After the children made their request, the experimenter pretended to confer with the puppet and then told the children: "Mrs. Rossi said that she will surely give you a candy. But, you know, she's a bit old, and she likes it when children are VERY, very nice. Ask her again EVEN MORE NICELY for the candy." Regardless of how they formed their second request, the children were given candy.

Two main findings emerged from this task: (1) Older children (3 years 5 months to 4 years) used more varied forms to express requests and were, in general, more indirect than younger children (2 years 10 months to 3 years 5 months); and (2) both older and younger children were able to use a different and less direct form the second time they asked. Thus evidence suggests that children as young as 3 years of age know to use a less direct form when they are asked to be more polite. Between the ages of 3 and 6, children acquire a variety of different ways of being less direct. Bates also asked the children in her study to judge the politeness of different forms of request and found developmental increases in children's ability to discriminate different forms as being different in politeness. For the most part, the forms produced at a younger age in response to the request to ask "even more nicely" were also the forms that were recognized as polite at a younger age.

Children's child-directed speech Another aspect of children's sociolinguistic skill that has been studied in some detail is the modifications children make when talking to listeners who are even younger than themselves. Again,

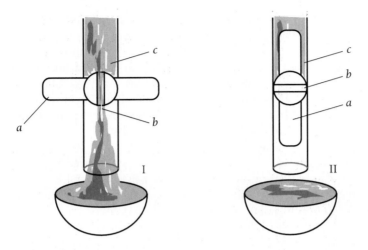

Figure 5.3   Diagram of water tap used in Piaget's study of children's communication skill
Source: From Piaget, 1926.

a review of the evidence begins with Piaget's (1926) description of children as relatively incompetent. One example of Piaget's research is a study in which 6-year-old children were shown a diagram of a water tap (illustrated in Figure 5.3) and given an explanation of how the tap worked. The children were then required to explain how the tap worked to a peer. Piaget found children's explanations of the water tap to be inadequate in several ways. The children did not order their explanations properly or explain causal connections between elements in the explanation in a way that would ensure listener comprehension (Shatz & Gelman, 1973). (Compare the adult's and child's explanations presented in Box 5.7.) Piaget attributed the poor quality of children's explanations to their egocentrism. Because children cannot consider the perspective of others, they cannot make their messages fit their listeners' needs.

Although the inadequacy of even 6-year-olds' mechanical explanations is not in doubt, the explanation in terms of egocentrism now seems wrong. Children may not be able to put together a clear explanation, but it is not because they don't know that different listeners need different messages. When children's talk to other children is examined in the contexts of less difficult tasks or more naturalistic settings, there is evidence that children do adjust their speech depending on their listener's ability. They talk differently to peers than to adults, and they talk differently to younger children than to peers (see Figure 5.4).

Shatz and Gelman (1973) asked 4-year-olds to explain to their mothers and to 2-year-olds how a toy dumping station worked. They found that the

---

Box 5.7   Adult's and child's explanation of the water tap in Figure 5.3

Adult's:

1. Look, these two pictures (I and II) are drawings of a tap.

2. This here (*a*) is the handle of the tap.

3. To turn it off, look, you have to do this with your fingers (move the finger on diagram I and show the result on diagram II). Then it is like this (diagram II).

4. You see (diagram I), when the handle is turned on like this (point to *a* and make horizontal movement), then the canal (point to *b*, call it also the little hole, door, or passage) is open.

5. Then the water runs out (point to *b* in diagram I).

6. It runs out because the canal is open.

7. Look, here (diagram II), when the handle is turned off (point to *a* and make a vertical movement), then the canal (point to *b*; can also be called the hole or door or passage) is also shut.

8. The water can't get through, you see? (point to *c*). It is stopped.

9. It can't run out, because the canal (point to *b*) is closed.

Child's:

You see, this way (diagram I) it is open. The little pipe (*c*) finds the little pipe (*b*) and then the water runs out. There (diagram II) it is shut and it can't find the little pipe that runs through. The water comes this way (diagram I, (*c*)) it comes in the little pipe. It is open, and there (II) it is shut. Look, you can't see the little pipe any more (II) it is lying down, then the water comes this way (*c*) and wouldn't find the little pipe any more.

Source: From Piaget, 1926.

4-year-olds' speech to the adult and to the 2-year-old differed on a number of dimensions. Speech to adults had a longer MLU and more frequently included complex constructions. Speech to 2-year-olds more frequently included devices to secure and direct the listener's attention such as *Hey, Look,* and *Watch*. Sachs and Devin (1976) recorded 4-year-olds in free play with their mother, a peer, a baby (between 1 and 2½ years old), and while talking to a doll. They also found

Figure 5.4   The ability to modify one's speech when talking to even younger children is part of a 4-year-old's communicative competence.

modifications in the 4-year-olds' speech to the baby and to the baby doll. The fact that the children made similar speech adjustments in talking to the doll and to a real baby suggests that the adjustments in speech to the baby are the result of children's knowledge of how to talk to babies, not feedback from the babies themselves.

Children speak differently to 2-year-olds than either to peers or to adults, but children do not speak to 2-year-olds in the same way that adults do. Several studies compared the infant-directed speech of children between 2 and 5 years to mothers' infant-directed speech and found that when children talk to younger children, there is less talk overall; and the speech that is addressed to the young child is more directive, has a higher frequency of attention-getting devices and repetitions, has a lower frequency of questions, and is, in general, less attuned to the young child (Dunn & Kendrick, 1982; Mannle & Tomasello, 1987; Tomasello & Mannle, 1985; Vandell & Wilson, 1987). Tomasello and Mannle (1985) also found that when older siblings interacted with younger siblings, they spent less time than mothers did sharing the attentional focus of the young child. The suggested sources

suggest that these acknowledgments, which actually interrupt the children's speech, have the effect of stopping the children from talking on at length; and of course fewer requests for description would also work in the same direction of eliciting shorter narratives.

Among many African American groups, adults' narratives have a structure different from the structure typical of white, middle-class narratives. Not surprisingly, the narrative development of children in those communities follows a different path. On the basis of her research with school-aged African American and white children in northern California and in Boston, Michaels (1983) described the differences in the following way. The narratives told among white, middle-class groups tend to be tightly organized around a single topic. This type of narrative structure has been referred to as **topic centered.** In contrast, the narratives told among African Americans are more likely to consist of a loosely related set of personal anecdotes. This type of narrative structure has been referred to as **topic associating.**

Heath's (1983) description of the narratives told by African Americans in the rural southeastern United States also fits the topic-associating label. In addition, Heath describes narratives as "performances." Good verbal performers within this speech community are skilled at telling narratives in a way that secures and sustains an audience's attention. Stories are often told in a poemlike structure, and the nonverbal embellishments that accompany the story are an important part of the performance. Exaggerating the facts to make the story more interesting is also part of good verbal performance. By the standards of this speech community, the narrative about hair cutting in Box 5.6 would not be judged as very good. A good story performance by a 5-year-old in this community is illustrated in Box 5.9. In this example, a 5-year-old boy named Teegie is describing and demonstrating riding his new tricycle.

The child who told the story in Box 5.9 is skilled in the narrative style of his sociocultural group. He has learned a very different style of storytelling than did the little girl who told the story about her sister cutting her own hair. The contrast between these children illustrates two points: (1) Children acquire the stylistic aspects of language use of their own speech community, in addition to acquiring the grammar and vocabulary of the language they hear, and (2) by the age of 5 years, children from different speech communities use language very differently.

What we are discussing here is children's successful achievement of the communicative competencies that are valued in their environment. As long as we are talking about Samoan children learning register variation or Japanese children learning a specifically Japanese style of narrative production, the

---

Box 5.9   Example of African American narrative style from a 5-year-old

Zoom. (*racing part-way down the hill, and then falling down*)

Zoom, zoom, zoom, zoom, zoom, zoom, zoom, zoom, zoom, zoom.

Hi ay. (*walking back up the hill, as though he were on a tottering bicycle*)

Hi ay, ay, ay, ay, ay, ay.

Teegie got (*continuing to trudge up the hill with exaggerated motions of a tired old man*)

A bike

A new bike

A bike to ride

See Teegie bike?

Source: From Heath, 1983, pp. 173–174.

achievement of these competencies at 5 years is the successful conclusion of the developmental story (although, of course, development may continue after the age of 5 years). However, when we are talking about North American white and African American children acquiring group-specific styles of language use, the achievement of these competencies at the age of 5 years is not an unmitigated success. And although it may be the end of one story, it is also the beginning of a different story. At the age of approximately 5 years, both white children and African American children begin formal schooling, and the children need to use the oral language skills they have acquired at home in a new setting. A substantial body of research has documented that the way language is used in U.S. classrooms is more similar to the way it is used in white middle-class homes than it is to the way language is used by other groups. Thus the successful achievement of a minority style of language use places minority children at a disadvantage in school. We will pursue this topic further in Chapter 6, when we take up the topic of children's transition from home to school.

Early gender differences in language use

The observation that men and women use language in different ways is of interest to more people than just language researchers; it was even the subject of a best-selling book (Tannen, 1990). Gender differences include some domains of vocabulary knowledge (how many male readers of this book know the meanings of the words *mauve, puce,* and *ecru?*), articulation (men tend to say "somethin'" and "workin'"; women more frequently pronounce the final *ing*), and grammar (women's speech is more grammatically correct than men's) (Lakoff, 1975). However, the area of greatest gender difference is in conversational style. The question we consider here is, What aspects of **gender-typed** discourse style are evidenced in preschoolers?

Several studies suggest that there are gender differences in language use in children as young as 3 years old. Preschool boys tend to be more assertive and demanding in their conversational style, whereas preschool girls tend to be more polite and cooperative. For example, Esposito (1979) found that boys interrupted girls twice as frequently as girls interrupted boys. Sachs (1987) found that boys tended to use simple imperatives in talking to their partner in pretend play (such as *Lie down, Get the heart thing, Gimme your arm*). Girls in the same situation used fewer simple imperatives and instead used language that included the other child in planning (such as *Let's sit down and use it, OK, and I'll be the doctor for my baby and you be the doctor for your baby*).

Given these gender differences in preschoolers' conversational style, perhaps it is not surprising that there are more disputes when preschool boys interact than when preschool girls interact. And, when conflict arises, boys handle it differently than girls do. Amy Sheldon (1990) videotaped same-sex triads of preschool girls and boys at a day care center. She observed that when the boys had conflicts, they frequently issued directives and made threats. The girls, in contrast, tended more to try to negotiate a settlement. Looking at interaction in single-gender and gender-mixed triads, Killen and Naigles (1995) also found that girls used more talk oriented toward conflict resolution than boys did. In addition, Killen and Naigles found that children's discourse style differed depending on the group's gender composition. Children's discourse was less gender-stereotyped in mixed-sex groups than in same-sex groups. Together these descriptions of gender-differentiated language use suggest that the early development of communicative competence includes both the development of gender-specific style and, as we saw earlier with the study of children's child-directed speech, the development of the ability to modify language use based on properties (in this case the gender) of one's conversational partners. There is also evidence that communicative style becomes more strongly gender-typed during middle childhood. We will return to this topic in Chapter 6.

THEORETICAL ISSUES CONCERNING THE DEVELOPMENT OF COMMUNICATIVE COMPETENCE

Explanations of the development of communicative competence

Having described the "what" and "when" of children's development of pragmatic, discourse, and sociolinguistic skills, we now need to ask how and why those developments occur.

Influences on pragmatic development   How do children learn what you can do with words? One possibility is that the urge to communicate with others is an innate characteristic of human beings. When this communicative urge becomes mature, children look for a means of communication and find it in the sounds people make. This view accommodates the data from Bell and Ainsworth's (1972) study that maternal responsiveness influences communicative development. This view can also accommodate the evidence that communicative competence still develops in cultures in which mothers do not treat infants as communicative beings (Heath, 1983; Ochs, 1988; and see Lieven, 1994, for a review). If the urge to communicate is innate, then maternal responsiveness may help children realize the communicative value of sounds, but it is not essential for that discovery. The evidence of a maturational change at age 9 to 10 months [labeled the development of secondary intersubjectivity by Trevarthen and Hubley (1978)] also fits the view that there is something innate in children that matures, thereby enabling communication.

A slightly more complex version of an account that accepts innate characteristics proposes that the prerequisites to the development of communication can be separated into social and cognitive components. According to such a view, children may be inherently social organisms, but using language for social interaction also depends on cognitive developments. This view would be consistent with the idea that what matures at age 9 to 10 months is the cognitive capacity to handle a three-term interaction, such as one that includes a speaker, a listener, and a referent. This separation of cognitive and social prerequisites further fits the evidence that babies are socially responsive from around the age of 8 weeks, although not intentionally communicative until the age of 9 to 10 months.

Unpacking the social and cognitive prerequisites to communication also helps explain the developments that occur after age 10 months and after the milestone of secondary intersubjectivity is passed. We can make distinctions among types of communicative intent, such as the distinction between intentions to achieve goals and intentions to meet other minds proposed by Shatz (1983b). According to this view, children between the ages of 10 months and 3 years have intentions to achieve goals. However, they cannot have intentions to meet other minds until they achieve the cognitive understanding that others have minds, sometime between the ages of 3 and 5 years.

Bloom (1993b) proposed a different explanation of the function of early language. She disagrees with the idea that children's early communicative intentions are primarily to achieve goals. She suggests, instead, that the primary function of children's speech is to express the contents of their minds. Children do not have to learn this function, nor do they need a theory of mind in order to seek the state of "being together" with another person. For babies, natural expressions of emotion communicate their mental states. However, as children develop cognitively and their mental states become more complicated, children need language to continue to maintain intersubjectivity with another.

At a more mundane level, explaining how children learn what you can do with words also entails explaining the development of the multiple functions of language, such as referring, requesting, and so on. Nelson (1973) addressed this question in her discussion of referential and expressive styles of language use. Nelson's proposal was that children have their own intrinsic cognitive tendencies—to be interested in objects or to be interested in the social world—and that the functions mothers attribute to language influence children's notions of what language is for. Nelson, then, proposes both an internally based cognitive influence and an externally based influence—the model adults provide.

The influence of adult models on children's acquisition of language function is also part of controversial proposals regarding differences in language function associated with socioeconomic status. That is, it has been suggested that adults in different socioeconomic strata use language for different purposes; therefore children's development of language function also differs by socio-economic stratum (Bernstein, 1970, 1981; Hymes, 1961; Tough, 1982). For example, Tough (1982) found that mothers with higher education used language to analyze and reflect on experience more than did mothers with minimal levels of education, and this same difference in the use to which language is put was observed in their children between the ages of 3½ and 7 years.

Influences on the development of discourse skill ~talking~   In trying to explain the development of discourse skill, we can similarly talk about social and cognitive influences and the role of experience. Participating in conversation depends on an interest in social interaction; it also depends on cognitive ability. The first proposed relation between cognitive ability and conversational skill we discussed was Piaget's proposal that children have very limited conversational skills because they are egocentric. Although research since Piaget suggests that his view underestimates both children's conversational abilities and their cognitive abilities, newer research indicates that children's ability to participate in conversation does depend on their level of cognitive development. According to a structural view of the cognitive prerequisites to conversational skill, children must reach a certain cognitive level, such as the ability not to be egocentric, in order for certain conversational skills to be possible. If children haven't reached the requisite cognitive level, then their conversational skills are accordingly limited (Shatz, 1983a).

It is also possible to think of the cognitive requirements of conversation as process requirements (Shatz, 1983a). According to this view, conversation places multiple demands on children's cognitive capacity. Children's ability to participate in conversation depends on how many demands are simultaneously being made and on their current processing capacity. The processing capacity notion can account for evidence that children's conversational skill is not consistent at any point in development but instead fluctuates, depending on task demands. For example, Bloom, Rocissano, and Hood (1976) found children's utterances were syntactically more advanced when children initiated conversations than when they responded to another's prior speech. According to the researchers, the work of holding in mind what the previous speaker said in order to make one's utterance relevant takes up processing capacity that could otherwise be used to produce a grammatically more complex utterance. There are other examples of children's variable communicative performance depending on the demands of the task (Shatz, 1983a).

The contribution of experience to the development of discourse skill seems to be of two sorts. On the one hand, children clearly learn what they hear. For example, children learn the narrative style of their culture and they learn that "What time is it?" is responded to with a number. On the other hand, there is evidence that the development of conversational skill is also influenced by what children's circumstances require of them. For example, Dunn and Shatz (1989) found that children with older siblings develop the ability to intrude into the conversation between the older sibling and the mothers. Between 2 and 3 years of age, the younger children's intrusions become more frequently relevant to the ongoing conversation and more frequently successful at gaining the child entry into the conversation. Additional evidence that children learn the communicative competencies the situation requires may be the finding that later-born children produce more contingent responses in conversation than same-aged first-born children do, even though their linguistic skills are not more advanced (Hoff-Ginsberg, 1995).

Influences on sociolinguistic development   Like the other aspects of communicative competence, sociolinguistic competence also has social and cognitive prerequisites. Using language in a manner appropriate to the social situation depends on awareness of the relevant social variables and the ability to take those variables into account in crafting messages. As with other aspects of communicative competence, the development of sociolinguistic competence probably also depends on children observing what others do.

Explicit teaching is one source of influence that is more obvious with respect to sociolinguistic development than to other aspects of communicative and linguistic competence. Parents (and others) instruct children in the appropriate use of language (Say "Please."), prompt children (What's the magic word?) and directly praise children for appropriate speech and reprimand them for socially inappropriate speech (Becker, 1990; Ely & Gleason, 1995). A clear and frequently cited illustration of direct instruction in language use comes from Gleason and Weintraub (1976), who observed mothers and older siblings explicitly coaching young children in the routine of saying "trick-or-treat" as they made their rounds on Halloween.

A less explicit means of language socialization is for adults to engage children in the kind of verbal interaction that demands particular competencies. For example, Eisenberg (1986) and Miller (1986) described adults' teasing of young children in Mexicano families and in white, working-class families. One of the mothers in Miller's study explained that the purpose of the teasing was to prepare the children to stand up for themselves in real-life disputes.

Perhaps the most subtle form of language socialization is the sort suggested by Reese and Fivush (1993) in their study of parents' elicitations of children's narratives. According to Reese and Fivush, mothers' efforts at eliciting past-event descriptions from their children not only helps their children acquire the skill of producing narratives but also communicates to the children that narratives are valued in the culture. In like manner, but with different outcomes, the interrupting that Japanese mothers do and the attention that African American audiences pay to children like Teegie (Box 5.9) let children in these cultures know what kind of verbal performance is valued.

In summary, it appears that the development of communicative competence has multiple sources of influence. Biologically based social and cognitive capacities mature, making communication interesting and possible. Responsive communicative partners support the development of some communicative skills, and the need to communicate in less supportive environments may foster the development of other skills. Children observe the communicative behaviors of those around them and reproduce them, and sometimes communicative skills are explicitly taught. Each of the foregoing statements, although probably true, is also very vague. In the previous chapter on syntax, we didn't pretend that a statement to the effect that some things mature and other things are learned from experience constitutes an adequate theory of the development of syntax. And we shouldn't pretend that this summary is adequate as an account of the development of communicative competence.

Part of the problem of devising a precise theory of the development of communicative competence is that there isn't a body of theoretical work that describes the end state of development with the same degree of precision (if not unanimity) that there is for the several domains of linguistic competence. Part of the problem is also that communicative competence seems, to many, to be simpler and therefore less problematic for the child. Put another way, people see grammar as more obviously complicated and difficult for children to figure out than are things like politeness and register variation, and so we have higher standards for what counts as an adequate theory of grammar acquisition. Another notion that follows from this (perhaps mistaken) notion that communication is simple and obvious and grammar is complicated is the theoretical view that communication provides the foundation for the acquisition of grammar. We turn to this topic next.

The relation between the development of language function and language structure

Language function as the basis of language structure   There are several proposals for how the communicative function of language might be related to children's acquisition of language structure. The proposals that make the strongest claim for a connection between language function and language structure are those that entail a **functionalist theory of language.** According to functionalist theories, the structure of language itself has a functional basis, and therefore the grammatical categories and rules that children must acquire are associated with functionally based categories. For example, Bates and MacWhinney (1982) argued that the grammatical category of the subject of a sentence tends to be correlated with the communicative role of "topic." The acquisition claim that goes along with such a proposal is that children "exploit the correlation between form and function to 'crack the code' of their native language" (Bates and MacWhinney, 1982, p. 184). The reasonableness of this proposal depends on whether the grammar of languages can indeed be described in functional terms, and there are linguistic theories of this sort (see, for example, Foley & Van Valin, 1984). However, such theories are completely rejected by some notable others, including Noam Chomsky.

Language function as the gateway to language structure   Another functionalist theory of language acquisition shares the notion that children use language function to "crack the code" but differs in allowing that the grammar achieved may not be reducible to a functionally based system. According to such a view, language function serves "as a wedge into a grammar that ultimately will be purely formal" (Budwig, 1991, p. 2). Although this notion does not entail assumptions about the functional basis of language structure, it does entail some assumptions. In particular, the notion that children use function to gain entry into the formal system assumes that there are correlations between function and form

7.   *gramma*

for children to use and that function is somehow obvious to the child. Some research suggests that children are sensitive to form/function correspondences in language. For example, Choi (1991) found that Korean children under the age of 2 years used different sentence-ending suffixes depending on whether the sentence they were producing was a statement or a request. However, there is nothing remotely like evidence that children's sensitivity to form/function correspondences (or even perfect sensitivity to the form/function correspondences that exist) is sufficient to account for the acquisition of grammar.

Communication as the motivation for acquiring language structure

The weakest sort of claim for a role of language function in children's acquisition of language structure is that the need to communicate motivates the language acquisition process. For example, Glucksberg, Krauss, and Higgins (1975) suggested that the need to be understood is "a source of pressure" on children to be explicit in their messages. This hypothesis is similar to Bloom's (1993) proposal that language is acquired in order to express what one is thinking.

If the need to be understood by others is what drives language acquisition, that, then, raises the question of the role these others play in motivating language acquisition. Bloom (1993) described mothers' willingness to create shared understandings as an essential ingredient in the language acquisition process. Not necessarily in conflict with this notion, Golinkoff (1983) suggested that when children fail to be understood, the failure prompts them to find new and better ways of communicating. In the same vein, Tomasello and his colleagues (Mannle & Tomasello, 1987) suggested that fathers and siblings, who are less skilled than mothers at figuring out the meaning behind children's immature sentences, place communicative pressure on children that promotes their language development.

Communicative pressure as the source of communicative development

The proposals just described suggest that the need to communicate fuels the acquisition of language form. Alternatively, it has been suggested that communicative pressure shapes communicative development but not linguistic development. For example, taking a somewhat different position from Mannle and Tomasello (1987), Barton and Tomasello (1994) proposed that interaction with fathers and siblings promotes skills that are communicative rather than purely linguistic. This proposal is supported by the evidence that younger siblings learn to interject themselves into others' conversations (Dunn & Shatz, 1989) and that later-born children are more skillful than first-born children are at producing contingent replies with minimal linguistic resources (Hoff-Ginsberg, 1995). There is another example of children's learning communicatively relevant but not particularly linguistic skills that their environment demands. Children who live in cultures in which children are not talked to may learn to pay attention to speech among others instead. This must be true to a certain extent or only Western middle-class children would learn to talk. Ochs (1988) offers anecdotal support for the idea that children who are not actively solicited to engage in conversation become particularly good at paying attention to the conversations that go on around them. Ochs observed that her Samoan research assistants, who grew up in such an environment, were much better at hearing background conversations on audiotape than she was.

There are other cases in which linguistic skills develop far in advance of communicative skills. One group for whom this is true is children with autism. We will discuss language in individuals with autism in some detail in Chapter 7. Here we will illustrate the phenomenon of dissociable communicative and linguistic development with a case report of one child who was not autistic but who did show a huge discrepancy between his linguistic knowledge and his communicative competence. In a report entitled "Language without Communication," Blank, Gessner, and Esposito (1979) described a 3-year-old boy whose command of grammar and semantics were appropriate for his age, but whose sociocommunicative skills were severely deficient. For example, in interaction with his parents, this child typically either did not respond at all to his parents' speech or produced a completely unrelated response. When his mother asked, in the context of a pretend game about driving, "Are you going to go in and say hi to daddy?", the child replied, "O.K., here we are in the garage." Further evidence that this child's difficulties were communicative and not linguistic was his inability to understand nonverbal communicative signals, such as a pointing gesture. The cause of this child's communicative inability is not known, but this case is a striking demonstration of the potential independence of language and communicative development.

SUMMARY

People use language to communicate. The successful use of language for communicating requires knowing more than the phonology, the lexicon, and the morphosyntactic rules of one's language. Other competencies involved in communication include understanding the functions of language (pragmatics), knowing how to participate in conversation and relate a past event (discourse knowledge), and knowing how to use language in a manner that is appropriate to the social situation and is valued by your social group (sociolinguistic knowledge).

In the first five years of life, as children are acquiring language, they are also developing communication skills. At birth, infants are not communicative. Although adults may be able to interpret babies' cries and smiles, babies do not produce these cries and smiles with communicative intent. The first evidence of intentional communication appears around the age of 10 months when, for example, babies start to request help from others in obtaining objects. By the time children are 1 year old, they can be quite communicative, using the few words in their vocabularies along with intonation and gesture to perform such communicative functions as referring to objects, requesting objects, refusing something that is offered to them, and so on. As children's language abilities progress, language becomes the primary vehicle of communicative acts.

Conversational skill also begins to develop during the second year of life as children learn such mechanics of verbal interaction as turn taking, initiating topics, repairing miscommunication, and responding contingently. Initially, children's conversations with adults are very asymmetrical, with adults doing the work of building conversations around children's contributions. As children's conversational skills develop, the relative burdens carried by the adult and child in sustaining conversation become more equal. As children start to produce descriptions of past events in conversation, often in response to adults' questions and with adults' help, a new type of discourse—the narrative—begins to develop. Preschool children also talk to each other, although their lack of conversational skill sometimes limits the success of peer conversations. Children seem interested in conversations with each other from the age of 2 years, and they show some ability to adapt their speech to their listeners' needs from at least the age of 4 years. However, children's conversations tend to be disjointed compared to adult conversations, and children's dialogue is often intermixed with each participant's private speech.

The development of sociolinguistic skill also begins early in the course of language development. Two-year-old children use language differently depending on the social situation. For example, in Samoa, where different speech registers are appropriate in different social situations, 2-year-olds use some aspects of the appropriate register, depending on the setting. In role play, 5-year-olds also demonstrate an awareness that people in different roles—for example, mothers and fathers—use language differently.

Another aspect of sociolinguistic development that is well under way by the age of 5 years is the development of the style of language use of one's social group. For example, white middle-class North American children, Japanese children, and some African American children learn to produce very different sorts of narratives, in accordance with the kind of narrative that is valued in their social group. As a second example, preschool boys and girls already differ in the ways they use language in conversation.

The factors that influence the development of communicative competence include social and cognitive development, exposure to adult models of language use and, sometimes, direct instruction. Normally, the development of communicative competence and the development of language proceed together. However, the correlation between the development of communicative skills and language skills is not perfect, even among normally developing children. For example, a late talker may be a very skillful communicator using nonverbal means. Cases of atypical development reveal even more clearly the potential dissociation of communicative and linguistic development.

KEY TERMS

linguistic competence	secondary intersubjectivity
communicative competence	turn-taking
pragmatic knowledge	protoconversation
discourse knowledge	active dialogues
sociolinguistic knowledge	scaffolding
speech act	collective monologues
illocutionary force	egocentric
locution	private speech
perlocution	language play
intentionality	topics
conversations	referential communication
narrative	topic-centered narrative style
registers	topic-associating narrative style
dialects	gender-typed language
language socialization	theory of mind
primary intersubjectivity	functionalist theory of language

REVIEW QUESTIONS

1. Define the distinction between linguistic competence and communicative competence.
2. List and define the kinds of knowledge that constitute communicative competence.
3. Describe the course of speech act development.
4. Why is the period around age 9 months considered a major milestone in communicative development? What changes occur in the child?
5. What role does prelinguistic interaction play in the development of communicative competence and in the development of linguistic competence? What claims have been made and what is the evidence?
6. Explain the difference between the instrumental and expressive functions of language. How does this distinction figure in discussions of early language development?

7. What does the Piagetian view of preschool children as egocentric imply about their conversational and sociolinguistic skills?

8. What are the kinds and functions of private speech?

9. Describe the conversational skills of the 2- to 3-year-old. What can children do at this age, and in what ways do they still fall short of adult competence?

10. Describe the narrative skills of the 2- to 3-year-old.

11. Describe the sociolinguistic skills of the 2- to 3-year-old.

12. What is the difference between the narrative style that is typical of middle-class 5-year-olds and the narrative style that is characteristic of nonmainstream African American children of that age? What is the significance of this difference?

13. How does the language use of preschool boys and girls differ?

14. What are the sources of influence on the development of communicative competence? Illustrate each with an example.

15. What are the possible relations between the development of the communicative functions of language and the development of language structure? What sort of evidence would you need to test these proposals?

6 Language Development after Early Childhood

Myself prunes quickly. (Alissa, 9½ years, referring to her skin that is wrinkled from being in the swimming pool)

I'll go get eaten. (Alissa, 9½ years, after being told to "get washed, get dressed, and do whatever else you have to do to get ready")

Thank you for peanut buttering my toast. (Alissa, 13 years)

Between birth and the age of 5 years, children change from nonlinguistic infants to young persons with the linguistic means to express themselves and join the social world. By the age of 5 years, children have mastered the essentials of language, and if language development stopped at that point, humans would still be a linguistic species. However, language development continues after early childhood. In this chapter, we will discuss some of the developments that occur during middle childhood and adolescence. We will return to the topics of previous chapters, this time discussing later developments in phonology, the lexicon, grammar, and the development of communicative competence. Later developments in the domain of communicative competence will be considered under the headings of discourse development (including conversation and narratives), the development of communication skills, and sociolinguistic development. Following that discussion, we will consider a new topic that is particularly relevant during the school-age years—the acquisition of literacy. We will not consider the processes of reading and writing per se, but we will ask how children's oral language development may be related to the acquisition of literacy. Last, we will discuss changes in language that occur in adulthood and old age.

The use of 5 years as the dividing line between early and later language development is not entirely arbitrary. In its early years, the field of language development focused on the acquisition of syntax and found that children can produce most types of complex sentences by the age of 4 or 5 years. This finding—that 5-year-olds can produce all the types of linguistic structures that adults can—led to the widespread assumption that the process of language development is essentially complete by 5 years. Attention to later language development is a more recent phenomenon in the history of the field.

Historical explanations aside, there seems to be another difference between developments that occur before and after age 5 years. In discussing early development, we made the assumption that all children reach the same endpoint. That assumption is true if we define the endpoint of language development as knowing the phonology, the basic lexicon, and the grammar of a language, along with rules for socially appropriate language use. In discussing developments after age 5 years, however, it quickly becomes apparent that we are often talking about developments that are achieved to different degrees by different speakers. Put another way, all normal children learn to talk, but they do not all achieve the same size vocabulary, the same narrative skill, or the same ability to sustain a conversation. We will begin our discussion of later developments in each component of language by picking up where we left off in previous chapters—at the level of development most children reach at the age of 5 years.

LATER PHONOLOGICAL DEVELOPMENT

By 5 years of age, children have essentially mastered the phonology of their language. Lingering difficulty in articulating some of the later-acquired phones is the only overt sign that phonological development has not reached adult levels. However, children's phonological skills can and do change beyond early childhood.

During middle childhood, children get better at coordinating speech production. They become more fluent in producing complex sequences of sounds and multisyllabic words (Vihman, 1988b). With respect to speech perception, children continue to improve in their ability to understand speech under noisy circumstances up to the age of 15 years. These improvements in comprehension come from children's increased ability to use knowledge of the phonetic patterns of the language, in addition to semantic and grammatical knowledge, to help identify words in a less-than-clear signal (Vihman, 1988b; see also Grunwell, 1986).

In addition to these incremental changes in phonological ability, two new kinds of changes in children's phonology can occur during the school-age years. Exposure to peers who speak a dialect different from the dialect spoken at home can alter the sound of children's speech, and learning to read an alphabetic writing system affects children's phonological awareness.

The acquisition of an accent

In the course of early language acquisition, children acquire the particular accent of their caregivers. However, a person's accent is not permanently fixed, even once phonological development is complete. Imagine a family from England who moves to the United States. If we talked to the members of this family five years after their move, we would probably find that the children's speech is noticeably Americanized and that the parents' speech is less changed. This example illustrates that a phonological system can change after early childhood but that it doesn't always change, despite exposure to a new phonological system. The questions that this example raises are, What causes changes in a phonological system once that system is acquired? and What limits the likelihood of change?

Peer influence   Part of the explanation for changes in accent after early childhood is the influence of peers. We can see evidence of this influence in a careful study of families who were in the same position as our imaginary British family. Payne (1980) studied families who moved to the Philadelphia area from other regions of the country. Vowels are different in Philadelphia than they are elsewhere; for example, *merry* and *Murray* and *ferry* and *furry* sound the same. Payne studied the acquisition of this Philadelphia dialect in transplanted families, focusing on one family with four children. When this family moved to Philadelphia, the children were 3, 5, 6, and 8 years old. Payne examined the children's speech five years later, when they were 8, 10, 11, and 13, respectively, and she found that the 10- and 11-year-old had the strongest Philadelphia accents. The 8- and the 13-year old had fewer features of the Philadelphia dialect. The explanation Payne offered for this finding was that the age of maximum sensitivity to peer influence is between 4 and 14 years. The 10- and 11-year-old had spent five of those years in Philadelphia and only one or two of those years elsewhere. In contrast, the 13-year-old had spent four of those years in another location, and the 8-year-old had spent some of the Philadelphia years at home, exposed to the mother's dialect. Applying this explanation to our imaginary British family, we would say that the children's accent changed more than the parents' did because the children were more subject to the influence of peers.

Sometimes adolescents' phonology changes not as a result of moving to a new area but as a result of moving in new social circles. As the adolescent's social world becomes the peer group, adolescents come to talk the way members of their particular peer group do. Eckert (1988) studied the speech of Detroit-area adolescents and found that some vowel sounds differed between adolescents who defined themselves as "Jocks" and those who defined themselves as "Burnouts." Hewitt (1982) described a phenomenon common among black adolescents of Caribbean descent who were born in and live in London. These native Londoners adopt a Jamaican Creole speech for the first time in their lives when they are teenagers. The use of this dialect expresses their black identity, their affiliation with their peer group, and their cultural difference from the larger society. The Jamaican style of speech persists among these adolescents despite the fact (or because of the fact) that it has less prestige in the wider community and is not preferred by the black parents. The social significance of speech in this particular dialect is such that white adolescents who become friends with blacks also sometimes adopt Jamaican pronunciation (Hewitt, 1982).

According to Labov (1970), the influence of peers on dialect is one stage of sociolinguistic development. Labov proposed that up to the age of 5 years, children acquire the basic grammar and lexicon of their language, normally under the influence of parents. Between the ages of 5 and 12 years, children learn the dialect of their peer group. The peer group dialect may be quite different from, and less prestigious than, the mainstream form of the target language, especially for minority children. By the age of 14 or 15, adolescents start to move away from the peer group dialect and toward the more prestigious form of speech, especially in formal situations. The extent to which minority-dialect speakers master and use the mainstream form of speech as adults depends, in part, on the level of education they achieve (Labov, 1970; Romaine, 1984).

The influence of prestige, social pressure, and identity   The peer influence on dialect is not the automatic result of exposure to a new style of speech. Other influences include the prestige associated with a particular dialect (within the peer group), social pressure, and identity. Sometimes these other factors can counteract peer influence. For example, Labov (1972b) described cases in which teenagers born in Athens to Turkish immigrant families spoke in the Istanbul dialect of their parents because, according to Labov, "The strength and prestige of Istanbul family ties and the value of Istanbul identification seem to have been great enough to resist (peer) pressures" (p. 307). On the other hand, Labov (1972b) also cites the case of Swiss-German women who change their dialect as young adults when they marry and move to another village where they would be ridiculed for their native dialect. The role of identity in the dialect one speaks is also illustrated by Labov's finding that among lifelong residents of Martha's Vineyard, Massachusetts, the extent to which people have the characteristic accent of the region is related to their sociopolitical views about the encroachment of the tourism industry on the life and economy of the island. Those individuals who are more resistant to change have stronger regional accents. However, accent is not entirely a matter of exposure and identity. Speakers with strong foreign or regional accents sometimes find it very difficult to lose their unwanted accents. (See Flege, 1992, for a discussion of purely phonological processes that underlie the resilience of some foreign accents.) We will return to the relation of language and identity later in this chapter when we discuss sociolinguistic development.

The development of phonological awareness

In Chapter 2, we made the point that all competent speakers/hearers know the phonology of their language, even though they are not aware of that knowledge. So, for example, all speakers pluralize *bug* with [z] and *bike* with [s], although most speakers couldn't say why. However, adults do have some conscious awareness of the sounds that make up the speech they hear.

What is phonological awareness?   How many syllables are in the word *psycholinguistics*? Think of a word that rhymes with *cat*. Think of a word that begins with the same sound as *cat*. How many sounds are in the word *cat*? To answer these questions, we have to analyze the sounds that make up words. Children show some ability to do this kind of phonological analysis from the age of 2 years, but important developments in **phonological awareness** occur after early childhood.

The developmental course of phonological awareness   If you ask preschool children to tap out the number of syllables in a multisyllabic word, about 50% of 4- and 5-year-olds and 90% of 6-year-olds can do so (Liberman, Shankweiler, Fischer, & Carter, 1974). Young children also show awareness that a syllable can be further analyzed in two constituents: the **onset,** which consists of the initial consonant or consonant cluster, and the **rime,** which consists of the vowel plus any following consonants (Treiman, 1985). So, for example, the /k/ in *cat* is the onset and /æt/ is the rime. Naturalistic evidence of young children's awareness of onsets and rime can be found in the sound play that 2-year-olds produce, in dialogue or in soliloquies. For example, children have been observed to produce spontaneous rhymes, such as the following from a 2½-year-old girl:

> Ilk silk tilk
> I eat kasha with milk.
> Ilks-silks-tilks
> I eat kashas with milks. (Chukovsky, 1963, p. 63)

There is also experimental evidence of children's phonological awareness. For example, Treiman (1985) found that 4-year-olds can identify onsets. She introduced children to a puppet, telling the children that the puppet had a "favorite sound" (such as [f]). She then asked the children to listen to both nonsense and real words and to judge which of the words the puppet would like. The 4-year-olds in Treiman's study could correctly identify syllables like [fol] and [fir] as beginning with [f]. MacLean, Bryant, and Bradley (1987), using the same sort of task, found that a "considerable portion" of 3-year-olds were able to detect both onsets and rimes.

Syllables, onsets, and rimes are the smallest units most preschool children can identify. A 3-year-old can hear that the word *cat* is made up of *c* + *at* but not that *at* is made up of *a* + *t*. And Treiman (1985) found that 4-year-old children had a harder time recognizing initial consonants when they were part of clusters. For example, the [f] in syllables such as [flo] and [fri] were less recognizable than the [f] in syllables such as [fol]. Liberman and associates (1974) found that no 4-year-olds and only 17% of 5-year-olds were able to tap out the number of phonemes in words. By age 6 years, 70% of children could analyze a word in its constituent phonemes. In sum, some phonological awareness develops early, although sensitivity to phonemes is a later development than sensitivity to syllables, onsets, and rimes. At least in Western societies, where most of the research has been conducted, children's phonemic awareness shows rapid increase after the age of 5 years.

The significance of phonological awareness   It is interesting that children develop some awareness of the internal phonological structure of words even though speaking does not require it, and some researchers have suggested that this ability is part of the language acquisition capacity with which children are innately endowed (Mann, 1986, 1991; Mattingly, 1984). However, the huge volume of research that exists on phonological awareness was not aimed at investigating this innate capacity but rather had a more applied motive. The goal of such research is, for the most part, to understand the prerequisites to reading. It has been well established that phonological awareness is related to success in reading. Children who do well on tests of phonological awareness before first grade become better readers than do children who do poorly on tests of phonological awareness. Children who have difficulty reading demonstrate poor phonological awareness even at the age of 10 years (for reviews of this literature, see Adams, 1990; Goswami & Bryant, 1990; Wagner & Torgesen, 1987).

What causes phonological awareness?   There is evidence that both experience and innate characteristics influence the development of phonological awareness. In terms of experience, Mann (1991) suggested that a variety of **secondary language activities** that involve manipulation of the sounds of language, such as songs and word games, may contribute to the development of phonological awareness. Goswami and Bryant (1990) argue that early experience hearing nursery rhymes is another contributor. MacLean and associates (1987) found that 3-year-olds who knew more nursery rhymes also showed higher levels of awareness of onsets and rimes, even when effects of IQ and socioeconomic status were removed; and those children who knew more nursery rhymes at age 3 were better readers at age 6 (Bryant, Bradley, MacLean, & Crossland, 1989). However, Bryant and colleagues measured children's *knowledge* of nursery rhymes, not children's *exposure* to nursery rhymes. It could be that children who are better at remembering nursery rhymes are so because of their phonological skills.

The secondary activity of reading may itself be the biggest cause of phonological awareness. To the extent that this is true, the correlation between phonological awareness and reading acquisition indicates that phonological awareness is a consequence of reading more than that it is a precondition for reading (Wimmer, Landerl, Linortner, & Hummer, 1991). Evidence that phonological awareness, perhaps particularly the awareness of phonemes, depends on learning to read comes from studies that find very low levels of phonemic awareness in adult illiterates (Morais, Cary, Alegria, & Bertelson, 1979) and in Chinese adults, who read a logographic system in which characters stand for meanings instead of an alphabetic system in which characters stand for phonemes (Read, Zhang, Nie, & Ding, 1986).

On the other hand, some children do show awareness of phonemes before learning to read. And, unlike alphabet-illiterate adults, Japanese children who are not learning an alphabetic system show some phonemic awareness (Mann, 1986). Furthermore, children all over the world (many without benefit of literacy) invent secret languages, like pig latin, that depend on the manipulation of phonemes. The incidence of children's spontaneous abilities, combined with the lack of phonological awareness in alphabet-illiterate adults, suggests that phonemic awareness can develop without reading instruction; but in the absence of reading an alphabetic system, this capacity for phonological analysis is lost in adulthood (Mann, 1986, 1991).

Experience in secondary language activities is not the only determinant of phonological awareness. Some children develop phonemic awareness more readily than others, and children who develop phonological awareness easily tend to be successful at learning to read (Wimmer et al., 1991). Thus early phonological awareness may predict reading achievement because children who develop phonological awareness without reading instruction are those who will develop further awareness from instruction most readily.

Genetics may also play a role in children's potential for phonological awareness. For example, in pairs of identical twins, if one twin has particular difficulty with phonological awareness tasks, the other twin is also likely to have difficulty (Goswami & Bryant, 1990). There also may be a reciprocal relationship between phonemic awareness and reading, such that some awareness is important for beginning reading, but progress in reading then enables progress in phonemic awareness, which enables further progress in reading, and so on (Perfetti, Beck, Bell, & Hughes, 1987).

LATER LEXICAL DEVELOPMENT

The transition young children make from knowing no words to knowing words is dramatic and has captured a substantial amount of research attention. The lexical accomplishments of older children seem, in contrast, to be less interesting. However, vocabulary growth continues after early childhood, at an even more rapid pace than during the preschool years (Anglin, 1993). We will consider three phenomena that characterize lexical development after early childhood: (1) growth in vocabulary size, (2) growth in knowledge of word formation processes, and (3) the increasing ability and importance of being able to learn new words from context. We will also consider the relation between vocabulary growth and reading.

Growth in vocabulary size

Once a child's vocabulary outstrips a caregiver's ability to keep records, it is impossible to compile a list of all the words a child knows. The technique used to estimate children's vocabularies in the school-age years is to take

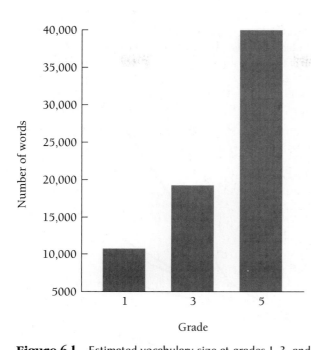

Figure 6.1 Estimated vocabulary size at grades 1, 3, and 5

Source: From "Vocabulary Development: A Morphological Analysis," by J. M. Anglin, Society for Research in Child Development, 58, Serial No. 238. Copyright © 1993 The Society for Research in Child Development, Inc. Reprinted by permission.

a sample of entries from a dictionary, ask the children to define those words, calculate the percentage of words in the sample that the child knows, and then use that percentage to estimate how many of the dictionary entries the child would know—if you had the time and wherewithal to conduct such a test.

The most recent study to estimate vocabulary size in school-age children is by Anglin (1993). Anglin sampled ⅟₅₉₅th (that is, 434) of the estimated 258,601 entries in an unabridged dictionary. Then, in an orally administered multiple-choice test, he asked first-, third-, and fifth-graders to give definitions of those words. (Actually, he tested them on only 196 of the 434 that fifth-graders had an at least remote chance of knowing.) The average number of words the children knew at each grade level were 17, 32, and 67, respectively. Multiplying these raw scores by 595 yields the estimates of vocabulary size shown in Figure 6.1.

Children's vocabularies increased by 9000 words from first to third grade and by 20,000 words from third to fifth grade. What accounts for this increase in rate of vocabulary growth? Anglin suggested that the answer lies in the analysis of the children's vocabularies by type of word. There were five types of words on Anglin's test: (1) root words (like *closet* and *flop*), (2) inflected

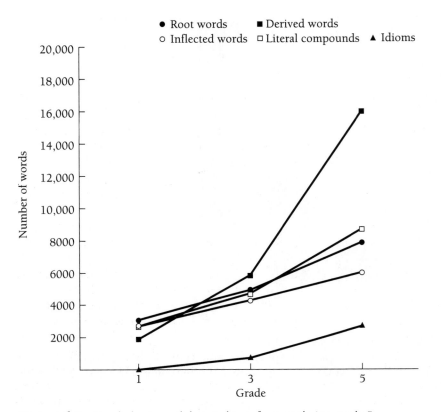

Figure 6.2 Vocabulary growth by word type from grade 1 to grade 5

Source: From "Vocabulary Development: A Morphological Analysis," by J. M. Anglin, Society for Research in Child Development, 58, Serial No. 238. Copyright © 1993 The Society for Research in Child Development, Inc. Reprinted by permission.

words, which are roots plus a grammatical inflection (*boys, soaking,*) (3) derived words, which are roots plus an affix (*sadness: sad + ness; preacher: preach + er*), (4) compounds (*payday, milk cow*), and (5) idioms (*lady's slipper:* a kind of orchid; *carrying on:* misbehavior).

As Figure 6.2 shows, the bigger increase from third to fifth grade compared to first to third grade is in the category of derived words. Remember, the test that produced these results was a multiple-choice recognition test. Anglin suggested that the dramatic growth between third- and fifth-grade children's ability to recognize derived words did not reflect an increase in the number of words known but rather an increase in the children's ability to figure out words they had never heard before, using their knowledge of root and affix meanings. An important part of lexical development in the school years, then, is the development of the morphological knowledge that allows children to decipher what new words mean.

Learning word formation processes

Compounding and derivational morphology   Imagine I showed you a picture of a birdlike creature and said, "This is a wug. What would you call a very tiny wug?" (A wuggie, wuglet, or wugling?) "What would you call a house that a wug lives in?" (A wughouse, wuggery, or wughut?) Or, what would you say if asked, "What would you call a man whose job is to zib?" (A zibber?) These questions may sound familiar to you because they are like other questions Berko (1958) asked of 4- to 7-year old children, who knew that the plural of *wug* is *wug/z/* and that the past tense of *rik* is *rik/t/.*

The children in Berko's study had a harder time with these new questions than they did with providing plural and past-tense forms. (Adults provided the answers given in parentheses above.) The questions above tap knowledge about **derivational morphology.** The tasks of forming plurals and past-tense forms require knowledge of **inflectional morphology.** The difference between the two kinds of morphology is that inflectional morphemes add to a word, but they don't make it into a different word. However, when a derivational morpheme is added to a word, a new word is formed. There is an easy test for determining whether a morphological ending is inflectional or derivational: you can add inflectional endings after derivational ones, but not vice versa (Aitchison, 1987). So, two people who zib for a living are zibbers, not zibser. Knowing derivational morphology is knowing how to build (derive) new words by adding morphemes to other words, or knowing how to interpret newly encountered words by recognizing their component parts. Creating *wughouse* by combining two existing words is an example of another **word-formation process,** called **compounding.**

Developing knowledge of compounding and derivational morphology
Preschool children have been known to coin novel words, as in *Is Anna going to babysitter me?* and *Try to be more rememberful, mom.* (Clark, 1995; see also Becker, 1994; Bowerman, 1985). These lexical innovations show that preschoolers have figured out something about the processes of word formation. However, other data reveal that full control over compounding and derivational morphology is acquired only gradually during later childhood and shows variability even among adults.

Compounding appears to be the earliest acquired word formation process. Forty-seven percent of Berko's subjects showed some productive control of word compounding. Very few of the 4- to 7-year-olds in Berko's (1958) study could produce derived words. Similarly, Clark and Hecht (1982) found that when asked questions such as, "What could we call someone who gives things?" 3-year-olds were likely to produce compounds like *giveman*, whereas 5-year-olds consistently used the *-er* suffix to derive forms like *giver*.

Although the first signs of the ability to form compounds may appear early, even adults do not always have full control over the compounding process. In his developmental study, Derwing (1976) found that only 70% of adult subjects showed full control of compounding when asked to generate compounds with nonsense words. In another study of adults, Gleitman and Gleitman (1979) revealed that some adults will abandon their knowledge of how compounds are formed under some circumstances. The researchers asked adults to paraphrase straightforward word combinations that included a compound (such as *a black bird-house* or a *black-bird house*) and to paraphrase odd combinations such as *bird house-black* and *house-bird glass*. Although all adults consistently interpreted the straightforward combinations in accordance with the structural principle that makes a bird-house a kind of house and a black-bird a kind of bird, there were individual differences in the interpretation of the odd combinations. Adult subjects who were doctoral candidates tended to interpret the compounds according to the structural principle, even if the resultant interpretation was somewhat far-fetched. For example, if a house-black must be a kind of black, then a bird house-black might be a "blackener of houses who is a bird." Similarly, if a house-bird must be a kind of bird, then a house-bird glass could be "a very small drinking cup used by a canary." In contrast, adult subjects who were clerical workers tended to ignore the structural rule and to come up with more plausible interpretations, so that a bird house-black was "a black bird who lives in the house" and a house-bird glass was "a bird that is made of glass." (Quotations are from participants in Gleitman and Gieitman's 1979 study.)

Knowledge of derivational morphology appears later than knowledge of word compounding. In the same study that tested the ability to produce compounds with nonsense words, Derwing (1976) also tested the productive use of derivational morphology in speakers from preschoolers through adults. He found that derivational morphology shows a protracted course of development, with even 17-year-olds not showing full productive control over all morphemes when asked to inflect nonsense stems (Derwing & Baker, 1986). His results are presented in Table 6.1. Tyler and Nagy (1989) similarly found increases in knowledge of derivational morphology up through eighth-graders (who were the oldest children they studied).

Where does knowledge of derivational morphology come from?   The learning process that underlies this protracted development is, according to Derwing and Baker, one of inducing generalizations from input. In their words, "The learning of a morphological rule, surely, depends critically on the

Table 6.1 **Percentage of children and adults able to correctly use word formation processes with nonsense stems**

Process	Preschool years	Early school years	Middle school years	Junior high/ high school	Adult
Agentive + *er*	7	63	80	86	96
Compounding	47	50	65	79	70
Adjective + *y*	0	30	55	86	100
Instrumental + *er*	7	35	45	64	59
Adverb + *ly*	0	13	20	79	81
Diminutive + *ie*	7	5	10	14	33

Source: From "Research on the Acquisition of English Morphology," by B. L. Derwing and W. J. Baker. In P. Fletcher & M. Garman (Eds.), *Language Acquisition,* pp. 209–223. Copyright © 1979 and reprinted with the permission of Cambridge University Press.

discovery of at least a small set of words that succumb to a common morphological analysis" (Derwing & Baker, 1986, p. 327).

On the other hand, there is something about morphological processes that children seem to know at a fairly young age, and that evidence is used to argue that some constraints on morphology are innate. Children know that inflectional morphemes are added to words after derivational morphemes, not the other way around. Peter Gordon (1985) discovered that if you ask 3- to 5-year-old children, "What do you call someone who eats rats?" the children will come up with *rat-eater* and not *rats-eater*, because you can't have a plural inside a compound. By the same token, children will say that someone who eats mice is a *mice-eater* (not *mouse-eater*) because, although *mice* is a plural, it is not formed by an inflectional process.

Gordon argues that this evidence supports a highly nativist view of the development of morphology because it shows that children obey a distinction—between inflections and derivations—that is not provided in input. The finding that children are willing to coin the term *mice-eater* but not *rats-eater* has also been cited in support of the argument (discussed in Chapter 4) that irregular plural forms are stored in the mental lexicon as rote-learned wholes, whereas regular plurals are formed by the application of a rule (see Marcus et al., 1992; Pinker, 1990).

Learning new words in context

The value of knowing word formation processes notwithstanding, most words have to be learned. In Chapter 3, we spent a great deal of time discussing how it is possible for young children to figure out what newly encountered words refer to. In this chapter, we add evidence that with increasing age, children seem to improve their ability to pick up new words. We discuss what this ability to learn words from context consists of, and we consider the role that exposure to new words through reading plays in children's later vocabulary development.

Quick incidental learning   Mabel Rice and her colleagues presented children with new words embedded in an ongoing narration of a cartoon (such as *An artisan comes down the road*). They found that 5-year-olds were capable of picking up new words from this incidental exposure, but 3-year-olds learn almost nothing (Rice, 1990; Rice, Buhr, & Nemeth, 1990; Rice & Woodsmall, 1988). Rice coined the acronym QUIL (for Quick Incidental Learning) for this ability, which seems to emerge only after children have been in the business of learning words for a couple of years. We know from other research that 3-year-olds are capable of fast mapping if they hear a word and see a referent. Thus, this finding of the later emergence of QUIL suggests that, to notice words and identify referents, children aged 3 years and under may be more dependent than older children on certain features of mother/child interaction—such as mothers' following their children's attentional focus and explicitly labeling objects (see Chapter 3). (The children in Rice's studies were American. It would be interesting to see whether 3-year-olds in Samoa, where mothers don't adapt their speech to children the way American mothers do, might be better at incidental word learning.)

In any case, it is certainly a good thing for vocabulary development that children do become able to pick up words from context without explicit labeling, because that is almost the only way children encounter new words after the preschool years. After early childhood, a majority of children learn most of their words by figuring out the meaning of new words from the context in which they are used.

The process of learning words from context   Although we do not have developmental data that tell us how the ability to pick up words from context increases after the age of 5 years, it is clear that the process is complex and that there are differences among children (and probably also among adults) in how able they are to do this. According to Sternberg (1987), the process of learning words from context involves identifying all the relevant information in the context, combining the relevant cues to converge on a definition of an unknown word, and drawing on background knowledge. Consider, for example, the following passage from Sternberg (1987):

> Although for the others the party was a splendid success, the couple there on the blind date was not enjoying the festivities in the least. An *acapnotic,* he disliked her smoking; and when he removed his hat, she, who preferred "ageless" men, eyed his increasing *phalacrosis* and grimaced. (p. 91)

To determine from the context what the words *acapnotic* and *phalacrosis* mean, you need to figure out that disliking smoking is a clue to the meaning of *acapnotic;* and her preference for ageless men and that his phalacrosis showed when he removed his hat are clues to the meaning of *phalacrosis.* If you know that baldness is a condition of aging, that helps too.

On the other hand, research has shown that explicit teaching of vocabulary is an effective means of building a stock of known words (Pressley, Levin, & McDaniel, 1987). The fact that vocabulary can be explicitly taught, combined with the fact that most new words are encountered in context, is the source of some disagreement over how to help school-age children increase their vocabularies. Sternberg (1987) has argued that the focus should be on helping children get better at making use of context. Others have argued that, although contextual approaches are useful for inferring what a newly encountered word means, explicit instruction is the best way for building a vocabulary of remembered words (Pressley et al., 1987). In fact, explicit vocabulary instruction is part of many classrooms (McKeown & Curtis, 1987).

Reading and vocabulary development   When educators debate how best to help children build their vocabularies, the issue is not only that a large vocabulary is a desirable end in and of itself. It is also true that vocabulary knowledge and reading skill are strongly related (for example, Chall, Jacobs, & Baldwin, 1990; McKeown & Curtis, 1987; Stanovich, 1986). Two directions of influence seem to underlie the well-established relation between vocabulary and reading. First, the more words you know, the better able you will be to understand what you read (Stanovich, 1986). In addition, the same skills that got you a big vocabulary in the first place (being able to figure things out from the context) are useful for reading comprehension (Sternberg, 1987). The relation between reading skill and vocabulary size also works in the other direction

(Stanovich, 1986). Good readers will have bigger vocabularies because good readers read more, and reading is a major source of exposure to new words. There is strong evidence that the amount of reading children do predicts their vocabulary size (Cunningham & Stanovich, 1991). Consistent with the evidence that exposure to words through reading and the ability to learn new words in context are the crucial influences on vocabulary development after early childhood, Gathercole and associates (1992) found that the influence of phonological memory skills on vocabulary development subsides after the age of 5.

LATER SYNTACTIC DEVELOPMENT

When we left the 4- to 5-year-old children at the end of Chapter 4, they appeared to have mastered the grammar of the language. The sentences that 5-year-olds produce are no longer missing elements that would be in adults' sentences, and 5-year-olds' sentences include a variety of long, complex constructions. However, syntactic development is not over at age 5. There are clear developmental changes in the frequency of complex constructions, such as expanded noun phrases, adverbial clauses, subordinate clauses, and so on. (See Scott, 1988, for a description of these quantitative developmental changes.) In this chapter, we will focus on two qualitative changes in children's syntax that occur after the age of 5 years. One change is in the ability to interpret coreference relations in complex sentences. The other is children's development of syntactic devices for linking successive utterances together into longer stretches of discourse.

Understanding coreference relations in complex sentences

Problems children have with coreference   Certain sentence constructions cause difficulty for most 5-year-olds, such as the following:

Sentence	Difficulty
John is easy to see.	Who is easy to see and who does the seeing?
John promised Bill to go.	Who does the going?
John asked Bill what to do.	Who does the doing?
He knew that John was going to win the race.	To whom does *he* refer?

All the interpretive difficulties in these sentences concern who is being referred to. In linguistic terminology, the problem is in interpreting the **coreference relations** in these sentences.

Carol Chomsky (1969) studied comprehension of these sentence forms in children aged 5 to 10 years, and on the basis of her data she countered the then-prevailing view that language acquisition was complete by the age of 5. She claimed that 5-year-old children have not acquired all the structural principles of the grammar, and they rely, as younger children do, on strategies that look to meaning, context, or surface properties of the sentence for clues to sentence interpretation. For example, Chomsky found that children often interpret the noun phrase that is closest to the verb as the subject of that verb. She termed this the **Minimal Distance Principle (MDP).** Like the strategies that younger children use to interpret sentences they cannot fully analyze, the MDP works for many sentences that children are likely to hear (*John threw the ball. The ball rolled into the street.*). However, it yields the wrong interpretation when applied to sentences like *John promised Bill to go.* Although there are huge individual differences, with some children mastering nearly all forms by age 5 years, some children do not master interpretation of these structures until age 9 years (Chomsky, 1969).

We could stop our discussion of coreference relations at this point, simply offering the evidence that children's grammars are not fully adultlike even at the age of 5. In fact, this conclusion is where the matter rested for many years after Carol Chomsky's work. Syntax development after age 5 years received very little research attention until the 1980s, when the theory of Universal Grammar proposed by Noam Chomsky (Carol Chomsky's husband) made the source of difficulty in the above sentences central to linguistic theory and to the Universal Grammar approach to language acquisition.

Remember, according to the Universal Grammar approach, UG is innate in all children. Furthermore, according to current UG theory (which is the Government and Binding theory (GB) first proposed by Chomsky, 1981), there is a component of UG that handles coreference relations. Thus there is a seeming contradiction—UG is innate, UG handles the interpretation of coreference relations, yet children (who are held to have UG in their heads) have difficulty interpreting coreference relations. To follow how the question of children's interpretation of coreference relations has been studied in recent years, it is necessary to introduce some elements of the Government and Binding theory that is the current theory of Universal Grammar.

Before we do that however, it should be pointed out that many of the phenomena discussed in Chapter 4 are also studied within a GB framework, even though that framework was not presented there. For example, describing the nature of children's early sentences as thematically based combinations of lexical categories (Radford, 1990, 1995) comes from a GB framework (although an essentially similar claim about the semantic basis of early word combinations can be made without the GB vocabulary). Similarly, the research on children's understanding of the difference in possible interpretations between sentences such as *When did the boy say he fell* versus *When did the boy say how he fell* is conducted within a GB framework. We introduced this latter phenomenon in Chapter 4 without much linguistic discussion simply to illustrate that children know complex and subtle aspects of syntax. In the next section on children's understanding of coreference relations in complex sentences, we will go a little further than we did in Chapter 4 in describing the linguistic framework behind the research.

Government and Binding theory   In the following paragraphs, we will walk through the GB account of the syntactic knowledge that underlies adults' interpretation of coreference relations and the current proposals for the source of children's difficulties. We will do so with as little syntactic detail as possible, providing further references for the interested and intrepid to pursue.

Consider the following sentence from Hsu, Cairns, Eisenberg, and Schlisselberg (1989):

(1) The zebra told the deer to jump over the fence.

When asked to act out this sentence with toys, both children and adults reliably make the deer do the jumping (Chomsky, 1969; Goodluck, 1981). However, given a different type of sentence, such as

(2) The zebra touched the deer after jumping over the fence.

adults interpret the sentence as meaning that the zebra did the jumping, but many children interpret the sentence as meaning that the deer did the jumping (Chomsky, 1969; Goodluck, 1981; Hsu, Cairns, & Fiengo, 1985).

The question for psychologists and linguists concerns what is inside the heads of adults and children that leads to their different interpretations. As Carol Chomsky observed in 1969, children seem to behave in accordance with a principle that says that the noun phrase closest to the verb is the subject of that verb (the MDP). Because *the deer* is closer to *jump* than *the zebra* is in both sentences, children interpret both sentences as indicating that the deer is doing the jumping. This principle works for sentence (1). However, MDP does not work as a general linguistic principle, as sentence (2) illustrates. Therefore, the Minimal Distance Principle cannot be the rule adults apply. The question then becomes, What principle do adults use and how do children get it?

To explain adults' interpretation of coreference relations, we need to make explicit that each sentence above contains a null element (or, in GB terminology, an empty category). Following linguistic convention, we will call this element PRO. Thus the sentences are represented as

(1)

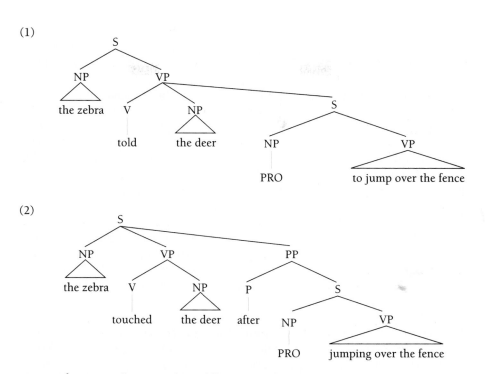

(2)

Figure 6.3 Tree diagrams of two different sentence constructions

Source: From "Control and Coreference in Early Child Language," by J. R. Hsu et al., Journal of Child Language, 16, p. 600. Copyright © 1989 and reprinted with the permission of Cambridge University Press.

The zebra told the deer PRO to jump over the fence.

The zebra touched the deer after PRO jumping over the fence.

The question then becomes, What does PRO refer to? or, in the language of GB theory, What controls PRO? The answer is that PRO is controlled by the closest noun phrase—not closest in terms of the linear order of words in the sentence but in terms of sentence constituents that have particular structural relations to each other. That is, PRO refers to the closest noun phrase that has a *c(constituent)-commanding* relation to PRO.

Now all we need to do is define **c-command,** but to do that we have to analyze the sentences into their constituent structures. Figure 6.3 illustrates the structure of sentences (1) and (2) using the **tree diagram** convention of linguistics. The definition of c-command is in terms of these tree diagrams. One branching node of the tree c-commands another if the branching node that immediately dominates it dominates the second also. In (1), the node immediately above *the deer* is also above PRO, so *the deer* c-commands PRO, and PRO refers to *the deer*. In (2), the node immediately above *the deer* is not above PRO; but the node above *the zebra* is. In (2), *the zebra* c-commands PRO, and PRO refers to the zebra.

According to Government and Binding theory, the linguistic principles just outlined (the principle of control, the structural c-command relations that are part of the definition of control, and other principles that are part of GB theory) are part of what every adult knows about the grammar of language. This linguistic knowledge underlies interpretation of coreference relations in a wide range of sentence forms. Although this knowledge is much more complicated than the MDP, it has the advantage of working for all coreference relations, and so it seems reasonable to attribute this knowledge to adults. (Exactly how well GB theory works as currently formulated is debated within linguistics; see Goodluck, 1981; Sherman & Lust, 1993; and references cited therein for those arguments. For the present purpose of understanding the developmental question, we will accept GB theory as the correct account of adults' underlying knowledge.) The question we need to ask now is, How do we account for the child data?

Explanations of children's nonadultlike performance   Why children interpret coreference relations differently than adults do and how children eventually achieve adultlike interpretations are at present open and actively researched questions. We will not go through the details of specific studies here but instead will outline the types of answers that have been proposed.

According to one view, children do not have the adult system, and their system is based on **sentence interpretation strategies** that depend on the meaning or pragmatics of surface features of the sentence, rather than on purely linguistic principles. Sometimes these strategies lead to nonadultlike interpretations. Only after the age of 5 years are the adult structural principles acquired. This is the kind of explanation of her data that Carol Chomsky proposed in 1969, in pre–Government and Binding days, and it has also been proposed more recently by others (Goodluck, 1991; Hsu et al., 1985).

Karmiloff-Smith has also argued that children's performance is based on nonadultlike interpretation procedures (Karmiloff-Smith, 1986). Her argument is part of a broader one she makes about the nature of syntactic development and the changes that occur after age 5 years. According to Karmiloff-Smith, at the age of about 5 years, children have built up a series of procedures for language use and understanding, but these procedures are not yet organized into a coherent system. For this reason, children's performance is neither adultlike nor consistent. Between the ages of 5 and 8 years, children actively work on establishing a coherent system. In Karmiloff-Smith's terminology, language becomes a **"problem-space"** for children as they analyze their collection of procedures and integrate them into a single coherent system.

Karmiloff-Smith does not assume that the adult system is the one described by GB theory, but her arguments about syntactic development after the age of 5 have application to the data on children's interpretation of coreference relations. Karmiloff-Smith argues that some change in children's linguistic understanding between 5 and 8 years must occur in order to explain that before the age of 8, children's interpretation of sentences can be influenced by the specifics of the experimental task; but that after age 8, children, like adults, are able to interpret sentences as abstract objects out of context. That ability is achieved only as a result of the children's active work on their internal linguistic systems.

This kind of explanation is, of course, anathema to theorists who consider language the result of an innate, language-specific module. Other proposals work within the assumptions of Universal Grammar to explain why children do not perform in accordance with GB theory principles. According to the **maturation hypothesis,** the child's system is initially not adultlike but becomes so as the result of maturation. The principles underlying interpretation of coreference relations happen to emerge late in the course of development (Borer & Wexler, 1987). In contrast, the **continuity hypothesis** asserts that all the adult grammatical principles are there from the start; children's nonadultlike performance is attributed to difficulty in obeying those principles in experimental tasks. This latter account, like other strategy-based explanations for children's performance, suggests that children sometimes base their sentence interpretation on nonlinguistic factors. However, this interpretation saves continuity of the grammar in the face of noncontinuity of performance by asserting that the grammatical principles are always there, just not always used (Grimshaw & Rosen, 1990; Sherman & Lust, 1993). In support of the continuity hypothesis, Grimshaw and Rosen (1990) argue that if children didn't have the principles at all, one would expect errors that children do not in fact make, such as producing sentences that violate binding principles. That is, children do not say things like *John promised Bill to go* meaning that Bill will do the going. Last, some propose that the syntactic principles of the grammar are present at the outset and that all the nonadultlike aspects of children's performance are due either to (1) incomplete knowledge of semantics or the lexicon (McDaniel, Cairns, & Hsu, 1990/1991; Sherman & Lust, 1993) or (2) misanalysis of the structure of the sentences (McDaniel & Cairns, 1990).

For the reader who may have gotten lost in some of the syntactic details in the foregoing account, there are two points to get out of this discussion. One is an understanding of the GB approach to studying language acquisition. That approach, in broad outline, consists of taking the principles of Government and Binding theory as a description of the endpoint of development and asking when children show evidence that they have these principles. Where children show nonadultlike performance, the challenge is to explain why that should be the case if the principles are innate. A second point to be gleaned from this taste of the GB approach is that the structural knowledge all adults have is extremely complex and not obvious, even to college students with years of language experience. Thus accounting for how such knowledge could be acquired is a serious challenge for theoretical approaches that exclude innateness. Having made those points, we turn now to a discussion of a later-developing syntactic skill that does not require GB terminology for its description.

Developing the syntactic means of discourse cohesion

Syntactic development after the age of 5 years includes acquiring the means for using syntactic devices to link multiple utterances together. The change in productive language this acquisition allows can be illustrated with two stories collected by Karmiloff-Smith (1986). Children between 4 and 9 years old were asked to tell a story from a picture book with no text. The story involved a balloon vendor and a boy. A 4-year-old produced the following narrative:

> There's a little boy in red. He's walking along and he sees a balloon man and he gives him a green one and he walks off home and it flies away into the sky so he cries. (Karmiloff-Smith, 1986, p. 471)

The problem here is in the use of pronouns. Without the book, a listener can't tell to whom the different *he's* refer. Each clause by itself— *he sees a balloon man* and *he gives him a green one*—is grammatical, and the pronouns refer appropriately to referents in the picture being described. However, the listener can't tell whether the person referred to by *he* is the same from one sentence to the next. (The heavy use of *and* to link clauses together is also typical of the narratives produced by children this age; Peterson & McCabe, 1988.)

In contrast, a 9-year-old produced the following story:

> A little boy is walking home. He sees a balloon man. The balloon man gives him a green balloon so he happily goes off home with it, but the balloon suddenly flies out of his hand and so he starts to cry. (Karmiloff-Smith, 1986, p. 472)

In this story, not only can the listener tell to whom the *he's* refer, but also the use of pronouns makes the story flow by linking one utterance to the next. Both the 4-year-old and the 9-year-old use the linguistic device of pronominalization (that is, using pronouns to refer to things). The difference between them is that the 4-year-old uses pronouns only to refer to things in the world, whereas the 9-year-old uses pronouns to refer to things in other sentences, thereby creating a cohesive narrative. In sum, according to Karmiloff-Smith, the 4- and

5-year-olds' grammar is a grammar for producing sentences. After the age of 8, children use their grammars for producing text. The question of how children develop the ability to produce long spans of connected text is the topic of the section on narrative development.

LATER DISCOURSE DEVELOPMENT

Long spans of connected utterances produced by several speakers are conversations; when produced by a single speaker, they are monologues. The most studied form of monologue is the narrative, or story. In the next two sections, we will pick up our discussion of discourse development where we left off in Chapter 5, and we will discuss later developments in conversation and narrative production.

Conversation

Most studies of conversation among children past the age of 5 years examine conversation as a social phenomenon (as in the study of friendship) or as a sociolinguistic phenomenon (as in the study of styles of speech particular to certain social groups). We will discuss the sociolinguistic research in a later section of this chapter. Here we will ask whether any developmental trends in conversation during the school-age years are separate from the socio-linguistic phenomenon of learning to talk the way members of your social group do.

Bruce Dorval and Carol Eckerman (1984) asked this question by creating groups of acquainted peers using students from second grade, fifth grade, ninth grade, and twelfth grade and young adults. After listening to tape recordings of the conversations of five different groups at each age level (each group consisting of three males and three females), Dorval and Eckerman described developmental changes that continue trends seen in the younger children's conversations. That is, with increasing age, children's contributions to conversation are more frequently relevant to the current topic, and, no doubt as a result, the length of continuous dialogue the groups can maintain increases. Figures 6.4 and 6.5 illustrate some of Dorval and Eckerman's results. The biggest developmental changes in children's ability to sustain conversation come between second and fifth grade. However, there are other later changes in the quality of conversation that are not revealed in the figures. For example, although the frequency of related turns increased only slightly from fifth to twelfth grade, the kind of related turn changed significantly. Fifth-graders' related turns were more likely to be factually related to the prior turn, whereas twelfth-graders and adults more frequently responded to the feelings or attitudes expressed by the previous speaker (Dorval & Eckerman, 1984).

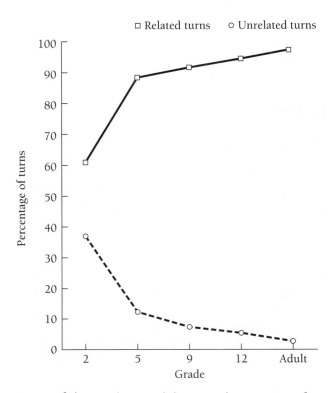

Figure 6.4 Developmental changes in the percentage of turns in group conversation that are related and unrelated to the conversational topic

Source: Based on data in Dorval and Eckerman, 1984.

We should point out that there is no single kind of adultlevel conversation that is the endpoint of development. The kinds of conversations that adults have differ depending on who is talking, what they are talking about, and a host of other variables.

Narratives

A narrative is a description of a real or fictional past event, and there are many different kinds, or **genres,** of narratives. Narratives can recount a past event that one has personally experienced, describe a type of event such as seeing the dentist or attending a birthday party (these are called **scripts**), or tell a story. The demands on the speaker in each narrative genre are somewhat different, and even the understanding that these genres differ is only gradually achieved. Judith Hudson and Lauren Shapiro (1991) asked preschoolers, first-graders, and third-graders to produce examples of each type of narrative and found that

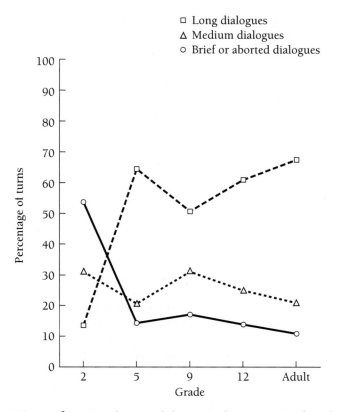

Figure 6.5   Developmental changes in the percentage of speaker turns occurring in brief, medium, and long dialogues. Dialogues were defined as a sequence of turns on the same topic and were categorized as brief or aborted (between I and I0 turns), medium (between II and 30 turns), and long (3I+ turns).

Source: Based on data in Dorval and Eckerman, 1984.

preschoolers' stories, scripts, and personal narratives were hardly distinguishable from each other. First-graders produced reasonably good examples of personal narratives and scripts, but their stories were incomplete. Third-graders told better stories than first-graders did, although even the third-graders' stories were not adultlike in structure.

Telling a story seems to be the most demanding narrative genre, and research on children's abilities to tell stories makes it clear that this skill takes a long time to develop. In the rest of this section, we will consider what a good story consists of, we will describe developmental changes in the stories that children tell, and we will consider what developments underlie children's changing narrative abilities. (The interested reader is referred to research that focuses on children's abilities to tell personal narratives—Fivush, Gray, & Fromhoff, 1987; Hudson, 1990; Lucariello & Nelson, 1987; McCabe & Peterson, 1991; and scripts—Fivush & Slackman, 1986; Hudson & Nelson, 1986; Nelson & Gruendel, 1986.)

What makes a story good? A variety of research suggests that good stories must have the properties of coherence and cohesion. **Coherence** refers to the structure of a story; the sequence of events must be related to each other in a meaningful way (Shapiro & Hudson, 1991). **Cohesion** refers to the use of linguistic devices to link sentences together. The development of the ability to tell stories is the development of coherence and cohesion in narrative production.

The development of story coherence   Stories have a structure, and telling a coherent story requires knowing what that structure is. The term **story grammar** has been used to refer to the structure all stories follow. Although different researchers have proposed somewhat different grammars, most agree on the following: (1) A story consists of a *setting* and one or more *episodes* (Johnston, 1982, based on Stein & Glenn, 1979); (2) the setting includes both the *place* (once upon a time in a faraway kingdom) and the *characters* (there lived a girl named Cinderella, with her stepmother and three ugly stepsisters); and (3) each episode includes an *initiating event* (an announcement of a ball to which all the eligible young maidens of the land are invited), a *problem* or an obstacle (nothing to wear and no means of transportation), and a *resolution* of the problem (action by the Fairy Godmother; actually, the full story of Cinderella has several episodes). Accounts of past events that do not have this structure are judged by adults to be either poor stories (McCabe & Peterson, 1984) or not stories at all (Stein, 1988).

A variety of different methods have been employed to elicit stories from children in order to examine the development of story structure. Perhaps the most straightforward is simply to ask children to make up a story. Studies employing this method have found a clear developmental progression in the structure of the stories children tell. Often, young children's stories are descriptions of past events that are more like fragments of a story than a united whole. For example, although 5-year-olds' stories are likely to have setting information and some initiating event, they often leave episodes unresolved (Nelson & Gruendel, 1981). By the age of 6 years, children are usually able to produce a single-episode story that includes all the major story components (Kemper, 1984). From age 6 to 10 years, children develop the ability to produce stories with multiple coordinated events and embedded events. Another developmental change is the inclusion of reference to the internal motivations or mental states of the actors in a story. Two-year-olds' stories tend to contain actions alone, with no account of why those actions

Box 6.1 Developmental changes in the structural complexity of children's fantasy narratives

Level 1 stories (typical of 3-year-olds):

Consists of a series of associated events without the structure of a story.

> A little duck went swimming. Then the crab came. A lobster came. And a popsicle was playing by itself.

Level 3 stories (typical of 6-year-olds):

Contains major plot elements but reference to internal states and motivations tend to be absent. Stories tend to contain only a single episode.

> Once there was a little girl. She went walking in the woods and soon it was dark. It was so dark that she couldn't find her way back home. She cried and cried. An owl heard her and asked if she was lost. She said yes. The owl said he would help her find her way home. He flew up in the air and looked around. After finding out which way to go he said, "Okay, follow me." Then he led the girl out of the woods and showed her the way home. When she got back home she was so happy. She gave the friendly owl a kiss and thanked him and told her parents she would never go walking in the woods again by herself. The end.

Level 5 stories (typical of 9-year-olds):

Episodes are well developed and a story often consists of multiple episodes. Internal motivations are included.

> Once Batman and Robin were in a haunted house. Robin fell through a trap door in the floor and landed in an underground river. Robin pressed his magic watch to signal Batman for help. Batman heard the signal and looked all over the house for Robin. Then he saw the trap door. He lowered a rope from his Bat belt and pulled Robin out of the water. Then they heard a scream. They thought it was a girl, but it was Spiderman. They looked around and the screams seemed to come from the attic.

(continued)

Box 6.1 *(continued)*

Batman and Robin ran up to the attic to save the girl but Spiderman was hiding behind the door waiting for them. When they came in Spiderman threw an extra strong Spider net over them. They tried to get out but they couldn't. "I've got you now," he said. "I'm going to kill you, and Wonderwoman and I are going to take your Batmobile and live in your Bat Cave." But Batman told him that he had a special key for the Batmobile and Bat Cave. And when Spiderman came over to get the key Batman hit him right in the face and knocked him down. Then Batman and Robin got out of the net and beat up Spiderman and put him in jail so he wouldn't bother them anymore. The end.

Source: From "The Development of Structural Complexity in Children's Fantasy Narratives," by G. J. Botvin and B. Sutton-Smith, 1977, *Developmental Psychology, 13,* 377–388. Copyright © 1977 American Psychological Association. Reprinted with permission.

were produced. Mention of internal motives begins around age 8 but is not consistently present until much later (for example, Hudson & Shapiro, 1991; Kemper, 1984).

Botvin and Sutton-Smith (1977) elicited fantasy narratives from 220 children between 3 and 12 years old and scored the narratives in terms of structural complexity. They found that with increasing age, children's stories included an increasing number of story-grammar components. The types of stories typical for 3-year-olds, 6-year-olds, and 9-year-olds are described in Box 6.1.

Another technique for eliciting stories from children is to provide children with a sequence of pictures and ask them to tell the story that is happening in the pictures. One sequence of pictures that has been used in several studies of children's narrative development is a wordless book by Mercer Mayer, entitled *Frog, Where Are You?* (Mayer, 1969). The story in this book begins with a pet frog escaping, after which a sequence of misadventures befall a boy and his dog as they search for and eventually find the missing frog. This book has been used by at least 150 different researchers studying children acquiring 50 different languages (Berman & Slobin, 1994). Although you might think that providing children with the story in pictures would eliminate developmental differences in plot structure, that doesn't happen. As was the case for spontaneous stories, preschoolers tend not to be able to tell a coherent story, and even 10-year-olds' stories are not quite adultlike.

Ruth Berman (1988) elicited "frog stories" from Hebrew speakers aged 3, 4, 5, 7, 9, 11 years and adult. She found that 3- and 4-year-olds tended to describe each picture individually. From school-age up, children organized the events into longer stretches and made reference to the goal of finding the frog. However, only adults organized the entire sequence of events into a single whole. Using the same picture book and similar age groups of English speakers in Australia, Gillian Wigglesworth (1993) similarly found a developmental increase in the size of the span of discourse that children can organize into a coherent and cohesive whole.

The development of linguistic cohesion   A good narrative is more than just an assemblage of the necessary components of a story. If we think of each element in a narrative as expressed by a clause, then creating a narrative requires linking the clauses together. Adults make use of a variety of linguistic devices for linking clauses into a single cohesive piece. These devices for creating discourse cohesion include conjunctions, relative clauses, and pronouns used to refer to previously introduced characters (anaphoric reference) (Halliday & Hasan, 1976).

Children as young as 3 years do use conjunctions and pronouns (Bruner & Lucariello, 1989; Levy, 1989); however, full control over these devices is not complete even by the age of 8 years. With respect to conjunctions, children first rely heavily on the coordinating conjunction *and* to link clauses. Peterson and McCabe (1988) describe *and* as serving as "discourse glue." Between the ages of 5 and 10 years, children develop the use of other conjunctions, first temporal conjunctions (then), followed by causal conjunctions (because), and later subordination conjunctions (while).

With respect to pronominalization, Karmiloff-Smith (1986) describes children as going through three developmental stages. As we discussed in reference to grammatical development earlier in this chapter, children under the age of 5 years tend not to use pronominalization to link utterances. Given the task of telling a story from a sequence of pictures, children under 5 years tend to describe each picture individually. Pronouns are used to refer to referents in the pictures, not to referents in previous sentences. In the second stage, from 5 to 8 years, children use what Karmiloff-Smith terms a **thematic subject strategy,** in which the main character of the story is always referred to with a pronoun and all the other characters are referred to with nominal forms (for example, the boy is *he,* and the other characters are *the dog, the frog,* but not *he*). Only at the third stage, after the age of 8 years, do children employ what is known as full **anaphoric reference,** in which pronouns are used to maintain reference to characters (such as *The boy woke up. He looked for his frog.*) and nominal forms are used to introduce new characters or to switch reference (*The boy woke up. The frog was gone.*). Although other research confirms this basic order of development, the age at which children use anaphoric reference may depend on the task, the language, and the individual child. For example, Bamberg (1987)—who was actually the first to use the frog book, in his 1985 dissertation—allowed children to hear the story several times before telling it, and he found anaphoric reference in German-speaking children under age 5. Wigglesworth (under review) found individual differences in the strategy that narrators adopted that depended not only on their age but also on the complexity of the referencing task at that particular point in the story.

There are other linguistic devices, in addition to conjunctions and pronominalization, that narrators can use to serve their literary ends. A skillful narrative does not simply present events in linear order. Rather, the events are packed into hierarchical constructions, and narrators have choices among linguistic means of packaging. For example, narrators can choose different aspectual forms (*The boy looked* versus *The boy was looking*), and they can use relative clauses to create the foreground or background for different events or characters. Learning to produce narratives includes learning the particular linguistic devices the language makes available to serve these expressive functions. In general, young children's narratives tend to be more similar to each other's than to older children's and adults' (given the same story to tell) because young children use fewer expressive options (Berman & Slobin, 1994). Box 6.2 presents examples of frog stories told by children of different ages.

What underlies narrative development?   Producing a coherent and cohesive narrative requires both knowledge of the structure of a story and control over the linguistic devices that produce cohesion. Telling a story also requires knowledge about the world. To invent a story with a goal, an obstacle, and a resolution, you need to know something about goals, about the kinds of things that can present obstacles, and about the ways that obstacles can be overcome (Shapiro & Hudson, 1991). Finally, telling a story is a communicative act that requires consideration of the listener's knowledge and ability to understand.

Narrative development continues into late childhood and even into adulthood, because the separate knowledges on which narrative production depends take a long time to acquire and because the task of coordinating these various knowledge structures, linguistic devices, and communicative considerations is substantial. There is evidence that the cognitive demands of the storytelling task interfere with children's ability to tell a story, even when the children have the component competencies. For example, Shapiro and Hudson (1991) used a picture-eliciting task with 4- and 6-year-olds and found that the children used more sophisticated linguistic devices to achieve cohesion when the pictures provided the goal, the obstacle, and the solution than when the pictures provided only a sequence of events and the children had to invent these story components. The task of producing a narrative, like the task of participating in conversation, makes both content and processing demands of the speaker. When the processing demands exceed their capacity, children make

---

Box 6.2 Developmental changes in picture-elicited narratives

The narrators are describing an episode in which a boy climbs a tree, the boy causes an owl to emerge from a hole in the tree, and the owl causes the boy to fall (Berman & Slobin, 1994, pp. 13–14).

5-year-old:

> And then he goes up there. An then an owl comes out and he falls.

5-year-old (more advanced):

> And the boy was looking through the tree when a owl came out and bammed him on the ground.

9-year-old:

> The owl came out of its tree, and scared the little boy. The little boy fell.

> (Note reference to internal state, *scared.*)

Adult (translated from German):

> Poor Tom has also not found the frog in the tree, but has scared an owl to death, who now comes flying out of the tree and scared Tom so much that he loses his grip on the tree and falls splat on his back, falls down on the ground.

---

trade-offs (although not necessarily consciously), so that the use of linguistic devices to achieve cohesion is more sophisticated when less effort is required to achieve coherence (see also Shatz, 1985).

Although there clearly are developmental changes in narrative production, there is also clearly not a single endpoint that all speakers achieve. In this chapter, we have considered only the development of the minimal adult-level ability to produce a narrative. We haven't considered how great authors develop their skills or even what distinguishes great stories from ordinary ones. That topic is more central to the discipline of literary theory but has also been considered by psychologists who study language (see Bruner, 1986; Winner, Gardner, Silberstein, & Meyer, 1988).

LATER DEVELOPMENT OF COMMUNICATION SKILLS

In Chapter 5, regarding communication skills in preschoolers, we discussed findings from the two research approaches taken in studying children's communicative abilities: experimental and naturalistic. Experimental studies give children a task such as describing one picture so that a listener can identify it in an array of pictures. Such studies typically find that children give informationally inadequate messages. Furthermore, when 5-year-olds as listeners are given inadequate information, they are likely to go ahead and act anyway rather than request more information (Flavell, Speer, Green, & August, 1981).

Naturalistic studies found evidence of greater communicative competence in children's spontaneous behavior than researchers had observed in experimental settings (for example, Keenan, 1974; Shatz & Gelman, 1973). These findings presented a challenge to some of the stronger conclusions that had been drawn from laboratory work, such as the conclusion that preschoolers are so egocentric that they are incapable of considering the listener's perspective. But if egocentrism is not the explanation for children's communicative failures, something else must be. In laboratory referential communication tasks, children in the early elementary school years often fail to communicate. The evidence of naturalistic abilities in preschoolers leaves unanswered the question of why 5-year-old speakers produce such communicatively inadequate messages and 5-year-old listeners tolerate them.

Comprehension monitoring

Part of the explanation of 5-year-olds' communicative difficulties seems to be that 5-year-olds do not realize when a message is inadequate. In studies where children are asked to assess the quality of incomplete or ambiguous messages, researchers typically find that children in kindergarten and early elementary grades overestimate the message quality (for example, Markman, 1977; Robinson, 1981). Children tend to think that the messages they were given were fine when, by design, they were not. The process of message evaluation is also referred to as **comprehension monitoring.** When children are given inadequate directions, they act anyway because they don't realize that they don't understand.

In a major investigation of the development of comprehension monitoring, Flavell, Spear, Green, and August (1981) gave kindergarteners and second-graders the task of making buildings with blocks according to instructions that they were told had been previously tape-recorded by a 12-year-old named

Kiersten. Sometimes the instructions were clear, and sometimes they were contradictory, incomplete, or impossible to execute with the blocks available. Flavell and colleagues (1981) found that second-graders were more likely than kindergarteners to express difficulty in following the inadequate instructions, evidenced by producing puzzled facial expressions, replaying the tape, or saying something to the experimenter.

In addition, after the children finished each building (following Kiersten's instructions), they were asked two questions: (1) Did they think their building looked exactly like the one that Kiersten built or might it look different? and (2) Did they think that Kiersten had done a good or bad job of telling them how to make a building exactly like hers? The kindergarteners were more likely than the second-graders to say that their building looked exactly like Kiersten's (even when the instructions were too inadequate to guarantee that), and they were more likely to say that Kiersten had done a good job even when she hadn't. In another study, Beal and Flavell (1983) found that the ability to evaluate messages improves from preschool through first grade, although even first-graders had difficulty. This inability to evaluate messages may go a long way toward explaining the communication failures children in the early elementary grades experience. If you don't know that message is inadequate, then as a speaker you don't know you need to revise it and as a listener you don't know to request more information.

Message repair

Realizing that a message is inadequate is crucial to the ability to repair it, but simply telling children that their messages are inadequate is not sufficient to elicit repairs. Several studies using a referential communication task have looked at children's ability to repair messages when either the experimenter or another child asks for more information (Alvy, 1968; Glucksberg & Krauss, 1967; Karabenick & Miller, 1977; Peterson, Danner, & Flavell, 1972). These studies find that children's performance is better when the task is to describe familiar, easily labeled items (Karabenick & Miller, 1977) than when the stimuli are abstract, difficult to describe figures (Glucksberg & Krauss, 1967). However, these studies also suggest that children from age 5 to 7 years are successful at providing more information to repair an inadequate message less than half the time, even under the best of circumstances (Karabenick & Miller, 1977).

In contrast, if the children themselves realize that a message is inadequate, they are far more successful at message repair. Beal (1987) gave first- and second-grade children road maps that were drawn with colored felt pens on posterboard, and she gave them directions for driving a toy car on the map to particular locations. The messages (like Kiersten's block building instructions) were sometimes conflicting or ambiguous. In this study, first-graders recognized only half of the inadequate messages, whereas second-graders recognized over two-thirds. When both first- and second-graders were asked to "fix up" the messages they recognized as inadequate, they were almost always able to do so. In sum, the evidence suggests that comprehension monitoring is a major component of communication skill, which raises the question of what underlies the development of comprehension monitoring. Why can't young children evaluate messages, and what develops during the school years that allows improvement in this ability?

Children's theory of mind

To answer these questions about what underlies the later changes in children's communication skill, we refer back to the development that was at the heart of early communicative development—the development of the child's theory of mind.

Communication depends on understanding (1) that mental entities such as knowledge, thoughts, and beliefs exist and (2) that others may not share your knowledge, thoughts, and beliefs; (3) that the information in one mind can come to be shared if it is transmitted in a message, but (4) that messages have to include all the information to be transferred (Beal, 1988). What develops in children, according to Beal (1988), is the understanding that the message is the vehicle for transmitting information. Preschool children seem not to understand this, instead assuming that "individuals will understand one another as long as a message is produced and received" (Beal, 1988, p. 316). It isn't until children understand that messages don't automatically represent the speaker's intended meaning that children can revise their own messages and request others to revise theirs.

As was the case for many of the later developments discussed, there is no single endpoint that all adults reach in the development of communication skills. As adults we may understand that knowing something and successfully communicating that knowledge are two different things, but we are not always sufficiently attentive to the task of communicating or sufficiently skillful at putting our ideas into words. There is no age at which communication is always successful. Computer programmers write documentation that is un-decipherable to the novice. Even college professors are occasionally less than perfectly clear.

On the listener's side, communicative development is also a long process with no single endpoint. As the material presented becomes more complicated, monitoring one's own comprehension becomes more difficult. Markman (1979) asked third- through sixth-graders to read essays that contained inconsistencies such as *There is absolutely no light at the bottom of the ocean. Some fish that live at the bottom of the ocean know their food by its color. They will only eat red fungus.* Markman found that a sizeable proportion of 12-year-olds judged such essays as comprehensible.

The implication of Markman's finding hits very close to home for many college students. In comprehension monitoring experiments, the messages are deliberately made inadequate to guarantee that comprehension is impossible. However, adult listeners may fail to comprehend an adequate message for a variety of reasons, including inattention, lack of background knowledge, unfamiliarity with the vocabulary used, and so on. College students are often in that position, but if they are adequately monitoring their comprehension of the material they are encountering, they can ask for more information. It's thinking that you understand when you really don't that gets you into trouble. College students are not the only ones who suffer from the problem of fallible comprehension monitoring. Most adults have experiences that force them to realize that even though they thought they understood the laws, the instructions, or the directions they were given, they in fact did not (Markman, 1979).

LATER SOCIOLINGUISTIC DEVELOPMENT

In middle childhood and adolescence, peers become more important than parents as agents of socialization. At the same time that the peer group is the social world of the adolescent, the major developmental task is to establish an individual identity. Both the effort to establish one's identity and the importance of the peer group affect language use during this period.

Language and identity

As we discussed earlier under the heading of phonological development, young children first speak the way their parents do but then change their style of speech to imitate their peers when they become adolescents. Phonological changes are only part of the changes that occur when adolescents adopt their peer group's dialect. Every generation has slang words and expressions that serve to distinguish adolescent users from both younger children and adults (Cooper & Anderson-Inman, 1988). Things that were "totally awesome" in 1990 were "cool" in 1970, "hip" in 1950, and "swell" before that. Adolescents not only talk alike in general, they talk in the style of their particular peer group, as do adults. There is a particular style of talk and specific jargon (vocabulary) used by doctors, bowlers, CB-radio users, and many other groups defined by occupation or recreational activity (Chaika, 1980).

As teenagers come to participate in and derive their identity from groups outside the family, their speech comes to resemble the speech of these groups. Sometimes the adoption of the peer group's speech style is quite conscious and deliberate. One black adolescent who began to use Jamaican Creole speech explained, "I feel black and I'm proud of it, to speak like that. That's why, when I talk it, I feel better than when I'm talking like now . . . " (Hewitt, 1982, p. 89).

The phenomenon of adolescents' adopting a style of speech that strongly indicates their minority group membership has also been observed among African Americans in New York City (Labov, 1972b) and among Chicanos in the American southwest (Ryan, 1979). It also sometimes happens that nonminority adolescents come to speak in a style associated with a minority group, if that minority group is the dominant peer group in the community (Saville-Troike, 1982). One example is the white Londoner described by Hewitt (1982) who acquired Jamaican Creole. Other examples include Puerto Rican adolescents in New York City and Mexican Americans in Chicago who do not learn the English their teachers use in the classroom but instead learn the black vernacular spoken by their peers (Wolfram, 1973, cited in Saville-Troike, 1982). However, for adolescents who already speak English, adopting the variety of English used by the peer group does not necessarily involve losing competence in the variety of English spoken at home. Adolescents, like adults, can switch their style of speech to fit the social context.

Verbal dueling

Among preadolescents and adolescents, language is a common weapon in ritualized contests. Most attention has been paid to the verbal contests of males, which are typically quite obscene. For example, throughout Turkey, teenage boys engage in **verbal duels** that follow the principles that (1) the goal is to force one's opponent into a female, passive role (in the verbally created scenario), and (2) the final word in the retort must rhyme with the final word in the initial insult (Dundes, Leach, & Ozkok, 1972). These duels can go back and forth as long as the duelers have the skill to keep responding within the constraints of the game. Although it is difficult to appreciate the rhyme without knowing Turkish, the following example illustrates the general tone of these insults:

> Speaker A: *Ayi.* (You bear.) (That's an insult in Turkey.)
> Speaker B: *Sana girsin keman yayi.* (May the bow of a violin enter your anus.)

Ritual insults among African American male adolescents, known as "playing the dozens," "sounding," "signifying," or "joning" (rhymes with toning; Britt, 1993), are familiar to many Americans, although the rules for their use may not be well known outside the African American community. In the 1960s, these insults took the form of rhymed couplets, typically with obscene content such as,

> Iron is iron, and steel don't rust, But your momma got a pussy like a Greyhound bus. (Labov, 1972a; see also Abrahams, 1962)

Now, 20 years later, these insults have been pared down to one-liners, such as:

> Your momma's so fat, when she sits around the house she sits AROUND the house.

> Your momma's so black, when she wears orange lipstick she looks like a cheeseburger. (M. Ginsberg, personal communication, 1994)

And then there's this classic:

> Your momma's so poor, I saw her kicking a can of beans down the street and when I asked her what she was doing, she said, "Moving." (Britt, 1993)

There are rules governing the content of these insults and their use in discourse. In terms of content, the insults must be about someone else (typically the mother), not the person the insult is addressed to. The insult typically refers to appearance, age, poverty, or sexual promiscuity, and, most important, the insult must not literally be true. Guaranteeing the falsity of insults depends in part on shared knowledge. For example, the insult that your mother is a prostitute would not be addressed to a boy whose mother really was a prostitute. Falsity is also ensured by making the insults so extreme as to be literally impossible. These insults are exchanged in dyads or triads, typically in front of an audience that expresses its evaluation of each insult. The recipient of an insult must never deny the insult but should counter with a related insult. For example, Labov (1972a) observed the following exchange:

Speaker A: Your momma's a truck driver!
Speaker B: Your father sell crackerjacks!
Speaker A: Your mother LOOK like a crackerjack!

There was no related comeback to this last insult, and the sounding went off in another direction.

Girls also have verbal contests, although they are perhaps a less central feature of female interaction than of male interaction. Gilmore (1986) described "steps," a performance of chorally chanted rhymes combined with footsteps and hand claps that is played by 8- to 11-year-old African American girls in Philadelphia. Girls take turns stepping out of line to perform individually. Each girl adds something original in her rendition, and creative performers are recognized for their virtuosity (Gilmore, 1986). Among white girls in the 1950s, jump-rope and ball-bouncing games also had verbal components. For example, one girl would bounce a ball and recite the rhyme

A my name is (a girl's name beginning with A),
and my husband's name is (a boy's name beginning with A).
We come from (a place name beginning with A),
and we sell (something beginning with A).

This continued for every letter in the alphabet. A girl held the floor until she missed the ball or was unable to fill in the blank without missing a beat. Perhaps it is a sign of social progress that in 1994 such games are unknown to many white middle-class preadolescent girls and that girls (both black and white) do sometimes compete with each other and with boys in ritualized insults (Britt, 1993; A. Ginsberg, 1994, personal communication). As verbal dueling moves into the mainstream, the content is changing from its earlier focus on poverty and blackness. White middle-class children use "put downs" (as they are called in those circles), such as:

You're so slow it takes you an hour to make Minute Rice.

You're so slow it takes you 2 hours to watch *60 Minutes.*

You're so fat that when you stand on the scale, it says, "One at a time, please." (A. Ginsberg, personal communication)

The acquisition of gender-differentiated conversational styles

Adult men and women have clear differences in the way they participate in conversations with each other. Women are more likely than men to ask questions, to make utterances that encourage responses, and to make use of positive minimal responses such as *mm-hmm* (Fishman, 1978). In contrast, men are more likely than women to interrupt, to ignore the comments of the other speaker, to control the topic of conversation, and to make direct declarations of fact or opinion (Fishman, 1978). One explanation of these differences is that they simply reflect the difference in social power held by men and women (West & Zimmerman, 1977). Another is that the un-assertive style of women's speech reflects the personalities women are socialized to have (see Maltz & Borker, 1982, for further elaboration). However, Daniel Maltz and Ruth Borker (1982) have offered another explanation of these gender differences in conversational style that locates the source in the socializing role of the peer group during middle childhood and adolescence.

Men and women participate in conversation in different ways because, according to Maltz and Borker (1982), they learned to converse in different cultures. For boys, the culture was that of the preadolescent and adolescent male peer group; for girls, it was that of the preadolescent and adolescent female peer group. Studies of boys' peer groups find that boys tend to play in large groups that include boys of different social status and even different ages, and that within the group there is a hierarchical structure with some boys on top and others on the bottom. Nondominant boys are not excluded, although they may be treated badly. The status hierarchy is in constant flux. As Maltz and Borker describe it, "The social world of boys is one of posturing and counterposturing. In this world speech is used in three major ways: (1) to assert one's position of dominance, (2) to attract and maintain an audience, and (3) to assert oneself when other speakers have the floor" (Maltz & Borker, 1982, p. 207).

The social world of girls is different. Girls play in small groups or pairs, and the groups tend to be homogeneous in terms of the social status and age of the group members. Nondominant girls have to find other nondominant girls to play with. Within the group, however, play is cooperative and activities are generally noncompetitive. Instead of jockeying for position within a group, as boys must, girls compete for membership in exclusive friendships (Brooks-Gunn & Matthews, 1979; Eder & Hallinan, 1978; Lever, 1976, cited in Maltz & Borker, 1982). According to Maltz and Borker (1982), the social world of girls is one of "shifting alliances and indirect expressions of conflict" (p. 207). Friendships are made and broken with language (Lever, 1976). Sharing secrets cements a relationship; telling secrets breaks off a relationship. While a pair or small group lasts, the function of language is to create and maintain a relationship among equals. This includes criticizing and arguing in ways that don't threaten, not acting "bossy," and accurately interpreting others' indirect signals so that you don't mistakenly think that you are accepted by the group only to have your secrets revealed.

As a result of experiencing these different socializing pressures in childhood, men and women have different cultural rules for how to carry on a conversation. When speakers from different cultures meet and interact, miscommunication can occur. For example, women use language in conversation simply to keep the conversation going. Women's conversation maintenance devices include minimal responses such as "mm-hmm," which indicate that they are listening, and questions, which simply request that the other speaker keep talking. Men, in contrast, don't use language for conversational maintenance. When men say "mm-hmm" it means that they agree, and when they ask a question, it is a request for information. Women (incorrectly) take men's lack of minimal responses as a sign that the men are not listening and are irritated that their questions elicit advice when what they wanted was supportive talk. Men (incorrectly) take women's *mm-hmm*'s to mean agreement, and find it irritating that women don't answer their questions.

THE ACQUISITION OF LITERACY

Children in literate cultures not only become speakers and hearers of a language, they also become readers and writers. In this section, we consider what these two language developments might have to do with each other. We will not discuss the development of reading and writing per se, although they are certainly important developments that have also been studied (see, for example, Martlew, 1986; Nelson, 1988; Perera, 1986). Rather, we will consider the relation between oral language development (the subject of the rest of this book) and the development of the ability to read and write language.

Literacy and human nature

We can start with some facts about literacy that do not depend on psycholinguistic research and that argue that achieving literacy is not a natural next step after oral language has been acquired. One such fact is that every human society has language, but many human societies, historically and currently, have no written language (Anderson, 1989). Another fact is that the transmission of literacy requires considerably more effort than does the transmission of spoken language. The transmission of oral language from generation to generation requires only normal human interaction, whereas the transmission of literacy is usually the result of formal instruction in school. This is not to deny that there are considerable environmental supports for the acquisition of spoken language. It may well be that instruction in language is embedded in the nature of human interaction. And it is also true that some children figure out how to read on their own, without formal instruction. Still, there is a huge difference between oral language and literacy in the degree of deliberate instruction that cultures provide and in the rate of successful acquisition in the absence of such instruction.

Finally, using language to communicate is so much a part of human nature that children who are not exposed to language will invent their own means of communication, and new languages have been created many times in the course of human history when people who shared no common language were placed together (see the section in Chapter 9 on the development of creole languages). In contrast, writing seems to have been invented only a few times in the course of history, and an alphabetic writing system in which one symbol corresponds to one sound was invented only once (Adams, 1990; Anderson, 1989). In sum, literacy seems less intrinsic to human nature than oral language does.

It should be pointed out that not everyone agrees with the foregoing argument. In particular, the **whole-language approach** to teaching reading is based on the assumption that reading is as natural as talking and that if children were immersed in written communication—and if the written form were the only way to communicate—then children might learn to read and write as easily as they learn to speak and understand oral language. From that point of view, the only explanation of why oral language is universal and literacy is not is that oral communication is more convenient than written communication.

However, there is no culture that has only written language. Children always learn to talk first, and when children learn to read and write, they are learning a system that builds on the oral language they already know. Furthermore, children are not always successful at learning to read. The fact that reading is difficult for some children, but seems logically related to the oral language skills they have already acquired, has prompted researchers to search for correlates of literacy achievement (typically reading achievement) in measures of children's oral language ability. A large part of the motivation for research in this area has been the effort to understand why low-income children consistently lag behind children from higher socioeconomic strata (SES) in reading achievement. Thus, scientific questions about the factors that contribute to the acquisition of literacy have historically been intertwined with social policy questions about how to guarantee literacy for all. We can start to address these questions by first dealing separately with two parts of the scientific question: (1) What aspects of oral language skill are related to literacy? and (2) What experiences contribute to developing those skills? As we find answers to what underlies the development of literacy, we can try to apply those answers to explaining the differences in literacy achievement that are related to socioeconomic status.

Literacy and oral language skills

If we return to the linguists' separation of oral language skill into the components of phonology, the lexicon, grammar, and language use, we can start to outline an answer to the question of how oral language and reading achievement are related, component by component.

Phonological awareness and reading   As we discussed earlier in this chapter, phonological awareness and success at learning to read are highly correlated, although the direction of causation underlying that correlation is complicated. Phonological awareness is an oral language skill in the sense that it is an ability to analyze sound sequences. However, it is unknown whether the development of phonological awareness is related to the development of the ability to produce or understand spoken language.

Vocabulary, grammar, and reading   Children's vocabulary knowledge is also a strong correlate of reading achievement (Chall et al., 1990). However, whereas phonological awareness is an important predictor early in the course of reading development, vocabulary seems to be most important in the middle elementary years. Chall and associates (1990) suggest that this change in the

Box 6.3   Characteristics of decontextualized language use

1. Distance between the sender and receiver

2. Use of complex syntactic structure

3. Permanency of the information

4. Autonomous (rather than interactive) establishment of truth

5. Explicitness of reference

6. High degree of cohesion

Source: From Snow, 1983; and Tannen, 1982.

Table 6.2   Types of contextualized and decontextualized oral and written language

	Oral language	*Written language*
Contextualized	Face-to-face conversation about the here-and-now	Menus, labels, some signs
Decontextualized	Narratives and lectures	Almost all written language

oral-language correlates of reading is the result of the fact that the process of reading itself changes with development. In the beginning stages, reading is primarily a process of word recognition and decoding—hence the importance of phonological skills. In the middle elementary years, when the mechanics of reading have been mastered, the focus of reading shifts to understanding the message. Children who have not acquired the vocabulary used in the material they are assigned at this level will be at a disadvantage. Grammar is less strongly related to reading than to either phonological skills or vocabulary (Chall et al., 1990).

Again, proponents of the whole-language theory of reading would disagree. They argue that uncovering meaning is central at all stages of reading. This argument about whether searching for meaning or learning to decode is the best way to describe (and teach) reading is related to the functionalist/formalist argument about oral language development discussed in Chapter 5. The functionalist approach and the whole-language approach view acquisition of the form (spoken or written) as the inevitable outcome of the function (trying to communicate). In contrast, the formalist approach to language and the phonetic approach to reading take the view that the medium of communication has structural components whose mastery is not guaranteed simply by immersion in the medium and the urge to communicate.

Language use and reading Skill at one sort of language use—decontextualized language use—may be an important precursor to literacy. In **decontextualized language use,** the words stand on their own. (Other characteristics are summarized in Box 6.3.) In contrast, in **contextualized language use,** the nonlinguistic context supports the interpretation of the linguistic message. Spoken language is often contextualized, as in the case of face-to-face conversation about the here-and-now; or it may be decontextualized, as in the case of narratives. Written language is almost always decontextualized. The relation between the form of language (oral or written) and decontextualized language use is presented in Table 6.2.

According to this account, skill at decontextualized oral language use provides an important bridge from oral language to literacy (Snow, 1983). The crucial variable for children in terms of oral language preparation for literacy is in their use of decontextualized language. As we discussed in Chapter 5, the ability to produce decontextualized speech (as in narrative production) emerges first in conversation and receives significant support from children's conversational partners (see also McNamee, 1987); and some caregivers have conversational styles that provide better support than others for the use of decontextualized language in conversation. For that reason, some children will meet the task of acquiring literacy better prepared than others. In addition to engaging in conversation, families can also prepare their children for literacy through book reading. Book reading is a hugely important source of exposure to decontextualized oral language. The frequency with which children are read books as preschoolers is one of the best predictors of children's early literacy achievement (Teale, 1984; Wells, 1985).

Children's development of decontextualized language use is far from complete when they enter school. Ideally, the school setting itself is one that not only requires decontextualized language use but also supports its development. In much the same way that mothers aid their young children's narrative development by asking supportive questions, so teachers can provide scaffolding for children's talk in school.

Sarah Michaels (1981, 1983) studied teacher/child interaction during sharing time (also known as circle time or show-and-tell) to find out how teachers help children acquire competence at this form of decontextualized language use. She found that when the child's discourse style matched the teacher's discourse style, the teachers were good at asking questions or making

Figure 6.6   Sharing time (or show-and-tell) gives children the opportunity to develop skill at decontextualized language use.

comments in the right places to help the child produce a better narrative. However, when the child's narrative style differed from the teacher's, the teachers were not very good at providing scaffolding. White, middle-class teachers were not very helpful to African American children who were producing topic-associating rather than topic-centered narratives (see Chapter 5 for more discussion of these narrative types). As Michaels (1981) points out, the problem is not simply one of prejudice or of not accepting a different narrative style. If the teacher is unable to follow the story, then the teacher cannot ask appropriately focused questions. The unfortunate result for minority children is that they do not get the same support for developing skill at decontextualized language use, and therefore do not get the same preparation for literacy, as their mainstream counterparts do (see Ely & Gleason, 1995, for additional discussion).

Emergent literacy

Acquiring literacy includes learning how to read and write, but literacy is more than just having these skills. Literacy is a tool that can be used for different functions, and the functions served by literacy vary depending on culture and socioeconomic status. Literacy activities in some homes may be minimal—reading labels, signs, and the Bible. They may also include reading newspapers, magazines, and books, or reading and writing may be integral to the way one earns one's living. Acquiring literacy, in this more anthropological view, includes learning the functions of literacy (see for example, Heath, 1982; Schieffelin & Gilmore, 1986; Wagner, 1993).

Children observe the literacy activities of those around them and learn about literacy well before they learn how to read. This early knowledge about literacy that is separate from actually knowing how to read has been termed **emergent literacy.** When children are read to from an early age, they learn that books are for reading, they learn how to hold a book and turn pages, they learn that words and stories are contained in the print on the page, and they learn that print (in English) is read from left to right (Goodman, 1984; Snow & Ninio, 1986). Children with this experience know more about literacy than children without this experience do, separate from any differences between children in knowing how to read. The focus on children's emergent literacy is part of a widening of focus in the research on literacy, from viewing reading and writing as skills that individuals acquire to seeing literacy as a function and product of culture.

Explaining SES-related differences in reading achievement

The foregoing analysis of how the components of oral language skill relate to reading provides part of the explanation of the SES-associated differences in reading achievement that are consistently observed. There are SES-associated differences in children's vocabulary, and SES-associated differences in reading become greater during the middle-school years when vocabulary is most strongly related to reading (Chall et al., 1990). Experience being read to also varies as a function of socioeconomic status, and thus differences in early exposure to books and in the skill at decontextualized language use that book reading fosters are likely to explain part of the SES-associated differences in literacy achievement. And mismatch between the style of language use valued at home and the style of language use the school expects often makes the school environment less supportive of literacy for low-SES minority children than for middle-class children.

On the other hand, several sources of evidence suggest that mismatch between home and school language use cannot be the whole explanation for the lower reading and general school achievement of low-income children.

Working-class, low-income children who come from the same culture and speak the same dialect as their middle-class counterparts do still do less well in school (Chandler, Argyris, Barnes, Goodman, & Snow, 1986). Some of this "poverty gap" can be accounted for in terms of the literacy experiences that homes provide. Lee and Croninger (1993) found that the difference in literacy achievement between poor and middle-class eighth-graders was partly explained by home environment measures, such as the books in the home and family use of the public library. Thus SES-related differences in the centrality of literacy activities may be a continuing source of SES-related differences in children's literacy achievement.

In sum, evidence suggests that language and literacy are separate skills that share some common and mutually reinforcing components. The areas of greatest mutual influence are vocabulary and decontextualized language use. The ability to isolate sounds in the speech stream is also crucial for learning to read an alphabetic writing system such as English, and this ability is fostered by reading instruction. Some evidence suggests that oral language experience in secondary language activities such as nursery rhymes also fosters that sort of phonological ability. The recent focus on emergent literacy suggests that there may also be important precursors to literacy acquisition that are separate from the language skills that literacy requires.

LANGUAGE CHANGE IN ADULTHOOD AND OLD AGE

Throughout most of adulthood, one's language knowledge and language skills stay relatively constant. The most obvious change is that adults continue to learn new words as long as they continue to be exposed to new words. Also, language skills can be improved in adulthood if one works on it. For example, college professors may get better at giving a coherent lecture, and writers may continue to develop their writing style.

Other changes that happen with age seem to be less dependent on specific effort or experiences and are more a part of the normal aging process. Elderly adults typically experience word-finding difficulties, and they are less able to understand and produce some types of complex grammatical constructions. Narrative skill, in contrast, appears to improve in older adults. Before we discuss these changes, two other factors that affect language in many older adults at least deserve mention. First, most adults who live in modern industrialized society experience some hearing loss as a result of a lifetime of exposure to noise, and hearing loss creates communicative problems. Second, older adults are more likely than younger people to suffer strokes and to have Alzheimer's disease or other forms of dementia, all of which affect language. Aphasia (loss of language) resulting from stroke is discussed in Chapter 9 on the biological bases of language. (For further information on language changes associated with Alzheimer's disease and dementia, see, for example, Obler, 1983; Obler & Albert, 1980.)

Decrements in word-finding abilities

The decrement in language skill that older adults are most likely to be aware of is difficulty in retrieving names for things. Research has demonstrated that this common self-perception is correct. **Word-finding ability** can be measured using *The Boston Naming Test,* which contains pictures of 85 objects ranging from common ones, such as *tree* and *bed,* to less frequent ones, such as *yoke* and *trellis.* Adults' performance on this test improves between the ages of 30 and 50 years, holds steady among 60-year-olds, and then declines among 70-year-olds. People in their seventies also show more variability than younger people, with institutionalized adults showing the poorest performance (Goodglass, 1980). The decline in naming performance consists of both more errors in naming and longer latencies to name. Elderly adults often produce circumlocutions, which describe the item but do not name it (such as *the thing you unlock a door with* instead of *key).* Similar findings are obtained when adults are asked to name actions (Obler & Albert, 1985).

Changes in grammatical performance

Between 50 and 90 years of age, adults' ability to produce, imitate, and understand some complex structures declines. Sentences with a single clause (one subject and one predicate), such as (1) below, are structurally less complex than sentences with two or more clauses, such as sentence (2):

(1) Alice saw the Cheshire Cat.

(2) Alice saw the Cheshire Cat after the baby turned into a pig.

Some sentences with two clauses are more complex—or at least more difficult to process—than are other sentences with two clauses, depending on how the clauses are arranged. Sentences like (3) below,

(3) After the baby turned into a pig, Alice saw the Cheshire Cat.

demand more of working memory than sentence (2) does, because in (3) the first clause needs to be held in memory while the second clause is being processed. Sentence (2) is referred to as a right-branching sentence (after the sort of tree diagram that describes it) and (3) is left branching.

Several studies by Susan Kemper and her colleagues demonstrate that, compared to young adults, the elderly are less likely to produce multiclause sentences, particularly left-branching ones; they are less able to imitate such sentences; and they are less able to extract information from them. Kemper, Kynette, Rash, O'Brien, and Sprott (1989) elicited oral and written language samples from young adults (18 to 28 years old) and elderly adults (60 to 92 years old). They found an age-related decline in the syntactic complexity of both oral and written language, which was attributable to the loss of left-branching clauses. Kemper and associates also looked for changes over an individual's life span by analyzing diary entries made by individuals over a 70-year period, from the time the individuals were in their early twenties until well into their eighties. In these diary entries, Kemper (1987a) found the same change in syntactic complexity that Kemper and colleagues (1989) found in their cross-sectional comparison. Seventy- and 80-year-olds produced fewer sentences with embedded clauses, especially left-branching embeddings, than they did when they were younger. In other studies, Kemper also documented that older adults are less able than younger adults to imitate left-branching sentences (Kemper, 1986) and to recall information presented in left-embedded subordinate clauses (Kemper, 1987b).

This age-related decline in the ability to produce and process left-branching complex sentences is the result, according to Kemper, of the well-documented age-related decline in working-memory capacity. The young and elderly adults tested by Kemper and associates (1989) were given a test of memory capacity (the backward digit span test from the Weschler Adult Intelligence Scale). The researchers found that performance on the memory capacity test predicted use of multiclause sentences and left-branching structures, and that differences in memory capacity accounted for the differences between the age groups. Furthermore, in a longitudinal follow-up of those adults, Kemper, Kynette, and Norman (1992) found that those adults whose memory capacity declined most over the next three years also showed the most decline in the syntactic complexity of their sentences.

This explanation has something in common with accounts described earlier of children's narrative development and children's communication skill. The common feature is the notion that using language makes both content demands (that is, you must know the grammar of the language) and process demands on the speaker/hearer. When the process demands are overwhelming, the sophistication of the output (in this case its grammatical complexity) declines.

The alternative to such a process account is to say instead that elderly adults actually lose grammatical knowledge, and such proposals have been made. The general form of such proposals is known as the **regression hypothesis,** according to which language decline in old age mirrors language acquisition in early childhood, as pieces of the grammar are lost in the reverse order in which they were acquired (see Emery, 1985 and Grodzinsky, 1990, for recent proposals). In reviewing the evidence for the regression hypothesis, Kemper (1992) argues that the particular changes that occur in old age violate many predictions of that hypothesis. For example, although older adults show some loss of grammatical morphemes, the order in which particular morphemes are lost does not parallel the order in which those morphemes are acquired. Furthermore, according to Kemper, processing accounts can explain some apparent regressions, such as the return to simpler sentence structure.

Changes in narrative performance

Older adults may have word-finding problems, and the decline in working-memory capacity may limit the syntactic complexity of their sentences, but older adults still tell the best stories. Lorraine Obler (1980) studied tale-tellers in a Palestinian village and found that the most proficient were all in their sixties or older. Mergler, Faust, and Goldstein (1985) also found that stories told by older adults are preferred by listeners and are remembered better than are stories told by young adults.

Figure 6.7   The best storytellers are often older adults—despite age-related declines in some other language skills.

Kemper (1990) asked whether the superiority of older adults' narratives would also be evidenced in longitudinal changes in diary entries. Kemper analyzed the coherence of diary entries using a story-grammar-based coding system, and she analyzed the use of linguistic cohesive devices. She found that cohesion declined in the elderly; specifically, the use of pronouns that had unclear referents increased. However, the structural complexity of the narratives increased with age. Older adults' diary entries were more likely to be full stories with settings, goals, motivating internal states, actions taken toward the goal, and a summarizing ending. Also, older adults' diary entries were judged to be more interesting by experienced English teachers. Apparently, being restricted by a limited memory capacity doesn't hurt one's ability to structure a story; and syntactically simple sentences, and even a few ambiguous pronominal references, don't detract from a good story.

SUMMARY

By the age of 5 years, children have mastered the essentials of language, but language development does not stop at that point. Each component of language—phonology, the lexicon, grammar, and communicative competence—continues to develop during middle childhood and adolescence.

Phonological development during middle childhood includes the mastery of some late-acquired sounds and includes increases in phonological awareness, particularly the ability to segment words into their component phonemes. The growth of phonological awareness is probably due in large part to the influence of reading instruction. During middle childhood and adolescence, some aspects of children's phonology may change as children shift from speaking the language as spoken by parents to using the language variety that is spoken by their peers.

Lexical development after the age of 5 years consists of continuing to add new words to one's vocabulary and of learning the derivational morphology of the language. Knowing derivational morphology allows children to interpret newly encountered words using their knowledge of root and affix meanings. During middle childhood, the ability to ascertain the meaning of new words from their contexts of use becomes important to vocabulary development. This ability and the exposure to new words through reading are important influences on vocabulary growth after early childhood.

The grammatical complexity of children's language continues to increase after age 5 years, not so much because new aspects of the grammar are being acquired, but because complex constructions are being produced more frequently. However, two sorts of qualitative grammatical developments occur during middle childhood. At age 5, children still have difficulty interpreting the coreference relations in complex sentences. Exactly how to account for this is an intensively researched and hotly debated issue. Another grammatical change after age 5 years is the development of the use of grammatical devices, such as pronominal reference, to link sentences together.

The ability to use grammatical devices to produce cohesive text is part of the change that occurs in children's narrative ability during middle childhood and adolescence. The plot structure of children's narratives also becomes increasingly complex with development.

Perhaps the most obviously nonadultlike aspect of children's language skills at 5 years is their referential communication skills. As speakers, 5-year-olds tend to produce informationally inadequate messages; and as listeners, 5-year-olds tend to not recognize when messages are inadequate. Children's communication skills improve significantly during the early elementary school years as their ability to recognize when a message is inadequate improves, but the task of producing informationally adequate messages is often difficult for adults as well. (For an illustration of this difficulty, see the instructions for assembly that came with your most recent stereo or computer purchase.)

Although the major events of phonological, lexical, and grammatical development occur in early childhood, middle childhood and adolescence are the prime period of sociolinguistic development. As the peer group becomes their social world, children start to learn their peer group's style of language use. During the ages when children largely play in sex-segregated groups, they learn gender-specific styles of conversation. If the peer group uses a low-prestige variety of speech, preadolescents and adolescents may adopt that vernacular. Language is sometimes the vehicle of competition as teenagers engage in verbal duels.

Middle childhood is the period when literacy develops. The acquisition of literacy has precursors in oral language development. Familiarity with decontextualized oral language use prepares children for the decontextualized nature of written language; and in middle childhood, vocabulary size is also predictive of reading achievement. Phonological awareness, although not required for speaking, is an important oral language skill for learning the sound/letter correspondences of an alphabetic system.

Adulthood is characterized more by language stability than by language change, although vocabulary often continues to grow and discourse skills may continue to develop. Old age is associated with some language decrement. Older adults experience word-finding difficulties, and the grammatical complexity of the sentences elderly adults produce and can understand declines, probably as a result of decreases in memory abilities. Narrative skills seem to be the one area where increasing age continues to be associated with improved skills. Studies of diaries kept by American adults and of tales told by Palestinian storytellers find that old people produce the most interesting narratives.

This chapter is not an exhaustive survey of language development after early childhood. Areas of development that have been the subject of research but were not covered here include the processes of reading and writing, the development of figurative language—metaphors, puns, irony, proverbs—and the development of literary understanding (Bruner, 1985; Winner, 1988). Another topic relevant to later language development but barely mentioned in this chapter is language use in school. (For information on classroom discourse, see Cazden, 1988; Green & Harker, 1988; Wells, 1986; and Wilkinson, 1982.)

KEY TERMS

phonological awareness

onset

rime

secondary language activities

derivational morphology

inflectional morphology

word formation process

compounding

coreference relations

Minimal Distance Principle (MDP)

c-command

tree diagram

sentence interpretation strategies

language as a "problem-space"

maturation hypothesis

continuity hypothesis

genres

scripts

coherence

cohesion

story grammar

thematic subject strategy

anaphoric reference

comprehension monitoring

theory of mind

verbal duels

whole-language approach

decontextualized language use

contextualized language use

emergent literacy

word-finding ability

regression hypothesis

REVIEW QUESTIONS

1. What is phonological awareness? What factors influence the development of phonological awareness? Why is phonological awareness important?

2. What is derivational morphology? What is the developmental course of the acquisition of derivational morphology? How does increasing knowledge of derivational morphology affect recognition vocabulary?

3. Vocabulary knowledge influences reading achievement and reading achievement influences vocabulary knowledge. Explain how these reciprocal influences work.

4. What does it mean to say that 5-year-olds do not always obey all the binding principles of the language when they interpret coreference relations in complex sentences? Why is this an issue?

5. Children's narratives change with development, both in their coherence and cohesiveness. Explain what this means.

6. What is comprehension monitoring? Why is the development of comprehension monitoring important for the development of communication skill?

7. How is children's theory of mind related to comprehension monitoring and to message repair?

8. Describe and explain examples of the influence of peers on the acquisition of dialect and of gender-typed language use.

9. What aspects of oral language development are related to literacy? What else seems to be important for the development of literacy?

10. Is there a parallel between the whole-language approach to reading and the functionalist approach to syntax discussed in Chapter 5?

11. What are the changes in language associated with old age? What are two possible explanations of changes in grammatical performance?

7 Language Development in Special Populations

Lo and behold, they find him . . . with a lady. Then they found him and another frog. But then lo and behold he knew why his . . . frog had ran away. It was time for him . . . to have children. And lo and behold . . . some frogs came out of the bushes. And there the boy and his dog are walking away. The boy got another frog. There they are walking away.

(The closing of a narrative told by a 10-year-old with Williams syndrome, a form of mental retardation that largely spares language functions; from Reilly, Klima, & Bellugi, 1990, p. 387)

The focus of this book thus far has been on describing and explaining the typical course of language development in children. In this chapter, we turn to a consideration of language development in populations of children who are atypical in language development. Included are children who have conditions such as deafness, blindness, mental retardation, or autism that affect their ability to acquire language. In addition, some children have difficulty acquiring language but appear to be normal in all other aspects of their development. These children are referred to as having specific language impairment.

There are two reasons for studying language development in populations other than typically developing children. One is the applied research motive discussed in Chapter 1; understanding how language development may be affected by other conditions should help provide a basis for designing programs to help such children optimize their language development. There is also a basic research motivation for studying language development in different populations; it allows us to ask how different human abilities contribute to the language acquisition process. For example, studying language development in deaf children can help us discover whether language depends on the auditory-vocal channel or whether language is a function of the human brain that can make use of other channels if the typical channel is unavailable. Studying language development in blind children can address questions about the role of the extralinguistic context in language development.

Children who are deaf or blind have normal mental abilities, although their access to information is impaired. What about children who have different mental endowments? Remember, one of the major issues in the field of language development concerns the extent to which language is separate from other cognitive abilities. Looking at language development in children who are mentally retarded provides insights into how language development is affected by general cognitive limitations. Looking at language development in children with autism, who have their own distinctive constellation of mental abilities and limitations, also sheds light on the extent to which the ability to acquire language depends on other human abilities.

Last, children who seem to develop typically in every respect except in language challenge us to identify what aspect of human ability is necessary for language development but not for anything else.

LANGUAGE DEVELOPMENT AND DEAFNESS

Approximately 1 in 1000 children is born with a severe hearing loss (Carrel, 1977), and some children who are able to hear at birth lose their hearing in infancy, before they have acquired language. In this section, we consider what language development is like for these **prelingually deaf** children, and we consider what the course of their language development can tell us about the process of language acquisition more generally.

By limiting our discussion of language development in deaf children in this way, we are excluding cases in which hearing loss occurs after language has been acquired. In such cases linguistic competence remains, although communication is impaired (Mogford-Bevan, 1993). We also are excluding children with mild to moderate hearing loss, who can hear spoken language with the use of hearing aids and whose success at language development is predicted to a large degree by how much hearing ability remains (Meadow, 1980). Another excluded topic that deserves at least brief mention is the effect of intermittent hearing loss on language development. Many young children have repeated middle ear infections or periodic fluid buildup in the middle ear that cause temporary hearing impairment. A substantial body of research has investigated whether these conditions are associated with language delay. Although a definitive answer hasn't yet been found, a recent review of the literature concludes that if any language delays are associated with this type of intermittent hearing loss, those delays are small, subtle, and probably temporary (Klein & Rapin, 1993).

The focus of this section is on the population of children who cannot hear—even with hearing aids—the spoken language around them. The primary determinant of the course of language development for these prelingually deaf children is the language environment to which they are exposed. One possible environment is exposure to **sign language,** the manual language used in the deaf community. This is the situation for the approximately 10% of deaf children who have a deaf parent. These "deaf of deaf" are exposed to sign language from infancy, and for these children, the story of their language development is the story of the acquisition of sign language as a first language.

For the 90% of deaf children who do not have a deaf parent, their language environment typically depends on the advice given to parents by those who specialize in the education of deaf children. For most of this century, the advice that has been given is to use the **oralist method,** in which deaf children are intensively coached in producing speech and trained in reading lips. Parents traditionally were discouraged from using any gestural communication system with their deaf children in the belief (which now appears to be mistaken) that using gestures or acquiring sign language would interfere with the children's acquiring a spoken language. More recently, the purely oralist approach has been supplanted by the **total communication** approach to deaf education. The goal of total communication approaches is the same as that of oralist approaches—mastery of spoken English. In total communication approaches (and there are several different ones), oral language is combined with some signing or gestural system. For deaf children who are not exposed to sign and who are trained in one of these methods, the story of their language development is the story of **oral language development** in the deaf.

The "deaf of hearing" who are orally educated provide two other topics of interest. One is the "home sign" gestural system that such children invent to communicate with those around them. Another is their later acquisition—after early childhood—of sign language. Most deaf individuals, even those who are orally educated, meet other deaf individuals who know sign, and so they acquire sign language, to some degree, later in life. We begin our description of language development in deaf children with the topic of sign language development in children who are exposed to sign from infancy. We then move to a discussion of oral and sign language development in children whose parents cannot communicate with them in sign.

The acquisition of sign language in early childhood

Sign languages are real languages   Before discussing the acquisition of sign language, it is important to dispel the common myth that sign language is simply pantomime and not a language at all. Several decades of linguistic analyses of sign languages have clearly established that sign languages are languages. (There are several different sign languages in the world, just as there are many different spoken languages.) The majority of the linguistic work has analyzed **American Sign Language (ASL),** which is used in the United States and the English-speaking provinces of Canada (Klima & Bellugi, 1979; Stokoe, Casterline, & Croneberg, 1965). This work has revealed (1) that ASL has a lexicon, (2) that lexical items in ASL are made up of a finite and discrete number of sublexical components (such as handshape and place of articulation) that are equivalent to phonemes in spoken language, and (3) that ASL has a grammar.

One way in which ASL differs slightly from spoken languages is that some signs are iconic—that is, they physically resemble their referents. For example, the sign TREE looks something like a tree waving in the wind. Also, ASL uses pointing, for example, pointing to the addressee means YOU and pointing to self means ME or I. However, many signs are completely arbitrary or have their iconic source so far back in history that it is of little present use. For example, the sign for GIRL in ASL may have originated as an imitation of tying a bonnet (Litowitz, 1987). Some examples of signs are illustrated in Figure 7.1. So, for the most part, acquiring a vocabulary in a sign language is the same task of learning arbitrary symbol-meaning connections that it is for spoken language. And learning the grammar of ASL is the same task of learning a productive system for expressing meanings with combinations of words and grammatical morphemes that it is for spoken language.

The course of sign language development   For deaf children who have a deaf parent and who are exposed to sign language from birth, the course of sign language development is essentially like the course of the development of spoken language. Children pass through the same stages in the same order. Infants exposed to ASL produce manual babbling, followed by single-sign productions, followed by multisign combinations, followed by morphological

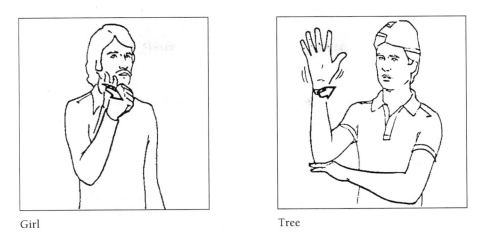

Girl   Tree

Figure 7.1   Examples of signs in American Sign Language

development and more complex syntax (Bellugi, van Hoek, Lillo-Martin, & O'Grady, 1993; Newport & Meier, 1985; Petitto, in press).

There is also evidence that similar processes underlie the acquisition of both sign and spoken languages. Children acquiring ASL make overregularization errors in their use of morphological markers, producing forms analogous to *goed* or *holded*. Like children acquiring spoken languages, children acquiring ASL persist in their errors and ignore parental corrections, even though parental corrections sometimes involve the parent's actually molding the child's handshape (Bellugi et al., 1993). What is perhaps most striking is that children acquiring ASL make pronoun reversal errors at the same age that children acquiring spoken language do. This error is striking because the signs for pronouns are points, and both deaf and hearing children use pointing gestures to communicate before they have acquired language. Yet the fact that ASL is physically similar in this aspect to prelinguistic communication seems to give it no advantage in acquisition. It seems as if acquiring a linguistic system is a separate enterprise from using prelinguistic communicative gestures, even when the modality is the same (Petitto, 1987, in press).

The timing of sign language development   It is widely agreed that ASL has all the structural features of a language and that its developmental course is like the developmental course of spoken languages. Furthermore, it is agreed that the timing of major milestones, beginning with the onset of two-word combinations at approximately 18 to 22 months of age, is the same as the timing of those milestones in the acquisition of spoken language.

One area of disagreement about the course of sign language acquisition concerns the age at which children produce their first word. (Because signs have

the same lexical status as spoken words, ASL researchers use the term *word*.)
Several reports in the literature indicate that children acquiring ASL produce their
first word at a younger age than do children acquiring a spoken language
(Bonvillian, Orlansky, & Novack, 1983; Folven & Bonvillian, 1991; Prinz & Prinz,
1979; Schlesinger & Meadow, 1972). This claim has been widely accepted and
has been interpreted as reflecting the earlier maturation of the motor system
involved in producing gestures—and perhaps the greater salience of gestured
over spoken input for infants (Newport & Meier, 1985).

However, Laura Petitto (1988, in press) claimed that the timing of *all*
milestones in sign and spoken language development are equivalent, including
the appearance of the first word. She argued that in attributing signs to very
young infants, researchers have actually overinterpreted the **nonlinguistic
gestures** all children make. In a clever (and somewhat sneaky) demonstration
of this point, Petitto (1988) showed a researcher who is deaf a videotape of a
10-month-old boy and told the researcher to record every time she thought the
little boy signed. Unknown to the researcher, this 10-month-old was a hearing
child who had not been exposed to sign and who therefore was no more likely
to produce signs than a 10-month-old in Boston is likely to produce words in
Chinese. However, the little boy did produce a natural repertoire of gestures,
reaching, pointing, grasping, and opening and closing his hand. The researcher
who watched the videotape reported that the child produced nearly 100 signs.
This point about the timing of first words in sign language acquisition remains
controversial, but it is clear that deafness is not an obstacle to acquiring
language—as long as that language is available through the eyes.

Oral language development in deaf children

Deafness is a severe obstacle to acquiring a spoken language, and the story of
oral language development in prelingually deaf children is typically not a
success story. Although some deaf individuals do learn to lip-read and to speak,
most achieve only limited success. Producing speech is also difficult for
prelingually deaf children. One report estimates that 15 to 55% of orally educated
deaf people achieve intelligible speech (Jensema, Karchmer, & Trybus, 1978).
More important than the difficulty deaf people have in reading lips and talking
is the difficulty that prelingually deaf children have in acquiring language
through oral means. Many researchers have argued that oralism fails to provide
most deaf children with any effective native language. Although there has been
less time to evaluate the success of total communication programs, the evidence
to date suggests that total communication also has its limitations. Some argue
that total communication is more effective than purely oral programs, but
the conclusions are mixed (for example, see Moores, 1978; Wood & Wood,
1992). According to Johnson, Liddell, and Erting (1992), both oral and total

communication programs deprive deaf children of the opportunity to fully acquire any language. The specifics of what deaf children do and do not acquire in oral language development is best described separately for phonological, semantic, and syntactic development.

Phonological development   Deaf infants sound very much like hearing infants in the first months of life. Deaf infants cry and coo and even begin to babble. (This is true for deaf infants exposed to sign as well.) However, by the babbling stage, deaf infants differ from hearing infants in both the quantity and quality of sound production (Stoel-Gammon & Otomo, 1986), and deaf infants do not produce the canonical clear syllabic babbling typical of hearing 9- and 10-month-olds (Oller, Eilers, Bull, & Carney, 1985). Some orally trained deaf children do seem to develop a phonological system. For example, these children do things like reduce consonant clusters when they produce words (such as pronouncing *school* as /kul/), showing evidence of phonological processes similar to those seen in the early productions of hearing children. Orally trained deaf children may also show some phonological awareness. For example, they can use lip-read information to identify rhymes (Dodd, 1987). As we discussed in Chapter 6, phonological awareness is related to reading skill, and thus the phonological awareness that orally trained deaf children achieve may help them learn to read, although that is not clear (Mayberry & Wodlinger-Cohen, 1987). In general, the level of literacy achieved by deaf children who have hearing parents is low. The average reading level of deaf high school graduates is roughly the third- or fourth-grade level (Johnson, Liddell, & Erting, 1989).

Semantic development   There is not a great deal of research on the topic of semantics in the oral language of deaf children, perhaps because semantic development tends to be the focus of studies of early language development, and there is not a great deal of language development occurring in young deaf children. For example, Gregory and Mogford (1981) set out to describe vocabulary development in the oral language of deaf children under the age of 4 years, and they had to exclude the most profoundly deaf children in their sample because there was so little vocabulary to describe.

Two studies suggest that semantic development is similar in deaf and hearing children, although both studies are of the expression and representation of meaning, not of language per se. Skarakis and Prutting (1977) found that 2- to 4-year-old deaf toddlers used their speech and gestures to express the same communicative intents (such as to greet, to request) present in the early speech of hearing children (see Chapter 5 for a discussion of the communicative functions of early language). Also, Tweney, Hoeman, and Andrews (1975) found, using a card sorting task, that 16- to 18-year-old deaf adolescents categorized words into hierarchical structures similar to those of hearing subjects.

> **Box 7.1   Examples of sentences produced by orally educated deaf students between the ages of 10 and 18 years**
>
> The cat under the table.
> John sick.
> The girl a ball.
> Tom has pushing the wagon.
> Beth made candy no.
> Beth threw the ball and Jean catch it.
> John goes to fishing.
> Bill liked to played baseball.
> Jim wanted go.
> Who a boy gave you a ball?
> Who TV watched?
> The dog chased the girl had on a red dress.

Source: From Quigley and King, 1980.

Syntactic development   In prelingually deaf children who are orally educated, syntactic development is delayed, and the endpoint of syntactic development typically falls far short of normal language competence (Mogford, 1993). A variety of syntactic errors are characteristic of the language produced by orally educated deaf children, even after the age of 10 years (Quigley & King, 1980). The syntactic abilities of hearing-impaired 18-year-olds fall below those of hearing 10-year-olds (Quigley, Power, & Steinkamp, 1977). Box 7.1 illustrates the kind of construction orally educated deaf adolescents produce. The particular type of syntactic errors made by deaf adolescents (educated with either oral or total communication methods) suggests that most deaf children do not fully acquire the grammar of the language (de Villiers, de Villiers, & Hoban, 1994).

The creation of home sign systems by deaf children

Children who are born deaf to parents who cannot sign and who have been discouraged from learning sign language are in the same situation as the two children whom King Psammetichus sent off to be raised by a shepherd who was not to talk to them. The "deaf of hearing" are linguistic isolates. Although they typically live in families that love and care for them, their caregivers cannot communicate with them in a language they can perceive. It has long been known that deaf children in such a situation spontaneously use gestures to communicate (Lane, 1984; Lenneberg, 1964); these gestures are known as **home sign.** Susan Goldin-Meadow and her colleagues (Feldman, Goldin-Meadow, & Gleitman, 1978; Goldin-Meadow, 1982; Goldin-Meadow & Mylander, 1984) studied the home sign systems created by several deaf children to ask the same question that King Psammetichus did: What sort of language does the brain create if it is not given an existing language to learn?

The answer suggested by Goldin-Meadow's findings is that deaf children invent a lexicon of signs to stand for actions and attributes (for example, a pantomimed action, such as a fist held at the mouth to mean "eat"); and they point to refer to people, places, and things. The children also combine these points and signs into "sign sentences" that express the same semantic relations found in hearing children's speech and that have a consistent ordering (for example, the sign for the object being acted on typically precedes the sign for the action, as in *bicycle-pedal, apple-eat*) (Goldin-Meadow, 1982). However, deaf children do not invent a full language, complete with morphology and complex syntax. (We consider what circumstances are necessary for the creation of a full language in the next chapter.)

The acquisition of sign language after early childhood

Deaf children educated by purely oral or by total communication methods typically do not learn sign language at home, nor are they instructed in it at school. However, many deaf children are eventually exposed to sign language when they meet other deaf children, some of whom have deaf parents and have been exposed to sign language from infancy. Historically, many children's first exposure to sign occurred when they were sent to residential schools for the deaf. It is interesting to ask about the sign language acquisition of children in this situation, for both practical (it is the situation for many deaf people) and theoretical reasons. What happens if a child is essentially languageless for many years and is then exposed to language after the age when most children acquire their native language?

Elissa Newport studied adult members of the deaf community in Philadelphia, Pennsylvania. All these adults, who ranged in age from 35 to 70 years, used sign in their everyday communications and had done so for more than 30 years. Some of these adults had acquired ASL as infants from their deaf parents. Some had first been exposed to ASL when they started attending the Pennsylvania School for the Deaf between the ages of 4 and 6 years. And some were first exposed to ASL only after the age of 12, when they entered school as teenagers, or later, when they made friends with people from that school or married someone from that school.

Newport (1990) administered a battery of comprehension and production tests to assess how well these deaf adults had mastered the grammar of ASL. Her results are depicted in Figure 7.2. Adults who were first exposed to ASL after

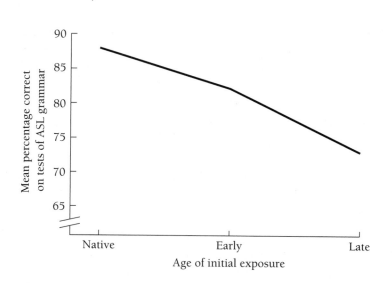

Figure 7.2   Effects of age of first exposure on mastery of American Sign Language
Source: From Psychology, Fourth Edition, by Henry Gleitman. Copyright © 1995, 1991, 1986, 1981 by W. W. Norton & Company, Inc. Reprinted by permission of W. W. Norton & Company, Inc.

early childhood—even after 30 years of using the language every day—did not perform as well as the adults who were exposed to ASL as infants. Exposure after the age of 12 resulted in lower performance than exposure at 4 to 6 years. The particular aspect of the grammar affected was morphology. All the adults had mastered the basic word order of ASL, but only the infant learners had mastered grammatical morphology.

Implications of research on language development in deaf children

So, what have we learned from this review of the literature on language development in the deaf? With respect to the applied question of deaf education, we have learned that deaf children are not handicapped in their ability to acquire language if the language is presented in the visual mode. Thus the optimal situation for language development is to be born to deaf parents who are themselves native speakers of sign. However, the issue of deaf education is complicated by two other facts. One is that 90% of deaf children do not have that option because they are born to hearing parents. The second is that language development is usually not the only goal that parents and educators have for deaf children; usually, the ability to participate in the hearing world and the acquisition of literacy are also goals, and these goals are not automatically achieved when a sign language is acquired.

The problem is somewhat simplified by two other conclusions that emerge from the literature. One is that purely oral methods, and even total communication approaches, result in limited success at oral language acquisition. Thus choosing these routes to the exclusion of sign language for the prelingually deaf child means limiting the level of language competence the child can achieve. To put it plainly, successful oral language acquisition is not really an option for prelingually deaf children. Another conclusion that emerges from the literature is that sign language acquisition does not interfere with what the child can accomplish via oral means (Wilbur, 1979); so, even if the goal is to become as orally competent as possible, there is no reason to deprive the deaf child of access to sign language.

There is a new and developing technology that may change this conclusion. A device, called a **cochlear implant,** can bypass the damaged cells in the ear and directly stimulate the auditory nerve. This device must be surgically implanted inside the cochlea—the part of the inner ear where sound is converted to neural signals. This implanted device receives signals that are picked up by a microphone worn behind the ear and that are processed for transmission by a small externally worn device. Cochlear implants have proven to be helpful to postlingually deafened adults (Owens, 1989), but how well they can work for the prelingually deaf is an open question at this point (see Owens & Kessler, 1989).

However, the potential of cochlear implants to "cure" deafness raises a political issue for many people. Some members of the Deaf* community argue that deafness is not a disability in need of a cure. Rather, deaf people constitute a culture that is defined, in large measure, by their shared language. Proponents of the "deafness as culture" view agree that there are hardships associated with being Deaf, but they see these hardships as resulting from the fact that they are a linguistic minority that is discriminated against rather than as an intrinsic feature of deafness (Dolnick, 1993; Lane, 1984; and see also Padden & Humphries, 1988, for a discussion of Deaf culture). Proponents of this view object to both oralist (or total communication) methods of education and to cochlear implants because the goal of these approaches is to make the deaf like the hearing rather than to promote Deaf culture. The controversy that surrounded the 1994 Miss America—who was deaf but who communicated orally rather than in sign language—is an illustration of the tensions this issue generates.

Studies of deaf individuals have also yielded information that advances our understanding of language acquisition in general. The similarities between the course of sign language development in deaf children exposed to sign from birth and spoken language development in hearing children suggest that the human capacity for language is not tied to the aural-oral channel (Petitto, in press). Language is a property of the human brain, not of the mouth and ears. The

---

*It is a convention to use the lowercase *deaf* to refer to the audiological condition and the uppercase *Deaf* to refer to a group of people who share a culture.

specific similarities in the acquisition of personal pronouns in sign and spoken language combined with the evidence that the similarity of the signs to prelinguistic pointing gestures doesn't help their acquisition as signs suggest that language development is not the next step after gestures in some continuous course of communicative development. This evidence suggests, in contrast, discontinuity between prelinguistic and linguistic communication (Petitto, 1987). Acquiring a formal grammatical system is a separate cognitive enterprise from figuring out how to communicate, even though, once acquired, that formal system is very useful for communication (see the discussion in Chapter 5 on the relation between communication and language).

Finally, the data on ASL competence in adults with different language learning experiences suggest that there are **maturational constraints** on language acquisition. That is, normal language acquisition culminating in full linguistic competence occurs only when exposure to language begins early in life. (This issue will come up again in Chapter 8 on second language learning and in Chapter 9 on the biological foundations of language.)

LANGUAGE DEVELOPMENT AND BLINDNESS

Perhaps the first question to consider in discussing language development in blind children is why it should be any different from language development in sighted children. After all, blind children can hear and talk. However, blind children's access to nonverbal communication and to the nonverbal context of communication is limited to what can be perceived through senses other than vision. Many arguments assert that language development builds on nonverbal communication (for example, Bates, Camaioni, & Volterra, 1975; Bruner, 1977; see also Chapter 5 on the role of prelinguistic interaction in the development of communication) and that language development depends on accessing the meaning of sentences from the observable nonlinguistic context (see Chapter 4 on semantic bootstrapping). Therefore, the language development of blind children provides an interesting test of these arguments.

Clearly, blindness does affect communicative interaction and some aspects of language development. Remember from earlier chapters that joint attention between speaker and listener is important for both effective communication in the short run and successful language development in the long run. With blind children, achieving joint attention is more difficult because the usual routes of eye gaze and pointing are blocked (Fraiberg, 1977; Urwin, 1978). Phonological development is also affected by blindness. Blind children make more errors than sighted children in producing speech sounds that have highly visible articulatory movements (such as /b/, /m/, /f/), but they are not different from sighted children in their production of speech sounds produced by nonvisible articulatory movements (such as /t/, /k/, /h/). This suggests that visual information, such as lip configuration, contributes to phonological development in sighted children (Mills, 1987). (This finding is also consistent with the evidence that deaf children can acquire some aspects of phonology on the basis of lipreading; see Dodd, 1987.)

With respect to vocabulary, blind children have been reported to have fewer words for objects that can be seen but not touched, such as *moon* or *flag,* and more words for things associated with auditory change, such as *piano, drum,* and *bird* (Bigelow, 1987). Also, several studies have indicated that blind children are less likely than sighted children to overgeneralize their words (such as calling a horse *doggie*) (Mills, 1993). In fact, blind children often fail to appropriately generalize words, using new words as names for specific referents rather than as names for categories (Dunlea, 1989), which suggests that visually accessible information plays a role in learning the extensions of categories.

The only reported difference between blind and sighted children in the rate of grammatical development is a delay in blind children's acquisition of verbal auxiliaries—the "helping verbs" such as *can, will, do* (Landau & Gleitman, 1985). Landau and Gleitman observed this delay in a study of three blind children and suggested that the cause for the delay was in the nature of the mothers' speech. Landau and Gleitman found that the mothers of the blind children used more direct imperatives (such as *Take the doll*) and fewer yes/no questions (such as *Can you take the doll?*) than did mothers talking to sighted children. Other studies of sighted children's language development have found that high rates of imperatives and low rates of yes/no questions in mothers' speech are associated with children's slower acquisition of auxiliaries (Newport, Gleitman, & Gleitman, 1977; see also Chapter 4).

With respect to style of language use, several studies have reported that blind children show a greater use of social routines and unanalyzed, formulaic speech than sighted children do (Dunlea, 1984; Kekelis & Andersen, 1984; Mills, 1993; Perez-Pereira & Castro, 1992; Peters, 1994). For example, Peters (1995) described a blind child who, at 2½ years, used the form *Didja* (from *Did you*) to introduce sentences about something that just happened. Examples of such sentences and their meanings include

Didja find it. (= I found it.)

Didja dump it out. (= I dumped it out.)

Didja burp. (= I burped.)

Peters (1994) suggests that because blind children are more dependent than sighted children are on speech as a means of social interaction, they are motivated to adopt a "pick it up and use it before you have time to analyze it" (Peters, 1994, p. 200) approach to language.

Blindness also affects conversational interaction. Adults talking to blind children tend to initiate topics more than adults talking to sighted children do; and when blind children introduce topics, they tend to be self-oriented topics (Kekelis & Andersen, 1984). Also, young blind children have difficulty understanding the conversations that go on around them, leading to frustration and sometimes to behavioral problems (Gleitman & Gleitman, 1991).

These differences notwithstanding, the course of language development is remarkably unimpeded by blindness. Blind children who have no other handicapping condition babble, produce first words, produce word combinations, and acquire syntax and morphology on essentially the same timetable as do sighted children. The difficulty that blind children experience in generalizing both word meaning and language use suggests that visual information plays a role in language development. However, the essential success of blind children's language acquisition reveals that language acquisition cannot be simply a process of mapping sounds onto the things and actions to which they refer. Otherwise, the unavailability of referents would pose greater problems for blind children than it does. In fact, it was the successful language acquisition of one blind child studied by Landau and Gleitman (1985) that led to the proposal that children use information in the syntactic structure of sentences as a significant source of information about what verbs mean (see discussion of the syntactic bootstrapping hypothesis in Chapter 3).

LANGUAGE DEVELOPMENT AND MENTAL RETARDATION

A variety of different conditions result in mental retardation, which is defined by the American Psychiatric Association as "significantly subaverage general intellectual functioning . . . that is accompanied by significant limitations in adaptive functioning" (American Psychiatric Association, 1994, p. 39). Persons with mental retardation form a very heterogeneous group, and different forms of mental retardation have different consequences for language development. The question of how language development is affected by mental retardation is of interest for obvious applied reasons and because it allows researchers to ask how general intellectual functioning is related to language development. If acquiring language is just one more thing humans do with their general intellectual capacity, then impairment in general intellectual capacity should impair language development, and it should do so to the same degree that general capacities are impaired. On the other hand, if language is a separate capacity (the term **autonomy** is often used to refer to this idea of separateness), then there should be some independence, or **dissociation,** of general intelligence and language ability. In this section, we will cover the topic of language development and mental retardation selectively, focusing first on persons with Down syndrome, second on the condition known as Williams syndrome, and last on a few individual case studies that have particular relevance for this theoretical issue. (A more comprehensive treatment of language and mental retardation is available in Rosenberg & Abbeduto, 1993.)

Figure 7.3 Down syndrome is a form of mental retardation that typically results in delayed language development. Individuals with Down syndrome become quite competent communicators, but their vocabulary and the grammatical complexity of their speech are usually below typical adult levels.

Language development in children with Down syndrome

Down syndrome is a chromosomal abnormality, present in approximately 1 in 800 newborns, that accounts for approximately one-third of the moderately to severely mentally retarded population (Rondal, 1993). (See Figure 7.3.) Both the severity of mental retardation and the language development of persons with Down syndrome vary considerably, and some individuals with Down syndrome achieve typical adult-level linguistic competence. However, most do not (Fowler, Gelman, & Gleitman, 1994), and despite the individual differences that exist, it is possible to describe some general characteristics of language development in individuals with Down syndrome.

In children with Down syndrome, language development is delayed relative to chronological age but is consistent with mental age up to the age of 3 or 4 years. After the age of 4, language in children with Down syndrome starts to lag even behind mental age (Miller, 1987). In the separate components of language development in children with Down syndrome, we find the following developmental courses: Although babbling occurs on a relatively normal time-table, phonological development after infancy is substantially delayed. Phonological processes that are typical of normally developing toddlers (such as final consonant deletion and cluster reduction) continue into adolescence and adulthood (Chapman, 1995). Most adults with Down syndrome have some difficulty producing intelligible speech, probably in part because of structural abnormalities of the mouth and tongue associated with the condition (Rondal, 1993).

Lexical development starts late and proceeds slowly in children with Down syndrome. They typically produce their first word around 24 months—approximately one year later than typically developing children but on schedule, so to speak, with respect to mental age. By the time children with Down syndrome are 6 years old, they are more than three years behind typically developing children, and their language lags behind their mental age. That is, a child with Down syndrome who is 6 years old and has a mental age of 3 years is likely to have a smaller vocabulary than an average 3-year-old child.

Grammatical development in children with Down syndrome is also delayed, even relative to mental age, and shows an extremely protracted course of growth. Children with Down syndrome cover the same course of grammatical development as typically developing children do, but the children with Down syndrome take 12 years to do what most children accomplish in 30 months (Fowler et al., 1994). For many individuals with Down syndrome, language development comes to a halt at the age of 12; Stage III, or an MLU of about 3.0, is as far as they get. Fowler (1988) suggests that an IQ over 50 may be necessary for progress beyond that point. Most individuals with Down syndrome do not have IQs above 50, and they fail to fully master the grammatical morphology or complex syntax of English (Fowler et al., 1994). What this degree of grammatical impairment means is that the average 12-year-old with Down syndrome, who has a mental age of no more than 6 years (that would be an IQ of exactly 50), produces speech with the grammatical complexity of the speech of a typically developing child who is 2½ to 3 years old (Fowler et al., 1994).

However, two other observations temper this conclusion that the language development of individuals with Down syndrome stops at the level of a typically developing 3-year-old. As Fowler and associates (1994) noted, 12-year-old children with Down syndrome who have these limited grammatical skills seem, on the surface, to be more competent communicators than the typical 3-year-old. Also, Chapman (1995) found that individuals with Down syndrome do show increases in the grammatical complexity of their speech after the age of 12, when their language is assessed in narrative production. These results suggest that individuals with Down syndrome may have a unique constellation of pragmatic abilities and inabilities. Studies of pragmatic competence in persons with Down syndrome have found that some early developing pragmatic skills, such as turn taking in conversation, seem relatively unimpaired (Rosenberg & Abbeduto, 1993). However, individuals with Down syndrome perform poorly in referential communication tasks, have difficulty with the kinds of form-function mappings that need to be controlled in order to mark politeness appropriately, and they have difficulty controlling reference in narrative production (Rosenberg & Abbeduto, 1993).

What does the language development of individuals with Down syndrome suggest for the role of general cognition in language? On the one hand, the fact that language development is delayed is consistent with the idea that general cognitive factors are involved. On the other hand, the language development of persons with Down syndrome is even more delayed than their cognitive development, suggesting that cognitive development cannot be the only relevant factor. Part of the problem in using the evidence from children with Down syndrome to explain how general cognitive functioning and language development may be related is that the typically available measure of cognitive development is mental age as assessed by an IQ test. IQ tests provide a useful overall measure of mental functioning, but they may not be sufficiently fine-grained to identify the components of mental functioning that would be interestingly related to language acquisition. This is a problem that is true for the study of other special populations as well.

Language development in children with Williams syndrome

Individuals with **Williams syndrome** are—by general IQ measures—as mentally retarded as individuals with Down syndrome (Bellugi, Wang, & Jernigan, 1994). Unlike individuals with Down syndrome, however, persons with Williams syndrome speak in long, grammatically complex sentences, use a rich vocabulary, and can tell coherent and complex stories. Williams syndrome is a rare disorder, but the striking contrast between the severe cognitive deficits and the unusual language abilities that characterize individuals with Williams syndrome make the study of Williams syndrome central to issues about the dissociability of language and cognition.

The psycholinguistic study of Williams syndrome came about in a rather unusual way. The impetus came from the mother of a child with Williams syndrome. The mother had read a magazine article about Noam Chomsky that expressed Chomsky's theory that there is a "language organ" separate from the rest of human mental abilities. Believing that Dr. Chomsky would be interested in her daughter's unusual language abilities, the mother called him up at his office at the Massachusetts Institute of Technology. Chomsky is a theoretical linguist who studies sentences, not children, and he resides in Massachusetts, whereas the mother and daughter lived in San Diego. So Chomsky referred the mother to Ursula Bellugi, who was one of Roger Brown's first students in developmental psycholinguistics and who is the director of the Laboratory for Cognitive Neuroscience at the Salk Institute for Biological Studies in California.

And so it came to pass that late one evening, when Dr. Bellugi was alone in her office and answering her own phone—which laboratory directors of institutes do not usually do—the phone rang and the caller announced to Dr. Bellugi that "Noam Chomsky told me to call you" (Bellugi, personal communication, February 1995). The mother, and subsequently the child herself, convinced Bellugi that Williams syndrome was of interest, and now not only this child but many other children with Williams syndrome have been studied intensively.

The first individuals with Williams syndrome to be studied ranged in age from 11 years to young adulthood. They all displayed a striking discrepancy between their language skills and their level of general cognitive functioning. Although the IQs of individuals with Williams syndrome range from 40 to 70—roughly the same range as individuals with Down syndrome—these individuals give the impression of being even more verbal and more conversational than typically developing children (Singer, Bellugi, Bates, Jones, & Rossen, in press). Adolescents with Williams syndrome tell coherent and complex stories with great emotional expression (Reilly, Klima, & Bellugi, 1990). They use advanced and unusual vocabulary in their spontaneous speech—words like *surrender, nontoxic, commentator,* and *brochure*—and, when asked, they are capable of providing appropriate definitions of these terms. Their spontaneous language is grammatically complex in terms of both grammatical morphology and sentence structure, although with occasional errors of overgeneralizing morphology (Bellugi et al., 1993). The contrast between the language and nonlinguistic skills of individuals with Williams syndrome is illustrated in Figure 7.4, which presents a drawing and a verbal description produced by an 18-year-old with Williams syndrome who was asked to draw an elephant.

Later research on Williams syndrome explored the early stages of language development, and it became apparent that Williams syndrome is associated with language delay—at least initially (Singer, et al., in press; Thal, Bates, & Bellugi, 1989). Children with Williams syndrome are as delayed as children with Down syndrome, who have similar IQs in early vocabulary development. However, when grammar begins to emerge, children with Williams syndrome diverge from the developmental course followed by children with Down syndrome, showing more advanced grammatical development than IQ-matched children with Down syndrome (Bellugi et al., 1994; Singer et al., in press). However, the language impairment that was seen as a delay in early language development is not completely left behind once grammatical development begins. Even in adolescence, some impairments of language are associated with Williams syndrome. On standardized tests of language, these adolescents score at or above their mental age but not at the level of their chronological age.

a.

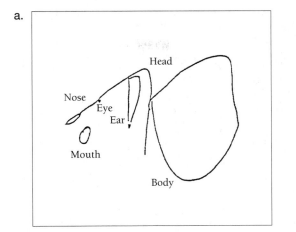

b.

And what an elephant is, it is one of the animals. And what the elephant does, it lives in the jungle. It can also live in the zoo. And what it has, it has long gray ears, fan ears, ears that can blow in the wind. It has a long trunk that can pick up grass, or pick up hay. . . If they're in a bad mood it can be terrible. . . If the elephant gets mad it could stomp; it could charge, like a bull can charge. They have long big tusks. They can damage a car. . . It could be dangerous. When they're in a pinch, when they're in a bad mood it can be terrible. You don't want an elephant as a pet. You want a cat or a dog or a bird. . .

Figure 7.4   Response of an adolescent with Williams syndrome who was asked to describe an elephant

Source: From "Williams Syndrome: An Unusual Neuropsychological Profile," by U. Bellugi et al. In S. H. Froman and J. Grafman (Eds.), Atypical Cognitive Deficits in Developmental Disorders, pp. 25–56. Copyright © 1994 Dr. Ursula Bellugi, The Salk Institute for Biological Studies, La Jolla, CA. Used by permission.

The great emotion with which they tell stories that initially seems so impressive appears aberrant on further examination. These individuals tell stories with the same high level of dramatic expression no matter how many times they've told the same story and no matter who the audience is (Reilly et al., 1990).

Williams syndrome clearly presents a very different picture from that of Down syndrome. In Down syndrome, language abilities are more impaired than cognitive abilities; in Williams syndrome, language abilities are much less impaired than cognitive abilities. Bellugi and associates have argued on this basis that language acquisition is a separate mental function from other cognitive functions—that language and cognition are dissociable. On the other hand, even in the case of Williams syndrome, language is not completely unaffected by mental retardation.

Case studies of individuals with mental retardation who have high-level language skills

There are some other, widely discussed cases of persons who are severely mentally retarded but who have remarkable linguistic abilities. The woman known in the literature as "D. H." has cognitive deficits so severe that she is unable to put three pictures in correct order to tell a story, she has difficulty

---

Box 7.2   Speech sample from D. H., a woman with chatterbox syndrome and a measured IQ of 44

Researcher: So how long have you been here then?

D. H.: Two and a half years.

Researcher: Uh-huh.

D. H.: And Dad's getting fed up with moving around. He thinks it's time that I settle down—to school, which is fair enough. To him, it . . . he feels it's going to ruin my whole life if I don't settle down sometime.

Researcher: Uh-huh.

D. H.: So I'm gonna have to, at some point settle down, somewhere,

Researcher: Uh-huh.

D. H.: somehow. Mum didn't mind me moving about, but Dad objected to it because he knew it was bothering me and it was bothering my school work.

Source: From Cromer, 1994.

naming the seasons of the year, and her IQ has been measured at 44. Yet D. H. can talk up a storm. She not only talks a great deal, but her speech is fluent and grammatically correct (Cromer, 1994). Box 7.2 shows an example of her speech in conversation with the psycholinguist who studied her, Richard Cromer.

D. H. demonstrates what is known as **chatterbox syndrome.** This syndrome has been described in other subjects as well, but D. H. is the individual who has been most carefully studied. Another mentally retarded individual with remarkable language abilities is the woman known in the scientific literature as "Laura" (Yamada, 1990). At the age of 16, Laura performed at the level of a 3- to 4-year-old on most cognitive tests, but she was able to produce sentences such as these:

> She does paintings, this really good friend of the kids who I went to school with last year and really loved.

> He was saying that I lost my battery powered watch that I loved.

On the basis of cases such as D. H. and Laura, some have argued that the ability to acquire grammar is separate from other nonlinguistic cognitive functions and in fact is separate from the mental ability that underlies the acquisition of semantics and pragmatics; this is the argument for the **modularity** of syntax (Cromer, 1994; Curtiss, 1988; Yamada, 1990). However, others have argued for a less sweeping conclusion (Shatz, 1994). Cases in which severe mental retardation is combined with good grammatical abilities make it clear that language need not be as affected as other mental faculties. On the other hand, neither D. H. nor Laura performed at normal levels on a battery of standardized language tests. Therefore, it is not quite accurate to describe the syntactic ability of these individuals as completely spared. And, as suggested earlier in the description of individuals with Down syndrome, we do not have a complete understanding of these individuals' cognitive abilities. It's not that these individuals haven't been fully tested; rather, the current state of the art in cognitive assessment limits what we know about these individuals' cognitive functioning. In fact, the content of what Laura and D. H. say suggests that they must have some cognitive abilities that are not typical of individuals with such low IQs.

In sum, mental retardation affects language development. However, the degree of mental retardation present does not straightforwardly predict how language development will be affected. In Down syndrome, language development is more affected than other cognitive skills, as evidenced by the fact that children with Down syndrome show lower-level language skills than typically developing children of the same mental age do. However, there are also syndromes and individuals in which impressive spontaneous speech is present despite severe mental retardation. However we are ultimately to explain the ability to talk, we will have to account for both these sorts of discrepancies between nonlinguistic cognitive ability and language ability.

LANGUAGE DEVELOPMENT AND AUTISM

Autism is a severe disorder that always involves impaired language and communication. The characteristic features of autism are impaired social development, delayed and deviant language, insistence on sameness, and onset before age 30 months (Rutter, 1978). That definition includes a wide range of levels of functioning, and for a discussion on language development, it is necessary to distinguish between lower- and higher-functioning persons with autism.

Language in lower-functioning persons with autism

Approximately 80% of autistic individuals score in the mentally retarded range on nonverbal tests of intelligence (Konstantareas, 1993). Those with the more severe cognitive impairments (the lower-functioning persons with autism who comprise about 50% of the autistic population) either do not speak at all or have **echolalic speech.** Echolalic speech is the meaningless repetition of a word or word group previously produced by another speaker (Fay, 1993). In

immediate echolalia, a child might respond to a question by repeating the question or the last word of the question. In **delayed echolalia,** chunks of previously heard utterances are produced much later. Although these echolalic chunks do not seem to have literal meaning for the autistic individual, they may serve communicative functions, such as maintaining social interaction (Prizant, 1983).

Although efforts have been made to teach language skills to such lower-functioning persons with autism, there have been no clear successes. Practitioners of an intensive behavioral approach, in which children are rewarded for appropriate communicative behavior and occasionally punished for inappropriate behavior, have had mixed results (Lovaas, 1987; Lovaas & Smith, 1988), and even their claims of success have been questioned (Schopler, Short, & Mesibov, 1989). However, some success has been reported for simultaneous communication programs that combine speech with manual signs (Konstantareas, 1993).

For a few years, it appeared that the technique of facilitated communication would enable otherwise low-functioning persons with autism to communicate. In facilitated communication, an individual with autism spells out messages on a keyboard while a facilitator steadies the person's arm. Great successes were initially reported with formerly mute individuals, seeming to write poetry and heart-wrenching accounts of life with their handicap (Biklen, 1990). However, facilitated communication turned out to be a modern-day version of the classic Clever Hans story. Clever Hans was a horse who appeared to be able to solve simple arithmetic problems and who communicated his answers by stomping his hoof the appropriate number of times. However, researchers finally detected that Clever Hans was completely unable to do arithmetic, but he was very good at reading the subtle nonverbal cues in facial expression and body posture his audience inadvertently provided when he reached the correct answer. When the audience didn't know the answer, neither did Clever Hans. Similarly, when subjected to close scientific scrutiny, facilitated communication turned out to be bogus; individuals with autism could answer questions only when the facilitators knew the answers. Thus the messages that appeared to come from the individuals with autism were actually coming from the facilitators, although the facilitators were unaware that they were actually directing the arm movements of the autistic individuals whose communication they thought they were only facilitating (Regal, Rooney, & Wandas, 1994; Shane, 1993; Smith, Haas, & Belcher, 1994).

Language in higher-functioning persons with autism

Higher-functioning individuals with autism, who have less severe general intellectual impairment, do acquire language. However, even in these individuals, language development is both delayed and deviant. The prosodic features of the speech produced by persons with autism are almost always odd, often sounding mechanical (Fay, 1993). In contrast, semantics seems less impaired. Compared to mental-aged matched children without autism, children with autism show both similar vocabulary growth (Tager-Flusberg, Calkins, Nolin, Baumberger, Anderson, & Chadwick-Dias, 1990) and similar understandings of word meanings (Tager-Flusberg, 1985). One semantic difference is that children with autism do not use words that refer to mental states, such as *believe, figure, idea,* and *guess* (Tager-Flusberg, 1993). Syntactic development in children with autism is slower than in normal children but follows a similar course (Tager-Flusberg, 1981, 1989).

It is in the area of communicative competence, rather than linguistic competence, that individuals with autism show the most clear and significant impairment. Even infants with autism differ from normal infants in their nonverbal communicative behaviors. They rarely produce the pointing gestures that typically developing children start to use to achieve joint attention around the age of 9 months; and even at age 4 years, their joint attention skills are markedly deficient (Loveland & Landry, 1986; Sigman, Mundy, Sherman, & Ungerer, 1986). Children with autism have difficulty with speaker roles in discourse, and they make pronoun reversal errors. They also have difficulty responding appropriately to indirect requests, which they tend to interpret literally (Paul & Cohen, 1985).

It is difficult to have a successful conversation with an individual with autism. Conversations tend to be limited to a small number of topics—those that are of special interest to the individual with autism (Tager-Flusberg, 1993)—and the nonautistic listener has a hard time learning much from such conversation (Paul, 1987). As stated in Chapter 5, as children's linguistic skills develop, their conversational skills normally develop as well. So, as children acquire language, they become more responsive conversational partners. This responsiveness is shown in an increase in the frequency of contingent responses (responses related to the topic of the other speaker's prior utterance) and an increase in the proportion of contingent responses that add new information (Bloom, Rocissano, & Hood, 1976). That developmental pattern does not hold for children with autism. Their linguistic skills improve with age, but their conversational skills do not. Therefore, even when high-functioning persons with autism have mastered the grammar of their language, they do not use those linguistic skills to contribute new relevant information to the ongoing discourse. They also do not ask questions that would elicit new information (Tager-Flusberg, 1993).

Individuals with autism seem to illustrate the dissociability of language and communication. High-functioning persons with autism acquire language, but they seem never to be fully communicative. It has been argued that the underlying deficit in autism is the lack of a theory of mind (Baron-Cohen,

Tager-Flusberg, & Cohen, 1993). And, recall from Chapter 5, it has been argued that understanding other people's minds is prerequisite to true communicative behavior. If both arguments are correct, they converge on an explanation of the communicative deficits observed in individuals with autism. That is, individuals with autism who are not mentally retarded can and do acquire the phonology, the lexicon, and the grammar of language. However, they never use that language normally because they lack the social understanding of other minds that underlies human communication.

SPECIFIC LANGUAGE IMPAIRMENT

Who is "specifically language impaired"?

For some children, language development is difficult, even in the absence of any clear sensory or cognitive disorder. Such children begin to talk and to understand spoken language later than other children. They have smaller vocabularies than other children of the same age, and they have difficulty acquiring grammar. The *Diagnostic and Statistical Manual of Mental Disorders* (DSM-IV) (American Psychiatric Association, 1994) uses the term **developmental language disorder** to label this condition, but among speech-language clinicians and researchers, the most frequently used term is **specific language impairment.** Another term for this condition, which is used more by Europeans, is **developmental dysphasia.** Estimates of the incidence of developmental dysphasia or specific language impairment (SLI) range from 1 child in 1000 affected (Leonard & Schwartz, 1985) to 3 to 5% of children (Johnston, 1993), depending on the criteria used.

Children who are diagnosed as having specific language impairment are a heterogeneous group. They all have delayed language in common, but the specifics of the language difficulties may vary from child to child. Identifying subcategories of language impairment is one topic of current research (see Miller & Klee, 1995). Furthermore, because SLI is diagnosed by exclusion (that is, no hearing impairment, no mental retardation, and so on), children labeled SLI may differ in the causes of their impairment. However, it is an interesting fact that some general characterizations of language impairment are possible, and it is to those general characteristics that we now turn.

Characteristics of language development in children with specific language impairment

Developmental delay   The most obvious feature of the language development of children with specific language impairment is that it is delayed, and often production is more delayed than comprehension. According to one definition, children have specific language impairment if their productive language is 1 year behind normal development and their comprehension is 6 months behind (Stark & Tallal, 1981). Many children with SLI are more delayed than that. It is not difficult to find 5-year-old children with SLI whose productive language is like that of typically developing 3-year-olds. The delayed development that characterizes SLI shows up in every area of language—phonology, semantics, syntax, and pragmatics (Leonard, 1979; Menyuk, 1993).

Delay or deviance?   One question that arises in characterizing the language of children with SLI is whether their language is only delayed or whether it is also deviant. The argument for pure delay is that children with SLI produce the same kinds of grammatical structures, use the same kinds of phonological processes, use the same kinds of vocabulary, and so on as that typically developing children do—they just do so later in the course of development. It is clear that this characterization of SLI as delayed language development accounts for a great deal of the difference between the language of children with SLI and that of typically developing children.

However, it has also been suggested that the language of (at least some) children with SLI is deviant in addition to being delayed. One argument for deviance refers to examples of errors made by children with SLI that are different in kind from errors that typically developing children make (for example, Grimm & Weinert, 1990). Another argument for deviance proposes that children with SLI (again, at least some) go about acquiring language in fundamentally different ways than typically developing children do (for example, M. Gopnik, 1990, 1994; van der Lely, 1994).

The question of whether to characterize the language development of children with SLI as delayed or deviant has theoretical implications. The underlying cause one can posit is different depending on whether the children are thought of as following the same progression as typically developing children do, albeit more slowly, or whether they are thought of as acquiring language in a different way. If their language is simply delayed, then explanations of SLI in terms of impairments in the ability to process input are possible. On the other hand, proposals that children with SLI have deviant grammars are more compatible with the view that a specifically linguistic deficit is at the core of SLI. We will explore these explanations of SLI in more detail in the next section. Before turning to proposed causes of SLI, however, there is one more view on the delay or deviance issue to consider.

Asynchrony   A potential resolution to the delay versus deviance conflict comes from the recognition that language development consists of development in many subsystems of language—syntax, morphology, semantics, and so on. Within each subsystem, children with SLI may follow the typical developmental course, although with delay. However, various subsystems may be delayed to

---

Box 7.3   A story told by a 4½-year-old child with SLI

The man got on the boat. He jump out the boat. He rocking the boat.
He drop his thing. He drop his other thing. He tipping over. He fell
off the boat.

Source: From Lindner and Johnston, 1992.

differing degrees, thus disrupting the usual synchrony of the various components of language development and producing a pattern of language competencies not seen in typically developing children.

An illustration of the notion of developmental asynchrony comes from the
well-established finding that when children with SLI are compared to typically
developing children with the same MLU, the children with SLI have deficiencies
in **morphology** (Johnston & Schery, 1976; Leonard, Bortolini, Caselli, McGregor, & Sabbadini, 1992; Steckol & Leonard, 1979). That is, children with SLI fail
to use word endings such as the verb endings that mark tense or person. This
type of language use is illustrated in the speech sample presented in Box 7.3.

When morphology is delayed relative to syntax, children produce
sentences unlike those typically developing children produce at any age, such
as 6- or 7-word telegraphic sentences. Remember from Chapter 4, children
typically start to acquire morphology when they start combining words, so that
by the time children produce sentences 6 and 7 words long, they are no longer
telegraphic speakers. It is not clear yet whether the notion of asynchrony will
solve the delay versus deviance issue. However, competing accounts of the
cause of SLI pay close attention to the fact that children with SLI are not equally
impaired in all aspects of language. Furthermore, the acquisition of grammatical
morphology, at least for children with SLI acquiring English, seems to be
particularly difficult. Cross-linguistic research has led to contradictory conclusions to whether it is morphology per se that is difficult or whether properties
of English morphology are the source of the difficulty. We will review this
research in some detail when we discuss causes of specific language
impairment.

What causes specific language impairment?

The language environment of children with SLI   Because children with
specific language impairment seem to be unimpaired in every other regard, it
was thought at one time that the cause of SLI might reside in the environment
rather than in the child. To test this hypothesis, numerous studies have

investigated the nature of the speech that parents (usually mothers) address to children with SLI. These studies have found some differences between the speech that mothers address to children with SLI and the speech that mothers address to typically developing children. The most consistent findings are that mothers of children with SLI are more directive of their children and they do proportionately more of the work of initiating and maintaining dialogue (Grimm, 1993). However, these characteristics of mothers' speech seem to be reactions to the conversational passivity of the children with SLI, rather than independent traits in the mothers (Grimm, 1993).

Two major reviews of the literature on the linguistic environment of children with SLI have concluded that the environment is not the explanation for the children's language difficulty (Lederberg, 1980; Leonard, 1987). These reviews argue that mothers of children with SLI modify their speech to suit their children's abilities in the same way that mothers of typically developing children do. On the other hand, other evidence suggests that, in modifying their speech to suit their children's diminished language abilities, mothers of children with SLI may be presenting less useful language input to their children than mothers of typically developing children do (Grimm, 1993; Nelson, Welsh, Camarata, Butkovsky, & Camarata, 1995); for example, Nelson and associates (1995) found that mothers of children with SLI provided fewer responses that were expansions of the child's previous utterance. However, such data suggest merely that the communicative environment of children with SLI may exacerbate their language difficulties. There is no evidence that the input to children with SLI explains their initial problems. Thus whatever the cause of SLI turns out to be, it seems clear that it is a property of the children who have language impairment, not a property of their environments.

Genetic factors in specific language impairment   There is evidence that whatever the cause of specific language impairment turns out to be, it is likely to be something that has a genetic basis. Problems with language acquisition run in families. Neils and Aram (1986) compared the incidence of language disorders in the immediate families of children with and without language impairment. They found that, on average, 20% of the family members of children with language impairment also had some language impairment, compared to a 3% incidence of language impairment among the family members of unimpaired children. Other studies have also found what is referred to as a **familial concentration** of specific language impairment (Ludlow & Dooman, 1992; Tallal, Ross, & Curtiss, 1989; Tomblin, 1989). Tomblin's data, graphed in Figure 7.5, show that children with language impairment have more family members who also show language impairment than do typically developing children. The most dramatic evidence of genetically transmitted language impairment is the case of one family in which language impairment has been observed over three generations in 16 out of 30 family members (Gopnik & Crago, 1991; Vargha-Khadem,

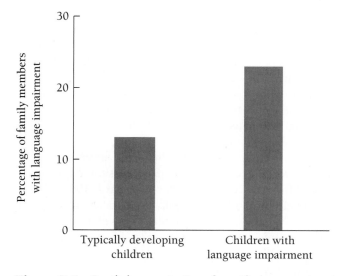

Figure 7.5   Familial concentration of specific language impairment
Source: Based on data in Tomblin, 1989.

Watkins, Alcock, Fletcher, & Passingham, 1995). In this family, the inheritance pattern suggests that a single dominant gene is at work (Gopnik & Crago, 1991).

However, a single gene or even some other genetic basis cannot be identified for all cases of specific language impairment. Not all persons who are specifically language impaired show exactly the same deficits as the members of the family studied by Gopnik and Crago (1991) in which the genetic basis is clear. In addition, although children with SLI are more likely than typically developing children to come from families in which other members have language impairment, not all children with SLI come from families with such a history. One study of 89 children with SLI found that 70% had a family history of language disorder; 30% did not (Tallal, Townsend, Curtiss, & Wulfeck, 1991). Furthermore, the children with SLI who did have a family history of language impairment were not different from the other children with SLI in their language skills or IQ.

Nonlinguistic cognition in children with SLI   One explanation of specific language impairment that has been and continues to be entertained is that SLI results from deficits in nonlinguistic cognition. On this account, specific language impairment is not so specific after all. Several studies have tested this hypothesis by comparing children with SLI to typically developing children on nonlinguistic cognitive measures. The criteria for diagnosing SLI produce a bias against finding differences between children with SLI and typically developing children on cognitive measures, because any child who scored below age level on an IQ test would not be diagnosed as specifically language impaired. Despite this bias, some differences have been found by studies that looked outside of IQ test–type measures of cognitive functioning.

Children diagnosed as having specific language impairment have shown deficits in a variety of cognitive areas, including symbolic functioning, mental imagery, hierarchical planning, hypothesis testing, and reasoning (for summaries, see Johnston, 1988, 1992; Kahmi, 1993). Additionally, Weismer (1985) found evidence that children with language impairment have difficulty drawing inferences from stories, even when the stories are presented in a sequence of pictures with no words. Although the evidence that children with SLI as a group show cognitive deficits in some areas is not in doubt, it is not clear how this evidence explains what causes specific language impairment. That is, it is not clear how these cognitive deficits would explain the language impairments with which they are correlated (Johnston, 1988; Leonard, 1987).

Another proposal is that deficits in **phonological memory** contribute to language impairment. Imagine a task in which you must repeat unfamiliar sequences of sounds (think of trying to catch an unusual name the first time you hear it). This task requires you to temporarily store in memory the phonological properties of the stimulus that was presented to you. The aspect of memory that allows you to do this is phonological memory (Baddeley, 1986). As we discussed in Chapters 3 and 6, there is evidence that 4- and 5-year-old children who are good at this sort of task tend to have bigger vocabularies than do otherwise equivalent children who are not as good at this task, suggesting that phonological memory is involved in the normal process of language acquisition (Gathercole & Baddeley, 1989). Both Gathercole and Baddeley (1990) and Bishop (1995) found that children with specific language impairment were worse at this task than typically developing children were. Furthermore, Bishop (1995) found that this deficit was heritable (has a genetic basis) and can be found even in children whose language impairment was resolved through speech-language therapy. Together these findings suggest that language acquisition depends on phonological memory and that language impairment results when phonological memory is deficient. However, no one is claiming that deficiencies in phonological memory explain all specific language impairment.

Linguistic accounts of specific language impairment   Rather than looking at something else such as cognition or memory to explain language impairment, linguistic approaches look to linguistic analyses of the speech that individuals with language impairment produce (and comprehension data as well) for clues to the source of their disability. There are a variety of such linguistically based accounts of SLI, but they all start from the same basic

---

Box 7.4   Examples of sentences produced by a 16-year-old with specific language impairment

Then he went home and tell mother—his mother—tell what he doing
  that day.
Then about noontime those guy went in and eat and warm up.
That boy climbing a rope to get to the top the rope.
He want play that violin.
Those men sleeping.
That man in a dark room.
Can I play with violin?

Source: From Weiner, 1974.

datum—that specific language impairment, at least for children trying to acquire English, seems to cause particular difficulty with grammatical morphology. The sentences that English-speaking children with SLI produce are correct in their use of word order (subjects precede verbs, which precede direct objects), showing that the children (or adults) have mastered the basic phrase structure of the language. However, the sentences they produce are characteristically missing many function words and word endings. This deficit is illustrated in the language sample in Box 7.3 and even more dramatically in the sample in Box 7.4.

One linguistically based account tries to explain the particular difficulties children with SLI have in terms of impairment in some aspect of the grammar or grammar acquisition mechanism believed to be innate in all of us. For example, Gopnik (1990) proposed the **missing features hypothesis** to account for the errors produced by the 16 family members with language impairment she studied. According to this hypothesis, the innate grammar of these individuals was missing a piece—the notion that certain features, such as number (for nouns) and tense (for verbs) must be marked. More recently, Gopnik (1994, in press) endorsed a different view, termed the **missing rule hypothesis** (Crago & Allen, 1994). This view postulates that affected members of this family have difficulty learning the implicit linguistic rules that govern the use of grammatical morphology (such as marking number and tense). So, for example, where unimpaired children hear *walk* and *walked* and *jump* and *jumped* and then build a rule for forming the past tense, children with language impairment never use those regularities to form a rule. As a result, they often omit these obligatory markers in their speech.

Gopnik and her colleagues have begun research exploring the extent to which the kinds of language problems seen in these family members are characteristic of other people with specific language impairment. However, there is huge disagreement in the field over exactly how to characterize what is wrong with the affected members of this family. In contrast to Gopnik's claim of a very language-specific impairment, another research group that has also studied this family found evidence of language disability beyond the inability to form rules. They also found general cognitive deficits (as indicated by IQ tests) in the family members with language impairment (Vargha-Khadem et al., 1995).

Another linguistic account of the deficit that underlies specific language impairment asserts that children with SLI are impaired in their ability to mark agreement relations. That is, they have particular problems getting the linguistic details right in cases where one element controls the form of another element (Clashen, 1989; Rice, 1994; Rice & Oetting, 1993). This explanation would account for errors like *He jump out . . .* , in which the verb does not agree with its subject.

Not all proposals motivated by linguistic analyses of the speech of children with SLI conclude that some piece of innate linguistic equipment is damaged. An alternative view is based on evidence that the degree to which children with language impairment experience difficulty with grammatical morphology depends on the nature of the language the children are trying to acquire. Specific language impairment is not unique to English-speaking countries; there are German, Italian, and Hebrew speakers with language impairment as well. However, the details of language impairment do vary depending on the language. Research investigating the language abilities of children with language impairment acquiring German (Lindner & Johnston, 1992), Italian (Leonard, McGregor, & Allen, 1992), and Hebrew (Dromi, Leonard, & Shteiman, 1993) found that morphology is less impaired than it is for English-speaking children. One possible explanation of this finding, according to Leonard and his colleagues, is in the morphological differences between English and these other languages (Dromi et al., 1993; Leonard et al., 1992). In English, morphology is sparse; word order does most of the work in conveying meaning. In German, in contrast, morphology is richer and plays a greater role. This **sparse morphology hypothesis** suggests that the functional role of morphology is relevant to its ease of acquisition, even for children with language impairment.

On the other hand, German-speaking children do show impairment of grammatical morphology relative to syntax (Clashen, 1989; Lindner & Johnston, 1992). Perhaps most dramatically, Crago and Allen (1994) described a child with SLI who produced completely uninflected verb forms (no endings at all) even though she was acquiring a language in which morphology does all the work and word order does no work in conveying semantic relations. (The language was Inuktitut, which is spoken by the Inuit of northern Canada.) Such evidence suggests that specific language impairment may make normal acquisition of morphology impossibly difficult, no matter how important morphology is in the language being acquired (for a review of this literature, see also Fletcher & Ingram, 1995).

The phonological salience hypothesis   Although it is true that children with specific language impairment have particular difficulty with grammatical morphology, not all grammatical morphemes are equally difficult for children with SLI. Leonard (Leonard, Sabbadini, Volterra, & Leonard, 1988; Leonard, 1989) suggested that the explanation of why some morphemes are more difficult than others lies in the **phonological salience** of these morphemes in the speech stream. The morphemes that cause difficulty for children with SLI tend to be unstressed syllables of short duration relative to adjacent syllables (such as *is* in *He is going*) or not to be whole syllables at all (such as the third person *s* on verbs). Leonard describes such morphemes as having **low phonetic substance.** If this account is true, then children with SLI acquiring different languages should show different areas of difficulty depending on what morphemes have low phonetic substance in the target language. Like the sparse morphology hypothesis, the low phonetic substance hypothesis is consistent with some data, but it does not adequately explain all the cross-linguistic data on specific language impairment (Crago & Allen, 1994; Leonard et al., 1992). Leonard and colleagues (1992) concluded that "for most SLI children, the precise factors accounting for the special problems in morphology remain to be discovered" (p. 175).

Specific language impairment as a temporal processing disorder
Imagine you were given the following task to perform: You are sitting in front of a metal box with two panels mounted on it—sort of like a typewriter with two giant keys. Now you hear two tones, first a low frequency tone and then a higher frequency tone, and you are instructed that the left panel goes with the low tone and the right panel goes with the higher tone. Now you hear a pair of tones in sequence—either low-low, low-high, high-low, or high-high. The task is to repeat the sequence you hear in panel pressings—left-left, left-right, right-left, or right-right. This repetition task doesn't appear to be very difficult, and it also doesn't appear on the face of it, that being able to do it should be very important. However, this task is quite difficult for some children, and children who find this task difficult are quite likely to be children who have difficulty acquiring language.

In a series of studies spanning 20 years, Paula Tallal and her colleagues established that children with specific language impairment have difficulty with this task when the interval between tones is very short. When the tones are separated by more than 400 milliseconds (.4 second), children with SLI and typically developing children perform similarly on this task. However, when the sequences are presented rapidly, children with language impairment cannot do it. In fact, children with language impairment appear to have a hard time even telling if two tones presented in rapid sequence are two different tones or two presentations of the same tone (Tallal, 1978).

On the basis of such findings, Tallal has proposed that the deficit underlying SLI is a deficit in processing rapidly presented stimuli. Tallal, Stark, and Mellits (1985) found the same sort of deficit with visually presented stimuli, suggesting that the deficit is not modality-specific. The idea suggested by this proposal is that processing speech depends on processing rapidly sequenced acoustic stimuli. Children with impairment in that sort of processing will have difficulty conducting the analysis of speech that language acquisition requires.

Evidence from Leonard and associates (1992) suggests that this kind of processing deficit could account for the particular problems with grammatical morphology that characterize SLI. The low phonetic substance positions in the speech stream that make grammatical morphemes difficult to acquire also make sounds difficult to identify for children with SLI, but not for typically developing children. Using a discrimination procedure developed by Stark and Tallal, Leonard and associates found that children with SLI could discriminate one vowel from another (such as [i] versus [u]). However, the children with SLI could not discriminate between two sequences of sounds that differed only in an unstressed syllable ([dab i ba] versus [dab u ba]) or in a final consonant ([das] versus [da]). Typically developing children could make all three discriminations.

What is specific language impairment?

The search for the underlying cause of specific language impairment has certainly increased our knowledge of the disorder. As a result of this research, we can describe with some precision which aspects of language are likely to be affected and to what degree. We know that, as a group, children with SLI are likely to be different from children who are acquiring language typically in a number of other ways. For example, children with SLI show non-linguistic cognitive deficits, deficits of phonological memory, and difficulty in discriminating and sequencing rapidly presented stimuli. However, the investigation of SLI has not resulted in identifying a single cause of the disorder.

In a radical proposal, Leonard (1987, 1991) suggested that there is no cause of specific language impairment because there is no such thing as specific language impairment. Instead, he argues, children labeled as SLI simply represent the low end of the distribution of language acquisition ability. Language ability varies in the population, as does every other ability. The child with limited musical ability is not called music impaired, nor is the uncoordinated child called sports impaired. Neither should the child with limited language acquisition ability be termed language impaired.

This proposal concerns more than just labeling. It is a claim that there may not be an underlying pathology that causes language impairment. In Leonard's words,

> many children given the label of SLI are not impaired in the sense of being damaged but rather are much less skilled than their peers in such acts as extracting regularities in the speech they hear, registering the conversational contexts in which these regularities occur, examining these regularities for word-referent associations and evidence of phonological and grammatical rules, and using these associations and rules to formulate utterances of their own. (1987, p. 33)

This is not to say that such children should not be treated. Whatever the explanation of the difficulty some children have acquiring language, those children need help in overcoming their problems with language because of the importance of language skills to academic, social, and occupational success.

SUMMARY

For a variety of reasons, language development in some children does not proceed in its typical fashion. Deafness makes the acquisition of spoken language difficult, if not impossible. However, deaf children who are exposed to sign language in infancy acquire that language according to the same developmental course as hearing children acquire spoken language. Blindness has far less severe consequences for language acquisition. Blind children sometimes fail to appropriately generalize the meanings of words, such as using object labels as if they were names for particular referents rather than as names for categories. Blind children also frequently rely on rote-memorized formulaic speech to participate in conversation. However, grammatical development is relatively unaffected by blindness.

Mental retardation has different consequences for language development, depending on the type and severity of the mental retardation. Individuals with Down syndrome typically show language development that is delayed not only in relation to chronological age but even relative to mental age. Although individuals with Down syndrome are conversationally competent, most do not achieve normal adult-level linguistic competence. In contrast, some individuals with other forms of mental retardation, including Williams syndrome, display language skills that far exceed their nonlinguistic mental abilities.

Autism is always associated with some degree of both language delay and language deviance. Approximately 50% of autistic individuals either do not speak or produce only echolalic speech, in which previously heard utterances are parroted with seemingly little comprehension. Higher-functioning autistic individuals do acquire language, but their eventual competence is almost never normal. The most significant language impairment in autistic individuals is in communicative competence. Although high-functioning autistic individuals may acquire normal vocabulary and grammar, they usually fail to use their language for normal communicative interaction.

Some children who seem typical in all other respects nonetheless have difficulty acquiring language. A great deal of research has been directed toward describing the nature of such specific language impairment (SLI) and finding its underlying cause. Children with SLI differ in the nature of their difficulties and, quite likely, in the cause of their difficulties. Nonetheless, some generalizations are possible. As a group, children with SLI have more trouble acquiring grammatical morphology than acquiring syntax or vocabulary—although those may be delayed as well. With respect to the cause of the difficulties, it seems clear that the cause lies not in the children's environments but in some characteristic of the children themselves. Furthermore, at least for some children with SLI, that characteristic is likely to have a genetic basis, because SLI runs in families. Several hypotheses about the nature of the underlying deficit have been proposed, including deficits in nonlinguistic cognition, deficits in innate grammar, and deficits in the ability to perceive, store, and/or process language input.

Each of the hypotheses concerning the underlying cause of SLI has some empirical support, but so far no single hypothesis has been able to account for the full range of phenomena that characterize SLI. It has also been proposed that the search for an underlying deficit is misguided. That is, children who are labeled SLI may not have anything wrong with them per se; they simply represent the lower end of the range of human ability to acquire language in the same way that other children represent the low end of the range in musical or athletic ability. Even if this proposal is true, the central importance of language skills to academic and occupational success (unlike musical or athletic ability) makes efforts at remediation crucial.

The study of language development in atypical populations provides information about those populations. It also provides information with the potential to shed light on typical language development. For example, the fact that the course of sign language development in deaf children is the same as the course of spoken language development in hearing children tells us that the human capacity for language is not specific to one modality. The fact that blind children have difficulty generalizing the meanings of object labels but are unimpeded in their acquisition of grammar tells us that visual information is more important for forming conceptual categories than for forming grammatical categories and learning the rules that operate over those grammatical categories.

The course and eventual outcomes of language development in people with different forms of mental retardation tell us that language development does not proceed in lockstep with the development of other mental abilities. Language development may lag behind nonlinguistic cognition, as it does in persons with Down syndrome; or language development may exceed nonlinguistic cognitive abilities, as it does in persons with Williams syndrome. Similarly, the relatively spared linguistic competence in individuals with autism, combined with severe social and communicative deficits, tells us that different human abilities are dissociable to some extent. In particular, the language of autistic individuals tells us that acquiring the vocabulary and grammar of language neither depends on nor results in normal communicative interaction. Finally, children with specific language impairment challenge the field to identify just what are the abilities that underlie the human capacity to acquire language.

KEY TERMS

prelingually deaf

sign language

oralist method

total communication

oral language development

American Sign Language (ASL)

nonlinguistic gestures

home sign

cochlear implant

maturational constraints

autonomy (of grammar)

dissociation (of general cognition and language)

Down syndrome

Williams syndrome

chatterbox syndrome

modularity (of syntax)

autism

echolalic speech

immediate echolalia

delayed echolalia

developmental language disorder

specific language impairment

developmental dysphasia

grammatical morphology

familial concentration

phonological memory

missing features hypothesis

missing rule hypothesis

sparse morphology hypothesis

phonological salience

low phonetic substance

REVIEW QUESTIONS

1. What do researchers hope to learn from studying language development in atypical populations?

2. What is the typical outcome of oral language development in the profoundly deaf?

3. What are "home sign" systems, and what does their form and existence imply about the human capacity for language?

4. Describe and contrast the language skills that are typical of individuals with Down syndrome and Williams syndrome.

5. What sort of relation between language development and cognitive skill is consistent with the evidence from both the Down syndrome and Williams syndrome populations?

6. What do the language skills of high-functioning individuals with autism look like? What might explain this pattern of strengths and weaknesses?

7. What are some characteristic features of language development in children with specific language impairment?

8. There are many proposals concerning the nature of the disorder that underlies the symptoms seen in SLI. List and briefly explain each.

9. List one thing that has been learned about normal language development from the study of each of the atypical populations described in this chapter.

10. What does the study of language development in these special populations suggest with regard to the three big issues in the field: (1) the innateness of language, (2) the relation between language and general cognition, and (3) the relation between language development and the development of communication?

8 Learning More Than One Language: Second Language Learning and Bilingual Development

Emir (age 4): I can speak Hebrew and English.

Danielle (age 5): What's English?

(from de Villiers & de Villiers, 1978)

Up to this point we have been discussing children's acquisition of one language—whichever one children are exposed to from birth. In this chapter,* we turn our attention to the phenomenon of learning more than one language. Many people learn a second language after they have achieved competence in the first. The field that studies this learning process is the field of **second language acquisition,** or **second language learning.** Some people are exposed to two or more languages from birth and learn them simultaneously. The simultaneous acquisition of two languages is referred to as **bilingual development.** In this chapter, we will first discuss the field of second language learning and then, more briefly, the topic of bilingual development.

SECOND LANGUAGE LEARNING: OVERVIEW

The phenomena the field of second language learning tries to explain are captured in the following scenario: Imagine we were to place a normal, 4-year-old, Russian-speaking child in a home where only English was spoken and leave this child there for two years. Other things being equal, we would return to find that the child had become a 6-year-old native speaker of English. In all likelihood, the child would be bilingual in both Russian and English, but the point is that the child would be nativelike in English, very probably indistinguishable from other, 6-year-old native English speakers. Now imagine we were to do the same with an adult, placing a 24-year-old native speaker of Russian in an English-speaking environment. Two years later, we would most likely not find a 26-year-old nativelike English speaker. The chances are great that—even if the individual had spent a large part of the two years studying English—we would find an adult who was readily identifiable as a nonnative English speaker. His or her pronunciation would probably be marked by an identifiable Russian accent, and his or her speech would exhibit

---

Box 8.1   Facts that a theory of L2 acquisition must explain

1. L2 learning is less successful than L1 learning.
2. To some extent, discrepancies between L2 competence and L1 competence are predictable.
3. The differences between L2 learning and L1 learning are more pronounced in adults and older children than they are in young children.

---

*This chapter was written by Fred Eckman and Erika Hoff-Ginsberg.

syntactic and lexical characteristics different from native English speakers' speech and similar to the speech of other adult, Russian-speaking English learners.

This imaginary scenario, with its probable outcome, illustrates three facts that theories of second language acquisition try to explain. First, in learning a second language (often abbreviated **L2**), adult learners generally do not attain nativelike proficiency, despite their best efforts. Second, the ways in which second language proficiency falls short of native proficiency (also known as proficiency in **L1**) are systematic and somewhat consistent across second language learners. Third, children are better at second language learning than adults are. These facts, which any theory of second language acquisition must explain, are listed in Box 8.1.

Historical background

Although scholars have been interested in the nature of foreign language learning and language teaching for centuries, the field of second language acquisition as it is now conceptualized is only about 30 or 40 years old. Forty years ago, the focus of the field was on the applied question of how best to teach foreign languages. The goals of this pedagogically oriented research were to identify areas of difficulty in learning the target language and to develop teaching methods to overcome these difficulties. More recently, the field has established itself as a separate discipline that asks basic research questions about why second language learning takes place the way it does (White, 1996).

Second language learning as a multidisciplinary field

Like the field of children's language development, the study of second language acquisition touches issues related to several disciplines. The field of linguistics is central among disciplines that study second language learning, but it is not alone. The facts listed in Box 8.1 have been studied from a wide variety of perspectives, with biological, sociological, and psychological explanations being offered. The field of education is also involved in the study of second language learning because second languages are very often taught in classroom settings.

In this chapter, we will begin with the linguistic and psychological work that focuses on the advantage children seem to have over adults in learning a second language. (Biological explanations of this phenomenon will be discussed in Chapter 9.) Next, we will turn to the largely linguistic work that addresses the fact (1) that second language learning is less successful than first language learning and (2) that the particulars of the difficulties are somewhat predictable based on the native language of the second language learners. We will see, as we did in the study of first language acquisition, how changes in linguistic theory have caused changes in the kinds of explanations of second language learning that have been pursued. Then, we will turn to accounts of second language learning that focus on the sociological processes involved, as learning a new language also involves becoming a member of a new culture. We will conclude the discussion of second language learning with the research that focuses on the applied question of how best to teach second languages. In a final section, we will briefly review the questions asked and the answers proposed regarding the process of bilingual development.

THE ROLE OF AGE IN SECOND LANGUAGE LEARNING

The critical period hypothesis

We saw in Chapter 7 that deaf adults who were first exposed to sign language as adolescents or young adults never achieved the native competence of deaf adults who learned sign language from infancy (Newport, 1990). This evidence supports the notion that early childhood is a period when humans are better at language learning than they ever will be again. This notion is known as the critical period hypothesis, meaning that childhood is the **critical period** for language learning. It is commonly believed among laypersons that there is a critical period for second language learning, a belief based largely on the common observation that children in immigrant families learn the new language more successfully than the adults do.

This common observation is not, however, conclusive evidence of a critical period for second language learning. One of the problems with using this observation as data is the possibility that the children and the adults do not have an equal opportunity to be exposed to the new language. In particular, the children go to school, which requires them to speak the new language and which exposes them to native speakers. In contrast, the adults must find work that does not require substantial language skills. Also, the children's impressive competence is based on comparison to other children, whereas the adults' seeming lack of competence is compared to native adult speakers' facility. What is necessary are studies of the sort Newport did with American Sign Language, looking at speakers who vary in the age of first exposure to a second language and controlling or testing for effects of differences in the opportunity to learn. We turn now to descriptions of such studies, first in the area of phonological competence in the second language and then in the area of syntactic competence.

Effects of age on L2 phonology   Oyama (1976) analyzed the English pronunciation of 60 Italian immigrants according to two variables, age at arrival (6 to 20 years) and number of years in the United States (5 to 18 years). Two tape-recorded samples of each participant's speech were made: the reading of a short paragraph and the recounting of a short anecdote. Equal-length speech samples for each person were then scored by two native-speaker judges according to a five-point scale, ranging from *no foreign accent* to *heavy foreign accent*. The results showed a strong effect of the age-at-arrival variable and no effect for the number of years in the United States.

In a different study, Oyama (1978) studied 60 Italian immigrants' English comprehension, also according to age at arrival and number of years in the country. These individuals, who ranged in age from 14 to 37 years, fell into three groups with respect to age of arrival: those who were between the ages of 6 and 10, those between the ages of 11 and 15, and those between the ages of 16 and 20. Half of the participants had spent between 5 and 11 years in the United States, and half had lived in the country between 12 and 20 years. These individuals were tested on 12 short sentences, 5 to 7 words long, which were recorded by an adult, female speaker of American English. Four copies of these recordings were made, each with different amounts of noise on the tape—sort of like static on a radio station. The result ranged, in the judgment of a pretested native speaker, from sentences that were completely unintelligible to sentences that were fully intelligible. The participants were instructed to listen to each sentence and to repeat what they had understood. This technique was intended to tap an array of linguistic knowledge the participant would need to use to understand the sentence. The results showed that those individuals who began learning English before the age of 11 had comprehension scores comparable to native English speakers. Later arrivals did less well, and those who arrived after the age of 16 showed considerably lower comprehension scores relative to native speakers.

Effects of age on L2 syntax   Patkowski (1980) studied L2 learners' ultimate attainment of English syntax by testing 67 immigrants according to a measure of global syntactic proficiency. Two native-speaker judges rated written transcripts of 5-minute portions of two oral interviews conducted with each participant. Patkowski also used a questionnaire to gather other information on the participants, including the age at arrival (the age at which L2 acquisition began), years in the United States, informal exposure to English, and formal instruction in English. Patkowski's participants could be described as being in an ideal position to learn a second language; they were all educated professionals who had resided in the country for at least 6 years, and they would all, presumably, be motivated to learn the second language. However, the results of the study showed that the only factor strongly associated with the level of syntactic proficiency was age at arrival. No correlations were found for other variables.

These findings were replicated and extended by Johnson and Newport (1989) in a study conducted with 46 native speakers of Chinese or Korean who spoke English as a second language. A group of 23 native English speakers served as a control group. The authors obtained grammatical judgments on 276 sentences involving 12 different rules of English grammar. Approximately half

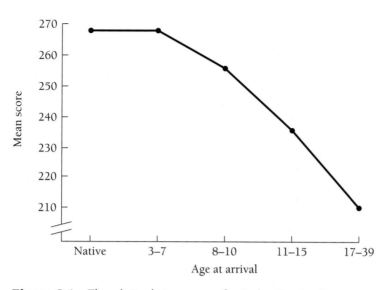

Figure 8.1   The relation between age of arrival and syntactic competence in L2

Source: From "Critical Period Effects in Second Language Learning," by J. Johnson and E. Newport, 1989, Cognitive Psychology, 21, 60–99. Copyright © 1989 Academic Press, Inc. Reprinted with permission.

the test sentences were grammatical and half were ungrammatical. The results showed that those who began learning English in the United States at an early age did significantly better than those who began later. These findings are in accord with those of Oyama and Patkowski and are presented in Figure 8.1.

Johnson and Newport were able to refine these results even further. The authors divided their participants into two groups according to age at exposure, with each group containing an equal number of individuals. The first group consisted of early arrivals—individuals who had arrived in the country between the ages of 3 and 15—and the second group consisted of the late arrivals—those who came to the country between the ages of 17 and 39. At the same time, the authors were also able to control for the number of years the participants had spent in the United States—an average of 9.8 years for the early arrivals and 9.9 years for the late arrivals. For the early arrivals, there was a correlation between age of arrival and eventual syntactic competence, but there was no significant correlation for the group that began learning English between the ages of 17 and 39. Thus, age at arrival appears to make a difference only within the age range from 3 to 15. Beyond 15 years of age, being younger confers no advantage in second language learning.

In another analysis of these data, Johnson and Newport further divided the early arrivals into three groups according to age at arrival: those arriving between ages 3 and 7, between ages 8 and 10, and between ages 11 and 15. The researchers found that, although the performances of these three groups were statistically different from each other, there was no difference in performance between native speakers and participants whose age at arrival was between 3 and 7. These findings suggest that if children are immersed in a second language before the age of 7, they will be able to achieve nativelike fluency; however, children who begin learning a second language even very soon after this age will show a decline in overall performance.

Two other results of the Johnson and Newport study are worth mentioning. First, the data indicated that the variance on the test scores of the early arrival group was small, whereas the variance for the late arrivals was quite large. Thus, for individuals arriving before age 15, there are relatively few individual differences in the ability to learn language; success in learning is predicted almost entirely by the age at which it begins. For the older group, however, although later age of acquisition precludes achieving near-native fluency, large individual differences exist within the diminished level of ability.

The second noteworthy finding of this study concerns the role of experiential and attitudinal factors in explaining the participants' performance. Johnson and Newport found two significant attitudinal factors: self-consciousness and American identification. Motivation, on the other hand, was not a significant factor. Although these findings suggest that, in addition to age at arrival, self-consciousness and American identification might also affect language learning, the authors caution about inferring a direct causal link between these attributes and language learning until more work has been done on possible mediating variables. The role of such variables will come up again in this chapter when we discuss the acculturation model of second language learning.

The preceding studies address the effect of age at arrival on the eventual linguistic competence achieved by second language learners. These studies did not look at the course of language learning. When the course of second language learning is studied, findings reveal that younger learners are not faster learners initially. Snow and Hoefnagel-Höhle (1978) studied the acquisition of Dutch as a second language by English speakers who moved to the Netherlands. The subjects ranged in age from 3 years to adult. Beginning within six months of the English speakers' arrival in the Netherlands, Snow and Hoefnagel-Höhle tested their participants' mastery of Dutch using a variety of measures of pronunciation, vocabulary, grammar, and text comprehension. Contrary to the prediction of the critical period hypothesis, Snow and Hoefnagel-Höhle found that the youngest children scored the lowest on every test, and the 12- to 15-year-olds showed the most rapid acquisition. Thus the advantage that children have in second language acquisition is not in how quickly they learn a new language but in how nativelike their ultimate mastery can become. Given those differences in ultimate mastery, however, it seems fair to conclude that maturational differences between children and adults account at least in part for the facts outlined in Box 8.1. Most L2 researchers would agree with this conclusion. What is not agreed on, however, is exactly how these maturational differences affect the language learning process. We consider briefly only two possibilities.

What underlies the critical period?

One possible interpretation of the research on the maturational effects of the critical period is that maturation affects the mechanism by which language is acquired. According to this view, a human's ability to acquire a language is diminished with age because the language faculty either ceases to operate or becomes less accessible after the critical period has ended. As a consequence, older language learners must use other cognitive mechanisms to acquire a language, and these other mechanisms are not as well suited to the task.

Another possibility is that the language learning mechanism stays the same, and the effect of the critical period pertains only to the ultimate outcome of acquisition. According to this view, differences between child and adult language learners are not attributed directly to the internal mechanism for learning languages but to other cognitive, social, or linguistic differences. These other factors could include the presence of the native language or the development of certain negative attitudes toward the target language or target culture.

A third possible interpretation of the critical period research is that it shows that not all aspects of the target language are equally affected by maturation. This idea is supported by the results from Johnson and Newport's study, which showed that a second language does not become completely unlearnable for adults but found that some aspects of the target language grammar presented more difficulty than others. Also, the effects of maturation may be more severe for phonology than for other aspects of second language acquisition. (Again, other accounts of the critical period will be described in Chapter 9.)

However one interprets the data regarding the critical period hypothesis, it is clear that this hypothesis can provide only a partial explanation for the facts of second language learning listed in Box 8.1. The hypothesis gives no insight, for example, into the way in which adults' second language acquisition is similar to or different from children's first language acquisition. To answer these remaining questions about L2 acquisition, analysts must look at other factors involved. On this note, we turn now to the role of the native language.

THE ROLE OF THE NATIVE LANGUAGE IN SECOND LANGUAGE LEARNING

One of the clearest differences between first and second language acquisition is that in the latter, the learner always knows another language, whereas in the former, this is not the case. Therefore, a potentially viable explanation for why second language acquisition generally produces a result different from that in first language acquisition is that the learner's native language affects the learning of the second language. This influence is known as **language transfer,** and several explanations of language transfer have been proposed.

A behavioral account: The contrastive analysis hypothesis

Claims of the contrastive analysis hypothesis   The earliest approach to the role of the native language in second language acquisition was the **contrastive analysis hypothesis,** developed in the work of Lado (1957). The fundamental claim of this hypothesis is that what an L2 learner finds difficult about virtually any aspect of a given target language is a function of the similarities and differences between the learner's native language and the language being learned. More specifically, where the native and target languages differ, the contrastive analysis hypothesis predicts the learner will experience difficulty, and where the native and target languages are similar, the hypothesis asserts that the learner will find no difficulty: "Those elements that are similar to his native language will be simple for him, and those items that are different will be difficult" (Lado, 1957, p. 2).

On both an intuitive and an empirical level, the hypothesis makes a good deal of sense, and it derives support from various kinds of evidence.

Arguments supporting the contrastive analysis hypothesis   Intuitively, it seems highly reasonable that when we learn something new, such as how to play a different musical instrument, how to do a job we have never done before, or how to play a new sport, those aspects of learning that are most unfamiliar to what we already know are going to cause the most difficulty. And because it is often possible to identify certain foreign accents as associated with specific language backgrounds, it seems plausible that one's native language would influence the way one speaks a foreign language.

On an empirical level, this view of L2 learning seems viable and has engendered a good deal of interest, largely because it can be formulated as a hypothesis that can be tested in a very straightforward manner. In any given language learning situation, a linguist first formulates a description of the two languages in question and then compares those descriptions to determine areas of similarity and difference. Now, if we assume that the difficulty an L2 learner has with another language is directly reflected in the errors the learner makes, then the kinds of facts that would falsify the hypothesis become clear. The hypothesis is supported if the learner makes errors only in the areas of difference between the native and target languages, and makes no (or relatively few) errors in the areas where the two languages are similar. Alternatively, if the learner evinces difficulty in the areas of similarity or shows no difficulty with the differences between the languages, the hypothesis is disconfirmed.

Suppose the language learning situation in question involves a native Spanish speaker learning English. Linguistic analyses of these two languages reveal that one phonological difference between English and Spanish is that English has both /s/ and /z/ as phonemes and Spanish has only /s/. In other words, English has many words, such as *sip* and *zip, busing* and *buzzing,* and *peace* and *peas,* where the only pronunciation difference between each of these pairs of words is the presence of /s/ versus /z/; Spanish, on the other hand, has no such pairs. Spanish has words—such as *sopa* ("soup"), *Peso* ("peso"), and *mas* ("more")—that contain /s/ in initial, medial, and final positions; but Spanish has no words with /z/ in these positions. Now, given these differences between Spanish and English, it follows from the contrastive analysis hypothesis that Spanish speakers learning English should have significant difficulty in pronouncing English words containing the phoneme /z/. Therefore, the observation that Spanish-speaking learners of English pronounce words such as *zone, freeze* and *phrase* as [son], [fris], and [fres], respectively, each with a corresponding [s] sound, would support the contrastive analysis hypothesis.

Consider another example from the same language learning situation, one involving syntax. For present purposes, we focus on two differences in sentence structure between Spanish and English: (1) Spanish allows the omission of subject pronouns in sentences, but English does not; and (2) in Spanish, the negative element is placed preverbally, but in English, the negative always occurs after the auxiliary verb. These two aspects of Spanish syntax are illustrated in Box 8.2.

Because the differences in question pertain to pronominal subjects and negation, that is where the difficulty should arise. And, indeed, English learners whose native language is Spanish do sometimes produce sentences like the one in Box 8.2: "No is possible to do that." Such sentences reflect both of the syntactic differences between Spanish and English—preverbal negation and the absence of a pronominal subject.

The second language acquisition literature has documented numerous examples, such as the phonological and syntactic cases discussed above, from

---

Box 8.2   Aspects of Spanish syntax that cause errors by Spanish-speaking learners of English as a second language

Spanish form: *No es posible hacer eso.*
English form: "It is not possible to do that."
            (neg is possible to do that)
Common error: "No is possible to do that."

a large number of studies involving many different language learning situations. These facts leave little doubt that a learner's native language affects the acquisition of a second language and that many learner errors can be traced to the first language. The contrastive analysis hypothesis, however, says much more than this; it claims that differences between the native and target languages are both necessary and sufficient to explain the difficulty that L2 learners have. It is here that the hypothesis runs into trouble.

Problems with the contrastive analysis hypothesis   Although there is significant support for the contrastive analysis hypothesis both anecdotally and empirically, the hypothesis has encountered difficulty on two different fronts, one theoretical and the other empirical. The contrastive analysis hypothesis ran into problems on theoretical grounds because it was based on the school of American structural linguistics, which had very heavy leanings toward behavioral psychology. The hypothesis viewed language as a set of habits and conceptualized the influence of the native language on second language learning as the interference of old habits in the acquisition of a new habit. The Chomskyan revolution, which changed the way that linguistics regarded language from a set of habits to a system of rules, left the contrastive analysis hypothesis based on a discarded assumption (Dulay & Burt, 1974).

However, the rejection of the hypothesis has turned out, on reflection, to be a bit harsh and premature. Although the behavioral view of language may have been discredited, it does not necessarily follow that the basic thrust of the contrastive analysis hypothesis is unsound. To the contrary, subsequent work has shown that some of the ideas behind the hypothesis can be reformulated within a modern linguistic framework. If knowing a language is knowing a system of rules, then perhaps the native language rules affect the learning of the target language rules. Indeed, as we will see later, there is a place for native language interference or transfer within the newer approaches to second language learning.

More serious for the contrastive analysis hypothesis, however, were the empirical problems it encountered. Although there was certainly ample evidence that native language interference plays a role in explaining second language acquisition, several empirical studies raised a number of doubts as to just how significant that role is. The contrastive analysis hypothesis itself claimed that differences between the active and target languages were both necessary and sufficient to explain learner difficulty. What became apparent, however, was that these differences, although necessary, were not sufficient. Two of the earliest studies that called the hypothesis into question were by Duškova (1969), who studied native Czech speakers learning English, and by Sciarone (1970), who looked at Dutch-speaking learners of French.

Duškova obtained data from 50 Czech-speaking university students who knew English well enough to read the scientific literature in their field and to converse in English on a topic about which they knew. After eliciting L2 English data from these students, Duškova noted that, although many of their errors could be accounted for through L1 interference, a large number of their errors had little, if any, connection to the native language. The students made many errors on constructions in which English and Czech do not differ. Instead, the errors these students made seemed to result from their trying to work out the various subsystems of English morphology and syntax. Sciarone (1970) reported similar kinds of problems in accounting for the errors of Dutch speakers learning French. His participants had difficulty with aspects of French that are similar to Dutch, and they did not have difficulty with some French constructions that are different from anything in Dutch.

Thus, although both studies reported learner errors that were attributable to the native language, each study also reported errors on structures where the native and target languages did not differ. Furthermore, both studies found areas in which the languages differed that did not seem to cause difficulty for the learners. On the basis of these kinds of facts, it became clear that native language interference was limited as an explanation for L2 errors. The task then became one of determining how to predict which type of native and target language differences would cause learning difficulty and which would not.

A linguistic universals account

The fact that some differences between the native and target language cause learning difficulty whereas others do not was potentially a significant problem for any proposal that the native language is the source of errors in the target language. The general facts in this area seemed clear, but a hypothesis that asserts that *some* differences between the native and target languages cause learning difficulty—without specifying which differences were problematic and which were not—has no explanatory value. Therefore the task at hand was to propose principles whereby one could determine which differences would cause difficulty and which would not.

A reasonable place to look for such principles is in the area of language universals. Because such principles are applicable to all languages, they are independent of any particular language and therefore might be able to shed light on which kinds of language differences would likely cause learning difficulty. A central concept to this approach is the notion of **markedness,** which describes the relative generality or naturalness of some linguistic unit. The concern in attempting to characterize notions such as "generality" and "naturalness" is that linguists, being native speakers of at least one language, are apt to reflect their own cultural or linguistic bias. To prevent ethnocentric considerations from intruding on any formulations of naturalness or generality, linguists developed the notion of markedness. Markedness is a construct derived from work on **language universals** and **linguistic typology,** which looks for commonalities among the world's languages.

Markedness and language typology   Linguists who describe some aspect of a language actually have two goals in mind. The first is to describe the particular language being studied; the second is to describe the nature of human language in general. Thus, for example, a linguist who sets out to describe the way in which a particular language indicates singular and plural (number), also has the goal of describing how such an account fits in with the description of number in other languages. The linguist wants to know which aspects of number are particular to the language in question, which aspects are similar to the way number is indicated in at least some other languages, and which aspects, if any, are universal across all languages.

In attempting to analyze languages from a universal standpoint, linguists have found it insightful to describe languages in terms of types. For example, consider again the formation of singular and plural. Investigations have found that not all languages use a morpheme, as English does (such as the *s* in *cats*) to indicate that a noun is plural, even when the meaning of that noun is plural. For example, the Chinese word for "cat" is *mao,* and this word does not add a plural suffix or prefix when more than one cat is indicated, as shown by the examples in Box 8.3.

If we group languages according to whether they indicate singular or plural, we can conceive of four logically possible types of languages. However, only three of these types of languages actually exist: type A, which includes languages with no singular or plural morpheme, such as Chinese; type B, languages with both a singular and a plural morpheme, such as Zulu (for example, *umfana* for "boy," *abafana* for "boys"); and type C, those with a plural morpheme but no singular morpheme, such as English. The other logically possible language—one having a singular morpheme but no plural—has never been found and is presumed not to exist. These language types are summarized in Table 8.1.

Box 8.3   Example of plurality in Chinese

Chinese form	*Literal English translation*
mao	cat
yizhi mao	one cat
sanzhi mao	three cat

Table 8.1   Occurrence of singular and plural morphemes across languages

Language type	Example	Singular morpheme	Plural morpheme
A	Chinese	No	No
B	Zulu	Yes	Yes
C	English	No	Yes
D	None	Yes	No

Thus, Table 8.1 represents a typology of languages with respect to the occurrence of a singular and plural morphemes. What is important is that even though neither morpheme is universal, we can still make a universal statement about the occurrence of these morphemes—namely, that a language may have a plural morpheme without having a singular one, but no language will have a singular morpheme without also having a plural. The notion of markedness is directly derivable from this generalization. We say that the occurrence of the plural is unmarked relative to the singular and that the occurrence of the singular is marked relative to the plural because indicating the plural is a more frequently occurring property of language than indicating the singular. "Unmarked" always refers to structures that are more frequent or more generally occurring relative to other structures, and "marked" refers to constructions that are relatively less frequent. Another way to think of the notion of markedness is that the unmarked way of doing things is the default for languages. If a language indicates number, it will indicate the default first—the plural—and only if it has two structures for indicating number will it also indicate the singular.

The concept of markedness can be applied to any kind of linguistic unit or representation. In phonology, for example, we can show that certain sounds are marked relative to others, and that phonemic contrasts in some positions are marked relative to that same contrast in another position. Typological research has shown that if a language has voiced fricatives—sounds such as /v/ or /z/—in its phonemic inventory, it also has voiceless fricatives—sounds such as /f/ or /s/. However, the reverse is not true. Thus, the presence of voiced fricatives in a language implies the presence of voiceless fricatives, but not vice versa, making voiced fricatives marked relative to voiceless fricatives.

Markedness can also be applied straightforwardly to syntactic constructions. Research has shown that the presence of certain sentence types in a language implies the presence of certain other types, but not vice versa. For example, languages such as English and Japanese have passive sentences (sentences in which the noun undergoing the action is the subject of the sentence) in which it is possible to express the agent of the action, as in the following sentence:

The building was demolished by a wrecking crew.

Alternatively, it is also possible to leave the agent unspecified, as in

The building was demolished.

Other languages, such as Arabic and Greek, do not have passive sentences with expressed agents but allow only passives without agents. Furthermore, there is no known language that has passives with agents but lacks passives without agents. Therefore, passives with agents imply, and are marked relative to, passives without agents.

It is important to remember that, according to this view of markedness, a structure is always unmarked or marked relative to some other structure, never absolutely or in isolation. This markedness relationship is determined on the basis of a universal implicational statement. In the generalization "if a language has structure A, it also necessarily has structure B, but not vice versa," A is the implying structure and is therefore marked relative to structure B, and B is the implied structure and is therefore unmarked relative to structure A. It is also important to note that not all constructions are marked or unmarked relative to others. Whether a markedness relationship exists between two structures is a function of whether the occurrence of one of the stuctures in a language implies the occurrence of the other. If no such implication exists, then no markedness relationship exists. Given this concept of typological markedness, we return to the main theme and discuss how this construct has been applied in second language acquisition.

The markedness differential hypothesis The principle of markedness offered a potential solution to some of the inadequacies of the contrastive analysis hypothesis. Recall that studies showed that although native language interference could account for some of the errors L2 learners made, there were many that could not be attributed to the first language. The task then became to identify which types of native and target language differences would cause difficulty, and which would not. Eckman (1977) proposed that the difficulty an L2 learner will have can be predicted on the basis of the differences between the native and target languages and the markedness relations that obtain among these differences. This hypothesis is known as the **markedness differential hypothesis.** It asserts that a target structure that is both different and relatively more marked than the corresponding native language structure will be difficult; a target structure that is different but not more marked will not be difficult. Moreover, the relative degree of difficulty among the native and target language differences corresponds directly to the relative degree of markedness among these differences.

The markedness differential hypothesis makes three claims. The first is that L2 difficulty can be predicted on the basis of two considerations: the differences between the native and target languages and the markedness relationships that hold within those areas of difference. Specifically, those target language structures that are both different and relatively more marked than the corresponding structures in the native language are predicted to be difficult. The second claim of this hypothesis is that the degree of difficulty among the native and target language differences will correspond directly to the degree of markedness. Finally, the hypothesis predicts that those target language differences that are not more marked will not be difficult.

From this discussion, it should be clear that the markedness differential hypothesis and the contrastive analysis hypothesis have the same goal—the prediction of difficulty in second language acquisition—and both hypotheses claim that such predictions depend to some extent on the differences between the native and target languages. The two hypotheses differ, however, in whether factors other than these differences must be considered. The contrastive analysis hypothesis claims that such differences are both necessary and sufficient for the prediction of L2 difficulty, whereas the markedness differential hypothesis claims that these differences are necessary but not sufficient. Consequently, the latter hypothesis does not claim that all differences between the native and target languages will cause difficulty; rather, only those differences where a markedness relationship obtains should produce problems.

To illustrate the predictions that the markedness differential hypothesis generates, consider a syntactic example involving types of relative clauses, which are illustrated by the sentences in Box 8.4. A relative clause is a sentence contained within a larger sentence that is used to modify a noun phrase. The italicized portions of the sentences in Box 8.4 are relative clauses. These relative clauses differ from each other in terms of the function of the relative pronoun (who, whom, whose) in its own clause. For example, the relative pronoun *who* in the first sentence is the subject of its own clause, whereas the relative pronoun *whom* in the second sentence is the object of the verb *telephoned* in its clause.

Not all languages have the full range of relative clauses shown in Box 8.4. Instead, there is a markedness relationship that corresponds to the order in which the clauses are listed in Box 8.4. A language that has a relative clause of type 6 in the list, in which the relative pronoun functions as the object of a comparative, also has relative clauses of type 5, in which the relative pronoun is a possessive, and so on, with the least marked relative clause being that exemplified in type 1, in which the relative pronoun is the subject of its clause.

Given a markedness relationship among the different relative clauses, the

---

Box 8.4 Examples of English relative clauses

1. The parole officer *who scheduled the drug test* is my sister.
2. The parole officer *whom the lawyer telephoned* was not available.
3. The parole officer *to whom the court assigned the case* was overworked.
4. The parole officer *with whom the judge corresponded* was on vacation.
5. The parole officer *whose client left town* was angry.
6. The parole officer *who the prisoners are older than* must gain their confidence.

---

markedness differential hypothesis predicts that the difficulty associated with the various relative clause types should follow accordingly, and this is what L2 studies of relative clauses have shown. For example, Hyltenstam (1984) found that the difficulty learners of Swedish as a second language experienced with relative clauses generally corresponded to the degree of markedness. In a different study, Gass (1979) argued that less marked relative clauses in the native language were more likely than more marked ones to be transferred by the learner into the target language. Both of these results are consistent with the markedness differential hypothesis.

To summarize, typological markedness has been incorporated into second language acquisition research to address some of the problems encountered by the contrastive analysis hypothesis. Researchers using markedness as a measure of difficulty in L2 learning could specify, on principled grounds, which differences between the native and target languages would cause difficulty and which would not. However, markedness may not be the entire explanation for influences of L1 on L2 acquisition.

A cognitive account

Kellerman (for example, 1978, 1986) proposed another way in which speakers' native languages influence their second language acquisition. According to Kellerman, all speakers have beliefs concerning which constructions in their native language should be directly translatable into another language and which constructions should not be. For example, if you are a native English speaker you might expect that you could translate the sentence *The boy kicked the ball* into just about any other language simply by knowing the translation of each word and the rules for putting the words together in the new language. In contrast, you wouldn't expect to be able to use that method of direct translation with a sentence like *The old man kicked the bucket* (Gass & Selinker, 1994). These differing beliefs about how different aspects of one's native language are either language neutral or language specific should explain why some aspects cause interference in second language acquisition and others do not.

Kellerman investigated the role of native speakers' intuitions about the relative translatability or transferability of certain lexical items in two well-known studies, one involving the Dutch verb *breken* ("to break") and the other concerning different meanings of the noun *oog,* meaning "eye." In the first study, Kellerman (1978) gave native Dutch speakers 17 sentences containing various meanings of the verb *breken.* In the first stage, he asked the speakers to divide the sentences into groups in which the meaning of the verb was similar. What he found was that the speakers had a notion of the relative "coreness" of any given meaning of *breken.* For example, in the Dutch equivalents of the sentences

He broke his leg.

The cup broke.

the meaning of the verb is considered to be core; whereas in the sentences

She broke his heart.

His voice broke when he was thirteen.

the meaning is thought to be noncore. Thus, a use of *breken* was considered a core meaning if the sense of the verb was more literal, more concrete, and perceived to occur more frequently. In the second stage of the experiment, Kellerman asked 81 university-age Dutch learners of English to say which of the 17 sentences they would translate into English using the verb *break.* Kellerman found clear differences among the speakers about which sentences could be translated with *break,* and the rank order for the translatability correlated strongly with the speakers' notions about core and noncore.

In the second study, Kellerman (1986) tested 35 university-age, first-year Dutch students of English on the various uses of *oog,* such as for the human eye, the eye of a potato, an electronic eye, the eye of a needle, and several others. The students were given three forced-choice preference tests in which they were to choose between pairs of the different senses of *oog* with respect to translatability, similarity, and frequency. The translatability test asked the students to choose on the basis of whether the particular sense of *oog* would be translated as *eye* in English, the similarity test asked for a choice on how similar the meaning was to "human eye," and the frequency test sought to determine how frequent the participants believed the usage was in everyday language. The results showed that the students' judgments on similarity and frequency could be used to approximate their judgments on transferability. The results of these experiments led Kellerman to conclude that native speakers' intuitions about the "semantic space" of lexical items can be used to predict transferability; that is, these judgments act as a constraint on the kinds of items that are likely to be transferred.

Another constraint on L1 transfer, also discussed by Kellerman, is what he termed **psychotypology,** or the language learner's perception of how closely related the native and target languages are. The hypothesis is that learners will be more likely to transfer a construction to a target language that is perceived as being closer to the native language than to a target language that is perceived as more distant. Thus, native Dutch speakers are much more likely to transfer native structures when they are learning German, a language that is perceived as being close to Dutch, than they will when they are studying English, which is perceived as more distant from Dutch.

We can draw several points from these discussions about the role of the native language in second language acquisition. The first is that virtually every researcher in second language acquisition ascribes some weight to the native language in explaining how second languages are acquired. All L2 theorists, in other words, allow for the possibility that at least some learner errors may be attributable to characteristics of the learner's first language. And although it is fair to state that no one currently subscribes to the contrastive analysis hypothesis, in which all errors were explained in terms of native and target language differences, it is equally fair to say that no one completely discounts the influence of the native language.

The second point is that, in keeping with more recent linguistic theory, second language acquisition theory has taken a more mentalistic view of transfer, or cross-linguistic influence, than the contrastive analysis hypothesis does. Under the behaviorist view of the contrastive analysis hypothesis, considerations involving the language learner were virtually excluded; ease and difficulty were predicted solely on the basis of the native and target languages. Within the generative grammar approach, on the other hand, these notions are seen as involving cognitive processes, connected either with the notion of the relative difficulty associated with a given structure or with certain intuitions that native speakers have, rather than as a behavioral construct or as a matter of rote learning. Thus, native language transfer is best viewed as a multifaceted process that can be affected by other principles, including markedness, universality, coreness of meaning, and relative "psychological distance" between languages; and that transfer has the potential to affect all aspects of the language—pronunciation, grammar, and vocabulary.

Finally, because native language transfer is one of the tenets of virtually every serious approach to second language acquisition, transfer can be viewed as the default explanation; whatever *can* be explained by transfer *is* explained by transfer. The import of this conclusion is that it becomes necessary to formulate additional principles of second language acquisition only if native language transfer is not an adequate explanation. Therefore, part of the description and justification of any principle of second language acquisition is to show how this principle goes beyond transfer.

In the remainder of this chapter, we will see that second language researchers view native language transfer as only one factor in explaining second language learning. Many additional principles have been proposed to help explain why second language learning is different from first language acquisition, and these proposals must be justified theoretically and supported empirically. In the next section, we consider a proposal that explains L2 acquisition in terms of the mechanisms of learning.

SECOND LANGUAGE ACQUISITION AS RULE LEARNING

The Chomskyan revolution that gave rise to the modern field of research on first language acquisition also gave rise to a new approach to the study of second language learning. Researchers reasoned that if a language is characterized as a set of rules, as Chomsky then argued, it follows that the task of learning a second language is to acquire a new set of rules. The process of acquiring these rules was thought to be the same process involved in first language acquisition. Dulay and Burt (1975) coined the term **creative construction** to describe this process (Bialystok, 1991).

This approach led researchers to collect a new sort of data on second language learning. One of the first studies carried out within the rule-learning approach to second language acquisition was by Richards (1971). Although allowing for the possibility that some L2 learners' errors can be explained by native language interference, Richards argued that many L2 errors—indeed the more interesting ones—do not arise from such interference but instead stem from the nature of rule learning. On the basis of a compendium of errors gathered from numerous L2 learners from many different language backgrounds, Richards demonstrated that, in trying to acquire the target language rule system, the learner mislearns these rules, just as a child L1 learner does. According to this approach, L2 learners' errors reflect the various rule-learning strategies used in the acquisition of a second language. This framework for explaining L2 data, which came to be known as **error analysis,** held that much of the difficulty in L2 learning came not from the learner's native language but from the learner's trying to sort out the various complexities and intricacies of the language being learned.

From this groundbreaking work by Richards, the next major development was to raise the question of the "reality" of the rule system the learner internalizes. The reasoning was as follows: The L2 utterances of the second language learner are systematic; even when learners make errors and produce nontargetlike forms, the errors themselves reveal a certain regularity. This systematicity of the L2 utterances begs explanation. Thus, the reasoning continued, there must be a system underlying these utterances, but which system is it? One possibility, of course, is that the learner is using the native language's system. This is not a viable possibility because if the learner were to use the native system, then the L2 utterances should reflect the structures of the native language. Although this is true in some cases, it simply does not account for other situations in which learners' utterances do not reflect transfer. Another possibility is that the learner is using the target language. If this is true, then the learner would presumably perform like a native speaker and produce targetlike utterances, which is also clearly not the case. The conclusion was that the L2 learners must be using their own system, a set of rules that is separate from both the native and the target languages. This system, ultimately termed an **interlanguage,** was proposed independently, in one form or another, in work by Corder (1967), Nemser (1971), and Selinker (1972).

Consider the example of a common pronunciation error made by Spanish speakers acquiring English. These L2 learners typically pronounce the word *big* as "bik" and *Bob* as "Bop," but the question is, Why? The answer can't be that native Spanish speakers have difficulty producing the sounds [g] and [b] because Spanish also has these sounds. Furthermore, the same speakers who say "bik" instead of "big" can pronounce the [g] when they say "bigger." The typical pattern of native Spanish speakers' pronunciation of English words is presented in Table 8.2. The key word here is *pattern*; the errors in pronunciation are systematic, and they are typical of native Spanish speakers learning English.

Table 8.2 Pronunciation of English words typical of native speakers of Spanish

Target word	L2 pronunciation	Target word	L2 pronunciation
big	[bɪk]	tag	[taek]
bigger	[bigər]	rob	[rap]
Bob	[bap]	bad	[baet]
Bobby	[babi]	wet	[wɛt]
sick	[sɪk]	wetter	[wɛtər]
sickest	[sɪkəst]	prepay	[pripe]
red	[rɛt]		

So the questions are, What is the pattern, and Why do Spanish speakers in particular show this pattern?

The answer to the first question is that Spanish learners of English systematically pronounce English words that end in the voiced consonants, [b d g], with the corresponding voiceless sounds, [p t k]. The reason for this error pattern is suggested by a comparison of the phonological properties of English and Spanish. In English, the sounds [p t k b d g] can occur at the beginning, in the middle, and at the end of words. Spanish, in contrast, has restrictions on where these sounds can occur. In Spanish, the voiceless sounds [p t k] can occur in initial and medial positions but not in word-final position, and the voiced sounds [b d g] can occur only initially but not medially or finally. (This is actually an oversimplification, because the voiced sounds can occur medially after certain consonants, as in *hombre* ("man") and *desde* ("since"), but this distinction is not relevant for our purposes.) Most important for our example is the fact that none of these sounds can occur word-finally in Spanish; that is, there are no words in Spanish that end with the sounds [p t k b d g].

How do these facts about English and Spanish explain the pronunciation errors we observe? One possible explanation is L1 interference. Because the learner's native language does not have words ending in the sounds [b d g], we might expect such words to present difficulty. This explanation seems viable until we consider the fact that the learner is substituting word-final sounds— [p t k]—that also do not occur in that position in the native language. Thus, when confronted with a target pronunciation that is nonnativelike, the learner produces a result that is also nonnativelike. Why should this happen?

The explanation we propose is that the learner has acquired an inter-language rule that pronounces all word-final consonants as voiceless—a rule that is not part of the grammar of either the native or the target language. Consider the following facts: First, the learner's performance as represented in Table 8.2 is systematic; it appears to be rule-governed behavior and so could be described by a rule. Second, some of the pronunciations reveal that the learner does know that at least some of the target words contain a word-final consonant. Specifically, some words are related in that one member of the pair is formed by adding a suffix to the other, as in the words *big* and *bigger*. What is particularly interesting about these related words is that they show that the learner "knows" that *big* contains a final [g] sound because she pronounces this [g] in the word *bigger*. Thus, although our learner pronounces *big* as [bɪk], she pronounces *bigger* in a targetlike manner as [bɪgər]. The same pattern is revealed by the related forms *Bob*, pronounced as [bap], with a final voiceless sound, and *Bobby*, pronounced as the targetlike form [babi]. We can account for this regularity by postulating that our learner has acquired the first pronunciation rule listed in Box 8.5, which derives the above pronunciations as shown in the derivation in item 2.

The important point to be made is that the rule of final devoicing cannot be part of either the native or the target language. Such a rule could not be part

---

Box 8.5   The interlanguage rule that underlies the pattern in native Spanish speakers' pronunciation of English

1. *Rule of final devoicing:* All word-final consonants are pronounced as voiceless.

2. *Derivation of interlanguage pronunciation:*

	Word *big*	*Word* *bigger*
Phonemic form	/bɪg/	/bɪgər/
Apply final devoicing	bɪk	bɪgər
Pronunciation	[bɪk]	[bɪgər]

---

of English because English has many words that end in final voiced consonants (such as rib, field, bag); if the grammar of English contained this rule, all words would be pronounced with a final voiceless consonant. Similarly, Spanish grammar does not have this rule either, for two reasons. First, as we pointed out above, because [b d g] do not occur word-finally in Spanish words, there would be very little for such a rule to apply to. Second, although most Spanish words end in a vowel, some word-final consonants are permitted, including the sound [ð] (pronounced like the "th" in *the*), which is voiced. Thus, final devoicing is not justified as a rule for either the native or the target language, but it is motivated on the basis of the subject's L2 pronunciations. Consequently, we posit this rule as part of the interlanguage.

One of the few, uncontroversial pieces of "conventional wisdom" in second language acquisition theory is that second language learners internalize an interlanguage—their own set of rules that they use to speak and understand the target language. There is essentially no disagreement about this claim among researchers in the field. The interlanguage hypothesis fits in well with a large portion of the previous findings about second language acquisition and helps explain several facts of L2 learning.

The construct of an interlanguage constitutes one of the major breakthroughs in second language acquisition theory for two reasons. First, it ties together in one package much of the research on the systematicity of learners' errors and the idea of language acquisition as rule learning. The idea behind this concept is that L2 learners internalize their own version of the target language; when exposed to the L2 data (and very possibly also given instruction in the target language), the learners construct a system—an interlanguage—which, to whatever extent possible, enables them to speak and understand the target language. The construct of interlanguage also captures the idea that second languages are languages in their own right. Although they may not be spoken within fixed geographical borders or have a large literature written in them (as is most often the case with "normal" languages), interlanguages are nevertheless human languages. If this is true, then one can reasonably ask whether they obey the same principles other languages do. It is to this question that we now turn.

THE ROLE OF UNIVERSAL GRAMMAR IN SECOND LANGUAGE ACQUISITION

Thus far we have been discussing how the Chomskyan notion of language acquisition as rule learning, which inspired the early research on children's syntactic development in their first language, also influenced the study of second language acquisition. More recently, the Chomskyan notion of Universal Grammar has inspired research on first language acquisition, and, similarly, the notion that Universal Grammar (UG) plays a role in L2 learning has become the basis for research in the field of second language learning. We will begin discussion of the UG approach to second language acquisition with a review of the central tenets of the theory.

Principles and parameters in Universal Grammar

Recall from Chapter 4 that the position of the UG approach to language acquisition is that all human languages conform to a single set of principles. The differences among languages are differences in the settings of parameters that are also universal. Parameters can be thought of as principles with more than one option available; the task of the language learner is to determine, on the basis of the available input, which particular option is appropriate for the language being learned. According to this view, the bulk of the structure of language is provided innately by UG. The L1 learner's task is merely that of setting parameters.

A particularly interesting aspect of the UG (or the principles and parameters) approach, at least from a theoretical viewpoint, is the claim that parameter settings relate clusters of structural properties. That is, parameter settings do not describe merely a single difference between any two languages; rather, they relate several differences. In terms of first language acquisition, this view makes the extremely interesting claim that, by virtue of a child's determining the setting of one parameter, the child has actually acquired several structures, perhaps without ever having been exposed to those structures.

Before we turn our attention to the hypothesis that principles of UG play a significant role in L2 acquisition, two important points need to be made. First, principles of UG do not cover all aspects of language, only those thought to be describable in terms of general or universal principles. Consequently, many aspects of language lie outside the boundaries of UG and, as such, would have to be learned on the basis of the available input. Not all variation, in other words, is describable in terms of parameters. For example, the regular past-tense ending on English verbs, -ed, would not be part of UG, and English-learning children would have to work out the various past-tense endings. There is, in fact, evidence that children go through a period of sorting out the past-tense endings. The second point that needs to be made is that the theory of Universal Grammar is a hypothetical construct, the details of which are still being worked out. Many of the principles and parameters that have been proposed represent hypotheses in the process of being tested and revised. Thus, which principles and parameters are part of UG and which particular structures are related by a given parameter are empirical questions about which hypotheses can be made and tested. Bearing these points in mind, we turn our attention to the proposal that UG plays an interesting role in L2 acquisition.

Universal Grammar and second language acquisition

The proposal that Universal Grammar is involved in second language acquisition claims that the grammars of interlanguages are constructed according to the principles of UG in the same way that grammars of primary languages are. This position raises some serious questions for researchers. At first glance, the claim that UG has a role to play in L2 learning (henceforth referred to as the UG position) seems to run directly counter to a number of facts discussed at the outset of this chapter—in particular, that children and adults seem to have different endpoints with respect to language learning. Whereas young children learning a language virtually always end up with nativelike competence, adult learners rarely do. Proponents of the UG position would therefore have to explain why, if both L1 and L2 learners are guided by UG, adults as a rule fall short of becoming native speakers. Would it not be reasonable, as some have suggested (for example, Wong Fillmore, 1991), to explain these child/adult differences in language learning by hypothesizing that UG is available for language acquisition during childhood, and then after it has served this function, it is no longer accessible for language learning later in life, forcing adults to use a different, less efficient cognitive mechanism for language learning?

The proponents of the UG position answer this question negatively. They maintain that it is not necessary to explain child/adult differences in language learning in terms of the presence or absence of UG. White (1989) argued that " . . . there may indeed be a critical period without the end resulting in the loss of UG" (p. 44). In other words, proponents of this position do not deny that there are child/adult differences in language learning; they merely reject the claim that such differences must be explained in terms of access versus nonaccess to UG. Proponents of the UG position emphasize that it does not necessarily follow from their position that first and second language acquisition should be exactly the same, only that interlanguage grammars will follow the same principles and constraints that UG imposes on L1 grammars. Therefore, to determine the role of UG in L2 acquisition, it is necessary to scratch the surface of interlanguage grammars and look for evidence of UG principles.

Ultimately, the question reduces to an empirical one: Is there evidence that UG principles function in interlanguage grammars? This topic has been vigorously debated in the second language acquisition literature. It is not our purpose here to try to resolve the issue, or even to add to the discussion. Rather, the goal of the remainder of this section is to outline, using as an example a study by White (1990), how one would go about arguing the UG position.

Second language acquisition as parameter resetting

At issue is how to construct an argument showing that UG is involved in L2 acquisition. Assume a language learning situation in which the native and target languages differed in the setting of a UG parameter. The task of the learners would be twofold: First, learners would have to recognize that the native and target languages differed with respect to this parameter; second, learners would have to learn the parameter setting of the target language. The mechanism by which acquistition would take place is that in the early stages of acquisition, stage 1, the interlanguage would take on the parameter setting of the native language—in other words, at stage 1, this setting would be transferred into the interlanguage. At a later stage, say stage 2, the learner may recognize that the parameter of the interlanguage needs to be reset to agree with the target language setting. Presumably, the learner must have access to UG to accomplish such a resetting, because only the native language value of the parameter would be available from the native language.

What would constitute evidence that this mechanism of acquisition— namely, the resetting of a parameter in the interlanguage—was actually taking place? Recall that one of the interesting aspects of parameters is that they account for several connected differences between languages, not just a single difference. At stage 1, because the native language setting has been transferred to the interlanguage, we should be able to observe as part of the interlanguage utterances all the structures that are consistent with the native language setting of the parameter. At stage 2, on the other hand, the parameter has been reset to that of the target language, and the interlanguage should contain all those structures that are consistent with the target language setting of the parameter. This notion of second language acquisition as **parameter resetting** requires hypothesizing that L2 learners have access to UG in formulating their interlanguage. Otherwise, we could not explain either why the interlanguages had one set of constructions at stage 1 and then a different set at stage 2 or how L2 learners had access to a parameter setting that was not part of the grammar of their L1.

Box 8.6   Sentences showing the placement of adverbs, negatives, and subject-auxiliary inversion in English and French

1. John often kisses Mary.
2. *Jean souvent embrasse Marie. (often kisses)
   "John often kisses Mary."
3. Jean embrasse souvent Marie.
4. Jean n'aime pas Marie. (likes neg[†])
   "John does not like Marie."
5. *John likes not Mary.
6. Aime-t-elle Jean? (likes she)
   "Does she like John?"
7. *Likes she John?
8. Does she like John?

---

*Denotes an ungrammatical construction.

[†]"Neg" means "negation."

This hypothesis was directly tested by White (1990) in an investigation of the effects of different sorts of input on the acquisition of English by native speakers of Canadian French. French and English differ with respect to a parameter known as the **verb movement parameter.** To follow the logic of White's experiment, we need to understand the several differences between French and English associated with this verb movement parameter (Pollock, 1989). The placement of adverbs relative to verbs is different in these two languages. As the sentences in Box 8.6 show, adverbs such as *often* cannot occur between the verb and direct object in English, whereas their equivalent can in French; and adverbs such as *souvent* ("often") cannot occur between the subject and verb in French, but their equivalent can in English.

Details aside, this difference between languages follows from a parameter of UG which either allows or does not allow movement of the verb relative to other constituents in the sentence. According to this proposal, the position of the adverb in French follows from the fact that French allows the verb to move whereas English does not. According to this view, the principle that allows verbs to move is innately specified as part of UG, and as such, does not have to be learned. What does have to be learned by children, however, is whether the language they are acquiring is of the French type, which permits verb movement, or of the English type, which does not.

Two other structures are associated with this parameter: one that pertains to negative placement and the other to yes/no questions. Languages like French, which permit verb movement, also allow postverbal negation, as shown in sentence 4 of Box 8.6; English-type languages, which do not allow verbs to move, do not permit postverbal negation. And as shown in sentence 6, French allows pronouns and subjects to be inverted to form yes/no questions, whereas sentence 7 demonstrates that English allows no such inversion. This fact is also hypothesized to be a consequence of the verb movement parameter.

Given this background, we can now understand the logic of White's (1990) study. White's experiment involved dividing the learners into two groups; one group was instructed only on the placement of the adverb in English, and the other group received instruction on question formation. The hypothesis was that the instruction would trigger both groups of learners to reset the value of the verb movement parameter in their respective interlanguages to the English value. But because the parameter not only relates the position of the adverb but also pertains to the formation of questions, the group that was instructed only on questions should also "learn" about the placement of adverbs without being directly exposed to instruction adverbs.

White's participants were five classes of fifth- and sixth-grade native French speakers (average age 11 and 12 years, respectively) who were in the beginning stages of learning English. These students were divided into two groups, one consisting of 1 fifth-grade class and 2 sixth-grade classes and the other containing 1 fifth-grade and 1 sixth-grade class. Both groups were given a pretest on adverb placement in English. The first group was then given instruction on adverb placement for a period of 5 hours over a week, with a subsequent 2 hours of follow-up instruction. The second group was instructed for a corresponding amount of time on question formation. Instruction for both groups was done using a set of specially prepared and tightly controlled instructional materials. After the period of instruction was complete, the groups were given two posttests—one the first day after instruction was completed and the other five weeks later. Both groups were tested only on adverb placement using three types of tests. The first test was a grammaticality judgment task in which the participants had to indicate which sentences in a story had the wrong word order. The second was a written preference test in which the participants had to indicate which of a pair of sentences was correct. The third test was a manipulation task, using cards with words on them that could be used to form sentences. The students were given the randomly shuffled cards and asked to arrange them into an English sentence; they were then asked whether another sentence could also be made with the same cards.

Unfortunately for the UG position, the results did not support the hypothesis. The scores on the pretest indicated that all the students thought that English sentences in which the adverb occurred between the verb and direct object (as in sentence 1 of Box 8.6) were grammatical. In UG terms, all the participants thought that English had the same value for the verb movement parameter that French has, and they therefore transferred this setting into the interlanguage. However, the scores from the posttest indicated that only the learners who were instructed on the placement of adverbs learned that English sentences like sentence 2 in Box 8.6 are ungrammatical. Those learners who received instruction only on English question formation did not recognize the ungrammaticality of this sentence type, contrary to what the UG hypothesis predicted. Consequently, there was no evidence from White's study to support the claim that the participants were able to access UG in their acquisition of English.

At present, the UG position in second language acquisition remains an open question and a much debated issue. Opponents of the position point to the fact that both anecdotal and experimentally gathered data indicate that the tacit knowledge L2 learners have about the target language does not approach that of native speakers. Proponents of the UG position have several possible responses to their claims, short of simply capitulating. One response is to claim that the methodology of a particular study was flawed and therefore did not serve as a good test of the hypothesis. Alternatively, it could be argued that because the principles of UG are themselves hypotheses that are still being worked out, the study tested a structure that is not encompassed by UG; therefore, one does not have a valid test of UG's role in L2 acquisition until one has a defensible principle of UG.

To summarize, in this section we have considered one of the recent strands of research in L2 acquisition—the hypothesis that UG governs second language acquisition. We have outlined the motivation for this hypothesis and the rationale behind how one would test it. The UG position is consistent with previous findings of second language acquisition research in several areas: (1) the systematicity of learner errors, (2) the idea that universal principles may give insights into interlanguages, and (3) the possibility that the native language may influence the learning of the target language. The last finding is clearly the most surprising, because it is easy to jump to the conclusion that an approach to L2 learning that proceeds from a universalist position would not be able to handle L1 interference. We have seen in the discussion above that this is simply not true. The influence of the native language is reflected (by hypothesis) in the transfer of the native parameter settings in the early stages of the interlanguage.

At present, the available evidence from empirical studies is inconclusive and the issue must remain open. However, the fact that proponents of the UG position have not been able to make their case does not detract from the interest of their ideas. If the proponents of this position could demonstrate that UG in fact governed L2 acquisition, then they would have united two seemingly disparate phenomena—L1 and L2 acquisition—under a single framework.

AN ACCULTURATION MODEL OF SECOND LANGUAGE LEARNING

Learning a second language involves coming into contact with people who speak another language and who are members of another culture. Thus the process of learning a second language is not just a process of acquiring a new vocabulary and new phonological and grammatical rules. It is also a social and psychological process of making contact with and ultimately joining another social group. In other words, the process of second language learning is a process of **acculturation.** Research on second language learning done from this acculturation model of L2 acquisition focuses on the influence of social and psychological factors in second language learning.

Much of the current work in this area stems from studies carried out by Gardner and Lambert (1959, 1972), who looked at the proficiency of English-speaking high school students learning French in Canada. They found that overall proficiency was significantly influenced by the intensity of the learners' motivation. Gardner and Lambert further identified two kinds of motivational orientation: **integrative motivation,** in which the student was interested in learning the language in order to associate with members of the target culture; and **instrumental motivation,** in which the student was less interested in integrating with the target culture and more interested in learning the language for utilitarian reasons, such as getting ahead in his or her profession. Gardner and Lambert found that, other things being equal, learners with an integrative motivation were generally more successful and that an integrative orientation was better at sustaining the long-term effort needed to gain proficiency in a second language.

In line with this work, Schumann (1978, 1987, 1993) proposed the **acculturation model** for second language acquisition. The major claim of this model is that L2 learning, as one aspect of acculturation, is controlled by the degree to which the learner acculturates to the target language group. Schumann defined *acculturation* as the learner's social and psychological integration into the target language group. According to Schumann, it is possible to place any given L2 learner on a continuum that ranges from socially and psychologically distant to socially and psychologically proximate with respect to speakers of the target language. The hypothesis is that learners will acquire the target language only to the degree to which they acculturate.

Schumann listed several social and affective variables involved in acculturation. Included in the social variables were what he called social dominance patterns. To the extent that one of the groups involved in the language contact situation is politically, culturally, economically, or technologically superior to the other group, then the two groups are socially distant and second language acquisition will be impeded. An example of this situation would be colonization.

Because the colonizing group is usually seen to be politically, economically, and technologically dominant to the colonized group, those two strata of the society would be socially distant; and, according to the hypothesis, little if any language learning would occur in the colonizing group.

Affective variables pertain to individuals. Among the affective factors that Schumann discussed for second language acquisition was motivation, and here he appealed to the two major motivational orientations outlined by Gardner and Lambert (1972)—integrative and instrumental. Schumann saw learners with an integrative motivation to learn the target language as being more acculturated. Instrumentally motivated learners would be expected to integrate with the target culture only to the extent that their instrumental goals were satisfied.

The acculturation model makes an interesting and plausible claim about second language acquisition—specifically, that L2 proficiency is a function of certain social and psychological variables affecting the learner. It's also important to note that the Johnson and Newport (1989) study, discussed earlier in this chapter, found that only two factors other than age at arrival in the United States were significant in accounting for L2 proficiency, and both factors concerned affect: self-consciousness and American identification.

Despite the plausibility of the acculturation model, the major problem with the hypothesis is that there is no evidence to support the claim that these affective variables actually *cause* L2 proficiency. The research supports only the conclusion that these variables *correlate* with L2 proficiency. In fact, one could make a reasonable case that the causal effect is in the opposite direction—that proficiency in the second language causes the acculturation. This line of argument would claim that acculturation is the result of meaningful contact with speakers of the target language, and that such contact is possible only if the learner is proficient enough in the language to interact with the target group. Research finding a correlation between proficiency and acculturation would support this cause-and-effect relationship equally as well as the claim that it is the acculturation that causes the L2 proficiency. Yet another possibility is that both the affective variables and the second language proficiency could actually be caused by some other variable, such as amount of exposure to the target culture. The point is simply that although the acculturation model has uncovered some interesting facts, the explanation of these facts must await further research.

The acculturation model for second language acquisition is in line with the other approaches we have considered in that it addresses the different end states in first and second language acquisition. It hypothesizes that children and adults are subject to different social and psychological variables in learning a language. Although such a proposal is certainly plausible and may ultimately turn out to be defensible, the existing research establishes only a correlational, rather than a causal, connection between these variables and language acquisition.

SECOND LANGUAGE PEDAGOGY

Having reviewed the basic research that seeks to understand the process of second language acquisition, we now turn to the applied research in the field that focuses on **pedagogy,** or how to teach a second language. Learning a second language in a tutored environment is very often the norm, and, as one might expect, a number of issues have arisen over the years regarding exactly how second languages should be taught.

A distinction relevant to a discussion of pedagogy is the difference between learning a foreign language and learning a second language. If the language is being taught or learned in a situation in which the target language is the ambient language outside the classroom, then the term **second language learning** applies; if, alternatively, the student is exposed to the target language only in the classroom, and the language is not the ambient language outside the classroom, then the relevant term is **foreign language learning.** For example, a native speaker of Russian learning English in the United States as part of a university program for international students is learning English as a second language. If this same student were studying English in his or her native country, then this student would be learning English as a foreign language.

Because the context of the language learning has implications for the instructional methods used, it ultimately bears on the various issues surrounding how languages should be taught. In a foreign language situation, the students more often than not constitute a linguistically homogeneous group, and the teacher knows both the target language and the native language of the learners. In a second language context, however, the situation is vastly different. The students are most likely immigrants or international students from different native language backgrounds, and it is highly unlikely that the teacher knows the native languages of all the students. As a consequence, instruction in a second language learning situation must always be in the target language, whereas in a foreign language context, the teacher usually has the option of using either the target language or the students' native language.

The issue we will consider is how the grammar of the target language should be taught. This topic, in one form or another, has been debated in the United States for at least the last century (Diller, 1978).

Structural approaches to second language teaching

During the 1950s and 1960s, L2 pedagogy consisted largely of grammar teaching. The widely employed audiolingual method used a series of drill and pattern practices designed to teach the grammatical structures of the target language. The 1970s saw, in some measure as a reaction against the audiolingual method of teaching, the rise of proposals that second language teaching should focus less on the structural aspects of the language and more on the communicative functions.

A communicative approach to language teaching

At the center of much of the recent debate on this topic is a proposal by Stephen Krashen (1985 and elsewhere), which can be classified as a communicative approach to language teaching that explicitly claims that it is not necessary to teach the grammar of the target language. All that is necessary, Krashen states, is to provide the learner with the right kind of input.

The approach to teaching second languages that follows from this claim is the **natural approach,** put forth by Krashen and Terrell (1983) and based on a model of second language acquisition known as the input hypothesis (Krashen, 1985). The five basic hypotheses of this model are

1. The acquisition-learning hypothesis
2. The natural order hypothesis
3. The monitor hypothesis
4. The input hypothesis
5. The affective filter hypothesis

The **acquisition-learning hypothesis** claims that second language learners are capable of internalizing two, independent kinds of knowledge of the L2: acquired knowledge and learned knowledge. **Acquired knowledge** of the target language is the result of subconscious processes, whereas **learned knowledge** is the result of conscious processes. According to Krashen (1985), "Acquisition is a subconscious process identical in all important ways to the process utilized by children in acquiring their first language . . ." (p. 1). In contrast, "Learning refers to 'explicit' knowledge of rules, being aware of them and being able to talk about them" (Krashen & Terrell, 1983, p. 26). These two kinds of knowledge are also used under different conditions. Acquired knowledge, being much more tacit than learned knowledge, is readily available to the learner for speaking or understanding the target language in normal conversation. Learned knowledge, however, is much more explicit and is not usable under the time pressures of normal conversation.

One justification for postulating these two separate kinds of knowledge about the target language is the need to account for different kinds of learner performance. A well-known occurrence in the L2 classroom is that a learner will correctly use a certain structure within the instructional context set up by the teacher, but moments later, outside of class, the learner will use an incorrect construction in place of the one that has just been practiced. The acquisition-learning hypothesis explains this behavior as the learner having "learned" but not "acquired" the construction in question.

The second major tenet of Krashen's theory is the **natural order hypothesis,** which claims that L2 learners acquire the rules of the target language in a well-defined, invariant order. This hypothesis, which pertains only to acquisition and not to learning, claims further that the order in which the rules are acquired is independent of the order in which they are taught in language classes, and largely independent of the order in which the rules may be revealed in the input.

The **monitor hypothesis** maintains that learning (as opposed to acquisition) has only one function—as a monitor, or editor, that operates only under very well-defined conditions. It operates when the learner is focused on the form of the utterance (as opposed to, say, the content), and when the learner has the time for such focus: "Our ability to produce utterances in another language comes from our acquired competence, from our subconscious knowledge. Learning, conscious knowledge, serves only as an editor, or Monitor" (Krashen, 1985, p. 1).

The **input hypothesis,** which is the central tenet of Krashen's model, claims that L2 learners acquire the target language by receiving comprehensible input at the $i + 1$ level, where i indicates the present competency level of the learner and the numeral 1 indicates a level just beyond the learner's current stage of acquisition: "We progress along the natural order . . . by understanding input that contains structures at our next 'stage'—structures that are a bit beyond our current level of competence" (Krashen, 1985, p. 2). The thrust of this hypothesis is that learners acquire a second language by receiving input that is simultaneously understandable yet slightly beyond the learner's current level of knowledge. Presumably, the learners use what has already been acquired along with the context to understand the input that is slightly beyond their level. According to this model, comprehensible input is necessary for acquisition, but it is not sufficient. What is needed in addition is for the learner to be receptive to the input.

The final hypothesis of this model, the **affective filter hypothesis,** asserts that learners may have different attitudes about the target language or culture, or about the learning situation itself, that affect how much of the input actually "gets through" and can be processed for acquisition. According to Krashen, "The acquirer needs to be 'open' to the input. The 'affective filter' is a mental block that prevents acquirers from fully utilizing the comprehensible input they receive for language acquisition" (Krashen, 1985, p. 3). Clearly, the affective filter hypothesis draws heavily on the acculturation model and other work on L2 learners' motivation and attitudes toward the target language.

Krashen's model of second language learning has attracted significant attention and has also engendered a good deal of discussion. One of the areas in which the debate has been vigorous concerns the role of explicit instruction in the acquisition of the target language's grammar. The issue revolves around

Krashen's distinction between acquisition and learning; the natural question to ask is whether there is any interface between these two types of knowledge. Can learned knowledge become acquired knowledge? Can a given construction be learned so well that it becomes part of acquisition? Krashen's response is no: "As argued in several places . . . [this] theory of second language acquisition . . . is a 'no-interface' position with respect to the relationship between acquisition and learning. Learned competence cannot directly become acquired competence" (Krashen, 1985, p. 38).

At the heart of the issue is what follows from this no-interface position. If the no-interface position is correct, much of the instruction that takes place in traditional language classrooms does not affect acquired knowledge. But fostering acquired knowledge is the true goal of instruction. Under the no-interface view, then, the role of the instructor in the L2 classroom should be to present the learners with comprehensible input at the appropriate level and to conduct the class in such a way that the students' affective filters are as low as possible.

One effect of Krashen's model has been to call into question some of the traditional assumptions about the role of grammar teaching in L2 acquisition. At the center of the issue is the relationship between explicit and implicit knowledge and how they are internalized. For Krashen, acquired knowledge is obtained unconsciously, which in turn severely reduces or eliminates altogether the need for explicit grammatical instruction. It is important to note, however, that the view that second language learners have both explicit and implicit L2 knowledge—a view that is generally accepted in the field—does not necessarily entail accepting the no-interface position. For many L2 researchers, the no-interface position does not adequately account for the relationship between explicit and implicit knowledge. However, even for those who do not fully accept Krashen's model, it has had the effect of causing them to question the traditional methods for teaching grammatical rules and to rethink how grammar should be taught. One proposal that has come out of this reexamination of grammar teaching is Piennemann's teachability hypothesis.

The teachability hypothesis

According to Piennemann (1985), instruction in the grammar of a second language must be sensitive to the natural sequence in which structures are acquired under more naturalistic circumstances. The **teachability hypothesis** claims that instruction will be successful in teaching a learner a structure that represents new development in the L2 only if the learner is "ready" for this structure. Learners are considered "ready" to learn a particular structure if their interlanguage is close to the point at which that structure would be acquired in a natural, untutored situation. The idea behind the hypothesis is that instruction is successful only when the necessary prerequisites for learning have been developed (which is assumed to be the case in naturalistic L2 acquisition). This hypothesis, while denying the no-interface position, is consistent with Krashen's input and natural order hypotheses.

A number of other researchers have taken the position that comprehensible input is necessary but not sufficient for L2 acquisition. At issue is not whether L2 learners should be provided with comprehensible input, but rather how this input should be presented and, more important, whether it is possible to enhance the input so as to draw the learners' attention to certain constructions, leading to a concomitant increase in acquisition (Sharwood Smith, 1991).

Doughty (1991) conducted one of the more interesting experimental studies designed to test the effectiveness of providing learners explicit grammatical instruction compared to simply providing learners with comprehensible input. In this study, Doughty used 20 participants from various native-language backgrounds, all of whom were intermediate-level students enrolled in an intensive English as a second language program. The structure used in the study was relative clauses; improvement in knowledge about relativization from pretest to posttest was compared among the three groups and was taken to reflect the relative effectiveness of the different kinds of instruction.

All instruction for the students was done on computers. The participants were randomly assigned to one of three groups. One group, the meaning-oriented group, received help with lexical items and was given strategies for clarifying sentences. A second group, the rule-oriented group, received help in the form of explicit grammatical rules and the manipulation of the relative clauses on the screen. The third, control, group simply reread the passage. The findings were that both experimental groups outperformed the control group in the test on relative clauses, and the meaning-oriented group did better than the rule-oriented group in understanding the content of the texts. The finding that both groups that received some kind of instruction did better in learning the syntactic structure than the control group led Doughty (1991) to conclude that instruction does make a difference.

To summarize, applied research in language pedagogy is a major focus of work within the field of second language learning because there is a major difference in the way first and second languages are learned; the latter are often taught in a classroom setting, whereas the former are acquired naturalistically during childhood. Over the years, views have changed as to the role of explicit grammatical instruction in the successful teaching and learning of a second language. The audiolingual method emphasized the importance of grammatical instruction in the form of drills and practice. More recent approaches to L2 instruction place more importance on the communicative aspects of language and have incorporated this view into instruction. The natural approach, which is based on Krashen's model of second language acquisition, makes a distinction between learned (explicit) knowledge and acquired (implicit) knowledge, and argues that explicit instruction benefits only learned knowledge. This view, however, has been debated; and although there is no current approach to second language pedagogy that advocates grammatical instruction as its primary focus, several approaches have a place for explicit instruction.

BILINGUAL DEVELOPMENT

In the last section of this chapter, we switch our attention from the process of learning a second language after native language acquisition is complete or well underway to the process of learning two languages simultaneously. The literature on bilingual development is much smaller than the literature on second language learning, in both the number of studies reported and the number of subjects studied. Many studies are based on the diary record of a single child, often the child of a linguist. The best known of these diary studies is still Werner Leopold's four-volume study (1939–1949) of his daughter's bilingual development of English and German. Another strand of research in the history of the study of bilingualism is composed of larger-scale studies of children in immigrant families. The focus of such studies was typically on documenting the children's skill in the majority language, not on the children's development of both languages (for more discussion of the history of the field, see Bialystok, 1991b; Hakuta, 1986).

The circumstances of bilingual development

Contrary to what one might conclude from the relative paucity of research on the subject, bilingual development is not a rare phenomenon. By some estimates, roughly half the world's children are exposed to more than one language (de Houwer, 1995; Hakuta, 1986). The details of the circumstances for those children vary enormously. Probably the most common circumstance is that of children of immigrant parents. In this case, one language is spoken in the home, but the dominant culture and the schools use another. Another circumstance is that in which the community and the country are themselves bilingual environments. In such circumstances, a child's language experience can be quite complex. For example, de Houwer (1995) described the following possible situation for a child who lives in the Flemish region of Belgium, where Dutch is the official language but French—the official language of the other half of Belgium—is spoken in many places:

> (The child) goes to a French-medium music school on Wednesday afternoons and a Dutch-speaking preschool on weekday mornings. . . . the paternal grandparents address the child in Dutch, while the

> maternal grandparents use French. However, the child sees the maternal grandparents every weekday afternoon, and the paternal grandparents only on Sundays. The child's babysitters, who spend approximately three waking hours a week with the child, use exclusively French, and the children that the child regularly plays with also only speak French. . . . (p. 224)

Finally, for some children, the environment may be entirely monolingual except for one parent who is a native speaker of a foreign language. In this case, the child will become bilingual only if the foreign-born parent talks to that child in his or her native language. If this language is not understood or spoken by anyone else in the environment, doing so requires a conscious decision and often a concerted effort by the parent.

Bilingualism is the subject of both basic and applied research. The basic research questions concern (1) how language develops in children who are simultaneously learning two languages, and (2) what the course of bilingual development can tell us about the nature of the language acquisition process. The applied questions are motivated by the varied circumstances of bilingualism. Educators and policy makers in countries with substantial immigrant populations are understandably concerned about how best to ensure children's acquisition of the majority language and about the effects on children of learning more than one language. In countries with large immigrant populations, the question of how to handle such children in the educational system is a hot political issue. Parents who can choose whether or not to expose their children to two languages worry both how best to accomplish this goal and also whether doing so is in their child's best interest. In this chapter, we will focus on the psycholinguistic questions that have been raised by the study of bilingual development. (For discussion of the social and political issues that surround bilingualism in the United States, see Bialystok & Cummins, 1991; Hakuta, 1986; Ridge, 1981. For advice on raising bilingual children, see Arnberg, 1987; Harding & Reilly, 1987; Saunders, 1988.)

Language differentiation in bilingual development

Imagine that you are an infant trying (albeit unconsciously) to figure out the system that underlies the speech addressed to you. How would you know if you needed to figure out one or two systems to account for all your input? In a very influential study of bilingual development, Volterra and Taeschner (1978) proposed that bilingual children start by constructing a single system in which one lexicon contains the words in both languages and one system of rules applies. Later, bilingual children distinguish two lexicons but apply the same syntactic rules to both languages; and only in a third stage, which is achieved around the age of 3 years, do the children have two, fully differentiated systems.

Two kinds of evidence have been the basis for the argument of an initial single system. One kind of evidence comes from the child's vocabulary. If children know different words in each language rather than knowing two sets of words for a single set of meanings, this lack of overlap or of cross-language synonyms is taken as evidence of a single, undifferentiated lexicon. The second kind of evidence is **language mixing.** If children produce utterances using words from both languages, this is taken as evidence of a failure to differentiate the two systems. It is clear that children learning two languages simultaneously do acquire somewhat different vocabularies in their two languages and that they do mix languages in production. However, work since Volterra and Taeschner has suggested a different interpretation of these facts.

With respect to vocabulary, the argument is that children have enough cross-language synonyms in their vocabularies—an average of 30% during the period between 8 and 30 months (Pearson, Fernández, & Oller, 1995)—to suggest that they are building two systems. Furthermore, given that the children hear their two languages from different people in different contexts, it is not surprising that they would learn somewhat different words (Pearson & Fernández, 1994; Pye, 1986). With respect to language mixing, Meisel (1989) argued that using words from two languages in a single utterance does not necessarily mean the child fails to differentiate between the two languages. Language mixing could be the result of the child's reaching into one language for a word that he or she doesn't know in the other language (Genesee, 1989). If the person the child is speaking with knows both languages, this is an appropriate communicative strategy. Another argument against interpreting language mixing as evidence of language confusion is that, according to Meisel (1989), children mix lexical items but tend to keep the rules of grammar separate. For example, children learning French and German simultaneously do not incorrectly combine French words in German word order or vice versa. The earliest evidence for two separate systems could come from studies of the phonological development of children exposed to two languages. Here, the data are the scantiest, but two studies have argued for the early establishment of separate sound systems (Deuchar, 1989, and Ingram, 1981, both cited by de Houwer, 1995).

In contrast to the notion of language mixing as evidence of confusion is the proposal that language mixing is evidence of sociolinguistic skill. Adults who know two languages often mix languages for communicative effect (Goodz, 1989). When language mixing is not seen as a sign of confusion between two systems, it is given a different name—**code switching.** Studies of bilingual children's code switching have found that children as young as age 2 years use their two languages in contextually sensitive ways (Lanza, 1992). Other evidence that refutes the notion that language mixing reflects language confusion is that bilingual children may learn to code switch by observing their parents doing so. Despite the fact that parents raising their children bilingually are advised not to switch languages when talking to their children, they often do. Goodz (1989) found that even parents who claim to adhere to the "one parent–one language" principle mix languages. (This widely circulated bit of advice does not have a body of research behind it but seems to have come from a linguist colleague of Louis Ronjat, whose daughter was the subject of the first diary study of bilingual development; see Reich, 1986; Ronjat, 1913.)

Bilingualism's effects on the development of each language

If children are learning two languages at the same time, do they learn each language more slowly, and does one language interfere with the other? Because the research base is still small, the literature provides only the barest outlines of answers to these questions. Reviews of the literature by Lindholm (1980) and de Houwer (1995) concluded that in both the course and the rate of development, "bilingual and monolingual development are highly similar" (de Houwer, 1995, p. 244). However, this conclusion is largely based on comparing case studies of bilingual children's development to descriptions of monolingual development taken from other studies. The children of linguists—who provide the data for most of the case studies—are, by and large, an advantaged group. Thus it could be that bilingual development causes some delay in the development of each language but not so much as to cause these children to be outside the normal range of variation in rate of language development.

Studies of vocabulary development have directly compared bilingual and monolingual development, and the answer these studies provide is mixed. Studies of children 5 years old and older have found that bilingual children have smaller comprehension vocabularies in each of their languages than do monolingual children of the same age (Ben-Zeev, 1977; Rosenblum & Pinker, 1983; Umbel, Pearson, Fernández, & Oller, 1992). In contrast, Pearson, Fernández, and Oller (1993), who followed children from the age of 8 to 30 months, found that bilingual children had comprehension vocabularies in each language that were comparable to monolinguals' vocabularies. However, in spontaneous speech production, these same children had smaller vocabularies in each of their languages than did their monolingual age-mates, although their total vocabularies in the two languages were comparable to monolinguals' vocabulary sizes (Pearson et al., 1993).

There are two extreme possibilities with respect to the effects of bilingualism on the development of each language. One possibility is that children can learn two languages as easily as one; the other is that learning two languages is so difficult that simultaneous exposure to two languages in infancy should be avoided. It is possible to find expression of both extreme positions. The research on bilingual development makes it clear that simultaneous acquisition of two languages is possible, but the research also suggests that the notion that two languages are as easy to learn as one may be overstated (Pearson, Fernández, Lewedeg, and Oller, in press). One point that research on bilingual development makes clear is that input plays a role in language acquisition (de Houwer, 1995). Not only do children learn the particular languages to which they are exposed, they appear to learn them in some measure to the degree that they are exposed to them. Very few children get exactly equal amounts of input in two languages, and Pearson et al. report that the percentage of exposure to each language has a large effect on the success of bilingual development. Among children exposed both to Spanish and English in the largely Cuban community of southern Florida, Pearson found that children were not likely to become competent users of Spanish if Spanish constituted less than 25% of their input.

Bilingualism and cognitive development

The last question about bilingualism that we will address concerns the effects of bilingual development on cognitive development. During the 1930s and 1940s, several studies compared immigrant bilingual children to nonimmigrant (and usually more economically advantaged) monolingual children and found consistently poorer performance among the immigrant children. There were, at the time, two competing explanations of these findings: (1) that the immigrants were genetically inferior, and (2) that their bilingualism was to blame. Within the field of psychology, the environmental argument won the day, leading to conclusions like Yoshioka's (1929): "Bilingualism in young children is a hardship and devoid of apparent advantage" (quoted in Hakuta, 1986, p. 30).

This view was overturned by the findings of a study of French-English bilingual children in Canada (Peal & Lambert, 1962), a study that corrected the major flaws of the previous work. In Peal and Lambert's study, the children were balanced bilinguals (relatively equal in their mastery of both languages), unlike the immigrant children who tended to be more competent in their parents' language. The children were also from the same social class as the monolinguals to whom they were compared. Peal and Lambert found, for the balanced, middle-class sample they studied, that bilinguals performed better than monolinguals on a range of cognitive tests. They concluded, in stark contrast to earlier conclusions, that the bilingual child is

> a youngster whose wider experiences in two cultures have given him advantages that a monolingual does not enjoy. Intellectually his experience with two language systems seems to have left him with

a mental flexibility, and superiority in concept formation, and a more diversified set of mental abilities. . . . (quoted in Palij & Homel, 1987, p. 133)

Subsequent studies have also found that bilingualism is associated with certain cognitive advantages. For example, Ben-Zeev (1977) compared middle-class, 5- to 8-year-old children who were bilingual in Hebrew and English to middle-class monolingual speakers of Hebrew and of English. The children were administered several nonverbal and verbal tests. In one test, the children were presented with a physical array of nine different-size cylinders arranged in a 3 × 3 matrix. The children's task was to explain the pattern in the matrix and then transpose it. In another task, the children were told they were playing a game in which an airplane was called a "turtle," and then the child was asked things like "Can the turtle fly?" and "How does the turtle fly?" Ben-Zeev found that the bilingual children were better than the monolingual children both at explaining the pattern in the matrix and at answering questions in the "turtle" example. She concluded that exposure to two languages causes children to develop a mental facility for "seeking out the rules and for determining which are required by the circumstances" (pp. 1017–1018). Other research on the abilities of bilingual children suggests that bilingual development fosters the development of **metalinguistic awareness,** or awareness of how language works. One caution, however, must be raised about the interpretation of these more recent findings. Children who become balanced bilinguals may be a select group. We simply do not know how many children who are exposed to two languages fail to become bilingual, and thus we don't really know how select such samples may be (Diaz, 1983).

SUMMARY

Researchers in second language acquisition seek to explain why second language learning is generally less successful than first language acquisition, why the difficulties second language learners encounter are somewhat consistent and predictable, and why children are more successful than adults at acquiring a second language. Although these facts are well established, there is disagreement about how to explain them.

One area of research has focused on the effect of age on second language learning. Although initially older adolescents and adults learn a new language more rapidly than young children, young children ultimately achieve more nativelike proficiency in the phonology and syntax of the target language than adult learners. These findings suggest that there is a critical period for language acquisition.

Another area of research has focused on the influence of the native language on second language learning. An early approach that described the influence of the native language in behaviorist terms has been supplanted by more recent work that seeks to account for the influence of native language transfer using universal principles of language, such as markedness, as well as other, more cognitive bases.

In keeping with some of the advances made in linguistic theory over the last few decades, second language theorists have also adopted the approach that second languages are rule-governed systems. This approach has led to the idea that second languages are in fact languages in their own right. Termed *inter-languages,* these systems developed by the learner account for why learner performance in the second language is generally systematic, even if that performance contains characteristic errors not found in the speech of natives.

One of the recent advances in linguistic theory is the claim that human beings are endowed with an innate language faculty. This language learning mechanism, called a Universal Grammar, contains all the principles necessary to form the grammar of any human language. Some have proposed that Universal Grammar also plays a significant role in second language learning. This claim has consequences that can be empirically tested.

The acculturation model attempts to explain why language acquisition is different in children and adults in terms of differences in attitudes toward the target language and culture. Also factored into this model is the motivation that a learner has for learning the target language; in general, an integrative motivation, in which the learner seeks to associate with the target language culture, has been shown to correlate most strongly with second language proficiency. Finally, one of the major differences between first and second language acquisition is the fact that second languages are very often learned in a classroom situation, at least in U.S. culture.

Although often a second language is learned later in life, some children learn two languages simultaneously. Research on bilingual development suggests that children can successfully acquire two languages at the same time with minimal confusion or delay in the syntactic realm. The data with respect to vocabulary development is more mixed, with some evidence that bilingual children have smaller vocabularies in each of their languages than monolingual children do, even though they have equivalent-size total vocabularies. Research also suggests that there are some advantages associated with bilingualism on certain measures of cognitive ability and in metalinguistic awareness.

KEY TERMS

second language acquisition	L2
second language learning	L1
bilingual development	critical period

language transfer

contrastive analysis hypothesis

markedness

language universals

language typology

markedness differential hypothesis

psychotypology

creative construction

error analysis

interlanguage

parameter resetting

verb movement parameter

acculturation

integrative motivation

instrumental motivation

acculturation model

pedagogy

foreign language learning

natural approach

acquisition-learning hypothesis

natural order hypothesis

monitor hypothesis

input hypothesis

affective filter hypothesis

teachability hypothesis

language mixing

code switching

metalinguistic awareness

REVIEW QUESTIONS

1. Outline the ways in which second language learning differs from first language learning, both in the circumstances of learning and in the outcome.

2. In what ways are young children better and worse in second language learning than older children and adults?

3. What are the possible explanations of a critical period for second language learning? How are they different from the possible explanations of a critical period for first language learning?

4. What is "behavioral" about the contrastive analysis hypothesis? How are the markedness differential hypothesis and the psychotypology hypothesis less behavioral?

5. Contrast the notion of language transfer with the notion of creative construction. What would be an empirical test of these two positions?

6. According to the Universal Grammar approach, how is the process of second language acquisition different from the process of first language acquisition?

7. Contrast the different influences of the native language on second language learning according to the contrastive analysis hypothesis, the markedness differential hypothesis, the psychotypology hypothesis, and the Universal Grammar approach.

8. What is the difference between acquired knowledge and learned knowledge, according to Krashen, and what implications does this distinction have for second language pedagogy?

9. What is the question of language differentiation in bilingual development about? What is the relevant evidence?

10. Can children learn two languages as easily as one?

11. What are the effects of bilingual development on nonlinguistic aspects of development?

9 Biological Bases of Language Development

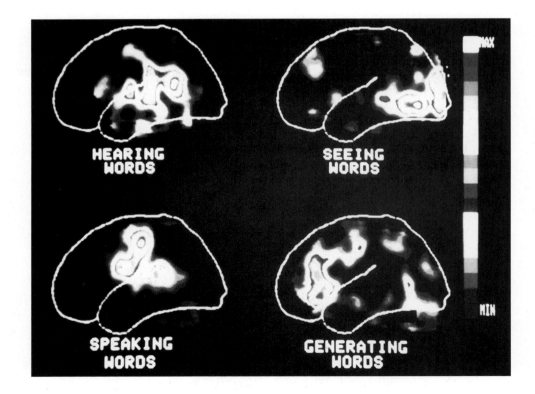

DRINK EAT ME NIM (Signed by a chimpanzee trained in
American Sign Language, from Terrace, 1979)

Wherever there are humans, there is language. Just as fish swim and birds (with a few exceptions) fly, humans talk. The capacity of fish to swim and birds to fly rests on biological properties of those animals. Fish have streamlined bodies; birds have wings. So too, the human capacity for language depends on human biology. The purpose of this chapter is to explore the biological bases of language.

We begin the discussion by providing evidence that language is a universal characteristic of the human species. It's not only that all humans talk; in the absence of a fully-formed language to learn from adults, human children will invent a language. We are referring, in this case, not to the relatively primitive home sign systems that isolated deaf children invent, but to full-fledged languages that communities of children invent. We present the evidence of the universality of language in this chapter because any behavior that is universal in a species is likely to have a biological basis (Lenneberg, 1967). However, it has been argued that universality does necessarily implicate biology. Language could be universal because it is the best solution to the problem of how to communicate, and all humans manage to find that best solution (Bates, 1984). Of course, humans must have some biologically provided equipment that enables them to figure out this best solution. The issue here, once again, concerns the language specificity of the capacities that underlie the universality of language. Does biology merely provide the equipment for solving the problem of how to communicate, or does biology actually specify the nature of the solution?

Following the discussion of the universality of language, we will turn to a discussion of particular biological structures and processes that underlie language. As we shall see, the ability to produce the sounds of language depends on the structure of the human vocal tract. However, if the oral-aural channel is blocked—as in the case of deafness—the human capacity for language finds another means of expression. Thus the crucial biological structure underlying language is the brain. Research examining patterns of language impairment associated with brain damage and patterns of brain activity associated with performing different tasks has begun to reveal how the brain is organized to perform its linguistic functions.

We will then turn to the topic of the development of brain organization, discussing both developmental changes in the normal organization of language functions in the brain and changes in the brain's capacity to recover function after injury.

After presenting evidence that language is universal in the human species and that the human capacity for language is intimately connected with the nature of the human brain, we will then turn to the question of whether language is uniquely human. There are two ways to examine this question. One is to look at the naturally occurring communication systems of other species and determine whether they have the characteristics of language. The other, which has been undertaken several times, is to try to teach a human language to another species. Finally, we will ask where the human capacity for language came from. Just as there is an evolutionary story that explains how fish acquired the capacity to swim and birds the capacity to fly, the human capacity for language has an evolutionary history.

LANGUAGE AS A HUMAN UNIVERSAL

The premise with which we began this chapter—that wherever there are people, there is language—depends on the fact that all humans (barring impairment) are capable of learning language. But when we compare language in humans to flying in birds or swimming in fish, we really mean something more. We mean that language is not merely something that humans *can* do if exposed to the right conditions; rather, language is something that humans *cannot help doing*.

Language creation

Is language part of human nature? Does language emerge even in the absence of a model for children to learn? We already discussed the home sign systems invented by deaf children in Chapter 7, and we concluded that although these inventions had some characteristics of language, they also lacked the grammatical complexity of true languages. There are, however, cases where true languages seem to be invented by a whole community of speakers.

Pidgins Sometimes historical circumstance throws together people who share no common language. To communicate in this situation, people invent a language that typically uses the lexical items from one or more of the contact languages but that has its own, very primitive grammar. Such languages are called **pidgins,** and they have arisen many times in history. For example, Hawaiian Pidgin English arose on the sugar cane plantations in Hawaii during the early part of this century when immigrant workers from Japan, Korea, and the Philippines came together; they shared no language with each other or with the English speakers for whom they worked (Bickerton, 1981, 1984). Another example is Russenorsk, which arose when Russian and Norwegian fishermen needed to communicate with each other (Todd, 1974). These are not isolated examples. There are over 100 pidgin languages currently in use (Romaine, 1988). Most pidgins are structurally simple, although if used over many generations, they do evolve, as all languages change (Aitchison, 1983; Sankoff & Laberge, 1973).

Creoles When children are born into a community in which a pidgin language is the common means of communication, the children acquire that pidgin as their native language. When children learn a pidgin, they add to it. They do not merely acquire the simple language they hear; rather, they create

---

Box 9.1   Examples of utterances in Hawaiian Pidgin English

1. Ifu laik meiki, mo beta make time, mani no kaen hapai.
   (If like make, more better die time, money no can carry.)
   "If you want to build (a temple), you should do it just before you die—you can't take it with you!"
2. Aena tu macha churen, samawl churen, haus mani pei.
   (And too much children, small children, house money pay.)
   "And I had many children, small children, and I had to pay the rent."

Source: From Bickerton, 1990.

a new language that is grammatically more complex. Usually we think of children as acquiring language, rather than the other way around. A **creole,** in contrast, results when a language acquires children (Sankoff & Laberge, 1973). A creole is usually defined as a language that once was a pidgin but that subsequently became a native language for some speakers (Todd, 1974). Thus creolization is a process that creates new languages. It is unknown how many of the world's languages originated in this way because the evidence is lost to prehistory, but there is evidence that Swahili may be the result of contact between Arabic and Bantu languages (Todd, 1974).

The process of creolization does tell us something about the biological basis of language. First, creolization suggests that the existence of language in a community does not depend on someone importing a language for the community to learn. People can invent their own. (In pidgins, the vocabulary is borrowed from one of the contact languages, but the grammar is not, as the example in Box 9.1 shows.) Furthermore, when children acquire the language, they add some grammatical features that are universal characteristics of human languages. Creoles that arose independently in different places nonetheless have similar characteristics. The shared features of independently arising creoles suggest that the human mind tends to construct only certain kinds of languages (Gee, 1993; and see Todd, 1974).

Not everyone agrees with the foregoing view of the origin of pidgins and creoles. For example, some argue that the similarities among different creoles do not necessarily result from properties of the human mind but from the common uses to which all languages are put (Jourdan, 1991) or from the fact that many creoles have been influenced by the same language (Muysken, 1988; and see Todd, 1974). For example, many creoles show the influence of either English or Portuguese because of Britain's history as a colonial power and because the Portuguese historically were worldwide seafarers and traders. It is difficult to

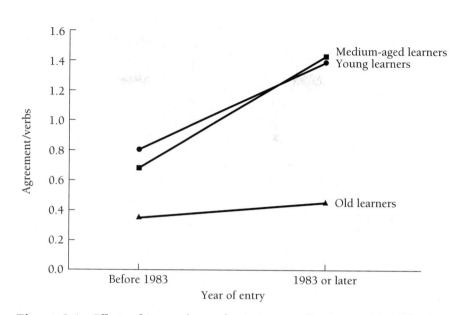

Figure 9.1 Effects of year and age of entry on use of verb agreement inflections in Nicaraguan Sign Language

Source: From "The Development of Nicaraguan Sign Language via the Language Acquisition Process," by A. Senghas. In D. MacLaughlin & S. McEwen (Eds.), Proceedings of BUCLD, 19, 543–552, published by Cascadilla Press. Copyright © 1995 Ann Senghas. Reprinted with permission.

settle arguments about the origin of creoles as long as the processes under dispute occurred a long time ago. What would really be informative would be to watch a pidgin develop into a creole.

The development of Nicaraguan sign language   A new language creating much interest is developing right now in Nicaragua. The setting for this event is the public schools for the deaf that the government of Nicaragua opened in 1978, enabling deaf children in that country to come together for the first time. These deaf children typically had their own idiosyncratic home sign systems when they entered the school, but they had no shared language. Now a new sign language is developing in the Nicaraguan schools for the deaf and in the deaf community that has arisen because of them. Ann Senghas has studied changes in this evolving language (Senghas, 1995), and she has found that individuals who learned the language in its early years of evolution have structurally less complex signing than do individuals who learned the language more recently. For example, signers who entered the school in its early years use fewer verb inflections and are less likely to mark verb agreement relations than are signers who entered the school later and acquired the more recent version of the language. It is also interesting to note that the same features that distinguish the early version from the more evolved version of the language also distinguish older learners from younger learners. One example of Senghas's findings is presented in Figure 9.1.

This evidence that children who entered the school as 4- or 5-year-olds acquired a structurally richer language than did older learners who entered at the same time is consistent with Newport's (1990) findings (discussed in Chapter 7) that deaf individuals who acquired American Sign Language as children showed better mastery of the grammar of ASL than did deaf individuals who acquired ASL as adults. The convergence of these findings—along with evidence that the process of creolization depends on children—suggests that children, not adults, contain within them the engine that drives both language acquisition and language creation.

The common basis of language creation and acquisition

Evidence that both language acquisition and language creation is done best by children suggests that the same capacity may underlie both processes. Some researchers have argued that this capacity is specific to language, and others have argued that it consists of general cognitive mechanisms.

One outline of a language-specific capacity is the **language bioprogram hypothesis** proposed by the linguist Derek Bickerton. Bickerton (1981, 1984, 1988) argued that humans are endowed with an innate skeletal or "core" grammar that constitutes "part or all, of the human species-specific capacity for syntax" (Bickerton, 1984, p. 178). Normally, in the process of language acquisition, input in the target language causes the language-learning child to modify and add to this bioprogram. In the absence of a full-fledged target language, the bioprogram builds a language using the available input to fill out the core grammar. Evidence for Bickerton's proposal consists of his analysis of a few creole languages and his claim of similarities between creoles and child language, both of which have been called into question (for example, Aitchison, 1983; Corne, 1984; Goodman, 1984). However, the general idea that the same language-specific inborn ability underlies both language acquisition and language creation is quite consistent with the nativist approach to language acquisition (Pinker, 1994; Senghas, 1995).

There is, however, an alternative point of view. It is possible to accept the proposal that creolization, language creation, and language acquisition all reflect the same process without accepting the idea that this process is language-specific. Bates (1984) argued that both language creation and language acquisition result from nonlinguistic cognitive mechanisms seeking a solution to communicating. Meier (1984) also argued that general cognitive mechanisms could underlie creolization and language acquisition. According to Meier, a process similar to creolization occurs when deaf children acquire sign language from parents who are not themselves native signers. Newport (1982) described differences in the linguistic competence of first- and second-generation signers that show structural additions similar to some of the changes that Senghas (1995) described. In particular, second-generation signers have analyzed the morphological structure of words that first-generation signers use only as frozen forms. However, Newport (1982) explains this change as a result of the way children analyze form-meaning relations in their input, which, in turn, is similar to the way children analyze patterns in other cognitive domains.

In sum, the evidence clearly argues that language is an intrinsic part of human nature. Humans are not just *able* to learn language; by nature, they create language. Furthermore, this capacity to create language seems to belong especially to children. There is disagreement, however, over how best to characterize this aspect of children's nature. At the crux of the disagreement is the by now familiar issue of whether the human capacity for language (in this case language creation) is specific to language or is a manifestation of humans' social and cognitive capacities. We will leave that question for the moment and turn to a description of the anatomical structures that serve this capacity—the vocal tract and, more important, the brain.

THE HUMAN VOCAL TRACT AND LANGUAGE

The capacity to produce speech depends on the structure and the functioning of the human vocal tract, which is illustrated in Figure 9.2. Speech is produced when air from the lungs exits the larynx and is filtered by the vocal tract above the larynx. We can change the pitch of the sound we produce by tightening or loosening the vocal folds in the larynx. We can further change the sound that comes out of our mouths by changing the shape of the vocal tract above the larynx (or, strictly speaking, the **supralaryngeal vocal tract**).

Although the structures in our vocal tract serve other purposes—biting, chewing, swallowing, taking in air—these structures have features that seem better suited for speaking than for their other functions. Human teeth are even and upright, which is not necessary for eating but is useful for producing certain sounds, such as [s] and [f]. The human lips and tongue also have properties that are useful for rapidly producing different sounds but are not particularly necessary for anything else (Aitchison, 1989). The most notably speech-specific feature of the human vocal tract is the position of the larynx. In humans, compared to other mammals, the larynx is low. Although this feature is good for producing speech sounds, it comes at a cost. Because our larynx is low, food from our mouths can fall into the trachea, and we run the risk of choking to death. Other animals have a higher larynx, and they can close off the passage for air into the lungs. Thus other animals can breathe through their nose and drink at the same time; humans cannot. Changes in the shape of the mouth that go along with the lower larynx also account for the frequent human problem of overcrowded teeth and impacted wisdom teeth (Lieberman, 1991).

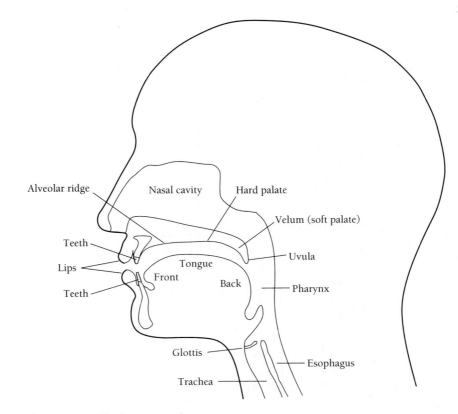

Figure 9.2 The human vocal tract

These life-threatening disadvantages that come with a vocal tract that is good for speech suggest that speech must have been very useful to the first hominids who had it. It must have given them a survival advantage that more than compensated for the risk of death from infected teeth and choking on food. It is possible to look at fossils to see when the hominid vocal tract first had a shape that would have supported modern speech. According to Philip Lieberman (1984, 1991), no hominid before Cro-Magnon was capable of producing the range of sounds in modern languages. Lieberman suggests that the advantage of having language may explain why the Cro-Magnon survived and their nonlinguistic contemporaries, the Neanderthal, did not.

THE HUMAN BRAIN AND LANGUAGE

A human vocal tract alone is not sufficient for language (and the existence of sign languages shows that it is not even necessary). Language requires a human

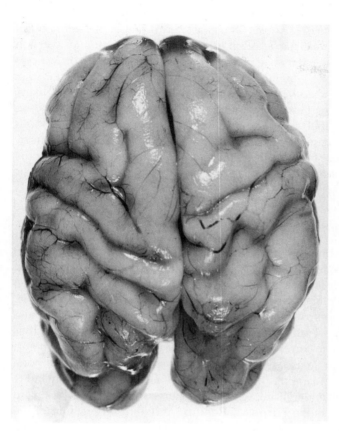

Figure 9.3   The human brain viewed from above. (In this photo, the front of the brain is at the top.) The physical appearance of the human brain does not reveal what the brain does or how it does it. The field of neurolinguistics is devoted to the study of what structures in the brain are involved in language processing and language acquisition and how those structures serve their linguistic functions.

brain. In this section, we describe what is known as the **functional architecture** of the brain—how the brain is organized to do what the brain does. To the untrained observer, the human brain appears to be an undifferentiated, wrinkly mass (see Figure 9.3). The only obvious structural feature is a fissure that divides the brain on its longer axis into two halves. Somewhere within this mass of tissue is the physical basis of the human capacity for language. Researchers who study the brain and language hope that **neurolinguistic** investigations will tell us not only where language resides in the brain but also what it is about our brain that makes language possible.

One question that neurolinguistic investigations might answer is whether we have a "language organ" (to use Chomsky's term) that is in the brain but separate from the rest of it. This question is really the neuroanatomical version of the question of whether language is a separate, isolated ability or just one manifestation of humans' general cognitive capacity. Another question that studies of the brain might answer is whether language itself is one thing or many things. That is, are syntax, semantics, and pragmatics different competencies in the brain or only in the theories of the linguists who study language? Questions of what are separate competencies are addressed in neurolinguistics in part by examining whether these functions are carried out by different parts of the brain. To understand the research in this area, we need to begin with some basic neuroanatomy.

Some basic neuroanatomy

The appearance of the brain as an undifferentiated mass is misleading. The brain actually has different parts that perform different functions. When you look at an intact brain, what you see is the outer layer—the **cerebral cortex.** Hidden underneath the large cortex are the **subcortical** parts of the brain. Roughly speaking, the cortex controls higher mental functions, such as reasoning and planning, and subcortical structures control more primitive functions, such as eating and breathing. The cortex itself is divided into two cerebral hemispheres; in most individuals, the area of the cortex that sits over the ear (the temporal lobe) is larger in the left cerebral hemisphere than in the right (Geschwind & Levitsky, 1968). The left and right cerebral hemispheres are connected by a band of nerve fibers known as the **corpus callosum.** An interesting feature of the human nervous system, which will be important to understanding some of the research on the brain and language, is that each cerebral hemisphere is connected to the opposite side of the body. As a result of these **contralateral connections,** the right side of the brain controls the left side of the body, and vice versa. Also, information coming in to sense receptors (the eyes, ears, and so on) from the right side of the body goes directly to the left cerebral hemisphere, and vice versa. (There are also same-side or **ipsilateral connections,** but these are not as strong as the contralateral connections.) These, then, are the basic outlines of the organ that neurolinguists study: two cerebral hemispheres connected to the rest of the body by contralateral fibers, connected to each other by the corpus callosum, and sitting on top of subcortical structures. How can we find out what these different parts do?

Methods of neurolinguistic investigation

A relatively primitive but extremely useful way to examine what different parts of the brain do is to study patients who have suffered injuries to different parts of their brains and determine what functions are impaired as a result. This technique is known as the **lesion method**—lesions being localized areas of damaged brain tissue. The goal of the lesion method is to correlate bits of missing brain with bits of missing psychological functioning (Damasio, 1988). Some individuals have a severed corpus callosum but an otherwise undamaged brain. These patients are called **split-brain** patients, and studying them provides a unique window on how each hemisphere functions.

Other methods are used to study healthy, intact individuals. For example, **dichotic listening tasks** utilize the fact that the contralateral connections from the ears to the brain are stronger than the ipsalateral connections. Experimenters can present two stimuli simultaneously and ask which one is perceived. If the information presented to the left ear wins the competition to be processed, we can infer that the processing occurs in the right hemisphere. If the information presented to the right ear wins out, the processing must occur in the left hemisphere (Kimura, 1967).

Another way to study the intact brain at work is to place electrodes on the scalp and monitor the electrical activity below the surface. These electrodes detect voltage fluctuations. The voltage fluctuations associated with the presentation of particular stimuli or the performance of particular tasks are known as **event-related brain potentials (ERPs).** The location of ERPs associated with different mental activities is taken as a clue to the area of the brain responsible for those activities (Caplan, 1987; Neville, 1995a). In recent years, a variety of **brain imaging techniques** have been developed that enable researchers to monitor individuals as they perform different tasks. For example, for **positron emission tomography (PET scans),** subjects inhale low-level radioactive gas or are injected with glucose that has been tagged with a radioactive substance; then computerized images can be obtained indicating which regions of the brain have the greatest blood flow or are using the most energy as individuals perform different tasks (Caplan, 1987; Raichle, 1994; Witelson, 1987). Another brain imaging technique, **magnetic resonance imaging (MRI),** does not require the administration of a radioactive substance and can provide images of activity in the brain that result from patterns of blood flow and oxygen consumption (Raichle, 1994).

Although the details of the neurolinguistic research are technically difficult for those outside of neurology and the findings from this research are not wholly consistent, it is possible to draw some broad conclusions about the neurological bases of language. One conclusion is that the job of supporting language is not evenly distributed across the whole brain; rather, it is concentrated in the left cerebral hemisphere—in that part of the left temporal lobe that is larger than the corresponding area on the right. This evidence is consistent with the idea that there is a somewhat isolable "language organ." If we push further into the literature and ask just what this "language organ" does, the research suggests that it carries out the grammatical functions of language and that the grammatical aspects of linguistic functioning are, at the neurological level, somewhat separable from the semantic and pragmatic aspects. With this general picture in mind, we turn now to the research that suggests this picture and to some of the complicating details.

Language as a left-hemisphere function

Evidence from brain injury and aphasia   In 1861, the French physician Paul Broca reported to the Anthropological Society of Paris on a patient known as "Tan" because that single syllable was all he could say. Tan survived with this condition of near total mutism for more than 20 years, although he also developed paralysis on the right side of his body in his later years. When Broca examined Tan's brain in autopsy, he found a lesion on the left side caused by a fluid-filled cyst. Broca subsequently reported on many more cases in which patients who had lost "the faculty of articulate language" (as Broca's words are often translated) all had left-hemisphere damage (see Caplan, 1987, for a full historical account).

The condition in which language functions are severely impaired is known as **aphasia.** Broca's basic observation that loss of language is typically a result of brain injury to the left but not the right hemisphere still stands today (Caplan, 1987; Goodglass, 1993). Damage to the right cerebral hemisphere tends to cause different problems, particularly in processing visual-spatial information (Springer & Deutsch, 1981; Witelson, 1987). In broad terms, there seems to be a division of labor between the left and right hemispheres of the cerebral cortex: The left hemisphere is specialized for language (and some other things); the right hemisphere is specialized for processing visual-spatial information. This state of affairs, in which one hemisphere is more important than the other for particular competencies, is known as **functional asymmetry** (Bullock, Liederman, & Todorovic, 1987).

Although Broca concluded that "We speak with the left hemisphere," we can now modify that conclusion to say that the left hemisphere processes language—regardless of whether it is spoken or not. Bellugi, Poizner, and Klima (1989) studied deaf signers who had suffered strokes that damaged portions of either their left or their right hemisphere. The researchers found that left-hemisphere damage resulted in aphasia for signers just as it does for users of a spoken language. Furthermore, even though sign language uses a visual-spatial modality, signers with right hemisphere damage were not aphasic. Thus the specialization of the left hemisphere is for language, regardless of modality.

Aphasia is a very general term. There are, in fact, many different kinds of aphasia. Some individuals with aphasia have difficulty producing speech, and the speech they do produce seems to lack grammatical structure. Instead, their speech tends to consist of short strings of content words—nouns and verbs—without grammatical morphemes. This syndrome is termed **Broca's**

Box 9.2   Example of speech produced by a patient with Broca's aphasia

Yes . . . ah . . . Monday . . . er . . . Dad and Peter H . . . (his own name), and Dad . . . er . . . hospital . . . and ah . . . Wednesday . . . Wednesday, nine o'clock . . . and oh . . . Thursday . . . ten o'clock, ah doctors . . . two . . . an' doctors . . . and er . . . teeth . . . yah.

Source: From Goodglass, 1979, p. 256.

aphasia. Other individuals with aphasia have no trouble producing speech, but the speech they produce makes no sense. This syndrome is termed **Wernicke's aphasia.** When patients with Wernicke's aphasia speak, either they use words that are wrong for the meaning they are trying to express or they use made-up, meaningless words. The speech of Wernicke's aphasics has been described as "syntactically full but semantically empty" (Blumstein, 1988, p. 203). Examples of the speech of patients with Broca's and Wernicke's aphasia are presented in Boxes 9.2 and 9.3. When one function can be disrupted without affecting another, we say these two functions are **dissociable.** In fact, there are many more different types of aphasia than just these two. (For more detailed descriptions of aphasia in adults, see Blumstein, 1988; Caplan, 1987; Goodglass, 1993.) The significance of the different aphasic syndromes for psycholinguistics is that they suggest that language is multifaceted, not only from the linguist's point of view but also in the brain.

A great deal of research has been directed toward trying to relate the particular type of aphasia with the particular location of brain damage within the left hemisphere. For example, Broca's aphasia is typically associated with damage to the front part of the left hemisphere, near the part of the cortex that controls movement—an area known as **Broca's area.** Wernicke's aphasia is typically associated with damage to a region more posterior than Broca's area, which lies next to the primary auditory cortex—**Wernicke's area.** These areas are mapped in Figure 9.4. The association between the location of left-hemisphere damage and the particular sort of resulting language impairment inspired hypotheses that Broca's area was the seat of grammar and Wernicke's area the seat of meaning. The current view, however, is that the neuroanatomical division of labor is not nearly as neat as this (Caplan, 1987; Zurif, 1995). First, the kinds of deficits shown by individual patients usually are not clear examples of one type of aphasia or another but are more mixed. Second, the particular location of injury associated with particular deficits is variable across patients. Currently, there is consensus that language functions are concentrated in the left hemisphere, but there is little agreement on how components of language

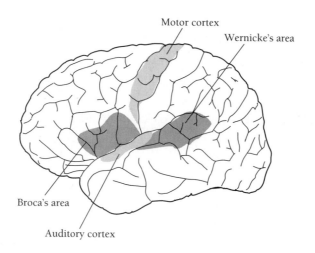

Motor cortex

Wernicke's area

Broca's area

Auditory cortex

Figure 9.4   Language areas of the brain

Box 9.3   Example of speech produced by a patient with Wernicke's aphasia

The patient is responding to the question, "How are you today?": "I feel very well. My hearing, writing been doing well. Things that I couldn't hear from. In other words, I used to be able to work cigarettes I didn't know how . . . Chesterfeela, for 20 years I can write it."

Source: From Goodglass, 1993, p. 86.

function might be localized within the language regions of the left hemisphere (Pinker, 1995).

Evidence from split-brain patients   Another source of evidence that language is a left-hemisphere function is found in individuals with a severed corpus callosum. This surgical procedure is performed as a treatment for severe epilepsy that has not responded to other measures. Severing the connections between the two hemispheres seems to stop the spread of the electrical activity that accompanies seizures, and the seizures are reduced or eliminated (Gazzaniga, 1983). Patients who have had this surgery have an intact left hemisphere and an intact right hemisphere; thus each hemisphere can still perform its normal functions. But because the corpus callosum is severed, there

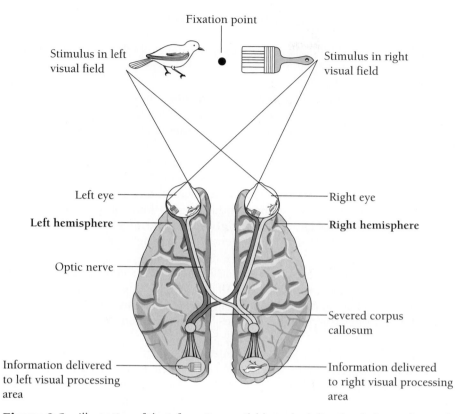

Figure 9.5   Illustration of the information available to the left and right hemispheres of a split-brain patient.

is no communication between the two hemispheres. These split-brain individuals have little difficulty functioning in daily life, but in experimental settings they provide researchers with the opportunity to study what each hemisphere does alone.

Split-brain patients have been tested in experimental situations in which a picture is presented only in the left half of the visual field—that is, to the left of a center fixation point. Because the connections from the left half of each retina go to the right hemisphere, only the right hemisphere knows what is on the picture. The information available in this situation to each cerebral hemisphere of a split-brain patient is illustrated in Figure 9.5. Split-brain patients in this situation typically cannot say what they saw. However, they are able to draw what they saw with their left hand (the one connected to the right hemisphere). The interpretation given to the inability of split-brain patients to indicate verbally what was presented to the left visual field is that the hemisphere that knows what's out there, the right hemisphere, cannot talk; and the left hemisphere, which can talk, doesn't know what's out there.

Evidence from studies of undamaged adults   It is also possible to demonstrate that the left hemisphere is the locus of language activity in healthy, intact individuals. Imagine you are in an experiment in which you are wearing a headset, and syllables such as "ba" or "ga" are presented either to your left ear or to your right ear. Your task is to report what you hear. As you can probably imagine, this presents no problem. Now, what if the experimenter simultaneously presents "ba" to one ear and "ga" to the other? What would you hear? Doreen Kimura conducted this kind of dichotic listening experiment with adults and found a **right-ear advantage**—subjects reported more of the syllables that were presented to the right ear than to the left ear (Kimura, 1967).

This basic finding of a right-ear advantage for speech stimuli has been replicated many times (see Bryden & Allard, 1978; Springer & Deutsch, 1981), and it suggests that the part of the brain most directly connected to the right ear (the left hemisphere) is primarily responsible for processing speech stimuli (See Figure 9.6).

Research using either scalp electrodes to measure event-related potentials or brain imaging techniques to measure cortical activity has also found greater left-hemisphere activity associated with language processing (Ingvar & Schwartz, 1974; Mazziotta & Metter, 1988; Molfese, Freeman, & Palermo, 1975; Phelps & Mazziotta, 1985; Wood, Goff, & Day, 1971).

If the left hemisphere is primarily responsible for processing language, the next question is why. It could be that the left hemisphere is specialized for language; however, some research suggests another possibility. Research with trained musicians suggests that it is the kind of processing rather than the kind of stimulus that determines the hemispheric advantage. Bever and Chiarello (1974) found that experienced musicians showed a right-ear (left-hemisphere) advantage for music, whereas naive listeners showed a left-ear (right-hemisphere) advantage for music. The explanation offered is that trained musicians process language in a more analytical way than naive listeners do, and that analytical processing engages the left hemisphere.

In sum, research from the study of the brain injuries associated with aphasia, from the study of split-brain patients, and from the study of functional asymmetries in intact adults all point to the conclusion that language is a left-hemisphere function. Some researchers have suggested that the left hemisphere's specialization may not be for language per se but for the kind of mental processing that language requires. It has been suggested that what the left hemisphere is really specialized for is analytical, serial processing—the

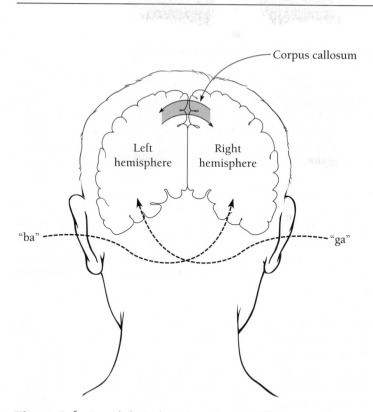

Figure 9.6 In a dichotic listening test, two different stimuli are presented simultane-ously, one to each ear, and the listener is asked to report what was presented. Because the dominant neural connections are contralateral, information from the right ear reaches the left hemisphere before information from the left ear does, and vice versa. (The infor-mation presented to the left ear goes first to the right hemisphere and then must cross through the corpus callosum to reach the left hemisphere, and vice versa.) Thus if the listener reports hearing the stimulus presented to right ear, the researcher infers that the left hemisphere is responsible for processing that stimulus. If the listener reports hearing the stimulus that was presented to the left ear, then the right hemisphere must be responsible for processing.

detailed processing of information that is received in a structured sequence (Bever & Chiarello, 1974; Bradshaw & Nettleton, 1981). Because language re-quires that kind of processing, language functions are carried out by the left hemisphere. In contrast, the right hemisphere is specialized for holistic pro-cessing—processing that is less analytic and handles multiple inputs presented simultaneously. Because visual-spatial tasks require holistic processing of in-formation, they are carried out by the right hemisphere (Bever & Chiarello, 1974).

Language as not exclusively a left-hemisphere function

Sometimes damage to the left cerebral hemisphere does not result in aphasia, and sometimes damage to the right cerebral hemisphere does. This finding suggests that for some individuals, language may not be exclusively a left-hemisphere function. In some people, usually people who are left-handed, language is controlled by the right hemisphere. Also, the right hemisphere apparently shares language functions with the left hemisphere, and it does so more for some individuals than for others, and (on average) more in women than in men.

Right hemisphere contributions to language   The right cerebral hemisphere makes some contribution to normal language functioning, even in individuals who show the typical left-hemisphere dominance for language. Evidence for this functioning is manifest in language impairments associated with right-hemisphere damage.

Right-hemisphere lesion patients sometimes produce abnormal intonation contour when they speak, and they may have difficulty recognizing the emotional tone of an utterance (Caplan, 1987). Right-hemisphere damaged patients have difficulty understanding jokes, understanding sarcasm, interpreting figurative language, and following indirect requests (Weylman, Brownell, & Gardner, 1988). These difficulties suggest that the right hemisphere may be involved in the pragmatic aspects of language use (Weylman et al., 1988), although not in the "core" psycholinguistic capacities (Caplan, 1987). Studies of event-related potentials in intact patients show that the right hemisphere is activated by semantic processing, whereas the left hemisphere is activated primarily by syntax processing (Neville, Nicol, Barss, Forster, & Garrett, 1991). In sum, studies of what the right hemisphere contributes to language when the left hemisphere is intact indicate that the right hemisphere is involved in semantics and pragmatics but that syntax is the province of the left hemisphere.

Another question about the linguistic functions of the right hemisphere concerns what the right hemisphere could do if it had to, as in cases of left-hemisphere damage. Again, the answer seems to be that the right hemisphere has some semantic and pragmatic competence, but it has limited syntactic (and phonological) abilities. This answer comes from studies of patients who have had their left hemispheres removed (because of severe pathology) and from studies of the language capacity of the right hemisphere in split-brain patients (Baynes & Gazzaniga, 1988; Dennis, 1980; Gazzaniga, 1983; Zaidel, 1985). This finding converges well with the findings from event-related potential studies that show more right-hemisphere involvement in language for individuals who learned language late (as did Newport's deaf signers; Neville, 1995a) and with the evidence that these late language learners are not quite as good at syntax as are those who learned language in infancy

(Johnson & Newport, 1989; Newport, 1990). We will return to the question of the right hemisphere's capacity for language when we discuss the case of Genie—a child who acquired what language she did relatively late in life and who seems to have done so with her right hemisphere.

Individual and sex-related differences If you should ever need brain surgery, your neurosurgeon will want to be especially careful to avoid damaging the language centers in your brain. You would probably be given the **Wada test,** in which a barbiturate is injected into one carotid artery, temporarily inactivating one hemisphere. In the Wada test, the patient is awake and can be tested to discover whether the inactive hemisphere is involved in language. The reason your doctor would do the Wada test instead of just checking a neurolinguistic text before operating is that everybody's brain is different.

The standard description of the left hemisphere as the seat of language functions is true for most people (between 80% and 98%, depending on the source of the estimate), but it is not true for everyone, and the degree of dominance is not always the same (Bryden, Hecaen, & DeAgostini, 1983; Caplan, 1987; Milner, 1974). People who are left-handed (but still left-hemisphere dominant) and even people who are right-handed but have left-handed family members may show more bilateral participation in language (Caplan, 1987). Also, women show more bilateral participation in language than men do (McGlone, 1980). Even within the left hemisphere, there are individual differences in where language functions are represented, although the causes and consequences of individual differences in brain organization are open questions at this point (Goodglass, 1993).

BRAIN DEVELOPMENT AND LANGUAGE DEVELOPMENT

The foregoing data establish a reasonably clear picture of how language is represented in the adult brain: in most people, language is primarily controlled by the left cerebral hemisphere, and the left hemisphere seems particularly specialized for grammar. We turn now to questions concerning how that adult organization is reached.

The development of the left-hemisphere specialization for language

The hypotheses Traditionally, there have been two competing views on the development of the left-hemisphere specialization for language in the adult brain. One view, termed the **equipotentiality hypothesis,** holds that the left hemisphere is not specialized for language at birth. Rather, the left and right hemispheres have equal potential for acquiring language (Bishop, 1983, 1988;

Lenneberg, 1967). This hypothesis has often been interpreted to mean that language is initially represented in both hemispheres and shifts to the left hemisphere only with maturation. Given that interpretation, one would expect that measures of dichotic listening performance, measures of brain activity during language processing, and the effects of brain injury on children should show a different and less lateralized pattern than would the corresponding data from adults. However, it is also possible to interpret equipotentiality more narrowly—to mean that the right hemisphere only *has the potential* to serve language, not that it normally does (Satz, Strauss, & Whitaker, 1990).

The opposite view regarding the ontogeny of cerebral lateralization is termed the **invariance hypothesis.** According to this view, the left hemisphere has the adult specialization for language from birth; nothing about lateralization changes with development. This view predicts that data from children—on lateralization of language processing and on effects of brain damage—should look much like the data from adults. (For fuller discussions of these two hypotheses, see Kinsbourne, 1993; Satz & Lewis, 1993; Satz et al., 1990; Witelson, 1987.) We turn now to the data that address these hypotheses.

Evidence from processing studies with children   When researchers study the processing of speech stimuli in children—using the same methods to assess lateralization of function that are used with adults—they find evidence of left-hemisphere specialization beginning in infancy. For example, Molfese, Freeman, and Palermo (1975) presented spoken syllables, spoken words, and nonspeech sounds to three groups of children: infants under 10 months old, children between 4 and 11 years old, and adults. Using scalp electrodes, Molfese and associates recorded the left- and right-hemisphere electrophysiological activity associated with presentation of each kind of stimulus. As expected, they found that most of the participants showed greater left-hemisphere activity in response to the speech sounds and greater right-hemisphere activity in response to nonspeech sounds. And, what is important for the developmental question, they found that the proportion of the children who showed this lateralization of speech sound processing remained constant from infancy to adulthood. This basic finding has been replicated many times (Molfese & Betz, 1988).

Asymmetries of function in children have also been found using dichotic listening tasks. Children as young as $2\frac{1}{2}$ years have shown a right-ear advantage for verbal stimuli, as adults do (Hiscock, 1988). Further investigations have tried to identify what it is about the speech stimuli that elicits left-hemisphere activity in infants. Using a dichotic listening procedure (modified for use with infants), Best (1988) found a right-ear advantage for consonants but not for vowels. Best suggested that it is the rapidly changing acoustic properties of consonants—in contrast to the steady-state acoustic properties of vowels—that evoke the left-hemisphere response. This finding is consistent with the notion that the left-hemisphere specialization for language is really specialization for serial processing.

In sum, research on hemispheric differences in language processing in children suggests that the left hemisphere is specialized for language from as early an age as infants can be tested (including preterm infants). However, this is not to say that the infant brain is the same as the adult brain, it is not. In fact, the human brain does not reach its mature state until after the age of 15 (Neville, 1991); and although there is asymmetry from birth, the degree of that asymmetry changes with development (Witelson, 1987). Results such as those from Molfese and colleagues (1975) show constancy only in the proportion of participants who show left-hemisphere dominance for language. Results on the degree of dominance are a different and considerably more complicated matter. However, there is substantial evidence that the degree of lateralization of function increases with development, and we will come back to this fact shortly. First we review one other source of data used to address questions about the development of cerebral asymmetry.

Evidence from childhood aphasia There are fewer studies of childhood aphasia than of aphasia in adults, because the strokes and war-related gunshot injuries that are the primary cause of aphasia in adults affect children less frequently. Thus the data on childhood aphasia are sketchier than the data on adulthood aphasia, and the picture that emerges is subject to different interpretations.

At one time, aphasia in children was thought to be equally likely to result from left- or right-hemisphere damage and that, unlike adults, children could recover completely from aphasia. If this were true, it would certainly support the equipotentiality theory, and a very famous argument to this effect was made by Eric Lenneberg in 1967. Although Lenneberg still deserves credit for being one of the first to see that biological data could inform studies of language development, more recent data on childhood aphasia largely contradict the equipotentiality view.

In the first aphasia study to establish that language is a left-hemisphere function for children as well as for adults, Woods and Teuber (1978) looked at 65 children who suffered unilateral brain damage to either the left or the right hemisphere. They found that aphasia almost always followed left-hemisphere injury and rarely followed right-hemisphere injury, just as is the case for adults. Woods and Teuber argued that earlier reports of aphasia following right-hemisphere injury described cases that occurred before antibiotics were used, and that the aphasias that were observed following right hemisphere injury were actually caused by bacterial infections that affected the whole brain.

In the first research to question the notion that children fully recover from aphasia, Woods and Carey (1979) administered a battery of tests to adolescents and adults who had suffered from aphasia in childhood but who seemingly had recovered from their symptoms. These "recovered" individuals scored below normal controls on these tests, leading Woods and Carey to conclude that when left-hemisphere damage causes aphasia in childhood, it leaves "significant residual impairment" (p. 409). More recent studies have confirmed this finding (Aram, Ekelman, Rose, & Whitaker, 1985; Vargha-Khadem, O'Gorman, & Watters, 1985). The most widely accepted interpretation of the newer aphasia evidence is that it agrees with the electrophysiological data and dichotic listening studies in suggesting left-hemisphere specialization for language from birth (for a contrary view, see Bishop, 1983, 1988).

Also like the processing data, however, the data on childhood aphasia suggest that the immature brain is not organized in quite the same way as the adult brain. Childhood aphasia differs from adulthood aphasia in several ways. The type of aphasia that children experience following left-hemisphere damage is different. Children are more likely to suffer nonfluent (Broca-type) aphasia, whereas Wernicke's aphasia is more common in adults. This difference suggests that within the left hemisphere, there are developmental changes in how language functions are organized (see also Satz & Lewis, 1993; Stiles & Thal, 1993). Also, recovery from aphasia is faster and more nearly complete in children than in adults; and for children, some evidence suggests that the earlier the damage occurs, the better the recovery (Vargha-Khadem et al., 1985).

Evidence from brain injury prior to language   So far, we have talked about the effects of left-hemisphere damage on children who have already acquired language. What happens when the left hemisphere is damaged prior to language acquisition? If the left hemisphere not only controls language processing but is also responsible for language acquisition, then left-hemisphere damage should severely impair the child's ability ever to acquire language. And, similarly, if the left hemisphere is solely responsible for language acquisition, then right-hemisphere damage should not affect language development.

Studies that have followed the language development of children who suffered left-hemisphere damage either in utero or in the first few months of life find the following general pattern: Although language development is initially delayed—in some cases by more than a year—children seem to catch up, and after a few years their language is essentially comparable to that of other children of their same age (Feldman, Holland, Kemp, & Janosky, 1992; Levy, Amir, & Shalev, 1992; Satz & Lewis, 1993; Stiles & Thal, 1993). Although these children with left-hemisphere lesions seem to catch up during the normal period of language development, subtle impairments in their language abilities, particularly in syntax and morphology, are found later. Thus children with early left-hemisphere damage manage to seem comparable to their peers when they are all still developing language; but the ultimate language achievement of children with prelinguistic left-hemisphere damage seems limited in the same way that the ultimate recovery from aphasia following left-hemisphere damage is limited.

When children who suffered right-hemisphere damage before acquiring language are followed longitudinally, we obtain a finding that does not parallel the aphasia data. Although right-hemisphere damage is not likely to cause loss of language function in children who have acquired language, right-hemisphere damage prior to language acquisition causes delays in language development (Feldman et al., 1992; Thal et al., 1991). Somehow, the right hemisphere seems to be more involved in language acquisition than in language processing after acquisition is accomplished. (This may not be as mysterious as it sounds. This finding suggests that processing speech after language is acquired uses the left hemisphere, but figuring out what people are saying and how they are saying it when you have not yet acquired language uses strategies that include right-hemisphere processing.)

In sum, the data on the lateralization of language in children suggest a position somewhere between equipotentiality and invariance. On the side of invariance, the data suggest that the left hemisphere is specialized for language from birth. On the side of equipotentiality (if not true equipotentiality, at least more nearly equal potential of both hemispheres), the degree of asymmetry increases with development, and the ability of the right hemisphere to take over language functions for a damaged left hemisphere is greater in children than in adults. But why does the degree of asymmetry change, and why do children recover from aphasia better than adults do? We'll start with the question about developmental changes in the ability to recover from aphasia.

Basic processes in neurological development

Neural plasticity in childhood   That children recover language after left-hemisphere damage more rapidly and more fully than adults suggests that something must be different in children's brains. One thing that children's brains have more of than adults' brains is **plasticity.** Plasticity is the ability of parts of the brain to take over functions they ordinarily would not serve (Witelson, 1987). Brain tissue does not regenerate once it is damaged. Thus when children with left-hemisphere damage recover language function, it must be that other areas of the brain are taking over the functions previously carried out by the damaged portions of the left hemisphere. Although there is some plasticity in the adult brain, there is more in the child's.

The greater plasticity of the immature brain is the basis for children's better, if not perfect, recovery from aphasia. Evidence of subtle syntactic impairments even after recovery from childhood aphasia suggests that the right hemisphere is never quite as good as the left at some aspects of language. Although the plasticity of the immature brain allows one part to take over the work of another, there remain telltale signs that the right hemisphere is doing a job that it is not as well suited for as the left hemisphere is. What we have suggested to this point then, is that children recover better from left-hemisphere damage than adults do because the right hemisphere can take over, and we refer to this capacity as plasticity. But plasticity only gives a label to the phenomenon; it doesn't explain it. We now turn to the question of what gives the immature brain its greater plasticity, and in so doing we start to find an explanation of why children have a greater capacity to recover from aphasia.

Where does plasticity come from?   The source of the great plasticity of the immature brain is quite likely in the initial redundancy in the neural architecture. The picture of brain development that emerges from recent work in developmental neurobiology is one in which the brain grows synaptic connections from the period of fetal development through the first 2 years of life, reaching a point at which there is a great deal of redundancy in the connections in the brain. After age 2, brain development consists primarily of losing connections (Huttenlocher, 1994). As connections are lost, redundancy is lost, and thus particular functions come to be located in specifically dedicated areas rather than throughout the brain (Neville, 1995a).

For this sort of developmental process to work, there must be a way to ensure that only redundant connections and not needed ones are lost. This is accomplished by the activity of the young brain influencing which connections are lost and which remain. A variety of evidence suggests that connections that are used become fixed or **stabilized,** and unused connections are eliminated. Unlike the early empiricists' notion of experience producing tracings on a blank slate, neurophysiological evidence suggests that huge numbers of tracings are innately provided and that the absence of experience structures the brain by erasing some of them (for fuller discussions, see Bertenthal & Campos, 1987; Greenough, Black, & Wallace, 1987; Huttenlocher, 1994; Neville, 1991; and Witelson, 1987). Another metaphor used to describe the influence of experience on brain organization describes experience as a sculptor, shaping the brain by removing the portions it doesn't need (Kolb, 1989).

Changes in functional asymmetry   This account of brain development as moving from an initial state of redundant capacity throughout the brain to one of nonredundant and hence localized function explains the difference between children and adults in recovery from aphasia. But it does not explain the developmental increase in asymmetry of function. In fact, if children use their right hemispheres for language, why is the right hemisphere's capacity for language ever lost? Shouldn't the bilateral activity associated with language in very young children have the effect of preserving both hemispheres for language functions? The plasticity explanation explains only why an unused right hemisphere loses its language capacity; something else is needed to explain why the use of the right hemisphere for language declines.

There are two proposals for what changes in children to account for the increasing lateralization of language functions to the left hemisphere. One is that the brain changes; the other is that the children acquire grammar. The kind of brain change that would account for a shift of language to the left hemisphere is the maturation of those areas of the brain that serve language in the adult (see Satz, Strauss, & Whitaker, 1990). According to this account, the child initially uses both hemispheres more because the language centers in the left hemisphere aren't ready yet. (One would expect, then, that young children would be limited in their linguistic abilities, and indeed this seems to be the case.)

The second proposed explanation of increasing asymmetry of function is that the brain doesn't change, but children change the way that they process language. As children come to process language in a way that makes use of what the left hemisphere has been ready to do all along, they use the left hemisphere more. According to this account, the increase in left-hemisphere specialization is a by-product or secondary manifestation of language development (see Witelson, 1977, 1987). Mills, Coffey, and Neville (1993, 1994) found a close correspondence between the acquisition of grammar in children and an increase in left-hemisphere language processing. Whether it is the acquisition of grammar that causes the shift to the left hemisphere or a change in the left hemisphere that causes the acquisition of grammar remains to be seen (Neville, 1995b).

Whatever the cause, under normal circumstances, the child by age 2 has begun to acquire grammar and is predominantly using the left hemisphere to process language. Daily use of the left hemisphere for language appears to stabilize language in the left hemisphere and allows the redundant right-hemisphere capacity to be eliminated. If the left hemisphere is damaged early in life, the right hemisphere still has the capacity to take over language functions, but at some point in development that capacity no longer exists. Biology appears to set a deadline by which connections must be used or lost.

The critical period hypothesis

The notion that there is a biologically determined period during which language acquisition must occur, if it is to occur at all, is known as the critical period hypothesis. Nature provides many examples of biologically determined deadlines, the best known of which is probably the critical period for imprinting in birds. Some species of birds walk as soon as they hatch. Chicks and ducklings, for example, will follow the first moving thing they see, and then they will follow it forevermore. Normally, the first thing a baby sees when it hatches is its mother, with the result that chicks and ducklings then follow their mothers everywhere. When this occurs, the chicks and ducklings are said to be imprinted on their mother. Imprinting cannot happen any time; it must occur within a few hours after hatching. [This requirement is not always absolute, and the term **sensitive period** is sometimes substituted for *critical period* (Lieberman, 1993).] There are well-documented human examples of critical periods as well. For example, some cells in the brain respond to input from both eyes in the normal adult, but if these cells fail to receive input from two eyes during the first year or two of life, they lose this capacity. Thus, the features common to all examples of critical or sensitive periods are these: some environmental input is necessary for normal development, but biology determines when the organism is responsive to that input. That period of responsivity is the critical period.

Overview of evidence for the critical period hypothesis   In Chapter 7, we presented evidence from the study of deaf individuals' acquisition of American Sign Language, and in Chapter 8 we presented evidence from the study of second language learning; both argued that there is a critical period for language acquisition. In this chapter, we present one more source of evidence for the critical period hypothesis, and we consider possible biological bases for the critical period.

The source of evidence we discuss here are the findings from studies of "wild" children, such as Victor of Aveyron, whose case we discussed in Chapter 1. There are other cases of wild children who were discovered at different ages. If it is true that discovery before a certain age allowed such language-deprived children to learn language but that discovery after a certain age did not, that would be evidence for a critical period for language acquisition. However, very few cases of "wild children" are well documented, and of those that are, not all the children survived long enough to learn language. Furthermore, when such children fail to acquire language, as was the case for Victor, we cannot be sure whether the failure was due to the late start or whether the child might have been impaired in some way to begin with. Reviewing the evidence in 1967, Lenneberg came to the conclusion that "The only safe conclusions to be drawn from the multitude of reports is life in dark closets, wolves' dens, forests, or sadistic parents' backyards is not conducive to good health and normal development" (p. 142).

There is one success story among such children. In the 1930s, a 6½-year-old child named Isabelle was discovered living hidden away in a dark room with only her deaf-mute mother for contact. (Isabelle, it seems, was illegitimate.) After her discovery, Isabelle was trained intensively to speak, and she did learn to talk. Isabelle's success makes it clear that she was cognitively normal, but her deprivation was also less extreme than that of the other cases of "wild" children. Furthermore, we do not have the sort of psycholinguistic details about Isabelle we would like. Although at 8½ she was described as having "a normal IQ" and "not easily distinguished from ordinary children of her age" (Brown, 1958, p. 192), no one administered the tests of linguistic competence that would allow fine-grained comparisons of her language competence with that of children with normal experience. There is, however, a modern case of a "wild child" who was discovered after linguistics and neurology were sufficiently advanced to allow us to ask questions that were not asked of the earlier cases.

The case of Genie In 1970, a woman who is known to most of the world only as "Genie's mother" was looking for the office of services for the blind in downtown Los Angeles. She was nearly blind, was seeking help for herself, and had only recently managed to escape virtual captivity by her mentally ill husband. By mistake, she entered the general social services office. She brought with her her 13-year-old daughter, Genie. The eligibility worker at the social services office noticed the small, frail-looking child with a strange gait and posture and called her supervisor, who, after questioning Genie's mother, called the police. The police took Genie into custody and admitted her into the hospital for severe malnutrition (Curtiss, 1977; Rymer, 1993).

The story of Genie's background that was eventually revealed was horrific. From the time Genie was 20 months old until her mother's escape when she was 13, Genie spent her time alone, strapped to a potty chair in a small bedroom. She was fed hurriedly, with minimal interaction and no talk. If Genie made any noise, her father would beat her with a large piece of wood he kept in the room for that purpose. Like the Wild Boy of Aveyron before her, Genie had no language when she was discovered. Also like Victor of Aveyron, Genie was immensely interesting to the scientific community. The story of Genie's life and treatment both before and after her discovery have been described by Curtiss (1977) and by Rymer (1993). We shall confine ourselves here to the investigation of Genie's language development, described by Susan Curtiss in her dissertation and subsequent papers (Curtiss, 1977, 1985, 1988, 1989).

Genie did not talk at all when she was first discovered. Four years later, she scored in the range of a normal 5-year-old on standardized vocabulary tests. She combined words into complex utterances, and she could express meanings. However, her language was far from normal. As the examples of Genie's speech in Box 9.4 show, her vocabulary and semantic skills far exceeded her syntactic skills. Her grammar was deficient in both production and comprehension. In production, her utterances were telegraphic, lacking most grammatical morphemes. In comprehension tests, she failed to understand passive constructions and distinctions marked by tense, and she had other difficulties as well.

Another fact about Genie's language might be related to her grammatical limitations. Dichotic listening tests showed that language was a right-hemisphere activity for Genie. In fact, the nature of her grammatical limitations has been compared to the grammatical deficiencies of patients who have recovered language after surgical removal of the left hemisphere. One possible explanation of this phenomenon is that Genie was exposed to language too late for the normal process of acquisition of language as a left-hemisphere function.

Box 9.4 Examples of Genie's utterances

Mama wash hair in sink.
At school scratch face.
I want Curtiss play piano.
Like go ride yellow school bus.
Father take piece wood. Hit. Cry.

Source: Curtiss, 1977.

She acquired language with the right hemisphere, and—as we have seen in the aphasia data—the right hemisphere is not as good at language as the left.

Genie's conversational competence was also extremely limited, and she often ignored the speech addressed to her. As Curtiss (1977) described it:

> Verbal interaction with Genie consists mainly of someone's asking Genie a question repeatedly until Genie answers, or of Genie's making a comment and someone else's responding to it in some way.... Except for those instances where Genie exerts control over the topic through repetition, verbal interaction with Genie is almost always controlled and/or "normalized" by the person talking to Genie, not by Genie. (p. 233)

Curtiss attributes this conversational incompetence to Genie's lack of early socializing experience.

The study of Genie is certainly more informative than earlier reports on isolated children. Evidence that language was a right-hemisphere function for Genie suggests that by age 13, a left hemisphere that has never been used for language has lost that capacity. However, interpretation of Genie's outcome is still hampered by the fact that we do not know with certainty that Genie was a normal child except for her experiences. Once, when Genie was seen by a doctor as an infant, she was diagnosed as mentally retarded. But there was never any follow-up to see whether that pediatrician's impression was correct, and even before Genie was totally isolated, she had something less than an ideal environment. Susan Curtiss, who worked most closely with Genie, is vehement in her disagreement with the possibility that Genie could be retarded (Rymer, 1993), but we simply do not know for sure.

In sum, the evidence on recovery from aphasia, on the effects of late exposure to language, and on the role of children in language creation presented earlier suggest that children have a language capacity that adults do not. Thus

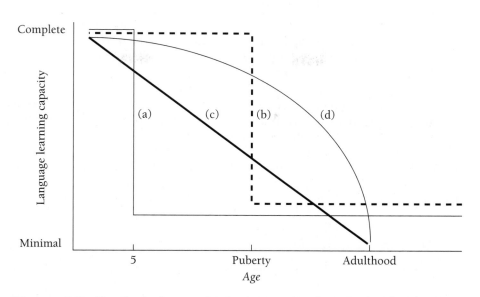

Figure 9.7 Hypothesized age-related changes in the capacity for language acquisition: (a) full capacity ending abruptly at age 5 years, (b) full capacity ending abruptly at puberty, (c) gradually declining capacity, (d) capacity declining at an increasing rate

the data support the hypothesis that there is a critical—or at least sensitive—period for language acquisition.

The data are less clear on exactly when this critical period ends. Bates (1993) suggested that the capacity for recovery from aphasia is greatest up to age 5 years, and declines after that. Krashen (1973) has also suggested 5 years as the end of the period of maximum language capacity. Lenneberg (1967) proposed puberty as the deadline, and Newport's (1990) data indicate a more gradual decline in language learning capacity. As a final possibility, Witelson (1987) suggested that an increasing negative slope characterizes age-related changes in the capacity to recover from brain damage. These four different functions are graphed in Figure 9.7. With respect to why the critical period ends, it is difficult to know which biological processes to invoke as explanation without being certain of just what the age-related function is that needs explanation. The loss of unused neural capacity is probably at least part of the reason early linguistic ability is lost, but it may not be the full account (for fuller discussions, see Johnson & Newport, 1989; Krashen, 1973; Lenneberg, 1967; Newport, 1990; Witelson, 1987).

An interesting possibility Newport (1991) suggested is that young children are better than adults are at learning language because their cognitive abilities are limited. The argument Newport makes is that it is easier to figure out the structure of language if you analyze small chunks than if you analyze longer stretches of speech. Because of children's perceptual and memory limitations, small chunks are all that children can extract from input and store in memory. Adults, in contrast, extract and store larger chunks, thereby giving themselves a more difficult analytical task. Newport refers to this argument as the **"less is more" hypothesis.** This hypothesis also receives support from computer simulations of language acquisition done within the connectionist approach, which found that the computer was more successful if fed shorter sequences as input (Elman, 1993). However, this hypothesis does not necessarily exclude the possibility that other, biological changes also contribute to the critical period for language acquisition.

LANGUAGE AND OTHER SPECIES

The natural communication systems of other species

Other animals besides humans communicate with each other. If we want to know whether language is uniquely human, we need to ask whether these other communication systems should be counted as languages too. To answer that question, we need to describe the communication systems used by other species, and we need to define language.

In describing the communication systems of other species, we will be selective rather than trying to survey the field. We will start with our closest relatives in the animal kingdom—primates. It is logical to think that the species most closely related to humans would be most likely to share the characteristic of having language. However, we will see that it is fairly easy to reject that possibility. We will then turn to research on more distant relations. Complex communication systems can be found among insects, and the development of song in some birds shares some features with language development in humans. However, we will see here, too, that fundamental features of human language are lacking in even the most sophisticated communication systems of other species.

What constitutes a language?   Human language is a vehicle for communication. But, as we discussed in Chapter 5, the fact that some activity is interpretable doesn't make it language. Crucial features of language are *reference* (symbols that stand for things) and *syntax* (a productive system for combining symbols to express new meanings). Another feature of human language is *intentionality*.

Communication among primates   One of the more sophisticated communication systems among primates that has been studied is the calls of the East

African vervet monkey. These monkeys produce a distinct alarm call for each of three different predators; there is a "leopard" call, an "eagle" call, and a "snake" call. Vervet monkeys also respond differently to these distinct calls. They run into trees when they hear the "leopard" call, they look up or run into bushes when they hear the "eagle" call, and they stand on their hind legs and look around when they hear the snake call (Seyfarth & Cheney, 1993). Seyfarth and Cheney have argued that these calls are more than expressions of excitement; they also serve to denote things in the environment. In the absence of any decontextualized uses, though, it is not clear that we would want to credit the monkeys with the capacity for reference. In terms of the other criteria for language, Seyfarth and Cheney do not argue for syntax, and they make it clear that there is no evidence that the monkeys produce their calls with the intent to modify the mental state of their listener (remember from Chapter 5, that is the kind of intentionality that underlies truly communicative behavior). Less is known about the naturally occurring communication system of our closer relatives among primates, although it is clear that chimpanzees do communicate via calls, facial expressions, and gestures (Goodall, 1986; Marler & Tenaza, 1977).

Nobody has argued that there is a naturally occurring communication system in primates equivalent to a human language. The strongest argument made, based on the most generous accounts of primate communication systems, is for continuity. As anthropologist Richard Leakey put it, the continuity view holds that "spoken language [is] merely an extension and enhancement of cognitive capacities to be found among our ape relatives" (Leakey & Lewin, 1992, p. 240). We have again the issue of whether language is unique or part of general cognition. In that regard, it may be instructive to look at the communication systems in other species that are very distant relatives of humans. We would not credit birds or insects with a great deal of general intelligence, yet when we look at birds and insects we find extremely complex communication systems.

The birds and the bees   Bees do not communicate by making noises; they dance. After a bee finds a source of nectar, it returns to the hive and does a dance that communicates the location of the food source to the other bees. Different dances are used for nearby versus distant food sources; and if the source is distant, the dance also indicates the direction of the food source. Richer food sources cause the bee to dance longer and harder, which in turn more strongly arouses the other bees (Von Frisch, 1962). As effective and sophisticated as this system is, it fails to meet virtually every criterion for being a language. It does exceed the primate systems that have been documented as having some limited productivity. A bee can communicate a new message that has never been produced before (such as distant food at a 65° angle from the sun), but it can communicate only the location of food sources. Thus it does not have the vast productivity that characterizes human language.

Some species of birds use their songs to communicate. The relevance of bird song to language development is not so much in the properties of the song (although see Snowdon, 1993) but in how the song is acquired (Marler, 1970; Nottebohm, 1970). Not all birds are songbirds, and not all songbirds show the same developmental pattern. But there are many species of songbirds in which the development of the songs that males produce to attract mates and maintain territories requires exposure to adult birds who model the song (in contrast, for example, to chimpanzees who seem not to learn their gestures or calls from adults; Tomasello, Call, Nagell, Olguin, & Carpenter, 1994). The parallels between the acquisition of song in birds and language in humans are more specific than simply the requirement of an adult model. Both have early stages prior to the appearance of the adult form—babbling in humans and what is termed subsong in birds. Both birds and humans need to be able to hear their own early productions for normal development, although deafening after acquisition does not have the same deleterious effect as deafening before acquisition. For both birds and humans, there are critical periods during which the ability to learn is at its maximum. And finally, both the production of song and speech are lateralized in the left hemisphere of the brain.

In sum, research on the communication systems of other species has revealed more complex communication systems in a number of species than many would have thought. And it is certainly true that the study of animal communication has contributed to defining the criterial attributes of human language; lists much longer than *reference, syntax,* and *intentionality* have been proposed (Hockett, 1960; and see Bradshaw, 1993). In this later regard, some might claim that revising the definition of language while you are asking whether another species has it is not quite fair. It's something like raising the high jump bar as soon as someone gets close to clearing it. However, another way of looking at it is to say that the study of animal communication reveals, by way of contrast, what is unique about human language; and if there were nothing unique, comparison to animal systems would reveal that too. Raising the bar is precisely how to find out whether one high jumper has an ability the others do not. If we set the bar at reference, syntax, and intentionality, only humans can clear it successfully.

So what light on the biological nature of the human capacity for language has been shed by this very brief foray into comparative psychology? Although not everyone would agree, a circumspect interpretation of the evidence leads to the conclusion that what humans do naturally is hugely different from anything our closest relatives seem to do. Richard Leakey, who is better known for his work on human origins, argues that "vervet 'language' is not so far removed from rudimentary human language" (Leakey & Lewin, 1992, p. 243). However, it is not at all clear just what this means, given that no normal human over the age of 3 years speaks anything that could be termed "rudimentary human language." Another implication can be found in the sophistication of bee dancing and the parallels between the development of birdsong and human language—that the complexity of a species' communication system is not a function of how close the species is to humans on the phylogenetic scale, nor is it a function of the species' general intellectual capacity. Rather, biology seems to separately equip species with communication systems that serve their needs. (For an account of how the developmental facts about birdsong are adaptive, see Nottebohm, 1970.) Whether that is the correct account of human language is an open question. We will address the issue of how our linguistic capacity might have been shaped by adaptation in the final section of this chapter. Before that, there is one more animal language topic to consider.

The acquisition of human language by other species

Just because no other species has anything equal to human language doesn't mean another animal couldn't acquire language if it were exposed to language in the right sort of supportive environment. This is the logic behind a set of efforts, undertaken several times, to teach language to a member of another species. Like many other areas of language research, these animal language experiments have been the source of huge controversy. Unlike many controversies, which are confined to academic circles, the animal language controversy plays out in newspapers, magazines, and television. In the following sections, we will review the history of attempts to teach language to apes. The ape experiments constitute the majority of animal language experiments, and they are the most nearly successful. The meaning of the carefully chosen words *nearly successful* should become apparent in the next few pages. (For discussion of the linguistic capacities of dolphins and parrots, see Premack, 1986; Roitblat, Herman, & Nachtigall, 1993.)

Efforts to teach chimpanzees to speak   The first efforts to teach human language to a chimpanzee used spoken English as the target language. In the 1930s, the Kelloggs raised an infant chimp, Gua, in their home, along with their infant son Donald. The chimp wore diapers, slept in a crib, and was in every way treated like a human child. The result was that although Gua's motor development outpaced Donald's, only Donald learned to talk. In the 1940s and 1950s, another intrepid couple, the Hayes, raised an infant chimp named Viki in their home, but, unlike the Kelloggs, the Hayes actively tried to teach Viki to produce words. After 6½ years, Viki could approximate the sounds of "mama," "papa," "cup," and "up."

It is clear that these efforts to get a chimpanzee to talk were failures, but it is not clear that these efforts were fair tests of the linguistic capacity of the species.

Chimpanzees have a vocal tract that makes speech production essentially impossible. But the question of interest in these studies is not whether chimps have the articulatory apparatus for speech but whether they have the brain for language.

Signing apes   The next efforts avoided the problem of speech and capitalized on chimpanzees' manual dexterity by employing American Sign Language as the target language. In 1966, Beatrice and Allan Gardner, faculty members at the University of Nevada in Reno, acquired a wild-born infant female chimp (Wallman, 1992). The chimp was named Washoe, after the county in Nevada where the Gardners lived. Washoe lived in a trailer in the Gardners' backyard, and she was cared for by the Gardners and by University of Nevada students. Everyone who interacted with Washoe was instructed to use only sign language, both with Washoe and among themselves in Washoe's presence. In addition, Washoe was actively taught signs by physically molding her hands into the proper shape and by drilling her and rewarding her for correct usage. After four years of this sort of language experience and language training, Washoe had learned to produce 132 signs and had been observed to produce many sign combinations. (At that point, Washoe grew rather large to handle in a trailer, and she was moved to the Institute for Primate Studies at the University of Oklahoma.) Washoe could correctly label a variety of objects and could sign MORE FRUIT, WASHOE SORRY, PLEASE TICKLE.

It seemed at the time that some great chasm had been bridged. Humans were not only talking to animals, animals were talking to humans. In 1972, Francine Patterson, a graduate student at Stanford, began a similar sign language project with a lowland gorilla named Koko. A *Nova* television program was made about these signing apes, and it is hard not to be amazed and impressed by the phenomenon of an animal producing a sign in a human language. Certainly the Gardners and Patterson were impressed. They have both claimed that their animals learned a human language. Patterson has claimed that Koko not only understands "everything that you say to her" (meaning in English), but she also communicates via her sign language skills "about the way animals view the world" (Patterson, 1985, p. 1, cited in Wallman, 1992). Patterson has also been very media savvy, and Koko has appeared on major network television programs and in *National Geographic* magazine, and she has even graced the pages of the "Weekly Reader"—a widely read newsletter for elementary school children. It is not surprising, then, that the belief that chimpanzees and gorillas can learn a human language is widespread.

However, careful analysis of just what the apes do suggests that the linguistic abilities of even our closest relatives are quite limited. During the 1970s, when stories of talking apes filled the airways and impressed enough psychologists to be reported in introductory textbooks, there were always some dissenting voices (see Seidenberg & Petitto, 1979). But the true unmasking of the

Figure 9.8   Chimpanzees have been successfully taught to use signs of American Sign Language to communicate with humans. However, the chimpanzees' accomplishments always fall short of full acquisition of the language. Just what the differences are between chimpanzee and human linguistic abilities and what they mean is a matter of considerable debate.

supposed linguistic accomplishments of apes came in 1979 from a group of researchers who set out, as the Gardners did, to teach American Sign Language to a chimpanzee.

The chimpanzee that was the focus of this ASL project was named Nim Chimpsky, an allusion to a well-known linguist. Project "Nim" was started by Herbert Terrace at Columbia University in New York City. (Terrace and Nim are pictured in Figure 9.8.) No backyards in Manhattan could accommodate a trailer, so Nim spent the first 21 months of his life raised in a private home, sleeping in a hammock in the dining room. For two years after that, he lived in splendor on the northern edge of New York City in a mansion that had been bequeathed to Columbia. As with Washoe, Nim's caretakers used sign language in interactions with him, and they also actively molded Nim's signs. Like Washoe, Nim learned over 100 signs and produced many sign combinations. A sample of these is presented in Box 9.5.

Box 9.5 Examples of sign combinations produced by the chimpanzee "Nim"		
2-sign combinations	*3-sign combinations*	*4-sign combinations*
play me	play me Nim	eat drink eat drink
me Nim	eat me Nim	eat Nim eat Nim
tickle me	grape eat Nim	banana Nim banana Nim
more eat	me Nim eat	banana me eat banana
eat drink	finish hug Nim	play me Nim play

Source: From Terrace, 1979.

However, closer examination both of Nim's "sentences" and of the circumstances under which they were produced revealed that Nim's language acquisition was very different from a human child's. The first problem with Nim's language can be seen simply by looking at the length and nature of the multisign utterances Nim produced. From the time that Nim started regularly producing sign combinations until his departure two years later, the average length of his utterances hovered between 1.1 and 1.6 signs. Unlike children, whose MLUs increase with development, Nim did not increase his mean utterance length. To compare Nim's changes in MLU with those of hearing children acquiring English and deaf children acquiring ASL, see Figure 9.9. Also, even when Nim produced a long utterance—as he sometimes did—it was highly repetitive. Children's utterances get longer because children express more content in each utterance, but Nim's long utterances tended to say the same thing over and over. This can be seen in many of the 4-sign combinations in Box 9.5 and is abundantly clear in Nim's longest-ever utterance, GIVE ORANGE ME GIVE EAT ORANGE ME EAT ORANGE GIVE ME EAT ORANGE GIVE ME YOU.

The other problem with Nim's language is that he didn't produce his utterances by himself. Close inspection of the videotaped interaction between Nim and his teachers revealed that Nim's utterances were very dependent on his teachers' previous utterances. In fact, 90% of Nim's utterances were either imitations, reductions, or expansions of prior utterances produced by his human interlocutor. The extent to which Nim's utterances depended on the teachers' signing is suggested by an interaction that happened to be captured in a sequence of still shots taken by an automatically advancing camera. In this sequence, Nim produced the multisign utterance ME HUG

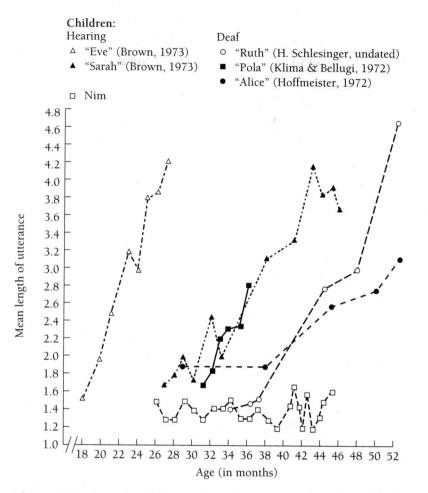

Children:

Hearing

△ "Eve" (Brown, 1973)

▲ "Sarah" (Brown, 1973)

□ Nim

Deaf

○ "Ruth" (H. Schlesinger, undated)

■ "Pola" (Klima & Bellugi, 1972)

● "Alice" (Hoffmeister, 1972)

Figure 9.9 Age-related changes in mean utterance length for two hearing children, three deaf children (learning ASL), and one chimpanzee (also "learning" ASL)

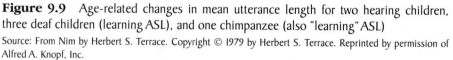

Source: From Nim by Herbert S. Terrace. Copyright © 1979 by Herbert S. Terrace. Reprinted by permission of Alfred A. Knopf, Inc.

CAT. In the frame where Nim is signing ME, the teacher is signing YOU. In the frame where Nim is signing CAT, the teacher is signing WHO (Terrace, 1979; Terrace, Petitto, Sanders, & Bever, 1979). Thus it appears that Nim produced the appearance of signing combinations with inadvertent support from his teachers.

Having found this problem with their own chimpanzee, Terrace and associates then analyzed the publicly available tapes of Washoe and Koko (one was a show produced for public television and the other a film produced by the

Gardners), and they found the same phenomenon. The sign combinations Washoe produced were always preceded by a similar utterance or by a prompt from her teacher; all of Koko's signs were signed first by the teacher (Terrace et al., 1979).

The researchers who worked with Nim came to the conclusion that chimpanzees cannot acquire a human language. Syntax was not the only way in which the chimps' use of ASL differed from the language competence of children. Although Nim had 125 signs, only a few were used regularly, and these tended to occur only in particular contexts. Basically, Nim signed to request food and other objects. Also, Nim's conversational use of signing was inappropriate. Unlike children who master turn taking even before mastering language, Nim frequently signed while his teachers were signing. Although the limited use of signs might be attributed to chimps' limited range of interests, and although their lack of conversational skill might not be a fatal flaw, syntax and reference are criterial features of language. The analyses of Terrace and associates make it clear that neither Nim, Washoe, nor Koko achieved syntax. Laura Petitto, one of Nim's teachers, argued that chimps also lack reference. She wrote:

> For Nim, meaning seemed to have no role outside of the specific association between a form and its referent that had been explicitly taught to him. I had not succeeded in bringing him to the water fountain as Annie Sullivan had done for Helen Keller. For Nim, signs did not *refer;* he did not have words—signs, or names—for things. (Petitto, 1988, p. 189)

Artificial language projects   Other attempts to teach language to chimpanzees have used experimenter-invented languages. David Premack taught the chimp Sarah a system that made use of metal chips on a magnetized board. Each chip had an arbitrary color, shape, and meaning, and there were rules for ordering the chips. After long and arduous training, Sarah learned to do things like request an apple by producing a sequence such as "Mary give apple Sarah" and to correctly respond to the instructions "Sarah insert banana pail apple dish" (meaning put the banana in the pail and the apple in the dish). Because Sarah was never exposed to full human language, it is not fair to judge her accomplishments against that criterion. However, it is clear that what she did accomplish is less than language, and Premack's more recent work has focused on Sarah's and other chimps' cognitive as opposed to linguistic skills.

At the Yerkes Regional Primate Center in Atlanta, Georgia, chimpanzees have been taught a language that uses a vocabulary of abstract symbols, called lexigrams, that can be combined according to a grammar that operates over semantically based categories. Lana, the first chimp taught this language (dubbed Yerkish), learned to produce and respond to sequences of symbols, but even her trainers made very limited claims for her accomplishments. What Lana learned was essentially a repertoire of rote-learned sequences associated with different situations and rewards (Savage-Rumbaugh et al., 1993; Wallman, 1992).

Language in a bonobo   The next major development in the animal language controversy came when researchers at the Yerkes center began to work with a different species of chimpanzee—the bonobo. Bonobos seem more similar to humans than do the common chimpanzees that had been the subjects of previous experiments. For example, bonobos engage in upright posture more frequently, and they use eye contact, gesture, and vocalization in communication more frequently than common chimps do (Savage-Rumbaugh et al., 1993).

In 1981, Sue Savage-Rumbaugh began to teach the lexigrams of Yerkish to an adult bonobo chimpanzee named Matata. However, Matata was a complete failure at learning symbol use. The surprise development that reopened the debate about the linguistic capacity of apes came from Matata's son. While Matata was being trained, her infant son Kanzi was allowed to tag along; and without anybody paying any attention to him, Kanzi not only learned the lexigrams his mother failed to master; he also acquired some ability to understand spoken English.

Kanzi's accomplishments are the basis of current claims made by Savage-Rumbaugh and her colleagues at Yerkes that chimpanzees—at least bonobos— are capable of both reference and syntax. In support of the claim for referentiality, Savage-Rumbaugh, McDonald, Sevcik, Hopkins, and Rupert (1986) cite Kanzi's performance on a vocabulary test and examples of his lexigram use in naturalistic exchanges. In the vocabulary test, Kanzi did a good job of matching lexigrams both to pictures of the objects that the lexigrams stand for and to spoken words. In interaction with his trainers, Kanzi used the lexigrams.

Although Kanzi clearly could do some things with the lexigrams he knew, the question is how to characterize what he did and the nature of the underlying knowledge. To illustrate, Kanzi would use the lexigram for *strawberry* when he wanted to go to the place where strawberries are found, when he was asking for a strawberry to eat, and when shown a picture of strawberries. On the basis of this sort of variety in the contexts in which the lexigram *strawberry* was produced, Savage-Rumbaugh and associates argued that Kanzi used *strawberry* to refer. Seidenberg and Petitto (1987) disagreed, pointing out that outside the testing context, all Kanzi's uses of *strawberry* resulted in his getting to eat strawberries. According to Seidenberg and Petitto, lexigrams for Kanzi functioned as instruments for achieving goals rather than as symbols. (As we discussed in Chapter 5, this kind of use characterizes children's prelinguistic gestures and perhaps some of their early language use, but it certainly does not characterize the end state of language development.)

The argument that bonobos are capable of syntax rests on evidence from tests of Kanzi's comprehension of spoken English (Savage-Rumbaugh et al.,

1993). In this case, Savage-Rumbaugh and colleagues explicitly compared Kanzi's comprehension abilities to those of a 2-year-old human child. Comprehension was tested by presenting the subject with commands, such as "Give Sue the bubbles," "Put the rubber band on the soap," "Go to the oven and get the tomato," and "Go get the carrot that's outdoors." Care was taken that many different objects were available so that correct responding depended on sentence understanding. Many of the sentences were presented in blind trials in which the researcher communicated to the subject from behind a one-way mirror and thus could not inadvertently cue the correct response. The results showed that Kanzi did about as well as the 2-year-old child, producing correct responses to the first presentation on 59% of trials, compared to the child's 54% correct.

Tapes of Kanzi's performance have been shown at academic conferences and on public television, and it is hard not be impressed by the sight of a chimpanzee responding correctly to somewhat improbable commands. Again, however, the problem lies in what to make of this accomplishment. Tomasello (1994) argues that none of the sentences presented to Kanzi require much syntactic competence to figure out. The comparison with the 2-year-old child doesn't help this problem, because by many accounts, a 2-year-old child's syntactic knowledge is quite limited. Ultimately, the problem is that we know the child will go on to acquire language and would, if tested at maturity, do better than 54% correct. Kanzi was 8 years old when he was tested, and 59% correct is probably as high a score as he will ever achieve.

Why can't chimpanzees acquire language? What do humans have in our brains that makes us the only linguistic species? What do chimpanzees lack that makes language unattainable for them? This is perhaps the most interesting thing to be learned from efforts to teach language to chimpanzees. Not unexpectedly, different and contradictory answers to this question have been proposed. However, there is one point of surprising agreement: the problem is not that chimpanzees lack intelligence. Both observations of chimps in the wild and laboratory experiments suggest to many observers that chimpanzees are highly intelligent. Although these impressions of chimpanzees' intellectual abilities do not constitute a fine-grained analysis of chimpanzee cognition, chimpanzees are clearly capable of learning concepts and of solving problems (see Petitto, 1988). As Seidenberg and Petitto (1987) put it, "Apes present a paradox: Why should an animal so demonstrably intelligent exhibit such dismal linguistic abilities?" (p. 284).

One possible explanation of why apes fail at language is that language is the expression of a domain-specific mental faculty that humans have and apes do not. But if humans' language-specific capacity is the capacity for syntax (the Universal Grammar argument and the bioprogram hypothesis would be versions of such a proposal), then we are still left with a paradox. The absence of innate

Universal Grammar would prevent any other animal from fully acquiring a human language, but that absence wouldn't explain why chimpanzees, for example, don't do more with what they have. Premack (1986) argued that chimps have the conceptual ability to support a semantically based grammar of the sort often attributed to 2-year-old children. And some interpretations of Kanzi's accomplishments would grant him that level of linguistic achievement. So why don't bonobos in the wild have a communication system that makes use of a semantically based grammar?

One answer proposed by Savage-Rumbaugh and associates (1993) is that maybe they do. Maybe, their argument goes, if we looked more closely than anyone has so far at the naturally occurring communication system among bonobos, we would find something like a semantically based grammar. But the researchers also suggest that chimpanzees may be limited in language by their limited production abilities. Chimpanzees cannot produce the number of discriminably different sounds that humans can (nor can they produce the finely articulated gestures of fully competent signers). According to Savage-Rumbaugh and associates (1993), "Kanzi's ability to understand human speech suggests that, if apes could produce human-like sounds, they might well invent and utilize a language that would be similar to our own, although probably considerably simpler" (p. 107).

Seidenberg and Petitto (1987) offered a different explanation of what humans have that chimpanzees lack. Remember, Seidenberg and Petitto do not credit Kanzi with reference, and they claim that it is the inability to achieve that naming insight that accounts for chimpanzees' linguistic limitations. On this view, the human language-specific capacity is not just syntactic; it also includes reference. Chimps are not capable of either learning a human language or creating their own because they are incapable of understanding that things have names.

One final proposal is that what chimpanzees lack is culture. By culture, we don't mean museums and the ballet; rather, we use a very narrow definition: culture as socially transmitted behavior. It may seem odd to bring this up now, near the end of a chapter on the biological bases of language, but language in humans is also a cultural phenomenon. It is definitely a socially transmitted behavior. Human language acquisition depends on the human capacity to learn from other people. Even human language invention depends on more than one participant. As Shatz (1994b) pointed out, social isolates—such as Genie or Victor, the wild boy of Aveyron—did not invent languages, although linguistic isolates who have potential communicative partners do. A great deal of research suggests that the chimpanzee's ability to learn through interaction with others—that is, for the social transmission of behavior—is extremely limited (Tomasello et al., 1994; Wrangham, McGrew, de Waal, & Heltne, 1994). Chimpanzees certainly imitate behaviors they observe, and chimpanzees can learn from human instruction. What chimpanzees do not seem to do is figure things out in collaboration with others (chimpanzee or human). The reason they do not, according to Tomasello and associates (1994), is that they do not have the capacity for the sort of intersubjectivity that collaborative learning requires. That is, chimpanzees cannot conceive of another individual's thoughts about something else.

By this account, what keeps language out of the reach of chimpanzees is neither a lack of general intelligence nor the absence of a language-specific mental capacity; it is the lack of the social/cognitive ability to learn through interaction with others. By some accounts the crucial component of this social/cognitive ability to learn from others (and also the ability to teach, which chimpanzees also seem not to do) depends on the ability to attribute mental states to others. What chimpanzees may lack, then, is a theory of mind (Cheney, 1995). Premack (1986) similarly argued that language is only one difference between humans and chimpanzees and concluded that language exists "as an instrument for consummating unique human social dispositions" (p. 155).

THE ORIGIN OF THE HUMAN CAPACITY FOR LANGUAGE

If language is a biologically based characteristic of the human species, then it has an evolutionary history. Just as we can ask how the giraffe got its long neck and how humans came to walk on two feet, we can ask how humans came to have the capacity for language. As Cosmides and Tooby (1994) put it, "The human brain did not fall out of the sky, an inscrutable artifact of unknown origin, . . . [rather, it acquired its] particular functional organization through the process of evolution" (pp. 85–86). The idea that we can learn about some aspect of human psychology by considering its evolutionary origins is part of a relatively new approach known as **evolutionary psychology** (see Barkow, Cosmides, & Tooby, 1992).

If we accept the central assertion of evolutionary psychology—that the brain, no less than the body, was shaped by evolution—then it would seem logical to think that we could look to those disciplines that have figured out evolution for at least the outlines of an account of the origins of language. However, the disciplines that claim to have something to say about evolution are in the middle of their own great debate (see Eldredge, 1995), and there are proposed accounts of the origin of language from very different points of view. (Note that there is no scientific disagreement about *whether* evolution occurred, only about *how* it occurred.)

In the following section, we will briefly outline the positions that have been taken on how the capacity for language evolved. As we will see, this last topic touches on two major issues that have appeared repeatedly in discussions of how children learn to talk. One is the issue of whether acquiring language is one thing that humans do with their general cognitive abilities or whether it reflects a domain-specific, modular ability. The other concerns the relation of language development to the social communicative functions that language serves.

Language as an adaptation

The standard neo-Darwinian account of evolution explains species' features as adaptations to the circumstances in which they live and compete for survival. Thus fish have streamlined bodies to more effectively move through the water, giraffes have long necks to reach leaves that other animals cannot, and so on. Evolution is not purposeful, but evolution selects features because they serve a useful purpose. Applied to the human capacity for language, the adaptationist view is that humans have language because having language gave some of our hominid ancestors an advantage in survival and reproduction over those who did not have language; thus natural selection resulted in the evolution of the capacity for language. Two very different views of the human capacity for language share the view that language evolved as an adaptation to circumstances in which communication conferred a selective advantage. The issue among differing adaptationist accounts concerns what sort of thing resulted from this selection for the capacity to communicate.

The modular view   One view is that the nature of the human adaptation to circumstances in which communication conferred an advantage is a complex, special-purpose mechanism—a modular language faculty (Pinker & Bloom, 1990). The notion that a special-purpose, complex mechanism was selected to serve its particular function is certainly in accord with the standard neo-Darwinian account of how other complex systems evolved; the eye evolved for vision, the heart for pumping blood, so why not parts of the left cerebral hemisphere for language? This account of language as a special-purpose adaptation is also consistent with the evolutionary psychology approach, according to which *all* mental capacities are special-purpose faculties designed by evolution to serve specific functions. According to this view, the mind is not some generally useful, all-purpose tool. Rather, the mind is like a Swiss army knife with many different special-purpose tools. (For an argument as to why evolution would result in that sort of mental organization, see Barkow, Cosmides, & Tooby, 1992.)

The nonmodular view   It is possible, however, to accept the insight from evolutionary psychology that human abilities have an evolutionary history without accepting that the result of evolution is necessarily a bundle of different special-purpose devices. Barring some huge mutation, evolution has to work with the material that is there. So even if language conferred an advantage on those who had it and they survived to pass on their genes in greater numbers because of it, language did not necessarily emerge from this evolutionary process as a domain-specific capacity.

Instead, language may have been made possible by "quantitative changes in the size, power, and interactive potential of preexisting components" (Bates, Thal, & Marchman, 1991, p. 35). As Elizabeth Bates has often put it, language is "a new machine built out of old parts" (Bates et al., 1991, p. 35). There is, according to this view, no language module separate from the rest of the human brain. Lieberman (1975) argues in a similar vein that human language is the result of converging changes in several mental capacities; he nominates automatization, cognitive ability, and encoding. Lieberman assigns particular importance to the evolution of the supralaryngeal vocal tract to account for the particular form human language takes. (Indeed, there are other accounts that suggest hominid communication was gestural before it became vocal; see Corballis, 1992; Kimura, 1979.)

Although the differences between the modular and nonmodular adaptationist positions are huge and involve a central issue in the field of psycholinguistics (domain specificity), these views share one assertion: whatever it is that underlies language, humans have that capacity because having language was advantageous on the savannah some 200,000 years ago (estimate from Corballis, 1992). Language is useful only to a species whose members are interested in communicating with each other. And a system as complex as human language is more useful than calls and hoots only if the interacting members of the species are interested in exchanges of information more complex than food locations and predator warnings. The readily observable facts that humans are extremely interested in talking about other humans and that managing interpersonal relations is at the core of managing human society may be what gives human language its particular characteristics. Thus both the nonmodular and modular adaptationist accounts of the origin of language assign a central role to the social nature of our hominid ancestors. (For an argument for how the demands of human communication require the structural complexity of human language, see Pinker & Bloom, 1990.)

Nonadaptationist accounts of the origin of language

Adaptation isn't always the correct account of how things came to be the way that they are. The fact that we use some part of our brain or our anatomy to serve a particular function doesn't mean that that physical structure was selected for in evolution to serve that function. Such a view has been dubbed "Panglossian," after Voltaire's fictional character Dr. Pangloss, according to whom "Everything is made for the best purpose. Our noses were made to carry spectacles, so we have spectacles" (quote from Eldredge, 1995). The adaptationist position that humans have language because language was selected for through evolutionary history has been criticized as Panglossian (Gould & Lewontin, 1979).

The alternative view is that the capacity for language was selected for other purposes, and then it was recruited for language—much the way our nose has other reasons for its shape, even though it is useful for supporting eyeglasses. A nonadaptationist account of the origin of the capacity for language would be one that invokes other selection pressures that operated to increase the size and power of the brain (a generally better brain being a generally useful thing to have). Then, having gotten so much larger in the service of general improvement in its old functions, the brain was also able to perform new functions. This view of language as a by-product of design for other purposes has been suggested by Gould and Lewontin (1979). Interestingly, something similar was suggested by Chomsky. Although Chomsky certainly rejected the idea that language could be served by general cognitive capacities, he did suggest that language may well be the result of changes that occurred for other reasons.

> These skills may well have arisen as a concomitant of structural properties of the brain that developed for other reasons. Suppose that there was selection for bigger brains, more cortical surface, hemispherical specialization for analytic processing, or many other structural properties that can be imagined. The brain that evolved might well have all sorts of special properties that are not individually selected; there would be no miracle in this, but only the normal workings of evolution. We have no idea, at present, how physical laws apply when 10^{10} neurons are placed in an object the size of a basketball, under the special conditions that arose during human evolution. (Chomsky, 1982, p. 321)

SUMMARY

This chapter presented a variety of evidence that (1) argues that language is a biological phenomenon and (2) describes what we know about language as a biological phenomenon. The claims and the evidence that supports them include the following:

- Language is universal in the human species. Not only do all human societies have language, but in situations where there is no target language to learn, humans in interaction will spontaneously create language.

- The capacity for language is served by physical structures (in the vocal tract and in the brain) that seem, to a certain extent at least, to be specifically dedicated to their linguistic functions. In most mature adults, language functions are carried out primarily by the left cerebral hemisphere. The core feature of the left-hemisphere specialization for language appears to be its role in grammatical processing.

• Language development occurs in a developing organism. Although some form of left-hemisphere specialization for language is present from birth, developmental changes occur in both the potential and the actual organization of language functions in the brain. With respect to potential, the immature right cerebral hemisphere has a capacity to take over language functions if the left hemisphere is damaged. That capacity (or plasticity) is largely absent in the mature brain. With respect to brain organization in the absence of damage, certain developmental changes in the brain, and probably also in how language is processed, consolidate language functions in the left hemisphere, starting from an initial state of more nearly equal bilateral involvement.

• Evidence supports the notion of a critical period for language development. Children acquire language easily and fully; adults, who are past the critical period for language acquisition, do not. The evidence on creolization suggests that the capacity children have that underlies the ability to learn a language also underlies the special role children play in the creolization process.

• The human capacity for language is species-specific. The results of research on the naturally occurring communication systems of other animals and the results of experiments that have attempted to teach a human language to another primate suggest that language is uniquely human. Most interesting, the comparisons of the human's to the ape's capacity for language begin to provide a basis for hypotheses about the nature of the uniquely human characteristic that accounts for language.

KEY TERMS

pidgins

creoles

language bioprogram hypothesis

supralaryngeal vocal tract

functional architecture (of the brain)

neurolinguistics

cerebral cortex

subcortical (brain structures)

corpus callosum

contralateral connections

ipsalateral connections

lesion method

split-brain patients

dichotic listening tasks

event-related brain potentials (ERPs)

brain imaging techniques

positron emission tomography (PET scans)

magnetic resonance imaging (MRI)

aphasia

functional asymmetry

Broca's aphasia

Wernicke's aphasia

dissociable (functions)

Broca's area

Wernicke's area

right-ear advantage

Wada test

equipotentiality hypothesis

invariance hypothesis

plasticity

stabilization (of function)

sensitive period

"less is more" hypothesis

evolutionary psychology

REVIEW QUESTIONS

1. How is the phenomenon of creolization relevant to (a) making the argument that language is part of human nature, and (b) understanding language acquisition?

2. What does it mean to claim that the human vocal tract is specialized for language, and what evidence supports that claim?

3. What does it mean to claim that the human brain is specialized for language, and what evidence supports that claim?

4. Outline the evidence that language is a left-hemisphere function in adults.

5. What is the role of the right hemisphere in normal language functioning?

6. What is the evidence that the left hemisphere is specialized for language in children?

7. Children recover from aphasia more quickly and more completely than adults do. Why would this be?

8. With development, language becomes increasingly lateralized to the left hemisphere. What might account for this phenomenon?

9. What is neural plasticity, and what causes its decline?

10. What is meant by the critical period hypothesis, and what is the evidence for this hypothesis?

11. What questions can be addressed by the study of animal communication systems and by the study of attempts to teach a human language to another primate? What answers does the evidence suggest?

12. What are the main points of disagreement among the several proposed accounts of the evolution of language?

13. For each of the following phenomena, provide an explanation that (a) is consistent with the view that the processes underlying language are general cognitive processes, and (b) that language depends on specifically linguistic capacities: creolization, localization of language in the left hemisphere, the critical period, the evolution of language.

Glossary

acculturation model   The view of second language learning that focuses on language learning as part of learning the culture of the group that speaks that language.

acquisition-learning hypothesis   The claim that there is a distinction between acquiring a second language, which happens unconsciously, and learning a second language, which involves the conscious learning of explicit rules.

active dialogue   An interaction that has the turn-taking structure of conversation but is nonverbal. This term is used to describe some interactions between prelinguistic infants and their caretakers.

action strategy   The strategy of responding to speech by doing something (that is, with action). This strategy is often used by young children when they only partially understand what is said to them.

adaptation   A characteristic that an organism possesses because the forces of natural selection operating during that organism's evolution made that particular characteristic advantageous. For example, long necks are adaptations that gave giraffes an advantage in reaching food and spotting predators. It has been proposed that the capacity for language is an adaptation that humans have because the ability to communicate gave humans a survival advantage.

affective filter hypothesis   The hypothesis that the second language learner's attitude toward the target language or culture acts as a filter determining how much input actually gets through to be processed for acquisition.

allophones   Acoustically different speech sounds (phones) that are not functionally different (that is, are the same phoneme) in a particular language. For example [p] and [pʰ] are allophones of the phoneme /p/ in English.

American Sign Language (ASL)   The manual language used by the deaf in the United States and the English-speaking provinces of Canada. It is not a system of pantomime; rather, it shares the same structural features as other natural languages.

analytical approach   An approach to language acquisition that is more characteristic of some children than of others. It involves breaking down the speech stream into its component parts (words and—within words—phonemes) and figuring out the system for productively combining those components parts. (see also **holistic approach**)

anaphoric reference   The use of pronouns to maintain reference to previously mentioned characters. (For example, John hit the ball, and then *he* ran to first base.)

aphasia   Any of a range of language disorders caused by brain damage.

articulatory phonetics   The system of describing speech sounds in terms of how they are produced.

autism   A disorder, with an onset before the age of 30 months, that involves severe social and communicative impairment and may or may not be accompanied by mental retardation.

autonomy (of grammar)   The proposal that the structure of language is separate from and cannot be explained in terms of anything else about language, such as its meaning or communicative function. (see also **formalism**)

behaviorism   The theoretical perspective that seeks to explain behavior in terms of factors external to the mind. (see **cognitivism**)

bilingual development   The simultaneous acquisition of two languages from infancy.

bioprogram   See **language bioprogram hypothesis.**

bound morphemes   Morphemes that cannot stand alone, but rather are attached to word stems (such as *-ed* to indicate past tense; *-s* to indicate plural). (see also **free morphemes**)

brain imaging techniques   Techniques that show the relative levels of activity of different parts of the brain during performance of a particular task. Positron emission tomography (PET scans) and magnetic resonance imaging (MRI) are examples of these techniques.

Broca's aphasia   The condition in which the ability to produce speech is severely impaired due to brain damage.

Broca's area   An area in the front portion of the left temporal lobe of the brain that is involved in language functioning.

canonical babbling   A reduplicated series of the same consonant-vowel combination in clear syllables (such as da-da). (see also **reduplicated babbling**)

canonical forms   Whole-word sound patterns that young children sometimes use as a basis for pronouncing new words.

categorical perception   The perception of stimuli that vary along a physical continuum as belonging to discrete categories. (see also **phoneme boundary effect**)

c-command   Constituent command; a structural relation between elements in a sentence. This notion is part of the Government and Binding theory of language.

cerebral cortex   The outer layer of the brain that controls higher mental functions, such as reasoning and planning.

chatterbox syndrome   A disorder characterized by severe mental retardation but remarkable linguistic abilities.

child-directed speech   The speech that adults and older children address to younger children. It has certain typical characteristics that distinguish it from adult-directed speech. (also referred to as **infant-directed speech** and **motherese**).

CHILDES   Child Language Data Exchange System; a computer program for the analysis of transcripts, and an archive of previously collected transcripts of children's speech.

closed-class words   Words from categories such as determiners (for example, *a, the*), auxiliaries (for example, *can, would*), and prepositions (for example, *on, over*). These categories share the characteristics that they serve grammatical functions (for example, determiners mark the beginnings of noun phrases) and that speakers cannot readily invent new words to add to these categories—in contrast to categories such as noun and verb that readily admit newly coined words. (see also **functional categories** and **open-class words**)

cochlear implant   A device surgically implanted in the cochlea that allows a deaf individual to perceive sound by bypassing damaged cells in the ear and directly stimulating the auditory nerve.

code switching   Changing from one type of language use to another, such as switching from a formal to an informal register when talking to people of different status. The term is also used to describe the switching between two languages that bilinguals do, when that switching is done for communicative purposes.

cognitive model of phonological development   The proposal that children try to sound like adults and actively work on figuring out how to do so.

cognitive science   An interdisciplinary field including psychology, linguistics, philosophy, computer science, and neuroscience devoted to understanding how the mind works.

cognitivism   The theoretical perspective that seeks to explain behavior in terms of processes that occur inside the mind.

coherence   The meaningful relation of sequences of events within the structure of a story.

cohesion   The use of linguistic devices to link sentences together in longer stretches of discourse.

collective monologues   A type of pseudoconversation engaged in by preschool children. The children take turns speaking, but each speaker's contribution to the conversation has little to do with the content of what other speakers are saying.

combinatorial speech   Speech in which words are combined in utterances (in contrast to single-word utterances).

communicative competence   The ability to use language in socially appropriate ways for communicative purposes.

complex sentence   A sentence that contains more than one clause

compounding   The creation of a single new word by combining two existing words (such as birdhouse).

comprehension monitoring   The evaluation of one's own understanding. Young children seem to accept and act on inadequate messages in part because they don't realize that they don't understand.

concept   A mental category that includes individual exemplars of that concept. For example, the concept "dog" includes all examples of things that are dogs. Words with different meanings encode different concepts.

connectionism   A theoretical perspective that holds that thinking consists of activating connections in a network; thinking is the process of activation spreading in this network along paths determined by the strengths of the connections.

connectionist model   A type of model of how a phenomenon, such as some aspect of language acquisition, could be accomplished by a device that consists of a network of interconnected nodes. Typically such models are implemented as computer programs, and the ability of the computer program to mimic human language development is taken as evidence of the plausibility of a connectionist account of language acquisition. (see also **connectionism**)

constraints on word learning   Internal biases that, by hypothesis, limit the number of possible meanings of new words children must consider.

constructivism   A view of development that holds that language (or any form of knowledge) is constructed by the child using inborn mental equipment that operates over information provided by the environment.

context-bound word use   Word use that is tied to particular contexts.

contextualized language use   Language use in which the nonlinguistic context supports interpretation of the language; speech about the here-and-now.

continuity assumption   The theoretical position that it should be assumed children have the same kind of grammar adults do unless the evidence proves otherwise.

continuity hypothesis   The proposal that the nature of children's linguistic knowledge is not different in kind—although perhaps in degree—from adults' linguistic knowledge.

contralateral connections   A feature of the human nervous system in which the primary connections from the brain to the body are from each hemisphere of the brain to the opposite side of the body. (see also **ipsilateral connections**)

contrastive analysis hypothesis   The hypothesis that the source of difficulty in second language learning is interference from the first language. This hypothesis is premised on the behaviorist view of language as a set of habits and proposes that, to the extent that the second language is different from the first, old habits will interfere with the learning of new habits.

conversations   Stretches of talk that involve two or more people.

cooing   Vowellike sounds that babies produce when they appear to be happy and contented.

corpus callosum   A band of nerve fibers that connects the right and left hemispheres of the brain.

creative construction   The hypothesis that second language learning, like first language learning, is a process of constructing rules.

creoles   Languages that develop when children acquire a pidgin language as their native language and that are grammatically more complex than pidgins.

critical period hypothesis   The theory that there is a biologically determined period during which language acquisition must occur.

decontextualized language use   Language use in which the words stand on their own without support from the nonlinguistic context.

delayed echolalia   The meaningless repetition of chunks of previously heard utterances.

derivational morphology   The process that creates new words by adding certain suffixes or prefixes (derivational morphemes) to existing words (such as dance + er = dancer; sad + ness = sadness).

descriptive rules   Rules that describe speakers' linguistic knowledge (in contrast to **prescriptive rules**).

developmental approach   The approach to research on language development that attempts to answer the question, "What is the course of language development and how can we explain it?" (see also **learnability**)

developmental dysphasia   See **developmental language disorder.**

developmental language disorder   A delay in language development in the absence of any clear sensory or cognitive disorder (as labeled in the *Diagnostic and Statistical Manual of Mental Disorders,* 4th ed); also referred to as **specific language impairment** or **developmental dysphasia.**

developmental psycholinguistics   The modern study of language development.

dialects   Variations within a language that are a function of the speaker, as opposed to being a function of the setting.

dichotic listening task   An experimental procedure in which two auditory stimuli are presented simultaneously (one to each ear). The purpose is to infer which cerebral hemisphere is responsible for processing the stimuli on the basis of which stimulus the listener perceives.

discourse cohesion   The connectedness of the separate utterances in a longer stretch of discourse, such as a narrative.

discourse knowledge   The knowledge that underlies the ability to use language in units larger than a sentence (such as conversation and narratives).

dishabituation   Renewed interest in a stimulus. (see also **habituation**)

dissociable   The characteristic of many cognitive and linguistic functions that one function can be affected without the other being affected—at least, not to the same degree. For example, some forms of mental retardation severely affect nonlinguistic cognition yet leave language skills relatively spared.

dissociation (of general cognition and language)   The idea that general intellectual and language capacities are separate entities that develop somewhat independently of each other.

distinctive feature   A phonetic feature (such as voicing) that creates a phonemic distinction between two speech sounds. (see also **phonemes**)

Down syndrome   A chromosomal abnormality that causes moderate to severe mental retardation and typically affects language development.

echolalic speech   see **immediate echolalia** and **delayed echolalia.**

egocentric   A characteristic of preschool children, according to the developmental theory of Jean Piaget, that makes them unable to consider what a situation is like from the point of view of another person.

emergent literacy   Early knowledge about literacy separate from knowing how to read or write.

empiricism   A view of development that asserts that the mind at birth is a blank slate and all knowledge and reason come from experience.

equipotentiality hypothesis   The hypothesis that at birth both hemispheres of the brain have equal potential for acquiring language.

error analysis   The process of studying second language acquisition by using as data the errors that L2 (second language) learners make.

event-related brain potentials (ERPs)   A measure of brain activity. Electrodes placed on the scalp record voltage fluctuations in the brain as the individual perceives or responds to presented stimuli. These voltage fluctuations are electrical potentials associated with the experimenter-controlled events, and the location of the potentials is taken as evidence of where in the brain the processing of that event occurred.

evolutionary psychology   The approach to the study of human mental functioning that attempts to understand human cognitive abilities by considering their adaptive function and evolutionary history.

expansion stage   A stage of prespeech phonological development immediately prior to the emergence of babbling. Infants at this stage, typically between 16 and 30 weeks, produce a variety of speech sounds but no true syllabic babbling.

expressive language style   A style of vocabulary development in which early lexicons contain relatively fewer object labels and relatively more words that serve social functions than do the early lexicons of children with a referential language style. (see also **referential language style**)

familial concentration   The rate of occurrence of a particular characteristic (such as specific language impairment) within a family. High familial concentration suggests a genetic basis.

fast mapping   The ability to learn a new word on the basis of a single exposure to that word.

foreign language learning   Learning a second language that is not spoken in the ambient community.

formalism   The view that the structure of language is arbitrary and cannot be explained in terms of the meanings language conveys or the communicative functions language serves.

free morphemes   Morphemes that stand alone as words. (see also **bound morphemes**)

fricatives   A category of consonants produced by partially obstructing the flow of air, such as [f] and [s].

functional architecture (of the brain)   How the brain is organized to serve the functions it performs.

functional asymmetry   The characteristic of the human brain in which each hemisphere serves different functions.

functional categories   The term used in Government and Binding Theory to refer to words such as auxiliaries, prepositions, and determiners (articles) that do not carry thematic content but rather serve primarily grammatical functions. (see **closed-class words** and **lexical categories**)

functionalism   The theory that the structure of language has a basis in the communicative functions language serves.

functionalist theory of language acquisition   The theory that children can discover the structure of language by virtue of the correspondence between that structure and the communicative functions for which children are trying to use language.

genders   Categories of nouns that take different forms of articles and grammatical morphemes, such as the plural marker.

gender-typed discourse style   Differences in language use that depend on the gender of the speaker.

Government and Binding (GB) theory   The theory of Universal Grammar proposed by Noam Chomsky (1981). It is the basis of the principles and parameters theory of language acquisition. (see also **principles and parameters theory**)

grammar   The rules that describe the structure of a language.

grammatical morphemes   Words and word endings that mark grammatical relations, such as articles, prepositions, auxiliary verbs, and noun and verb endings.

habituation   Apparent loss of interest in a repeatedly presented stimulus.

head-turn technique   An experimental procedure, used to test when infants perceive two sounds as different, that relies on conditioning the infant to produce a head turn when a repeatedly presented sound changes. Typically used with infants 5½ months and older.

high-amplitude sucking (HAS) technique   An experimental procedure, used to test when infants perceive two sounds as different, that relies on the infant first habituating to one sound and then showing dishabituation when a new sound is presented. Typically used with infants under 5½ months old.

holistic approach   An approach to language acquisition that is more characteristic of some children than others and that consists of memorizing large, unanalyzed chunks of speech. (see also **analytical approach**)

home sign   Gestural communication systems that deaf children often invent to communicate if they are not exposed to a sign language.

iconic (signs)   Signs in a manual language, such as American Sign Language, that resemble the object they stand for.

illocutionary force   The intended function of a speech act (such as to request or promise).

immediate echolalia   The meaningless repetition of a word or word group immediately after hearing it produced by another speaker.

infant-directed speech   Speech addressed to infants that has certain typical characteristics that differ from the characteristics of speech addressed to adults (also referred to as **child-directed speech** or **motherese**).

inflectional morphology   The system of morphemes that are added to words of particular grammatical classes, such as the markers of tense that are added to verbs or the plural marker that is added to nouns.

input hypothesis   The hypothesis that the relevant experience for second language acquisition is input in the target language that is just slightly beyond the learner's current level.

instrumental motivation   Interest in learning a second language for utilitarian purposes, such as job advancement.

integrative motivation   Interest in learning a second language for the purpose of associating with members of the culture in which that language is spoken.

intentionality   The purpose or goal in the mind of the speaker.

interactionism   A view of development that, although acknowledging there must be some innate characteristics of the mind that allow for language development, places greater emphasis on the nature of the language-learning environment of the child.

interlanguage   The second language learner's version of the target language. Interlanguages are internally consistent grammatical systems that may differ from the target language's grammar as acquired by native speakers.

invariance hypothesis   The theory that holds that the left hemisphere of the brain has the adult specialization for language from birth.

ipsilateral connections   The nervous system connections between each hemisphere of the brain and the same side of the body. The primary connections in the nervous system are contralateral. (see also **contralateral connections**)

jargon   Sequences of variegated babbling that have the intonation contour of sentences.

L1   Abbreviation for first, or native, language.

L2   Abbreviation for second language.

language bioprogram hypothesis   The hypothesis proposed by Bickerton (1981) that humans possess a biologically based, innate linguistic capacity that includes a skeletal grammar. By hypothesis, this capacity underlies both children's language acquisition and the process of creolization and accounts for similarities between child language and creoles.

language mixing   The phenomenon, which occurs in bilinguals, of using words from two different languages within a single utterance or conversation.

language play   Activities such as rhyming, alliteration, and punning that manipulate the sound of language.

language socialization   The process by which children learn the socially appropriate use of language in their communities.

language transfer   Influences of the native language on second language learning.

language typology   The study of commonalities among the world's languages that describes languages in terms of types.

language universals   Features of language that are true for all human languages.

lateralization of function   The specialization of each hemisphere of the brain for different functions.

learnability approach   The question of whether language, or some aspect of language, could in fact be learned by children. If language is not learnable, then it must be innate. The learnability approach to the study of language acquisition focuses on explaining how language could be learned, in contrast to the developmental approach, which focuses on explaining the course of language development. (see also **developmental approach**)

left cerebral hemisphere   The hemisphere of the brain that is specialized for processing language, among other things.

lesion method   The method of investigating the functions performed by different areas of the brain by correlating impaired function with the location of damage to the brain.

"less is more" hypothesis   The hypothesis (proposed by Newport, 1990) that children's smaller short-memory spans (compared to adults') facilitate language acquisition by giving children smaller chunks of language to analyze.

lexical categories   The term in Government and Binding Theory for categories of words, such as noun and verb, that carry thematic content. (see also **open-class words** and **functional categories**)

lexical development   Learning the words of a language.

lexical organization   The way in which the mental lexicon represents the relation between words and meanings.

linguistic competence   The ability to produce and understand well-formed, meaningful sentences.

linguistic perception (receptive phonology)   The perception of speech sounds in terms of the phonological categories of the language, including the ability to discriminate words based on contrasting sounds.

linguistic relativity hypothesis   See **Whorfian hypothesis.**

Linguistics and Language Behavior Abstracts   An index to articles on language and language-related fields in 1500 journals.

linking rules   The regular ways in which thematic roles (such as agent and affected object) are mapped onto syntactic categories (such as subject and direct object) in all languages. According to Pinker (1989), these regularities are part of children's innate linguistic knowledge and crucially contribute to the acquisition of syntax.

locution   The linguistic form of a speech act (such as declarative or imperative).

low phonetic substance   See **phonological salience hypothesis.**

magnetic resonance imaging (MRI)   A technique for assessing the location of activity in the brain by detecting where blood flow and oxygen consumption are greatest.

manner of articulation   How the airflow is obstructed as a consonant is produced.

mapping problem   The logical problem of learning word meanings that arises as a result of an infinite number of hypotheses about word meaning being consistent with information in the nonlinguistic context of use.

marginal babbling   The long series of sounds that infants produce just before they begin to produce canonical babbling. This kind of sound production is typical around 5 and 6 months of age.

markedness   The relative generality of some linguistic unit. A structure that is more common across the world's languages is unmarked relative to a structure that is less common.

markedness differential hypothesis   The hypothesis that the native language will interfere with second language learning whenever a structure in the second language is more marked than the corresponding native language structure.

maturation hypothesis   A theory of language development that holds that the child's system is not adultlike to begin with but becomes so as the result of maturation.

maturational constraints   The notion that the maturational status of an organism places limits on what the organism can learn. (see also **critical period hypothesis**)

mean length of utterance (MLU)   A common measure of grammatical development. It is the average length of the utterances in a sample spontaneous speech, usually counted in terms of the number of morphemes.

mental lexicon   The knowledge of words that speakers of a language possess; the dictionary in the head.

metalinguistic awareness   The conscious awareness of how language works.

Minimal Distance Principle (MDP)   An immature strategy for sentence interpretation that treats the noun phrase closest to the verb as the subject of that verb.

missing features hypothesis   The theory that explains specific language impairment as the result of a deficit in the innate grammar of individuals with specific language impairment; the nature of that deficit pertaining to the marking of features such as plural, past tense, and so on. This theory, originally proposed by Gopnik (1990), has been supplanted by the missing rule hypothesis. (see also **missing rule hypothesis**)

missing rule hypothesis   The theory that explains specific language impairment in terms of the difficulty individuals with specific language impairment have learning the rules that govern the use of grammatical morphology.

modularity   The cognitive theory that holds that the ability to develop language is a self-contained module in the mind, separate from other aspects of mental functioning.

modularity of syntax   The idea that the ability to acquire grammar is separate from other nonlinguistic cognitive functions and from the mental ability to acquire semantics and pragmatics.

monitor hypothesis   The hypothesis that learned knowledge (of a second language) is available only as a monitor, or editor, and that this monitor can be used only when the speaker is focused on the form instead of on the content of what the speaker is saying. When the speaker is not focused on the form, only acquired, not learned, knowledge influences the form of the utterances produced.

morpheme   The smallest element in a language that carries meaning. **Free morphemes** are words; **bound morphemes** are prefixes, suffixes, and, in some languages, infixes. (see also **word**)

morphology   A system of rules for combining the smallest units of language into words.

motherese   The kind of speech that mothers (and others) produce when talking to infants and young children. It is characterized by higher pitches, a wider range of pitches, longer pauses and shorter phrases than speech addressed to adults (also referred to as **infant-** or **child-directed speech**).

mutual exclusivity assumption   A word-learning constraint according to which children assume that objects can have only a single name.

naming insight   The realization that words name objects and that all objects have names.

narratives   Verbal descriptions of past events that are longer than a single utterance.

nativism   The view that knowledge is innate, as opposed to being learned from experience.

natural approach   An approach to second language teaching, predicated on the tenets of Krashen's input hypothesis, that subscribes to the view that it is not necessary to explicitly teach a second language; it is sufficient to provide the learner with the right kind of input.

natural order hypothesis   The hypothesis that second language learners acquire the rules of the target language in a necessary, invariant order that is not a function of the order in which those rules may be taught to them.

negative evidence   Evidence that a sentence is ungrammatical—in contrast to positive evidence that a sentence is grammatical. All the sentences that children hear are positive evidence of possible constructions in the language. Negative evidence would be feedback or correction when the child produces an ungrammatical sentence. The availability of negative evidence in children's input is a matter of some controversy.

neuroanatomy   The study of the parts of the brain and their functions.

neurolinguistics   The study of the brain and language.

nominals   Words that label things; common nouns.

nonlinguistic gestures   Gestures produced by both deaf and hearing children that are not part of a language system (such as reaching and waving).

onset   The initial consonant or consonant cluster of a syllable.

open-class words   Words from the categories of noun, verb, adjective, adverb; labeled "open class" because new nouns, verbs, adjectives, and adverbs can readily be coined and added to the language. (see also **closed-class words**)

oral language development   The development of spoken, as opposed to gestural or written, language.

oralist method   An approach to language education for the deaf that focuses on the development of the ability to produce speech and read lips.

order-of-mention strategy   A strategy for interpreting sentences in which the listener assumes that the event mentioned first happened first. This strategy results in the correct interpretation for a sentence such as *The dog bit the man before the man shouted* but in the wrong interpretation for *The dog bit the man after the man shouted*.

overextensions   A type of error in children's early word usage that seems to reflect an overly inclusive meaning in the mind of the child (such as referring to all four-legged animals as "doggie"). (see also **underextensions**)

overgeneralizations   Overly general rules that children might infer from the speech they hear.

overregularizations   Overapplications of rules to irregular parts of the language (such as pluralizing *foot* as *foots*).

parameter   A feature of Universal Grammar that handles the variation among languages. For example, pro-drop is a parameter that has the value + for languages that allow omission of subjects (such as Italian and Spanish) and that has the value − for languages that require that the subject be expressed (such as English).

parameter resetting   The process, hypothesized by some to be part of second language acquisition, of changing the parameter settings in the interlanguage grammar to agree with those of the target language.

parameter setting   The process of determining which set of options, which by hypothesis are specified in Universal Grammar, applies to the target language.

pedagogy   The study and practice of teaching.

perlocution   The effect of a speech act on the listener.

phoneme boundary   The location on a continuum of change in some acoustic property of a sound where the listener's perception of the sound changes from one phoneme to another. (see also **phoneme boundary effect**)

phoneme boundary effect   The phenomenon in which the same acoustic difference (such as a 20 msec. difference in VOT) is perceptible if the two stimuli are on either side of a phoneme boundary (as in /b/ versus /p/) but is not perceptible if the two stimuli are within the range of variation perceived as one phoneme. (see also **categorical perception**)

phonemes   Speech sounds that signal a difference in meaning in a particular language.

phones   Speech sounds, such as [p], [p], and [b], used by any language.

phonetic features   Characteristics of how speech sounds are produced that are used to describe differences and similarities among speech sounds. For example [b] and [p] differ in the feature of voicing.

phonological awareness   Conscious awareness of the phonological properties of language, such as the ability to count the number of syllables in a word and to identify rhymes.

phonological bootstrapping hypothesis   The hypothesis that language learning children find and use clues to the syntactic structure of language in phonological properties of the speech they hear. (see also **prosodic bootstrapping hypothesis**)

phonological development   The development of the sounds and sound patterns of a language.

phonological idioms   Words that children pronounce in a very adultlike manner while still incorrectly producing other words that use the same sounds.

phonological knowledge   Knowledge of the sounds and sound patterns of a language.

phonological memory   The function of short-term memory responsible for the temporary storage of the sound of a stimulus.

phonological processes   Rules that map sounds in the target language to sounds in young children's limited production repertoires. Phonological processes that are common to many children give young children's speech typical features, such as pronouncing *r*'s as *w*.

phonological salience hypothesis   The theory that explains specific language impairment as a result of difficulty perceiving parts of the speech signal that have low phonological salience (such as unstressed syllables of short duration).

pidgins   Structurally simple languages that arise when people who share no common language come into contact.

pivot grammar   A grammar in which a few function, or "pivot," words are combined with a larger category of content words, or "open," words. Braine (1963) proposed that such a grammar underlies children's first two-word combinations.

place of articulation   The location where the airflow is obstructed as a consonant is produced.

plasticity   The ability of parts of the brain to take over functions they normally would not serve. There is much more plasticity in the child's brain than in the adult's.

pragmatic knowledge   The knowledge that enables speakers to use language for communicative purposes in ways that are socially appropriate in their community.

pragmatic principles   Principles about how words are used that, by hypothesis, help children figure out the meaning of newly encountered words.

pragmatics   Language use.

prelingually deaf   The characteristic of having become deaf prior to acquiring language.

prerepresentational phonology   The period of phonological development during which children have mental representations for the sounds of whole words but not for individual speech sounds. (see also **representational phonology**)

prescriptive rules   Rules of grammar that define how language *should* be used, as taught in writing classes and specified in style manuals. For example, the rules that prohibit splitting infinitives and ending sentences with prepositions are prescriptive rules. (see also **descriptive rules**)

primary intersubjectivity   The ability to relate to an object or to another person but not to both at the same time. (see also **secondary intersubjectivity**)

principle of contrast   A pragmatic principle that, by hypothesis, leads children to assume that different words have different meanings.

principle of conventionality   A pragmatic principle that, by hypothesis, leads children to assume that words are used by all speakers to express the same meaning—that is, that word meaning is a convention.

principles and parameters theory   The theory that the child has innate knowledge of universal grammar, consisting of principles that hold true for every language, and a set of options, or parameters, that have to be filled in by experience. (see also **Government and Binding Theory** and **Universal Grammar**)

private speech   Speech produced for one's self (as opposed to for another listener).

probable-event strategy   A strategy for sentence interpretation that children use when they do not fully understand the meaning carried by the structure of the sentence. In using this strategy, children use their knowledge of what events are likely in the world and apply it to the incomplete meaning they glean from the sentence. Such a strategy is likely to yield a misinterpretation of a sentence like "The man bit the dog."

"problem-space"   The description of language as a "problem-space" for children is used, by Karmiloff-Smith (for example, 1986) to capture the notion that children analyze the linguistic system they are acquiring in its own right, separate from the usefulness of language for communication.

productivity or generativity of language   The characteristic of all human languages by which they make use of a finite repertoire of sounds to produce a potentially infinite number of sentences.

prosodic bootstrapping hypothesis   The hypothesis that language learning children find and use clues to syntactic structure of language in the prosodic characteristics of the speech they hear. (see also **phonological bootstrapping hypothesis**)

prosody   The intonation contour of speech, including pauses and changes in stress and pitch.

protoconversations   Patterns of interaction in which mothers alternate vocalizations with silent pauses and look at their babies when the babies vocalize.

prototypes   Central category members that are the basis for word meaning (other items belong to that category by virtue of their "family resemblance" to the prototype).

protowords   Idiosyncratic sound sequences that children use with consistent meaning but that are not clearly derived from words in the target language.

PsychLit   A computer accessible form of Psychological Abstracts—an index to a large number of journals, books, and book chapters in psychology and related fields.

psychotypology   The language learner's perception of the relation between the native and the target language. Second language learners may be more likely to transfer native language constructions to the target language if they perceive the languages to be closely related.

reduplicated babbling   Babbling that consists of repeating the same syllable over and over (such as da-da-da-da). This is characteristic of infant sound production around 8 to 10 months of age. (see also **canonical babbling**)

reference   The notion of words as symbols that stand for their referents.

referential communication   A communication task in which the speaker must indicate to a listener which item to select out of an array of items.

referential language style   A style of vocabulary development in which a child's early lexicon is heavily dominated by object labels. (see also **expressive language style**)

referential word use   Word use that is not bound to one particular context.

registers   Styles of language use associated with particular social settings.

regression hypothesis   A theory that attributes language decline in old age to the loss of pieces of grammar in reverse of the order in which they were learned in childhood.

relational meanings   The relation between the referents of the words in a word combination (for example, possession is indicated by *Daddy's shirt*).

representational phonology   The stage of phonological development in which the child first has a mental representation of the phonemes in the target language. Prior to this stage, children represents the sounds of words as whole words or in syllabic units. (see also **prerepresentational phonology**)

right cerebral hemisphere   The hemisphere of the brain that is specialized for processing visual-spatial information.

right-ear advantage   The relatively greater probability that stimuli presented to the right ear in a dichotic listening test will be perceived by the listener. Typically there is a right-ear advantage for linguistic stimuli, which suggests that the left cerebral hemisphere is primarily responsible for processing linguistic stimuli.

rime   The vowel plus any final consonants in a syllable; syllables are comprised of an onset and a rime.

scaffolding   A term used to describe the support for children's language use that more competent speakers sometimes provide. Examples of scaffolding include routinized formats for interaction and leading questions that adults ask, both of which enable children to perform at a more advanced level than they could on their own.

scripts   Mental representations of events.

second language acquisition   The acquisition of a language after the native language has already been acquired. In Krashen's theory of second language learning, *acquisition* refers to the unconscious process of coming to know a second language, whereas *learning* refers to the conscious process.

second language learning   See **second language acquisition.**

secondary intersubjectivity   The ability to relate to another person about an object. Infants first appear to be capable of secondary intersubjectivity around the age of 9 or 10 months. (see also **primary intersubjectivity**)

secondary language activities   Language activities that involve the manipulation of the sounds of language, such as rhymes and word games.

semantic bootstrapping   The theory that the correspondence between semantic and syntactic categories provides the language learning child entry into the grammatical system.

semantic feature hypothesis   A theory of word meaning and word learning according to which the meaning of a word can be defined in terms of a list of discrete components (features), and acquiring a word consists of learning that list.

semantic organization   The organization of meaning expressed in a language, as distinct from cognitive organization.

semantically based grammar   A grammar in which rules operate over meaning-based categories such as agent, action, location, and so on.

sensitive period   A term sometimes used instead of *critical period* to indicate that the ability to acquire language may be greatest during a particular period of development but that language acquisition later is not impossible.

sentence interpretation strategies   Strategies used to interpret sentences before having achieved the grammatical competence necessary for full comprehension.

social/cognitive view   The view that the starting point of language acquisition is provided by general cognition, as are the mechanisms of language development. The requisite experience for language acquisition is social interaction with other speakers.

social interactionism   A view of development that holds that a crucial aspect of language learning experience is social interaction with another person.

sociolinguistic knowledge   The knowledge of how language use varies as a function of changes in speaker status, gender, setting, and so on.

sociolinguistics   The study of how language use varies as a function of sociological variables such as status, culture, and gender.

socio-pragmatic cues   Cues to the meaning of new words that children find in the way words are used in social interaction. For example, children take a speaker's eye gaze as a cue to what the speaker is referring to.

sparse morphology hypothesis   The theory that explains specific language impairment by suggesting that the functional role of the morphology of a language is relevant to its ease of acquisition. Languages in which the morphological system does relatively little grammatical work, such as English, will cause particular problems for children with specific language impairment.

specific language impairment   See **developmental language disorder.**

speech acts   Utterances as behaviors; the notion that talking is "doing things with words."

speech samples   Video-recorded or tape-recorded records of spontaneous speech used to assess children's language development.

speech segmentation   The mental process of separating the speech stream into separate words.

split-brain patients   Patients who have had their corpus callosum severed (usually to relieve epileptic seizures).

stabilization (of function)   The process whereby some neural pathways become permanently committed to serve particular functions while other, unused neural circuits, lose their capacity.

stops   Consonant sounds that are produced by completely closing the vocal tract at some point and then releasing the air to pass through the vocal tract, as in [p] and [k].

story grammar   The abstract structure of a story.

subcortical structures   Structures of the brain beneath the cerebral cortex that control primitive functions, as opposed to higher mental processes.

supralaryngeal vocal tract   The vocal tract located above the larynx that is responsible for the production of speech sounds.

syntactic bootstrapping hypothesis   The hypothesis that children find and use clues to the meaning of new words in the syntactic structure of the sentences in which new words are encountered.

syntactically based grammar   A grammar in which rules operate over formal categories, such as nouns and verbs. These formal categories are not defined in terms of their meaning or their communicative function.

syntax   A system of rules for building phrases out of words (that belong to particular grammatical categories, such as noun and verb) and for building sentences out of these constituent phrases.

tadpole-frog problem   The problem of accounting for the change from a semantically based system to a syntactically based system if one describes children's grammars as semantically based (this change is compared to the metamorphosis that tadpoles undergo to become frogs). (See also **semantically based grammar** and **syntactically based grammar**)

taxonomic assumption   The child's assumption that words label categories of things of the same kind (taxonomic categories). This assumption is proposed as one word learning constraint that helps children learn the meaning of new words.

teachability hypothesis   The claim that there is a natural order in which structures in a second language must be acquired and that instruction will be successful only if it occurs close to the time the learner would acquire the structure in a naturalistic setting.

telegraphic speech   Speech, typical of 2-year-old children, that includes primarily content words and omits such grammatical morphemes as determiners and endings on nouns and verbs. So named because the result sounds like sentences adults use in writing telegrams.

thematic subject strategy   A storytelling strategy in which the main character of the story is always referred to with a pronoun and all other characters are referred to with nominal forms.

theory of mind   The theory that other persons have minds and that mental contents such as beliefs and intentions guide their behavior. Adults operate according to this theory; children must develop this theory.

topic   What a sentence or longer unit of discourse is about.

topic-associating narrative style   A style of describing past events that consists of a related set of personal anecdotes. This style is typical among some African Americans.

topic-centered narrative style   A style of describing past events that tends to be tightly organized around a single topic. This style is typical among middle-class European Americans.

total communication   An approach to language education for the deaf in which oral language is combined with a signing or gestural system.

transitional forms   Utterances such as vertical constructions that children produce between producing single-word and clear two-word utterances.

tree diagram   A convention of linguistics used to illustrate the structure of sentences.

turn taking   Verbal or nonverbal patterned interactions that occur between two parties.

underextensions   Using words with a range of meanings narrower than the meaning of the word in the target language (such as using *car* to refer only to cars seen from a window). (see also **overextensions**)

Universal Grammar (UG)   The set of principles and parameters that describes the structure of all languages of the world; hypothesized by some to be part of the child's innate knowledge. (see also **principles and parameters theory**)

variegated babbling   Strings of nonreduplicated syllables.

vegetative sounds   Sounds that accompany biological functions, such as breathing, sucking, and burping.

verb movement parameter   The feature of Universal Grammar that, by hypothesis, handles the fact that in some languages, such as English, adverbs cannot occur between the verb and direct object, negative markers cannot follow verbs, and verbs and pronouns cannot be inverted; whereas in other languages, such as French, all these constructions are possible.

verbal dueling   Ritualized contests in which language is used as the weapon.

vocal play   The activity of producing a variety of different consonant and vowel sounds that is typical of infants between 16 and 30 weeks.

voice onset time (VOT)   The time lag in the production of a consonant between the release of air and the beginning of vocal cord vibration. Consonants with a VOT greater than 25 milliseconds are perceived as voiceless (such as [p]) and VOTs less than 25 milliseconds are perceived as voiced (such as [b]).

voicing   A feature of sound production in which the vocal cords vibrate as air is released in the production of a consonant. [b] and [g] are voiced consonants; [p] and [k] are voiceless.

Wada test   A test performed (typically before brain surgery) in which a barbiturate is injected into one of the carotid arteries, temporarily inactivating one hemisphere and thereby allowing a test of the functions carried out by the unaffected hemisphere.

Wernicke's aphasia   The condition in which patients speak rapidly and fluently but without meaning as a result of damage to part of the left hemisphere of the brain.

Wernicke's area   An area in the left hemisphere of the brain, located next to the primary auditory cortex, that is responsible for language functions.

wh- questions   Questions that begin with who, what, where, why, when, or how.

whole-language approach   An approach to teaching reading based on the idea that if children are exposed to print and are motivated to extract meaning from print, then the mechanics of reading will be acquired naturally without explicit instruction in sound-letter correspondences.

whole-object assumption   A word learning constraint according to which children assume that a new word refers to a whole object, not to a part or property of an object.

Whorfian hypothesis   The hypothesis that language influences thought and, therefore, that differences among languages might cause differences in the cognition of speakers of those languages.

Williams syndrome   A rare disorder that produces severe mental retardation but leaves language functions largely intact.

word-finding ability   The ability to retrieve names for things from memory.

word-formation processes   Processes, such as forming compounds and adding suffixes, that enable generation of new words. (see also **derivational morphology** and **compounding**)

word order strategy A strategy for sentence interpretation in which the thing mentioned first is taken to be the subject and the thing mentioned second is taken to be the object of the verb. This yields correct interpretations for active sentences such as *The kitty bumps the swing* but incorrect interpretations for passive sentences such as *The swing was bumped by the kitty.*

word spurt The increase in the rate at which children acquire new words; it occurs some time around the achievement of a 50-word vocabulary, or about 18 months of age.

words Sound sequences that symbolize meaning and that can stand alone. (see also **morpheme**)

yes/no questions Questions that can be answered with a yes or a no.

References

ABRAHAMS, R. D. (1962). "Playing the dozens." *Journal of American Folklore, 75,* 209–220.

ABRAHAMSEN, A. A. (1977). *Child language: An interdisciplinary guide to theory and research.* Baltimore, MD: University Park Press.

ADAMS, M. J. (1990). *Beginning to read: Thinking and learning about print.* Cambridge, MA: MIT Press.

AITCHISON, J. (1983). On roots of language. *Language & Communication, 3,* 83–97.

AITCHISON, J. (1987). *Words in the mind.* Oxford: Basil Blackwell.

AKHTAR, N., CARPENTER, M., & TOMASELLO, M. (1996). The role of discourse novelty in early word learning. *Child Development, 67,* 635–645.

AKSU-KOC, A. A., & SLOBIN, D. I. (1985). The acquisition of Turkish. In D. I. Slobin (Ed.), *The crosslinguistic study of language acquisition: Vol. 1. The data* (pp. 839–880). Hillsdale, NJ: Erlbaum.

ALLEN, R., & SHATZ, M. (1983). "What says meow?" The role of context and linguistic experience in very young children's responses to *what*-questions. *Journal of Child Language, 10,* 321–335.

ALTENBERG, E., & VAGO, R. (1983). Theoretical implications of an error analysis of second language phonology. *Language Learning, 33,* 427–447.

ALVY, K. T. (1968). Relation of age to children's egocentric and cooperative communication. *Journal of Genetic Psychology, 112,* 275–286.

AMERICAN PSYCHIATRIC ASSOCIATION (1994). *Diagnostic and statistical manual of mental disorders* (4th ed.). Washington, DC: Author.

ANDERSEN, E. S. (1986). The acquisition of register variation by Anglo-American children. In B. B. Schieffelin & E. Ochs (Eds.), *Language socialization across cultures* (pp. 153–161). Cambridge: Cambridge University Press.

ANDERSEN, E. S. (1990). *Speaking with style: The socio-linguistic skill of children.* London: Routledge.

ANDERSON, J. M. (1989). Writing systems. In W. O'Grady, M. Dobrovolsky, & M. Aronoff (Eds.), *Contemporary linguistics: An introduction* (pp. 358–382). New York: St. Martin's Press.

ANGLIN, J. M. (1993). Vocabulary development: A morphological analysis. *Monographs of the Society for Research in Child Development, 58,* No. 10.

ANSELMI, D., TOMASELLO, M., & ACUNZO, M. (1986). Young children's responses to neutral and specific contingent queries. *Journal of Child Language, 13,* 135–144.

ARAM, D. M. (1988). Language sequelae of unilateral brain lesions in children. In F. Plum (Ed.), *Language, communication, and the brain* (pp. 171–198). New York: Raven Press.

ARAM, D. M., & EISELE, J. A. (1992). Plasticity and recovery of higher cognitive functions following early brain injury. In I. Rapin & S. J. Segalowitz (Eds.), *Handbook of neuropsychology: Vol. 6. Section 10: Child neuropsychology (Part 1)* (pp. 73–92). Amsterdam: Elsevier.

ARAM, D. M., EKELMAN, B. L., ROSE, D. F., & WHITAKER, H. A. (1985). Verbal and cognitive sequelae following unilateral lesions acquired in early childhood. *Journal of Clinical and Experimental Neuropsychology, 7,* 55–78.

ARNBERG, L. (1987). *Raising children bilingually: The pre-school years.* Clevedon, Avon: Multilingual Matters.

ASTINGTON, J. W. (1993). *The child's discovery of the mind.* Cambridge, MA: Harvard University Press.

ASTINGTON, J. W., HARRIS, P. L., & OLSON, D. R. (1988). *Developing theories of mind.* New York: Cambridge University Press.

ATKINSON, M. (1992). *Children's syntax.* Cambridge, MA: Blackwell Publishers.

AUSTIN, J. L. (1962). *How to do things with words.* Oxford: Oxford University Press.

BABY TALK. (1984). In *NOVA.* The Open University.

BACCHINE, S., KUIKEN, F., & SCHOONEN, R. (1995). Generalizability of spontaneous speech data: The effect of occasion and place on the speech production of children. *First Language, 15,* 131–150.

BADDELEY, A. D. (1986). *Working memory.* Oxford: Oxford University Press.

BALDWIN, D. (1991). Infants' contribution to the achievement of joint reference. *Child Development, 62,* 875–890.

BALDWIN, D. (1993). Infants' ability to consult the speaker for clues to word reference. *Journal of Child Language, 20,* 395–419.

BAMBERG, M. (1987). *The acquisition of narratives.* Berlin: Mouton de Gruyter.

BARKOW, J. H., COSMIDES, L., & TOOBY, J. (1992). *The adapted mind: Evolutionary psychology and the generation of culture.* New York: Oxford University Press.

BARON-COHEN, S., TAGER-FLUSBERG, H., & COHEN, D. J. (1993). *Understanding other minds: Perspectives from autism.* Oxford: Oxford University Press.

BARRETT, M. D. (1986). Early semantic representations and early word usage. In S. A.

Kuczaj & M. D. Barrett (Eds.), *The development of word meaning* (pp. 39–67). New York: Springer-Verlag.

BARRETT, M. (1995). Early lexical development. In P. Fletcher & B. MacWhinney (Eds.), *The handbook of child language* (pp. 362–392). Oxford: Basil Blackwell.

BARTON, D. (1975). Statistical significance in phonemic perception experiments. *Journal of Child Language, 2,* 297–298.

BARTON, D. (1976). The role of perception in the acquisition of phonology. Ph.D. thesis, University of London. (Reprinted by the Indiana University Linguistics Club, 1978). Cited in M. M. Vihman (1988a). Early phonological development. In J. Bernthal & N. Bambson (Eds.), *Articulation and phonological disorders, 2nd Edition* (pp. 60–109). New York: Prentice-Hall.

BARTON, D. (1978). The discrimination of minimally-different pairs of real words by children aged 2;3 to 2;11. In N. Waterson & C. Snow (Eds.), *The development of communication* (pp. 255–261). New York: Wiley.

BARTON, M. E., & TOMASELLO, M. (1994). The rest of the family: The role of fathers and siblings in early language development. In C. Gallaway & B. J. Richards (Eds.), *Input and interaction in language acquisition* (pp. 109–134). Cambridge: Cambridge University Press.

BATES, E. (1975). Peer relations and the acquisition of language. In M. Lewis & L. Rosenblum (Eds.), *Friendship and peer relations* (pp. 259–292). New York: Wiley.

BATES, E. (1976). *Language and context: The acquisition of pragmatics.* New York: Academic Press.

BATES, E. (1979). The emergence of symbols: Ontogeny and phylogeny. In W. A. Collins (Ed.), *Children's language and communication: The Minnesota Symposia on Child Psychology: Vol. 12* (pp. 121–155). Hillsdale, NJ: Erlbaum.

BATES, E. (1984). Bioprograms and the innateness hypothesis. *Behavioral and Brain Sciences, 7,* 188–190.

BATES, E. (1993). Comprehension and production in early language development (Commentary on Language comprehension in ape and child by Savage-Rumbaugh et al.). *Monographs of the Society for Research in Child Development, 58* (3–4, Serial No. 233).

BATES, E., BENIGNI, L., BRETHERTON, I., CAMIONI, L., & VOLTERRA, V. (1979). *The emergence of symbols: Cognition and communication in infancy.* New York: Academic Press.

BATES, E., BRETHERTON, I., & SNYDER, L. (1988). *From first words to grammar: individual differences and dissociable mechanisms.* Cambridge: Cambridge University Press.

BATES, E., CAMIONI, L., & VOLTERRA, V. (1975). The acquisition of performatives prior to speech. *Merrill-Palmer Quarterly, 21,* 205–226.

BATES, E., DALE, P., & THAL, D. (1995). Individual differences and their implications for theories of language development. In P. Fletcher & B. MacWhinney (Eds.), *The handbook of child language* (pp. 96–151). Oxford: Basil Blackwell.

BATES, E., & ELMAN, J. L. (1993). Connectionism and the study of change. In M. H.

Johnson (Ed.), *Brain development and cognition: A reader* (pp. 623–642). Cambridge, MA: Basil Blackwell.

BATES, E., & MacWHINNEY, B. (1982). Functionalist approaches to grammar. In L. Gleitman & E. Wanner (Eds.), *Language acquisition: The state of the art* (pp. 173–218). Cambridge: Cambridge University Press.

BATES, E., MARCHMAN, V., THAL, D., FENSON, L., DALE, P., REZNICK, J. S., REILLY, J., & HARTUNG, J. (1994). Developmental and stylistic variation in the composition of early vocabulary. *Journal of Child Language, 21,* 85–124.

BATES, E., THAL, D., & MARCHMAN, V., (1991). Symbols and syntax: A Darwinian approach to language development. In N. A. Krasnegor, D. M. Rumbaugh, R. L. Schiefelbusch, & M. Studdert-Kennedy (Eds.), *Biological and behavioral determinants of language development* (pp. 29–66). Hillsdale, NJ: Lawrence Erlbaum.

BATESON, M. C. (1975). Mother-infant exchanges: The epigenesis of conversational interaction. In D. Aaronson & R. W. Rieber (Eds.), *Developmental psycholinguistics and communication disorders* (pp. 101–112). Annals of the New York Academy of Science, Vol. 263.

BAYNES, K., & GAZZANIGA, M. S. (1988). Right hemisphere language: Insights into normal language mechanisms? In F. Plum (Ed.), *Language, communication, and the brain* (pp. 117–126). New York: Raven.

BEAL, C. R. (1987). Repairing the message: Children's monitoring and revision skills. *Child Development, 58,* 401–408.

BEAL, C. R. (1988). Children's knowledge about representations of intended meaning. In J. W. Astington, P. L. Harris, & D. R. Olson (Eds.), *Developing theories of mind* (pp. 315–325). Cambridge: Cambridge University Press.

BEAL, C. R., & FLAVELL, J. H. (1983). Young speakers' evaluations of their listener's comprehension in a referential communication task. *Child Development, 54,* 148–153.

BECHTEL, W. (1993). Knowing how to use language: Developing a rapprochement between two theoretical traditions. In H. L. Roitblat, L. M. Herman, P. E. Nachtigall (Eds.), *Language and communication: Comparative perspectives* (pp. 65–83). Hillsdale, NJ: Erlbaum.

BECHTEL, W., & ABRAHAMSEN, A. (1991). *Connectionism and the mind.* Cambridge, MA: Basil Blackwell Publishers.

BECKER, J. A. (1982). Children's strategic use of requests to mark and manipulate social status. In S. Kuczaj (Ed.), *Language development: Language, thought, and culture* (pp. 1–33). Hillsdale, NJ: Erlbaum.

BECKER, J. A. (1990). Processes in the acquisition of pragmatic competence. In G. Conti-Ramsden & C. E. Snow (Eds.), *Children's language: Vol. 7* (pp. 7–24). Hillsdale, NJ: Lawrence Erlbaum.

BECKER, J. A. (1994). 'Sneak-shoes,' 'sworders' and 'nose-beards': A case study of lexical innovation. *First Language, 14,* 195–212.

BEHREND, D. A. (1990). Constraints and development: A reply to Nelson (1988). *Cognitive Development, 5,* 313–330.

BEHREND, D. A. (1995). Processes involved in the initial mapping of verb meanings. In

M. Tomasello & W. E. Merriman (Eds.), *Beyond names for things: Young children's acquisition of verbs* (pp. 251–276). Hillsdale, NJ: Erlbaum.

BEHREND, D. A., ROSENGREN, K. S., & PERLMUTTER, M. (1992). The relation between private speech and parental interactive style. In R. M. Diaz & L. E. Berk (Eds.), *Private speech: From social interaction to self-regulation* (pp. 85–100). Hillsdale, NJ: Erlbaum.

BELL, S., & AINSWORTH, M. (1972). Infant crying and maternal responsiveness. *Child Development, 43,* 1171–1190.

BELLUGI, U., MARKS, S., BIHRLE, A., & SABO, H. (1993). Dissociation between language and cognitive functions in Williams syndrome. In D. Bishop & K. Mogford (Eds.), *Language development in exceptional children* (pp. 177–189). Hove, England: Erlbaum.

BELLUGI, U., POIZNER, H., & KLIMA, E. (1989). Language, modality and the brain. *Trends in Neurosciences, 12,* 380–388.

BELLUGI, U., VAN HOEK, K., LILLO-MARTIN, D., & O'GRADY, L. (1993). The acquisition of syntax and space in young deaf signers. In D. Bishop & K. Mogford (Eds.), *Language development in exceptional children* (pp. 132–149). Hove, England: Erlbaum.

BELLUGI, U., WANG, P. P., & JERNIGAN, T. L. (1994). Williams syndrome: An unusual neuropsychological profile. In S. H. Froman & J. Grafman (Eds.), *A typical cognitive deficits in developmental disorders: Implications for brain function* (pp. 23–56). Hillsdale, NJ: Erlbaum.

BENEDICT, H. (1979). Early lexical development: Comprehension and production. *Journal of Child Language, 6,* 183–200.

BEN-ZEEV, S. (1977). The influence of bilingualism on cognitive strategy and cognitive development. *Child Development, 48,* 1009–1018.

BERK, L. E. (1992). Children's private speech: An overview of theory and the status of research. In R. M. Diaz & L. E. Berk (Eds.), *Private speech: From social interaction to self-regulation* (pp. 17–54). Hillsdale, NJ: Erlbaum.

BERKO, J. (1958). The child's learning of English morphology. *Word, 14,* 150–177.

BERKO, J., & BROWN, R. (1960). Psycholinguistic research methods. In P. H. Mussen (Ed.), *Handbook of research methods in child development* (pp. 517–557). New York: Wiley.

BERMAN, R. A. (1986). A crosslinguistic perspective: Morphology and syntax. In P. Fletcher & M. Garman (Eds.), *Language acquisition (2nd ed.)* (pp. 429–447). Cambridge: Cambridge University Press.

BERMAN, R. A. (1988). On the ability to relate events in narrative. *Discourse Processes, 11,* 469–497.

BERMAN, R. A., & SLOBIN, D. I. (1994). *Relating events in narrative: A crosslinguistic developmental study.* Hillsdale, NJ: Erlbaum.

BERNSTEIN, B. B. (1970). A socio-linguistic approach to social learning. In F. Williams (Ed.), *Language and poverty* (pp. 25–61). Chicago: Markham.

BERNSTEIN, B. B. (1981). Elaborated and restricted codes: Their social origins and some consequences. In K. Danziger (Ed.), *Readings in child socialization* (pp. 165–186). Oxford: Pergamon Press.

BERTENTHAL, B. I., & CAMPOS, J. J. (1987). Commentary—New directions in the study of early experience. *Child Development, 58,* 560–567.

BEST, C. T. (1988). The emergence of cerebral asymmetries in early human development: A literature review and a neuroembryological model. In D. L. Molfese & S. J. Segalowitz (Eds.), *Brain lateralization in children: Developmental implications* (pp. 5–34). New York: The Guilford Press.

BEST, C. T. (1994). The emergence of native-language phonological influences in infants: A perceptual assimilation model. In J. C. Goodman & H. C. Nusbaum (Eds.), *The development of speech perception: The transition from speech sounds to spoken words* (pp. 167–224). Cambridge, MA: MIT Press.

BEVER, T. G., & CHIARELLO, R. J. (1974). Cerebral dominance in musicians and nonmusicians. *Science, 185,* 537–539.

BIALYSTOK, E. (1991a). Metalinguistic dimensions of bilingual language proficiency. In E. Bialystok (Ed.), *Language processing in bilingual children* (pp. 113–141). Cambridge: Cambridge University Press.

BIALYSTOK, E. (1991b). *Language processing in bilingual children.* Cambridge: Cambridge University Press.

BIALYSTOK, E., & CUMMINS, J. (1991). Language, cognition, and education of bilingual children. In E. Bialystok (Ed.), *Language processing in bilingual children* (pp. 222–232). Cambridge: Cambridge University Press.

BICKERTON, D. (1981). *Roots of language.* Ann Arbor, MI: Karoma.

BICKERTON, D. (1984). The language bioprogram hypothesis. *The Behavioral and Brain Sciences, 7,* 173–221.

BICKERTON, D. (1988). Creole languages and the bioprogram. In F. J. Newmeyer (Ed.), *Linguistics: The Cambridge survey: Vol II* (pp. 268–284). Cambridge: Cambridge University Press.

BICKERTON, D. (1990). *Language and species.* Chicago: University of Chicago Press.

BIGELOW, A. (1987). Early words of blind children. *Journal of Child Language, 14,* 47–56.

BIJELJAC-BABIC, BERTONCINI, J., & MEHLER, J. (1993). How do 4-day-old infants categorize multisyllabic utterances? *Development Psychology, 29,* 711–721.

BIKLEN, D. (1990). Communication unbound: Autism and praxis. *Harvard Educational Review, 60,* 291–314.

BIRDWHISTELL, R. L. (1970). *Kinesics and context: Essays on body motion communication.* Philadelphia: University of Pennsylvania Press.

BISHOP, D. V. M. (1983). Linguistic impairment after hemidecortication for infantile hemiplegia? A reappraisal. *Quarterly Journal of Experimental Psychology, 35,* 199–207.

BISHOP, D. V. M. (1988). Can the right hemisphere mediate language as well as the left? A critical review of recent research. *Cognitive Neuropsychology, 5,* 353–367.

BISHOP, D. V. M. (1995). Nonword repetition as a phenotypic marker for inherited language impairment. Paper presented at the 16th Symposium on Research in Child Language Disorders, University of Wisconsin-Madison, June 2–3.

BLANK, M., & ALLEN, D. A. (1976). Understanding "why": Its significance in early intelligence. In M. Lewis (Ed.), *Origins of Intelligence* (pp. 259–278). New York: Plenum.

BLANK, M., GESSNER, M., & ESPOSITO, A. (1979). Language without communication: A case study. *Journal of Child Language, 6,* 329–352.

BLOOM, L. (1973). *One word at a time.* The Hague: Mouton.

BLOOM, L. (1991). *Language development from two to three.* Cambridge: Cambridge University Press.

BLOOM, L. (1993a). Language acquisition and the power of expression. In H. L. Roitblat, L. M. Herman, & P. E. Nachtigall (Eds.), *Language and communication: Comparative perspectives* (pp. 95–114). Hillsdale, NJ: Erlbaum.

BLOOM, L. (1993b). *The transition from infancy to language: Acquiring the power of expression.* Cambridge: Cambridge University Press.

BLOOM, L., LAHEY, M., HOOD, L., LIFTER, K., & FIESS, K. (1980). Complex sentences: Acquisition of syntactic connectives and the semantic relations they encode. *Journal of Child Language, 7,* 235–261.

BLOOM, L., LIFTER, K., & HAFITZ, J. (1980). Semantics of verbs and the development of verb inflections in child language. *Language, 56,* 386–412.

BLOOM, L., LIGHTBOWN, P., & HOOD. L. (1975). Structure and variation in child language. *Monographs of the Society for Research in Child Development, 40* (2, Serial No. 160).

BLOOM, L., ROCISSANO, L., & HOOD, L. (1976). Adult-child discourse: Developmental interaction between information processing and linguistic knowledge. *Cognitive Psychology, 8,* 521–552.

BLOOM, L., TINKER, E., & MARGULIS, C. (1993). The words children learn: Evidence against a noun bias in early vocabularies. *Cognitive Development, 8,* 431–450.

BLUMSTEIN, S. E. (1988). Linguistic deficits in asphasia. In F. Plum (Ed.), *Language, communication, and the brain* (pp. 199–214). New York: Raven Press.

BOHANNON, J. N., & STANOWICZ, L. (1988). The issue of negative evidence: Adult responses to children's language errors. *Developmental Psychology, 24,* 684–689.

BONVILLIAN, J. D., ORLANSKY, M. D., & NOVACK, L. L. (1983). Developmental milestones: Sign language acquisition and motor development. *Child Development, 54,* 1435–1445.

BORER, H., & WEXLER, K. (1987). The maturation of syntax. In T. Roeper & E. Williams (Eds.), *Parameters in linguistic theory* (pp. 123–172). Dordrecht: Reidel.

BORNSTEIN, M. H., & TAMIS-LᴇMONDA, C. S. (1989). Maternal responsiveness and cognitive development in children. In M. H. Bornstein (Ed.), *Maternal responsiveness: Characteristics and consequences* (pp. 49–61). San Francisco: Jossey-Bass.

BOTVIN, G. J., & SUTTON-SMITH, B. (1977). The development of structural complexity in children's fantasy narratives. *Developmental Psychology, 13,* 377–388.

BOWERMAN, M. (1973). Structural relationships in children's utterances: Syntactic or semantic? In T. E. Moore (Ed.), *Cognitive development and the acquisition of language* (pp. 197–214). New York: Academic Press.

BOWERMAN, M. (1976). Semantic factors in the acquisition of rules for word use and sentence construction. In D. M. Morehead & A. E. Morehead (Eds.), *Normal and deficient child language.* Baltimore, MD: University Park Press.

BOWERMAN, M. (1978). The acquisition of word meaning: An investigation into some current conflicts. In N. Waterson & C. Snow (Eds.), *The development of communication* (pp. 263–287). Chichester: Wiley.

BOWERMAN, M. (1979). The acquisition of complex sentences. In P. Fletcher & M. Garman (Eds.), *Language acquisition* (pp. 285–306). Cambridge: Cambridge University Press.

BOWERMAN, M. (1985). Beyond communicative adequacy: From piecemeal knowledge to an integrated system in the child's acquisition of language. In K.E. Nelson (Ed.), *Children's language: Vol. 5* (pp. 369–398). Hillsdale, NJ: Erlbaum.

BOWERMAN, M. (1988). The 'no negative evidence' problem: How do children avoid constructing an overly general grammar? In V.A. Hawkins (Ed.), *Explaining language universals.* Oxford: Blackwell.

BOWERMAN, M. (1989). Learning a semantic system: What role do cognitive predispositions play? In M. L. Rice & R. H. Schiefelbusch (Eds.), *The teachability of language* (pp. 133–169). Baltimore: Paul Brookes.

BOWERMAN, M. (1990). Mapping thematic roles onto syntactic functions: Are children helped by innate linking rules? *Linguistics, 28,* 1253–1289.

BRADSHAW, G. (1993). Beyond animal language. In H. L. Roitblat, L. M. Herman, & P. E. Nachtigall (Eds.), *Language and communication: Comparative perspectives* (pp. 25–44). Hillsdale, NJ: Erlbaum.

BRADSHAW, J. L., & NETTLETON, N. C. (1981). The nature of hemispheric specialization in man. *The behavioral and brain sciences, 4,* 51–63.

BRAINE, M. D. S. (1963). The ontogeny of English phrase structure: The first phrase. *Language, 39,* 1–14.

BRAINE, M. D. S. (1976). Children's first word combinations. *Monographs of the Society for Research in Child Development, 41,* (1, Serial No. 164).

BRAINE, M. D. S. (1988). Modeling the acquisition of linguistic structure. In Y. Levy, I. M. Schlesinger, & M. D. S. Braine (Eds.), *Categories and processes in language acquisition* (pp. 217–259). Hillsdale, NJ: Erlbaum.

BRAINE, M. D. S. (1992). What sort of innate structure is needed to "bootstrap" into syntax? *Cognition, 45,* 77–100.

BRAINE, M. D. S. (1994). Is nativism sufficient? *Journal of Child Language, 21,* 9–32.

BRETHERTON, I., McNEW, S., SNYDER, L., & BATES, E. (1983). Individual differences at 20 months: Analytic and holistic strategies in language acquisition. *Journal of Child Language, 10,* 293–320.

BRINTON, B., FUJIKI, M., LOAB, D., & WINKLER, E. (1986). Development of conversational repair strategies in response to requests for clarification. *Journal of Speech and Hearing Research, 29,* 75–81.

BRITT, D. (1993). "If they're joning your mamma, it's just for fun." *Milwaukee Journal,* November 14, J5.

BROOKS-GUNN, J., & MATTHEWS, W. S. (1979). *He and she: How children develop their sex-role identity*. Englewood Cliffs, NJ: Prentice-Hall.

BROWN, R. (1957). Linguistic determinism and the part of speech. *Journal of Abnormal and Social Psychology, 55,* 1–5.

BROWN, R. (1958a). How shall a thing be called? *Psychological Review, 65,* 14–21.

BROWN, R. (1958b). *Words and things*. New York: Free Press.

BROWN, R. (1973). *A first language: The early stages*. Cambridge, MA: Harvard University Press.

BROWN, R. (1980). The maintenance of conversation. In D. R. Olson (Ed.), *The social foundations of language and thought* (pp. 187–210). New York: Norton.

BROWN, R., & FRASER, C. (1963). The acquisition of syntax. In C. N. Cofer & B. S. Musgrave (Eds.), *Verbal behavior and learning* (pp. 158–196). New York: McGraw-Hill.

BROWN, R., & HANLON, C. (1970). Derivational complexity and order of acquisition in child speech. In J. Hayes (Ed.), *Cognition and the development of language* (pp. 11–54). New York: Wiley.

BRUNER, J. (1977). Early social interaction and language acquisition. In H. R. Schaffer (Ed.), *Studies in mother-infant interaction* (pp. 271–289). London: Academic Press.

BRUNER, J. (1986). *Actual minds, possible worlds*. Cambridge, MA: Harvard University Press.

BRUNER, J., & LUCARIELLO, J. (1989). Monologue as narrative recreation of the world. In K. Nelson (Ed.), *Narratives from the crib* (pp. 73–97). Cambridge, MA: Harvard University Press.

BRYANT, P. E., BRADLEY, L., MacLEAN, M., & CROSSLAND, J. (1989). Nursery rhymes, phonological skills and reading. *Journal of Child Language, 16,* 407–428.

BRYDEN, M. P., & ALLARD, F. (1978). Dichotic listening and the development of linguistic processes. In M. Kinsbourne (Ed.), *Asymmetrical function of the brain* (pp. 392–404). Cambridge: Cambridge University Press.

BRYDEN, M. P., HECAEN, H., & DeAGOSTINI, M. (1983). Patterns of cerebral organization. *Brain and Language, 20,* 249–262.

BUDWIG, N. (1991). Introduction (to special issue on Functional Approaches to Child Language). *First Language, 11,* 1–5.

BUDWIG, N. (1995). *A developmental-functionalist approach to child language*. Mahwah, NJ: Erlbaum.

BULLOCK, D., LIEDERMAN, J., & TODOROVIC, D. (1987). Commentary—Reconciling stable asymmetry with recovery of function: An adaptive systems perspective on functional plasticity. *Child Development, 58,* 689–697.

BUTLER, S. (1980). The tum phenomenon. *Journal of Child Language, 7,* 428–429. (Original work published 1920)

CAPLAN, D. (1987). *Neurolinguistics and linguistic aphasiology: An introduction*. Cambridge: Cambridge University Press.

CAREY, S. (1978). The child as a word learner. In M. Halle, J. Bresnan, & G. A. Miller

(Eds.), *Linguistic theory and psychological reality* (pp. 264–293). Cambridge, MA: MIT Press.

CAREY, S. (1994). Does learning a language require the child to reconceptualize the world? In L. Gleitman & B. Landau (Eds.), *The acquisition of the lexicon* (pp. 143–168). Cambridge, MA: Elsevier/MIT Press.

CARREL, R. E. (1977). Epidemiology of hearing loss. In S. E. Gerber (Ed.), *Audiometry in infancy* (pp. 3–16). New York: Gruene & Stratten.

CARTER, A. (1978). The development of systematic vocalizations prior to words: A case study. In N. Waterson & C. E. Snow (Eds.), *The development of communication* (pp. 127–138). Chichester: Wiley.

CASELLI, M. C., BATES, E., CASADIO, P., FENSON, J., FENSON, L., SANDERL, L., & WEIR, J. (1995). A cross-linguistic study of early lexical development. *Cognitive Development, 10,* 159–199.

CAZDEN, C. B. (1988). *Classroom discourse: The language of teaching and learning.* Portsmouth, NH: Heinemann.

CHAIKA, E. (1980). Jargons and language change. *Anthropological Linguistics, 22,* 77–96.

CHAIKA, E. (1989). *Language: The social mirror* (2nd ed.). Cambridge: Newbury House.

CHALL, J. S., JACOBS, V. A., & BALDWIN, L. E. (1990). *The reading crisis: Why poor children fall behind.* Cambridge, MA: Harvard University Press.

CHANDLER, J., ARGYRIS, D., BARNES, W. S., GOODMAN, I. F., & SNOW, C. E. (1986). Parents as teachers: Observations of low-income parents and children in a homework-like task. In B. B. Schieffelin & P. Gilmore (Eds.), *The acquisition of literacy: Ethnographic perspectives* (pp. 171–187). Norwood, NJ: Ablex.

CHANEY, C. (1989). I pledge a legiance to the flag: Three studies in word segmentation. *Applied Psycholinguistics, 10,* 261–282.

CHAPMAN, R. S. (1978). Comprehension strategies in children. In J. F. Kavanaugh & W. Strange (Eds.), *Speech and language in the laboratory, school, and clinic* (pp. 308–327). Cambridge: MIT Press.

CHAPMAN, R. S. (1981). Exploring children's communicative intents. In J. F. Miller, *Assessing language production in children* (pp. 111–136). Austin, TX: Pro-Ed.

CHAPMAN, R. S. (1995). Language development in children and adolescents with Down syndrome. In P. Fletcher & B. MacWhinney (Eds.), *The handbook of child language* (pp. 641–663). Oxford: Blackwell Publishers.

CHAPMAN, R. S., & THOMPSON, J. (1980). What is the source of overextension errors in comprehension testing of two-year-olds? A response to Fregmen and Fay. *Journal of Child Language, 7,* 575–578.

CHENEY, D. L. (1995). Sociality without frills. *Science, 267,* 909–910.

CHERRY, L., & LEWIS, M. (1978). Differential socialization of girls and boys: Implications for sex differences in language development. In N. Waterson & C. Snow (Eds.), *The development of communication* (pp. 189–197). New York: Wiley.

CHOI, S. (1991). Early acquisition of epistemic meanings. *First Language, 11,* 93–120.

CHOI, S., & BOWERMAN, M. (1991). Learning to express motion events in English and Korean: The influence of language-specific lexicalization patterns. *Cognition, 41,* 83–121.

CHOMSKY, C. (1969). *The acquisition of syntax in children from 5 to 10.* Cambridge, MA: MIT Press.

CHOMSKY, N. (1957). *Syntactic structures.* The Hague: Mouton.

CHOMSKY, N. (1959). A review of B. F. Skinner's *Verbal Behavior. Language, 35,* 26–58.

CHOMSKY, N. (1965). *Aspects of the theory of syntax.* Cambridge, MA: MIT Press.

CHOMSKY, N. (1981). *Lectures on Government and Binding.* Dordrecht: Foris.

CHOMSKY, N. (1982). Discussion of Putnam's comments. In M. Piattelli-Palamarini (Ed.), *Language and learning: The debate between Jean Piaget and Noam Chomsky* (pp. 310–324). Cambridge, MA: Harvard University Press.

CHOMSKY, N. (1991). Linguistics and cognitive science: Problems and mysteries. In A. Kasher (Ed.), *The Chomskyan turn* (pp. 26–55). Cambridge, MA: Basil Blackwell.

CHOMSKY, N. (1993). On the nature, use, and acquisition of language. In A. I. Goldman (Ed.), *Readings in philosophy and cognitive science* (vol. C., pp. 511–534). Cambridge, MA: MIT Press. (Original work published 1987)

CHUKOVSKY, K. (1963). *From two to five.* Berkeley: University of California Press.

CLAHSEN, H. (1990/1991). Constraints on parameter setting: A grammatical analysis of some acquisition stages in German child language. *Language Acquisition, 4,* 361–391.

CLANCY, P. (1985). The acquisition of Japanese. In D. I. Slobin (Ed.), *The cross-linguistic study of language acquisition* (pp. 373–524). Hillsdale, NJ: Erlbaum.

CLANCY, P. (1986). The acquisition of communicative style in Japanese. In B. B. Schieffelin & E. Ochs (Eds.), *Language socialization across cultures* (pp. 213–250). Cambridge: Cambridge University Press.

CLARK, E. V. (1971). On the acquisition of the meaning of *before* and *after. Journal of Verbal Learning and Verbal Behavior, 10,* 266–275.

CLARK, E. V. (1973). What's in a word? On the child's acquisition of semantics in his first language. In T. E. Moore (Ed.), *Cognitive development and the acquisition of language* (pp. 65–110). New York: Academic Press.

CLARK, E. V. (1979). Building a vocabulary: Words for objects, actions, and relations. In P. Fletcher & M. Garman (Eds.), *Language acquisition* (pp. 149–160). Cambridge: Cambridge University Press.

CLARK, E. V. (1993). *The lexicon in acquisition.* Cambridge: Cambridge University Press.

CLARK, E. V. (1995). Later lexical development and word formation. In P. Fletcher & B. MacWhinney (Eds.), *The handbook of child language* (pp. 393–412). Oxford: Basil Blackwell.

CLARK, E. V., & HECHT, B. F. (1982). Learning to coin agent and instrument nouns. *Cognition, 12,* 1–24.

CLASHEN, H. (1989). The grammatical characterization of developmental dysphasia. *Linguistics, 27,* 897–920.

CONTI-RAMSDEN, G. (1994). Language interaction with atypical language learners. In C. Gallaway & B. J. Richards (Eds.), *Input and interaction in language acquisition* (pp. 183–196). Cambridge: Cambridge University Press.

COOPER, D., & ANDERSON-INMAN, L. (1988). Language and socialization. In M. A.

Nippold (Ed.), *Later language development: Ages nine through nineteen* (pp. 225–245). Austin, TX: Pro-Ed.

COOPER, R. P., & ASLIN, R. N. (1990). Preference for infant-directed speech in the first month after birth. *Child Development, 61,* 1584–1595.

COOPER, R. P., & ASLIN, R. N. (1994). Developmental differences in infant attention to the spectral properties of infant-directed speech. *Child Development, 65,* 1663–1677.

CORBALLIS, M. C. (1992). On the evolution of language and generativity. *Cognition, 44,* 197–226.

CORDER, S. P. (1967). The significance of learners' errors. *International Review of Applied Linguistics, 5,* 161–169.

CORNE, C. (1984). On the transmission of substratal features in creolisation. *Behavioral and Brain Sciences, 7,* 191–192.

CORRIGAN, R. (1979). Cognitive correlates of language: Differential criteria yield differential results. *Child Development, 50,* 617–631.

COSMIDES, L. (1989). The logic of social exchange: Has natural selection shaped how humans reason? Studies with the Wason selection task. *Cognition, 31,* 187–276.

COSMIDES, L., & TOOBY, J. (1994). Origins of domain specificity: The evolution of functional organization. In L. A. Hirschfeld & S. A. Gelman (Eds.), *Mapping the mind: Domain specificity in cognition and culture* (pp. 85–116). Cambridge: Cambridge University Press.

CRAGO, M. B., & ALLEN, S. E. M. (1994). Morphemes gone askew: Linguistic impairment in Inuktitut. McGill Working Papers in Linguistics, Vol. 10, Nos. 1 & 2.

CROMER, R. F. (1974). The development of language and cognition: The cognition hypothesis. In B. Foss (Ed.), *New perspectives in child development* (pp. 184–252). Harmondsworth, Middlesex: Penguin Books.

CROMER, R. F. (1994). A case study of dissociations between language and cognition. In H. Tager-Flusberg (Ed.), *Constraints on language acquisition: Studies of atypical children* (pp. 141–153). Hillsdale, NJ: Erlbaum.

CRYSTAL, D. (1986). Prosodic development. In P. Fletcher & M. Garman (Eds.), *Language acquisition (2nd ed.)* (pp. 174–197). Cambridge: Cambridge University Press.

CUNNINGHAM, A. E., & STANOVICH, K. E. (1991). Tracking the unique effects of print exposure in children: Associations with vocabulary, general knowledge, and spelling. *Journal of Educational Psychology, 83,* 264–274.

CURTISS, S. (1977). *Genie: A pscholinguistic study of a modern day "wild child."* New York: Academic Press.

CURTISS, S. (1985). The development of human cerebral lateralization. In D. F. Benson & E. Zaidel (Eds.), *The dual brain: Hemispheric specialization in humans* (pp. 97–116). New York: Guilford Press.

CURTISS, S. (1988). Abnormal language acquisition and the modularity of language. In F. Newmeyer (Ed.), *Linguistics: The Cambridge survey: Vol. II. Linguistic theory: Extensions and implications* (pp. 96–116). Cambridge: Cambridge University Press.

CURTISS, S. (1989). The independence and task-specificity of language. In M. H.

Bornstein & J. S. Bruner (Eds.), *Interaction in human development* (pp. 105–138). Hillsdale, NJ: Erlbaum.

CUTLER, A. (1994). Segmentation problems, rhythmic solutions. In L. Gleitman & B. Landau (Eds.), *The acquisition of the lexicon* (pp. 81–104). Cambridge, MA: Elsevier/MIT Press.

CUTLER, A. (1996). Prosody and the word boundary problem. In J. L. Morgan & K. Demuth (Eds.), *Signal to syntax: Bootstrapping from speech to grammar in early acquisition* (pp. 87–100). Mahwah, NJ: Erlbaum.

DALE, P. S. (1976). *Language development: Structure and function (2nd ed.)* Chicago: Holt, Rinehart & Winston.

DAMASIO, A. R. (1988). Concluding remarks: Neuroscience and cognitive science in the study of language and the brain. In F. Plum (Ed.), *Language, communication, and the brain* (pp. 275–282). New York: Raven Press.

DARWIN, C. (1877). A bibliographical sketch of an infant. *Mind, 2,* 285–294.

DAUGHERTY, K. G., & SEIDENBERG, M. S. (1994). Beyond rules and exceptions: A connectionist approach to inflectional morphology. In S. Lima, R. Corrigan, & G. Iverson (Eds.), *The reality of linguistic rules* (pp. 353–388). Philadelphia: Benjamins.

DE BOYSSON-BARDIES, B., HALLE, P., SAGART, L., & DURAND, C. (1989). A cross-linguistic-investigation of vowel formants in babbling. *Journal of Child Language, 16,* 1–17.

DE BOYSSON-BARDIES, B., SAGART, L., & DURAND, C. (1984). Discernable differences in the babbling of infants according to target language. *Journal of Child Language, 8,* 511–524.

DE BOYSSON-BARDIES, B., VIHMAN M., ROUG-HELLICHIUS, L., DURAND, C., LAND-BERG, I., & ARAO, F. (1992). Material evidence of infant selection from target language: A cross-linguistic study. In C. A. Ferguson, L. Menn, & C. Stoel-Gammon (Eds.), *Phonological development* (pp. 369–391). Timonium, MD: York Press.

DeCASPER, A. J., & FIFER, W. P. (1980). Of human bonding: Newborns prefer their mothers' voices. *Science, 208,* 1174–1176.

DeCASPER, A. J., & SPENCE, M. J. (1986). Prenatal maternal speech influences newborns' perception of speech sounds. *Infant Behavior and Development, 9,* 133–150.

DE HOUWER, A. (1995). Bilingual language acquisition. In P. Fletcher & B. MacWhinney (Eds.), *The handbook of child language* (pp. 219–250). Oxford: Basil Blackwell.

DEMETRAS, M. J., POST, K. N., & SNOW, C. E. (1986). Feedback to first language learners: The role of repetitions and clarification questions. *Journal of Child Language, 13,* 275–292.

DEMUTH, K. (1993). Issues in the acquisition of the Sesotho tonal system. *Journal of Child Language, 20,* 275–302.

DEMUTH, K. (1994). On the underspecification of functional categories in early grammars. In B. Lust, M. Suñer, & J. Whitman (Eds.), *Syntactic theory and first language acquisition: Cross-linguistic perspectives* (pp. 119–134). Hillsdale, NJ: Erlbaum.

DEMUTH, K. (1996). The prosodic structure of early words. In J. L. Morgan & K. Demuth

(Eds.), *Signal to syntax: Bootstrapping from speech to grammar in early acquisition* (pp. 171–186). Hillsdale, NJ: Erlbaum.

DENNIS, M. (1980). Capacity and strategy for syntactic comprehension after left and right hemidecortication. *Brain and Language, 7,* 153–169.

DERWING, B. L. (1976). Morpheme recognition and the learning of rules for derivational morphology. *The Canadian Journal of Linguistics, 21,* 38–66.

DERWING, B. L., & BAKER, W. J. (1979). Research on the acquisition of English morphology. In P. Fletcher & M. Garman (Eds.), *Language acquisition* (pp. 209–223). Cambridge: Cambridge University Press.

DERWING, B. L., & BAKER, W. J. (1986). Assessing morphological development. In P. Fletcher & M. Garman (Eds.), *Language acquisition, Second Edition* (pp. 326–338). Cambridge: Cambridge University Press.

DESCARTES, R. (1911). Trait de l'homme. (E. S. Haldane & G. R. T. Ross, Trans.). Cambridge: Cambridge University Press. (Original work published 1662)

DE VILLIERS, J. (1995a). Questioning minds and answering machines. In D. MacLaughlin & S. McEwen (Eds.), *Proceedings of the 19th Annual Boston University Conference on Language Development* (pp. 20–36). Somerville, MA: Cascadilla Press.

DE VILLIERS, J. (1995b). Empty categories and complex sentences: The case of wh-questions. In P. Fletcher & B. MacWhinney (Eds.), *The handbook of child language* (pp. 508–540). Oxford: Basil Blackwell.

DE VILLIERS, J. G., & DE VILLIERS, P. A. (1973). A cross-sectional study of the acquisition of grammatical morphemes in child speech. *Journal of Psycholinguistic Research, 2,* 267–278.

DE VILLIERS, J. G., & DE VILLIERS, P. A. (1978). *Language acquisition.* Cambridge: Harvard University Press.

DE VILLIERS, J., DE VILLIERS, P., & HOBAN, E. (1994). The central problem of functional categories in the English syntax of oral deaf children. In H. Tager-Flusberg (Ed.), *Constraints on language acquisition: Studies of atypical children* (pp. 9–48). Hillsdale, NJ: Erlbaum.

DE VILLIERS, J., & ROEPER, T. (1995). Relative clauses are barriers to *wh*-movement for young children. *Journal of Child Language, 22,* 389–405.

DE VILLIERS, P. (1988). Assessing English syntax in hearing-impaired children: Elicited production in pragmatically motivated situations. In R. R. Kretschmer & L. W. Kretschmer (Eds.), *Communication assessment of hearing-impaired children: From conversation to classroom. Journal of the Academy of Rehabilitative Audiology: Monograph Supplement, 21,* 41–71.

DIAZ, R. M. (1983). Thought and two languages: The impact of bilingualism on cognitive development. *Review of Research in Education, 10,* 23–54.

DIAZ, R. M., & BERK, L. E. (1992). *Private speech: From social interaction to self-regulation.* Hillsdale, NJ: Erlbaum.

DICKSON, W. P. (1981). *Children's oral communication skills.* New York: Academic Press.

DILLER, K. C. (1978). *The language teaching controversy.* Rowley, MA: Newbury House.

DODD, B. (1987). Lip-reading, phonological coding and deafness. In B. Dodd & R. Campbell (Eds.), *Hearing by eye: The psychology of lip-reading* (pp. 177–190). London: Erlbaum.

DOLNICK, E. (1993). Deafness as culture. *The Atlantic Monthly, 272,* 37–53.

DONEGAN, P. J., & STAMPE, D. (1979). The study of natural phonology. In D. A. Dinnsen (Ed.), *Current approaches to phonological theory* (pp. 126–173). Bloomington: Indiana University Press.

DORE, J. (1975). Holophrases, speech acts, and language universals. *Journal of Child Language, 2,* 20–40.

DORE, J. (1977). "Oh them sheriff": A pragmatic analysis of children's responses to questions. In S. Ervin-Tripp & C. Mitchell-Kernan (Eds.), *Child discourse* (pp. 139–164). New York: Academic Press.

DORE, J. (1978). Conditions for the acquisition of speech acts. In I. Markova (Ed.), *The social context of language* (pp. 87–112). Chichester: Wiley.

DORE, J., FRANKLIN, M. B., MILLER, R., & RAMER, A. L. H. (1976). Transitional phenomena in early language acquisition. *Journal of Child Language, 3,* 13–28.

DORVAL, B., & ECKERMAN, C. O. (1984). Developmental trends in the quality of conversation achieved by small groups of acquainted peers. *Monographs of the Society for Research in Child Development, 49* (Serial No. 206).

DOUGHTY, C. (1991). Second language instruction does make a difference. *Studies in Second Language Acquisition, 13,* 431–469.

DRESHER, B. E. (1996). Introduction to metrical and prosodic phonology. In J. L. Morgan & K. Demuth (Eds.), *Signal to syntax: Bootstrapping from speech to grammar in early acquisition* (pp. 41–54). Hillsdale, NJ: Erlbaum.

DREYFUS, H. L. (1988). The Socratic and Platonic basis of cognitivism. *AI and Society, 2,* 99–112.

DROMI, E. (1987). *Early lexical development.* Cambridge: Cambridge University Press.

DROMI, E., LEONARD, L. B., SHTEIMAN, M. (1993). The grammatical morphology of Hebrew-speaking children with specific language impairment: Some competing hypotheses. *Journal of Speech and Hearing Research, 36,* 760–771.

DULAY, H., & BURT, M. (1974). Natural sequences in child second language acquisition. *Language Learning, 24,* 37–53.

DULAY, H., & BURT, M. (1975). Creative construction in second language learning. In M. Burt & H. Dulay (Eds.), *New directions in second language learning, teaching and bilingual education* (pp. 21–32). Washington, DC: Teachers of English to Speakers of Other Languages.

DUNDES, A., LEACH, J. W., & OZKOK, B. (1972). The strategy of Turkish boys' verbal dueling rhymes. In J. J. Gumperz & D. Hymes (Eds.), *Directions in sociolinguistics: The ethnography of communication* (pp. 130–160). New York: Holt, Rinehart & Winston.

DUNHAM, P. J., DUNHAM, F., & CURWIN, A. (1993). Joint-attentional states and lexical acquisition at 18 months. *Developmental Psychology, 29,* 827–831.

DUNLEA, A. (1984). The relationship between concept formation and semantic roles:

Some evidence from the blind. In L. Feagans, C. Garvey, & R. Golinkoff (Eds.), *The origins and growth of communication* (pp. 224–243). Norwood, NJ: Ablex.

DUNLEA, A. (1989). *Vision and the emergence of meaning: Blind and sighted children's early language.* New York: Cambridge University Press.

DUNN, J., & KENDRICK, C. (1982). The speech of two- and three-year-olds to infant siblings: 'Baby talk' and the context of communication. *Journal of Child Language, 9,* 579–595.

DUNN, J., & SHATZ, M. (1989). Becoming a conversationalist despite (or because of) having an older sibling. *Child Development, 60,* 399–410.

DUSKOVA, L. (1969). On sources of errors in foreign language learning. *International Review of Applied Linguistics, 7,* 11–36.

ECHOLS, C. H. (1996). A role for stress in early speech segmentation. In J. L. Morgan & K. Demuth (Eds.), *Signal to syntax: Bootstrapping from speech to grammar in early acquisition* (pp. 151–170). Mahwah, NJ: Erlbaum.

ECHOLS, C. H., & NEWPORT, E. L. (1992). The role of stress and position in determining first words. *Language Acquisition, 2,* 189–220.

ECKERT, P. (1988). Adolescent social structure and the spread of linguistic change. *Language in Society, 17,* 183–207.

ECKMAN, F. (1977). Markedness and the contrastive analysis hypothesis. *Language Learning, 27,* 315–330.

EDER, D., & HALLINAN, M. T. (1978). Sex differences in children's friendships. *American Sociological Review, 43,* 237–250.

EILERS, R. E. (1980). Infant speech perception: History and mystery. In G. Yeni-Komshian, J. F. Kavanagh, & C. A. Ferguson (Eds.), *Child Phonology: Vol.2 Perception* (pp. 23–39). New York: Academic Press.

EILERS, R. E., & OLLER, D. K. (1976). The role of speech discrimination in developmental sound substitutions. *Journal of Child Language, 3,* 319–329.

EIMAS, P. D., SIQUELAND, E. R., JUSCZYK, P., & VIGORITO, J. (1971). Speech perception in infants. *Science, 171,* 303–306.

EISENBERG, A. (1985). Learning to describe past experiences in conversation. *Discourse processes, 8,* 177–204.

EISENBERG, A. (1986). Teasing: Verbal play in two Mexicano homes. In B. B. Schieffelin & E. Ochs (Eds.), *Language socialization across cultures* (pp. 182–198). Cambridge: Cambridge University Press.

ELDREDGE, N. (1995). *Reinventing Darwin: The great debate at the high table of evolutionary theory.* New York: Wiley.

ELMAN, J. L. (1993). Learning and development in neural networks: The importance of starting small. *Cognition, 48,* 71–99.

ELY, R., & GLEASON, J. B. (1995). Socialization across contexts. In P. Fletcher & B. MacWhinney (Eds.), *The handbook of child language* (pp. 251–270). Oxford: Basil Blackwell.

ELY, R., & McCABE, A. (1994). The language play of kindergarten children. *First Language, 14,* 19–36.

EMERY, O. (1985). Language and aging. *Experimental Aging Research, 11,* 3–60.

ERVIN-TRIPP, S. (1976). Is Sybil there? The structure of some American English directives. *Language in Society, 5,* 25–66.

ERVIN-TRIPP, S. (1977). Wait for me roller skate. In S. Ervin-Tripp & C. Mitchell-Kernan (Eds.), *Child discourse* (pp. 165–188). New York: Academic Press.

ERVIN-TRIPP, S. (1978). Some features of early child-adult dialogues. *Language in Society, 7,* 357–373.

ESPOSITO, A. (1979). Sex differences in children's conversations. *Language and Speech, 22,* 213–220.

FAY, W. H. (1993). Infantile autism. In D. Bishop & K. Mogford (Eds.), *Language development in exceptional circumstances* (pp. 190–202). Hillsdale, NJ: Erlbaum.

FEE, J., & INGRAM, D. (1982). Reduplication as a strategy of phonological development. *Journal of Child Language, 9,* 41–54.

FELDMAN, H. H., GOLDIN-MEADOW, S., & GLEITMAN, L. R. (1978). Beyond Herodotus: The creation of language by linguistically deprived deaf children. In Locke, A. (Ed.), *Action, gesture, and symbol: The emergence of language* (pp. 351–414). London: Academic Press.

FELDMAN, H. H., HOLLAND, A. L., KEMP. S. S., & JANOSKY, J. E. (1992). Language development after unilateral brain injury. *Brain and Language, 42,* 89–102.

FENSON, L., DALE, P. S., REZNICK, J. S., BATES, E., THAL, D. J., & PETHICK, S. J. (1994). Variability in early communicative development. *Monographs of the Society for Research in Child Development, 59,* (Serial No. 242).

FERGUSON, C. A. (1979). Phonology as an individual access system: Some data from language acquisition. In C.J. Fillmore, D. Kempler, & W. S-Y. Wang (Eds.), *Individual differences in language ability and language behavior.* New York: Academic Press.

FERGUSON, C. A., & FARWELL, C. B. (1975). Words and sounds in early language acquisition. *Language, 51,* 439–491.

FERNALD, A. (1985). Four-month-old infants prefer to listen to motherese. *Infant Behavior and Development, 8,* 181–195.

FERNALD, A. (1989). Intonation and communicative intent in mothers' speech to infants: Is the melody the message? *Child Development, 60,* 1497–1510.

FERNALD, A. (1992). Human maternal vocalizations to infants as biologically relevant signals: An evolutionary perspective. In J. H. Barkow, L. Cosmides, & J. Tooby (Eds.), *The adapted mind: Evolutionary psychology and the generation of culture* (pp. 391–428). New York: Oxford University Press.

FERNALD, A., & KUHL, P. K. (1987). Acoustic determinants of infant preference for motherese speech. *Infant Behavior and Development, 10,* 279–293.

FERNALD, A., & McROBERTS, G. (1995). Infants' developing sensitivity to language-typical word order patterns. Paper presented at the 20th Annual Boston University Conference on Child Language Development, Boston, MA.

FERNALD, A., & McROBERTS, G. (1996). Prosodic bootstrapping: A critical analysis of the argument and the evidence. In J. L. Morgan & K. Demuth (Eds.), *Signal to syntax:*

Bootstrapping from speech to grammar in early acquisition (pp. 249–262). Mahwah, NJ: Erlbaum.

FERNALD, A., & MORIKAWA, H. (1993). Common themes and cultural variations in Japanese and American mothers' speech to infants. *Child Development, 64,* 637–656.

FERNALD, A., & SIMON, T. (1984). Expanded intonation contours in mothers' speech to newborns. *Developmental Psychology, 20,* 104–113.

FERNALD, A., TAESCHNER, T., DUN, J., PAPOUSEK, M., DE BOYSSON-BARDIES, B., & FUKUI, I. (1989). A cross-language study of prosodic modifications in mothers' and fathers' speech to preverbal infants. *Journal of Child Language, 16,* 477–501.

FERRIER, L. J. (1978). Some observations of error in context. In N. Waterson & C. Snow (Eds.), *The development of communication* (pp. 301–309). Chichester: Wiley.

FEY, M., & GANDOUR, J. (1982). Rule discovery in early phonology acquisition. *Journal of Child Language, 9,* 71–82.

FISHER, C., HALL, D. G., RAKOWITZ, S., & GLEITMAN, L. (1994). When it is better to receive than to give: Syntactic and conceptual constraints on vocabulary growth. In L. Gleitman & B. Landau (Eds.), *The acquisition of the lexicon* (pp. 333–376). Cambridge, MA: MIT Press/Elsevier.

FISHMAN, P. M. (1978). Interaction: The work women do. *Social Problems, 25,* 397–406.

FIVUSH, R. (1991). The social construction of personal narratives. *Merrill-Palmer Quarterly, 37,* 59–81.

FIVUSH, R., GRAY, J. T., & FROMHOFF, F. A. (1987). Two-year-olds talk about the past. *Cognitive Development, 2,* 393–410.

FIVUSH, R., & SLACKMAN, E. (1986). The acquisition and development of scripts. In K. Nelson (Ed.), *Event knowledge: Structure and function in development* (pp. 71–96). Hillsdale, NJ: Erlbaum.

FLAVELL, J. H., SPEER, J. R., GREEN, F. L., & AUGUST, D. L. (1981). The development of comprehension monitoring and knowledge about communication. *Monographs of the Society for Research in Child Development, 46* (Serial No. 5).

FLEGE, J. E. (1992). Speech learning in a second language. In C. A. Ferguson, L. Menn, & C. Stoel-Gammon (Eds.), *Phonological development: Models, research, implications* (pp. 565–604). Timonium, MD: York Press.

FLETCHER, P., & INGRAM, R. (1995). Grammatical impairment. In P. Fletcher & B. MacWhinney (Eds.), *The handbook of child language* (pp. 603–622). Oxford: Blackwell Publishers.

FODOR, J. A. (1983). *The modularity of mind.* Cambridge, MA: MIT Press.

FOLEY, W., & VAN VALIN, R. (1984). *Functional syntax and universal grammar.* Cambridge: Cambridge University Press.

FOLVEN, R. J., & BONVILLIAN, J. D. (1991). The transition from nonreferential to referential language in children acquiring American Sign Language. *Developmental Psychology, 27,* 806–816.

FORRESTER, M. A. (1988). Young children's polyadic conversation monitoring skills. *First Language, 8,* 201–226.

FOSTER, S. H. (1986). Learning discourse topic management in the preschool years. *Journal of Child Language, 13,* 231–250.

FOWLER, A. E. (1988). Determinants of rate of language growth in children with Down syndrome. In L. Nadel (Ed.), *The psychobiology of Down syndrome.* Cambridge, MA: MIT Press.

FOWLER, A. E., GELMAN, R., & GLEITMAN, L. R. (1994). The course of language learning in children with Down syndrome: Longitudinal and language level comparisions with young normally developing children. In H. Tager-Flusberg (Ed.), *Constraints on language acquisition: Studies of atypical children* (pp. 91–140). Hillsdale: Erlbaum.

FOWLES, B., & GLANZ, M. E. (1977). Competence and talent in verbal riddle comprehension. *Journal of Child Language, 4,* 433–452.

FRAIBERG, S. (1977). *Insights from the blind: Comparative studies of blind and sighted infants.* New York: Basic Books.

FREGMEN, A., & FAY, D. (1980). Overextensions in production and comprehension: A methodological clarification. *Journal of Child Language, 7,* 205–211.

FRENCH, L. A. (1988). The development of children's understanding of "because" and "so." *Journal of Experimental Child Psychology, 45,* 262–279.

FRENCH, L. A., LUCARIELLO, J., SEIDMAN, S., & NELSON, K. (1985). The influence of discourse content and context on preschoolers' use of language. In L. Galda & A. Pellegrini (Eds.), *Play, language and stories.* Norwood, NJ: Albex.

FRENCH, L. A., & NELSON, K. (1985). *Young children's knowledge of relational terms: Some ifs, ors and buts.* New York: Springer-Verlag.

FROMKIN, V., & RODMAN, R. (1988). *An introduction to language* (4th ed.). New York: Holt, Rinehart & Winston.

FURROW, D. (1984). Social and private speech at two years. *Child Development, 55,* 355–362.

FURROW, D., & LEWIS, S. (1987). The role of the initial utterance in contingent query sequences: Its influence on responses to requests for clarification. *Journal of Child Language, 14,* 467–479.

GALLAGHER, T. M. (1977). Revision behaviors in the speech of normal children developing language. *Journal of Speech and Hearing Research, 20,* 303–318.

GALLAGHER, T. M., & CRAIG, H. K. (1978). Structural characteristics of monologues in the speech of normal children: Semantic and conversational aspects. *Journal of Speech and Hearing Research, 21,* 103–117.

GALLAWAY, C., & RICHARDS, B. J. (1994). *Input and interaction in language acquisition.* Cambridge: Cambridge University Press.

GARDNER, H. (1980). Cognition comes of age. In M. Piattelli-Palmarini (Ed.), *Language and learning: The debate between Jean Piaget and Noam Chomsky* (pp. xix–xxxvi). Cambridge, MA: Harvard University Press.

GARDNER, H. (1985). *The mind's new science: A history of the cognitive revolution.* New York: Basic Books.

GARDNER, R. C., & LAMBERT, W. E. (1959). Motivational variables in second language acquisition. *Canadian Journal of Psychology, 13,* 266–272.

GARDNER, R. C., & LAMBERT, W. E. (1972). *Attitudes and motivation in second-language learning.* Rowley, MA: Newbury House Publishers.

GARNICA, O. (1973). The development of phonemic speech perception. In T. E. Moore (Ed.), *Cognitive development and the acquisition of language* (pp. 215–222). New York: Academic Press.

GARVEY, C. (1975). Requests and responses in children's speech. *Journal of Child Language, 2,* 41–63.

GARVEY, C., & HOGAN, R. (1973). Social speech and social interaction: Egocentrism revisited. *Child Development, 44,* 562–568.

GASS, S. (1979). Language transfer and universal grammatical relations. *Language Learning, 29,* 327–345.

GASS, S., & SELINKER, L. (1994). *Second language acquisition: An introductory course.* Hillsdale, NJ: Erlbaum.

GATHERCOLE, S. E., & BADDELEY, A. D. (1989). Evaluation of the role of phonological STM in the development of vocabulary in children: A longitudinal study. *Journal of Memory and Language, 28,* 200–213.

GATHERCOLE, S. E., & BADDELEY, A. D. (1990). Phonological memory deficits in language disordered children: Is there a causal connection? *Journal of Memory and Language, 29,* 336–360.

GATHERCOLE, S. E., WILLIS, C. S., EMSLIE, H., & BADDELEY, A. D. (1992). Phonological memory and vocabulary development during the early school years: A longitudinal study. *Developmental Psychology, 28,* 887–898.

GATHERCOLE, V. C. (1989). Contrast: A semantic constraint? *Journal of Child Language, 16,* 685–702.

GAZZANIGA, M. S. (1983). Right hemisphere language following brain bisection: A twenty-year perspective. *American Psychologist, 38,* 525–537.

GEE, J. P. (1993). *An introduction to human language: Fundamental concepts in linguistics.* Englewood Cliffs, NJ: Prentice-Hall.

GELBART, B., & SOEDERBERGH, R. (Eds.) (Annual publication). *Bibliography of child language.* Stockholm: Child Language Institute, Stockholm University.

GELMAN, R., & BAILLARGEON, R. (1983). A review of some Piagetian concepts. In P. Mussen (Ed.), *Handbook of child development: Cognitive development; Vol. 3* (pp. 167–230). New York: Wiley.

GELMAN, S. A., & MARKMAN, E. M. (1985). Implicit contrast in adjectives vs. nouns: Implications for word-learning in preschoolers. *Journal of Child Language, 12,* 125–145.

GELMAN, S. A., & TAYLOR, M. (1984). How two-year-old children interpret proper and common names for unfamiliar objects. *Child Development, 55,* 1535–1540.

GENESEE, F. (1989). Early bilingual development: One language or two? *Journal of Child Language, 16,* 161–180.

GENTNER, D. (1978). On relational meaning: The acquisition of verb meaning. *Child Development, 49,* 988–998.

GENTNER, D. (1982). Why nouns are learned before verbs: Linguistic relativity versus natural partitioning. In S. A. Kuczaj (Ed.), *Language development: Syntax and semantics*. Hillsdale, NJ: Erlbaum.

GERKEN, L. A., LANDAU, B., & REMEZ, R. E. (1990). Function morphemes in young children's speech perception and production. *Developmental Psychology, 27,* 204–216.

GERKEN, L. A., & McINTOSH, B. J. (1993). The interplay of function morphemes and prosody in early language. *Developmental Psychology, 29,* 448–457.

GESCHWIND, N., & LEVITSKY, W. (1968). Human brain: Left-right asymmetries in temporal speech region. *Science, 161,* 186–187.

GILLIS, S., & DE SCHUTTER, G. (1986). Transitional phenomena revisited: Insights into the nominal insight. In B. Lindblom & R. Zetterstrom (Eds.), *Precursors of early speech* (pp. 127–142). New York: Stockton Press.

GILMORE, P. (1986). Sub-rosa literacy: Peers, play, and ownership in literacy acquisition. In B. B. Schieffelin & P. Gilmore (Eds.), *The acquisition of literacy: Ethnographic perspectives* (pp. 155–168). Norwood, NJ: Ablex.

GINSBERG, E. H. (1976). The influence of conceptual difficulty on children's comprehension of temporal language. Unpublished Master's thesis. Rutgers-The State University of New Jersey.

GLEASON, J. B. (1973). Code switching in children's language. In T. E. Moore (Ed.), *Cognitive development and the aquisition of language* (pp. 159–168). New York: Academic Press.

GLEASON, J. B. (1992). Language acquisition and socialization. University lecture, Boston University, MA.

GLEASON, J. B., & WEINTRAUB, S. (1976). The acquisition of routines in child language. *Language in Society, 5,* 129–136.

GLEITMAN, H. (1995). *Psychology (4th ed.)* New York: Norton.

GLEITMAN, H., CASSIDY, K., MASSEY, C., & SCHMIDT, H. (1995). *Instructors resource manual with classroom demonstrations: Gleitman's Psychology, 4th Edition*. New York: Norton.

GLEITMAN, H., & GLEITMAN, L. R. (1979). Language use and language judgement. In C. Fillmore, D. Kempler, & W. S-Y. Wang (Eds.), *Individual differences in language ability and language behavior* (pp. 103–129). New York: Academic Press.

GLEITMAN, L. R. (1981). Maturational determinants of language growth. *Cognition, 10,* 103–114.

GLEITMAN, L. R. (1990). The structural sources of verb meanings. *Language Acquisition, 1,* 3–55.

GLEITMAN, L. R., & GLEITMAN, H. (1991). Language. In H. Gleitman (Ed.), *Psychology* (pp. 333–390). New York: Norton.

GLEITMAN, L. R., & LANDAU, B. (1994). *The acquisition of the lexicon*. Cambridge, MA: MIT Press.

GLEITMAN, L. R., NEWPORT, E. L., & GLETIMAN, H. (1984). The current status of the motherese hypothesis. *Journal of Child Language, 11,* 43–79.

GLUCKSBERG, S., & KRAUSS, R. M. (1967). What do people say after they have learned how to talk? Studies of the development of referential communication. *Merrill-Palmer Quarterly, 13,* 309–316.

GLUCKSBERG, S., KRAUSS, R. M., & HIGGINS, E. (1975). The development of referential communication skills. In F. Horowitz (Ed.), *Review of child development research: Vol. 4* (pp. 305–346). Chicago: University of Chicago Press.

GOAD, H., & INGRAM, D. (1988). Individual variation and its relevance to a theory of phonological acquisition. *Journal of Child Language, 14,* 419–432.

GOLDFIELD, B. A., & REZNICK, J. S. (1990). Early lexical acquisition: Rate, content, and the vocabulary spurt. *Journal of Child Language, 17,* 171–184.

GOLDFIELD, B. A., & REZNICK, J. S. (1996). Measuring the vocabulary spurt: A reply to Mervis and Bertrand. *Journal of Child Language, 23,* 241–246.

GOLDIN-MEADOW, S. (1982). The resilience of recursion: A study of a communication system developed without a conventional language model. In E. Wanner & L. R. Gleitman (Eds.), *Language acquisition: The state of the art* (pp. 51–77). Cambridge: Cambridge University Press.

GOLDIN-MEADOW, S., & MYLANDER, C. (1984). Gestural communication in deaf children: The effects and noneffects of parental input on early language development. *Monographs of the Society for Research in Child Development, 49,* (Nos. 3–4).

GOLDIN-MEADOW, S., SELIGMAN, M. E. P., & GELMAN, R. (1976). Language in the two-year-old. *Cognition, 4,* 189–202.

GOLINKOFF, R. M. (1983). The preverbal negotiation of failed messages: Insights into the transition period. In R. M. Golinkoff (Ed.), *The transition from prelinguistic to linguistic communication.* Hillsdale, NJ: Erlbaum.

GOLINKOFF, R. M. (1986). "I beg your pardon?": The preverbal negotiation of failed messages. *Journal of Child Language, 13,* 455–476.

GOLINKOFF, R. M., ALIOTO, A., & HIRSH-PASEK, K. (1996). Infants' word learning is facilitated when novel words are presented in infant-directed speech and in either sentence-medial or sentence-final position. In D. Cahana-Arnitay, L. Hughes, A. Stringfellow, & A. Zukowske (Eds.), *Proceedings of the 20th Boston University Conference on Language Development.* Somerville, MA: Cascadilla Press.

GOLINKOFF, R. M., & GORDON, L. (1983). In the beginning was the word: A history of the study of language acquisition. In R. M. Golinkoff (Ed.), *The transition from prelinguistic to linguistic communication* (pp. 1–19). Hillsdale, NJ: Erlbaum.

GOLINKOFF, R. M., MERVIS, C. B., & HIRSH-PASEK, K. (1994). Early object labels: The case for a developmental lexical principles framework. *Journal of Child Language, 21,* 125–156.

GOODALL, J. (1986). *The chimpanzees of Gombe: Patterns of behavior.* Cambridge, MA: Harvard University Press.

GOODGLASS, H. (1979). Effect of aphasia on the retrieval of lexicon and syntax. In C. J. Fillmore, D. Kempler, & W. S-Y. Wang (Eds.), *Individual differences in language ability and language behavior* (pp. 253–260). New York: Academic Press.

GOODGLASS, H. (1980). Naming disorders in aphasia and aging. In L. Obler & M. Albert (Eds.), *Language and communication in the elderly* (pp. 37–46). Lexington, MA: D.C. Heath.

GOODGLASS, H. (1993). *Understanding aphasia*. New York: Academic Press.

GOODLUCK, H. (1981). Children's grammar of complement-subject interpretation. In S. L. Tavakolian (Ed.), *Language acquisition and linguistic theory* (pp. 139–166). Cambridge, MA: MIT Press.

GOODLUCK, H. (1991). *Language acquisition: A linguistic introduction*. Cambridge, MA: Basil Blackwell.

GOODMAN, J. C., & NUSBAUM, H. C. (1994). *The development of speech perception: The transition from speech sounds to spoken words*. Cambridge, MA: MIT Press.

GOODMAN, M. (1984). Are creole structures innate? *Behavioral and Brain Sciences, 7,* 193–194.

GOODMAN, Y. (1984). The development of initial literacy. In H. Goelman, A. Olberg, & F. Smith (Eds.), *Awakening to literacy*. Exeter, NH: Heinemann Educational.

GOODSITT, J. V., MORSE, P. A., Ver HOEVE, J. N., & COWAN, N. (1984). Infant speech recognition in multisyllabic contexts. *Child Development, 55,* 903–910.

GOODWIN, M. H. (1990). *He-said-she-said: Talk as social organization among black children*. Bloomington: Indiana University Press.

GOODZ, N. (1989). Parental language mixing in bilingual families. *Infant Mental Health Journal, 10,* 25–44.

GOPNIK, A. (1988). Three types of early word: The emergence of social words, names and cognitive relational words in the one-word stage and their relation cognitive development. *First Language, 8,* 49–70.

GOPNIK, A., & CHOI, S. (1990). Do linguistic differences lead to cognitive differences? A cross-linguistic study of semantic and cognitive development. *First Language, 10,* 199–215.

GOPNIK, A., & CHOI, S. (1995). Names, relational words, and cognitive development in English and Korean speakers: Nouns are not always learned before verbs. In M. Tomasello & W. E. Merriman (Eds.), *Beyond names for things: Young children's acquisition of verbs* (pp. 83–90). Hillsdale, NJ: Erlbaum.

GOPNIK, A., CHOI, S., & BAUMBERGER, T. (in press). Cross-linguistic differences in early semantic and cognitive development. *Developmental Psychology*.

GOPNIK, A., & MELTZOFF, A. N. (1984). Semantic and cognitive development in 15- to 21-month-old children. *Journal of Child Language, 11,* 495–513.

GOPNIK, A., & MELTZOFF, A. N. (1986). Relations between semantic and cognitive development in the one-word stage: The specificity hypothesis. *Child Development, 57,* 1040–1053.

GOPNIK, A., & MELTZOFF, A. N. (1987). The development of categorization in the second year and its relation to other cognitive and linguistic developments. *Child Development, 58,* 1523–1531.

GOPNIK, M. (1990). Feature-blind grammar and dysphasia. *Nature, 344,* 715.

GOPNIK, M. (1994). Theoretical implications of inherited dysphasia. In Y. Levy (Ed.), *Other children, other languages* (pp. 331–358). Hillsdale, NJ: Erlbaum.

GOPNIK, M., & CRAGO, M. B. (1991). Familial aggregation of a developmental language disorder. *Cognition, 39,* 1–50.

GORDON, P. (1985). Level-ordering in lexical development. *Cognition, 21,* 73–93.

GOSWAMI, U., & BRYANT, P. (1990). *Phonological skills and learning to read.* Hillsdale, NJ: Erlbaum.

GOULD, S. J., & LEWONTIN, R. C. (1979). The spandrels of San Marco and the Panglossian paradigm: A critique of the adaptationist programme. *Proceedings of the Royal Society of London, 205,* 581–598.

GREEN, J. L., & HARKER, J. O. (1988). *Multiple perspective analyses of classroom discourse.* Norwood, NJ: Ablex.

GREENOUGH, W. T., BLACK, J. E., & WALLACE, C. S. (1987). Experience and brain development. *Child Development, 58,* 539–559.

GREGORY, S., & MOGFORD, K. (1981). Early language development in deaf children. In B. Woll, J. Kyle, & M. Deuchar (Eds.), *Perspectives on British sign language and deafness* (pp. 218–237). London: Croom Helm.

GRICE, H. P. (1957). Meaning. *The Philosophical Review, 66,* 377–388.

GRICE, H. P. (1969). Utterer's meaning and intentions. *The Philosophical Review, 78,* 147–177.

GRICE, H. P. (1975). Logic and conversation. In P. Cole & J. Morgan (Eds.), *Speech acts: Syntax and semantics. Vol. 3.* (pp. 41–58). New York: Academic Press.

GRIESER, D. L., & KUHL, P. K. (1988). Maternal speech to infants in a tonal language: Support for the universal prosodic features in motherese. *Developmental Psychology, 24,* 14–20.

GRIESER, D. L., & KUHL, P. K. (1989). Categorization of speech by infants: Support for speech-sound prototypes. *Developmental Psychology, 25,* 577–588.

GRIMM, H. (1993). Patterns of interaction and communication in language development disorders. In G. Blanken, J. Dittmann, H. Grimm, J. D. Marshall, & C-W. Wallesch (Eds.), *Linguistic disorders and pathologies: An international handbook* (pp. 697–711). Berlin: Walter de Gruyter.

GRIMM, H., & WEINERT, S. (1990). Is the syntax development of dysphasic children deviant and why: New findings to an old question. *Journal of Speech and Hearing Research, 33,* 220–28.

GRIMSHAW, J., & ROSEN, S. (1990). Knowledge and obedience: The developmental status of the binding theory. *Linguistic Inquiry, 21,* 189–222.

GRODZINSKY, Y. (1990). *Theoretical perspectives on language deficits.* Cambridge, MA: MIT Press.

GROPEN, J., PINKER, S., HOLLANDER, M., & GOLDBERG, R. (1991). Affectedness and direct objects: The role of lexical semantics in the acquisition of verb argument structure. In B. Levin & S. Pinker (Eds.), *Lexical and conceptual semantics.* Cambridge, MA: Blackwell.

GRUNWELL, P. (1981). The development of phonology: A descriptive profile. *First Language, 3,* 161–191.

GRUNWELL, P. (1986). Aspects of phonological development in later childhood. In K. Durkin (Ed.), *Language development in the school years* (pp. 34–56). Cambridge, MA: Brookline Books.

GUNNAR, M. R., & MARATSOS, M. (1992). *Modularity and constraints in language and cognition: The Minnesota Symposia on Child Psychology: Vol. 25.* Hillsdale, NJ: Erlbaum.

HAKUTA, K. (1986). *Mirror of language: The debate on bilingualism.* New York: Basic Books.

HALL, D. G., WAXMAN, S. R., & HURWITZ, W. R. (1993). How two- and four-year-old children interpret adjectives and count nouns. *Child Development, 64,* 1651–1664.

HALLIDAY, M. A. K. (1975). *Learning how to mean.* London: Edward Arnold.

HALLIDAY, M. A. K., & HASAN, R. (1976). *Cohesion in English.* New York: Longman.

HALVORSEN, C. F., & WALDROP, M. F. (1970). Maternal behavior toward own and other preschool children: The problem of "ownness." *Child Development, 41,* 839–845.

HARDING, C. G., & GOLINKOFF, R. M. (1979). The origins of intentional vocalizations in prelinguistic infants. *Child Development, 50,* 33–40.

HARDING, E., & REILLY, P. (1987). *The bilingual family: A handbook for parents.* Cambridge: Cambridge University Press.

HARRINGTON, C. (1978). Bilingual education, social stratification, and cultural pluralism. *Equal Opportunity Review* (Summer). New York: ERIC Clearinghouse on Urban Education, Teachers College, Columbia University.

HARRIS, M., BARRETT, M., JONES, D., & BROOKES, S. (1988). Linguistic input and early word meaning. *Journal of Child Language, 15,* 77–94.

HARRIS, M., JONES, D., BROOKES, S., & GRANT, J. (1986). Relations between the non-verbal context of maternal speech and rate of language development. *British Journal of Developmental Psychology, 4,* 261–268.

HART, B., & RISLEY, T. R. (1995). *Meaningful differences in the everyday experience of young American children.* Baltimore: Paul H. Brookes.

HEATH, S. E. (1982). What no bedtime story means: Narrative skills at home and school. *Language in Society, 11,* 29–76.

HEATH, S. E. (1983). *Ways with words.* Cambridge, England: Cambridge University Press.

HEWITT, R. (1987). White adolescent creole users and the politics of friendship. In B. M. Mayor & A. K. Push (Eds.), *Language, communication, and education* (pp. 85–106). London: Croom Helm.

HIGGINSON, R., & MacWHINNEY, B. (1991). *CHILDES/BIB: An annotated bibliography of child language and language disorders.* Hillsdale, NJ: Erlbaum.

HIRSCHFELD, L. A., & GELMAN, S. A. (1994). *Mapping the mind: Domain specificity in cognition and culture.* Cambridge: Cambridge University Press.

HIRSH-PASEK, K., & GOLINKOFF, R. M. (1991). Language comprehension: A new look at some old themes. In N. A. Krasnegor, D. M. Rumbaugh, R. L. Schiefelbusch, & M. Studdert-Kennedy (Eds.), *Biological and behavioral determinants of language development* (pp. 301–320). Hillsdale, NJ: Erlbaum.

HIRSH-PASEK, K., & GOLINKOFF, R. M. (1996). *The origins of grammar: Evidence from early language comprehension.* Cambridge, MA: MIT Press.

HIRSH-PASEK, K., GOLINKOFF, R. M., & NAIGLES, L. (1996). Young children's use of syntactic frames to derive meaning. In K. Hirsh-Pasek & R. M. Golinkoff (Eds.), *The origins of grammar: Evidence from early language comprehension* (pp. 123–159). Cambridge, MA: MIT Press.

HIRSH-PASEK, K., KEMLER NELSON, D. G., JUSCZYK, P. W., WRIGHT CASSIDY, K., DRUSS, B., & KENNEDY, L. (1987). Clauses are perceptual units for young infants. *Cognition, 26,* 269–286.

HISCOCK, M. (1988). Behavioral asymmetries in normal children. In D. L. Molfese & S. J. Segalowitz (Eds.), *Brain lateralization in children: Developmental implications* (pp. 85–170). New York: Guilford Press.

HOCKETT, C. F. (1960). The origin of speech. *Scientific American, 203* (48), pp. 88–96.

HOEK, D., INGRAM, D., & GIBSON, D. (1986). Some possible causes of children's early word overextensions. *Journal of Child Language, 13,* 477–494.

HOFF-GINSBERG, E. (1985). Some contributions of mothers' speech to their children's syntax growth. *Journal of Child Language, 12,* 367–385.

HOFF-GINSBERG, E. (1986). Function and structure in maternal speech: Their relation to the child's development of syntax. *Developmental Psychology, 22,* 155–163.

HOFF-GINSBERG, E. (1987). Topic relations in mother-child conversation. *First Language, 7,* 145–158.

HOFF-GINSBERG, E. (1990). Maternal speech and the child's development of syntax: A further look. *Journal of Child Language, 17,* 337–346.

HOFF-GINSBERG, E. (1991). Mother-child conversation in different social classes and communicative settings. *Child Development, 62,* 782–796.

HOFF-GINSBERG, E. (1993). Early syntax is robust, but learning object labels depends on input. Paper presented at the Sixth International Congress for the Study of Child Language, Trieste, Italy.

HOFF-GINSBERG, E. (1994). Influences of mother and child on maternal talkativeness. *Discourse Processes, 18,* 105–117.

HOFF-GINSBERG, E. (1995). The independence of communication and grammar in development. In D. MacLaughlin & S. McEwen (Eds.), *Proceedings of the 19th Annual Boston University conference on language development* (pp. 303–312). Somerville, MA: Cascadilla Press.

HOFF-GINSBERG, E., & KRUEGER, W. (1991). Older siblings as conversational partners. *Merrill-Palmer Quarterly, 37,* 465–482.

HOFF-GINSBERG, E., & SHATZ, M. (1982). Linguistic input and the child's acquisition of language. *Psychological Bulletin, 92,* 3–26.

HOFF-GINSBERG, E., & TARDIF, T. (1995). Socioeconomic status and parenting. In M. H. Bornstein (Ed.), *Handbook of Parenting, Vol. II: Ecology and Biology of Parenting* (pp. 161–188). Mahwah, NJ: Erlbaum.

HOWES, M., SIGEL, M., & BROWN, F. (1993). Early childhood memories: Accuracy and affect. *Cognition, 47,* 95–119.

HSU, J. R., CAIRNS, H. S., EISENBERG, S., & SCHLISSELBERG, G. (1989). Control and coreference in early child language. *Journal of Child Language, 16,* 599–622.

HSU, J. R., CAIRNS, H. S., & FIENGO, R. W. (1985). The development of grammars underlying children's interpretation of complex sentences. *Cognition, 20,* 25–48.

HUDSON, J. A. (1990). The emergence of autobiographic memory in mother-child conversation. In R. Fivush & J. A. Hudson (Eds.), *Knowing and remembering in young children* (pp. 166–196). New York: Cambridge University Press.

HUDSON, J. A., & NELSON, K. (1984). Play with language: Overextensions as analogies. *Journal of Child Language, 11,* 337–346.

HUDSON, J. A., & NELSON, K. (1986). Repeated encounters of a similar kind: Effects of familiarity on children's autobiographic memory. *Cognitive Development, 1,* 232–271.

HUDSON, J. A., & SHAPIRO, L. R. (1991). From knowing to telling: The development of children's scripts, stories, and personal narratives. In A. McCabe & C. Peterson (Eds.), *Developing narrative structure* (pp. 89–136). Hillsdale, NJ: Erlbaum.

HUTTENLOCHER, J. (1974). The origins of language comprehension. In R. Solso (Ed.), *Theories in cognitive psychology* (pp. 331–368). New York: Erlbaum.

HUTTENLOCHER, J., HAIGHT, W., BRYK, A., SELTZER, M., & LYONS, T. (1991). Early vocabulary growth: Relation to language input and gender. *Developmental Psychology, 27,* 236–248.

HUTTENLOCHER, J., & SMILEY, P. (1987). Early word meanings: The case of object names. *Cognitive Psychology, 19,* 63–89.

HUTTENLOCHER, P. R. (1994). Synaptogenesis in human cerebral cortex. In G. Dawson & K. W. Fischer (Eds.), *Human behavior and the developing brain* (pp. 137–152). New York: Guilford Press.

HYAMS, N. (1986). *Language acquisition and the theory of parameters.* Boston: Reidel.

HYLTENSTAM, K. (1984). The use of typological markedness conditions as predictors in second language acquisition: The case of pronominal copies in relative clauses. In R. Andersen (Ed.), *Second Languages* (pp. 39–58). Rowley, MA: Newbury House Publishers.

HYMES, D. H. (1961). Functions of speech: An evolutionary approach. In F. C. Gruder (Ed.), *Anthropology and education* (pp. 55–83). Philadelphia: University of Pennsylvania Press.

HYMES, D. H. (1972). Models of the interaction of language and social life. In J. Gumperz & D. Hymes (Eds.), *Directions in sociolinguistics: The ethnography of communication* (pp. 35–71). New York: Holt, Rinehart & Winston.

INGRAM, D. (1986). Phonological development: Production. In P. Fletcher & M. Garman (Eds.), *Language acquisition* (2nd ed.) (pp. 223–239). Cambridge: Cambridge University Press.

INGRAM, D. (1988). Toward a theory of phonological acquisition. Paper presented at the Symposium on Research in Child Language Disorders, Madison, WI.

INGRAM, D. (1989). *First language acquisition: Method, description, and explanation.* Cambridge: Cambridge University Press.

INGRAM, D. (1995). The cultural basis of prosodic modifications to infants and children: A response to Fernald's universalist theory. *Journal of Child Language, 22,* 223–234.

INGVAR, D. H., & SCHWARTZ, M. S. (1974). Blood flow patterns induced in the dominant hemisphere by speech and reading. *Brain, 97,* 273–288.

JAKOBSON, R. (1968). *Child language, aphasia, and phonological universals* (R. Keiler, Trans.). The Hague: Mouton. (Original German version published 1941)

JAMES, S. (1993). Assessing children with language disorders. In D. K. Bernstein & E. Tiegerman (Eds), *Language and communication disorders in children (3rd ed.)* (pp. 185–228). New York: Merrill/Macmillan.

JENSEMA, C. J., KARCHMER, M. A., & TRYBUS, R. J. (1978). The rated speech intelligibility of hearing impaired children: Basic relationships and a detailed analysis (Series R., no. 6). Washington, DC: Office of Demographic Studies, Gallaudet College.

JOHNSON, J., & NEWPORT, E. (1989). Critical period effects in second language learning: The influence of maturational state on the acquisition of English as a Second Language. *Cognitive Psychology, 21,* 60–99.

JOHNSON, R. E., LIDDELL, S. K., & ERTING, C. J. (1989). Unlocking the curriculum: Principles for achieving access in deaf education. Gallaudet Research Institute Working Paper 89-3. Department of Linguistics and Interpreting and the Gallaudet Research Institute, Gallaudet University, Washington, DC.

JOHN-STEINER, V. (1992). Private speech among adults. In R. M. Diaz & L. E. Berk (Eds.), *Private speech: From social interaction to self-regulation* (pp. 285–296). Hillsdale, NJ: Erlbaum.

JOHNSTON, J. R. (1982). Narratives: A new look at communication problems in older language-disordered children. *Language, Speech, and Hearing Services in Schools, 13,* 145–155.

JOHNSTON, J. R. (1988). Specific language disorders in the child. In N. J. Lass, L. V. McReynolds, J. L. Norther, & D. E. Yoder (Eds.), *Handbook of speech-language pathology and audiology* (pp. 685–715). Toronto: B. C. Decker.

JOHNSTON, J. R. (1992). Cognitive abilities of language-impaired children. In P. Fletcher & D. Hall (Eds.), *Specific speech and language disorders in children: Correlates, characteristics and outcomes* (pp. 105–116). San Diego, CA: Singular Publishing Group, Inc.

JOHNSTON, J. R. (1993). Definition and diagnosis of language development disorders. In G. Blanken, J. Dittmann, H. Grimm, J. D. Marshall, & C-W. Wallesch (Eds.), *Linguistic disorders and pathologies: An international handbook* (pp. 574–585). Berlin: Walter de Gruyter.

JOHNSTON, J. R., & SCHERY, T. (1976). The use of grammatical morphemes by children with communication disorders. In D. Morehead & A. Morehead (Eds.), *Normal and deficient child language* (pp. 239–259). Baltimore: University Park Press.

JONES, S. (1993). *The language of genes: Solving the mysteries of our genetic past, present and future.* New York: Doubleday.

JOURDAN, C. (1991). Pidgins and creoles: The blurring of categories. *Annual Review of Anthropology, 20,* 187–209.

JUSCZYK, P. W., & DERRAH, C. (1987). Representation of speech sounds by young infants. *Developmental Psychology, 23,* 648–654.

JUSCZYK, P. W., FRIEDERICI, A. D., WESSELS, J. M. I., SVENKERUD, V. Y., & JUSCZYK, A. M. (1993). Infants' sensitivity to the sound patterns of native language words. *Journal of Memory and Language, 32,* 402–420.

KAMHI, A. G. (1993). Children with specific language impairment (developmental dyphasia): Perceptual and cognitive aspects. In G. Blanken, J. Dittmann, H. Grimm, J. D. Marshall, & C-W. Wallesch (Eds.), *Linguistic disorders and pathologies: An international handbook* (pp. 625–640). Berlin: Walter de Gruyter.

KARABENICK, J. D., & MILLER, S. A. (1977). The effects of age, sex, and listener feedback on grade school children's referential communication. *Child Development, 48,* 678–683.

KARMILOFF-SMITH, A. (1979). *A functional approach to child language.* Cambridge: Cambridge University Press.

KARMILOFF-SMITH, A. (1986). Some fundamental aspects of language development after age 5. In P. Fletcher & A. M. Garman (Eds.), *Language acquisition (2nd ed.)* (pp. 455–474). Cambridge: Cambridge University Press.

KARMILOFF-SMITH, A. (1992). *Beyond modularity: A developmental perspective on cognitive science.* Cambridge, MA: MIT Press.

KARZON, R. G. (1985). Discrimination of polysyllabic sequences by one- to four-month-old infants. *Journal of Experimental Child Psychology, 39,* 326–342.

KATZ, N., BAKER, E., & MACNAMARA, J. (1974). What's in a name? A study of how children learn common and proper names. *Child Development, 50,* 1–13.

KAY, D. A., & ANGLIN, J. M. (1982). Overextension and under extension in the child's expressive and receptive speech. *Journal of Child Language, 9,* 83–98.

KAYE, K. (1977). Toward the origin of dialogue. In H. R. Schaffer (Ed.), *Studies of mother-infant interaction.* London: Academic Press.

KAYE, K. (1979). The social context of infant development. Final report to the Spencer Foundation. In R. M. Golinkoff (Ed.), *The transition from prelinguistic to linguistic communication* (pp. 1–19). Hillsdale, NJ: Erlbaum.

KAYE, K., & CHARNEY, R. (1980). How mothers maintain "dialogue" with two-year-olds. In D. R. Olson (Ed.), *The social foundations of language and thought* (pp. 211–230). New York: Norton.

KEENAN, E. O. (1974). Conversational competence in children. *Journal of Child Language, 1,* 163–183.

KEENAN, E. O., & KLEIN, E. (1975). Coherency in children's discourse. *Journal of Psycholinguistic Research, 4,* 365–380.

KEKELIS, L. S., & ANDERSEN, E. S. (1984). Family communication styles and language development. *Journal of Visual Impairment and Blindness, 78,* 54–64.

KELLER, H. (1954). *The story of my life.* New York: Doubleday. (Original copyright 1902).

KELLERMAN, E. (1978). Giving learners a break: Native language intuitions as a source of predictions about transferability. *Working Papers on Bilingualism, 15,* 59–92.

KELLERMAN, E. (1986). An eye for an eye: Crosslinguistic constraints on the development of the L2 lexicon. In E. Kellerman & M. Sharwood Smith (Eds.), *Crosslinguistic influences in second language acquisition* (pp. 35–48). Elmsford, NY: Pergamon Press.

KELLY, M. (1996). The role of phonology in grammatical category assignments. In J. L. Morgan & K. Demuth (Eds.), *Signal to syntax: Bootstrapping from speech to grammar in early acquisition* (pp. 249–262). Mahwah, NJ: Erlbaum.

KEMLER NELSON, D. G., HIRSH-PASEK, K., JUSCZYK, P. W., & WRIGHT CASSIDY, K. (1989). How the prosodic cues in motherese might assist language learning. *Journal of Child Language, 16,* 55–68.

KEMPER, S. (1984). The development of narrative skills: Explanations and entertainments. In S. A. Kuczaj (Ed.), *Discourse development* (pp. 99–124). New York: Springer-Verlag.

KEMPER, S. (1986). Imitation of complex syntactic constructions by elderly adults. *Applied Psycholinguistics, 7,* 277–287.

KEMPER, S. (1987a). Life-span changes in syntactic complexity. *Journal of Gerontology, 42,* 232–238.

KEMPER, S. (1987b). Syntactic complexity and the recall of prose by middle-aged and elderly adults. *Experimental Aging Research, 13,* 47–52.

KEMPER, S. (1990). Adults' diaries: Changes made to written narratives across the life span. *Discourse Processes, 13,* 207–223.

KEMPER, S. (1992). Language and aging. In F. I. M. Craik & T. A. Salthouse (Eds.), *The handbook of aging and cognition* (pp. 213–270). Hillsdale, NJ: Erlbaum.

KEMPER, S., KYNETTE, C., & NORMAN, S. (1992). Age differences in spoken language. In R. West & J. Sinnott (Eds.), *Language, memory, and aging: Current research and methodology* (pp. 138–152). New York: Springer-Verlag.

KEMPER, S., KYNETTE, D., RASH, S., O'BRIEN, K., & SPROTT, R. (1989). Life-span changes to adults' language: Effects of memory and genre. *Applied Psycholinguistics, 10,* 49–66.

KERNAN, K. (1974). The acquisition of formal and colloquial styles of speech by Samoan children. *Anthropological Linguistics, 16,* 107–119.

KILLEN, M., & NAIGLES, L. R. (1995). Preschool children pay attention to their addressees: Effects of gender composition on peer disputes. *Discourse Processes, 19,* 329–346.

KIMURA, D. (1964). Left-right differences in the perception of melodies. *Quarterly Journal of Experimental Psychology, 16,* 355–358.

KIMURA, D. (1967). Functional asymmetry of the brain in dichotic listening. *Cortex, 3,* 163–178.

KIMURA, D. (1979). Neuromotor mechanisms in the evolution of human communication. In H. D. Steklis (Ed.), *Neurobiology of social communication in primates: An evolutionary perspective* (pp. 197–220). New York: Academic Press.

KING, M-C., & WILSON, A. C. (1975). Evolution at two levels in humans and chimpanzees. *Science, 188,* 107–115.

KINSBOURNE, M. (1993). Neurological aspects of language development disorders. In G. Blanken, J. Dittmann, H. Grimm, J. D. Marshall, & C.-W. Wallesch (Eds.), *Linguistic disorders and pathologies: An international handbook* (pp. 585–594). Berlin: Walter de Gruyter.

KLANN-DELIUS, G. (1981). Sex and language acquisition—Is there any influence? *Journal of Pragmatics, 5,* 1–25.

KLEE, T., & FITZGERALD, M. D. (1985). The relation between grammatical development and mean length of utterance in morphemes. *Journal of Child Language, 12,* 251–270.

KLEIN, S. K., & RAPIN, I. (1993). Intermittent conductive hearing loss and language development. In D. Bishop & K. Mogford (Eds.), *Language development in exceptional children* (pp. 96–109). Hove, England: Erlbaum.

KLIMA, E. S., & BELLUGI, U. (1967). Syntactic regularities. In J. Lyon & R. J. Wales (Eds.), *Psychological Papers*. Edinburgh: University Press.

KLIMA, E. S., & BELLUGI, U. (1979). *The signs of language*. Cambridge, MA: Harvard University Press.

KOHLBERG, L., YEAGER, J., & HJERTHOLM, E. (1968). Private speech: Four studies and a review of theories. *Child Development, 39,* 691–736.

KOLB, B. (1989). Brain development, plasticity, and behavior. *American Psychologist, 44,* 1203–1212.

KONSTANTAREAS, M. M. (1993). Language and communicative behavior in autistic disorder. In G. Blanken, J. Dittmann, H. Grimm, J. D. Marshall, & C-W. Wallesch (Eds.), *Linguistic disorders and pathologies: An international handbook* (pp. 804–824). Berlin: Walter de Gruyter.

KRASHEN, S. (1973). Lateralization, language learning and the critical period: Some new evidence. *Language Learning, 23,* 63–74.

KRASHEN, S. (1985). *The input hypothesis*. London: Longman.

KRASHEN, S., & TERRELL, T. (1983). *The natural approach*. Hayward, CA: The Alemany Press.

KUHL, P. K. (1976). Speech perception in early infancy: The acquisition of speech-sound categories. In S. K. Hirsh, D. H. Eldredge, I. J. Hirsh, & S. R. Silverman (Eds.), *Hearing and Davis: Essays honoring Hallowell Davis* (pp. 265–280). St. Louis: Washington University Press.

KUHL, P. K. (1980). Perceptual constancy for speech-sound categories in early infancy. In G. H. Yeni-Komshian, J. F. Kavanagh, & C. A. Ferguson (Eds.), *Child Phonology: Vol. 2. Perception* (pp. 41–66). New York: Academic Press.

KUHL, P. K. (1983). Perception of auditory equivalence classes for speech in early infancy. *Infant Behavior and Development, 6,* 263–285.

KUHL, P. K. (1987). Perception of speech and sound in early infancy. In P. Salapatek & L. Cohen (Eds.), *Handbook of Infant Perception* (pp. 275–382). New York: Academic Press.

KUHL, P. K., & MELTZOFF, A. N. (1988). Speech as an intermodal object of perception. In A. Yonas (Ed.), *Perceptual development in infancy: The Minnesota symposia on child psychology. Vol. 20* (pp. 235–266). Hillsdale, NJ: Erlbaum.

KUHL, P. K., & MILLER, J. D. (1975). Speech perception by the chinchilla: Voiced-voiceless distinction in alveolar plosive consonants. *Science, 190,* 69–72.

KUHL, P. K., WILLIAMS, K. A., LACERDA, F., STEVENS, K. N., & LINDBLOM, B. (1992). Linguistic experience alters phonetic perception in infants by 6 months of age. *Science, 255,* 606–608.

LABOV, W. (1970). Stages in the acquisition of standard English. In H. Hungerford, J. Robinson, & J. Sledd (Eds.), *English linguistics* (pp. 275–302). Glenview, IL: Scott Foresman.

LABOV, W. (1972a). *Language in the inner city.* Philadelphia: University of Pennsylvania Press.

LABOV, W. (1972b). *Sociolinguistic patterns.* Philadelphia: University of Pennsylvania Press.

LADO, R. (1957). *Linguistics across cultures.* Ann Arbor: University of Michigan Press.

LAKOFF, R. (1975). *Language and woman's place.* New York: Harper and Row.

LANDAU, B., & GLEITMAN, L. R. (1985). *Language and experience: Evidence from the blind child.* Cambridge, MA: Harvard University Press.

LANE, H. (1976). *The wild boy of Aveyron.* Cambridge, MA: Harvard University Press.

LANE, H. (1984). *When the mind hears.* New York: Random House.

LANZA, E. (1992). Can bilingual two-year-olds code switch? *Journal of Child Language, 19,* 633–658.

LAWRENCE, V., & SHIPLEY, E. F. (1996). Parental speech to middle and working class children from two racial groups in three settings. *Applied Psycholinguistics, 17.*

LAWSON, C. (1967). Request patterns in a two-year-old. Unpublished manuscript. Berkeley, CA.

LEAKEY, R., & LEWIN, R. (1992). *Origins reconsidered: In search of what makes us human.* New York: Doubleday.

LEDERBERG, A. (1980). The language environment of children with language delays. *Journal of Pediatric Psychology, 5,* 141–158.

LEE, V. E., & CRONINGER, R. G. (1993). The relative importance of home and school in the development of literacy skills for middle-grade students. Paper presented at the meetings of the Society for Research in Child Development, New Orleans, LA.

LENNEBERG, E. H. (1964). The capacity for language acquisition. In J. A. Fodor & J. J. Katz (Eds.), *The structure of language: Readings in the philosophy of language* (pp. 579–603). Englewood Cliffs, NJ: Prentice-Hall.

LENNEBERG, E. H. (1967). *Biological foundations of language.* New York: Wiley.

LEONARD, L. B. (1979). Language impairment in children. *Merrill-Palmer Quarterly, 25,* 205–232.

LEONARD, L. B. (1987). Is specific language impairment a useful construct? In S. Rosenberg (Ed.), *Advances in applied psycholinguistics, Vol. 1: Disorders of first language development* (pp. 1–39). Cambridge: Cambridge University Press.

LEONARD, L. B. (1989). Language learnability and specific language impairment in children. *Applied Psycholinguistics, 10,* 179–202.

LEONARD, L. B. (1991). Specific language impairment as a clinical category. *Language, Speech, and Hearing Services in Schools, 22,* 66–68.

LEONARD, L. B., BORTOLLINI, U., CASELLI, M. C., McGREGOR, K. K., & SABBADINI, L. (1992). Morphological deficits in children with specific language impairment: The status of features in the underlying grammar. *Language Acquisition, 2,* 151–179.

LEONARD, L. B., McGREGOR, K. K., & ALLEN, G. D. (1992). Grammatical morphology and speech perception in children with specific language impairment. *Journal of Speech and Hearing Research, 35,* 1076–1085.

LEONARD, L. B., NEWHOFF, M., & MESELAM, L. (1980). Individual differences in early child phonology. *Applied Psycholinguistics, 1,* 7–30.

LEONARD, L. B., SABBADINI, L., VOLTERRA, V., & LEONARD, J. S. (1988). Some influences on the grammar of English- and Italian-speaking children with specific language impairment. *Applied Psycholinguistics, 9,* 39–57.

LEONARD, L. B., & SCHWARTZ, R. G. (1985). Early linguistic development of children with specific language impairment. In K. E. Nelson (Ed.), *Children's language: Vol. 5* (pp. 291–318). Hillsdale, NJ: Erlbaum.

LEOPOLD, W. F. (1939–1949). *Speech development of a bilingual child: a linguist's record.* (Vols. 1–4). Evanston, IL: Northwestern University Press.

LEOPOLD, W. F. (1952). *Bibliography of child language.* Evanston, IL: Northwestern University Press.

LEVER, J. (1976). Sex differences in the games children play. *Social Problems, 23,* 478–487.

LEVY, E. (1989). Monologue as development of the text-forming function of language. In K. Nelson (Ed.), *Narratives from the crib* (pp. 123–170). Cambridge, MA: Harvard University Press.

LEVY, Y. (1983). It's frogs all the way down. *Cognition, 15,* 75–93.

LEVY, Y., AMIR, N., & SHALEV, R. (1992). Linguistic development of a child with a congenital, localised L. H. lesion. *Cognitive Neuropsychology, 9,* 1–32.

LI, C. N., & THOMPSON, S. A. (1977). The acquisition of tone in Mandarin-speaking children. *Journal of Child Language, 4,* 185–201.

LIBERMAN, I. Y., SHANKWEILER, D., FISCHER, F. W., & CARTER, B. (1974). Explicit syllable and phoneme segmentation in the young child. *Journal of Experimental Child Psychology, 18,* 201–212.

LIEBERMAN, D. A. (1993). *Learning: Behavior and cognition.* Pacific Grove, CA: Brooks/ Cole.

LIEBERMAN, P. (1975). *On the origins of language: An introduction to the evolution of human speech.* New York: Macmillan.

LIEBERMAN, P. (1984). *The biology and evolution of language.* Cambridge, MA: Harvard University Press.

LIEBERMAN, P. (1991). *Uniquely human: The evolution of speech, thought, and selfless behavior.* Cambridge, MA: Harvard University Press.

LIEVEN, E. V. M. (1994). Crosslinguistic and crosscultural aspects of language addressed to children. In C. Gallaway & B. J. Richards (Eds.), *Input and interaction in language acquisition* (pp. 56–73). Cambridge: Cambridge University Press.

LIMA, S., CORRIGAN, R., & IVERSON, G. (Eds.). (1994). *The reality of linguistic rules.* Philadelphia, PA: Benjamins.

LIMBER, J. (1973). The genesis of complex sentences. In T. Moore (Ed.), *Cognitive development and the acquisition of language* (pp. 169–186). New York: Academic Press.

LINDHOLM, K. J. (1980). Bilingual children: Some interpretations of cognitive and linguistic development. In K. E. Nelson (Ed.), *Children's language: Vol. 2* (pp. 215–266). New York: Gardner Press.

LINDNER, K., & JOHNSTON, J. R. (1992). Grammatical morphology in language-impaired children acquiring English or German as their first language: A functional perspective. *Applied Psycholinguistics, 13,* 115–129.

LITOWITZ, B. E. (1987). Language and the young deaf. In E. D. Mindel & M. Vernon (Eds.), *They grow in silence: Understanding deaf children and adults* (pp. 111–147). Boston: College Hill Press.

LOCKE, J. (1959). *An essay concerning human understanding.* (A. C. Fraser, Annot.). New York: Dover.

LOCKE, J. L. (1983). *Phonological acquisition and change.* New York: Academic Press.

LOCKE, J. L. (1993). *The child's path to spoken language.* Cambridge, MA: Harvard University Press.

LOCKE, J. L., & PEARSON, D. M. (1992). Vocal learning and the emergence of phonological capacity: A neurobiological approach. In C. A. Ferguson, L. Menn, & S. Stoel-Gammon (Eds.), *Phonological Development* (pp. 91–129). Timonium, MD: York Press.

LOVAAS, O. I. (1987). Behavioral treatment and normal educational and intellectual functioning in young autistic children. *Journal of Consulting and Clinical Psychology, 55,* 3–9.

LOVAAS, O. I., & SMITH, T. (1988). Intensive behavioral treatment for young autistic children. In B. B. Lahey & A. E. Kazdin (Eds.), *Advances in clinical psychology: Vol. II* (pp. 285–324). New York: Plenum.

LOVELAND, K. A., & LANDRY, S. H. (1986). Joint attention and language in autism and developmental language delay. *Journal of Autism and Developmental Disorders, 16,* 335–349.

LUCARIELLO, J. (1987). Concept formation and its relation to word learning and use in the second year. *Journal of Child Language, 14,* 309–332.

LUCARIELLO, J., & NELSON, K. (1987). Remembering and planning talk between mothers and children. *Discourse Processes, 10,* 219–235.

LUDLOW, C. L., & DOOMAN, A. G. (1992). Genetic aspects of idiopathic speech and language disorders. *Molecular Biology and Genetics, 25,* 979–994.

MACKEN, M. A., & FERGUSON, C. (1983). Cognitive aspects of phonological development: Model, evidence, and issues. In K. E. Nelson (Ed.), *Children's language: Vol. 4* (pp. 256–282). Hillsdale, NJ: Erlbaum.

MacLEAN, M., BRYANT, P. E., & BRADLEY, L. (1987). Rhymes, nursery rhymes and reading in early childhood. *Merrill-Palmer Quarterly, 33,* 255–282.

MacWHINNEY, B. (1978). The acquisition of morphophonology. *Monographs of the Society for Research in Child Development, 43,* (1, Serial No. 174).

MacWHINNEY, B. (1987). The competition model. In B. MacWhinney (Ed.), *Mechanisms of language acquisition* (pp. 249–308). Hillsdale, NJ: Erlbaum.

MacWHINNEY, B. (1991). *The CHILDES Project: Tools for analyzing talk.* Hillsdale, NJ: Erlbaum.

MacWHINNEY, B., BATES, E., & KLIEGL, R. (1984). Cue validity and sentence interpretation in English, German, and Italian. *Journal of Verbal Learning and Verbal Behavior, 23,* 127–150.

MacWHINNEY, B., & SNOW, C. (1985). The child language data exchange system. *Journal of Child Language, 12,* 271–296.

MALTZ, D. N., & BORKER, R. A. (1982). A cultural approach to male-female miscommunication. In J. J. Gumperz (Ed.), *Language and social identity* (pp. 196–216). Cambridge: Cambridge University Press.

MANDEL, D. R., JUSCZYK, P. W., & PISONI, D. B. (1995). Infants' recognition of the sound patterns of their own names. *Psychological Science, 6,* 314–317.

MANN, V. A. (1986). Phonological awareness: The role of reading experience. *Cognition, 24,* 65–92.

MANN, V. A. (1991). Are we taking too narrow a view of the conditions for development of phonological awareness? In S. A. Brady & D. P. Shankweiler (Eds.), *Phonological processes in literacy* (pp. 55–64). Hillsdale, NJ: Erlbaum.

MANNLE, S., & TOMASELLO, M. (1987). Fathers, siblings, and the bridge hypothesis. In K. Nelson & A. Van Kleeck (Eds.), *Children's language: Vol. 6* (pp. 23–42). Hillsdale, NJ: Erlbaum.

MARATSOS, M. (1983). Some current issues in the study of the acquisition of grammar. In J. Flavell and E. Markman (Eds.), *Carmichael's handbook of child psychology: Vol. 3* (pp. 709–786). New York: Wiley.

MARATSOS, M. (1988). Cross-linguistic analysis, universals, and language acquisition. In F. S. Kessel (Ed.), *The development of language and language researchers: Essays in honor of Roger Brown* (pp. 121–152). Hillsdale, NJ: Erlbaum.

MARATSOS, M. (1991). How the acquisition of nouns may be different from that of verbs. In Krasnegor, N. A., Rumbaugh, D. M., Schiefelbusch, R. L., & Studdert-Kennedy, M. (Eds.), *Biological and behavioral determinants of language development* (pp. 76–88). Hillsdale, NJ: Erlbaum.

MARATSOS, M. (1993). Discussant's remarks in the symposium "Issues in the acquisition of inflectional processes," presented at the meetings of the Society for Research in Child Development, New Orleans.

MARATSOS, M. P., & CHALKLEY, M. A. (1980). The internal language of children's syntax: The ontogenesis and representation of syntactic categories. In K. E. Nelson (Ed.), *Children's language: Vol. 2* (pp. 127–214). New York: Gardner Press.

MARCUS, G. F. (1993). Negative evidence in language acquisition. *Cognition, 46,* 53–85.

MARCUS, G. F. (1995). Children's overregularization of English plurals: A quantitative analysis. *Journal of Child Language, 22,* 447–460.

MARCUS, G. F., PINKER, S., ULLMAN, M., HOLLANDER, M., ROSEN T. J., & XU, F. (1992). Overregularization in language acquisition. *Monographs of the Society for Research in Child Development, 57,* (4, Serial No. 228).

MARKMAN, E. M. (1977). Realizing that you don't understand: A preliminary investigation. *Child Development, 48,* 986–992.

MARKMAN, E. M. (1979). Realizing that you don't understand: Elementary school children's awareness of inconsistencies. *Child Development, 50,* 643–655.

MARKMAN, E. M. (1989). *Categorization and naming in children: Problems of induction.* Cambridge, MA: MIT Press.

MARKMAN, E. M. (1991). The whole-object, taxonomic, and mutual exclusivity assumptions as initial constraints on word meanings. In S. A. Gelman & J. P. Byrnes (Eds.), *Perspectives on language and thought: Interrelations in development* (pp. 72–106). Cambridge: Cambridge University Press.

MARKMAN, E. M. (1992). Constraints on word learning: Speculations about their nature, origins and domain specificity. In M. R. Gunnar & M. Maratsos (Eds.), *Modularity and constraints in language and cognition: The Minnesota symposia on child psychology: Vol. 25* (pp. 59–103). Hillsdale, NJ: Erlbaum.

MARKMAN, E. M. (1994). Constraints on word meaning in early language acquisition. In L. Gleitman & B. Landau (Eds.), *The acquisition of the lexicon* (pp. 199–229). Cambridge, MA: MIT Press/Elsevier.

MARKMAN, E. M., & HUTCHINSON, J. E. (1984). Children's sensitivity to constraints on word meaning: Taxonomic vs. thematic relations. *Cognitive Psychology, 16,* 1–27.

MARKMAN, E. M., & WACHTEL, G. A. (1988). Children's use of mutual exclusivity to constrain the meanings of words. *Cognitive Psychology, 20,* 121–157.

MARLER, P. (1970). Birdsong and speech development: Could there be parallels? *American Scientist, 58,* 669–673.

MARLER, P., & TENAZA, R. (1977). Signalling behavior of apes with special reference to vocalization. In T. A. Sebeok (Ed.), *How animals communicate* (pp. 965–1033). Bloomington: Indiana University Press.

MARTINDALE, C. (1991). *Cognitive psychology.* Pacific Grove, CA: Brooks/Cole.

MARTLEW, M. (1986). The development of written language. In K. Durkin (Ed.), *Language development in the school years* (pp. 117–139). London: Croom Helm.

MATTINGLY, I. G. (1984). Reading, linguistic awareness and language acquisition. In J. Downing & R. Valtin (Eds.), *Linguistic awareness and learning to read* (pp. 9–25). New York: Springer-Verlag.

MAYBERRY, R., & WODLINGER-COHEN, R. (1987). After the revolution: Educational practice and the deaf child's communication skills. In E. D. Mindell & M. Vernon (Eds.), *They grow in silence: Understanding deaf children and adults* (pp. 149–185). Boston: College Hill Publishing.

MAYBERRY, R., WODLINGER-COHEN, R., & GOLDIN-MEADOW, S. (1987). Symbolic development in deaf children. In D. Chicchetti & M. Beeghly (Eds.), *Symbolic development in atypical children* (pp. 109–125). New Directions for Child Development, No. 36. San Francisco: Josey-Bass.

MAZZIOTTA, J. C., & METTER, E. J. (1988). Brain cerebral metabolic mapping of normal and abnormal language and its acquisition during development. In F. Plum (Ed.), *Language, communication, and the brain* (pp. 245–266). New York: Raven Press.

McCABE, A., & PETERSON, C. (1984). What makes a good story? *Journal of Psycholinguistic Research, 13,* 457–480.

McCABE, A., & PETERSON, C. (1991). Getting the story: A longitudinal study of parental styles in eliciting narratives and developing narrative skill. In A. McCabe & C. Peterson (Eds.), *Developing narrative structure* (pp. 217–253). Hillsdale, NJ: Erlbaum.

McCARTHY, D. (1930). The language development of the preschool child. *Institute of Child Welfare Monograph* (Serial No. 4). Minneapolis: University of Minnesota Press.

McCARTHY, D. (1954). Language development in children. In L. Carmichael (Ed.), *Manual of child psychology* (2nd ed.) (pp. 492–630). New York: Wiley.

McCARTNEY, K. (1984). Effect of quality of day care environment on children's language development. *Developmental Psychology, 20,* 244–260.

McDANIEL, D., & CAIRNS, H. S. (1990). Processing and acquisition of control structures by young children. In L. Frazier & J. de Villiers (Eds.), *Language processing and language acquisition* (pp. 311–322). Dordrect, Holland: Kluwer Academic.

McDANIEL, D., CAIRNS, H. S., & HSU, J. R. (1990/1991). Control principles in the grammars of young children. *Language Acquisition, 4,* 297–335.

McGLONE, J. (1980). Sex differences in human brain asymmetry: A critical survey. *Behavioral and Brain Sciences, 3,* 215–263.

McKEOWN, M. G., & CURTIS, M. E. (Eds.). (1987). *The nature of vocabulary acquisition.* Hillsdale, NJ: Erlbaum.

McNAMEE, G. D. (1987). The social origins of narrative skills. In M. Hickmann (Ed.), *Social and functional approaches to language and thought* (pp. 287–304). New York: Academic Press.

McSHANE, J. (1980). *Learning to talk.* Cambridge: Cambridge University Press.

McTEAR, M. (1985). *Children's conversation.* Oxford: Basil Blackwell.

MEADOW, K. P. (1980). *Deafness and child development.* Berkeley: University of California Press.

MEHLER, J., DUPOUX, E., NAZZI, T., & DEHAENE-LAMBERTZ, G. (1996). In J. L. Morgan & K. Demuth (Eds.), *Signal to syntax: Bootstrapping from speech to grammar in early acquisition* (pp. 101–116). Mahwah, NJ: Erlbaum.

MEHLER, J., JUSCZYK, P., LAMBERTZ, G., HALSTED, N., BERTONCINI, J., & AMIEL-TISON, C. (1988). A precursor of language acquisition in young infants. *Cognition, 29,* 143–178.

MEIER, R. P. (1984). Sign as creole. *Behavioral and Brain Sciences, 7,* 201–202.

MEISEL, J. M. (1989). Early differentiation of languages in bilingual children. In K. Hyltenstam & L. K. Obler (Eds.), *Bilingualism across the lifespan: Aspects of acquisition, maturity, and loss* (pp. 13–40). Cambridge: Cambridge University Press.

MENN, L., & STOEL-GAMMON, C. (1995). Phonological development. In P. Fletcher & B. MacWhinney (Eds.), *The handbook of child language* (pp. 335–360). Oxford: Basil Blackwell.

MENYUK, P. (1993). Children with specific language impairment (developmental dysphasia): Linguistic aspects. In G. Blanken, J. Dittmann, H. Grimm, J. D. Marshall, & C-W. Wallesch (Eds.), *Linguistic disorders and pathologies: An international handbook* (pp. 606–624). Berlin: Walter de Gruyter.

MENYUK, P., & MENN, L. (1979). Early strategies for the perception and production of words and sounds. In P. Fletcher & M. Garman (Eds.), *Language acquisition* (pp. 49–70). Cambridge: Cambridge University Press.

MENYUK, P., MENN, L., & SILBER, R. (1986). Early strategies for the perception and production of words and sounds. In P. Fletcher & M. Garman (Eds.), *Language acquisition* (2nd ed.) (pp. 198–222). Cambridge: Cambridge University Press.

MERGLER, N., FAUST, M., & GOLDSTEIN, M. (1985). Storytelling as an age-dependent skill. *International Journal of Aging and Human Development, 20,* 205–228.

MERRIMAN, W. E., & BOWMAN, L. L. (1989). The mutual exclusivity bias in children's word learning. *Monographs of the Society for Research in Child Development, 54* (Serial No. 220).

MERVIS, C. B., & BERTRAND, J. (1994). Acquisition of the novel name-nameless category principle. *Child Development, 65,* 1646–1662.

MERVIS, C. B., & BERTRAND, J. (1995). Early lexical acquisition and the vocabulary spurt: A response to Goldfield & Reznick. *Journal of Child Language, 22,* 461–468.

MERVIS, C. B., & LONG, L. M. (1987). Words refer to whole objects: Young children's interpretation of the referent of a novel word. Paper presented at the biennial meeting of the Society for Research in Child Development, Baltimore, MD.

MERVIS, C. B., & MERVIS, C. A. (1988). Role of adult input in young children's category evolution: An observational study. *Journal of Child Language, 15,* 257–272.

MERVIS, C. B., MERVIS, C. A., JOHNSON, K. E., & BERTRAND, J. (1992). Studying early lexical development: The value of the systematic diary method. In C. Rovee-Collier & L. P. Lipsitt (Eds.), *Advances in infancy research: Vol. 7* (pp. 291–379). Norwood, NJ: Ablex.

MICHAELS, S. (1981). "Sharing time": Children's narrative styles and differential access to literacy. *Language in Society, 10,* 423–442.

MICHAELS, S. (1983). The role of adult assistance in children's acquisition of literate discourse strategies. *Volta Review, 85,* 72–85.

MILLER, G. A. (1977). *Spontaneous apprentices: Children and language.* New York: Seabury.

MILLER, G. A. (1981). *Language and speech.* San Francisco: W. H. Freeman.

MILLER, J. D., WIER, C. C., PASTORE, R. E., KELLEY, W. J., & DOOLING, R. J. (1976). Discrimination and labeling of noise-buzz sequences with varying noise-lead times: An example of categorical perception. *Journal of the Acoustic Society of America, 60,* 410–417.

MILLER, J. F. (1987). Language and communication characteristics of children with Down syndrome. In S. M. Pueschel, C. Tingey, J. E. Rynders, A. C. Crocker, & D. M. Crutcher (Eds.), *New perspectives on Down syndrome* (pp. 233–262). Baltimore: Paul H. Brookes.

MILLER, J. F., & CHAPMAN, R. S. (1981). The relation between age and mean length of utterance. *Journal of Speech and Hearing Research, 24,* 154–161.

MILLER, J. F., & CHAPMAN, R. S. (1985). *SALT II: Systematic analysis of language transcripts.* Madison: Language Analysis Laboratory, Waisman Center on Mental Retardation and Human Development, University of Wisconsin-Madison.

MILLER, J. F., & KLEE, T. (1995). Computational approaches to the analysis of language impairment. In P. Fletcher & B. MacWhinney (Eds.), *The handbook of child language* (pp. 454–572). Oxford: Blackwell Publishers.

MILLER, J. L., & EIMAS, P. D. (1994). Observations on speech perception, its development, and the search for a mechanism. In J. C. Goodman & H. C. Nusbaum (Eds.), *The development of speech perception: The transition from speech sounds to spoken words* (pp. 37–56). Cambridge, MA: MIT Press.

MILLER, P. (1986). Teasing as language socialization and verbal play in a white working-class community. In B. B. Schieffelin & E. Ochs (Eds.), *Language socialization across cultures* (pp. 199–212). Cambridge: Cambridge University Press.

MILLER, P. J., & SPERRY, L. L. (1988). Early talk about the past: The origins of conversational stories of personal experience. *Journal of Child Language, 15,* 293–315.

MILLER, W., & ERVIN, S. (1964). The development of grammar in child language. In U. Bellugi & R. Brown (Eds.), The acquisition of language. *Monographs of the Society for Research in Child Development, 29,* 9–34.

MILLS, A. (1985). The acquisition of German. In D. I. Slobin (Ed.), *The crosslinguistic study of language acquisition: Vol. 1. The data* (pp. 141–254). Hillsdale, NJ: Erlbaum.

MILLS, A. (1987). The development of phonology in the blind child. In B. Dodd & R. Campbell (Eds.), *Hearing by eye: The psychology of lip-reading* (pp. 145–162). London: Erlbaum.

MILLS, A. (1993). Visual handicap. In D. Bishop & K. Mogford (Eds.), *Language development in exceptional children* (pp. 150–164). Hove, England: Erlbaum.

MILLS, D., COFFEY, S., & NEVILLE, H. (1993). Language acquisition and cerebral specialization in 20-month-old children. *Journal of Cognitive Neuroscience, 5,* 326–342.

MILLS, D., COFFEY, S., & NEVILLE, H. (1994). Changes in cerebral organization in infancy during primary language acquisition. In G. Dawson & K. Fischer (Eds.), *Human behavior and the developing brain.* New York: Guilford.

MILNER, B. (1974). Hemispheric specialization: Scope and limits. In F. O. Schmitt & F. G. Worden (Eds.), *The Neurosciences: Third Study Program* (pp. 75–89). Cambridge, MA: MIT Press.

MINAMI, M., & McCABE, A. (1995). Rice balls and bear hunts: Japanese and North American family narrative patterns. *Journal of Child Language, 22,* 423–446.

MOGFORD, K. (1993). Oral language acquisition in the prelinguistically deaf. In D. Bishop & K. Mogford (Eds.), *Language development in exceptional children* (pp. 110–131). Hove, England: Erlbaum.

MOGFORD-BEVAN, K. (1993). Language acquisition and development with sensory impairment: Hearing-impaired children. In G. Blanken, J. Dittmann, H. Grimm,

J. D. Marshall, & C-W. Wallesch (Eds.), *Linguistic disorders and pathologies: An international handbook* (pp. 660–679). Berlin: Walter de Gruyter.

MOLFESE, D. L., & BETZ, J. C. (1988). Electrophysiological indices of the early development of lateralization for language and cognition, and their implications for predicting later development. In D. L. Molfese & S. J. Segalowitz (Eds.), *Brain lateralization in children: Developmental implications* (pp. 171–190). New York: Guilford Press.

MOLFESE, D. L., FREEMAN, R. B., & PALERMO, D. S. (1975). The ontogeny of brain lateralization for speech and nonspeech stimuli. *Brain and Language, 2,* 356–368.

MOORES, D. F. (1978). Current research and theory with the deaf: Educational implications. In L. Liben (Ed.), *Deaf children: Developmental perspectives* (pp. 173–193). New York: Academic Press.

MORAIS, J., CARY, L., ALEGRIA, J., & BERTELSON, P. (1979). Does awareness of speech as a sequence of phones arise spontaneously? *Cognition, 7,* 323–331.

MORGAN, J. L. (1986). *From simple input to complex grammar.* Cambridge, MA: MIT Press.

MORGAN, J. L. (1990). Input, innateness, and induction in language acquisition. *Developmental Psychobiology, 23,* 661–678.

MORGAN, J. L., & DEMUTH, K. (1996). *Signal to syntax: Bootstrapping from speech to grammar in early acquisition.* Mahwah, NJ: Erlbaum.

MOWRER, O. (1960). *Learning theory and symbolic processes.* New York: Wiley.

MUELLER, E., BLEIER, M., KRAKOW, J., HEGEDUS, K., & COURNOYER, P. (1977). The development of peer verbal interaction among two-year-old boys. *Child Development, 48,* 284–287.

MUYSKEN, P. (1988). Are creoles a special type of language? In F. J. Newmeyer (Ed.), *Linguistics: The Cambridge survey: Vol. II. Linguistic theory: Extensions and implications* (pp. 285–301). Cambridge: Cambridge University Press.

NAIGLES, L. (1990). Children use syntax to learn verb meanings. *Journal of Child Language, 17,* 357–374.

NAIGLES, L. (1995). The use of multiple frames in verb learning via syntactic bootstrapping. *Cognition, 58,* 221–251.

NAIGLES, L., EISENBERG, A. R., & KAKO, E. T. (1992, November). Acquiring a language-specific lexicon: Motion verbs in English and Spanish. Lecture presented at the International Pragmatics Association Conference, Antwerp, Belgium.

NAIGLES, L., & GELMAN, S. (1995). Overextensions in comprehension and production revisited: Preferential-looking in a study of *dog, cat,* and *cow. Journal of Child Language, 22,* 19–46.

NAIGLES, L., & HOFF-GINSBERG, E. (1995). Input to verb learning: Evidence for the plausibility of syntactic bootstrapping. *Developmental Psychology, 31,* 827–837.

NEILS, J., & ARAM, D. M. (1986). Family history of children with developmental language disorders. *Perceptual and Motor Skills, 63,* 655–658.

NELSON, K. (1973). Structure and strategy in learning to talk. *Monographs of the Society for Research in Child Development, 1978, 38* (1 and 2, Serial No. 149).

NELSON, K. (1981). Individual differences in language development: Implications for development and language. *Developmental Psychology, 17,* 170–187.

NELSON, K. (1988). Constraints on word learning? *Cognitive Development, 3,* 221–246.

NELSON, K. (1989). *Narratives from the crib.* Cambridge, MA: Harvard University Press.

NELSON, K. (1990). Comment on Behrend's "Constraints and Development." *Cognitive Development, 5,* 331–339.

NELSON, K., & GRUENDEL, J. M. (1979). At morning it's lunchtime: A scriptal view of children's dialogues. *Discourse Processes, 2,* 73–94.

NELSON, K., & GRUENDEL, J. M. (1981). Generalized event representations: Basic building blocks of cognitive development. In A. L. Brown & M. E. Lamb (Eds.), *Advances in developmental psychology: Vol. 1* (pp. 131–158). Hillsdale, NJ: Erlbaum.

NELSON, K., & LUCARIELLO, J. (1985). The development of meaning in first words. In M. Barrett (Ed.), *Children's single-word speech.* New York: Wiley.

NELSON, K. E., DENNINGER, M. M., BONVILLIAN, J. D., KAPLAN, B. J., & BAKER, N. D. (1984). Maternal input adjustments and nonadjustments as related to children's linguistic advances and to language acquisition theories. In A. D. Pellegrini & T. D. Yawkey (Eds.), *The development of oral and written languages: Readings in developmental and applied linguistics* (pp. 31–56). New York: Ablex.

NELSON, K. E., WELSH, J., CAMARATA, S. M., BUTKOVSKY, L., & CAMARATA, M. (1995). Available input for language-impaired children and younger children of matched language levels. *First Language, 15,* 1–17.

NELSON, N. W. (1988). Reading and writing. In M. A. Nippold (Ed.), *Later language development: Ages nine through nineteen* (pp. 97–126). Boston: Little, Brown.

NEMSER, W. (1971). Approximate systems of foreign language learners. In J. C. Richards (Ed.), *Error analysis* (pp. 55–63). London: Longman.

NEVILLE, H. J. (1991). Neurobiology of cognitive and language processing: Effects of early experience. In K. R. Gibson & A. C. Petersen (Eds.), *Brain maturation and cognitive development: Comparative and cross-cultural perspectives* (pp. 355–380). New York: Aldine de Bruyter.

NEVILLE, H. J. (1995a). Developmental specificity in neurocognitive development in humans. In M. S. Gazzaniga (Ed.), *The cognitive neurosciences* (pp. 219–231). Cambridge: MIT Press.

NEVILLE, H. J. (1995b). Developmental specificity in neurocognitive development in humans. Presentation to the Symposium on Research in Child Language Disorders. Madison, WI.

NEVILLE, H. J., NICOL, J. L., BARSS, A., FORSTER, K. I., & GARRETT (1991). Syntactically based sentence processing classes: Evidence from event-related brain potentials. *Journal of Cognitive Neuroscience, 3,* 151–165.

NEWPORT, E. L. (1982). Task specificity in language learning? Evidence from speech perception and American Sign Language. In E. Wanner & L. R. Gleitman (Eds.), *Language acquisition: The state of the art* (pp. 450–486). Cambridge: Cambridge University Press.

NEWPORT, E. L. (1990). Maturational contraints on language learning. *Cognitive Science, 14,* 11–28.

NEWPORT, E. L. (1991). Contraining concepts of the critical period for language. In S. Carey & R. Gelman (Eds.), *The epigenesis of mind: Essays on biology and cognition* (pp. 111–130). Hillsdale, NJ: Erlbaum.

NEWPORT, E. L., GLEITMAN, H., & GLEITMAN, L. (1977). Mother, I'd rather do it myself: Some effects and noneffects of maternal speech style. In C. E. Snow & C. A. Ferguson (Eds.), *Talking to children: Language input and acquisition* (pp. 109–150). Cambridge: Cambridge University Press.

NEWPORT, E. L., & MEIER, R. P. (1985). The acquistion of American Sign Language. In D. I. Slobin (Ed.), *The cross-linguistic study of language acquisition: Vol. 1. The data* (pp. 881–938). Hillsdale, NJ: Erlbaum.

NOTTEBOHM, F. (1970). Ontogeny of birdsong. *Science, 167,* 950–956.

OBLER, L. K. (1980). Narrative discourse style in the elderly. In L. K. Obler & M. L. Albert (Eds.), *Language and communication in the elderly* (pp. 75–90). Lexington, MA: D. C. Heath.

OBLER, L. K. (1983). Language and brain dysfunction in dementia. In S. J. Segalowitz (Ed.), *Language functions and brain organization* (pp. 267–282). New York: Academic Press.

OBLER, L. K., & ALBERT, M. L. (Eds.). (1980). *Language and communication in the elderly.* Lexington, MA: D. C. Heath.

OBLER, L. K., & ALBERT, M. L. (1985). Language skills across adulthood. In J. E. Birren & W. K. Schaie (Eds.), *Handbook of the Psychology of Aging* (2nd ed.) (pp. 463–473). New York: Van Nostrand Reinhold.

OCHS, E. (1982). Talking to children in Western Samoa. *Language in Society, 11,* 77–104.

OCHS, E. (1988). *Culture and language development.* Cambridge: Cambridge University Press.

O'GRADY, W., DOBROVOLSKY, M., & ARONOFF, M. (1989). *Contemporary linguistics: An introduction.* New York: St. Martin's Press.

OLGUIN, R., & TOMASELLO, M. (1993). Twenty-five-month-old children do not have a grammatical category of verb. *Cognitive Development, 8,* 245–272.

OLLER, D. K. (1980). The emergence of the sounds of speech in infancy. In G. H. Yeni-Komshian, J. F. Kavanagh, & C. A. Ferguson. (Eds.), *Child Phonology: Vol. 1.* New York: Academic Press.

OLLER, D. K. (1986). Metaphonology and infant vocalizations. In B. Lindbloom & R. Zetterstrom (Eds.), *Precursors of early speech.* (pp. 21–35). New York: Stockton Press.

OLLER, D. K., EILERS, R. E., BASINGER, D., STEFFENS, M. L., & URBANO, R. (1995). Extreme poverty and the development of precursors to the speech capacity. *First Language, 15,* 167–189.

OLLER, D. K., EILERS, R. E., BULL, D. H., & CARNEY, A. E. (1985). Prespeech vocalizations of a deaf infant: A comparison with normal metaphonological development. *Journal of Speech and Hearing Research, 28,* 47–63.

OLLER, D. K., & LYNCH, M. P. (1992). Infant vocalizations and innovations in infraphonology: Toward a broader theory of development and disorders. In C. A. Ferguson,

L. Menn, & C. Stoel-Gammon (Eds.), *Phonological development: Models, research, implications* (pp. 509–538). Timonium, MD: York Press.

OLLER, D. K., & STEFFENS, M. L. (1994). Syllables and segments in infant vocalizations and young child speech. In M. Yavas (Ed.), *First and second language phonology* (pp. 45–61). San Diego: Singular Publishing Group.

OLLER, D. K., WIEMAN, L. A., DOYLE, W. J., & ROSS, C. (1976). Infant babbling and speech. *Journal of Child Language, 3,* 1–11.

OVIATT, S. L. (1982). Inferring what words mean: Early development in infants' comprehension of common object names. *Child Development, 53,* 274–277.

OWENS, E. (1989). Present status of adults with cochlear implants. In E. Owens & D. K. Kessler (Eds.), *Cochlear implants in young deaf children* (pp. 25–52). Boston: College Hill Publications.

OWENS, E., & KESSLER, D. K. (1989). *Cochlear implants in young deaf children.* Boston: College Hill Publications.

OYAMA, S. (1976). A sensitive period in the acquisition of a nonnative phonological system. *Journal of Psycholinguistic Research, 5,* 261–285.

OYAMA, S. (1978). The sensitive period and comprehension of speech. *Working Papers on Bilingualism, 16,* 1–17.

PADDEN, C., & HUMPHRIES, T. (1988). *Deaf in America: Voices from a culture.* Cambridge, MA: Harvard University Press.

PALIJ, M., & HOMEL, P. (1987). The relationship of bilingualism to cognitive development: Historical, methodological and theoretical considerations. In P. Homel, M. Palij, & D. Aaronson (Eds.), *Childhood bilingualism: Aspects of linguistic, cognitive, and social development* (pp. 131–148). Hillsdale, NJ: Erlbaum.

PATKOWSKI, M. (1980). The sensitive period for the acquisition of syntax in a second language. *Language Learning, 30,* 449–472.

PAUL, R. (1987). Communication. In D. J. Cohen, A. M. Donnellan, & R. Paul (Eds.), *Handbook of autism and pervasive developmental disorders* (pp. 61–84). New York: Wiley.

PAUL, R., & COHEN, D. J. (1985). Comprehension of indirect requests in adults with autistic disorders and mental retardation. *Journal of Speech and Hearing Research, 28,* 475–479.

PAYNE, A. (1980). Factors controlling the acquisition of the Philadelphia dialect by out-of-state children. In W. Labov (Ed.), *Locating language in time and space* (pp. 143–177). New York: Academic Press.

PEAL, E., & W. E. LAMBERT (1962). The relation of bilingualism to intelligence. *Psychological Monographs, 76* (27, Whole No. 546).

PEARSON, B. Z., & FERNÁNDEZ, S. C. (1994). Patterns of interaction in the lexical growth in two languages of bilingual infants and toddlers. *Language Learning, 44,* 617–653.

PEARSON, B. Z., FERNÁNDEZ, S. C., LEWEDEG, V., & OLLER, D. K. (in press). The relation of input factors to lexical learning by bilingual infants. (Ages 8 to 30 months). *Applied Psycholinguistics.*

PEARSON, B. Z., FERNÁNDEZ, S. C., & OLLER, D. K. (1993). Lexical development in bilingual infants and toddler: Comparison to monolingual norms. *Language Learning, 43,* 93–120.

PEARSON, B. Z., FERNÁNDEZ, S. C., & OLLER, D. K. (1995). Cross-language synonyms in the lexicons of bilingual infants: One language or two? *Journal of Child Language, 22,* 345–368.

PERERA, K. (1986). Language acquisition and writing. In P. Fletcher & M. Garman (Eds.), *Language acquisition* (2nd ed.) (pp. 494–518). Cambridge: Cambridge University Press.

PEREZ-PEREIRA, M., & CASTRO, J. (1992). Pragmatic functions of blind and sighted children's language: A twin case study. *First Language, 12,* 17–37.

PERFETTI, C. A., BECK, I., BELL, L., & HUGHES, C. (1987). Phonemic knowledge and learning to read are reciprocal: A longitudinal study of first-grade children. *Merrill-Palmer Quarterly, 33,* 283–320.

PETERS, A. M. (1983). *The units of language acquisition.* Cambridge: Cambridge University Press.

PETERS, A. M. (1986). Early syntax. In P. Fletcher & M. Garman (Eds.), *Language acquisition (2nd ed.)* (pp. 307–325). Cambridge: Cambridge University Press.

PETERS, A. M. (1994). The interdependence of social, cognitive, and linguistic development: Evidence from a visually impaired child. In H. Tager-Flusberg (Ed.), *Constraints on language acquisition* (pp. 195–219). Hillsdale, NJ: Erlbaum.

PETERS, A. M. (1995). Strategies in the acquisition of syntax. In P. Fletcher & B. MacWhinney (Eds.), *The handbook of child language* (pp. 462–483). Oxford: Basil Blackwell.

PETERSON, C. L., DANNER, R. W., & FLAVELL, J. H. (1972). Developmental changes in children's response to three indications of communicative failure. *Child Development, 43,* 1463–1468.

PETERSON, C. L., & McCABE, A. (1988). The connective *and* as discourse glue. *First Language, 8,* 19–28.

PETITTO, L. (1987). On the autonomy of language and gesture: Evidence from the acquisition of personal pronouns in American Sign Language. *Cognition, 27,* 1–52.

PETITTO, L. (1988). "Language" in the prelinguistic child. In F. S. Kessel (Ed.), *The development of language and language researchers: Essays in honor of Roger Brown* (pp. 187–222). Hillsdale, NJ: Erlbaum.

PETITTO, L. (1993). On the ontogenetic requirements for early language acquisition. In B. de Boysson-Bardies, S. de Schonen, P. W. Jusczyk, P. McNeilage, & J. Morton (Eds.), *Developmental neurocognition: Speech and face processing in the first year of life* (pp. 365–383). Dordrecht, Netherlands: Kluwer Academic Press.

PHELPS, M. E., & MAZZIOTTA, J. C. (1985). PET: Human brain function and biochemistry. *Science, 228,* 799–809.

PIAGET, J. (1926). *The language and thought of the child.* London: Routledge & Kegan Paul.

PIENNEMANN, M. (1985). Learnability and syllabus construction. In K. Hyltenstam &

M. Piennemann (Eds.) *Modelling and assessing second language acquisition*. Clevedon, Avon: Multilingual Matters.

PINE, J. M. (1994). Environmental correlates of variation in lexical style: Interactional style and the structure of the input. *Applied Psycholinguistics, 15,* 355–370.

PINE, J. M. (1995). Variation in vocabulary development as a function of birth order. *Child Development, 66,* 272–281.

PINE, J. M., & LIEVEN, E. V. M. (1990). Referential style at thirteen months: Why age-defined cross-sectional measures are inappropriate for the study of strategy differences in early language development. *Journal of Child Language, 17,* 625–632.

PINE, J. M., & LIEVEN, E. V. M. (1993). Reanalysing rote-learned phrases: Individual differences in the transition to multi-word speech. *Journal of Child Language, 20,* 551–573.

PINKER, S. (1984). *Language learnability and language development*. Cambridge, MA: Harvard University Press.

PINKER, S. (1989). *Learnability and cognition: The acquisition of argument structure*. Cambridge, MA: MIT Press.

PINKER, S. (1990). Language acquisition. In D. N. Osherson & H. Lasnik (Eds.), *Language: An invitation to cognitive science: Vol. 1* (pp. 199–242). Cambridge, MA: MIT Press.

PINKER, S. (1991). Rules of language. *Science, 253,* 530–535.

PINKER, S. (1994). *The language instinct: How the mind creates language*. New York: Morrow.

PINKER, S. (1995). Introduction. In M. S. Gazzaniga (Ed.), *The cognitive neurosciences* (pp. 851–853). Cambridge: MIT Press.

PINKER, S., & BLOOM, P. (1990). Natural language and natural selection. *Behavioral and Brain Sciences, 13,* 707–784.

PINKER, S., LEBEAUX, D. S., & FROST, L. A. (1987). Productivity and constraints in the acquisition of the passive. *Cognition, 26,* 195–267.

PINKER, S., & PRINCE, A. (1994). Regular and irregular morphology and the psychological status of rules of grammar. In S. Lima, R. Corrigan, & G. Iverson (Eds.), *The reality of linguistic rules* (pp. 321 to 352). Philadelphia, PA: Benjamins.

PITCHER, E. G., & PERLINGER, E. (1963). *Children tell stories: An analysis of fantasy*. New York: International Universities Press.

PLUNKETT, K. (1995). Connectionist approaches to language acquisition. In P. Fletcher & B. MacWhinney (Eds.), *The handbook of child language* (pp. 36–72). Cambridge, MA: Basil Blackwell.

PLUNKETT, K., & MARCHMAN, V. (1991). U-shaped learning and frequency effects in a multi-layered perceptron: Implications for child language acquisition. *Cognition, 38,* 43–102.

POLLOCK, J. Y. (1989). Verb movement, Universal Grammar and the structure of IP. *Linguistic Inquiry, 20,* 365–424.

PREMACK, D. (1971). Language in chimpanzees. *Science, 172,* 808–822.

PREMACK, D. (1986). *Gavagai! Or the future history of the animal language controversy*. Cambridge, MA: MIT Press.

PRESSLEY, M., LEVIN, J. R., & McDANIEL, M. A. (1987). Remembering versus inferring what a word means: Mnemonic and contextual approaches. In M. G. McKeown & M. E. Curtis (Eds.), *The nature of vocabulary acquisition* (pp. 107–128). Cambridge, MA: MIT Press.

PRINZ, P. M., & PRINZ, E. A. (1979). Simultaneous acquisition of ASL and spoken English (In a hearing child of a deaf mother and hearing father). Phase I: Early lexical development. *Sign Language Studies, 25,* 283–296.

PRIZANT, B. M. (1983). Language acquisition and communicative behavior in autism: Toward an understanding of the "whole" of it. *Journal of Speech and Hearing Disorders, 48,* 296–307.

PYE, C. (1986). One lexicon or two? An alternative interpretation of early bilingual speech. *Journal of Child Language, 13,* 591–594.

PYE, C. (1992). The acquisition of K'iche' Maya. In D. I. Slobin (Ed.), *Cross-linguistic studies of language acquisition: Vol. 3* (pp. 221–308). Hillsdale, NJ: Erlbaum.

PYE, C., INGRAM, D., & LIST, H. (1987). A comparison of initial consonant acquisition in English and Quiche. In K. E. Nelson & A. van Kleeck (Eds.), *Children's language: Vol. 6* (pp. 175–190). Hillsdale, NJ: Erlbaum.

QUARTZ, S. R. (1993). Neural networks, nativism, and the plausibility of constructivism. *Cognition, 48,* 223–242.

QUIGLEY, S. P., & KING, C. M. (1980). Syntactic performance of hearing impaired and normal hearing individuals. *Applied Psycholinguistics, 1,* 329–356.

QUIGLEY, S. P., POWER, D. J., & STEINKAMP, M. W. (1977). The language structure of deaf children. *The Volta Review, 79,* 73–84.

QUINE, W. V. O. (1960). *Word and object*. Cambridge: Cambridge University Press.

RADFORD, A. (1990). *Syntactic theory and the acquisition of English syntax: The nature of early child grammars of English*. Oxford: Basil Blackwell.

RADFORD, A. (1995). Phrase structure and functional categories. In P. Fletcher & B. MacWhinney (Eds.), *The handbook of child language* (pp. 483–507). Oxford: Basil Blackwell.

RAICHLE, M. E. (1994). Images of the mind: Studies with modern imaging techniques. *Annual Review of Psychology, 45,* 333–356.

RAPIN, I., & SEGALOWITZ, S. J. (1992). *Handbook of neuropsychology: Vol. 6. Section 10: Child neuropsychology (Part 1)*. Amsterdam: Elsevier.

RATNER, N. B. (1996). From "signal to syntax": But what is the nature of the signal? In J. L. Morgan & K. Demuth (Eds.), *Signal to syntax: Bootstrapping from speech to grammar in early acquisition* (pp. 135–150). Mahwah, NJ: Erlbaum.

RATNER, N., & BRUNER, J. (1978). Games, social exchange and the acquisition of language. *Journal of Child Language, 5,* 391–401.

RATNER, N. B., & PYE, C. (1984). Higher pitch in BT is not universal: Acoustic evidence from Quiche Mayan. *Journal of Child Language, 2,* 515–522.

READ, C., ZHANG, Y.-F., NIE, H.-Y., & DING, B.-Q. (1986). The ability to manipulate speech sounds depends on knowing alphabetic spelling. *Cognition, 24,* 31–44.

REES, N. S. (1978). Pragmatics of language: Applications to normal and disordered language development. In R. L. Schiefelbusch (Ed.), *Bases of language intervention: Vol. 1* (pp. 191–268). Baltimore: University Park Press.

REESE, E., & FIVUSH, R. (1993). Parental styles of talking about the past. *Developmental Psychology, 29,* 596–606.

REGAL, R. A., ROONEY, J. R., & WANDAS, T. (1994). Facilitated communication: An experimental investigation. *Journal of Autism and Developmental Disorders, 24,* 345–355.

REICH, P. A. (1986). *Language development.* Englewood Cliffs, NJ: Prentice-Hall.

REILLY, J., KLIMA, E. S., & BELLUGI, U. (1990). Once more with feeling: Affect and language in atypical populations. *Development and Psychopathology, 2,* 369–391.

RESCORLA, L. A. (1980). Overextension in early language development. *Journal of Child Language, 7,* 321–335.

RESCORLA, L. A. (1981). Category development in early language. *Journal of Child Language, 8,* 225–238.

REZNICK, J. S., & GOLDFIELD, B. A. (1992). Rapid change in lexical development in comprehension and production. *Developmental Psychology, 28,* 406–413.

RHEINGOLD, H. L., GEWIRTZ, J. L., & ROSS, H. W. (1959). Social conditioning of vocalizations in the infant. *Journal of Comparative and Physiological Psychology, 52,* 68–73.

RICE, M. L. (1990). Preschooler's QUIL: Quick incidental learning of words. In G. Conti-Ramsden & C. E. Snow (Eds.), *Children's language: Vol. 7* (pp. 171–196). Hillsdale, NJ: Erlbaum.

RICE, M. L. (1994). Grammatical categories of specifically language-impaired children. In R. Watkins & M. Rice (Eds.), *New directions in specific language impairment* (pp. 69–89). Baltimore: Brookes.

RICE, M. L., BUHR, J., & NEMETH, M. (1990). Fast mapping word-learning abilities of language-delayed preschoolers. *Journal of Speech and Hearing Disorders, 55,* 33–42.

RICE, M. L., & OETTING, J. B. (1993). Morphological deficits of children with SLI: Evaluation of number marking and agreement. *Journal of Speech and Hearing Research, 36,* 1249–1257.

RICE, M. L., & WOODSMALL, L. (1988). Lessons from television: Children's word learning when viewing. *Child Development, 59,* 420–429.

RICHARDS, B. (1990). *Language development and individual differences: A study of auxiliary verb learning.* Cambridge: Cambridge University Press.

RICHARDS, J. C. (1971). A non-contrastive approach to error analysis. *English Language Teaching, 25,* 204–219.

RIDGE, M. (1981). *The new bilingualism: An American dilemma.* Los Angeles: University of Southern California Press. Center for Study of the American Experience, The Annenberg School of Communications, University of Southern California.

ROBINSON, E. J. (1981). The child's understanding of inadequate messages and communication failure: A problem of ignorance or egocentrism? In W. P. Dickson (Ed.), *Children's oral communication skills* (pp. 167–188). New York: Academic Press.

ROITBLAT, H. L., HERMAN, L. M., & NACHTIGALL, P. E. (1993). *Language and communication: Comparative perspectives*. Hillsdale, NJ: Erlbaum.

ROMAINE, S. (1984). *The language of children and adolescents: The acquisition of communicative competence*. Oxford: Basil Blackwell.

ROMAINE, S. (1988). *Pidgin and creole languages*. New York: Longman.

RONDAL, J. A. (1993). Down's syndrome. In D. Bishop & K. Mogford (Eds.), *Language development in exceptional children* (pp. 165–176). Hove, England: Erlbaum.

RONDAL, J. A., GHIOTTO, M., BREDART, S., & BACHELET, J. F. (1987). Age-relation, reliability and grammatical validity of measures of utterance length. *Journal of Child Language, 14,* 433–446.

RONJAT, J. (1913). *Le développement du langage observé chez un enfant bilingue.* Paris: Champion.

ROSCH, E., MERVIS, C. B., GRAY, W. D., JOHNSON, D. M., & BOYES-BRAEM, P. (1976). Basic objects in natural categories. *Cognitive Psychology, 8,* 382–439.

ROSENBERG, S., & ABBEDUTO, L. (1993). *Language and communication in mental retardation: Development, processes, and intervention*. Hillsdale, NJ: Erlbaum.

ROSENBLUM, T., & PINKER, S. A. (1983). Word magic revisited: Monolingual and bilingual children's understanding of the word-object relationships. *Child Development, 54,* 773–780.

RUHLEN, M. (1976). A guide to the languages of the world. Language Universals Project, Stanford University, CA.

RUTTER, M. (1978). Language disorder and infantile autism. In M. Rutter & E. Schopler (Eds.), *Autism: A reappraisal of concepts and treatment* (pp. 85–104). New York: Plenum.

RYAN, E. B. (1979). Why do low-prestige language varieties persist? In H. Giles & R. N. St. Clair (Eds.), *Language and social psychology* (pp. 145–157). Baltimore: University Park Press.

RYMER, R. (1993). *Genie: A scientific tragedy*. New York: HarperCollins.

SACHS, J. (1983). Talking about there and then: The emergence of displaced reference in parent-child discourse. In K. E. Nelson (Ed.), *Children's language: Vol. 4* (pp. 1–28). Hillsdale, NJ: Erlbaum.

SACHS, J. (1987). Preschool boys' and girls' language use in pretend play. In S. U. Phillips, S. Steele, & C. Tanz (Eds.), *Language, gender and sex in comparative perspective* (pp. 178–188). Cambridge: Cambridge University Press.

SACHS, J., & DEVIN, J. (1976). Young children's use of age appropriate speech styles in social interaction and role-playing. *Journal of Child Language, 3,* 81–98.

SACHS, J., & TRUSWELL, L. (1978). Comprehension of 2-word instructions by children in the 1-word stage. *Journal of Child Language, 5,* 17–24.

SACKS, H., SCHEGLOFF, E. A., & JEFFERSON, G. (1974). A simplest systematics for the organization of turn-taking for conversation. *Language, 50,* 696–735.

SANDER, E. K. (1972). When are speech sounds learned? *Journal of Speech and Hearing Disorders, 37,* 55–63.

SANKOFF, G., & LABERGE, Z. (1973). On the acquisition of native speakers by a language. *Kivung, 6,* 32–47.

SATZ, P., & LEWIS, R. (1993). Acquired aphasia in children. In G. Blanken, J. Dittmann, H. Grimm, J. D. Marshall, & C-W. Wallesch (Eds.), *Linguistic disorders and pathologies: An international handbook* (pp. 646–659). Berlin: Walter de Gruyter.

SATZ, P., STRAUSS, E., & WHITAKER, H. (1990). The ontogeny of hemispheric specialization: Some old hypotheses revisited. *Brain and Language, 38,* 596–614.

SAUNDERS, G. (1988). *Bilingual children: From birth to teens.* Clevedon, Avon: Multilingual Matters.

SAVAGE-RUMBAUGH, E. S. (1991). Language learning in the Bonobo: How and why they learn. In N. A. Krasnegor, D. M. Rumbaugh, R. L. Schiefelbusch, & M. Studdert-Kennedy (Eds.), *Biological and behavioral determinants of language development* (pp. 209–234). Hillsdale, NJ: Erlbaum.

SAVAGE-RUMBAUGH, E. S., McDONALD, K., SEVCIK, R., HOPKINS, W., & RUPERT, E. (1986). Spontaneous symbol acquisition and communicative use by pygmy chimpanzees (Pan paniscus). *Journal of Experimental Psychology: General, 115,* 211–235.

SAVAGE-RUMBAUGH, E. S., MURPHY, J., SEVCIK, R. A., BRAKKE, K. E., WILLIAMS, S. L., & RUMBAUGH, D. M. (1993). Language comprehension in ape and child. *Monographs of the Society for Research in Child Development, 58* (3–4, Serial No. 233).

SAVILLE-TROIKE, M. (1982). *The ethnography of communication: An introduction.* Baltimore: University Park Press.

SCHIEFFELIN, B. B. (1979). Getting it together: An ethnographic approach to the study of the development of communicative competence. In E. Ochs & B. B. Schieffelin (Eds.), *Developmental pragmatics* (pp. 73–110) New York: Academic Press.

SCHIEFFELIN, B. B. (1985). The acqusition of Kaluli. In D. I. Slobin (Ed.), *The crosslinguistic study of language acquisition: Vol. 1. The data* (pp. 525–594). Hillsdale, NJ: Erlbaum.

SCHIEFFELIN, B. B., & GILMORE, P. (1986). *The acquisition of literacy: Ethnographic perspectives.* Norwood, NJ: Ablex.

SCHIEFFELIN, B. B., & OCHS, E. (1986). Language socialization. *Annual Review of Anthropology, 15,* 163–191.

SCHLESINGER, H. S., & MEADOW, K. P. (1972). *Sound and sign: Childhood deafness and mental health.* Berkeley: University of California Press.

SCHOEBER-PETERSON, D., & JOHNSON, C. J. (1989). Conversational topics of four-year-olds. *Journal of Speech and Hearing Research, 32,* 857–870.

SCHOEBER-PETERSON, D., & JOHNSON, C. J. (1991). Non-dialogue speech during preschool interactions. *Journal of Child Language, 18,* 153–170.

SCHOLNICK, E. K., & WING, C. S. (1991). Speaking deductively: Preschoolers' use of *If* in conversation and conditional reference. *Developmental Psychology, 27,* 249–258.

SCHOPLER, E., SHORT, A., & MESIBOV, G. (1989). Relation of behavioral treatment to "normal functioning": Comment on Lovaas. *Journal of Consulting and Clinical Psychology, 57,* 162–164.

SCHUMANN, J. (1978). The acculturation model for second language acquisition. In R. C. Gingras (Ed.), *Second-Language Acquisition and Foreign Language Teaching* (pp. 27–50). Washington, DC: Center for Applied Linguistics.

SCHUMANN, J. (1987). The expression of temporality in basilang speech. *Studies in Second Language Acquisition, 9,* 21–41.

SCHUMANN, J. (1993). Some problems with falsification: An illustration from SLA research. *Applied Linguistics, 14,* 295–306.

SCHWARTZ, R. (1983). Diagnosis of speech sound disorders in children. In Mertus & Weinberg (Eds.), *Diagnosis in Speech-Language Pathology* (pp. 113–149). Baltimore, MD: University Park Press.

SCHWARTZ, R., & LEONARD, L. (1982). Do children pick and choose? An examination of phonological selection and avoidance in early acquisition. *Journal of Child Language, 9,* 319–336.

SCIARONE, A. C. (1970). Contrastive Analysis: Possibilities and limitations. *International Review of Applied Linguistics, 8,* 115–131.

SCOLLON, R. (1979). A real early stage: An unzippered condensation of a dissertation on child language. In E. Ochs & B. B. Schieffelin (Eds.), *Developmental Pragmatics* (pp. 215–228). New York: Academic Press.

SCOTT, C. M. (1984). Adverbial connectivity in conversations of children 6 to 12. *Journal of Child Language, 11,* 423–452.

SEARLE, J. (1969). *Speech acts,* Cambridge, MA: University Press.

SEIDENBERG, M. S. (1992). Connectionism without tears. In S. Davis (Ed.), *Connectionism: Theory and practice* (pp. 84–122). New York: Oxford University Press.

SEIDENBERG, M. S. (1994). Language and connectionism: The developing interface. *Cognition, 50,* 385–401.

SEIDENBERG, M. S., & PETITTO, L. A. (1979). Signing behavior in apes: A critical review. *Cognition, 7,* 177–215.

SEIDENBERG, M. S., & PETITTO, L. A. (1987). Communication, symbolic communication, and language: Comment on Savage-Rumbaugh, McDonald, Sevcik, Hopkins, and Rupert (1986). *Journal of Experimental Psychology: General, 116,* 279–287.

SELINKER, L. (1972). Interlanguage. *International Review of Applied Linguistics, 10,* 209–231.

SELKIRK, E. (1996). The prosodic structure of function words. In J. L. Morgan & K. Demuth (Eds.), *Signal to syntax: Bootstrapping from speech to grammar in early acquisition* (pp. 187–214). Mahwah, NJ: Erlbaum.

SENGHAS, A. (1995). The development of Nicaraguan Sign Language via the language acquisition process. In D. MacLaughlin & S. McEwen (Eds.), *Proceedings of BUCLD 19, 543-552.* Somerville, MA: Cascadilla Press.

SEUREN, P. A. M. (1984). The bioprogram hypothesis: Facts and fancy. *The Behavioral and Brain Sciences, 7,* 208–209.

SEYFARTH, R. M., & CHENEY, D. L. (1993). Meaning, reference, and intentionality in the natural vocalizations of monkeys. In H. L. Roitblat, L. M. Herman, & P. E. Nachtigall (Eds.), *Language and communication: Comparative perspectives* (pp. 195–220). Hillsdale, NJ: Lawrence Erlbaum.

SHACHKIN, N. K. (1973). The development of phonemic speech perception in early childhood. In C. A. Ferguson & D. I. Slobin (Eds.), *Studies of child language development* (pp. 91–127). New York: Holt, Rinehart & Winston.

SHANE, H. (1993). The dark side of facilitated communication. *Topics in Language Disorders, 13,* ix–xv.

SHAPIRO, L. R., & HUDSON, J. A. (1991). Tell me a make-believe story: Coherence and cohesion in young children's picture-elicited narratives. *Developmental Psychology, 27,* 960–974.

SHARWOOD SMITH, M. (1991). Speaking to many minds: On the relevance of different types of language information for the L2 learner. *Second Language Research, 7,* 118–132.

SHATZ, M. (1978a). On the development of communicative understandings: An early strategy for interpreting and responding to messages. *Cognitive Psychology, 10,* 271–301.

SHATZ, M. (1978b). Children's comprehension of their mothers' question-directives. *Journal of Child Language, 5,* 39–46.

SHATZ, M. (1983a). Communication. In P. H. Mussen (Ed.), *Handbook of Child Psychology* (pp. 841–889). New York: Wiley.

SHATZ, M. (1983b). On transition, continuity, and coupling: An alternative approach to communicative development. In R. M. Golinkoff (Ed.), *The transition from prelinguistic to linguistic communication* (pp. 43–56). Hillsdale, NJ: Erlbaum.

SHATZ, M. (1985). A song without music and other stories: How cognitive process constraints influence children's oral and written narratives. In D. Schiffrin (Ed.), *Georgetown University Round Table on Language and Linguistics 1984* (pp. 313–324). Washington, D. C.: Georgetown University Press.

SHATZ, M. (1994a). Review article. (Review of *Laura: A case for the modularity of language* by J. E. Yamada and *First verbs: A case study of early grammatical development* by M. Tomasello) *Language, 70,* 789–796.

SHATZ, M. (1994b). *A toddler's life: Becoming a person.* New York: Oxford University Press.

SHATZ, M., & GELMAN, R. (1973). The development of communication skills: Modifications in the speech of young children as a function of listener. *Monographs of the Society for Research in Child Development, 38,* 1–37.

SHATZ, M., HOFF-GINSBERG, E., & MacIVER, D. (1989). Induction and the acquisition of English auxiliaries: The effects of differentially enriched input. *Journal of Child Language, 16,* 121–140.

SHATZ, M., & McCLOSKEY, L. (1984). Answering appropriately: A developmental perspective on conversational knowledge. In S. Kuczaj (Ed.), *Discourse development* (pp. 19–36). New York: Springer-Verlag.

SHATZ, M., & WATSON O'REILLY, A. (1990). Conversational or communicative skill?

A reassessment of two-year-olds' behaviour in miscommunication episodes. *Journal of Child Language, 17,* 131.

SHELDON, A. (1990). Pickle-fights: Gendered talk in preschool disputes. *Discourse Processes, 13,* 5–31.

SHERMAN, J. C., & LUST, B. (1993). Children are in control. *Cognition, 46,* 1–51.

SHIPLEY, E. F., SMITH, C. S., & GLEITMAN, L. (1969). A study in the acquisition of language: Free responses to commands. *Language, 45,* 322–342.

SHORE, C., O'CONNELL, B., & BATES, E. (1984). First sentences in language and symbolic play. *Developmental Psychology, 20,* 872–880.

SHRIBERG, L. D. (1986). PEPPER: Programs to examine phonetic and phonologic evaluation records. Hillsdale, NJ: Erlbaum.

SIGMAN, M., MUNDY, P., SHERMAN, T., & UNGERER, J. (1986). Social interactions of autistic, mentally retarded and normal children and their caregivers. *Journal of Child Psychology and Psychiatry, 27,* 647–656.

SINCLAIR-DE-ZWART, H. (1969). Developmental psycholinguistics. In D. Elkind & J. Flavell (Eds.), *Studies in cognitive development* (pp. 315–336). New York: Oxford University Press.

SINGER, N. G., BELLUGI, U., BATES, E., JONES, W., & ROSSEN, M. (in press). Contrasting profiles of language development in children with Williams and Down syndromes. *Developmental Neuropsychology.*

SKARAKIS, E. A., & PRUTTING, C. A. (1977). Early communication: Semantic functions and communicative intentions in the communication of the preschool child with impaired hearing. *American Annals of the Deaf, 122,* 382–391.

SKINNER, B. F. (1957). *Verbal behavior.* Englewood Cliffs, NJ: Prentice-Hall.

SLOBIN, D. I. (1972). *Leopold's bibliography of child language: Revised and augmented by D. I. Slobin.* Bloomington, IN: Indiana University Press.

SLOBIN, D. I. (Ed.). (1985). *The cross-linguistic study of language acquisition: Vols. 1 & 2.* Hillsdale, NJ: Erlbaum.

SLOBIN, D. I. (Ed.). (1992). *The crosslinguistic study of language acquisition: Vol. 3.* Hillsdale, NJ: Erlbaum.

SMITH, M. D., HAAS, P. J., & BELCHER, R. G. (1994). Facilitated communication: The effects of facilitator knowledge and level of assistance on output. *Journal of Autism and Developmental Disorders, 24,* 357–367.

SNOW, C. E. (1977). The development of conversation between mothers and babies. *Journal of Child Language, 4,* 1–22.

SNOW, C. E. (1983). Literacy and language: Relationships during the preschool years. *Harvard Educational Review, 53,* 165–189.

SNOW, C. E. (1988). The last word: Questions about the emerging lexicon. In M. D. Smith & J. L. Locke (Eds.), *The emergent lexicon: The child's development of a linguistic vocabulary* (pp. 341–353). San Diego: Academic Press.

SNOW, C. E. (1989). Understanding social interaction and language acquisition: Sentences are not enough. In M. H. Bornstein & J. S. Bruner (Eds.), *Interaction in human development,* (pp. 83–104). Hillsdale, NJ: Erlbaum.

SNOW, C. E., BARNES, W. S., CHANDLER, J., GOODMAN, I. F., & HEMPHILL, L. (1991). *Unfulfilled expectations: Home and school influences on literacy.* Cambridge, MA: Harvard Unviersity Press.

SNOW, C. E., & HOEFNAGEL-HÖHLE, M. (1978). The critical period for language acquisition: Evidence from second language learning. *Child Development, 49,* 1114–1128.

SNOW, C. E., & NINIO, A. (1986). The contracts of literacy: What children learn from learning to read books. In W. H. Teale & E. Sulzby (Eds.), *Emergent literacy: Writing and reading* (pp. 116–138). Norwood, NJ: Ablex.

SNOW, C. E., PERLMANN, R., & NATHAN, D. (1987). Why routines are different: Toward a multiple-factors model of the relation between input and language acquisition. In K. Nelson & A. van Kleeck (Eds.), *Children's language: Vol. 6* (pp. 65–98). Hillsdale, NJ: Erlbaum.

SNOWDON, C. T. (1993). Linguistic phenomena in the natural communication of animals. In H. L. Roitblat, L. M. Herman, & P. E. Nachtigall (Eds.), *Language and communication: Comparative perspectives* (pp. 175–194). Hillsdale, NJ: Erlbaum.

SNYDER, L., BATES, E., & BRETHERTON, I. (1981). Content and context in early lexical development. *Journal of Child Language, 8,* 565–582.

SOJA, N. N., CAREY, S., & SPELKE, E. S. (1991). Ontological categories guide young children's inductions of word meaning: Object terms and substance terms. *Cognition, 38,* 179–211.

SPRINGER, A., & DEUTSCH, G. (1981). *Left brain, right brain.* San Francisco: W. H. Freeman.

STAATS, A. W. (1971). Linguistic-mentalistic theory versus an explanatory S-R learning theory of language development. In D. I. Slobin (Ed.), *The ontogenesis of grammar* (pp. 103–152). New York: Academic Press.

STANOVICH, K. E. (1986). Matthew effects in reading: Some consequences of individual differences in the acquisition of literacy. *Reading Research Quarterly, 21,* 360–406.

STARK, R. E. (1986). Prespeech segmental feature development. In P. Fletcher & M. Garman (Eds.), *Language acquisition (2nd ed.)* (pp. 149–173). Cambridge: Cambridge University Press.

STECKOL, K., & LEONARD, L. (1979) The use of grammatical morphemes by normal and language-impaired children. *Journal of Communication Disorders, 12,* 291–301.

STEIN, N. L. (1988). The development of children's storytelling skill. In M. B. Franklin & S. Barten (Eds.), *Child language: A book of readings* (pp. 282–297). New York: Oxford University Press.

STEIN, N. L., & GLENN, C. G. (1979). An analysis of story comprehension in elementary school children. In R. O. Freedle (Ed.), *New directions in discourse processing: Vol. 2* (pp. 53–120). *Advances in discourse processes.* Norwood, NJ: Ablex.

STEMBERGER, J. P. (1992). A connectionist view of child phonology phonological processing without phonological processes. In C. A. Ferguson, L. Menn, & C. Stoel-Gammon (Eds.), *Phonological Development* (pp. 165–189). Timonium, MD: York Press.

STERN, C., & STERN, W. (1907). *Die Kindersprache.* Leipzig: Barth.

STERN, D. N. (1974). Mother and infant at play. In M. Lewis & L. Rosenblum (Eds.), *The origins of behavior* (vol. 1, pp. 187–213). New York: Wiley.

STERNBERG, R. J. (1987). Most vocabulary is learned from context. In M. G. McKeown & M. E. Curtis (Eds.), *The nature of vocabulary acquisition* (pp. 89–106). Hillsdale, NJ: Erlbaum.

STILES, J., & THAL, D. (1993). Linguistic and spatial cognitive development following early focal brain injury: Patterns of deficit and recovery. In M. H. Johnson (Ed.), *Brain development and cognition: A reader* (pp. 643–664). Oxford: Basil Blackwell.

STOEL-GAMMON, C., & COOPER, J. (1984). Patterns of early lexical and phonological development. *Journal of Child Language, 11,* 247–271.

STOEL-GAMMON, C., & OTOMO, K. (1986). Babbling development of hearing-impaired and normally hearing subjects. *Journal of Speech and Hearing Disorders, 51,* 33–41.

STOKOE, W. C., CASTERLINE, D. C., & CRONEBERG, C. G. (1965). *A dictionary of American Sign Language on linguistic principles.* Washington, DC: Gallaudet College Press.

SUGARMAN, S. (1984). The development of preverbal communication: Its contribution and limits in promoting the development of language. In R. L. Schiefelbusch & J. Pickar (Eds.), *The acquisition of communicative competence* (pp. 23–68). Baltimore, MD: University Park Press.

SUGARMAN-BELL, S. (1978). Some organizational aspects of preverbal communication. In I. Markova (Ed.), *The social context of language* (pp. 49–66). New York: Wiley.

TAGER-FLUSBERG, H. (1981). On the nature of linguistic functioning in early infantile autism. *Journal of Autism and Developmental Disorders, 11,* 45–56.

TAGER-FLUSBERG, H. (1985). The conceptual basis for referential word meaning in children with autism. *Child Development, 56,* 1167–1178.

TAGER-FLUSBERG, H. (1989). A psycholinguistic perspective on language development in the autistic child. In G. Dawson (Ed.), *Autism: Nature, diagnosis, and treatment* (pp. 92–115). New York: Guilford Press.

TAGER-FLUSBERG, H. (1993). What language reveals about the understanding of minds in children with autism. In S. Baron-Cohen, H. Tager-Flusberg, & D. J. Cohen (Eds.), *Understanding other minds: Perspectives from autism* (pp. 139–157). Oxford: Oxford University Press.

TAGER-FLUSBERG, H. (1994). Dissociations in form and function in the acquisition of language by autisitic children. In H. Tager-Flusberg (Ed.), *Constraints on language acquisition: Studies of atypical children* (pp. 175–194). Hillsdale, NJ: Erlbaum.

TAGER-FLUSBERG, H., CALKINS, S., NOLIN, T., BAUMBERGER, T., ANDERSON, M., & CHADWICK-DIAS, A. (1990). A longitudinal study of language acquisition in autistic and Down syndrome children. *Journal of Autism and Developmental Disorders, 20,* 1–21.

TALLAL, P. (1978) An experimental investigation of the role of auditory temporal processing in normal and disordered language development. In A. Caramazza & E. B. Zurif (Eds.), *Language acquisition and language breakdown* (pp. 25–61). Baltimore: Johns Hopkins University Press.

TALLAL, P., ROSS, R., & CURTISS, S. (1989). Familial aggregation in specific language impairment. *Journal of Speech and Hearing Disorders, 54,* 167–173.

TALLAL, P., STARK, R. E., & MELLITS, E. D. (1985). Identification of language-impaired children on the basis of rapid perception and reproduction skills. *Brain and Language, 25,* 314–322.

TALLAL, P., TOWNSEND, J., CURTISS, S., & WULFECK, B. (1991). Phenotypic profiles of language-impaired children based on genetic/family history. *Brain and Language, 41,* 81–95.

TANNEN, D. (1982). *Spoken and written language: Exploring orality and literacy.* Norword, NJ: Ablex.

TANNEN, D. (1990). *You just don't understand: Men and women in conversation.* New York: Morrow.

TARDIF, T. (1996). Nouns are not always learned before verbs: Evidence from Mandarin speakers' early vocabularies. *Developmental Psychology, 32,* 492–504.

TAYLOR, M., & GELMAN, S. A. (1988). Adjectives and nouns: Children's strategies for learning new words. *Child Development, 59,* 411–419.

TEALE, W. H. (1984). Reading to young children: Its significance for literacy development. In H. Goelman, A. Oberg, & F. Smith (Eds.), *Awakening to literacy* (pp. 110–121). Exeter: Heineman Education Books.

TEALE, W. H., & SULZBY, E. (1986). *Emergent literacy: Writing and reading.* Norwood, NJ: Ablex.

TEMPLIN, M. (1957). *Certain language skills in children.* University of Minnesota Institute of Child Welfare Monograph Series 26. Minneapolis: University of Minnesota Press.

TERRACE, H. S. (1979). *Nim.* New York: Knopf.

TERRACE, H. S., PETITTO, L. A., SANDERS, R. J., & BEVER, T. G. (1979). Can an ape create a sentence? *Science, 206,* 891–902.

THAL, D., BATES, E., & BELLUGI, U. (1989). Language and cognition in two children with Williams syndrome. *Journal of Speech and Hearing Research, 32,* 489–500.

THAL, D. J., MARCHMAN, V., STILES, J., ARAM, D., TRAUNER, D., NASS, R., & BATES, E. (1991). Early lexical development in children with focal brain injury. *Brain and Language, 40,* 491–527.

THOMPSON, J. R., & CHAPMAN, R. S. (1977). Who is 'Daddy' revisited: The status of two-year-olds' over-extended words in use and comprehension. *Journal of Child Language, 4,* 359–375.

TODD, L. (1974). *Pidgins and creoles.* London: Routledge & Kegan Paul.

TOMASELLO, M. (1992a). Author's response: On defining language: Replies to Shatz and Ninio. *Social Development, 1,* 159–162.

TOMASELLO, M. (1992b). *First verbs: A case study of early grammatical development.* Cambridge: Cambridge University Press.

TOMASELLO, M. (1994). Can an ape understand a sentence? A review of *Language comprehension in ape and child* by E. S. Savage-Rumbaugh et al. *Language & Communication, 14,* 377–390.

TOMASELLO, M., & AKHTAR, N. (1995). Two-year-olds use pragmatic cues to differentiate reference to objects and actions. *Cognitive Development, 10,* 201–224.

TOMASELLO, M., & BARTON, M. (1994). Learning words in non-ostensive context. *Developmental Psychology, 30,* 639–650.

TOMASELLO, M., CALL, J., NAGELL, K., OLGUIN, R., & CARPENTER, M. (1994). The learning and use of gestural signals by young chimpanzees: A trans-generational study. *Primates, 35,* 137–154.

TOMASELLO, M., FARRAR, M. J., & DINES, J. (1984). Children's speech revisions for a familiar and an unfamiliar adult. *Journal of Speech and Hearing Research, 27,* 359–363.

TOMASELLO, M., & KRUGER, A. (1992). Acquiring verbs in ostensive and non-ostensive context. *Journal of Child Language, 19,* 311–333.

TOMASELLO, M., & MANNLE, S. (1985). Pragmatics of sibling speech of one-year-olds. *Child Development, 56,* 911–917.

TOMASELLO, M., & MERRIMAN, W. E. (1995). *Beyond names for things: Young children's acquisition of verbs.* Hillsdale, NJ: Erlbaum.

TOMASELLO, M., & OLGUIN, R. (1993). Twenty-three-month-old children have a grammatical category of noun. *Cognitive Development, 8,* 451–464.

TOMASELLO, M., & TODD, J. (1983). Joint attention and lexical acquisition style. *First Language, 4,* 197–212.

TOMBLIN, J. B. (1989). Familial concentration of developmental language impairment. *Journal of Speech and Hearing Disorders, 54,* 287–295.

TOUGH, J. (1977). *The development of meaning.* London: Unwin Education Books.

TOUGH, J. (1982). Language, poverty, and disadvantage in school. In L. Feagans & D. C. Farran (Eds.), *The language of children reared in poverty: Implications for evaluation and intervention* (pp. 3–18). New York: Academic Press.

TREHUB, S. E. (1976). The discrimination of foreign speech contrasts by infants and adults. *Child Development, 47,* 466–472.

TREHUB, S. E. (1973). Infants' sensitivity to vowel and tonal contrasts. *Developmental Psychology, 9,* 91–96.

TREIMAN, R. (1985). Onsets and rimes as units of spoken syllabales: Evidence from children. *Journal of Experimental Child Psychology, 39,* 181–191.

TREVARTHEN, C., & HUBLEY, P. (1978). Secondary intersubjectivity: Confidence, confiding and acts of meaning in the first year. In A. Lock (Ed.), *Action, gesture and symbol: The emergence of language.* New York: Academic Press.

TWENEY, R. D., HOEMAN, H. W., & ANDREWS, C. E. (1975). Semantic organization in deaf and hearing subjects. *Journal of Psycholinguistic Research, 4,* 61–73.

TYLER, A., & NAGY, W. (1989). The acquisition of English derivational morphology. *Journal of Memory and Language, 28,* 649–667.

UMBEL, V. M., PEARSON, B. Z., FERNÁNDEZ, S. C., & OLLER, D. K. (1992). Measuring bilingual children's receptive vocabularies. *Child Development, 63,* 1012–1020.

UMIKER-SEBEOK, D. J. (1979). Preschool children's intraconversational narratives. *Journal of Child Language, 6,* 91–109.

URWIN, C. (1978). The development of communication between blind infants and their parents. In A. Lock (Ed.), *Action, gesture, and symbol: The emergence of language* (pp. 79–108). London: Academic Press.

VALIAN, V. (1986). Syntactic categories in the speech of young children. *Developmental Psychology, 22,* 562–579.

VALIAN, V. (1991). Syntactic subjects in the early speech of American and Italian children. *Cognition, 40,* 21–81.

VANDELL, D., & WILSON, K. (1987). Infants' interactions with mother, sibling, and peer: Contrasts and relations between interaction systems. *Child Development, 58,* 176–186.

VAN DER LELY, H. (1994). Canonical linking rules: Forward vs. reverse linking in normally developing and specifically language impaired children. *Cognition, 51,* 29–72.

VAN VALIN R. D. (1991). Functionalist linguistic theory and language acquisition. *First Language, 11,* 7–40.

VARGHA-KHADEM, F., O'GORMAN, A. M., & WATTERS, G. V. (1985). Aphasia and handedness in relation to hemispheric side, age at injury and severity of cerebral lesion during childhood. *Brain, 108,* 677–696.

VARGHA-KHADEM, F., WATKINS, K., ALCOCK, K., FLETCHER, P., & PASSINGHAM, R. (1995). Praxic and nonverbal cognitive deficits in a large family with a genetically transmitted speech and language disorder. *Proceedings of the National Academy of Sciences of the United States, 92,* 930–934.

VELLEMAN, S., MANGIPUDI, L., & LOCKE, J. L. (1989). Prelinguistic phonetic contingency. *First Language, 9,* 169–173.

VIHMAN, M. M. (1988a). Early phonological development. In J. Bernthal & N. Bambson, (Eds.), *Articulation and phonological disorders (2nd ed.)* (pp. 60–109). New York: Prentice-Hall.

VIHMAN, M. M. (1988b). Later phonological development. In J. Bernthal & N. Bambson (Eds.), *Articulation and phonological disorders (2nd ed.)* (pp. 110–144). New York: Prentice-Hall.

VIHMAN, M. M. (1993). Variable paths to early word production. *Journal of Phonetics, 21,* 61–82.

VIHMAN, M. M., VELLEMAN, S., & McCUNE, L. (1994). How abstract is child phonology? Toward an integration of linguistic and psychological approaches. In M. Yavas (Ed.), *First and second language phonology* (pp. 9–44). San Diego: Singular Publishing Group.

VOLTERRA, V., & TAESCHNER, T. (1978). The acquisition and development of language by bilingual children. *Journal of Child Language, 5,* 311–326.

VON FRISCH, K. (1962). Dialects in the language of the bees. *Scientific American, 207,* 79–87.

VYGOTSKY, L. (1962). *Thought and language.* Cambridge: MIT Press.

VYGOTSKY, L. (1978). In M. Cole, V. John-Steiner, S. Scribner, & E. Souberman (Eds.), *Mind in society: The development of higher mental processes.* Cambridge, MA: Harvard University Press. (Original work published 1930, 1933, 1935)

WAGNER, D. A. (1993). *Literacy, culture, and development: Becoming literate in Morocco*. Cambridge: Cambridge University Press.

WAGNER, R. K., & TORGESEN, J. K. (1987). The nature of phonological processing and its causal role in the acquisition of reading skills. *Psychological Bulletin, 101,* 192–212.

WALLMAN, J. (1992). *Aping language*. Cambridge: Cambridge University Press.

WARREN, A. R., & TATE, C. S. (1992). Egocentrism in children's telephone conversations. In R. M. Diaz & L. E. Berk (Eds.), *Private speech: From social interaction to self-regulation* (pp. 245–266). Hillsdale, NJ: Erlbaum.

WARREN, S. F., & REICHLE, J. (Eds.) (1992). *Causes and effects in communication and language intervention: Vol. 1*. Baltimore: Paul H. Brookes.

WAXMAN, S. R. (1994). The development of an appreciation of specific linkages between linguistic and conceptual organization. In L. Gleitman & B. Landau (Eds.), *The acquisition of the lexicon* (pp. 229–258). Cambridge, MA: MIT Press/Elsevier.

WAXMAN, S. R., & MARKOW, D. B. (1995). Words as invitations to form categories: Evidence from 12- to 13-month-old infants. *Cognitive Psychology, 29,* 257–303.

WEINER, P. (1974). A language-delayed child at adolescence. *Journal of Speech and Hearing Disorders, 39,* 202–212.

WEIR, R. H. (1962). *Language in the crib*. The Hague: Mouton.

WEISMER, S. E. (1985). Constructive comprehension abilities exhibited by language-disordered children. *Journal of Speech and Hearing Research, 28,* 175–184.

WELLMAN, H. M. (1990). *The child's theory of mind*. Cambridge, MA: MIT Press.

WELLMAN, H. M., & LEMPERS, J. D. (1977). The naturalistic communicative abilities of two-year-olds. *Child Development, 48,* 1052–1057.

WELLS, G. (1977). Language use and educational success: An empirical response to Joan Tough's 'The Development of Meaning' (1977). *Research in Education, 18,* 9–34.

WELLS, G. (1985). Preschool literacy-related activities and success in school. In D. R. Olson, N. Torrance, & A. Hildyard (Eds.), *Literacy, language, and learning* (pp. 229–255). Cambridge: Cambridge University Press.

WELLS, G. (1986). *The meaning makers: Children learning language and using language to learn*. Portsmouth, NH: Heinemann.

WERKER, J. F., GILBERT, J. H. V., HUMPHREY, K., & TEES, R. C. (1981). Developmental aspects of cross-language speech perception. *Child Development, 52,* 349–355.

WERKER, J. F., & PEGG, J. E. (1992). Infant speech perception and phonological acquisition. In C. A. Ferguson, L. Menn, & S. Stoel-Gammon (Eds.), *Phonological Development* (pp. 285–311). Timonium, MD: York Press.

WERKER, J. F., & POLKA, L. (1993). Developmental changes in speech perception: New challenges and new directions. *Journal of Phonetics, 21,* 83–101.

WERKER, J. F., & TEES, R. C. (1984). Cross-language speech perception: Evidence for perceptual reorganization during the first year of life. *Infant Behavior and Development, 7,* 49–63.

WERTSCH, J. (1985). *Vygotsky and the social formation of mind*. Cambridge: Harvard University Press.

WEST, C., & ZIMMERMAN, D. (1977). Women's place in everyday talk: Reflections on parent-child interaction. *Social Problems, 24,* 521–529.

WEXLER, D., & CULICOVER, R. (1980). *Formal principles of language acquisition.* Cambridge, MA: MIT Press.

WEYLMAN, S. T., BROWNELL, H. H., & GARDNER, H. (1988). "It's what you mean, not what you say": Pragmatic language use in brain-damaged patients. In F. Plum (Ed.), *Language, communication, and the brain* (pp. 229–244). New York: Raven Press.

WHITE, L. (1989). *Universal grammar and second language acquisition.* Philadelphia: John Benjamins.

WHITE, L. (1990). The verb movement parameter in second language acquisition. *Language Acquisition, 1,* 337–360.

WHITE, L. (1996). The tale of the ugly duckling (or: the coming of age of second language acquisition research). In D. Cahana-Arnitay, L. Hughes, A. Stringfellow, & A. Zukowske (Eds.), *Proceedings of the 20th Boston University Conference on Language Development.* Somerville, MA: Cascadilla Press.

WIGGLESWORTH, G. (1993, July). Individual approaches to the organization of narrative. Paper presented at the Sixth International Congress for the Study of Child Language. Trieste, Italy.

WILBUR, R. B. (1979). *American Sign Language and sign systems.* Baltimore: University Park Press.

WILCOX, M. J., & WEBSTER, E. J. (1980). Early discourse behavior: An analysis of children's responses to listener feedback. *Child Development, 51,* 1120–1125.

WILKINSON, L. D. (1982). *Communicating in the classroom.* New York: Academic Press.

WIMMER, H., LANDERL, K., LINORTNER, R., & HUMMER, P. (1991). The relationship of phonemic awareness to reading acquisition: More consequence than precondition but still important. *Cognition, 40,* 219–249.

WINNER, E. (1988). *The point of words: Children's understanding of metaphor and irony.* Cambridge, MA: Harvard University Press.

WINNER, E., GARDNER, H., SILBERSTEIN, L., & MEYER, C. (1988). Creating a world with words. In F. S. Kessel (Ed.), *The development of language and language researchers: Essays in honor of Roger Brown* (pp. 353–372). Hillsdale, NJ: Erlbaum.

WITELSON, S. F. (1977). Early hemisphere specialization and interhemispheric plasticity: An empirical and theoretical review. In S. J. Segalowitz & F. A. Gruber (Eds.), *Language development and neurological theory* (pp. 213–289). New York: Academic Press.

WITELSON, S. F. (1987). Neurobiological aspects of language in children. *Child Development, 58,* 653–688.

WOLFRAM, W. (1973). *Sociolinguistic aspects of assimiliation: Puerto Rican English in East Harlem.* Washington, DC: Center for Applied Linguistics.

WONG FILLMORE, L. (1991). Second-language learning in children: A model of language learning in social context. In E. Bialystok (Ed.), *Language processing in bilingual children* (pp. 49–69). Cambridge: Cambridge University Press.

WOOD, C. C. (1976). Discriminability, response bias, and phoneme categories in discrimination of voice onset time. *Journal of the Acoustical Society of America, 60,* 1381–1389.

WOOD, C. C., GOFF, W., & DAY, R. (1971). Auditory evoked potential during speech perception. *Science, 173,* 1248–1251.

WOOD, D., WOOD, H., & MIDDLETON, D. (1978). An experimental evaluation of four face-to-face teaching strategies. *International Journal of Behavioral Development, 1,* 131–147.

WOOD, H., & WOOD, D. (1992). Signed English in the classroom, IV. Aspects of children's speech and sign. *First Language, 12,* 125–145.

WOODS, B. T., & CAREY, S. (1979). Language deficits after apparent clinical recovery from childhood aphasia. *Annals of Neurology, 6,* 405–409.

WOODS, B. T., & TEUBER, H. L. (1978). Changing patterns of childhood aphasia. *Annals of Neurology, 3,* 273–280.

WRANGHAM, R. W., McGREW, W. C., DE WAAL, F. B. M., & HELTNE, P. G. (1994). *Chimpanzee culture.* Cambridge, MA: Harvard University Press.

XU, F., & CAREY, S. (1995). Do children's first object kind names map onto adult-like conceptual representations? In D. MacLaughlin & S. McEwen (Eds.), *Proceedings of the 19th Annual Boston University Conference on Language Development* (pp. 679–688). Somerville, MA: Cascadilla Press.

XU, F., & CAREY, S. (in press). Infants' metaphysics: The case of numerical identity. *Cognitive Psychology.*

YAMADA, J. E. (1990). *Laura: A case for the modularity of language.* Cambridge, MA: MIT Press.

YOSHIOKA, J. G. (1929). A study of bilingualism. *Journal of Genetic Psychology, 36,* 473–479.

ZAIDEL, E. (1985). Language in the right hemisphere. In D. F. Benson & E. Zaidel (Eds.), *The dual brain: Hemispheric specialization in humans* (pp. 205–232). New York: Guilford Press.

ZUKOW, P. G. (1990). Socio-perceptual bases for the emergence of language: An alternative to innatist approaches. *Developmental Psychobiology, 23,* 705–726.

ZURIF, E. B. (1995). Brain regions of relevance to syntactic processing. In L. R. Gleitman & M. Liberman (Eds.), *Language: An invitation to cognitive science, second edition: Vol. 1* (pp. 381–398). Cambridge: MIT Press.

Name Index

Subject Index

517

Photo Credits

Chapter 1: 0, © Kate Pietri. **Chapter 2: 30,** Photo Researchers, Inc.; **47,** photo reprinted with permission from P. K. Kuhl, University of Washington; **49,** photos reprinted with permission from P. K. Kuhl, University of Washington. **Chapter 3: 78,** courtesy of Anne Hoff; **90,** UPI Photo/Archive photos; **109,** © Erika Stone/Photo Researchers, Inc. **Chapter 4: 128,** © 1983 Tim Davis/Photo Researchers, Inc.; **171,** (*top*) © Harry Rogers/Photo Researchers, Inc., (*bottom*) © J. L. Lepore 1982/Photo Researchers, Inc.; **174,** (*left*) © Erika Stone/Photo Researchers, Inc., (*right*) Corel Professional Photos CD-ROM collection, "People." **Chapter 5: 184,** © Erika Stone/Photo Researchers, Inc.; **224,** courtesy of Anne Hoff; **226,** © Shirley Zeiberg/Photo Researchers, Inc. **Chapter 6: 242,** © Bob Krist/The Stock Market; **286,** © 1992 Peter Beck/The Stock Market; **291,** © Joseph Nettis/Photo Researchers, Inc. **Chapter 7: 296,** © Myrleen Ferguson/PhotoEdit; **311,** © Susan Woog Wagner/Photo Researchers, Inc. **Chapter 8: 334,** © 1980 Cynthia B. Matthews/The Stock Market. **Chapter 9: 380,** Marcus Raichle, M.D., Mallinckrodt Institute of Radiology at Washington University School of Medicine; **389,** Photo Researchers, Inc.; **415,** © Susan Kuklin 1977/Photo Researchers, Inc.

TO THE OWNER OF THIS BOOK:

We hope that you have found *Language Development* useful. So that this book can be improved in a future edition, would you take the time to complete this sheet and return it? Thank you.

School and address: _____

Department: _____

Instructor's name: _____

1. What I like most about this book is: _____

_____

_____

2. What I like least about this book is: _____

_____

_____

3. My general reaction to this book is: _____

_____

4. The name of the course in which I used this book is: _____

_____

5. Were all of the chapters of the book assigned for you to read? _____

   If not, which ones weren't? _____

6. In the space below, or on a separate sheet of paper, please write specific suggestions for improving this book and anything else you'd care to share about your experience in using the book.

_____

_____

_____

_____

_____

Optional:

Your name: _____ Date: _____

May Brooks/Cole quote you, either in promotion for *Language Development* or in future publishing ventures?

Yes: _____ No: _____

Sincerely,

Erika Hoff-Ginsberg

FOLD HERE

NO POSTAGE
NECESSARY
IF MAILED
IN THE
UNITED STATES

BUSINESS REPLY MAIL

FIRST CLASS   PERMIT NO. 358   PACIFIC GROVE, CA

POSTAGE WILL BE PAID BY ADDRESSEE

ATT: *Erika Hoff-Ginsberg* _____

Brooks/Cole Publishing Company
511 Forest Lodge Road
Pacific Grove, California 93950-9968

FOLD HERE